THE COMPLETE
POETICAL WORKS AND LETTERS OF
JOHN KEATS

Cambridge Edition

At Hampstead in 1819

BOSTON AND NEW YORK
HOUGHTON, MIFFLIN AND COMPANY
The Riverside Press, Cambridge
1899

EDITOR'S NOTE

THE period of Keats's poetical production was so brief, and he leaped so quickly into the possession of his poetical powers, that almost any arrangement of his works, which was orderly, would serve. Yet since Keats has left in all but a very few cases indication of the date of composition, and since even delicate intimations of poetic growth in the case of so rare a genius are worth attention, I have endeavored to make the arrangement as nearly chronological as the evidence, chiefly obtainable from Keats's letters, will permit. The head-notes disclose all instances where I have had to fall back on conjecture. The adoption of this order has compelled me to disregard the grouping of the volumes published by Keats and the posthumous publication by editors, but for the information of students a bibliographical note, setting forth the historical order of publication, is given in the Appendix.

The text of the poems published in Keats's three volumes has been carefully collated with copies of the first editions. I am indebted to Mr. F. H. Day for the opportunity of using the volumes of 1817 and 1820, and to Col. T. W. Higginson for *Endymion*. In reprinting the posthumous poems I have followed sometimes Lord Houghton in the *Life, Letters and Literary Remains of John Keats*, London, 1848, and the same editor's *Aldine* edition of 1876, sometimes Mr. Sidney Colvin in his *Letters of John Keats*, London, 1891, where so many of the poems are taken from Keats's own copy, and sometimes the text given by Mr. H. Buxton Forman in his careful four volume edition, London, 1883. There are a good many manuscripts, and these, together with the printed verses, have a variety of readings. All variations of consequence are noted in the Appendix; it was beyond the scope of this series to give every minute alteration. For an exhaustive statement, the curious student is referred to the invaluable edition by Mr. Forman. I have not deemed it indispensable to follow scrupulously the spelling and punctuation even of the poems whose publication was supervised by Keats, but I have not wilfully departed from either in accordance with any mere change of fashion; the spelling conforms to the accepted spelling of Keats's day; the capitalization is somewhat modified; the punctuation is studied with reference to the legibility of the passage.

For the prefatory notes I have been mainly indebted to Keats's letters, and have endeavored, as far as possible, to put the reader in possession of such light as Keats himself throws on his composition. I have also, in pursuance of the plan adopted for the arrangement of the poems, indicated in each instance the date, exactly or approximately. In accordance with the general scheme of the Cambridge editions, these prefatory notes are rarely critical; they are designed to be rather historical and bibliographical. In the preparation of these notes, as also of the Notes and Illustrations in the Appendix, I must again acknowledge my great indebtedness to Mr. Forman.

In undertaking to assemble Keats's *Complete Poetical Works*, I have been aware that I was including some things which neither Keats nor any one else would call poetical. Yet besides the contribution which verse makes to beauty, there is also the light which it throws on the poetical mind and character. And since the volume of Keats's production is not large, and much of his posthumous poetry is rightly classed with his own acknowledged work, it seemed best to give everything, but to make the natural discrimination between the poetry in the body of the volume and that which follows in the division, Supplementary Verse. The personality of Keats is so vivid, that just as his friends in his lifetime and after his death carefully garnered every scrap which he wrote, so the friends created by his life and his poetry may be trusted to know what his imperishable verse is, and yet will handle affectionately even the toys he played with.

Although I have endeavored to draw from Keats's letters such passages as throw direct light on his poetry, there yet remains an undefined scholia in the whole body of his familiar correspondence. No attentive reader of Keats's letters will fail to find in these unstudied, spontaneous expressions of the poet's mind a lambent light playing all over the surface of his poetry, and therefore it is not a wide departure from the scheme of this series of poets to include, in the same volume with Keats's poems, a collection also of his letters. This collection is complete, though one or two brief notes will not be found here, because already printed in the headings to poems. I have been dependent for the text mainly upon Mr. Colvin, supplemented by the minute garnering of Mr. Forman. I have to thank Mr. John Gilmer Speed for his courtesy in permitting the use of letters which he derived from the papers of his grandfather, George Keats.

CAMBRIDGE, August, 1899.

TABLE OF CONTENTS

✓ LETTERS

xii TABLE OF CONTENTS

NOTE. The frontispiece is a photogravure by John Andrew and Son from a painting made by Joseph Severn in his old age after the picture painted by him in his youth. The painting was in the possession of the late John W. Field, Esq., and is now the property of Williams College, by whose courtesy this copy was made.

The vignette is from a portrait by the same artist in the National Portrait Gallery, London.

BIOGRAPHICAL SKETCH

JOHN KEATS was born in Finsbury, London, on either the 29th or the 31st of October, 1795. He died in an apartment overlooking the Piazza di Spagna, Rome, February 23, 1821. Thus his life was a brief span of a few months more than twenty-five years, and as his first acknowledged verses were written in the autumn of 1813, and his last sonnet was composed in the autumn of 1820, his poetical career was seven years long. Within that time he composed the verses included in this volume, yet by far the largest portion may be referred to the three years 1818–1820, and if one distilled the whole, the precious deposit would be but a few hundred lines. For all that, perhaps because of it, and because Keats with his warm human passion wrote what is almost an autobiography in his letters, we are able to get a tolerably clear notion of his early training and associations, and to follow quite closely the development of his nature after he began to devote himself to poetry.

His father, Thomas Keats, was not a Londoner by birth, but came from the country to the town early, and was head hostler in a livery stable before he was twenty. He married Frances Jennings, the daughter of his master, who thereupon retired from business, leaving it in the hands of his son-in-law. The young couple lived over the stable at first, but when their family increased, they removed to a house in the neighborhood. John Keats was the first born. He had two brothers and a sister who grew to maturity. George Keats was sixteen months his junior; Thomas was four years younger, and Fanny, who was born in 1803, was a girl of ten when John Keats was making his first serious ventures in poetry.

The little that is known of Keats's parents is yet sufficient to show them persons of generous qualities and lively temperament. They were prosperous in their lives, and meant to better the condition of their children, so they sent the boys to good schools. The father died when John Keats was in his tenth year, and his mother shortly after married a man who appears to have been her husband's successor in business as well as in affections, but the marriage proved an unhappy one; there was a separation, and the stepfather scarcely came into the boy's life to affect him for good or for ill. He was still a school-boy, not yet fifteen, when his mother died, and he grieved for her with the force of a passionate nature that through a short life was to find various modes of expressing its keen sensibility.

As Keats went early to school, the influences which came most forcibly into his boyhood were from his brothers and schoolmates. Tom, the youngest brother, was always frail. George, who was nearer John's age, was like him in spirit and more robust. His recollections of his brothers, written after both Tom and John had died, are frank enough to make the relation undoubtedly truthful: —

'I loved him [John] from boyhood, even when he wronged me, for the good-ness of his heart and the nobleness of his spirit. Before we left school we quar-rélled often, and fought fiercely, and I can safely say and my schoolfellows will bear witness, that John's temper was the cause of all, still we were more attached than brothers ever are. From the time we were boys at school, where we loved, jangled and fought alternately, until we separated in 1818, I in a great measure relieved him by continual sympathy, explanation and inexhaustible spirits and good humor, from many a bitter fit of hypochondriasm. He avoided teasing any one with his miseries but Tom and myself, and often asked our forgiveness ; vent-ing and discussing them gave him relief.'

The school which the boys attended was kept by the Rev. John Clarke at En-field, and a son of Mr. Clarke was Charles Cowden Clarke, the 'ever young-hearted' as his happy-natured wife calls him, who was seven or eight years the senior of John Keats, but became his intimate friend and remained such through his life. Clarke's own reminiscence of his friend seems to fill out George Keats's sketch : —

'He was a favorite with all. Not the less beloved was he for having a highly pugnacious spirit, which when roused was one of the most picturesque exhibitions — off the stage — I ever saw. . . . His passion at times was almost ungoverna-ble ; and his brother George, being considerably the taller and stronger, used fre-quently to hold him down by main force, laughing when John was in one of his moods, and was endeavoring to beat him. It was all, however, a wisp-of-straw conflagration ; for he had an intensely tender affection for his brothers, and proved it upon the most trying occasions. He was not merely the favorite of all, like a pet prize-fighter, for his terrier courage ; but his highmindedness, his utter uncon-sciousness of a mean motive, his placability, his generosity, wrought so general a feeling in his behalf that I never heard a word of disapproval from any one, supe-rior or equal, who had known him.'

The reader will look in vain for any signs of a polemic nature in Keats's verse, but it is easy enough to find witness to his moodiness, as in such a sonnet as that beginning : —

'Why did I laugh to-night ? No voice will tell,'

and of the ungovernable passion there is evidence enough in his later life, though it took then another form. Yet the boyish impulsiveness which had its rude ex-pression in animal spirits turned in youth into a headlong eagerness for books before, during, and after school hours. According to Charles Cowden Clarke he won all the literature prizes of the school, and took upon himself for fun the trans-lation of the entire Æneid into prose. He read voraciously, and the same friend says : 'In my mind's eye I now see him at supper, sitting back on the form from the table, holding the folio volume of Burnet's *History of his Own Time* between himself and the table, eating his meal from behind it. This work, and Leigh Hunt's *Examiner*, which my father took in, and I used to lend to Keats — no

lt laid the foundation of his love of civil and religious liberty.' Still more
uite in its relation to his art was the intimate acquaintance he then formed with
ke's *Pantheon* and Lemprière's *Dictionary*.

he death of Keats's mother brought an interruption to his schooling.   The
dmother, who was still living, created a trust for the benefit of the Keats chil-
and committed its care to two guardians, one of whom, Mr. Richard Abbey,
he active trustee, and though the fund seems to have been reasonably suffi-
to protect the young people against the ordinary demands for a living, both
and George Keats seem always to have been sorely pinched for means.   Mr.
r at once removed John Keats from school and had him apprenticed to a
n, Mr. Hammond, for a term of five years.   Mr. Hammond lived at Edmon-
t far from Enfield, and Keats was wont to walk over to the Clarkes' once a
r oftener to see his friends and borrow books.

ras just fifteen when he began thus to equip himself for a place in the world,
r a little more than five years he was in training for the practice of medicine
rgery.   His apprenticeship to Mr. Hammond did not last as long as this, for
lentures were cancelled about a year before the term expired, but Keats then
p to London to continue his studies at St. Thomas's and Guy's hospitals.
sed with credit his examination as licentiate at Apothecaries' Hall, July 26,
and received an appointment at Guy's in the March following.   It does not
exactly when he abandoned his profession.   It may be said, with some
that he never actually abandoned it in intention; he held it in reserve as
ible resort, but it seems doubtful if he ever took up the practice for-
outside the walls of the hospital.   Once when his friend Charles Cowden
asked him about his attitude toward his profession, he expressed his grave
if he should go on with it.   'The other day,' he said to him, 'during
ture, there came a sunbeam into the room, and with it a whole troop of
res floating in the ray; and I was off with them to Oberon and fairy land.'
st operation,' he told another man, 'was the opening of a man's temporal
   I did it with the utmost nicety, but reflecting on what passed through my
t the time, my dexterity seemed a miracle, and I never took up the lancet.

nay be assumed that not later than the summer of 1816, when Keats was
ching his majority, he laid aside his instruments, never to resume them.   It
easy to reckon the contribution which these years of study and of brief
e in the medical art made to his intellectual, much less to his poetical
pment.   With his active mind he no doubt appropriated some facts — per-
re owe to his studies some lines in his verse, as that in 'Isabella,' where in
ing the Ceylon diver contributing to the brothers' wealth, he says : —

'For them his ears gush'd blood ; '

s more probable that, like many another young student, he went through his
rith sufficient fidelity to secure proper credit, but without any of that devo-

tion which is the only real 'learning by heart.' It is more to the purpose that during the years in which he was forming his mental habits, he was steadied by intellectual exercise while he was obeying instinctively the voice which was calling him more and more loudly.

The actual record of his poetry up to this date of the summer of 1816 is not extensive, but it is indicative of his growing power, of his taste in reading and observation, of his companionship, and most notably of his consciousness of the poetic spirit. Along with a few pieces like the lines 'To Some Ladies,' which show how little skill he had in making poetry a mere parlor maid, there are poems which show how he was struggling to do what other poets have done, as the lines 'To Hope' and the 'Ode' and 'Hymn to Apollo.' The lines 'To Hope,' with all their formal use of poetic conventions, have an interest from the attempt he makes at using the instrument he most highly valued in expressing his own moods and that youthful fervor which found a suburban Hampden in Leigh Hunt. His friendship with Hunt was in part founded on an admiration for the political hissing which Hunt and his friends kept up, and which was translated by his own independence of spirit into a valiant revolutionary sound, but more on an appreciation of Hunt's good taste in literature, his enjoyment of the Elizabethans and Milton, and his literary temper. Hunt was more of a public figure than Clarke or Reynolds, James Rice, Mathew, or any other of Keats's chosen companions, but the basis of Keats's friendship, apart from his brothers, was a community of literary taste more even than of literary production. It is a pleasure to get such glimpses as we do of this coterie exchanging books, revelling in their discovery of great authors who had been wrapped in the cerecloth of an antique speech, and celebrating their own admiration of these bards that 'gild the lapses of time.' It was not the *Examiner* that filled Keats's mind, it was Spenser and Milton, Chapman and Chaucer, and when he came away from Hunt's cottage, 'brimful of the friendliness' he there had found, it was of Lycidas and Petrarch and Laura that he sang as he fared on foot in the cool bleak air. In his 'Epistle to George Felton Mathew,' it is poetry and the brotherhood which springs from poetry that prompt the expression of friendship, and there is no prettier tale in literary friendship than that which shows Keats and Clarke sitting up through the night reading Chapman's Homer, and Keats in the morning sending his friend the well-turned sonnet which has been the key that unlocks Chapman to many readers.

These early verses thus are full of Keats's personal history, for he was living in the land of fancy and was rejoicing in the companionship of lovers of that land; but they are also witnesses to the feeling which he had for nature. It is true the flinging of himself on the grass, after being pent up in the city, is to read some 'debonair and gentle tale of love and languishment,' and a fair summer's eve suggests thoughts of Milton's fate and Sydney's bier; nevertheless, these expressions occur in the constricted sonnet. When Keats allows himself freedom and the rush of spontaneous emotion, as in the lines 'I stood tiptoe upon a little hill,' the reflection of nature in mythology and poetry is merely incidental to the joyous delight in nature itself, a delight so genuine that it almost covers from sight the half formal, half negligent beadroll of poetic subjects. Keats was born almost within sound of Bowbells, but his school days and early youth were spent in the rural environs of Enfield and Edmonton, and he escaped often from the city to Hampstead, not merely for companionship, but because there the nightingale sang, and there the walk in the woods or the stroll on the heath brought him face to face with the solitude which yielded indeed in his mind to pleasant converse, yet was, as he knew well, the direct road to converse with nature. Perhaps, in the lines, 'I stood tiptoe,' it is the close and loving observation of nature which first arrests one's attention, but a nearer scrutiny quickly reveals that imaginative rendering which lifts these lines far above the level of descriptive poetry. If in some of Wordsworth's sketches from nature written when he was of the same age one descries a profounder consciousness of human personality and a deeper sense of elemental relations, one is aware also of longer stretches of purely descriptive verse; with Keats there is an instant alchemy by which all sights and sounds are transmuted into the elements of a poetic world.

As this poem goes on it trembles into a half dreamy rapture of the poet away from all scenes into the world of visions, but it is in 'Sleep and Poetry,' written apparently at about the same time, that we discover a more precise witness to the poetic ideals now well formed in Keats's mind. The poet placed this piece last in his first printed volume, as if he intended to make it his personal apology. It is in part an impassioned plea for the freedom of imagination as against the artifices of the school of Pope, but even when thus half formally reciting his creed, Keats shows how little of the dogmatist there was in l nature, how little even of the critic, by the careless wandering of his own poem, and the unconscious expression of his own delight in everything that is beautiful in nature or art; so that as he writes his eye takes in the walls of the room where he lies, and he falls to versifying its contents. He thrills with the consciousness of being a poet, and flushes over the prospect of what he may do, yet at present what he does is rather the overflow of a poetic nature than the studied product of an artist.

The poems which precede 'Endymion' are many of them chiefly interesting for the hints they give thus of a nature which was gathering itself for a large leap. They are, as the reader will see, tentative excursions into the airy region, and they contain besides little witnesses to some of the important compelling influences which were forming Keats's mind. Thus the sonnets to Haydon illustrate Keats's recognition of Wordsworth, and also the great impression made upon him by the introduction which Haydon gave him to Greek art. They bear evidence, too, of his increasing study of Shakespeare and of his admiration for Milton, whose minor poems seem at this time to have exercised much influence over his style. Hunt's influence can be seen in the poems, but more indirectly than directly, for Hunt with his fine taste had done much to open the way to a return of lovers of poetry to the spacious days of Elizabeth. The poems are sometimes exercises, sometimes illuminations of a poetic mind, and they have a rare value to the student of poetry, as they disclose the mingling of great poetic traditions with the bursts of a poetic nature which was itself to add to the stock of great English verse.

There was about a year's space between Keats's abandonment of his profession and his occupation upon a long and serious poem. The group in this volume entitled 'Early Poems' gives the product of that period. That is, the pieces from 'I stood tiptoe upon a little hill' to the end of the section may be referred to this time, and the first one may fairly be taken as a sort of prologue to his adoption of a poetical life. When he was writing these poems he was living much with his brothers, to whom he was warmly attached, and was in a circle of ardent friends, men and women. He was an animated talker, with bursts of indignation, and a prey somewhat to moods of depression. His appearance has been described by many, and is thus summed up by Mr. Colvin: [1] 'A small, handsome, ardent-looking youth — the stature little over five feet; the figure compact and well turned, with the neck thrust eagerly forward, carrying a strong and shapely head set off by thickly clustering gold-brown hair; the features powerful, finished, and mobile; the mouth rich and wide, with an expression at once combative and sensitive in the extreme; the forehead not high, but broad and strong; the eyebrows nobly arched, and eyes hazel-brown, liquid-flashing, visibly inspired — "an eye that had an inward look, perfectly divine, like a Delphian priestess who saw visions."'

Keats was in London and its neighborhood during most of this year, but after the publication of his first volume of poems he went to the Isle of Wight and later to the seashore, and soon began to occupy himself with his serious labor of 'Endymion.' While he was working upon this poem he wrote but few verses. His letters, however, show him immersed in literature and the friendships which with him were so identified with literature, and kept, moreover, in a state of restlessness by what in homely phrase may be termed the growing pains of his poetic nature. 'I went to the Isle of Wight,' he writes to Leigh Hunt, May 10, 1817, 'thought so much about poetry, so long together, that I could not get to sleep at night; and, moreover, I know not how it was, I could not get wholesome food. By this means, in a week or so, I became not over capable in my upper stories, and set off pell mell for Margate, at least a hundred and fifty miles, because, forsooth, I fancied that I should like my old lodging here, and could contrive to do without trees. Another thing, I was too much in solitude and consequently was obliged to be in continual burning of thought, as an only recourse. However, Tom is with me at present, and we are very comfortable. . . . These last two days I have felt more confident. I have asked myself so often why I should be a poet more than other men, seeing how great a thing it is, — how great things are to be gained by it, what a thing to be in the mouth of Fame, — that at last the idea has grown so monstrously beyond my seeming power of attainment, that the other day I nearly consented with myself to drop into a Phaethon. Yet 't is a disgrace to fail, even in a huge attempt; and at this moment I drive the thought from me.'

These lines were written when Keats was deep in 'Endymion,' and with others

---

[1] *Keats* [Men of Letters Series]. By Sidney Colvin.

they intimate with some clearness how seriously Keats took himself, as the saying is. Much reading of great poetry had set standards for him rather than furnished models. It is not difficult to trace Keats's indebtedness to other poets, so far as words and turns of expression go, yet his confessed imitations show almost as conclusively as his original verse how incapable he was of merely reproducing out of the quarries of other poetry his own fair buildings. His was a nature possessed of poetic power, yet fed more than usual by great poetry. That he should have gone by turns to ancient mythology and mediæval romance for his themes, and have treated both in a spirit of romance, was due to a large artistic endowment, which bade him see both nature and humanity as subjects for composition, furnishing images to be delighted in. He was conscious of poetic genius, and never more so than when reading great poetry. In the presence of Shakespeare and Spenser he could exclaim, 'I too am a poet,' and this was no mere excitement such as hurries lesser men into clever copying, but an exhilaration which sent his pulses bounding as his own conceptions rose fair to view. It was obedience to this strong impulse to produce a great work of art which led him to sketch 'Endymion' and try his powers upon an attack on the very citadel of poetic beauty. Fame waved a wreath before him, yet it was not Fame but Poetry that really urged him forward. It is not unfair to translate even a confession of desire for fame into an acknowledgment of conscious power.

'Endymion' was published in the spring of 1818, and Keats's own attitude toward his work at this time is well expressed in the sonnet 'When I have fears that I may cease to be,' and in that written on sitting down to read King Lear once again. The very completion of his task set free new fancies, and there is a spontaneity in his occasional verse and in his letters which witnesses to a rapid maturing of power and a firmness of tread. The interesting letter to Reynolds of February 3, 1818, which contains a spirited criticism of Wordsworth and holds the Robin Hood verses, is quick with gay strength, and shows the poet alert and sane.

The publication of 'Endymion' was an important event to Keats and his circle. His earlier volume, the verses which he had since written and shown, and his own personality, had raised great expectations among his near friends and the few who could discern poetry without waiting for the poet to be famous; and now he was staking all, as it were, upon this single throw. The book was coarsely and roughly handled by the two leading reviews of the day, Blackwood's and the Quarterly. Criticism in those days was far from impersonal. A poet was condemned or praised, not for his work, but for his politics, the friends he associated with, his religion, and anything in his private life which might be known to the reviewer. Keats knew the worthlessness of much of this criticism, but he felt nevertheless keenly the hostility of what, rightly or wrongly, was looked upon as the supreme court in the republic of letters.

Under other circumstances he might have felt this even more keenly, and there appears to be evidence that he recurred afterward with bitterness to the attitude of the reviews; but just at this time other matters filled his mind. His brother,

George Keats, with his wife, went to America to try fortune in the new world, ar
Keats immediately afterward took a long walking tour in the north with his frier
Brown. His letters and the few poems of travel he wrote show how ardently l
threw himself into this acquaintance with a new phase of nature. But he was t
pass through experiences which entered more profoundly into life. In Decembe
of the same year, 1818, his brother Tom died. He had been his constant con
panion and nurse, and was with him at his death. Then, when his whole natui
was deeply stirred, he came to know and ardently to love a girl who by turns fa
cinated and repelled him, until he was completely enthralled, without apparentl
finding in her the repose which his restless nature needed.

Keats's first mention of Fanny Brawne scarcely prepares one for the inroad
made upon him by this personage during the rest of his short life. He went t
live with his friend Brown after Tom's death, and Mrs. Brawne became his nex
door neighbor. 'She is a very nice woman,' he writes, 'and her daughter senio
is I think beautiful and elegant, graceful, silly, fashionable and strange. W
have a little tiff now and then — and she behaves a little better, or I must hav
sheered off.' The passion which he conceived for Miss Brawne rapidly mounte
into a dominant place, and it is one of the marks of Keats's deeper nature, no
disclosed to his friends, intimate as he was with them, that for the two years whic
intervened before he left England a dying man, he carried this passion as a sort o
vulture gnawing at his vitals, concealed for the most part, though not wholly
Some overt expression it found, as in the 'Ode to Fanny,' the 'Lines to Fanny
and the verses addressed to the same person beginning: —

          'I cry your pity — mercy — love, ay love,'

and it may be traced, with little doubt, in those poems which emphasize his mood
such as the 'Ode to Melancholy' and the sonnet beginning: —

          'Why did I laugh to-night?'

and that also beginning: —

          'The day is gone, and all its sweets are gone.'

The letters contain infrequent allusions, except of course the posthumously pul
lished letters to the lady herself.

But with this overmastering passion to reckon with, the student of Keats ca
scarcely avoid regarding it as strongly influencing the poet's career during hi
remaining days. The turbulent experience of death and love acted upon a physici
organism predisposed to decay, and soon it was apparent that Keats was himsel
invaded by the disease of consumption, which had wasted his brother Tom. Bu
before this ravaging of his powers set in, that is, during the first half of 1819, whe
he was at once deepened by sorrow and excited by love, he wrote that great grou
of poems which begins with 'The Eve of St. Agnes' and closes with 'Lamia
If one takes as in some respects the high-water mark of his genius the mystic 'L
Belle Dame sans merci,' it is not perhaps too speculative a judgment which se
the keenest anguish of a passionate soul transmuted into terms of imperson;

poesy. There is no hectic flush about the poetry of this half year, but an increasing firmness of touch and rich, yet reserved imagination.

But great as his products were, he had not found his public, and the little property he had was slipping away, so that he was confronted by the fear of poverty as his weakness grew upon him. Nothing seemed to go well with him; his love affair brought him little else than exquisite pain. It is probable that on Keats's side the pride which was so dominant a chord in his nature forbade a man who could scarce support himself and felt the damp dews of decline chilling his vitality from seeking refuge in marriage with a girl who was in happier circumstance than he. He tried to turn his gifts into money by aiming at fortune with a play for the popular stage. He tried his hand at work for the periodicals. He even considered the possibility of returning to his profession of surgery for a livelihood. But all these projects failed him, and he turned with an almost savage and certainly sardonic humor to a scheme for flinging at the head of the public a popular poem. 'The Cap and Bells' is a melancholy example of what a great poet can produce who is consumed by a hopeless passion and wasted by disease.

Keats clung to his friends and wrote affectionate letters to his family. His brother George came over from America on a brief business visit, and was disturbed to find John so altered; and scarcely had George returned in January, 1820, than the poet had a sharp attack with loss of blood. He rallied as the spring came on, and early in the summer saw to the publication of his last volume, containing 'Hyperion, Isabella, The Eve of St. Agnes, Lamia,' and the 'Odes,' perhaps the most precious cargo carried in a vessel of this size in English literature in this century.

A month after the publication of the volume he was writing to Shelley, who had sent him an invitation to visit him in Pisa: 'There is no doubt that an English winter would put an end to me, and do so in a lingering, hateful manner. Therefore, I must either voyage or journey to Italy, as a soldier marches up to a battery.' In September he put himself into the hands of his cheerful and steadfast friend Severn the artist, and they took passage for Naples. It was when they were detained by winds off the coast of England that Keats wrote his last sonnet, with its veiled homage to Fanny Brawne, and in Naples Harbor he wrote to Mrs. Brawne in a feverish mood: 'I dare not fix my mind upon Fanny, I have not dared to think of her. The only comfort I have had that way has been in thinking for hours together of having the knife she gave me put in a silver case — the hair in a locket — and the pocket-book in a gold net. Show her this. I dare say no more.' And then there is the letter to Brown, with its agony of separation, in which he gives way to the torment of his love, with despair written in every line. It is difficult to say as one thinks of Keats's ashes whether the fire of passion or the fire of physical consumption had most to do with causing them.

It was in November, 1820, that the travellers reached Rome, and for a little while Keats could take short strolls on the Pincian Hill; but the fatal disease was making rapid progress, and on the 22d of February, 1821, he died, and three days later he was buried in the Protestant cemetery, where upon his gravestone may be read the words which Keats had said of himself : —

'Here lies one whose name was writ in water.'

In his first sonnet on Fame, Keats, in a saner mood, puts by the temptation which would withdraw him from the high serenity of conscious worth. In the second, wherein he seems almost to be seeing Fanny Brawne mocking behind the figure of Fame, he shows a more scornful attitude. There is little doubt that notwithstanding his close companionship with poets living and dead Keats never could long escape from the allurements of this 'wayward girl,' yet it may surely be said that his escape was most complete when he was fulfilling the highest law of his nature and creating those images of beauty which have given him Fame while he sleeps.

H. E. S.

POEMS

EARLY POEMS

In this group are included the contents of the volume *Poems by John Keats*, published in March, 1817, as well as certain poems composed before the publication of *Endymion*. The order followed is as nearly chronological as the evidence permits.

IMITATION OF SPENSER

Lord Houghton states, on the authority of the notes of Charles Armitage Brown, given to him in Florence in 1832, that this was the earliest known composition of Keats, and that it was written during his residence in Edmonton at the end of his eighteenth year, which would make the date in the autumn of 1813. The poem was included in the 1817 volume, which bore on its title-page this motto: —

What more felicity can fall to creature
Than to enjoy delight with liberty ?
Fate of the Butterfly. — SPENSER.

. . . .

Now Morning from her orient chamber came,
And her first footsteps touch'd a verdant hill;
Crowning its lawny crest with amber flame,
Silv'ring the untainted gushes of its rill;
Which, pure from mossy beds, did down distil,
And after parting beds of simple flowers,
By many streams a little lake did fill,
Which round its marge reflected woven bowers,
And, in its middle space, a sky that never lowers.

There the kingfisher saw his plumage bright,
Vying with fish of brilliant dye below;
Whose silken fins, and golden scales' light
Cast upward, through the waves, a ruby glow:
There saw the swan his neck of arched snow,

And oar'd himself along with majesty;
Sparkled his jetty eyes; his feet did show
Beneath the waves like Afric's ebony,
And on his back a fay reclined voluptuously.

Ah ! could I tell the wonders of an isle
That in that fairest lake had placed been,
I could e'en Dido of her grief beguile;
Or rob from aged Lear his bitter teen:
For sure so fair a place was never seen,
Of all that ever charm'd romantic eye:
It seem'd an emerald in the silver sheen
Of the bright waters; or as when on high,
Through clouds of fleecy white, laughs the cœrulean sky.

And all around it dipp'd luxuriously
Slopings of verdure through the glossy tide,
Which, as it were in gentle amity,
Rippled delighted up the flowery side;
As if to glean the ruddy tears, it tried,
Which fell profusely from the rose-tree stem !
Haply it was the workings of its pride,
In strife to throw upon the shore a gem
Outvying all the buds in Flora's diadem.

. . . .

ON DEATH

Assigned by George Keats to the year 1814, and first printed in Forman's edition, 1883.

Can death be sleep, when life is but a dream,
And scenes of bliss pass as a phantom by ?

The transient pleasures as a vision seem,
  And yet we think the greatest pain's to
    die.

How strange it is that man on earth should
    roam,
  And lead a life of woe, but not forsake
His rugged path; nor dare he view alone
  His future doom, which is but to awake.

TO CHATTERTON

First printed in *Life, Letters, and Literary
Remains*, but undated. Keats's admiration of
Chatterton was early and constant.

O CHATTERTON! how very sad thy fate!
  Dear child of sorrow — son of misery!
  How soon the film of death obscur'd that
    eye,
Whence Genius mildly flash'd, and high
    debate.
How soon that voice, majestic and elate,
  Melted in dying numbers!   Oh! how
    nigh
  Was night to thy fair morning.   Thou
    didst die
A half-blown flow'ret which cold blasts
    amate.
But this is past: thou art among the stars
  Of highest Heaven: to the rolling spheres
Thou sweetly singest: nought thy hymning
    mars,
  Above the ingrate world and human
    fears.
On earth the good man base detraction
    bars
  From thy fair name, and waters it with
    tears.

TO BYRON

The date of December, 1814, is given to this
sonnet by Lord Houghton in *Life, Letters, and
Literary Remains*, where it was first published.

BYRON! how sweetly sad thy melody!
  Attuning still the soul to tenderness,

As if soft Pity, with unusual stress,
Had touch'd her plaintive lute, and thou
    being by,
Hadst caught the tones, nor suffer'd them
    to die.
  O'ershadowing sorrow doth not make
    thee less
  Delightful: thou thy griefs dost dress
With a bright halo, shining beamily,
As when a cloud the golden moon doth veil,
  Its sides are ting'd with a resplendent
    glow,
Through the dark robe oft amber rays pre-
    vail,
  And like fair veins in sable marble flow;
Still warble, dying swan! still tell the tale,
  The enchanting tale, the tale of pleasing
    woe.

'WOMAN! WHEN I BEHOLD THEE FLIPPANT, VAIN'

In the 1817 volume, where this poem was
first published, with no title, it is placed at
the end of a group of poems which are thus
advertised on the leaf containing the dedication: 'The Short Pieces in the middle of the
Book as well as some of the Sonnets, were
written at an earlier period than the rest of
the Poems.'   In the absence of any documen-
tary evidence, it seems reasonable to place it
near the 'Imitation of Spenser' rather than
near 'Calidore.'

WOMAN! when I behold thee flippant, vain,
  Inconstant, childish, proud, and full of
    fancies;
  Without that modest softening that en-
    hances
The downcast eye, repentant of the pain
That its mild light creates to heal again:
  E'en then, elate, my spirit leaps, and
    prances,
  E'en then my soul with exultation dances
For that to love, so long, I've dormant
    lain:
But when I see thee meek, and kind, and
    tender,

Heavens ! how desperately do I adore
Thy winning graces; — to be thy defender
I hotly burn — to be a Calidore —
A very Red Cross Knight — a stout Le-
  ander —
Might I be loved by thee like these of
  yore.

Light feet, dark violet eyes, and parted
  hair;
  Soft dimpled hands, white neck, and
    creamy breast,
  Are things on which the dazzled senses
    rest
Till the fond, fixed eyes, forget they stare.
From such fine pictures, heavens ! I cannot
  dare
  To turn my admiration, though unpos-
    sess'd
  They be of what is worthy, — though not
    drest
In lovely modesty, and virtues rare.
Yet these I leave as thoughtless as a lark;
  These lures I straight forget, — e'en ere
    I dine,
Or thrice my palate moisten: but when I
  mark
  Such charms with mild intelligences
    shine,
My ear is open like a greedy shark,
  To catch the tunings of a voice divine.

Ah ! who can e'er forget so fair a being ?
  Who can forget her half-retiring sweets ?
  God ! she is like a milk-white lamb that
    bleats
For man's protection. Surely the All-see-
  . ing,
Who joys to see us with his gifts agree-
  ing,
  Will never give him pinions, who intreats
  Such innocence to ruin, — who vilely
    cheats
A dove-like bosom. In truth there is no
  freeing
One's thoughts from such a beauty; when
  I hear
  A lay that once I saw her hand awake,

Her form seems floating palpable, and near;
  Had I e'er seen her from an arbour take
A dewy flower, oft would that hand appear,
  And o'er my eyes the trembling moisture
    shake.

TO SOME LADIES

This and the poem following were included
in the 1817 volume. George Keats says further that it was 'written on receiving a copy
of Tom Moore's "Golden Chain" and a most
beautiful Dome shaped shell from a Lady.'
The exact title of Moore's poem is 'The
Wreath and the Chain,' and it will be readily
seen how expressly imitative these lines are of
Moore's verse in general. The poems are not
dated, but they are the first in a group stated
by Keats to have been 'written at an earlier
period than the rest of the Poems;' it is safe to
assume that they belong very near the beginning of Keats's poetical career. It is quite
likely that they were included in the volume a
few years later on personal grounds.

WHAT though while the wonders of nature
    exploring,
  I cannot your light, mazy footsteps at-
    tend;
Nor listen to accents, that almost adoring,
  Bless Cynthia's face, the enthusiast's
    friend:

Yet over the steep, whence the mountain-
    stream rushes,
  With you, kindest friends, in idea I rove;
Mark the clear tumbling crystal, its pas-
    sionate gushes,
  Its spray that the wild flower kindly
    bedews.

Why linger you so, the wild labyrinth
    strolling ?
  Why breathless, unable your bliss to de-
    clare ?
Ah ! you list to the nightingale's tender
    condoling,
  Responsive to sylphs, in the moon-beamy
    air.

'T is morn, and the flowers with dew are
     yet drooping,
   I see you are treading the verge of the
     sea:
And now! ah, I see it — you just now are
     stooping
   To pick up the keepsake intended for me.

If a cherub, on pinions of silver descending,
   Had brought me a gem from the fret-
     work of heaven;
And smiles, with his star-cheering voice
     sweetly blending,
   The blessings of Tighe had melodiously
     given;

It had not created a warmer emotion
   Than the present, fair nymphs, I was
     blest with from you;
Than the shell, from the bright golden
     sands of the ocean,
   Which the emerald waves at your feet
     gladly threw.

For, indeed, 't is a sweet and peculiar plea-
     sure,
   (And blissful is he who such happiness
     finds,)
To possess but a span of the hour of leisure,
   In elegant, pure, and aerial minds.

ON RECEIVING A CURIOUS SHELL AND A COPY OF VERSES FROM THE SAME LADIES

Hast thou from the caves of Golconda, a
     gem
   Pure as the ice-drop that froze on the
     mountain?
Bright as the humming-bird's green diadem,
   When it flutters in sunbeams that shine
     through a fountain?

Hast thou a goblet for dark sparkling wine?
   That goblet right heavy, and massy, and
     gold?

And splendidly mark'd with the s
     vine
   Of Armida the fair, and Rina
     bold?

Hast thou a steed with a mane rich
     ing?
   Hast thou a sword that thine
     smart is?
Hast thou a trumpet rich melodies bl
And wear'st thou the shield of th
     Britomartis?

What is it that hangs from thy sl
     so brave,
   Embroidered with many a spring
     flower?
Is it a scarf that thy fair lady gave
   And hastest thou now to that fai
     bower?

Ah! courteous Sir Knight, with la
     thou art crown'd;
   Full many the glories that brigh
     youth!
I will tell thee my blisses, which
     abound
   In magical powers to bless, and to

On this scroll thou seest written in
     ters fair
   A sun-beamy tale of a wreath
     chain:
And, warrior, it nurtures the prope
   Of charming my mind from the tr
     of pain.

This canopy mark: 't is the work o
   Beneath its rich shade did King
     languish,
When lovely Titania was far, far a
   And cruelly left him to sorrow,
     guish.

There, oft would he bring from l
     sighing lute
   Wild strains to which, spell-bou
     nightingales listen'd;

The wondering spirits of heaven were
    mute,
  And tears 'mong the dewdrops of morn-
    ing oft glistened.

In this little dome, all those melodies
    strange,
  Soft, plaintive, and melting, for ever will
    sigh;
Nor e'er will the notes from their tender-
    ness change ;
Nor e'er will the music of Oberon die.

So, when I am in a voluptuous vein,
  I pillow my head on the sweets of the
    rose,
And list to the tale of the wreath, and the
    chain,
Till its echoes depart; then I sink to re-
    pose.

Adieu, valiant Eric ! with joy thou art
    crown'd ;
  Full many the glories that brighten thy
    youth,
I too have my blisses, which richly abound
  In magical powers, to bless and to soothe.

WRITTEN ON THE DAY THAT MR. LEIGH HUNT LEFT PRISON

Either the 2d or 3d of February, 1815.
Charles Cowden Clarke, to whom Keats
showed the sonnet, writes in his recollections:
'This I feel to be the first proof I had received of his having committed himself in
verse ; and how clearly do I recollect the conscious look and hesitation with which he offered it ! There are some momentary glances
by beloved friends that fade only with life.'
The sonnet was printed in the 1817 volume.

WHAT though, for showing truth to flat-
    ter'd state,
  Kind Hunt was shut in prison, yet has
    he,
In his immortal spirit, been as free

As the sky-searching lark, and as elate.
Minion of grandeur ! think you he did
    wait ?
  Think you he nought but prison-walls
    did see,
  Till, so unwilling, thou unturn'dst the
    key ?
Ah, no ! far happier, nobler was his fate !
In Spenser's halls he strayed, and bowers
    fair,
  Culling enchanted flowers; and he flew
With daring Milton .through the fields of
    air:
  To regions of his own his genius true
Took happy flights. Who shall his fame
    impair
  When thou art dead, and all thy wretched
    crew ?

TO HOPE

Keats dates this poem in the volume of 1817,
February, 1815.

WHEN by my solitary hearth I sit,
  And hateful thoughts enwrap my soul in
    gloom;
When no fair dreams before my ' mind's
    eye ' flit,
  And the bare heath of life presents no
    bloom;
    Sweet Hope, ethereal balm upon me
    shed,
    And wave thy silver pinions o'er my
    head.

Whene'er I wander, at the fall of night,
  Where woven boughs shut out the moon's
    bright ray,
Should sad Despondency my musings
    fright,
  And frown, to drive fair Cheerfulness
    away,
    Peep with the moonbeams through the
    leafy roof,
    And keep that fiend Despondence far
    aloof.

Should Disappointment, parent of Despair,
  Strive for her son to seize my careless
    heart;
When, like a cloud, he sits upon the air,
  Preparing on his spell-bound prey to
    dart:
    Chase him away, sweet Hope, with
      visage bright,
    And fright him as the morning fright-
    ens night !

Whene'er the fate of those I hold most dear
  Tells to my fearful breast a tale of sorrow,
O bright-eyed Hope, my morbid fancy
    cheer;
  Let me awhile thy sweetest comforts
    borrow:
    Thy heaven-born radiance around me
      shed,
    And wave thy silver pinions o'er my
      head !

Should e'er unhappy love my bosom pain,
  From cruel parents, or relentless fair ;
O let me think it is not quite in vain
  To sigh out sonnets to the midnight air !
    Sweet Hope, ethereal balm upon me
      shed,
    And wave thy silver pinions o'er my
      head.

In the long vista of the years to roll,
  Let me not see our country's honour fade:
O let me see our land retain her soul,
  Her pride, her freedom; and not free-
    dom's shade.
    From thy bright eyes unusual bright-
      ness shed —
    Beneath thy pinions canopy my head !

Let me not see the patriot's high bequest,
  Great Liberty ! how great in plain attire!
With the base purple of a court oppress'd,
  Bowing her head, and ready to expire:
    But let me see thee stoop from hea-
      ven on wings
    That fill the skies with silver glitter-
      ings !

And as, in sparkling majesty, a star
  Gilds the bright summit of some gloomy
    cloud,
Brightening the half veil'd face of heaven
    afar:
  So, when dark thoughts my boding spirit
    shroud,
    Sweet Hope, celestial influence round
      me shed,
    Waving thy silver pinions o'er my head.

ODE TO APOLLO

The *Ode* and the *Hymn* which follows were
first printed by Lord Houghton in *Life, Letters
and Literary Remains ;* the former is there
dated February, 1815.

In thy western halls of gold
  When thou sittest in thy state,
Bards, that erst sublimely told
  Heroic deeds, and sang of fate,
With fervour seize their adamantine
    lyres,
Whose chords are solid rays, and twinkle
  radiant fires.

Here Homer with his nervous arms
  Strikes the twanging harp of war,
And even the western splendour warms,
  While the trumpets sound afar:
But, what creates the most intense sur-
    prise,
His soul looks out through renovated eyes.

Then, through thy Temple wide, melodi-
    ous swells
  The sweet majestic tone of Maro's lyre:
The soul delighted on each accent
    dwells, —
  Enraptur'd dwells, — not daring to re-
    spire,
The while he tells of grief around a funeral
    pyre.

'T is awful silence then again;
  Expectant stand the spheres;
  Breathless the laurell'd peers,

Nor move, till ends the lofty strain,
Nor move till Milton's tuneful thunders
cease,
And leave once more the ravish'd heavens
in peace.

Thou biddest Shakspeare wave his hand,
And quickly forward spring
The Passions — a terrific band —
And each vibrates the string
That with its tyrant temper best accords,
While from their Master's lips pour forth
the inspiring words.

A silver trumpet Spenser blows,
And, as its martial notes to silence flee,
From a virgin chorus flows
A hymn in praise of spotless Chastity.
'T is still!   Wild warblings from the
Æolian lyre
Enchantment softly breathe, and trem-
blingly expire.

Next thy Tasso's ardent numbers
Float along the pleasèd air,
Calling youth from idle slumbers,
Rousing them from Pleasure's lair: —
Then o'er the strings his fingers gently
move,
And melt the soul to pity and to love.

But when *Thou* joinest with the Nine,
And all the powers of song combine,
We listen here on earth:
The dying tones that fill the air,
And charm the ear of evening fair,
From thee, Great God of Bards, receive
their heavenly birth.

HYMN TO APOLLO

GOD of the golden bow,
And of the golden lyre,
And of the golden hair,
And of the golden fire,
Charioteer
Of the patient year,

Where — where slept thine ire,
When like a blank idiot I put on thy wreath,
Thy laurel, thy glory,
The light of thy story,
Or was I a worm — too low crawling, for
death ?
O Delphic Apollo !

The Thunderer grasp'd and grasp'd,
The Thunderer frown'd and frown'd;
The eagle's feathery mane
For wrath became stiffen'd — the sound
Of breeding thunder
Went drowsily under,
Muttering to be unbound.
O why didst thou pity, and for a worm
Why touch thy soft lute
Till the thunder was mute,
Why was not I crush'd — such a pitiful
germ ?
O Delphic Apollo !

The Pleiades were up,
Watching the silent air;
The seeds and roots in the Earth
Were swelling for summer fare;
The Ocean, its neighbour,
Was at its old labour,
When, who — who did dare
To tie, like a madman, thy plant round his
brow,
And grin and look proudly,
And blaspheme so loudly,
And live for that honour, to stoop to thee
now ?
O Delphic Apollo !

TO A YOUNG LADY WHO SENT ME A LAUREL CROWN

First printed by Lord Houghton in the *Life,
Letters and Literary Remains*, but undated.

FRESH morning gusts have blown away all
fear
From my glad bosom, — now from gloom
iness
I mount for ever — not an atom less

Than the proud laurel shall content my
   bier.
No ! by the eternal stars ! or why sit here
   In the Sun's eye, and 'gainst my temples
     press
   Apollo's very leaves, woven to bless
By thy white fingers and thy spirit clear.
Lo ! who dares say, 'Do this ?' Who dares
   call down
   My will from its high purpose ? Who
     say, 'Stand,'
Or 'Go ?' This mighty moment I would
   frown
   On abject Cæsars — not the stoutest
     band
Of mailèd heroes should tear off my crown :
   Yet would I kneel and kiss thy gentle
     hand !

SONNET

Published in the 1817 volume. Lord Houghton states that this sonnet ' was the means of
introducing Keats to Mr. Leigh Hunt's society.
Mr. Cowden Clarke had brought some of his
young friend's verses and read them aloud.
Mr. Horace Smith, who happened to be there,
was struck with the last six lines, especially
the penultimate, saying " what a well condensed
expression ! " and Keats was shortly after introduced to the literary circle.' This would
appear to fix the date as not later than the
summer of 1815.

How many bards gild the lapses of time !
   A few of them have ever been the food
Of my delighted fancy, — I could brood
Over their beauties, earthly, or sublime :
And often, when I sit me down to rhyme,
   These will in throngs before my mind
     intrude :
   But no confusion, no disturbance rude
Do they occasion ; 't is a pleasing chime.
So the unnumber'd sounds that evening
   store ;
   The songs of birds — the whisp'ring of
     the leaves —
   The voice of waters — the great bell
     that heaves

With solemn sound, — and thousand others
   more,
That distance of recognizance bereaves,
Make pleasing music, and not wild uproar.

SONNET

According to Charles Cowden Clarke, this
sonnet was written upon Keats first visiting
Hunt in the Vale of Health. It was published
in the 1817 volume.

KEEN, fitful gusts are whisp'ring here and
   there
   Among the bushes half leafless, and dry ;
   The stars look very cold about the sky,
And I have many miles on foot to fare.
Yet feel I little of the cool bleak air,
   Or of the dead leaves rustling drearily,
   Or of those silver lamps that burn on
     high,
Or of the distance from home's pleasant
   lair :
For I am brimful of the friendliness
   That in a little cottage I have found ;
Of fair-hair'd Milton's eloquent distress,
   And all his love for gentle Lycid drown'd ;
Of lovely Laura in her light green dress,
   And faithful Petrarch gloriously crown'd.

SPENSERIAN STANZA

WRITTEN AT THE CLOSE OF CANTO II.
BOOK V. OF 'THE FAERIE QUEENE'

Given by Lord Houghton in *Life, Letters and
Literary Remains*, who comments as follows :
' His sympathies were very much on the side
of the revolutionary Giant, who " undertook for
to repair " the " realms and nations run awry,"
and to suppress " tyrants that make men subject to their law," " and lordings curbe that
commons over-aw," while he grudged the legitimate victory, as he rejected the conserva-
tive philosophy, of the " righteous Artegall "
and his comrade, the fierce defender of privilege and order. And he expressed in this
ex post facto prophecy, his conviction of the

ultimate triumph of freedom and equality by
the power of transmitted knowledge.' No
date is assigned, and the verse may as well be
placed in the early period of Keats's acquaintance with Spenser and friendship with Leigh
Hunt.

In after-time, a sage of mickle lore
Yclep'd Typographus, the Giant took,
And did refit his limbs as heretofore,
And made him read in many a learned
    book,
And into many a lively legend look;
Thereby in goodly themes so training
    him,
That all his brutishness he quite for-
    sook,
When, meeting Artegall and Talus grim,
The one he struck stone-blind, the other's
eyes wox dim.

ON LEAVING SOME FRIENDS AT AN EARLY HOUR

Written, as Clarke intimates, in connection
with Keats's visits to Leigh Hunt in the Vale
of Health. Published in the 1817 volume.

Give me a golden pen, and let me lean
    On heap'd-up flowers, in regions clear
    and far;
Bring me a tablet whiter than a star,
Or hand of hymning angel, when 't is seen
The silver strings of heavenly harp atween:
And let there glide by many a pearly
    car,
Pink robes, and wavy hair, and diamond
    jar,
And half-discover'd wings, and glances
    keen.
The while let music wander round my ears,
    And as it reaches each delicious ending,
    Let me write down a line of glorious
    tone,
And full of many wonders of the spheres:
    For what a height my spirit is contend-
    ing !
'T is not content so soon to be alone.

ON FIRST LOOKING INTO CHAPMAN'S HOMER

It was Charles Cowden Clarke who was with
Keats when the friends made the acquaintance
of this translation of Homer by the Elizabethan poet. The two young men had sat up
nearly all one night in the summer of 1815 in
Clarke's lodging, reading from a folio volume
of the book which they had borrowed. Keats
left for his own lodgings at dawn, and when
Clarke came down to breakfast the next morning, he found this sonnet which Keats had
sent him.

Much have I travell'd in the realms of
    gold,
    And many goodly states and kingdoms
    seen;
    Round many western islands have I been
Which bards in fealty to Apollo hold.
Oft of one wide expanse had I been told
    That deep-brow'd Homer ruled as his
    demesne:
    Yet did I never breathe its pure serene
Till I heard Chapman speak out loud and
    bold:
Then felt I like some watcher of the skies
    When a new planet swims into his ken;
Or like stout Cortez when with eagle eyes
    He star'd at the Pacific — and all his
    men
Look'd at each other with a wild surmise —
    Silent, upon a peak in Darien.

EPISTLE TO GEORGE FELTON MATHEW

Mathew, who was of Keats's age, was his
companion when he first went to London. The
two had common tastes in literature and read
together, and Mathew also made essays in
writing, so that Keats, who was living much in
Elizabethan literature at the time, might easily
transfer in imagination some of the great deeds
of partnership to himself and his friend. It
is worth while to note Mathew's own recollection, thirty years later, of the contrast of him-

self with Keats: 'Keats and I, though about the same age, and both inclined to literature, were in many respects as different as two individuals could be. He enjoyed good health — a fine flow of animal spirits — was fond of company — could amuse himself admirably with the frivolities of life — and had great confidence in himself. I, on the other hand, was languid and melancholy — fond of repose — thoughtful beyond my years — and diffident to the last degree.' The epistle is dated November, 1815, in the volume of 1817, where it is the first of a group of three epistles with the motto from Browne's *Britannia's Pastorals*:

Among the rest a shepherd (though but young
Yet hartned to his pipe) with all the skill
His few yeeres could, began to fit his quill.

SWEET are the pleasures that to verse
 belong,
And doubly sweet a brotherhood in song;
Nor can remembrance, Mathew! bring to
 view
A fate more pleasing, a delight more true
Than that in which the brother Poets joy'd,
Who, with combinèd powers, their wit em-
 ploy'd
To raise a trophy to the drama's muses.
The thought of this great partnership dif-
 fuses
Over the genius-loving heart, a feeling
Of all that's high, and great, and good,
 and healing.   10

Too partial friend! fain would I follow
 thee
Past each horizon of fine poesy;
Fain would I echo back each pleasant note
As o'er Sicilian seas, clear anthems float
'Mong the light skimming gondolas far
 parted,
Just when the sun his farewell beam has
 darted:
But 't is impossible; far different cares
Beckon me sternly from soft 'Lydian airs,'
And hold my faculties so long in thrall,
That I am oft in doubt whether at all   20
I shall again see Phœbus in the morning:
Or flush'd Aurora in the roseate dawning!

Or a white Naiad in a rippling stream;
Or a rapt seraph in a moonlight beam;
Or again witness what with thee I 've seen,
The dew by fairy feet swept from the
 green,
After a night of some quaint jubilee
Which every elf and fay had come to see:
When bright processions took their airy
 march
Beneath the curvèd moon's triumphal
 arch.   30

But might I now each passing moment
 give
To the coy Muse, with me she would not
 live
In this dark city, nor would condescend
'Mid contradictions her delights to lend.
Should e'er the fine-eyed maid to me be
 kind,
Ah! surely it must be whene'er I find
Some flowery spot, sequester'd, wild, ro-
 mantic,
That often must have seen a poet fran-
 tic;
Where oaks, that erst the Druid knew, are
 growing,
And flowers, the glory of one day, are
 blowing;   40
Where the dark-leav'd laburnum's droop-
 ing clusters
Reflect athwart the stream their yellow
 lustres,
And intertwined the cassia's arms unite,
With its own drooping buds, but very white.
Where on one side are covert branches
 · hung,
'Mong which the nightingales have always
 sung
In leafy quiet: where to pry, aloof
Atween the pillars of the sylvan roof,
Would be to find where violet beds were
 nestling,
And where the bee with cowslip bells was
 wrestling.   50
There must be too a ruin dark and gloomy,
To say 'Joy not too much in all that's
 bloomy.'

Yet this is vain — O Mathew, lend thy
   aid
To find a place where I may greet the
   maid —
Where we may soft humanity put on,
And sit, and rhyme and think on Chatter-
   ton;
And that warm-hearted Shakspeare sent to
   meet him
Four laurell'd spirits, heavenward to en-
   treat him.
With reverence would we speak of all the
   sages
Who have left streaks of light athwart
   their ages: 60
And thou shouldst moralize on Milton's
   blindness,
And mourn the fearful dearth of human
   kindness
To those who strove with the bright golden
   wing
Of genius, to flap away each sting
Thrown by the pitiless world. We next
   could tell
Of those who in the cause of freedom fell;
Of our own Alfred, of Helvetian Tell;
Of him whose name to ev'ry heart 's a
   solace,
High - minded and unbending William
   Wallace.
While to the rugged north our musing
   turns,   70
We well might drop a tear for him, and
   Burns.

Felton! without incitements such as these,
How vain for me the niggard Muse to
   tease:
For thee, she will thy every dwelling grace,
And make ' a sunshine in a shady place: '
For thou wast once a flowret blooming
   wild,
Close to the source, bright, pure, and unde-
   fil'd,
Whence gush the streams of song: in
   happy hour
Came chaste Diana from her shady bower,
Just as the sun was from the east uprising;

And, as for him some gift she was devising,
Beheld thee, pluck'd thee, cast thee in the
   stream   82
To meet her glorious brother's greeting
   beam.
I marvel much that thou hast never told
How, from a flower, into a fish of gold
Apollo chang'd thee: how thou next didst
   seem
A black-ey'd swan upon the widening
   stream;
And when thou first didst in that mirror
   trace
The placid features of a human face:
That thou hast never told thy travels
   strange,   90
And all the wonders of the mazy range
O'er pebbly crystal, and o'er golden sands;
Kissing thy daily food from Naiads' pearly
   hands.

TO ——

A valentine written in 1816 by Keats for his
brother George to send to the lady Georgiana
Wylie, whom he afterward married, was later
expanded into the following lines. It was included in the 1817 volume. For the original
valentine see the Notes at the end of this
volume.

HADST thou liv'd in days of old,
O what wonders had been told
Of thy lively countenance,
And thy humid eyes that dance
In the midst of their own brightness;
In the very fane of lightness.
Over which thine eyebrows, leaning,
Picture out each lovely meaning:
In a dainty bend they lie,
Like to streaks across the sky,   10
Or the feathers from a crow,
Fallen on a bed of snow.
Of thy dark hair, that extends
Into many graceful bends:
As the leaves of Hellebore
Turn to whence they sprung before.
And behind each ample curl

Peeps the richness of a pearl.
Downward too flows many a tress
With a glossy waviness;   20
Full, and round like globes that rise
From the censer to the skies
Through sunny air. Add too, the sweet-
        ness
Of thy honied voice; the neatness
Of thine ankle lightly turn'd:
With those beauties scarce discern'd,
Kept with such sweet privacy,
That they seldom meet the eye
Of the little loves that fly
Round about with eager pry.   30
Saving when, with freshening lave,
Thou dipp'st them in the taintless wave;
Like twin water-lilies, born
In the coolness of the morn.
O, if thou hadst breathèd then,
Now the Muses had been ten.
Couldst thou wish for lineage higher
Than twin-sister of Thalia?
At least for ever, evermore
Will I call the Graces four.   40

Hadst thou liv'd when chivalry
Lifted up her lance on high,
Tell me what thou wouldst have been?
Ah! I see the silver sheen
Of thy broider'd, floating vest
Cov'ring half thine ivory breast:
Which, O heavens! I should see,
But that cruel destiny
Has plac'd a golden cuirass there;
Keeping secret what is fair.   50
Like sunbeams in a cloudlet nested
Thy locks in knightly casque are rested:
O'er which bend four milky plumes
Like the gentle lily's blooms
Springing from a costly vase.
See with what a stately pace
Comes thine alabaster steed;
Servant of heroic deed!
O'er his loins his trappings glow
Like the northern lights on snow.   60
Mount his back! thy sword unsheath!
Sign of the enchanter's death;
Bane of every wicked spell;

Silencer of dragon's yell.
Alas! thou this wilt never do:
Thou art an enchantress too,
And wilt surely never spill
Blood of those whose eyes can kill.

SONNET

Lord Houghton gives the date of 1816. It
appears in the Aldine edition of 1876.

As from the darkening gloom a silver dove
    Upsoars, and darts into the eastern light,
    On pinions that nought moves but pure
        delight,
So fled thy soul into the realms above,
Regions of peace and everlasting love;
    Where happy spirits, crown'd with cir-
        clets bright
    Of starry beam, and gloriously bedight,
Taste the high joy none but the blest can
        prove.
There thou or joinest the immortal quire
    In melodies that even heaven fair
Fill with superior bliss, or, at desire,
    Of the omnipotent Father, cleav'st the
        air
On holy message sent — What pleasure 's
        higher?
Wherefore does any grief our joy impair?

SONNET TO SOLITUDE

Published in *The Examiner*, 5 May, 1816, and
the first piece printed by Keats. It was re-
issued in the 1817 volume.

O SOLITUDE! if I must with thee dwell,
    Let it not be among the jumbled heap
    Of murky buildings; climb with me the
        steep, —
Nature's observatory, — whence the dell,
Its flowery slopes, its river's crystal swell,
    May seem a span; let me thy vigils keep
    'Mongst boughs pavilion'd, where the
        deer's swift leap
Startles the wild bee from the foxglove
        bell.

But though I 'll gladly trace these scenes
with thee,
  Yet the sweet converse of an innocent
mind,
  Whose words are images of thoughts re-
fin'd,
Is my soul's pleasure; and it sure must be
  Almost the highest bliss of human-kind,
When to thy haunts two kindred spirits flee.

SONNET

George Keats has a memorandum on this
sonnet, 'written in the Fields, June, 1816.'
Published in the 1817 volume.

To one who has been long in city pent,
  'T is very sweet to look into the fair
  And open face of heaven, — to breathe
a prayer
Full in the smile of the blue firmament.
Who is more happy, when, with hearts
content,
  Fatigued he sinks into some pleasant lair
  Of wavy grass, and reads a debonair
And gentle tale of love and languishment?
Returning home at evening, with an ear
  Catching the notes of Philomel, — an eye
Watching the sailing cloudlet's bright ca-
reer,
  He mourns that day so soon has glided
by:
E'en like the passage of an angel's tear
  That falls through the clear ether si-
lently.

TO A FRIEND WHO SENT ME SOME ROSES

The friend was Charles J. Wells, author of
the dramatic poem *Joseph and his Brethren*,
which was published in 1824, when it died almost at once and was recalled to life by a few
words printed by D. G. Rossetti in 1863, and has
since been reprinted for the curious. In Tom
Keats's copy book the sonnet is dated 29 June,
1816. It is included in the volume of 1817.

As late I rambled in the happy fields,
  What time the skylark shakes the tremu-
lous dew
From his lush clover covert; — when anew
Adventurous knights take up their dinted
shields:
I saw the sweetest flower wild nature yields,
  A fresh-blown musk-rose; 't was the first
that threw
    Its sweets upon the summer: graceful it
grew
As is the wand that Queen Titania wields.
And, as I feasted on its fragrancy,
  I thought the garden-rose it far excell'd:
But when, O Wells ! thy roses came to me,
  My sense with their deliciousness was
spell'd:
Soft voices had they, that with tender plea
  Whisper'd of peace, and truth, and
friendliness unquell'd.

SONNET

First printed by Lord Houghton in the *Life,
Letters and Literary Remains*, with the date
1816.

OH ! how I love, on a fair summer's eve,
  When streams of light pour down the
golden west,
  And on the balmy zephyrs tranquil rest
The silver clouds, far — far away to leave
All meaner thoughts, and take a sweet re-
prieve
  From little cares; to find, with easy quest,
  A fragrant wild, with Nature's beauty
drest,
And there into delight my soul deceive.
There warm my breast with patriotic lore,
  Musing on Milton's fate — on Sydney's
bier —
    Till their stern forms before my mind
arise:
Perhaps on wings of Poesy upsoar,
  Full often dropping a delicious tear,
    When some melodious sorrow spells
mine eyes.

'I STOOD TIPTOE UPON A LITTLE HILL'

'Places of nestling green, for poets made.'
LEIGH HUNT, *The Story of Rimini.*

Leigh Hunt, in *Lord Byron and Some of His Contemporaries*, says that 'this poem was suggested to Keats by a delightful summer's day as he stood beside the gate that leads from the Battery on Hampstead Heath into a field by Caen Wood;' but it is not needful for one to put himself into the same geographical position. It is more to the point to remember that when Keats wrote the lines which here follow he was living in the Vale of Health in Hampstead, happy in the association of Hunt and kindred spirits, and trembling with the consciousness of his own poetic power. He had not yet essayed a long flight, as in *Endymion;* but these lines indeed were written as a prelude to a poem which he was devising, which should narrate the loves of Diana, and it will be seen how, with circling flight, he draws nearer and nearer to his theme; but after all, his song ends with a half agitated and passionate speculation over his own poetic birth. The date of the poem, which is the first after the dedication, in the 1817 volume, was presumably in the summer of 1816, for Keats appears to have written promptly under the stimulus of momentary experience.

I STOOD tiptoe upon a little hill,
The air was cooling, and so very still
That the sweet buds which with a modest
   pride
Pull droopingly, in slanting curve aside,
Their scantly-leaved and finely tapering
   stems,
Had not yet lost those starry diadems
Caught from the early sobbing of the morn.
The clouds were pure and white as flocks
   new shorn,
And fresh from the clear brook; sweetly
   they slept
On the blue fields of heaven, and then there
   crept   10
A little noiseless noise among the leaves,
Born of the very sigh that silence heaves:
For not the faintest motion could be seen

Of all the shades that slanted o'er the green.
There was wide wand'ring for the greedi-
   est eye
To peer about upon variety;
Far round the horizon's crystal air to skim,
And trace the dwindled edgings of its brim;
To picture out the quaint and curious
   bending
Of a fresh woodland alley, never-ending; 20
Or by the bowery clefts, and leafy shelves,
Guess where the jaunty streams refresh
   themselves.
I gazed awhile, and felt as light and free
As though the fanning wings of Mercury
Had played upon my heels: I was light-
   hearted,
And many pleasures to my vision started;
So I straightway began to pluck a posey
Of luxuries bright, milky, soft, and rosy.

A bush of May flowers with the bees
   about them;
Ah, sure no tasteful nook could be without
   them;   30
And let a lush laburnum oversweep them,
And let long grass grow round the roots
   to keep them
Moist, cool, and green; and shade the vio-
   lets,
That they may bind the moss in leafy nets.

A filbert hedge with wild briar over-
   twined,
And clumps of woodbine taking the soft
   wind
Upon their summer thrones; there too
   should be
The frequent chequer of a youngling tree,
That with a score of light green brethren
   shoots
From the quaint mossiness of aged roots: 40
Round which is heard a spring-head of
   clear waters
Babbling so wildly of its lovely daughters
The spreading blue-bells: it may haply
   mourn
That such fair clusters should be rudely
   torn

From their fresh beds, and scattered
thoughtlessly
By infant hands, left on the path to die.

Open afresh your round of starry folds,
Ye ardent marigolds!
Dry up the moisture from your golden lids,
For great Apollo bids   50
That in these days your praises should be
sung
On many harps, which he has lately strung;
And when again your dewiness he kisses,
Tell him, I have you in my world of blisses:
So haply when I rove in some far vale,
His mighty voice may come upon the gale.

Here are sweet peas, on tiptoe for a
flight:
With wings of gentle flush o'er delicate
white,
And taper fingers catching at all things,
To bind them all about with tiny rings.   60

Linger awhile upon some bending planks
That lean against a streamlet's rushy banks,
And watch intently Nature's gentle doings:
They will be found softer than ring-dove's
cooings.
How silent comes the water round that bend;
Not the minutest whisper does it send
To the o'erhanging sallows: blades of grass
Slowly across the chequer'd shadows pass.
Why, you might read two sonnets, ere they
reach
To where the hurrying freshnesses aye
preach   70
A natural sermon o'er their pebbly beds;
Where swarms of minnows show their little
heads,
Staying their wavy bodies 'gainst the
streams,
To taste the luxury of sunny beams
Temper'd with coolness.   How they ever
wrestle
With their own sweet delight, and ever
nestle
Their silver bellies on the pebbly sand.
If you but scantily hold out the hand,

That very instant not one will remain;
But turn your eye, and they are there again.
The ripples seem right glad to reach those
cresses,   81
And cool themselves among the em'rald
tresses;
The while they cool themselves, they fresh-
ness give,
And moisture, that the bowery green may
live:
So keeping up an interchange of favours,
Like good men in the truth of their be-
haviours.
Sometimes goldfinches one by one will drop
From low-hung branches; little space they
stop;
But sip, and twitter, and their feathers
sleek;
Then off at once, as in a wanton freak: 90
Or perhaps, to show their black, and golden
wings,
Pausing upon their yellow flutterings.
Were I in such a place, I sure should pray
That nought less sweet, might call my
thoughts away,
Than the soft rustle of a maiden's gown
Fanning away the dandelion's down;
Than the light music of her nimble toes
Patting against the sorrel as she goes.
How she would start, and blush, thus to be
caught
Playing in all her innocence of thought.   100
O let me lead her gently o'er the brook,
Watch her half-smiling lips, and downward
look;
O let me for one moment touch her wrist;
Let me one moment to her breathing list;
And as she leaves me, may she often turn
Her fair eyes looking through her locks au-
burne.
What next?   A tuft of evening primroses,
O'er which the mind may hover till it dozes;
O'er which it well might take a pleasant
sleep,
But that 't is ever startled by the leap   110
Of buds into ripe flowers; or by the flitting
Of diverse moths, that aye their rest are
quitting;

Or by the moon lifting her silver rim
Above a cloud, and with a gradual swim
Coming into the blue with all her light.
O Maker of sweet poets, dear delight
Of this fair world, and all its gentle livers;
Spangler of clouds, halo of crystal rivers,
Mingler with leaves, and dew and tumbling
    streams,
Closer of lovely eyes to lovely dreams, 120
Lover of loneliness, and wandering,
Of upcast eye, and tender pondering !
Thee must I praise above all other glo-
    ries
That smile us on to tell delightful stories.
For what has made the sage or poet write
But the fair paradise of Nature's light ?
In the calm grandeur of a sober line,
We see the waving of the mountain pine;
And when a tale is beautifully staid,
We feel the safety of a hawthorn glade: 130
When it is moving on luxurious wings,
The soul is lost in pleasant smotherings:
Fair dewy roses brush against our faces,
And flowering laurels spring from diamond
    vases;
O'erhead we see the jasmine and sweet-
    briar,
And bloomy grapes laughing from green
    attire;
While at our feet, the voice of crystal
    bubbles
Charms us at once away from all our trou-
    bles:
So that we feel uplifted from the world,
Walking upon the white clouds wreath'd
    and curl'd.   140
So felt he, who first told, how Psyche
    went
On the smooth wind to realms of wonder-
    ment;
What Psyche felt, and Love, when their
    full lips
First touch'd; what amorous and fondling
    nips
They gave each other's cheeks; with all
    their sighs,
And how they kist each other's tremulous
    eyes:

The silver lamp, — the ravishment, — the
    wonder —
The darkness, — loneliness, — the fearful
    thunder;
Their woes gone by, and both to heaven up-
    flown,   149
To bow for gratitude before Jove's throne.
So did he feel, who pull'd the boughs
    aside,
That we might look into a forest wide,
To catch a glimpse of Fauns, and Dryades
Coming with softest rustle through the
    trees;
And garlands woven of flowers wild, and
    sweet,
Upheld on ivory wrists, or sporting feet:
Telling us how fair, trembling Syrinx fled
Arcadian Pan, with such a fearful dread.
Poor Nymph, — poor Pan, — how he did
    weep to find
Nought but a lovely sighing of the wind 160
Along the reedy stream; a half-heard strain,
Full of sweet desolation — balmy pain.

What first inspired a bard of old to sing
Narcissus pining o'er the untainted spring ?
In some delicious ramble, he had found
A little space, with boughs all woven round;
And in the midst of all, a clearer pool
Than e'er reflected in its pleasant cool,
The blue sky here, and there, serenely peep-
    ing
Through tendril wreaths fantastically creep-
    ing.   170
And on the bank a lonely flower he spied,
A meek and forlorn flower, with naught of
    pride,
Drooping its beauty o'er the watery clear-
    ness,
To woo its own sad image into nearness:
Deaf to light Zephyrus it would not move;
But still would seem to droop, to pine, to
    love.
So while the Poet stood in this sweet spot,
Some fainter gleamings o'er his fancy
    shot;
Nor was it long ere he had told the tale
Of young Narcissus, and sad Echo's bale. 180

Where had he been, from whose warm
   head outflew
That sweetest of all songs, that ever new,
That aye refreshing, pure deliciousness,
Coming ever to bless
The wanderer by moonlight? to him
   bringing
Shapes from the invisible world, unearthly
   singing
From out the middle air, from flowery
   nests,
And from the pillowy silkiness that rests
Full in the speculation of the stars.   189
Ah! surely he had burst our mortal bars;
Into some wond'rous region he had gone,
To search for thee, divine Endymion!

He was a Poet, sure a lover too,
Who stood on Latmus' top, what time
   there blew
Soft breezes from the myrtle vale below;
And brought in faintness solemn, sweet,
   and slow
A hymn from Dian's temple; while up-
   swelling,
The incense went to her own starry dwell-
   ing.
But though her face was clear as infant's
   eyes,   199
Though she stood smiling o'er the sacrifice,
The Poet wept at her so piteous fate,
Wept that such beauty should be deso-
   late:
So in fine wrath some golden sounds he won,
And gave meek Cynthia her Endymion.

Queen of the wide air; thou most lovely
   queen
Of all the brightness that mine eyes have
   seen!
As thou exceedest all things in thy shine,
So every tale, does this sweet tale of thine.
O for three words of honey, that I might
Tell but one wonder of thy bridal night!   210

Where distant ships do seem to show
   their keels,
Phœbus awhile delay'd his mighty wheels,

And turn'd to smile upon thy bashful eyes,
Ere he his unseen pomp would solem-
   nize.
The evening weather was so bright, and
   clear,
That men of health were of unusual cheer;
Stepping like Homer at the trumpet's
   call,
Or young Apollo on the pedestal:
And lovely women were as fair and warm,
As Venus looking sideways in alarm.   220
The breezes were ethereal, and pure,
And crept through half closed lattices to
   cure
The languid sick; it cool'd their fever'd
   sleep,
And soothed them into slumbers full and
   deep.
Soon they awoke clear-eyed: nor burnt
   with thirsting,
Nor with hot fingers, nor with temples
   bursting:
And springing up, they met the wond'ring
   sight
Of their dear friends, nigh foolish with
   delight;
Who feel their arms, and breasts, and kiss
   and stare,
And on their placid foreheads part the
   hair.   230
Young men and maidens at each other
   gaz'd,
With hands held back, and motionless,
   amaz'd
To see the brightness in each other's eyes;
And so they stood, fill'd with a sweet sur-
   prise,
Until their tongues were loos'd in poesy.
Therefore no lover did of anguish die:
But the soft numbers, in that moment
   spoken,
Made silken ties, that never may be broken.
Cynthia! I cannot tell the greater blisses
That follow'd thine, and thy dear shep-
   herd's kisses: 240
Was there a Poet born? — But now no
   more,
My wand'ring spirit must no further soar.

SLEEP AND POETRY

The last poem in the 1817 volume. Charles Cowden Clarke relates that 'it was in the library of Hunt's cottage, where an extempore bed had been put up for Keats on the sofa, that he composed the framework and many lines of this poem, the last sixty or seventy being an inventory of the art garniture of the room.' It may be assigned to the summer of 1816.

> As I lay in my bed slepe full unmete
> Was unto me, but why that I ne might
> Rest I ne wist, for there n' as erthly wight
> (As I suppose) had more of hertis ese
> Than I, for I n' ad sicknesse nor disese.
>   CHAUCER.

WHAT is more gentle than a wind in summer?
What is more soothing than the pretty hummer
That stays one moment in an open flower,
And buzzes cheerily from bower to bower?
What is more tranquil than a musk-rose blowing
In a green island, far from all men's knowing?
More healthful than the leafiness of dales?
More secret than a nest of nightingales?
More serene than Cordelia's countenance?
More full of visions than a high romance?
What, but thee, Sleep? Soft closer of our eyes!   11
Low murmurer of tender lullabies!
Light hoverer around our happy pillows!
Wreather of poppy buds, and weeping willows!
Silent entangler of a beauty's tresses!
Most happy listener! when the morning blesses
Thee for enlivening all the cheerful eyes
That glance so brightly at the new sunrise.

But what is higher beyond thought than thee?
Fresher than berries of a mountain-tree?
More strange, more beautiful, more smooth, more regal,   21

Than wings of swans, than doves, than dim-seen eagle?
What is it? And to what shall I compare it?
It has a glory, and nought else can share it:
The thought thereof is awful, sweet, and holy,
Chasing away all worldliness and folly:
Coming sometimes like fearful claps of thunder,
Or the low rumblings earth's regions under;
And sometimes like a gentle whispering   29
Of all the secrets of some wond'rous thing
That breathes about us in the vacant air;
So that we look around with prying stare,
Perhaps to see shapes of light, aerial limning;
And catch soft floatings from a faint-heard hymning;
To see the laurel wreath, on high suspended,
That is to crown our name when life is ended.
Sometimes it gives a glory to the voice,
And from the heart up-springs, rejoice! rejoice!
Sounds which will reach the Framer of all things,
And die away in ardent mutterings.   40

No one who once the glorious sun has seen,
And all the clouds, and felt his bosom clean
For his great Maker's presence, but must know
What 't is I mean, and feel his being glow:
Therefore no insult will I give his spirit,
By telling what he sees from native merit.

O Poesy! for thee I hold my pen,
That am not yet a glorious denizen
Of thy wide heaven — should I rather kneel
Upon some mountain-top until I feel   50
A growing splendour round about me hung,
And echo back the voice of thine own tongue?
O Poesy! for thee I grasp my pen,
That am not yet a glorious denizen

Of thy wide heaven; yet, to my ardent
    prayer,
Yield from thy sanctuary some clear air,
Smoothed for intoxication by the breath
Of flowering bays, that I may die a death
Of luxury, and my young spirit follow
The morning sunbeams to the great Apollo
Like a fresh sacrifice; or, if I can bear   61
The o'erwhelming sweets, 't will bring to
    me the fair
Visions of all places: a bowery nook
Will be elysium — an eternal book
Whence I may copy many a lovely saying
About the leaves, and flowers — about the
    playing
Of nymphs in woods, and fountains; and
    the shade
Keeping a silence round a sleeping maid;
And many a verse from so strange influence
That we must ever wonder how, and whence
It came. Also imaginings will hover   71
Round my fire-side, and haply there dis-
    cover
Vistas of solemn beauty, where I 'd wander
In happy silence, like the clear Meander
Through its lone vales; and where I found
    a spot
Of awfuller shade, or an enchanted grot,
Or a green hill o'erspread with chequer'd
    dress
Of flowers, and fearful from its loveliness,
Write on my tablets all that was permitted,
All that was for our human senses fitted.
Then the events of this wide world I 'd
    seize   81
Like a strong giant, and my spirit tease
Till at its shoulders it should proudly see
Wings to find out an immortality.

  Stop and consider! life is but a day;
A fragile dewdrop on its perilous way
From a tree's summit; a poor Indian's sleep
While his boat hastens to the monstrous
    steep
Of Montmorenci. Why so sad a moan?
Life is the rose's hope while yet unblown;
The reading of an ever-changing tale;   91
The light uplifting of a maiden's veil;

A pigeon tumbling in clear summer air;
A laughing school-boy, without grief or
    care,
Riding the springy branches of an elm.

  O for ten years, that I may overwhelm
Myself in poesy; so I may do the deed
That my own soul has to itself decreed.
Then I will pass the countries that I see
In long perspective, and continually   100
Taste their pure fountains. First the realm
    I 'll pass
Of Flora, and old Pan: sleep in the grass,
Feed upon apples red, and strawberries,
And choose each pleasure that my fancy
    sees;
Catch the white-handed nymphs in shady
    places,
To woo sweet kisses from averted faces, —
Play with their fingers, touch their shoul-
    ders white
Into a pretty shrinking with a bite
As hard as lips can make it: till agreed,
A lovely tale of human life we 'll read.   110
And one will teach a tame dove how it best
May fan the cool air gently o'er my rest;
Another, bending o'er her nimble tread,
Will set a green robe floating round her
    head,
And still will dance with ever-varied ease,
Smiling upon the flowers and the trees:
Another will entice me on, and on
Through almond blossoms and rich cinna-
    mon;
Till in the bosom of a leafy world
We rest in silence, like two gems upcurl'd
In the recesses of a pearly shell.   121

  And can I ever bid these joys farewell?
Yes, I must pass them for a nobler life,
Where I may find the agonies, the strife
Of human hearts: for lo! I see afar,
O'er-sailing the blue cragginess, a car
And steeds with streamy manes — the
    charioteer
Looks out upon the winds with glorious fear:
And now the numerous tramplings quiver
    lightly

Along a huge cloud's ridge; and now with
    sprightly   130
Wheel downward come they into fresher
    skies,
Tipt round with silver from the sun's bright
    eyes.
Still downward with capacious whirl they
    glide;
And now I see them on a green-hill's side
In breezy rest among the nodding stalks.
The charioteer with wond'rous gesture
    talks
To the trees and mountains; and there soon
    appear
Shapes of delight, of mystery, and fear,
Passing along before a dusky space
Made by some mighty oaks: as they would
    chase   140
Some ever-fleeting music, on they sweep.
Lo! how they murmur, laugh, and smile,
    and weep:
Some with upholden hand and mouth severe;
Some with their faces muffled to the ear
Between their arms; some, clear in youth-
    ful bloom,
Go glad and smilingly athwart the gloom;
Some looking back, and some with upward
    gaze;
Yes, thousands in a thousand different ways
Flit onward — now a lovely wreath of girls
Dancing their sleek hair into tangled curls;
And now broad wings. Most awfully in-
    tent   151
The driver of those steeds is forward bent,
And seems to listen: O that I might know
All that he writes with such a hurrying
    glow.

The visions all are fled — the car is fled
Into the light of heaven, and in their stead
A sense of real things comes doubly strong,
And, like a muddy stream, would bear
    along
My soul to nothingness: but I will strive
Against all doubtings, and will keep alive
The thought of that same chariot, and the
    strange   161
Journey it went.

Is there so small a range
In the present strength of manhood, that
    the high
Imagination cannot freely fly
As she was wont of old? prepare her
    steeds,
Paw up against the light, and do strange
    deeds
Upon the clouds? Has she not shewn us
    all?
From the clear space of ether, to the small
Breath of new buds unfolding? From the
    meaning
Of Jove's large eyebrow, to the tender
    greening   170
Of April meadows? here her altar shone,
E'en in this isle; and who could paragon
The fervid choir that lifted up a noise
Of harmony, to where it aye will poise
Its mighty self of convoluting sound,
Huge as a planet, and like that roll round,
Eternally around a dizzy void?
Ay, in those days the Muses were nigh
    cloy'd
With honours; nor had any other care
Than to sing out and soothe their wavy
    hair.   180

Could all this be forgotten? Yes, a
    schism
Nurtured by foppery and barbarism,
Made great Apollo blush for this his land.
Men were thought wise who could not un-
    derstand
His glories: with a puling infant's force
They sway'd about upon a rocking-horse,
And thought it Pegasus. Ah, dismal-soul'd!
The winds of heaven blew, the ocean
    roll'd
Its gathering waves — ye felt it not. The
    blue
Bared its eternal bosom, and the dew   190
Of summer nights collected still to make
The morning precious: beauty was awake!
Why were ye not awake? But ye were
    dead
To things ye knew not of, — were closely
    wed

To musty laws lined out with wretched
    rule
And compass vile: so that ye taught a
    school
Of dolts to smooth, inlay, and clip, and
    fit,
Till, like the certain wands of Jacob's wit,
Their verses tallied. Easy was the task:
A thousand handicraftsmen wore the mask
Of Poesy. Ill-fated, impious race !   201
That blasphem'd the bright Lyrist to his
    face,
And did not know it, — no, they went about,
Holding a poor, decrepid standard out,
Mark'd with most flimsy mottoes, and in
    large
The name of one Boileau !

                O ye whose charge
It is to hover round our pleasant hills !
Whose congregated majesty so fills
My boundly reverence, that I cannot trace
Your hallowed names, in this unholy place,
So near those common folk; did not their
    shames   211
Affright you ?   Did our old lamenting
    Thames
Delight you ? did ye never cluster round
Delicious Avon, with a mournful sound,
And weep ? Or did ye wholly bid adieu
To regions where no more the laurel grew ?
Or did ye stay to give a welcoming
To some lone spirits who could proudly
    sing
Their youth away, and die ? 'T was even
    so: 219
But let me think away those times of woe:
Now 't is a fairer season; ye have breathed
Rich benedictions o'er us; ye have wreathed
Fresh garlands: for sweet music has been
    heard
In many places; — some has been upstirr'd
From out its crystal dwelling in a lake,
By a swan's ebon bill; from a thick brake,
Nested and quiet in a valley mild,
Bubbles a pipe; fine sounds are floating
    wild
About the earth: happy are ye and glad.

These things are, doubtless; yet in truth
    we 've had   230
Strange thunders from the potency of song;
Mingled indeed with what is sweet and
    strong
From majesty: but in clear truth the themes
Are ugly clubs, the Poets Polyphemes
Disturbing the grand sea. A drainless
    shower
Of light is Poesy; 't is the supreme of
    power;
'T is might half slumb'ring on its own right
    arm.
The very archings of her eyelids charm
A thousand willing agents to obey,
And still she governs with the mildest sway:
But strength alone though of the Muses
    born   241
Is like a fallen angel: trees uptorn,
Darkness, and worms, and shrouds, and
    sepulchres
Delight it; for it feeds upon the burrs
And thorns of life; forgetting the great
    end
Of Poesy, that it should be a friend
To soothe the cares, and lift the thoughts
    of man.

    Yet I rejoice: a myrtle fairer than   248
E'er grew in Paphos, from the bitter weeds
Lifts its sweet head into the air, and feeds
A silent space with ever sprouting green.
All tenderest birds there find a pleasant
    screen,
Creep through the shade with jaunty flut-
    tering,
Nibble the little cuppèd flowers and sing.
Then let us clear away the choking thorns
From round its gentle stem; let the young
    fawns,
Yeanèd in after-times, when we are flown,
Find a fresh sward beneath it, overgrown
With simple flowers: let there nothing be
More boisterous than a lover's bended knee;
Nought more ungentle than the placid look
Of one who leans upon a closèd book;   262
Nought more untranquil than the grassy
    slopes

Between two hills. All hail, delightful
    hopes !
As she was wont, th' imagination
Into most lovely labyrinths will be gone,
And they shall be accounted poet kings
Who simply tell the most heart - easing
    things.
O may these joys be ripe before I die.

Will not some say that I presumptu-
    ously   270
Have spoken ? that from hastening disgrace
'T were better far to hide my foolish face ?
That whining boyhood should with rever-
    ence bow
Ere the dread thunderbolt could reach ?
    How !
If I do hide myself, it sure shall be
In the very fane, the light of Poesy :
If I do fall, at least I will be laid
Beneath the silence of a poplar shade ;
And over me the grass shall be smooth
    shaven ;
And there shall be a kind memorial
    graven.   280
But off, Despondence ! miserable bane !
They should not know thee, who athirst to
    gain
A noble end, are thirsty every hour.
What though I am not wealthy in the dower
Of spanning wisdom ; though I do not know
The shiftings of the mighty winds that
    blow
Hither and thither all the changing
    thoughts
Of man : though no great minist'ring rea-
    son sorts
Out the dark mysteries of human souls
To clear conceiving : yet there ever
    rolls   290
A vast idea before me, and I glean
Therefrom my liberty ; thence too I 've
    seen
The end and aim of Poesy. 'T is clear
As anything most true ; as that the year
Is made of the four seasons — manifest
As a large cross, some old cathedral's
    crest,

Lifted to the white clouds. Therefore
    should I
Be but the essence of deformity,
A coward, did my very eyelids wink
At speaking out what I have dared to
    think.   300
Ah ! rather let me like a madman run
Over some precipice ; let the hot sun
Melt my Dædalian wings, and drive me
    down
Convuls'd and headlong ! Stay ! an in-
    ward frown
Of conscience bids me be more calm awhile.
An ocean dim, sprinkled with many an
    isle,
Spreads awfully before me. How much
    toil !
How many days ! what desperate turmoil !
Ere I can have explored its widenesses.
Ah, what a task ! upon my bended
    knees,   310
I could unsay those — no, impossible !
Impossible !

            For sweet relief I 'll dwell
On humbler thoughts, and let this strange
    assay
Begun in gentleness die so away.
E'en now all tumult from my bosom fades :
I turn full-hearted to the friendly aids
That smooth the path of honour ; brother-
    hood,
And friendliness the nurse of mutual good.
The hearty grasp that sends a pleasant
    sonnet
Into the brain ere one can think upon it; 320
The silence when some rhymes are coming
    out ;
And when they 're come, the very pleasant
    rout:
The message certain to be done to-morrow.
'T is perhaps as well that it should be to
    borrow
Some precious book from out its snug
    retreat,
To cluster round it when we next shall
    meet.
Scarce can I scribble on ; for lovely airs

Are fluttering round the room like doves in
 pairs ;
Many delights of that glad day recalling,
When first my senses caught their tender
 falling.   330
And with these airs come forms of elegance
Stooping their shoulders o'er a horse's
 prance,
Careless, and grand — fingers soft and
 round
Parting luxuriant curls ; — and the swift
 bound
Of Bacchus from his chariot, when his eye
Made Ariadne's cheek look blushingly.
Thus I remember all the pleasant flow
Of words at opening a portfolio.

 Things such as these are ever harbingers
To trains of peaceful images : the stirs 340
Of a swan's neck unseen among the rushes :
A linnet starting all about the bushes :
A butterfly, with golden wings broad
 parted,
Nestling a rose, convuls'd as though it
 smarted
With over pleasure — many, many more,
Might I indulge at large in all my store
Of luxuries : yet I must not forget
Sleep, quiet with his poppy coronet :
For what there may be worthy in these
 rhymes
I partly owe to him : and thus, the
 chimes   350
Of friendly voices had just given place
To as sweet a silence, when I 'gan retrace
The pleasant day, upon a couch at ease.
It was a poet's house who keeps the keys
Of pleasure's temple. Round about were
 hung
The glorious features of the bards who
 sung
In other ages — cold and sacred busts
Smiled at each other. Happy he who trusts
To clear Futurity his darling fame !
Then there were fauns and satyrs taking
 aim   360
At swelling apples with a frisky leap
And reaching fingers, 'mid a luscious heap

Of vine leaves. Then there rose to view a
 fane
Of liny marble, and thereto a train
Of nymphs approaching fairly o'er the
 sward :
One, loveliest, holding her white hand
 toward
The dazzling sunrise : two sisters sweet
Bending their graceful figures till they meet
Over the trippings of a little child :
And some are hearing, eagerly, the wild 370
Thrilling liquidity of dewy piping.
See, in another picture, nymphs are wiping
Cherishingly Diana's timorous limbs ; —
A fold of lawny mantle dabbling swims
At the bath's edge, and keeps a gentle
 motion
With the subsiding crystal : as when ocean
Heaves calmly its broad swelling smooth-
 iness o'er
Its rocky marge, and balances once more
The patient weeds ; that now unshent by
 foam
Feel all about their undulating home. 380

Sappho's meek head was there half smiling
 down
At nothing ; just as though the earnest
 frown
Of over-thinking had that moment gone
From off her brow, and left her all alone.

 Great Alfred's too, with anxious, pitying
 eyes,
As if he always listened to the sighs
Of the goaded world ; and Kosciusko's,
 worn
By horrid suffrance — mightily forlorn.

 Petrarch, outstepping from the shady
 green,
Starts at the sight of Laura ; nor can
 wean   390
His eyes from her sweet face. Most happy
 they !
For over them was seen a free display
Of outspread wings, and from between them
 shone

The face of Poesy : from off her throne
She overlook'd things that I scarce could
    tell.
The very sense of where I was might well
Keep Sleep aloof : but more than that there
    came
Thought after thought to nourish up the
    flame
Within my breast ; so that the morning
    light
Surprised me even from a sleepless
    night ;   400
And up I rose refresh'd, and glad, and gay,
Resolving to begin that very day
These lines ; and howsoever they be done,
I leave them as a father does his son.

EPISTLE TO MY BROTHER
GEORGE

Written according to George Keats at Margate, August, 1816, and included in the 1817
volume.

FULL many a dreary hour have I past,
My brain bewilder'd, and my mind o'ercast
With heaviness ; in seasons when I've
    thought
No sphery strains by me could e'er be
    caught
From the blue dome, though I to dimness
    gaze
On the far depth where sheeted lightning
    plays ;
Or, on the wavy grass outstretch'd supinely,
Pry 'mong the stars, to strive to think di-
    vinely :
That I should never hear Apollo's song,
Though feathery clouds were floating all
    along   10
The purple west, and, two bright streaks
    between,
The golden lyre itself were dimly seen :
That the still murmur of the honey bee
Would never teach a rural song to me :
That the bright glance from beauty's eye-
    lids slanting
Would never make a lay of mine enchanting,

Or warm my breast with ardour to unfold
Some tale of love and arms in time of old.

But there are times, when those that love
    the bay,
Fly from all sorrowing far, far away ;   20
A sudden glow comes on them, nought
    they see
In water, earth, or air, but poesy.
It has been said, dear George, and true I
    hold it,
(For knightly Spenser to Libertas told it,)
That when a Poet is in such a trance,
In air he sees white coursers paw and
    prance,
Bestridden of gay knights, in gay apparel,
Who at each other tilt in playful quarrel ;
And what we, ignorantly, sheet-lightning
    call,
Is the swift opening of their wide portal, 30
When the bright warder blows his trumpet
    clear,
Whose tones reach nought on earth but
    Poet's ear.
When these enchanted portals open wide,
And through the light the horsemen swiftly
    glide,
The Poet's eye can reach those golden halls,
And view the glory of their festivals :
Their ladies fair, that in the distance seem
Fit for the silv'ring of a seraph's dream ;
Their rich brimm'd goblets, that incessant
    run
Like the bright spots that move about the
    sun ;   40
And, when upheld, the wine from each
    bright jar
Pours with the lustre of a falling star.
Yet further off are dimly seen their bowers,
Of which no mortal eye can reach the flow-
    ers ;
And 't is right just, for well Apollo knows
'T would make the Poet quarrel with the
    rose.
All that's reveal'd from that far seat of
    blisses,
Is, the clear fountains' interchanging kisses,
As gracefully descending, light and thin,

Like silver streaks across a dolphin's fin, 50
When he upswimmeth from the coral caves,
And sports with half his tail above the
 waves.

 These wonders strange he sees, and many
  more,
Whose head is pregnant with poetic lore.
Should he upon an evening ramble fare
With forehead to the soothing breezes bare,
Would he naught see but the dark, silent
 blue,
With all its diamonds trembling through
 and through ?
Or the coy moon, when in the waviness 59
Of whitest clouds she does her beauty dress,
And staidly paces higher up, and higher,
Like a sweet nun in holiday attire ?
Ah, yes ! much more would start into his
 sight —
The revelries, and mysteries of night:
And should I ever see them, I will tell you
Such tales as needs must with amazement
 spell you.

 These are the living pleasures of the
  bard:
But richer far posterity's award.
What does he murmur with his latest breath,
While his proud eye looks through the film
 of death ?   70
'What though I leave this dull and earthly
 mould,
Yet shall my spirit lofty converse hold
With after times. — The patriot shall feel
My stern alarum, and unsheath his steel;
Or in the senate thunder out my numbers,
To startle princes from their easy slumbers.
The sage will mingle with each moral theme
My happy thoughts sententious; he will
 teem
With lofty periods when my verses fire
 him,
And then I 'll stoop from heaven to inspire
 him.   80
Lays have I left of such a dear delight
That maids will sing them on their bridal
 night.

Gay villagers, upon a morn of May,
When they have tired their gentle limbs
 with play,
And form'd a snowy circle on the grass,
And plac'd in midst of all that lovely lass
Who chosen is their queen, — with her fine
 head
Crownèd with flowers purple, white, and ,
 red:
For there the lily, and the musk-rose, sigh-
 ing,   89
Are emblems true of hapless lovers dying:
Between her breasts, that never yet felt
 trouble,
A bunch of violets full blown, and double,
Serenely sleep: — she from a casket takes
A little book, — and then a joy awakes
About each youthful heart, — with stifled
 cries,
And rubbing of white hands, and sparkling
 eyes: .
For she 's to read a tale of hopes and fears;
One that I foster'd in my youthful years:
The pearls, that on each glist'ning circlet
 sleep,
Gush ever and anon with silent creep, 100
Lured by the innocent dimples.   To sweet
 rest
Shall the dear babe, upon its mother's
 breast,
Be lull'd with songs of mine.   Fair world,
 adieu !
Thy dales and hills are fading from my
 view:
Swiftly I mount, upon wide-spreading
 pinions,
Far from the narrow bounds of thy do-
 minions.
Full joy I feel, while thus I cleave the air,
That my soft verse will charm thy daugh-
 ters fair,
And warm thy sons !' Ah, my dear friend
 and brother,   109
Could I, at once, my mad ambition smother,
For tasting joys like these, sure I should be
Happier, and dearer to society.
At times, 't is true, I 've felt relief from
 pain

When some bright thought has darted
    through my brain:
Through all that day I've felt a greater
    pleasure
Than if I'd brought to light a hidden trea-
    sure.
As to my sonnets, though none else should
    heed them,
I feel delighted, still, that you should read
    them.
Of late, too, I have had much calm enjoy-
    ment,
Stretch'd on the grass at my best lov'd em-
    ployment   120
Of scribbling lines for you. These things
    I thought
While, in my face, the freshest breeze I
    caught.
E'en now I'm pillow'd on a bed of flowers
That crowns a lofty cliff, which proudly
    towers
Above the ocean waves. The stalks and
    blades
Chequer my tablet with their quivering
    shades.
On one side is a field of drooping oats,
Through which the poppies show their
    scarlet coats;   128
So pert and useless, that they bring to mind
The scarlet coats that pester human-kind.
And on the other side, outspread, is seen
Ocean's blue mantle, streak'd with purple,
    and green;
Now 't is I see a canvass'd ship, and now
Mark the bright silver curling round her
    prow.
I see the lark down-dropping to his nest,
And the broad-winged sea-gull never at rest;
For when no more he spreads his feathers
    free,
His breast is dancing on the restless sea.
Now I direct my eyes into the west,
Which at this moment is in sunbeams
    drest: 140
Why westward turn? 'T was but to say
    adieu!
'T was but to kiss my hand, dear George,
    to you!

TO MY BROTHER GEORGE

The first in the group of sonnets in the 1817
volume. A transcript by George Keats bears
the date 'Margate, August, 1816.'

MANY the wonders I this day have seen:
    The sun, when first he kist away the tears
    That fill'd the eyes of morn; — the lau-
        rell'd peers
Who from the feathery gold of evening
    lean; —
The ocean with its vastness, its blue green,
    Its ships, its rocks, its caves, its hopes,
        its fears, —
    Its voice mysterious, which whoso hears
Must think on what will be, and what has
    been.
E'en now, dear George, while this for you I
    write,
    Cynthia is from her silken curtains peep-
        ing
So scantly, that it seems her bridal night,
    And she her half-discover'd revels keep-
        ing.
But what, without the social thought of
    thee,
Would be the wonders of the sky and sea?

TO ——

There is no clue to the identity of the person addressed, and no date is affixed. It was
published in the 1817 volume, and there follows
the one addressed to his brother George.

HAD I a man's fair form, then might my
    sighs
    Be echoed swiftly through that ivory
        shell
    Thine ear, and find thy gentle heart; so
        well
Would passion arm me for the enterprise:
But ah! I am no knight whose foeman dies;
    No cuirass glistens on my bosom's swell;
    I am no happy shepherd of the dell
Whose lips have trembled with a maiden's
    eyes.

Yet must I dote upon thee, — call thee
    sweet,
  Sweeter by far than Hybla's honied roses
  When steep'd in dew rich to intoxica-
    tion.
Ah! I will taste that dew, for me 't is meet,
  And when the moon her pallid face dis-
    closes,
    I 'll gather some by spells, and incan-
      tation.

SPECIMEN OF AN INDUCTION
TO A POEM

  This poem was published in the 1817 volume
where it immediately precedes *Calidore*. Leigh
Hunt, when reviewing the volume on its appearance, speaks of the two poems as connected,
and in Tom Keats's copybook they are written
continuously. The same copy contains a memorandum 'marked by Leigh Hunt — 1816.'

Lo! I must tell a tale of chivalry;
For large white plumes are dancing in mine
    eye.
Not like the formal crest of latter days:
But bending in a thousand graceful ways;
So graceful, that it seems no mortal hand,
Or e'en the touch of Archimago's wand,
Could charm them into such an attitude.
We must think rather, that in playful mood,
Some mountain breeze had turned its chief
    delight,
To show this wonder of its gentle might. 10
Lo! I must tell a tale of chivalry;
For while I muse, the lance points slant-
    ingly
Athwart the morning air; some lady sweet,
Who cannot feel for cold her tender feet,
From the worn top of some old battlement
Hails it with tears, her stout defender sent:
And from her own pure self no joy dissem-
    bling,
Wraps round her ample robe with happy
    trembling.
Sometimes, when the good Knight his rest
    would take,
It is reflected, clearly, in a lake,   20

With the young ashen boughs, 'gainst
    which it rests,
And th' half-seen mossiness of linnets'
    nests.
Ah! shall I ever tell its cruelty,
When the fire flashes from a warrior's eye,
And his tremendous hand is grasping it,
And his dark brow for very wrath is knit?
Or when his spirit, with more calm intent,
Leaps to the honours of a tournament,
And makes the gazers round about the
    ring
Stare at the grandeur of the balancing? 30
No, no! this is far off: — then how shall I
Revive the dying tones of minstrelsy,
Which linger yet about long gothic arches,
In dark green ivy, and among wild larches?
How sing the splendour of the revelries,
When butts of wine are drunk off to the
    lees?
And that bright lance, against the fretted
    wall,
Beneath the shade of stately banneral,
Is slung with shining cuirass, sword, and
    shield?
Where ye may see a spur in bloody field. 40
Light-footed damsels move with gentle
    paces
Round the wide hall, and show their happy
    faces;
Or stand in courtly talk by fives and sevens:
Like those fair stars that twinkle in the
    heavens.
Yet must I tell a tale of chivalry:
Or wherefore comes that knight so proudly
    by?
Wherefore more proudly does the gentle
    knight,
Rein in the swelling of his ample might?

Spenser! thy brows are archèd, open, kind,
And come like a clear sunrise to my
    mind;   50
And always does my heart with pleasure
    dance,
When I think on thy noble countenance:
Where never yet was ought more earthly
    seen

Than the pure freshness of thy laurels
     green.
Therefore, great bard, I not so fearfully
Call on thy gentle spirit to hover nigh
My daring steps : or if thy tender care,
Thus startled unaware,
Be jealous that the foot of other wight
Should madly follow that bright path of
     light   60
Trac'd by thy lov'd Libertas; he will
     speak,
And tell thee that my prayer is very meek;
That I will follow with due reverence,
And start with awe at mine own strange
     pretence.
Him thou wilt hear; so I will rest in hope
To see wide plains, fair trees, and lawny
     slope:
The morn, the eve, the light, the shade, the
     flowers;
Clear streams, smooth lakes, and overlook-
     ing towers.

CALIDORE

A FRAGMENT

YOUNG Calidore is paddling o'er the lake ;
His healthful spirit eager and awake
To feel the beauty of a silent eve,
Which seem'd full loth this happy world to
     leave;
The light dwelt o'er the scene so linger-
     ingly.
He bares his forehead to the cool blue sky,
And smiles at the far clearness all around,
Until his heart is well nigh over wound,
And turns for calmness to the pleasant
     green
Of easy slopes, and shadowy trees that
     lean   10
So elegantly o'er the waters' brim
And show their blossoms trim.
Scarce can his clear and nimble eyesight
     follow
The freaks and dartings of the black-wing'd
     swallow,
Delighting much, to see it half at rest,

Dip so refreshingly its wings, and breast
'Gainst the smooth surface, and to mark
     anon,
The widening circles into nothing gone.

And now the sharp keel of his little boat
Comes up with ripple, and with easy
     float,   20
And glides into a bed of water-lilies:
Broad-leav'd are they, and their white can-
     opies
Are upward turn'd to catch the heavens'
     dew.
Near to a little island's point they grew;
Whence Calidore might have the goodliest
     view
Of this sweet spot of earth.   The bowery
     shore
Went off in gentle windings to the hoar
And light blue mountains : but no breath-
     ing man
With a warm heart, and eye prepared to scan
Nature's clear beauty, could pass lightly
     by   30
Objects that look'd out so invitingly
On either side.   These, gentle Calidore
Greeted, as he had known them long before.

The sidelong view of swelling leafiness,
Which the glad setting sun in gold doth
     dress;
Whence, ever and anon, the jay outsprings,
And scales upon the beauty of its wings.

The lonely turret, shatter'd, and outworn,
Stands venerably proud; too proud to
     mourn
Its long lost grandeur : fir-trees grow
     around,   40
Aye dropping their hard fruit upon the
     ground.

The little chapel, with the cross above,
Upholding wreaths of ivy; the white dove,
That on the windows spreads his feathers
     light,
And seems from purple clouds to wing its
     flight.

Green tufted islands casting their soft
    shades
Across the lake; sequester'd leafy glades,
That through the dimness of their twilight
    show
Large dock-leaves, spiral foxgloves, or the
    glow
Of the wild cat's-eyes, or the silvery stems
Of delicate birch-trees, or long grass which
    hems   51
A little brook.   The youth had long been
    viewing
These pleasant things, and heaven was
    bedewing
The mountain flowers, when his glad senses
    caught
A trumpet's silver voice.   Ah! it was
    fraught
With many joys for him : the warder's ken
Had found white coursers prancing in the
    glen:
Friends very dear to him he soon will see;
So pushes off his boat most eagerly,
And soon upon the lake he skims along, 60
Deaf to the nightingale's first under-song;
Nor minds he the white swans that dream
    so sweetly:
His spirit flies before him so completely.

And now he turns a jutting point of land,
Whence may be seen the castle gloomy, and
    grand:
Nor will a bee buzz round two swelling
    peaches,
Before the point of his light shallop reaches
Those marble steps that through the water
    dip:
Now over them he goes with hasty trip,
And scarcely stays to ope the folding
    doors: 70
Anon he leaps along the oaken floors
Of halls and corridors.

Delicious sounds! those little bright-eyed
    things
That float about the air on azure wings,
Had been less heartfelt by him than the
    clang

Of clattering hoofs;   into the court he
    sprang,
Just as two noble steeds, and palfreys twain,
Were slanting out their necks with loosen'd
    rein;
While from beneath the threat'ning port-
    cullis
They brought their happy burthens.   What
    a kiss,   80
What gentle squeeze he gave each lady's
    hand !
How tremblingly their delicate ankles
    spann'd !
Into how sweet a trance his soul was gone,
While whisperings of affection
Made him delay to let their tender feet
Come to the earth; with an incline so sweet
From their low palfreys o'er his neck they
    bent:
And whether there were tears of languish-
    ment,
Or that the evening dew had pearl'd their
    tresses,
He feels a moisture on his cheek, and
    blesses   90
With lips that tremble, and with glistening
    eye,
All the soft luxury
That nestled in his arms.   A dimpled hand,
Fair as some wonder out of fairy land,
Hung from his shoulder like the drooping
    flowers
Of whitest Cassia, fresh from summer
    showers:
And this he fondled with his happy cheek,
As if for joy he would no further seek;
When the kind voice of good Sir Clerimond
Came to his ear, like something from be-
    yond   100
His present being: so he gently drew
His warm arms, thrilling now with pulses
    new,
From their sweet thrall, and forward gently
    bending,
Thank'd Heaven that his joy was never
    ending;
While 'gainst his forehead he devoutly
    press'd

A hand Heaven made to succour the dis-
    tress'd;
A hand that from the world's bleak promon-
    tory
Had lifted Calidore for deeds of glory.

  Amid the pages, and the torches' glare,
There stood a knight, patting the flowing
    hair   110
Of his proud horse's mane: he was withal
A man of elegance, and stature tall:
So that the waving of his plumes would be
High as the berries of a wild ash-tree,
Or as the wingèd cap of Mercury.
His armour was so dexterously wrought
In shape, that sure no living man had
    thought
It hard, and heavy steel: but that indeed
It was some glorious form, some splendid
    weed,
In which a spirit new come from the
    skies   120
Might live, and show itself to human eyes.
'T is the far-fam'd, the brave Sir Gondi-
    bert,
Said the good man to Calidore alert;
While the young warrior with a step of
    grace
Came up, — a courtly smile upon his face,
And mailèd hand held out, ready to greet
The large-eyed wonder, and ambitious heat
Of the aspiring boy; who as he led
Those smiling ladies, often turned his head 130
To admire the visor arched so gracefully
Over a knightly brow; while they went by
The lamps that from the high-roof'd hall
    were pendent,
And gave the steel a shining quite tran-
    scendent.

  Soon in a pleasant chamber they are
    seated ;
The sweet-lipp'd ladies have already
    greeted
All the green leaves that round the window
    clamber,
To show their purple stars, and bells of
    amber.

Sir Gondibert has doff'd his shining steel,
Gladdening in the free, and airy feel
Of a light mantle; and while Clerimond 140
Is looking round about him with a fond
And placid eye, young Calidore is burning
To hear of knightly deeds, and gallant
    spurning
Of all unworthiness; and how the strong of
    arm
Kept off dismay, and terror, and alarm
From lovely woman: while brimful of this,
He gave each damsel's hand so warm a kiss,
And had such manly ardour in his eye,
That each at other look'd half-staringly;
And then their features started into
    smiles,   150
Sweet as blue heavens o'er enchanted isles.

Softly the breezes from the forest came,
Softly they blew aside the taper's flame;
Clear was the song from Philomel's far
    bower;
Grateful the incense from the lime-tree
    flower;
Mysterious, wild, the far heard trumpet's
    tone;
Lovely the moon in ether, all alone:
Sweet too the converse of these happy mor-
    tals,
As that of busy spirits when the portals
Are closing in the west; or that soft hum-
    ming   160
We hear around when Hesperus is coming.
Sweet be their sleep. . . .

EPISTLE TO CHARLES COWDEN CLARKE

  This epistle printed in the 1817 volume is
there dated September, 1816, when Clarke was
in his twenty-ninth year. He was by eight
years Keats's senior, and he lived till his nineti-
eth year.

OFT have you seen a swan superbly frown-
    ing,
And with proud breast his own white
    shadow crowning;

He slants his neck beneath the waters
    bright
So silently, it seems a beam of light
Come from the galaxy: anon he sports, —
With outspread wings the Naiad Zephyr
    courts,
Or ruffles all the surface of the lake
In striving from its crystal face to take
Some diamond water-drops, and them to
    treasure
In milky nest, and sip them off at lei-
    sure.   10
But not a moment can he there insure them,
Nor to such downy rest can he allure them;
For down they rush as though they would
    be free,
And drop like hours into eternity.
Just like that bird am I in loss of time,
Whene'er I venture on the stream of rhyme;
With shatter'd boat, oar snapt, and canvas
    rent,
I slowly sail, scarce knowing my intent;
Still scooping up the water with my fingers,
In which a trembling diamond never
    lingers.   20

   By this, friend Charles, you may full
    plainly see
Why I have never penn'd a line to thee:
Because my thoughts were never free, and
    clear,
And little fit to please a classic ear;
Because my wine was of too poor a savour
For one whose palate gladdens in the fla-
    vour
Of sparkling Helicon: — small good it were
To take him to a desert rude, and bare,
Who had on Baiæ's shore reclin'd at ease,
While Tasso's page was floating in a
    breeze   30
That gave soft music from Armida's
    bowers,
Mingled with fragrance from her rarest
    flowers:
Small good to one who had by Mulla's
    stream
Fondled the maidens with the breasts of
    cream;

Who had beheld Belphœbe in a brook,
And lovely Una in a leafy nook,
And Archimago leaning o'er his book:
Who had of all that's sweet tasted, and
    seen,
From silv'ry ripple, up to beauty's queen;
From the sequester'd haunts of gay Tita-
    nia,   40
To the blue dwelling of divine Urania:
One, who of late had ta'en sweet forest
    walks
With him who elegantly chats and talks —
The wrong'd Libertas, — who has told you
    stories
Of laurel chaplets, and Apollo's glories;
Of troops chivalrous prancing through a
    city,
And tearful ladies made for love, and pity:
With many else which I have never known.
Thus have I thought; and days on days
    have flown
Slowly, or rapidly — unwilling still   50
For you to try my dull, unlearned quill.
Nor should I now, but that I 've known you
    long;
That you first taught me all the sweets of
    song:
The grand, the sweet, the terse, the free,
    the fine:
What swell'd with pathos, and what right
    divine:
Spenserian vowels that elope with ease,
And float along like birds o'er summer
    seas:
Miltonian storms, and more, Miltonian ten-
    derness:
Michael in arms, and more, meek Eve's fair
    slenderness.
Who read for me the sonnet swelling
    loudly   60
Up to its climax, and then dying proudly?
Who found for me the grandeur of the
    ode,
Growing, like Atlas, stronger from its load?
Who let me taste that more than cordial
    dram,
The sharp, the rapier-pointed epigram?
Show'd me that epic was of all the king,

Round, vast, and spanning all, like Saturn's
    ring ?
You too upheld the veil from Clio's beauty,
And pointed out the patriot's stern duty;
The might of Alfred, and the shaft of
    Tell;   70
The hand of Brutus, that so grandly fell
Upon a tyrant's head. Ah! had I never
    seen,
Or known your kindness, what might I
    have been ?
What my enjoyments in my youthful years,
Bereft of all that now my life endears ?
And can I e'er these benefits forget ?
And can I e'er repay the friendly debt ?
No, doubly no; — yet should these rhym-
    ings please,
I shall roll on the grass with twofold ease;
For I have long time been my fancy feed-
    ing   80
With hopes that you would one day think
    the reading
Of my rough verses not an hour misspent;
Should it e'er be so, what a rich content !
Some weeks have pass'd since last I saw
    the spires
In lucent Thames reflected: — warm de-
    sires
To see the sun o'er-peep the eastern dim-
    ness
And morning shadows streaking into slim-
    ness,
Across the lawny fields, and pebbly water;
To mark the time as they grow broad, and
    shorter;
To feel the air that plays about the hills, 90
And sips its freshness from the little rills;
To see high, golden corn wave in the light
When Cynthia smiles upon a summer's
    night,
And peers among the cloudlet's jet and
    white,
As though she were reclining in a bed
Of bean blossoms, in heaven freshly shed.
No sooner had I stepp'd into these plea-
    sures,
Than I began to think of rhymes and mea-
    sures;

The air that floated by me seem'd to say
' Write ! thou wilt never have a better
    day.'   100
And so I did.   When many lines I 'd
    written,
Though with their grace I was not over-
    smitten,
Yet, as my hand was warm, I thought I 'd
    better
Trust to my feelings, and write you a letter.
Such an attempt required an inspiration
Of a peculiar sort, — a consummation; —
Which, had I felt, these scribblings might
    have been
Verses from which the soul would never
    wean;
But many days have past since last my
    heart   109
Was warm'd luxuriously by divine Mozart;
By Arne delighted, or by Handel mad-
    den'd;
Or by the song of Erin pierc'd and sad-
    den'd:
What time you were before the music
    sitting,
And the rich notes to each sensation fitting.
Since I have walk'd with you through shady
    lanes
That freshly terminate in open plains,
And revell'd in a chat that ceasèd not
When at night-fall among your books we
    got:
No, nor when supper came, nor after that, —
Nor when reluctantly I took my hat;   120
No, nor till cordially you shook my hand
Mid-way between our homes: — your ac-
    cents bland
Still sounded in my ears, when I no more
Could hear your footsteps touch the grav'ly
    floor.
Sometimes I lost them, and then found
    again;
You changed the foot-path for the grassy
    plain.
In those still moments I have wish'd you
    joys
That well you know to honour: — ' Life's
    very toys

With him,' said I, ' will take a pleasant
    charm;
It cannot be that ought will work him
    harm.'   130
These thoughts now come o'er me with all
    their might: —
Again I shake your hand, — friend Charles,
    good night.

TO MY BROTHERS

Though the poem is thus headed in the 1817
volume, where it is dated November 18, 1816,
it might as properly have the heading given it
in Tom Keats's copybook: 'Written to his
Brother Tom on his Birthday,' with the same
date.

SMALL, busy flames play through the fresh-
    laid coals,
    And their faint cracklings o'er our si-
        lence creep
    Like whispers of the household gods that
        keep
A gentle empire o'er fraternal souls.
And while, for rhymes, I search around the
    poles,
    Your eyes are fix'd, as in poetic sleep,
    Upon the lore so voluble and deep,
That aye at fall of night our care condoles.
This is your birth-day, Tom, and I rejoice
    That thus it passes smoothly, quietly:
Many such eves of gently whisp'ring noise
    May we together pass, and calmly try
What are this world's true joys, — ere the
    great Voice,
    From its fair face, shall bid our spirits fly.

ADDRESSED TO BENJAMIN
ROBERT HAYDON

The first of these two sonnets was sent by
Keats with this brief note: 'November 20,
1816. My dear Sir — Last evening wrought
me up, and I cannot forbear sending you the
following.' In his prompt acknowledgment
Haydon suggested the omission of the last four
words in the penultimate line, and proposed
sending the sonnet to Wordsworth. Keats re-

plied on the same day as his first note : ' Your
letter has filled me with a proud pleasure, and
shall be kept by me as a stimulus to exertion —
I begin to fix my eye upon one horizon. My
feelings entirely fall in with yours in regard to
the Ellipsis, and I glory in it. The Idea of
your sending it to Wordsworth put me out of
breath. You know with what Reverence I
would send my Well-wishes to him.' The pre-
sentation copy of the 1817 volume bears the
inscription ' To W. Wordsworth with the Author's sincere Reverence.' Both sonnets were
printed, but in the reverse order in the 1817
volume, and the ellipsis was preserved.

I

GREAT spirits now on earth are sojourning;
    He of the cloud, the cataract, the lake,
    Who on Helvellyn's summit, wide awake,
Catches his freshness from Archangel's
    wing:
He of the rose, the violet, the spring,
    The social smile, the chain for Freedom's
        sake:
    And lo ! — whose steadfastness would
        never take
A meaner sound than Raphael's whispering.
And other spirits there are standing apart
    Upon the forehead of the age to come;
These, these will give the world another
    heart,
    And other pulses. Hear ye not the hum
Of mighty workings in the human mart ?
Listen awhile ye nations, and be dumb.

II

HIGHMINDEDNESS, a jealousy for good,
    A loving-kindness for the great man's
        fame,
    Dwells here and there with people of no
        name,
In noisome alley, and in pathless wood:
And where we think the truth least under-
    stood,
    Oft may be found a ' singleness of aim,'
    That ought to frighten into hooded shame .
A money-mong'ring, pitiable brood.
How glorious this affection for the cause
    Of steadfast genius, toiling gallantly !

What when a stout unbending champion
    awes
Envy, and Malice to their native sty?
Unnumber'd souls breathe out a still ap-
    plause,
Proud to behold him in his country's eye.

TO KOSCIUSKO

First published in *The Examiner*, where it
is dated 'Dec., 1816.' It is included in the
1817 volume.

GOOD Kosciusko, thy great name alone
    Is a full harvest whence to reap high
    feeling;
It comes upon us like the glorious pealing
Of the wide spheres — an everlasting tone.
And now it tells me, that in worlds unknown,
    The names of heroes, burst from clouds
        concealing,
    Are changed to harmonies, for ever
        stealing
Through cloudless blue, and round each
    silver throne.
It tells me too, that on a happy day,
    When some good spirit walks upon the
        earth,
    Thy name with Alfred's, and the great
        of yore,
Gently commingling, gives tremendous
    birth
To a loud hymn, that sounds far, far away
    To where the great God lives for ever-
    more.

TO G. A. W.

Georgiana Augusta Wylie, who afterward
married George Keats. For other verses addressed to this lady see pp. 11, 240, 243.
    This sonnet in Tom Keats's copybook is
dated December, 1816; it was published in the
1817 volume.

NYMPH of the downward smile and side-
    long glance,
    In what diviner moments of the day
    Art thou most lovely? When gone far
        astray

Into the labyrinths of sweet utterance?
Or when serenely wand'ring in a trance
    Of sober thought? Or when starting
        away,
    With careless robe, to meet the morning
        ray,
Thou spar'st the flowers in thy mazy dance?
Haply 't is when thy ruby lips part sweetly,
    And so remain, because thou listenest:
But thou to please wert nurtured so com-
        pletely
    That I can never tell what mood is best.
I shall as soon pronounce which Grace more
    neatly
    Trips it before Apollo than the rest.

STANZAS

There is no date given to this poem by Lord
Houghton, who published it in the 1848 edition, and no reference occurs to it in the *Letters*.
It was probably an early careless poem, very
likely a set of album verses.

IN a drear-nighted December,
    Too happy, happy tree,
Thy branches ne'er remember
    Their green felicity:
    The north cannot undo them,
    With a sleety whistle through them;
    Nor frozen thawings glue them
        From budding at the prime.

In a drear-nighted December,
    Too happy, happy brook,
Thy bubblings ne'er remember
    Apollo's summer look;
    But with a sweet forgetting,
    They stay their crystal fretting,
    Never, never petting
        About the frozen time.

Ah! would 't were so with many
    A gentle girl and boy!
But were there ever any
    Writh'd not at passèd joy?
    To know the change and feel it,
    When there is none to heal it,

Nor numbèd sense to steal it,
Was never said in rhyme.

WRITTEN IN DISGUST OF VULGAR SUPERSTITION

In Tom Keats's copybook this sonnet is dated 'Sunday evening, Dec. 24, 1816.' Lord Houghton gives it in the Aldine edition, and heads it 'Written on a Summer Evening.' Possibly the seventh line may be adduced as evidence of the wintry season.

THE church bells toll a melancholy round,
  Calling the people to some other prayers,
  Some other gloominess, more dreadful cares,
More hearkening to the sermon's horrid sound.
Surely the mind of man is closely bound
  In some black spell; seeing that each one tears
  Himself from fireside joys, and Lydian airs,
And converse high of those with glory crown'd.
Still, still they toll, and I should feel a damp, —
  A chill as from a tomb, did I not know
That they are dying like an outburnt lamp;
  That 't is their sighing, wailing ere they go
  Into oblivion; — that fresh flowers will grow,
And many glories of immortal stamp.

SONNET

Published in the 1817 volume, but there is no evidence as to its exact date. It is the latest in order of the sonnets, immediately preceding *Sleep and Poetry*.

HAPPY is England! I could be content
  To see no other verdure than its own;
  To feel no other breezes than are blown
Through its tall woods with high romances blent:

Yet do I sometimes feel a languishment
  For skies Italian, and an inward groan
  To sit upon an Alp as on a throne,
And half forget what world or worldling meant.
Happy is England, sweet her artless daughters;
  Enough their simple loveliness for me,
    Enough their whitest arms in silence clinging:
  Yet do I often warmly burn to see
    Beauties of deeper glance, and hear their singing,
And float with them about the summer waters.

ON THE GRASSHOPPER AND CRICKET

Written December 30, 1816, on a challenge from Leigh Hunt, who printed both his and Keats's sonnets in his paper, *The Examiner*. Keats included the sonnet in his 1817 volume. Leigh Hunt's sonnet will be found in the NOTES AND ILLUSTRATIONS.

THE poetry of earth is never dead:
  When all the birds are faint with the hot sun,
  And hide in cooling trees, a voice will run
From hedge to hedge about the new-mown mead;
That is the Grasshopper's — he takes the lead
  In summer luxury, — he has never done
  With his delights; for when tired out with fun,
He rests at ease beneath some pleasant weed.
The poetry of earth is ceasing never:
  On a lone winter evening, when the frost
    Has wrought a silence, from the stove there shrills
The Cricket's song, in warmth increasing ever,
  And seems to one, in drowsiness half lost,
    The Grasshopper's among some grassy hills.

SONNET

Printed in *The Examiner*, February 23, 1817, and dated by Lord Houghton, when reprinting it, ' January, 1817.'

AFTER dark vapours have oppress'd our
        plains ʌ
    For a long dreary season, comes a day ι
    Born of the gentle South, and clears
        away ι
From the sick heavens all unseemly stains.ʌ
The anxious month, relieved its pains, ι
    Takes as a long-lost right the feel of
        May; ι
    The eyelids with the passing coolness
        play, ι
Like rose leaves with the drip of summer
    rains. ʌ
And calmest thoughts come round us; as,
    of leaves ι
    Budding, — fruit ripening in stillness, —
        Autumn suns ι
Smiling at eve upon the quiet sheaves, — c
Sweet Sappho's cheek, — a sleeping infant's
    breath, — ι
    The gradual sand that through an hour-
        glass runs, — ι
A woodland rivulet, — a Poet's death. ⟩

WRITTEN ON THE BLANK SPACE AT THE END OF CHAUCER'S TALE OF 'THE FLOURE AND THE LEFE'

Written in February, 1817, and published in *The Examiner*, March 16, 1817. There is a pleasant story that Charles Cowden Clarke had fallen asleep over the book, and woke to find this epilogue.

THIS pleasant tale is like a little copse:
    The honied lines so freshly interlace,
    To keep the reader in so sweet a place,
So that he here and there full-hearted
    stops;
And oftentimes he feels the dewy drops
    Come cool and suddenly against his face,
And, by the wandering melody, may trace
Which way the tender-legged linnet hops.
Oh! what a power has white simplicity !
    What mighty power has this gentle story !
    I, that do ever feel athirst for glory,
Could at this moment be content to lie
    Meekly upon the grass, as those whose
        sobbings
    Were heard of none beside the mournful
        robins.

ON SEEING THE ELGIN MARBLES

This and the following sonnet were printed in *The Examiner*, March 9, 1817, and reprinted in *Life, Letters and Literary Remains*.

MY spirit is too weak — mortality
    Weighs heavily on me like unwilling
        sleep,
    And each imagin'd pinnacle and steep
Of godlike hardship tells me I must die
Like a sick Eagle looking at the sky.
    Yet 't is a gentle luxury to weep
    That I have not the cloudy winds to
        keep,
Fresh for the opening of the morning's eye.
Such dim-conceivèd glories of the brain
    Bring round the heart an indescribable
        feud;
So do these wonders a most dizzy pain,
    That mingles Grecian grandeur with the
        rude
Wasting of old Time — with a billowy
    main —
A sun — a shadow of a magnitude.

TO HAYDON

(WITH THE PRECEDING SONNET)

HAYDON ! forgive me that I cannot speak
    Definitively of these mighty things;
    Forgive me, that I have not Eagle's
        wings —
That what I want I know not where to
    seek:

And think that I would not be over meek,
  In rolling out upfollow'd thunderings,
  Even to the steep of Heliconian springs,
Were I of ample strength for such a
    freak —
Think too, that all those numbers should
    be thine;
  Whose else? In this who touch thy
    vesture's hem ?
For when men star'd at what was most
    divine
  With browless idiotism — o'erwise
    phlegm —
Thou hadst beheld the Hesperean shine
  Of their star in the East, and gone to
    worship them.

TO LEIGH HUNT, ESQ.

This stood as dedication to the 1817 volume,
which was published in the month of March.
Charles Cowden Clarke makes the statement:
' On the evening when the last proof sheet was
brought from the printer, it was accompanied
by the information that if a " dedication to the
book was intended, it must be sent forthwith."
Whereupon he withdrew to a side table, and in
the buzz of a mixed conversation (for there
were several friends in the room) he composed
and brought to Charles Ollier, the publisher,
the dedication sonnet to Leigh Hunt.'

GLORY and loveliness have pass'd away;
  For if we wander out in early morn,
  No wreathèd incense do we see upborne
Into the east, to meet the smiling day:
No crowd of nymphs soft-voic'd and young,
    and gay,
  In woven baskets bringing ears of corn,
  Roses, and pinks, and violets, to adorn
The shrine of Flora in her early May.
But there are left delights as high as these,
  And I shall ever bless my destiny,
That in a time, when under pleasant trees
Pan is no longer sought, I feel a free,
A leafy luxury, seeing I could please
  With these poor offerings, a man like
    thee.

ON THE SEA

Sent in a letter to Reynolds, dated April 17,
1817. ' From want of regular rest,' Keats
says, ' I have been rather narvus, and the passage in Lear — " Do you not hear the sea ? " —
has haunted me intensely.' He then copies the
sonnet, which was published in The Champion,
August 17 of the same year. The letter was
written from Carisbrooke. He had been sent
away from London by his brothers a month
before, shortly after the appearance of his first
volume of Poems, and his letters show the
nervous, restless condition into which he had
been driven by that venture.

IT keeps eternal whisperings around
  Desolate shores, and with its mighty
    swell
  Gluts twice ten thousand caverns, till the
    spell
Of Hecate leaves them their old shadowy
    sound.
Often 't is in such gentle temper found,
  That scarcely will the very smallest shell
  Be mov'd for days from where it some-
    time fell,
When last the winds of Heaven were
    unbound.
O ye ! who have your eyeballs vex'd and
    tir'd,
  Feast them upon the wideness of the Sea;
  O ye ! whose ears are dinn'd with up-
    roar rude,
  Or fed too much with cloying melody, —
  Sit ye near some old cavern's mouth,
    and brood
Until ye start, as if the sea-nymphs quired !

LINES

First published, with the date 1817, in Life,
Letters and Literary Remains. It is barely
possible that this is the 'song' to which Keats
refers in a letter to Benjamin Bailey, dated
November 22, 1817, when he says: ' I am certain of nothing but the holiness of the Heart's
affections, and the truth of Imagination. What
the Imagination seizes as Beauty must be truth

— whether it existed before or not — for I
have the same idea of all our passions as of
Love: they are all, in their sublime, creative
of essential Beauty. In a word, you may know
my favourite speculation by my first Book, and
the little Song I sent in my last, which is a
representation from the fancy of the probable
mode of operating in these matters.'

UNFELT, unheard, unseen,
　　I 've left my little queen,
Her languid arms in silver slumber lying:
　　Ah ! through their nestling touch,
　　Who — who could tell how much
There is for madness — cruel, or comply-
　　　ing ?

Those faery lids how sleek !
Those lips how moist ! — they speak,
In ripest quiet, shadows of sweet sounds:
　　Into my fancy's ear
　　Melting a burden dear,
How 'Love doth know no fulness, and no
　　bounds.'

True ! — tender monitors !
I bend unto your laws:
This sweetest day for dalliance was born !
　　So, without more ado,
　　I 'll feel my heaven anew,
For all the blushing of the hasty morn.

ON ——

Published with the date 1817 by Lord
Houghton in *Life, Letters and Literary Remains*, but slightly varied in form when reprinted in the Aldine edition.

THINK not of it, sweet one, so; —
　　Give it not a tear;
Sigh thou mayst, and bid it go
　　Any — any where.

Do not look so sad, sweet one, —
　　Sad and fadingly;
Shed one drop, then it is gone,
　　Oh ! 't was born to die !

Still so pale ? then dearest weep;
　　Weep, I 'll count the tears,
For each will I invent a bliss
　　For thee in after years.

Brighter has it left thine eyes
　　Than a sunny rill;
And thy whispering melodies
　　Are more tender still.

Yet — as all things mourn awhile
　　At fleeting blisses;
E'en let us too; but be our dirge
　　A dirge of kisses.

ON A PICTURE OF LEANDER

This sonnet was printed in 1829 in *The Gem,
a Literary Annual*, edited by Thomas Hood.
It is not dated, but may fairly be assigned to
this time.

COME hither, all sweet maidens soberly,
　　Down-looking aye, and with a chasten'd
　　　light
Hid in the fringes of your eyelids white,
And meekly let your fair hands joined be,
As if so gentle that ye could not see,
　　Untouch'd, a victim of your beauty bright,
　　Sinking away to his young spirit's night,
Sinking bewilder'd 'mid the dreary sea:
'T is young Leander toiling to his death;
　　Nigh swooning, he doth purse his weary
　　　lips
　　　For Hero's cheek, and smiles against
　　　　her smile.
　　O horrid dream ! see how his body dips
　　　Dead-heavy; arms and shoulders gleam
　　　　awhile:
He 's gone; up bubbles all his amorous
　　breath !

ON LEIGH HUNT'S POEM, 'THE
STORY OF RIMINI'

Dated 1817 in the *Life, Letters and Literary
Remains*, and placed next after the preceding.

WHO loves to peer up at the morning sun,
    With half-shut eyes and comfortable
        cheek,
    Let him, with this sweet tale, full often
        seek
For meadows where the little rivers run;
Who loves to linger with that brightest one
    Of Heaven — Hesperus — let him lowly
        speak
    These numbers to the night, and star-
        light meek,
Or moon, if that her hunting be begun.
He who knows these delights, and too is
        prone
    To moralize upon a smile or tear,
Will find at once a region of his own,
    A bower for his spirit, and will steer
To alleys, where the fir-tree drops its cone,
    Where robins hop, and fallen leaves are
        sear.

SONNET

First published in *Life, Letters and Literary
Remains*, but dated 1817 in a manuscript copy
owned by Sir Charles Dilke. Keats sends it
as his 'last sonnet' in a letter to Reynolds
written on the last day of January, 1818.

WHEN I have fears that I may cease to
        be
    Before my pen has glean'd my teeming
        brain,
Before high piled books, in charactry,
    Hold like rich garners the full-ripen'd
        grain;
When I behold, upon the night's starr'd
        face,
    Huge cloudy symbols of a high romance,
And think that I may never live to trace
    Their shadows, with the magic hand of
        chance;
And when I feel, fair creature of an hour!
    That I shall never look upon thee more,
Never have relish in the faery power
    Of unreflecting love; — then on the shore
Of the wide world I stand alone, and think
Till Love and Fame to nothingness do sink.

ON SEEING A LOCK OF MILTON'S HAIR

'I was at Hunt's the other day,' writes
Keats to Bailey, January 23, 1818, 'and he
surprised me with a real authenticated lock of
Milton's Hair. I know you would like what I
wrote thereon, so here it is — *as they say of a
sheep in a Nursery Book*.' 'This I did,' he
adds, after copying the lines, 'at Hunt's at
his request — perhaps I should have done
something better alone and at home.' Lord
Houghton printed the verse in *Life, Letters
and Literary Remains*.

CHIEF of organic numbers !
    Old Scholar of the Spheres !
Thy spirit never slumbers,
    But rolls about our ears,
For ever and for ever !
O what a mad endeavour
        Worketh he,
Who to thy sacred and ennobled hearse
Would offer a burnt sacrifice of verse
        And melody.

How heavenward thou soundest,
    Live Temple of sweet noise,
. And Discord unconfoundest,
    Giving Delight new joys,
And Pleasure nobler pinions !
O, where are thy dominions ?
        Lend thine ear
To a young Delian oath, — ay, by thy soul,
By all that from thy mortal lips did roll,
And by the kernel of thine earthly love,
Beauty, in things on earth, and things above,
        I swear !
When every childish fashion
    Has vanish'd from my rhyme,
Will I, grey-gone in passion,
    Leave to an after-time,
        Hymning and harmony
Of thee, and of thy works, and of thy
        life;
But vain is now the burning and the strife,
Pangs are in vain, until I grow high-rife
        With old Philosophy,
And mad with glimpses of futurity !

For many years my offering must be hush'd;
  When I do speak, I'll think upon this
    hour,
Because I feel my forehead hot and flush'd.
  Even at the simplest vassal of thy
    power, —
  A lock of thy bright hair —
  Sudden it came,
And I was startled, when I caught thy name
  Coupled so unaware;
Yet, at the moment, temperate was my
  blood.
I thought I had beheld it from the flood.

ON SITTING DOWN TO READ 'KING LEAR' ONCE AGAIN

In a letter to his brothers, dated January 23, 1818, Keats says: 'I think a little change has taken place in my intellect lately — I cannot bear to be uninterested or unemployed, I, who for so long a time have been addicted to passiveness. Nothing is finer for the purposes of great productions than a very gradual ripening of the intellectual powers. As an instance of this — observe — I sat down yesterday to read King Lear once again: the thing appeared to demand the prologue of a sonnet, I wrote it, and began to read — (I know you would like to see it). So you see,' he goes on after copying the sonnet, 'I am getting at it with a sort of determination and strength, though verily I do not feel it at this moment.' The sonnet was printed in Life, Letters and Literary Remains.

O GOLDEN-TONGUED Romance, with se-
    rene lute !
  Fair plumèd Syren, Queen of far away !
  Leave melodizing on this wintry day,
Shut up thine olden pages, and be mute:
Adieu ! for once again the fierce dispute,
  Betwixt damnation and impassion'd clay,
  Must I burn through; once more humbly
    assay
The bitter sweet of this Shakespearean
    fruit:
Chief Poet ! and ye clouds of Albion,
  Begetters of our deep eternal theme !

When through the old oak forest I am gone,
  Let me not wander in a barren dream,
But when I am consumèd in the Fire,
  Give me new Phœnix-wings to fly at my
    desire.

LINES ON THE MERMAID TAVERN

In sending his *Robin Hood* verses to Reynolds (see next poem), Keats added the following, but from the tenor of his letter, it would appear that they had been written earlier and were sent at Reynolds's request. The poem was published by Keats in his *Lamia, Isabella, The Eve of St. Agnes, and other Poems*, 1820. The friends were then in full tide of sympathy with the Elizabethans, and would have been very much at home with Shakespeare, Jonson, and Marlowe at the Mermaid.

SOULS of Poets dead and gone,
What Elysium have ye known,
Happy field or mossy cavern,
Choicer than the Mermaid Tavern ?
Have ye tippled drink more fine
Than mine host's Canary wine ?
Or are fruits of Paradise
Sweeter than those dainty pies
Of venison ?   O generous food !
Drest as though bold Robin Hood   10
Would, with his maid Marian,
Sup and bowse from horn and can.

  I have heard that on a day
Mine host's sign-board flew away,
Nobody knew whither, till
An astrologer's old quill
To a sheepskin gave the story,
Said he saw you in your glory,
Underneath a new-old sign
Sipping beverage divine,   20
And pledging with contented smack
The Mermaid in the Zodiac.

  Souls of Poets dead and gone,
What Elysium have ye known,
Happy field or mossy cavern,
Choicer than the Mermaid Tavern ?

ROBIN HOOD

TO A FRIEND

The friend was J. H. Reynolds, who had sent Keats two sonnets which he had written on Robin Hood. Keats's letter, dated February 3, 1818, is full of energetic pleasantry on the poetry which ' has a palpable design upon us,' and concludes: 'Let us have the old Poets and Robin Hood. Your letter and its sonnets gave me more pleasure than will the Fourth Book of *Childe Harold*, and the whole of any-body's life and opinions. In return for your Dish of Filberts, I have gathered a few Catkins. I hope they'll look pretty.' Keats included the poem in his *Lamia, Isabella, The Eve of St. Agnes and other Poems*, 1820, with some trifling changes of text.

No! those days are gone away,
And their hours are old and gray,
And their minutes buried all
Under the down-trodden pall
Of the leaves of many years:
Many times have Winter's shears,
Frozen North, and chilling East,
Sounded tempests to the feast
Of the forest's whispering fleeces,
Since men knew nor rent nor leases. 10

No, the bugle sounds no more,
And the twanging bow no more;
Silent is the ivory shrill
Past the heath and up the hill;
There is no mid-forest laugh,
Where lone Echo gives the half
To some wight, amaz'd to hear
Jesting, deep in forest drear.

On the fairest time of June
You may go, with sun or moon, 20
Or the seven stars to light you,
Or the polar ray to right you;
But you never may behold
Little John, or Robin bold;
Never one, of all the clan,
Thrumming on an empty can
Some old hunting ditty, while
He doth his green way beguile

To fair hostess Merriment,
Down beside the pasture Trent; 30
For he left the merry tale,
Messenger for spicy ale.

Gone, the merry morris din;
Gone, the song of Gamelyn;
Gone, the tough-belted outlaw
Idling in the 'grenè shawe;'
All are gone away and past!
And if Robin should be cast
Sudden from his turfèd grave,
And if Marian should have 40
Once again her forest days,
She would weep, and he would craze:
He would swear, for all his oaks,
Fall'n beneath the dock-yard strokes,
Have rotted on the briny seas;
She would weep that her wild bees
Sang not to her — strange! that honey
Can't be got without hard money!

So it is; yet let us sing
Honour to the old bow-string! 50
Honour to the bugle horn!
Honour to the woods unshorn!
Honour to the Lincoln green!
Honour to the archer keen!
Honour to tight little John,
And the horse he rode upon!
Honour to bold Robin Hood,
Sleeping in the underwood!
Honour to Maid Marian,
And to all the Sherwood clan! 60
Though their days have hurried by,
Let us two a burden try.

TO THE NILE

Composed February 4, 1818, in company with Shelley and Hunt, who each wrote a sonnet on the same theme. It was first published by Lord Houghton in the *Life, Letters and Literary Remains*.

SON of the old moon-mountains African!
    Chief of the Pyramid and Crocodile!
    We call thee fruitful, and that very while

A desert fills our seeing's inward span;
Nurse of swart nations since the world
    began,
    Art thou so fruitful? or dost thou be-
    guile
Such men to honour thee, who, worn with
    toil,
Rest for a space 'twixt Cairo and De-
    can?
O may dark fancies err! They surely
    do;
    'T is ignorance that makes a barren waste
Of all beyond itself. Thou dost bedew
    Green rushes like our rivers, and dost
    taste
The pleasant sun-rise. Green isles hast
    thou too,
And to the sea as happily dost haste.

TO SPENSER

Printed in *Life, Letters and Literary Remains*, and undated. Afterward, when Lord
Houghton printed it in the Aldine edition of
1876, he noted that he had seen a transcript
given by Keats to Mrs. Longmore, a sister of
Reynolds, dated by the recipient, February 5,
1818. But Lord Houghton is confident that
the sonnet was written much earlier.

SPENSER! a jealous honourer of thine,
    A forester deep in thy midmost trees,
Did last eve ask my promise to refine
    Some English that might strive thine ear
    to please.
    But Elfin Poet, 't is impossible
For an inhabitant of wintry earth
    To rise like Phœbus with a golden quill
Fire-wing'd and make a morning in his
    mirth.
It is impossible to escape from toil
O' the sudden and receive thy spiriting:
    The flower must drink the nature of the
    soil
Before it can put forth its blossoming:
    Be with me in the summer days, and I
    Will for thine honour and his pleasure
    try.

SONG

WRITTEN ON A BLANK PAGE IN BEAU-
MONT AND FLETCHER'S WORKS, BE-
TWEEN 'CUPID'S REVENGE' AND
'THE TWO NOBLE KINSMEN'

First published in *Life, Letters and Literary
Remains*, and undated.

SPIRIT here that reignest!
Spirit here that painest!
Spirit here that burnest!
Spirit here that mournest!
    Spirit, I bow
    My forehead low,
Enshaded with thy pinions.
    Spirit, I look
    All passion-struck
Into thy pale dominions.

Spirit here that laughest!
Spirit here that quaffest!
Spirit here that dancest!
Noble soul that prancest!
    Spirit, with thee
    I join in the glee
A-nudging the elbow of Momus.
    Spirit, I flush
    With a Bacchanal blush
Just fresh from the Banquet of
    Comus.

FRAGMENT

Under the flag
Of each his faction, they to battle bring
Their embryo atoms.
                              MILTON.

Published in *Life, Letters and Literary Remains*, without date.

WELCOME joy, and welcome sorrow,
    Lethe's weed and Hermes' feather;
Come to-day, and come to-morrow,
    I do love you both together!
    I love to mark sad faces in fair weather;
And hear a merry laugh amid the thunder;

Fair and foul I love together.
Meadows sweet where flames are under,
And a giggle at a wonder;
Visage sage at pantomime;
Funeral, and steeple-chime;
Infant playing with a skull;
Morning fair, and shipwreck'd hull;
Nightshade with the woodbine kissing;
Serpents in red roses hissing;
Cleopatra regal-dress'd
With the aspic at her breast;
Dancing music, music sad,
Both together, sane and mad;
Muses bright, and muses pale;
Sombre Saturn, Momus hale; —
Laugh and sigh, and laugh again;
Oh, the sweetness of the pain !
Muses bright and muses pale,
Bare your faces of the veil;
Let me see; and let me write
Of the day, and of the night —
Both together : — let me slake
All my thirst for sweet heart-ache !
Let my bower be of yew,
Interwreath'd with myrtles new;
Pines and lime-trees full in bloom,
And my couch a low grass-tomb.

WHAT THE THRUSH SAID

In a long letter to Reynolds, dated February
19, 1818, Keats writes earnestly of the sources
of inspiration to a poet, and especially of the
need of a receptive attitude : ' Let us open our
leaves like a flower, and be passive and receptive; budding patiently under the eye of
Apollo and taking hints from every noble
insect that favours us with a visit — Sap will
be given us for meat, and dew for drink. I
was led into these thoughts, my dear Reynolds,
by the beauty of the morning operating on a
sense of Idleness. I have not read any Book
— the Morning said I was right — I had no
idea but of the Morning, and the Thrush said
I was right, seeming to say,' and then follows
the poem. It was first printed in *Life, Letters
and Literary Remains.*

O THOU whose face hath felt the Winter's
    wind,
Whose eye has seen the snow-clouds hung
    in mist,
And the black elm tops 'mong the freezing
    stars,
To thee the spring will be a harvest-time.
O thou, whose only book has been the light
Of supreme darkness which thou feddest on
Night after night when Phœbus was away,
To thee the Spring shall be a triple morn.
O fret not after knowledge — I have none,
And yet my song comes native with the
    warmth.
O fret not after knowledge — I have none,
And yet the Evening listens. He who sad-
    dens
At thought of idleness cannot be idle,
And he 's awake who thinks himself asleep.

WRITTEN IN ANSWER TO A SONNET ENDING THUS:—

' Dark eyes are dearer far
Than those that mock the hyacinthine bell '
          BY J. H. REYNOLDS.

Dated by Lord Houghton ' February, 1818,'
in *Life, Letters and Literary Remains,* where it
was first printed.

BLUE ! 'T is the life of heaven, — the do-
    main
    Of Cynthia, — the wide palace of the
    sun, —
The tent of Hesperus, and all his train, —
    The bosomer of clouds, gold, gray, and
    dun.
Blue ! 'T is the life of waters — ocean
    And all its vassal streams, pools num-
    berless,
May rage, and foam, and fret, but never can
    Subside, if not to dark blue nativeness.
Blue ! Gentle cousin of the forest-green,
    Married to green in all the sweetest
    flowers, —
Forget-me-not, — the blue bell, — and, that
    queen

Of secrecy, the violet: what strange
    powers
Hast thou, as a mere shadow! But how
    great,
When in an Eye thou art, alive with fate!

TO JOHN HAMILTON REYNOLDS

Undated, but placed by Lord Houghton directly after the preceding in *Life, Letters and Literary Remains.*

O THAT a week could be an age, and we
    Felt parting and warm meeting every
    week;
Then one poor year a thousand years would
    be,
    The flush of welcome ever on the cheek:
So could we live long life in little space,
So time itself would be annihilate,
So a day's journey in oblivious haze
    To serve our joys would lengthen and
    dilate.
O to arrive each Monday morn from Ind!
    To land each Tuesday from the rich Levant!
In little time a host of joys to bind,
    And keep our souls in one eternal pant!

This morn, my friend, and yester-evening
    taught
Me how to harbor such a happy thought.

THE HUMAN SEASONS

This sonnet was sent by Keats in a letter to Benjamin Bailey, from Teignmouth, March 13, 1818, and was printed the next year in Leigh Hunt's *Literary Pocket-Book*, but Keats did not include the verses in his 1820 volume.

FOUR Seasons fill the measure of the year;
    There are four seasons in the mind of
    man:
He has his lusty Spring, when fancy clear
    Takes in all beauty with an easy span:
He has his Summer, when luxuriously
    Spring's honied cud of youthful thought
    he loves
To ruminate, and by such dreaming high
    Is nearest unto heaven: quiet coves
His soul has in its Autumn, when his wings
    He furleth close; contented so to look
On mists in idleness — to let fair things
    Pass by unheeded as a threshold brook.
He has his Winter too of pale misfeature,
Or else he would forego his mortal nature.

ENDYMION

KEATS began this poem in the spring of 1817 and finished it and saw it through the press in just about a year. It is interesting to follow in his correspondence the growth of the poem. The subject in general had been in his mind at least since the summer of 1816, when he wrote *I stood tiptoe upon a little hill*, and the poem *Sleep and Poetry* hints also at the occupation of his mind, though through all the earlier and partly imitative period of his poetical growth he was drawn almost equally by the romance to which Spenser and Leigh Hunt introduced him, and the classic themes which his early studies, Chapman and the Elgin marbles, all conspired to make real. In April, 1817, he writes as one absorbed in the delights of poetry and stimulated by it to production. 'I find,' he writes to Reynolds from Carisbrooke, April 18, 'I cannot exist without Poetry — half the day will not do — the whole of it — I began with a little, but habit has made me a Leviathan. I had become all in a Tremble from not having written anything of late — the Sonnet overleaf [*On the Sea*] did me good. I slept the better last night for it — this morning, however, I am nearly as bad again. Just now I opened Spenser, and the first lines I saw were these —

"The noble heart that harbours virtuous
     thought,
And is with child of glorious great intent,
Can never rest until it forth have brought
Th' eternal brood of glory excellent."

. . . I shall forthwith begin my *Endymion*, which I hope I shall have got some way with by the time you come, when we will read our verses in a delightful place I have set my heart upon, near the Castle.'

He reported progress to his friends from time to time during the summer: the poem was his great occupation, and he had the alternate exhilaration and depression which such an undertaking naturally would produce in a temperament as sensitive as his; indeed, one is not surprised to find him near the end of September expressing himself to Haydon as tired of the poem, and looking forward to a Romance to which he meant to devote himself the next summer, for so did his mind swing back and forth, though in truth romance was always uppermost, whether expressed in terms of Grecian mythology or mediævalism. But the main significance of *Endymion*, as one traces the growth of Keats's mind, is in the strong impulse which possessed him to try his wings in a great flight. In a letter to Bailey, October 8, 1817, he quotes from his own letter to George Keats 'in the spring,' and thus at the very time of his setting forth on his great venture, the following notable passage : —

'As to what you say about my being a Poet, I can return no answer but by saying that the high idea I have of poetical fame makes me think I see it towering too high above me. At any rate I have no right to talk until *Endymion* is finished — it will be a test, a trial of my Powers of Imagination, and chiefly of my invention, which is a rare thing indeed — by which I must make 4000 lines of one bare circumstance, and fill them with Poetry: and when I consider that this is a great task, and that when done it will take me but a dozen paces towards the temple of fame — it makes me say: God forbid that I should be without such a task ! I have heard Hunt say, and I may be asked — "Why endeavour after a long Poem ? " To which I would answer, Do not the lovers of poetry like to have a little region to wander in, where they may pick and choose, and in which the images are so numerous that many are forgotten and found new in a second reading: which may be food for a week's stroll in summer? Do not they like this better than what they can read through before Mrs. Williams comes down stairs? a morning work at most.

'Besides, a long poem is a test of invention, which I take to be the polar star of Poetry, as Fancy is the sails, and Imagination the rudder. Did our great Poets ever write short Pieces? I mean in the shape of Tales — this same invention seems indeed of late years to have been forgotten as a poetical excellence — But enough of this; I put on no laurels till I shall have finished *Endymion*.'

Keats was drawing near the end of his task when he wrote to Bailey November 22: 'At present I am just arrived at Dorking — to change the scene, change the air and give me a spur to wind up my Poem, of which there are wanting 500 lines.' And at the end of the first draft is written 'Burford Bridge [near Dorking] November 28, 1817.' Early in January, 1818, Keats gave the first book to Taylor, who 'seemed,' he says, 'more than satisfied with it,' and to Keats's surprise proposed issuing it in quarto if Haydon would make a drawing for a frontispiece. Haydon, when asked, was more eager to paint a picture from some scene in the book, but proposed now to make a finished chalk sketch of Keats's head to be engraved for a frontispiece; for some unmentioned reason, this plan was not carried out.

Keats was copying out the poem for the printer, giving it in book by book and reading the proofs until April, when it was ready save the Preface. This with dedication and title-page he had sent to his Publishers March 21. They were as follows:

ENDYMION

A ROMANCE

By John Keats

'The stretched metre of an antique song.'
Shakspeare's Sonnets.

INSCRIBED,
WITH EVERY FEELING OF PRIDE AND REGRET
AND WITH 'A BOWED MIND'
TO THE MEMORY OF
THE MOST ENGLISH OF POETS EXCEPT SHAKSPEARE,
THOMAS CHATTERTON

PREFACE

IN a great nation, the work of an individual is of so little importance; his pleadings and excuses are so uninteresting; his 'way of life' such a nothing, that a Preface seems a sort of impertinent bow to strangers who care nothing about it.

A Preface, however, should be down in so many words; and such a one that by an eye-glance over the type the Reader may catch an idea of an Author's modesty, and non-opinion of himself — which I sincerely hope may be seen in the few lines I have to write, notwithstanding many proverbs of many ages old which men find a great pleasure in receiving as gospel.

About a twelvemonth since, I published a little book of verses; it was read by some dozen of my friends who lik'd it; and some dozen whom I was unacquainted with, who did not.

Now, when a dozen human beings are at words with another dozen, it becomes a matter of anxiety to side with one's friends — more especially when excited thereto by a great love of Poetry. I fought under disadvantages. Before I began I had no inward feel of being able to finish; and as I proceeded my steps were all uncertain. So this Poem must rather be considered as an endeavour than as a thing accomplished; a poor prologue to what, if I live, I humbly hope to do. In duty to the Public I should have kept it back for a year or two, knowing it to be so faulty; but I really cannot do so, — by repetition my favourite passages sound vapid in my ears, and I would rather redeem myself with a new Poem should this one be found of any interest.

I have to apologize to the lovers of simplicity for touching the spell of loneliness that hung about Endymion; if any of my lines plead for me with such people I shall be proud.

It has been too much the fashion of late to consider men bigoted and addicted to every word that may chance to escape their lips; now I here declare that I have not any particular affection for any particular phrase, word, or letter in the whole affair. I have written to please myself, and in hopes to please others, and for a love of fame; if I neither please myself, nor others, nor get fame, of what consequence is Phraseology.

I would fain escape the bickerings that all works not exactly in chime bring upon their begetters — but this is not fair to expect, there must be conversation of some sort and to object shows a man's consequence. In case of a London drizzle or a Scotch mist, the following quotation from Marston may perhaps 'stead me as an umbrella for an hour or so: 'let it be the curtesy of my peruser rather to pity my self-hindering labours than to malice me.'

One word more — for we cannot help seeing our own affairs in every point of view — should any one call my dedication to Chatterton affected I answer as followeth: 'Were I dead, sir, I should like a book dedicated to me.'

TEIGNMOUTH,
  March 19th, 1818.

This Preface was shown either before or after it was in type to Reynolds and other friends, and Reynolds objected to it in terms which may be inferred from the following letter which Keats wrote him April 9, 1818, and which is so striking a reflection of his mind, when contemplating his finished work, that it should be read in connection with the poem: —

' Since you all agree that the thing is bad, it must be so — though I am not aware there is anything like Hunt in it (and if there is, it is my natural way, and I have something in common with Hunt). Look it over again, and examine into the motives, the seeds, from which any one sentence sprung — I have not the slightest feel of humility toward the public — or to anything in existence, — but the eternal Being, the Principle of Beauty, and the Memory of Great Men. When I am writing for myself for the mere sake of the moment's enjoyment, perhaps nature has its course with me — but a Preface is written to the Public; a thing I cannot help looking upon as an Enemy, and which I cannot address without feelings of Hostility. If I write a Preface in a supple or subdued style, it will not be in character with me as a public speaker — I would be subdued before my friends, and thank them for subduing me — but among Multitudes of Men — I have no feel of stooping; I hate the idea of humility to them.

' I never wrote one single line of Poetry with the least Shadow of public thought.

' Forgive me for vexing you and making a Trojan horse of such a Trifle, both with respect to the matter in question, and myself — but it eases me to tell you — I could

not live without the love of my friends — I
would jump down Ætna for any great Public good — but I hate a mawkish Popularity.
I cannot be subdued before them; my Glory
would be to daunt and dazzle the thousand
jabberers about pictures and books. I see
swarms of Porcupines with their quills
erect "like lime-twigs set to catch my
wingèd book," and I would fright them away
with a torch. You will say my Preface is
not much of a Torch. It would have been
too insulting "to begin from Jove," and I
could not set a golden head upon a thing of
clay. If there is any fault in the Preface
it is not affectation, but an undersong of
disrespect to the Public. If I write another Preface, it must be without a thought
of those people — I will think about it. If it
should not reach you in four or five days, tell
Taylor to publish it without a Preface, and
let the Dedication simply stand "Inscribed
to the Memory of Thomas Chatterton."'
The next day he wrote to his friend, in-
closing a new draft: 'I am anxious you
should find this Preface tolerable. If there
is an affectation in it 't is natural to me.
Do let the Printer's Devil cook it, and let
me be as "the casing air." You are too
good in this matter — were I in your state,
I am certain I should have no thought but
of discontent and illness — I might though
be taught Patience: I had an idea of giving
no Preface; however, don't you think this
had better go? O, let it — one should not
be too timid — of committing faults.'

The Dedication stood as Keats proposed,
and the new Preface, which is as follows:

PREFACE

KNOWING within myself the manner in
which this Poem has been produced, it is
not without a feeling of regret that I make
it public.

What manner I mean, will be quite clear
to the reader, who must soon perceive great
inexperience, immaturity, and every error
denoting a feverish attempt, rather than a
deed accomplished. The two first books,
and indeed the two last, I feel sensible are
not of such completion as to warrant their
passing the press; nor should they if I
thought a year's castigation would do them
any good; — it will not: the foundations are
too sandy. It is just that this youngster
should die away: a sad thought for me, if
I had not some hope that while it is dwin-
dling I may be plotting, and fitting myself
for verses fit to live.

This may be speaking too presumptu-
ously, and may deserve a punishment: but
no feeling man will be forward to inflict
it: he will leave me alone, with the conviction that there is not a fiercer hell than
the failure in a great object. This is not
written with the least atom of purpose to
forestall criticisms of course, but from the
desire I have to conciliate men who are
competent to look, and who do look with a
zealous eye, to the honour of English literature.

The imagination of a boy is healthy, and
the mature imagination of a man is healthy;
but there is a space of life between, in which
the soul is in a ferment, the character undecided, the way of life uncertain, the
ambition thick-sighted: thence proceeds
mawkishness, and all the thousand bitters
which those men I speak of must necessarily
taste in going over the following pages.

I hope I have not in too late a day
touched the beautiful mythology of Greece,
and dulled its brightness: for I wish to try
once more, before I bid it farewel.

TEIGNMOUTH,
April 10, 1818.

BOOK I

A THING of beauty is a joy for ever:
Its loveliness increases; it will never
Pass into nothingness; but still will keep
A bower quiet for us, and a sleep
Full of sweet dreams, and health, and quiet
    breathing.
Therefore, on every morrow, are we wreath-
    ing
A flowery band to bind us to the earth,
Spite of despondence, of the inhuman dearth
Of noble natures, of the gloomy days,
Of all the unhealthy and o'er - darken'd
    ways   10
Made for our searching: yes, in spite of
    all,
Some shape of beauty moves away the pall
From our dark spirits. Such the sun, the
    moon,
Trees old and young, sprouting a shady
    boon
For simple sheep; and such are daffodils
With the green world they live in; and clear
    rills
That for themselves a cooling covert make
'Gainst the hot season; the mid-forest brake,
Rich with a sprinkling of fair musk-rose
    blooms: 19
And such too is the grandeur of the dooms
We have imagined for the mighty dead;
All lovely tales that we have heard or read:
An endless fountain of immortal drink,
Pouring unto us from the heaven's brink.

Nor do we merely feel these essences
For one short hour; no, even as the trees
That whisper round a temple become soon
Dear as the temple's self, so does the moon,
The passion poesy, glories infinite,   29
Haunt us till they become a cheering light
Unto our souls, and bound to us so fast,
That, whether there be shine, or gloom o'er-
    cast,
They alway must be with us, or we die.

Therefore 't is with full happiness that I
Will trace the story of Endymion.

The very music of the name has gone
Into my being, and each pleasant scene
Is growing fresh before me as the green
Of our own valleys: so I will begin
Now while I cannot hear the city's din;   40
Now while the early budders are just new,
And run in mazes of the youngest hue
About old forests; while the willow trails
Its delicate amber; and the dairy pails
Bring home increase of milk. And, as the
    year
Grows lush in juicy stalks, I 'll smoothly
    steer
My little boat, for many quiet hours,
With streams that deepen freshly into bow-
    ers.
Many and many a verse I hope to write,
Before the daisies, vermeil rimm'd and
    white,   50
Hide in deep herbage; and ere yet the bees
Hum about globes of clover and sweet peas,
I must be near the middle of my story.
O may no wintry season, bare, and hoary,
See it half-finish'd: but let Autumn bold,
With universal tinge of sober gold,
Be all about me when I make an end.
And now at once, adventuresome, I send
My herald thought into a wilderness:
There let its trumpet blow, and quickly
    dress   60
My uncertain path with green, that I may
    speed
Easily onward, thorough flowers and weed.

Upon the sides of Latmos was outspread
A mighty forest; for the moist earth fed
So plenteously all weed-hidden roots
Into o'erhanging boughs, and precious
    fruits.
And it had gloomy shades, sequestered
    deep,
Where no man went; and if from shepherd's
    keep
A lamb stray'd far a-down those inmost
    glens,
Never again saw he the happy pens   70
Whither his brethren, bleating with con-
    tent,

Over the hills at every nightfall went.
Among the shepherds, 't was believed ever,
That not one fleecy lamb which thus did sever
From the white flock, but pass'd unworrièd
By angry wolf, or pard with prying head,
Until it came to some unfooted plains
Where fed the herds of Pan: aye great his gains
Who thus one lamb did lose. Paths there were many,
Winding through palmy fern, and rushes fenny,   80
And ivy banks; all leading pleasantly
To a wide lawn, whence one could only see
Stems thronging all around between the swell
Of turf and slanting branches: who could tell
The freshness of the space of heaven above,
Edged round with dark tree-tops ? through which a dove
Would often beat its wings, and often too
A little cloud would move across the blue.

Full in the middle of this pleasantness
There stood a marble altar, with a tress 90
Of flowers budded newly; and the dew
Had taken fairy phantasies to strew
Daisies upon the sacred sward last eve,
And so the dawned light in pomp receive.
For 't was the morn: Apollo's upward fire
Made every eastern cloud a silvery pyre
Of brightness so unsullied, that therein
A melancholy spirit well might win
Oblivion, and melt out his essence fine
Into the winds: rain-scented eglantine 100
Gave temperate sweets to that well-wooing sun;
The lark was lost in him; cold springs had run
To warm their chilliest bubbles in the grass;
Man's voice was on the mountains; and the mass
Of nature's lives and wonders pulsed tenfold,
To feel this sun-rise and its glories old.

Now while the silent workings of the dawn   •
Were busiest, into that self-same lawn
All suddenly, with joyful cries, there sped
A troop of little children garlanded; 110
Who gathering round the altar seem'd to pry
Earnestly round as wishing to espy
Some folk of holiday: nor had they waited
For many moments, ere their ears were sated
With a faint breath of music, which ev'n then
Fill'd out its voice, and died away again.
Within a little space again it gave
Its airy swellings, with a gentle wave,
To light-hung leaves, in smoothest echoes breaking
Through copse-clad valleys, — ere their death, o'ertaking 120
The surgy murmurs of the lonely sea.

And now, as deep into the wood as we
Might mark a lynx's eye, there glimmer'd light
Fair faces and a rush of garments white,
Plainer and plainer showing, till at last
Into the widest alley they all past,
Making directly for the woodland altar.
O kindly muse ! let not my weak tongue faulter
In telling of this goodly company,
Of their old piety, and of their glee: 130
But let a portion of ethereal dew
Fall on my head, and presently unmew
My soul; that I may dare, in wayfaring,
To stammer where old Chaucer used to sing.

Leading the way, young damsels danced along,
Bearing the burden of a shepherd song;
Each having a white wicker, overbrimm'd
With April's tender younglings: next, well trimm'd,
A crowd of shepherds with as sunburnt looks
As may be read of in Arcadian books; 140
Such as sat listening round Apollo's pipe,

When the great deity, for earth too ripe,
Let his divinity o'erflowing die
In music, through the vales of Thessaly:
Some idly trail'd their sheep-hooks on the
    ground,
And some kept up a shrilly mellow sound
With ebon-tipped flutes: close after these,
Now coming from beneath the forest trees,
A venerable priest full soberly,
Begirt with minist'ring looks: alway his
    eye   150
Steadfast upon the matted turf he kept,
And after him his sacred vestments swept.
From his right hand there swung a vase,
    milk-white,
Of mingled wine, out-sparkling generous
    light;
And in his left he held a basket full
Of all sweet herbs that searching eye could
    cull:
Wild thyme, and valley-lilies whiter still
Than Leda's love, and cresses from the rill.
His aged head, crowned with beechen
    wreath,
Seem'd like a poll of ivy in the teeth   160
Of winter hoar. Then came another
    crowd
Of shepherds, lifting in due time aloud
Their share of the ditty. After them ap-
    pear'd,
Up-follow'd by a multitude that rear'd
Their voices to the clouds, a fair-wrought
    car,
Easily rolling so as scarce to mar
The freedom of three steeds of dapple
    brown:
Who stood therein did seem of great re-
    nown
Among the throng. His youth was fully
    blown,
Showing like Ganymede to manhood grown;
And, for those simple times, his garments
    were   171
A chieftain king's; beneath his breast, half
    bare,
Was hung a silver bugle, and between
His nervy knees there lay a boar-spear
    keen.

A smile was on his countenance; he seem'd
To common lookers-on, like one who
    dream'd
Of idleness in groves Elysian:
But there were some who feelingly could
    scan
A lurking trouble in his nether lip,
And see that oftentimes the reins would slip
Through his forgotten hands: then would
    they sigh,   181
And think of yellow leaves, of owlets' cry,
Of logs piled solemnly. — Ah, well-a-day,
Why should our young Endymion pine
    away!

Soon the assembly, in a circle ranged,
Stood silent round the shrine: each look
    was changed
To sudden veneration: women meek
Beckon'd their sons to silence; while each
    cheek
Of virgin bloom paled gently for slight fear.
Endymion too, without a forest peer,   190
Stood, wan, and pale, and with an awed
    face,
Among his brothers of the mountain chase.
In midst of all, the venerable priest
Eyed them with joy from greatest to the
    least,
And, after lifting up his aged hands,
Thus spake he: 'Men of Latmos! shepherd
    bands!
Whose care it is to guard a thousand flocks:
Whether descended from beneath the rocks
That overtop your mountains; whether
    come
From valleys where the pipe is never
    dumb;   200
Or from your swelling downs, where sweet
    air stirs
Blue harebells lightly, and where prickly
    furze
Buds lavish gold; or ye, whose precious
    charge
Nibble their fill at ocean's very marge,
Whose mellow reeds are touch'd with
    sounds forlorn
By the dim echoes of old Triton's horn:

Mothers and wives! who day by day pre-
pare
The scrip, with needments, for the moun-
tain air;
And all ye gentle girls who foster up
Udderless lambs, and in a little cup   210
Will put choice honey for a favour'd youth:
Yea, every one attend! for in good truth
Our vows are wanting to our great god
Pan.
Are not our lowing heifers sleeker than
Night-swollen mushrooms? Are not our
wide plains
Speckled with countless fleeces? Have
not rains
Green'd over April's lap? No howling sad
Sickens our fearful ewes; and we have had
Great bounty from Endymion our lord.
The earth is glad: the merry lark has
pour'd   220
His early song against yon breezy sky,
That spreads so clear o'er our solemnity.'

Thus ending, on the shrine he heap'd a
spire
Of teeming sweets, enkindling sacred fire;
Anon he stain'd the thick and spongy sod
With wine, in honour of the shepherd-god.
Now while the earth was drinking it, and
while
Bay leaves were crackling in the fragrant
pile,
And gummy frankincense was sparkling
bright
'Neath smothering parsley, and a hazy
light   230
Spread grayly eastward, thus a chorus
sang:

'O thou, whose mighty palace roof doth
hang
From jagged trunks, and overshadoweth
Eternal whispers, glooms, the birth, life,
death
Of unseen flowers in heavy peacefulness;
Who lov'st to see the hamadryads dress
Their ruffled locks where meeting hazels
darken;

And through whole solemn hours dost sit,
and hearken
The dreary melody of bedded reeds —
In desolate places, where dank moisture
breeds   240
The pipy hemlock to strange overgrowth;
Bethinking thee, how melancholy loth
Thou wast to lose fair Syrinx — do thou
now,
By thy love's milky brow!
By all the trembling mazes that she ran,
Hear us, great Pan!

'O thou, for whose soul-soothing quiet,
turtles
Passion their voices cooingly 'mong myrtles,
What time thou wanderest at eventide
Through sunny meadows, that outskirt the
side   250
Of thine enmossed realms: O thou, to whom
Broad-leaved fig-trees even now foredoom
Their ripen'd fruitage; yellow-girted bees
Their golden honeycombs; our village leas
Their fairest blossom'd beans and poppied
corn;
The chuckling linnet its five young unborn,
To sing for thee; low-creeping strawberries
Their summer coolness; pent-up butterflies
Their freckled wings; yea, the fresh-bud-
ding year
All its completions — be quickly near,   260
By every wind that nods the mountain pine,
O forester divine!

'Thou, to whom every faun and satyr
flies
For willing service; whether to surprise
The squatted hare while in half-sleeping
fit;
Or upward ragged precipices flit
To save poor lambkins from the eagle's
maw;
Or by mysterious enticement draw
Bewilder'd shepherds to their path again;
Or to tread breathless round the frothy
main,   270
And gather up all fancifullest shells
For thee to tumble into Naiads' cells,

And, being hidden, laugh at their out-peep-
   ing;
Or to delight thee with fantastic leaping,
The while they pelt each other on the
   crown
With silvery oak-apples, and fir-cones
   brown —
By all the echoes that about thee ring,
Hear us, O satyr king!

  'O Hearkener to the loud-clapping
    shears,
While ever and anon to his shorn peers   280
A ram goes bleating: Winder of the horn,
When snouted wild-boars routing tender
   corn
Anger our huntsman: Breather round our
   farms,
To keep off mildews, and all weather
   harms:
Strange ministrant of undescribed sounds,
That come a-swooning over hollow grounds,
And wither drearily on barren moors:
Dread opener of the mysterious doors
Leading to universal knowledge — see,
Great son of Dryope,   290
The many that are come to pay their vows
With leaves about their brows!

  'Be still the unimaginable lodge
For solitary thinkings; such as dodge
Conception to the very bourne of heaven,
Then leave the naked brain: be still the
   leaven,
That spreading in this dull and clodded
   earth
Gives it a touch ethereal — a new birth:
Be still a symbol of immensity;
A firmament reflected in a sea;   300
An element filling the space between;
An unknown — but no more: we humbly
   screen
With uplift hands our foreheads, lowly
   bending,
And giving out a shout most heaven-rend-
   ing,
Conjure thee to receive our humble Pæan,
Upon thy Mount Lycean!'

Even while they brought the burden to a
   close,
A shout from the whole multitude arose,
That linger'd in the air like dying rolls
Of abrupt thunder, when Ionian shoals   310
Of dolphins bob their noses through the
   brine.
Meantime, on shady levels, mossy fine,
Young companies nimbly began dancing
To the swift treble pipe, and humming
   string.
Aye, those fair living forms swam heavenly
To tunes forgotten — out of memory:
Fair creatures! whose young children's
   children bred
Thermopylæ its heroes — not yet dead,
But in old marbles ever beautiful.
High genitors, unconscious did they cull   320
Time's sweet first-fruits — they danced to
   weariness,
And then in quiet circles did they press
The hillock turf, and caught the latter end
Of some strange history, potent to send
A young mind from its bodily tenement.
Or they might watch the quoit-pitchers,
   intent
On either side; pitying the sad death
Of Hyacinthus, when the cruel breath
Of Zephyr slew him, — Zephyr penitent,
Who now, ere Phœbus mounts the firma-
   ment,   330
Fondles the flower amid the sobbing rain.
The archers too, upon a wider plain,
Beside the feathery whizzing of the shaft,
And the dull twanging bowstring, and the
   raft
Branch down sweeping from a tall ash top,
Call'd up a thousand thoughts to envelope
Those who would watch. Perhaps, the
   trembling knee
And frantic gape of lonely Niobe,
Poor, lonely Niobe! when her lovely young
Were dead and gone, and her caressing
   tongue   340
Lay a lost thing upon her paly lip,
And very, very deadliness did nip
Her motherly cheeks. Aroused from this
   sad mood

By one, who at a distance loud halloo'd,
Uplifting his strong bow into the air,
Many might after brighter visions stare:
After the Argonauts, in blind amaze
Tossing about on Neptune's restless ways,
Until, from the horizon's vaulted side,
There shot a golden splendour far and
  wide,   350
Spangling those million poutings of the
 brine
With quivering ore: 't was even an awful
 shine
From the exaltation of Apollo's bow;
A heavenly beacon in their dreary woe.
Who thus were ripe for high contemplating,
Might turn their steps towards the sober
 ring
Where sat Endymion and the aged priest
'Mong shepherds gone in eld, whose looks
 increased
The silvery setting of their mortal star.
There they discoursed upon the fragile
 bar   360
That keeps us from our homes ethereal;
And what our duties there: to nightly call
Vesper, the beauty-crest of summer wea-
 ther;
To summon all the downiest clouds together
For the sun's purple couch; to emulate
In minist'ring the potent rule of fate
With speed of fire-tail'd exhalations;
To tint her pallid cheek with bloom, who
 cons
Sweet poesy by moonlight: besides these,
A world of other unguess'd offices. 370
Anon they wander'd, by divine converse,
Into Elysium; vying to rehearse
Each one his own anticipated bliss.
One felt heart-certain that he could not
 miss
His quick-gone love, among fair blossom'd
 boughs,
Where every zephyr-sigh pouts, and endows
Her lips with music for the welcoming.
Another wish'd, 'mid that eternal spring,
To meet his rosy child, with feathery sails,
Sweeping, eye-earnestly, through almond
 vales: 380

Who, suddenly, should stoop through the
 smooth wind,
And with the balmiest leaves his temples
 bind;
And, ever after, through those regions be
His messenger, his little Mercury.
Some were athirst in soul to see again
Their fellow-huntsmen o'er the wide cham-
 paign
In times long past; to sit with them, and
 talk
Of all the chances in their earthly walk;
Comparing, joyfully, their plenteous stores
Of happiness, to when upon the moors, 390
Benighted, close they huddled from the
 cold,
And shared their famish'd scrips. Thus
 all out-told
Their fond imaginations, — saving him
Whose eyelids curtain'd up their jewels
 dim,
Endymion: yet hourly had he striven
To hide the cankering venom, that had
 riven
His fainting recollections. Now indeed
His senses had swoon'd off: he did not heed
The sudden silence, or the whispers low,
Or the old eyes dissolving at his woe, 400
Or anxious calls, or close of trembling
 palms,
Or maiden's sigh, that grief itself embalms:
But in the self-same fixed trance he kept,
Like one who on the earth had never stept.
Aye, even as dead-still as a marble man,
Frozen in that old tale Arabian.

Who whispers him so pantingly and
 close?
Peona, his sweet sister: of all those,
His friends, the dearest. Hushing signs
 she made,
And breathed a sister's sorrow to per-
 suade   410
A yielding up, a cradling on her care.
Her eloquence did breathe away the curse:
She led him, like some midnight spirit nurse
Of happy changes in emphatic dreams, .
Along a path between two little streams, —

Guarding his forehead, with her round
elbow,
From low-grown branches, and his foot-
steps slow
From stumbling over stumps and hillocks
small;
Until they came to where these streamlets
fall,
With mingled bubblings and a gentle
rush,   420
Into a river, clear, brimful, and flush
With crystal mocking of the trees and
sky,
A little shallop, floating there hard by,
Pointed its beak over the fringed bank;
And soon it lightly dipt, and rose, and sank,
And dipt again, with the young couple's
weight, —
Peona guiding, through the water straight,
Towards a bowery island opposite;
Which gaining presently, she steered light   430
Into a shady, fresh, and ripply cove,
Where nested was an arbour, overwove
By many a summer's silent fingering;
To whose cool bosom she was used to bring
Her playmates, with their needle broid-
ery,
And minstrel memories of times gone by.

So she was gently glad to see him laid
Under her favourite bower's quiet shade,
On her own couch, new made of flower
leaves,
Dried carefully on the cooler side of sheaves
When last the sun his autumn tresses
shook,   440
And the tann'd harvesters rich armfuls
took.
Soon was he quieted to slumbrous rest:
But, ere it crept upon him, he had prest
Peona's busy hand against his lips,
And still, a-sleeping, held her finger-tips
In tender pressure. And as a willow keeps
A patient watch over the stream that creeps
Windingly by it, so the quiet maid
Held her in peace: so that a whispering
blade
Of grass, a wailful gnat, a bee bustling   450

Down in the bluebells, or a wren light
rustling
Among sere leaves and twigs, might all be
heard.

O magic sleep! O comfortable bird,
That broodest o'er the troubled sea of the
mind
Till it is hush'd and smooth! O unconfined
Restraint! imprison'd liberty! great key
To golden palaces, strange minstrelsy,
Fountains grotesque, new trees, bespangled
caves,
Echoing grottoes, full of tumbling waves
And moonlight; aye, to all the mazy
world   460
Of silvery enchantment! — who, upfurl'd
Beneath thy drowsy wing a triple hour,
But renovates and lives? — Thus, in the
bower,
Endymion was calm'd to life again.
Opening his eyelids with a healthier brain,
He said: 'I feel this thine endearing love
All through my bosom: thou art as a dove
Trembling its closed eyes and sleeked
wings
About me; and the pearliest dew not brings
Such morning incense from the fields of
May,   470
As do those brighter drops that twinkling
stray
From those kind eyes, — the very home and
haunt
Of sisterly affection. Can I want
Aught else, aught nearer heaven, than such
tears?
Yet dry them up, in bidding hence all fears
That, any longer, I will pass my days
Alone and sad. No, I will once more raise
My voice upon the mountain-heights; once
more
Make my horn parley from their foreheads
hoar:
Again my trooping hounds their tongues
shall loll   480
Around the breathed boar: again I'll poll
The fair-grown yew-tree, for a chosen bow:
And, when the pleasant sun is getting low,

Again I'll linger in a sloping mead
To hear the speckled thrushes, and see feed
Our idle sheep.   So be thou cheered, sweet !
And, if thy lute is here, softly intreat
My soul to keep in its resolved course.'

   Hereat Peona, in their silver source,
Shut her pure sorrow-drops with glad ex-
    claim,   490
And took a lute, from which there pulsing
    came
A lively prelude, fashioning the way
In which her voice should wander.   'T was
    a lay
More subtle cadenced, more forest wild
Than Dryope's lone lulling of her child;
And nothing since has floated in the air
So mournful strange.   Surely some influ-
    ence rare
Went, spiritual, through the damsel's hand;
For still, with Delphic emphasis, she spann'd
The quick invisible strings, even though
    she saw   500
Endymion's spirit melt away and thaw
Before the deep intoxication.
But soon she came, with sudden burst, upon
Her self-possession — swung the lute aside,
And earnestly said: ' Brother, 't is vain to
    hide
That thou dost know of things mysterious,
Immortal, starry; such alone could thus
Weigh down thy nature.   Hast thou sinn'd
    in aught
Offensive to the heavenly powers ?   Caught
A Paphian dove upon a message sent ?   510
Thy deathful bow against some deer-herd
    bent,
Sacred to Dian ?   Haply, thou hast seen
Her naked limbs among the alders green;
And that, alas ! is death.   No, I can trace
Something more high perplexing in thy
    face !'

   Endymion look'd at her, and press'd her
    hand,
And said, ' Art thou so pale, who wast so
    bland
And merry in our meadows ?   How is this ?

Tell me thine ailment: tell me all amiss ! —
Ah ! thou hast been unhappy at the change
Wrought suddenly in me.   What indeed
    more strange ?   521
Or more complete to overwhelm surmise ?
Ambition is no sluggard: 't is no prize,
That toiling years would put within my
    grasp,
That I have sigh'd for: with so deadly gasp
No man e'er panted for a mortal love.
So all have set my heavier grief above
These things which happen.   Rightly have
    they done:
I, who still saw the horizontal sun
Heave his broad shoulder o'er the edge of
    the world,   530
Out-facing Lucifer, and then had hurl'd
My spear aloft, as signal for the chase —
I, who, for very sport of heart, would
    race
With my own steed from Araby; pluck
    down
A vulture from his towery perching; frown
A lion into growling, loth retire —
To lose, at once, all my toil-breeding fire,
And sink thus low ! but I will ease my
    breast
Of secret grief, here in this bowery nest.

   ' This river does not see the naked sky,
Till it begins to progress silverly   541
Around the western border of the wood,
Whence, from a certain spot, its winding
    flood
Seems at the distance like a crescent moon:
And in that nook, the very pride of June,
Had I been used to pass my weary eves;
The rather for the sun unwilling leaves
So dear a picture of his sovereign power,
And I could witness his most kingly hour,
When he doth tighten up the golden reins,
And paces leisurely down amber plains   551
His snorting four.   Now when his chariot
    last
Its beams against the zodiac-lion cast,
There blossom'd suddenly a magic bed
Of sacred ditamy, and poppies red:
At which I wondered greatly, knowing well

That but one night had wrought this flow-
ery spell;
And, sitting down close by, began to muse
What it might mean. Perhaps, thought I,
Morpheus,
In passing here, his owlet pinions shook;
Or, it may be, ere matron Night uptook 561
Her ebon urn, young Mercury, by stealth,
Had dipt his rod in it: such garland wealth
Came not by common growth. Thus on I
thought,
Until my head was dizzy and distraught.
Moreover, through the dancing poppies
stole
A breeze, most softly lulling to my soul;
And shaping visions all about my sight
Of colours, wings, and bursts of spangly
light;
The which became more strange, and
strange, and dim, 570
And then were gulf'd in a tumultuous swim:
And then I fell asleep. Ah, can I tell
The enchantment that afterwards befell?
Yet it was but a dream: yet such a dream
That never tongue, although it overteem
With mellow utterance, like a cavern
spring,
Could figure out and to conception bring
All I beheld and felt. Methought I lay
Watching the zenith, where the milky way
Among the stars in virgin splendour pours;
And travelling my eye, until the doors 581
Of heaven appear'd to open for my flight,
I became loth and fearful to alight
From such high soaring by a downward
glance:
So kept me steadfast in that airy trance,
Spreading imaginary pinions wide.
When, presently, the stars began to glide,
And faint away, before my eager view:
At which I sigh'd that I could not pursue,
And dropt my vision to the horizon's verge;
And lo! from opening clouds, I saw
emerge 591
The loveliest moon, that ever silver'd o'er
A shell for Neptune's goblet; she did
soar
So passionately bright, my dazzled soul

Commingling with her argent spheres did
roll
Through clear and cloudy, even when she
went
At last into a dark and vapoury tent —
Whereat, methought, the lidless-eyed train
Of planets all were in the blue again.
To commune with those orbs, once more I
raised 600
My sight right upward: but it was quite
dazed
By a bright something, sailing down apace,
Making me quickly veil my eyes and face:
Again I look'd, and, O ye deities,
Who from Olympus watch our destinies!
Whence that completed form of all com-
pleteness?
Whence came that high perfection of all
sweetness?
Speak, stubborn earth, and tell me where,
O where
Hast thou a symbol of her golden hair?
Not oat-sheaves drooping in the western
sun; 610
Not — thy soft hand, fair sister! let me
shun
Such follying before thee — yet she had,
Indeed, locks bright enough to make me
mad;
And they were simply gordian'd up and
braided,
Leaving, in naked comeliness, unshaded,
Her pearl round ears, white neck, and
orbed brow;
The which were blended in, I know not
how,
With such a paradise of lips and eyes,
Blush-tinted cheeks, half smiles, and faint-
est sighs,
That, when I think thereon, my spirit
clings 620
And plays about its fancy, till the stings
Of human neighbourhood envenom all.
Unto what awful power shall I call?
To what high fane? — Ah! see her hover-
ing feet,
More bluely vein'd, more soft, more whitely
sweet

Than those of sea-born Venus, when she
   rose
From out her cradle shell. The wind out-
   blows
Her scarf into a fluttering pavilion ;
'T is blue, and over-spangled with a million
Of little eyes, as though thou wert to shed,
Over the darkest, lushest bluebell bed, 631
Handfuls of daisies.' — 'Endymion, how
   strange !
Dream within dream ! ' — ' She took an
   airy range,
And then, towards me, like a very maid,
Came blushing, waning, willing, and afraid,
And press'd me by the hand: Ah ! 't was
   too much,
Methought I fainted at the charmed touch,
Yet held my recollection, even as one
Who dives three fathoms where the waters
   run
Gurgling in beds of coral: for anon, 640
I felt upmounted in that region
Where falling stars dart their artillery forth,
And eagles struggle with the buffeting
   north
That balances the heavy meteor-stone ; —
Felt too, I was not fearful, nor alone,
But lapp'd and lull'd along the dangerous
   sky.
Soon, as it seem'd, we left our journeying
   high,
And straightway into frightful eddies
   swoop'd;
Such as ay muster where gray time has
   scoop'd
Huge dens and caverns in a mountain's
   side: 650
There hollow sounds aroused me, and I
   sigh'd
To faint once more by looking on my bliss —
I was distracted; madly did I kiss
The wooing arms which held me, and did
   give
My eyes at once to death : but 't was to live,
To take in draughts of life from the gold
   fount
Of kind and passionate looks; to count,
   and count

The moments, by some greedy help that
   seem'd
A second self, that each might be redeem'd
And plunder'd of its load of blessed-
   ness. 660
Ah, desperate mortal ! I ev'n dared to press
Her very cheek against my crowned lip,
And, at that moment, felt my body dip
Into a warmer air: a moment more,
Our feet were soft in flowers. There was
   store
Of newest joys upon that alp. Sometimes
A scent of violets, and blossoming limes,
Loiter'd around us; then of honey cells,
Made delicate from all white-flower bells;
And once, above the edges of our nest, 670
An arch face peep'd, — an Oread as I
   guess'd.

   'Why did I dream that sleep o'erpower'd
   me
In midst of all this heaven ? Why not see,
Far off, the shadows of his pinions dark,
And stare them from me ? But no, like a
   spark
That needs must die, although its little
   beam
Reflects upon a diamond, my sweet dream
Fell into nothing — into stupid sleep.
And so it was, until a gentle creep,
A careful moving caught my waking
   ears, 680
And up I started: Ah ! my sighs, my tears,
My clenched hands; — for lo ! the poppies
   hung
Dew-dabbled on their stalks, the ouzel sung
A heavy ditty, and the sullen day
Had chidden herald Hesperus away,
With leaden looks: the solitary breeze
Bluster'd, and slept, and its wild self did
   tease
With wayward melancholy; and I thought,
Mark me, Peona ! that sometimes it brought
Faint fare-thee-wells, and sigh-shrilled
   adieus ! — 690
Away I wander'd — all the pleasant hues
Of heaven and earth had faded: deepest
   shades

Were deepest dungeons; heaths and sunny
glades
Were full of pestilent light; our taintless
rills
Seem'd sooty, and o'erspread with upturn'd
gills
Of dying fish; the vermeil rose had blown
In frightful scarlet, and its thorns outgrown
Like spiked aloe. If an innocent bird
Before my heedless footsteps stirr'd, and
stirr'd
In little journeys, I beheld in it   700
A disguised demon, missioned to knit
My soul with under darkness; to entice
My stumblings down some monstrous pre-
cipice:
Therefore I eager follow'd, and did curse
The disappointment. Time, that aged
nurse,
Rock'd me to patience. Now, thank gentle
heaven !
These things, with all their comfortings,
are given
To my down-sunken hours, and with thee,
Sweet sister, help to stem the ebbing sea
Of weary life.'

       Thus ended he, and both
Sat silent: for the maid was very loth   711
To answer; feeling well that breathed
words
Would all be lost, unheard, and vain as
swords
Against the enchased crocodile, or leaps
Of grasshoppers against the sun. She
weeps,
And wonders; struggles to devise some
blame;
To put on such a look as would say, *Shame
On this poor weakness !* but, for all her
strife,
She could as soon have crush'd away the
life
From a sick dove. At length, to break the
pause,   720
She said with trembling chance: 'Is this
the cause ?
This all ? Yet it is strange, and sad, alas !

That one who through this middle earth
should pass
Most like a sojourning demi-god, and leave
His name upon the harp-string, should
achieve
No higher bard than simple maidenhood,
Singing alone, and fearfully, — how the
blood
Left his young cheek; and how he used to
stray
He knew not where; and how he would
say, *nay*,
If any said 't was love: and yet 't was
love;   730
What could it be but love ? How a ring-
dove
Let fall a sprig of yew-tree in his path;
And how he died: and then, that love doth
scathe
The gentle heart, as northern blasts do
roses;
And then the ballad of his sad life closes
With sighs, and an alas ! — Endymion !
Be rather in the trumpet's mouth, — anon
Among the winds at large — that all may
hearken !
Although, before the crystal heavens
darken,
I watch and dote upon the silver lakes   740
Pictured in western cloudiness, that takes
The semblance of gold rocks and bright
gold sands,
Islands, and creeks, and amber-fretted
strands
With horses prancing o'er them, palaces
And towers of amethyst, — would I so tease
My pleasant days, because I could not
mount
Into those regions ? The Morphean fount
Of that fine element that visions, dreams,
And fitful whims of sleep are made of,
streams
Into its airy channels with so subtle,   750
So thin a breathing, not the spider's shuttle,
Circled a million times within the space
Of a swallow's nest-door, could delay a
trace,
A tinting of its quality: how light

Must dreams themselves be; seeing they 're
  more slight
Than the mere nothing that engenders
  them !
Then wherefore sully the entrusted gem
Of high and noble life with thoughts so
  sick ?
Why pierce high-fronted honour to the
  quick
For nothing but a dream ? ' Hereat the
  youth   760
Look'd up: a conflicting of shame and ruth
Was in his plaited brow: yet his eyelids
Widen'd a little, as when Zephyr bids
A little breeze to creep between the fans
Of careless butterflies: amid his pains
He seem'd to taste a drop of manna-dew,
Full palatable; and a colour grew
Upon his cheek, while thus he lifeful spake.

'Peona ! ever have I long'd to slake
My thirst for the world's praises: nothing
  base,   770
No merely slumberous phantasm, could
  unlace
The stubborn canvas for my voyage pre-
  pared —
Though now 't is tatter'd; leaving my bark
  bared
And sullenly drifting: yet my higher hope
Is of too wide, too rainbow-large a scope,
To fret at myriads of earthly wrecks.
Wherein lies happiness ? In that which
  becks
Our ready minds to fellowship divine,
A fellowship with essence; till we shine,
Full alchemized, and free of space. Be-
  hold   780
The clear religion of heaven ! Fold
A rose leaf round thy finger's taperness,
And soothe thy lips: hist, when the airy
  stress
Of music's kiss impregnates the free winds,
And with a sympathetic touch unbinds
Æolian magic from their lucid wombs:
Then old songs waken from enclouded
  tombs;
Old ditties sigh above their father's grave;

Ghosts of melodious prophesyings rave
Round every spot where trod Apollo's
  foot;   790
Bronze clarions awake, and faintly bruit,
Where long ago a giant battle was;
And, from the turf, a lullaby doth pass
In every place where infant Orpheus slept.
Feel we these things ? — that moment have
  we stept
Into a sort of oneness, and our state
Is like a floating spirit's. But there are
Richer entanglements, enthralments far
More self-destroying, leading, by degrees,
To the chief intensity: the crown of these
Is made of love and friendship, and sits
  high   801
Upon the forehead of humanity.
All its more ponderous and bulky worth
Is friendship, whence there ever issues forth
A steady splendour; but at the tip-top,
There hangs by unseen film, an orbed drop
Of light, and that is love: its influence
Thrown in our eyes genders a novel sense,
At which we start and fret: till in the end,
Melting into its radiance, we blend,   810
Mingle, and so become a part of it, —
Nor with aught else can our souls interknit
So wingedly: when we combine therewith,
Life's self is nourish'd by its proper pith,
And we are nurtured like a pelican brood.
Aye, so delicious is the unsating food,
That men, who might have tower'd in the
  van
Of all the congregated world, to fan
And winnow from the coming step of time
All chaff of custom, wipe away all slime 820
Left by men-slugs and human serpentry,
Have been content to let occasion die,
Whilst they did sleep in love's Elysium.
And, truly, I would rather be struck dumb,
Than speak against this ardent listless-
  ness:
For I have ever thought that it might bless
The world with benefits unknowingly;
As does the nightingale, up-perched high,
And cloister'd among cool and bunched
  leaves —   829
She sings but to her love, nor e'er conceives

How tiptoe Night holds back her dark-
gray hood.
Just so may love, although 't is understood
The mere commingling of passionate breath,
Produce more than our searching witness-
eth:
What I know not: but who, of men, can
tell
That flowers would bloom, or that green
fruit would swell
To melting pulp, that fish would have
bright mail,
The earth its dower of river, wood, and
vale,
The meadows runnels, runnels pebble-
stones,   839
The seed its harvest, or the lute its tones,
Tones ravishment, or ravishment its sweet,
If human souls did never kiss and greet?

' Now, if this earthly love has power to
make
Men's being mortal, immortal; to shake
Ambition from their memories, and brim
Their measure of content; what merest
whim,
Seems all this poor endeavour after fame,
To one, who keeps within his steadfast
aim
A love immortal, an immortal too.
Look not so wilder'd; for these things are
true   850
And never can be born of atomies
That buzz about our slumbers, like brain-
flies,
Leaving us fancy-sick. No, no, I'm sure,
My restless spirit never could endure
To brood so long upon one luxury,
Unless it did, though fearfully, espy
A hope beyond the shadow of a dream.
My sayings will the less obscured seem
When I have told thee how my waking
sight
Has made me scruple whether that same
night   860
Was pass'd in dreaming. Hearken, sweet
Peona!
Beyond the matron-temple of Latona,

Which we should see but for these dark-
ening boughs,
Lies a deep hollow, from whose ragged
brows
Bushes and trees do lean all round athwart,
And meet so nearly, that with wings out-
raught,
And spreaded tail, a vulture could not glide
Past them, but he must brush on every
side.
Some moulder'd steps lead into this cool
cell,
Far as the slabbed margin of a well,   870
Whose patient level peeps its crystal eye
Right upward, through the bushes, to the
sky.
Oft have I brought thee flowers, on their
stalks set
Like vestal primroses, but dark velvet
Edges them round, and they have golden
pits:
'T was there I got them, from the gaps and
slits
In a mossy stone, that sometimes was my
seat,
When all above was faint with mid-day
heat.
And there in strife no burning thoughts to
heed,
I'd bubble up the water through a reed;
So reaching back to boyhood: make me
ships   881
Of moulted feathers, touchwood, alder
chips,
With leaves stuck in them; and the Nep-
tune be
Of their petty ocean. Oftener, heavily,
When lovelorn hours had left me less a
child,
I sat contemplating the figures wild
Of o'er-head clouds melting the mirror
through.
Upon a day, while thus I watch'd, by flew
A cloudy Cupid, with his bow and quiver;
So plainly character'd, no breeze would
shiver   890
The happy chance: so happy, I was fain
To follow it upon the open plain,

And, therefore, was just going; when, be-
  hold !
A wonder, fair as any I have told —
The same bright face I tasted in my sleep,
Smiling in the clear well. My heart did
  leap
Through the cool depth. — It moved as if
  to flee —
I started up, when lo ! refreshfully,
There came upon my face, in plenteous
  showers,
Dew-drops, and dewy buds, and leaves, and
  flowers,   900
Wrapping all objects from my smother'd
  sight,
Bathing my spirit in a new delight.
Aye, such a breathless honey-feel of bliss
Alone preserved me from the drear abyss
Of death, for the fair form had gone again.
Pleasure is oft a visitant; but pain
Clings cruelly to us, like the gnawing sloth
On the deer's tender haunches: late, and
  loth,
'T is scared away by slow returning plea-
  sure.
How sickening, how dark the dreadful lei-
  sure   910
Of weary days, made deeper exquisite,
By a foreknowledge of unslumbrous hight !
Like sorrow came upon me, heavier still,
Than when I wander'd from the poppy
  hill:
And a whole age of lingering moments
  crept
Sluggishly by, ere more contentment swept
Away at once the deadly yellow spleen.
Yes, thrice have I this fair enchantment
  seen;
Once more been tortured with renewed life.
When last the wintry gusts gave over
  strife   920
With the conquering sun of spring, and
  left the skies
Warm and serene, but yet with moisten'd
  eyes
In pity of the shatter'd infant buds, —
That time thou didst adorn, with amber
  studs,

My hunting cap, because I laugh'd and
  smiled,
Chatted with thee, and many days exiled
All torment from my breast; — 't was even
  then,
Straying about, yet coop'd up in the den
Of helpless discontent, — hurling my lance
From place to place, and following at
  chance,   930
At last, by hap, through some young trees
  it struck,
And, plashing among bedded pebbles, stuck
In the middle of a brook, — whose silver
  ramble
Down twenty little falls through reeds and
  bramble,
Tracing along, it brought me to a cave,
Whence it ran brightly forth, and white
  did lave
The nether sides of mossy stones and
  rock, —
'Mong which it gurgled blithe adieus, to
  mock
Its own sweet grief at parting. Overhead,
Hung a lush screen of drooping weeds, and
  spread   940
Thick, as to curtain up some wood-nymph's
  home.
"Ah ! impious mortal, whither do I roam !"
Said I, low-voiced: "Ah, whither ! 'T is the
  grot
Of Proserpine, when Hell, obscure and hot,
Doth her resign; and where her tender
  hands
She dabbles, on the cool and sluicy sands:
Or 't is the cell of Echo, where she sits,
And babbles thorough silence, till her wits
Are gone in tender madness, and anon,
Faints into sleep, with many a dying tone
Of sadness. O that she would take my
  vows,   951
And breathe them sighingly among the
  boughs,
To sue her gentle ears for whose fair head,
Daily, I pluck sweet flowerets from their
  bed,
And weave them dyingly — send honey-
  whispers

Round every leaf, that all those gentle
    lispers
May sigh my love unto her pitying !
O charitable Echo ! hear, and sing
This ditty to her " — tell her " — So I stay'd
My foolish tongue, and listening, half
    afraid,   960
Stood stupefied with my own empty folly,
And blushing for the freaks of melancholy.
Salt tears were coming, when I heard my
    name
Most fondly lipp'd, and then these accents
    came:
" Endymion ! the cave is secreter
Than the isle of Delos. Echo hence shall
    stir
No sighs but sigh-warm kisses, or light
    noise
Of thy combing hand, the while it travel-
    ling cloys
And trembles through my labyrinthine
    hair."
At that oppress'd, I hurried in. — Ah !
    where   970
Are those swift moments ? Whither are
    they fled ?
I 'll smile no more, Peona; nor will wed
Sorrow, the way to death; but patiently
Bear up against it: so farewell, sad sigh;
And come instead demurest meditation,
To occupy me wholly, and to fashion
My pilgrimage for the world's dusky brink.
No more will I count over, link by link,
My chain of grief: no longer strive to find
A half-forgetfulness in mountain wind 980
Blustering about my ears: aye, thou shalt
    see,
Dearest of sisters, what my life shall be;
What a calm round of hours shall make
    my days.
There is a paly flame of hope that plays
Where'er I look: but yet, I 'll say 't is
    naught —
And here I bid it die. Have not I caught,
Already, a more healthy countenance ?
By this the sun is setting; we may chance
Meet some of our near-dwellers with my
    car.'

This said, he rose, faint-smiling like a
    star   990
Through autumn mists, and took Peona's
    hand:
They stept into the boat, and launch'd from
    land.

BOOK II

O SOVEREIGN power of love! O grief! O
    balm !
All records, saving thine, come cool, and
    calm,
And shadowy, through the mist of passed
    years:
For others, good or bad, hatred and
    tears
Have become indolent; but touching thine,
One sigh doth echo, one poor sob doth
    pine,
One kiss brings honey-dew from buried
    days.
The woes of Troy, towers smothering o'er
    their blaze,
Stiff - holden shields, far - piercing spears,
    keen blades,
Struggling, and blood, and shrieks — all
    dimly fades   10
Into some backward corner of the brain;
Yet, in our very souls, we feel amain
The close of Troïlus and Cressid sweet.
Hence, pageant history! hence, gilded
    cheat !
Swart planet in the universe of deeds !
Wide sea, that one continuous murmur
    breeds
Along the pebbled shore of memory !
Many old rotten - timber'd boats there
    be
Upon thy vaporous bosom, magnified
To goodly vessels; many a sail of pride, 20
And golden-keel'd, is left unlaunch'd and
    dry.
But wherefore this ? What care, though
    owl did fly
About the great Athenian admiral's mast?
What care, though striding Alexander past

The Indus with his Macedonian numbers?
Though old Ulysses tortured from his
  slumbers
The glutted Cyclops, what care? — Juliet
  leaning
Amid her window-flowers, — sighing, —
  weaning
Tenderly her fancy from its maiden snow,
Doth more avail than these: the silver
  flow   30
Of Hero's tears, the swoon of Imogen,
Fair Pastorella in the bandit's den,
Are things to brood on with more ardency
Than the death-day of empires. Fearfully
Must such conviction come upon his head,
Who, thus far, discontent, has dared to
  tread,
Without one muse's smile, or kind behest,
The path of love and poesy. But rest,
In chafing restlessness, is yet more drear
Than to be crush'd, in striving to uprear 40
Love's standard on the battlements of song.
So once more days and nights aid me along,
Like legion'd soldiers.

               Brain-sick shepherd-prince,
What promise hast thou faithful guarded
  since
The day of sacrifice? Or, have new sor-
  rows
Come with the constant dawn upon thy
  morrows?
Alas! 't is his old grief. For many days,
Has he been wandering in uncertain ways:
Through wilderness, and woods of mossed
  oaks;
Counting his woe-worn minutes, by the
  strokes   50
Of the lone wood-cutter; and listening
  still,
Hour after hour, to each lush-leaved rill.
Now he is sitting by a shady spring,
And elbow-deep with feverous fingering
Stems the upbursting cold: a wild rose tree
Pavilions him in bloom, and he doth see
A bud which snares his fancy: lo! but now
He plucks it, dips its stalk in the water:
  how!

It swells, it buds, it flowers beneath his
  sight;
And, in the middle, there is softly pight 60
A golden butterfly; upon whose wings
There must be surely character'd strange
  things,
For with wide eye he wonders, and smiles
  oft.

  Lightly this little herald flew aloft,
Follow'd by glad Endymion's clasped
  hands:
Onward it flies. From languor's sullen
  bands
His limbs are loosed, and eager, on he hies
Dazzled to trace it in the sunny skies.
It seem'd he flew, the way so easy was;
And like a new-born spirit did he pass 70
Through the green evening quiet in the sun,
O'er many a heath, through many a wood-
  land dun,
Through buried paths, where sleepy twi-
  light dreams
The summer time away. One track un-
  seams
A wooded cleft, and, far away, the blue
Of ocean fades upon him; then, anew,
He sinks adown a solitary glen,
Where there was never sound of mortal
  men,
Saving, perhaps, some snow-light cadences
Melting to silence, when upon the breeze 80
Some holy bark let forth an anthem sweet,
To cheer itself to Delphi. Still his feet
Went swift beneath the merry-winged
  guide,
Until it reach'd a splashing fountain's side
That, near a cavern's mouth, for ever
  pour'd
Unto the temperate air: then high it soar'd,
And, downward, suddenly began to dip,
As if, athirst with so much toil, 't would
  sip
The crystal spout-head: so it did, with
  touch
Most delicate, as though afraid to smutch, 90
Even with mealy gold, the waters clear.
But, at that very touch, to disappear

So fairy-quick, was strange!   Bewildered,
Endymion sought around, and shook each
   bed
Of covert flowers in vain; and then he flung
Himself along the grass.   What gentle
   tongue,
What whisperer, disturb'd his gloomy rest ?
It was a nymph uprisen to the breast
In the fountain's pebbly margin, and she
   stood
'Mong lilies, like the youngest of the
   brood.   100
To him her dripping hand she softly kist,
And anxiously began to plait and twist
Her ringlets round her fingers, saying:
   ' Youth !
Too long, alas, hast thou starved on the
   ruth,
The bitterness of love: too long indeed,
Seeing thou art so gentle.   Could I weed
Thy soul of care, by heavens, I would offer
All the bright riches of my crystal coffer
To Amphitrite; all my clear-eyed fish,
Golden, or rainbow-sided, or purplish,   110
Vermilion - tail'd, or finn'd with silvery
   gauze;
Yea, or my veined pebble-floor, that draws
A virgin light to the deep; my grotto-sands,
Tawny and gold, oozed slowly from far
   lands
By my diligent springs: my level lilies,
   shells,
My charming rod, my potent river spells;
Yea, every thing, even to the pearly cup
Meander gave me, — for I bubbled up
To fainting creatures in a desert wild.
But woe is me, I am but as a child   120
To gladden thee; and all I dare to say,
Is, that I pity thee; that on this day
I 've been thy guide; that thou must wander
   far
In other regions, past the scanty bar
To mortal steps, before thou canst be ta'en
From every wasting sigh, from every pain,
Into the gentle bosom of thy love.
Why it is thus, one knows in heaven above:
But, a poor Naiad, I guess not.   Farewell !
I have a ditty for my hollow cell.'   130

Hereat she vanish'd from Endymion's
   gaze,
Who brooded o'er the water in amaze:
The dashing fount pour'd on, and where
   its pool
Lay, half asleep, in grass and rushes cool,
Quick waterflies and gnats were sporting
   still,
And fish were dimpling, as if good nor ill
Had fallen out that hour.   The wanderer,
Holding his forehead, to keep off the burr
Of smothering fancies, patiently sat down;
And, while beneath the evening's sleepy
   frown   140
Glowworms began to trim their starry
   lamps,
Thus breathed he to himself: ' Whoso en-
   camps
To take a fancied city of delight,
O what a wretch is he ! and when 't is his,
After long toil and travelling, to miss
The kernel of his hopes, how more than
   vile :
Yet, for him there 's refreshment even in
   toil:
Another city doth he set about,
Free from the smallest pebble - bead of
   doubt   149
That he will seize on trickling honey-combs:
Alas, he finds them dry; and then he foams,
And onward to another city speeds.
But this is human life: the war, the deeds,
The disappointment, the anxiety,
Imagination's struggles, far and nigh,
All human; bearing in themselves this good,
That they are still the air, the subtle food,
To make us feel existence, and to show
How quiet death is.   Where soil is, men
   grow,   159
Whether to weeds or flowers; but for me,
There is no depth to strike in: I can see
Naught earthly worth my compassing; so
   stand
Upon a misty, jutting head of land —
Alone ?   No, no; and by the Orphean lute,
When mad Eurydice is listening to 't,
I 'd rather stand upon this misty peak,
With not a thing to sigh for, or to seek,

But the soft shadow of my thrice seen love,
Than be — I care not what. O meekest
   dove
Of heaven! O Cynthia, ten-times bright
   and fair!   170
From thy blue throne, now filling all the
   air,
Glance but one little beam of temper'd
   light
Into my bosom, that the dreadful might
And tyranny of love be somewhat scared!
Yet do not so, sweet queen; one torment
   spared,
Would give a pang to jealous misery,
Worse than the torment's self: but rather
   tie
Large wings upon my shoulders, and point
   out
My love's far dwelling. Though the play-
   ful rout   179
Of Cupids shun thee, too divine art thou,
Too keen in beauty, for thy silver prow
Not to have dipp'd in love's most gentle
   stream.
O be propitious, nor severely deem
My madness impious; for, by all the stars
That tend thy bidding, I do think the bars
That kept my spirit in are burst — that I
Am sailing with thee through the dizzy
   sky!
How beautiful thou art! The world how
   deep!
How tremulous-dazzlingly the wheels sweep
Around their axle! Then these gleaming
   reins,   190
How lithe! When this thy chariot attains
Its airy goal, haply some bower veils
Those twilight eyes? Those eyes! — my
   spirit fails —
Dear goddess, help! or the wide gaping
   air
Will gulf me — help!' — At this, with
   madden'd stare,
And lifted hands, and trembling lips, he
   stood;
Like old Deucalion mountain'd o'er the
   flood,
Or blind Orion hungry for the morn.

And, but from the deep cavern there was
   borne
A voice, he had been froze to senseless
   stone;   200
Nor sigh of his, nor plaint, nor passion'd
   moan
Had more been heard. Thus swell'd it
   forth: 'Descend,
Young mountaineer! descend where alleys
   bend
Into the sparry hollows of the world!
Oft hast thou seen bolts of the thunder
   hurl'd
As from thy threshold; day by day hast
   been
A little lower than the chilly sheen
Of icy pinnacles, and dipp'dst thine arms
Into the deadening ether that still charms
Their marble being: now, as deep pro-
   found
As those are high, descend! He ne'er is
   crown'd   211
With immortality, who fears to follow
Where airy voices lead: so through the
   hollow,
The silent mysteries of earth, descend!'

He heard but the last words, nor could
   contend
One moment in reflection: for he fled
Into the fearful deep, to hide his head
From the clear moon, the trees, and com-
   ing madness.

'T was far too strange, and wonderful
   for sadness;
Sharpening, by degrees, his appetite   220
To dive into the deepest. Dark, nor light,
The region; nor bright, nor sombre wholly,
But mingled up; a gleaming melancholy;
A dusky empire and its diadems;
One faint eternal eventide of gems.
Aye, millions sparkled on a vein of gold,
Along whose track the prince quick foot-
   steps told,
With all its lines abrupt and angular:
Out-shooting sometimes, like a meteor-star,
Through a vast antre; then the metal woof,

Like Vulcan's rainbow, with some mon-
    strous roof   231
Curves hugely: now, far in the deep abyss,
It seems an angry lightning, and doth hiss
Fancy into belief: anon it leads
Through winding passages, where sameness
    breeds
Vexing conceptions of some sudden change;
Whether to silver grots, or giant range
Of sapphire columns, or fantastic bridge
Athwart a flood of crystal.   On a ridge
Now fareth he, that o'er the vast beneath
Towers like an ocean-cliff, and whence he
    seeth   241
A hundred waterfalls, whose voices come
But as the murmuring surge.   Chilly and
    numb
His bosom grew, when first he, far away,
Descried an orbed diamond, set to fray
Old Darkness from his throne: 't was like
    the sun
Uprisen o'er chaos: and with such a stun
Came the amazement, that, absorb'd in it,
He saw not fiercer wonders — past the
    wit
Of any spirit to tell, but one of those   250
Who, when this planet's sphering time doth
    close
Will be its high remembrancers: who they ?
The mighty ones who have made eternal
    day
For Greece and England.   While astonish-
    ment
With deep-drawn sighs was quieting, he
    went
Into a marble gallery, passing through
A mimic temple, so complete and true
In sacred custom, that he well nigh fear'd
To search it inwards; whence far off ap-
    pear'd,
Through a long pillar'd vista, a fair shrine,
And, just beyond, on light tiptoe divine, 261
A quiver'd Dian.   Stepping awfully,
The youth approach'd; oft turning his
    veil'd eye
Down sidelong aisles, and into niches old:
And when, more near against the marble
    cold

He had touch'd his forehead, he began to
    thread
All courts and passages, where silence dead,
Roused by his whispering footsteps, mur-
    mur'd faint:
And long he traversed to and fro, to ac-
    quaint
Himself with every mystery, and awe; 270
Till, weary, he sat down before the maw
Of a wide outlet, fathomless and dim,
To wild uncertainty and shadows grim.
There, when new wonders ceased to float
    before,
And thoughts of self came on, how crude
    and sore
The journey homeward to habitual self !
A mad pursuing of the fog-born elf,
Whose flitting lantern, through rude nettle-
    brier,
Cheats us into a swamp, into a fire,
Into the bosom of a hated thing.   280

    What misery most drowningly doth sing
In lone Endymion's ear, now he has raught
The goal of consciousness ?   Ah, 't is the
    thought,
The deadly feel of solitude: for lo !
He cannot see the heavens, nor the flow
Of rivers, nor hill-flowers running wild
In pink and purple chequer, nor, up-piled,
The cloudy rack slow journeying in the
    west,
Like herded elephants; nor felt, nor prest
Cool grass, nor tasted the fresh slumberous
    air;   290
But far from such companionship to wear
An unknown time, surcharged with grief,
    away,
Was now his lot.   And must he patient stay,
Tracing fantastic figures with his spear ?
'No !' exclaim'd he, 'why should I tarry
    here ? '
No ! loudly echoed times innumerable.
At which he straightway started, and 'gan
    tell
His paces back into the temple's chief;
Warming and glowing strong in the belief
Of help from Dian: so that when again 300

He caught her airy form, thus did he plain,
Moving more near the while: ' O Haunter
    chaste
Of river sides, and woods, and heathy
    waste,
Where with thy silver bow and arrows keen
Art thou now forested ? O woodland
    Queen,
What smoothest air thy smoother forehead
    woos ?
Where dost thou listen to the wide halloos
Of thy disparted nymphs ?   Through what
    dark tree
Glimmers thy crescent ? Wheresoe'er it be,
'T is in the breath of heaven: thou dost
    taste   310
Freedom as none can taste it, nor dost
    waste
Thy loveliness in dismal elements;
But, finding in our green earth sweet con-
    tents,
There livest blissfully.   Ah, if to thee
It feels Elysian, how rich to me,
An exiled mortal, sounds its pleasant name !
Within my breast there lives a choking
    flame —
O let me cool 't the zephyr-boughs among !
A homeward fever parches up my tongue —
O let me slake it at the running springs ! 320
Upon my ear a noisy nothing rings —
O let me once more hear the linnet's note !
Before mine eyes thick films and shadows
    float —
O let me 'noint them with the heaven's
    light !
Dost thou now lave thy feet and ankles
    white ?
O think how sweet to me the freshening
    sluice !
Dost thou now please thy thirst with berry-
    juice ?
O think how this dry palate would rejoice !
If in soft slumber thou dost hear my voice,
O think how I should love a bed of
    flowers ! —   330
Young goddess ! let me see my native
    bowers !
Deliver me from this rapacious deep ! '

Thus ending loudly, as he would o'er-
    leap
His destiny, alert he stood: but when
Obstinate silence came heavily again,
Feeling about for its old couch of space
And airy cradle, lowly bow'd his face,
Desponding, o'er the marble floor's cold
    thrill.
But 't was not long; for, sweeter than the
    rill
To its old channel, or a swollen tide   340
To margin sallows, were the leaves he spied,
And flowers, and wreaths, and ready myrtle
    crowns
Upheaping through the slab: refreshment
    drowns
Itself, and strives its own delights to hide —
Nor in one spot alone; the floral pride
In a long whispering birth enchanted grew
Before his footsteps; as when heaved anew
Old ocean rolls a lengthened wave to the
    shore,
Down whose green back the short-lived
    foam, all hoar,
Bursts gradual, with a wayward indo-
    lence.   350

Increasing still in heart, and pleasant
    sense,
Upon his fairy journey on he hastes;
So anxious for the end, he scarcely wastes
One moment with his hand among the
    sweets:
Onward he goes — he stops — his bosom
    beats
As plainly in his ear, as the faint charm
Of which the throbs were born.   This still
    alarm,
This sleepy music, forced him walk tip-
    toe:
For it came more softly than the east could
    blow
Arion's magic to the Atlantic isles;   360
Or than the west, made jealous by the
    smiles
Of throned Apollo, could breathe back the
    lyre
To seas Ionian and Tyrian.

O did he ever live, that lonely man,
Who loved — and music slew not ? 'T is
    the pest
Of love, that fairest joys give most unrest;
That things of delicate and tenderest worth
Are swallow'd all, and made a seared
    dearth,
By one consuming flame: it doth immerse
And suffocate true blessings in a curse. 370
Half-happy, by comparison of bliss,
Is miserable. 'T was even so with this
Dew-dropping melody, in the Carian's
    ear ;
First heaven, then hell, and then forgotten
    clear,
Vanish'd in elemental passion.

    And down some swart abysm he had
    gone,
Had not a heavenly guide benignant led
To where thick myrtle branches, 'gainst
    his head
Brushing, awakened: then the sounds again
Went noiseless as a passing noontide
    rain 380
Over a bower, where little space he stood;
For as the sunset peeps into a wood,
So saw he panting light, and towards it
    went
Through winding alleys; and lo, wonder-
    ment !
Upon soft verdure saw, one here, one there,
Cupids a-slumbering on their pinions fair.

    After a thousand mazes overgone,
At last, with sudden step, he came upon
A chamber, myrtle-wall'd, embower'd high,
Full of light, incense, tender minstrelsy, 390
And more of beautiful and strange beside:
For on a silken couch of rosy pride,
In midst of all, there lay a sleeping youth
Of fondest beauty; fonder, in fair sooth,
Than sighs could fathom, or contentment
    reach:
And coverlids gold-tinted like the peach,
Or ripe October's faded marigolds,
Fell sleek about him in a thousand folds —
Not hiding up an Apollonian curve

Of neck and shoulder, nor the tenting
    swerve 400
Of knee from knee, nor ankles pointing
    light;
But rather, giving them to the fill'd sight
Officiously. Sideway his face reposed
On one white arm, and tenderly unclosed,
By tenderest pressure, a faint damask
    mouth
To slumbery pout; just as the morning
    south
Disparts a dew-lipp'd rose. Above his
    head,
Four lily stalks did their white honours
    wed
To make a coronal; and round him grew
All tendrils green, of every bloom and
    hue, 410
Together intertwined and trammell'd fresh:
The vine of glossy sprout; the ivy mesh,
Shading its Ethiop berries; and woodbine,
Of velvet-leaves and bugle-blooms divine;
Convolvulus in streaked vases flush;
The creeper, mellowing for an autumn
    blush;
And virgin's bower, trailing airily;
With others of the sisterhood. Hard by,
Stood serene Cupids watching silently.
One, kneeling to a lyre, touch'd the
    strings, 420
Muffling to death the pathos with his wings;
And, ever and anon, uprose to look
At the youth's slumber; while another took
A willow bough, distilling odorous dew,
And shook it on his hair; another flew
In through the woven roof, and fluttering-
    wise
Rain'd violets upon his sleeping eyes.

    At these enchantments, and yet many
    more,
The breathless Latmian wonder'd o'er and
    o'er;
Until impatient in embarrassment, 430
He forthright pass'd, and lightly treading
    went
To that same feather'd lyrist, who straight-
    way,

Smiling, thus whisper'd: 'Though from
    upper day
Thou art a wanderer, and thy presence
    here
Might seem unholy, be of happy cheer!
For 't is the nicest touch of human honour,
When some ethereal and high-favouring
    donor
Presents immortal bowers to mortal sense;
As now 't is done to thee, Endymion. Hence
Was I in no wise startled. So recline   440
Upon these living flowers. Here is wine,
Alive with sparkles — never, I aver,
Since Ariadne was a vintager,
So cool a purple: taste these juicy pears,
Sent me by sad Vertumnus, when his fears
Were high about Pomona: here is cream,
Deepening to richness from a snowy gleam;
Sweeter than that nurse Amalthea skimm'd
For the boy Jupiter: and here, undimm'd
By any touch, a bunch of blooming plums
Ready to melt between an infant's gums:
And here is manna pick'd from Syrian
    trees,   452
In starlight, by the three Hesperides.
Feast on, and meanwhile I will let thee
    know
Of all these things around us.' He did
    so,
Still brooding o'er the cadence of his lyre;
And thus: 'I need not any hearing tire
By telling how the sea-born goddess pined
For a mortal youth, and how she strove to
    bind
Him all in all unto her doating self.   460
Who would not be so prison'd? but, fond
    elf,
He was content to let her amorous plea
Faint through his careless arms; content to
    see
An unseized heaven dying at his feet;
Content, O fool! to make a cold retreat,
When on the pleasant grass such love, love-
    lorn,
Lay sorrowing; when every tear was born
Of diverse passion; when her lips and eyes
Were closed in sullen moisture, and quick
    sighs

Came vex'd and pettish through her nos-
    trils small.   470
Hush! no exclaim — yet, justly might'st
    thou call
Curses upon his head. — I was half glad,
But my poor mistress went distract and
    mad,
When the boar tusk'd him: so away she flew
To Jove's high throne, and by her plainings
    drew
Immortal tear-drops down the thunderer's
    beard;
Whereon, it was decreed he should be
    rear'd
Each summer-time to life. Lo! this is he,
That same Adonis, safe in the privacy
Of this still region all his winter-sleep.   480
Aye, sleep; for when our love-sick queen
    did weep
Over his waned corse, the tremulous
    shower
Heal'd up the wound, and, with a balmy
    power,
Medicined death to a lengthened drowsi-
    ness:
The which she fills with visions, and doth
    dress
In all this quiet luxury; and hath set
Us young immortals, without any let,
To watch his slumber through. 'T is well
    nigh pass'd,
Even to a moment's filling up, and fast
She scuds with summer breezes, to pant
    through   490
The first long kiss, warm firstling, to renew
Embower'd sports in Cytherea's isle.
Look! how those winged listeners all this
    while
Stand anxious: see! behold!' — This cla-
    mant word
Broke through the careful silence; for
    they heard
A rustling noise of leaves, and out there
    flutter'd
Pigeons and doves: Adonis something
    mutter'd,
The while one hand, that erst upon his
    thigh

Lay dormant, moved convulsed and gradu-
   ally
Up to his forehead. Then there was a
   hum   500
Of sudden voices, echoing, ' Come ! come !
Arise ! awake ! Clear summer has forth
   walk'd
Unto the clover-sward, and she has talk'd
Full soothingly to every nested finch:
Rise, Cupids ! or we 'll give the bluebell
   pinch
To your dimpled arms. Once more sweet
   life begin !'
At this, from every side they hurried in,
Rubbing their sleepy eyes with lazy wrists,
And doubling overhead their little fists
In backward yawns. But all were soon
   alive: 510
For, as delicious wine doth, sparkling, dive
In nectar'd clouds and curls through water
   fair,
So from the arbour roof down swell'd an air
Odorous and enlivening; making all
To laugh, and play, and sing, and loudly call
For their sweet queen: when lo ! the
   wreathed green
Disparted, and far upward could be seen
Blue heaven, and a silver car, air-borne,
Whose silent wheels, fresh wet from clouds
   of morn,
Spun off a drizzling dew, — which falling
   chill   520
On soft Adonis' shoulders, made him still
Nestle and turn uneasily about.
Soon were the white doves plain, with necks
   stretch'd out,
And silken traces lighten'd in descent;
And soon, returning from love's banish-
   ment,
Queen Venus leaning downward open-
   arm'd:
Her shadow fell upon his breast, and
   charm'd
A tumult to his heart, and a new life
Into his eyes. Ah, miserable strife,
But for her comforting ! unhappy sight, 530
But meeting her blue orbs ! Who, who
   can write

Of these first minutes ? The unchariest
   muse
To embracements warm as theirs makes
   coy excuse.

   O it has ruffled every spirit there,
Saving Love's self, who stands superb to
   share
The general gladness: awfully he stands;
A sovereign quell is in his waving hands;
No sight can bear the lightning of his bow;
His quiver is mysterious, none can know
What themselves think of it; from forth
   his eyes   540
There darts strange light of varied hues
   and dyes:
A scowl is sometimes on his brow, but who
Look full upon it feel anon the blue
Of his fair eyes run liquid through their
   souls.
Endymion feels it, and no more controls
The burning prayer within him; so, bent
   low,
He had begun a plaining of his woe.
But Venus, bending forward, said: ' My
   child,
Favour this gentle youth; his days are wild
With love — he — but alas ! too well I see
Thou know'st the deepness of his misery.
Ah, smile not so, my son: I tell thee true,
That when through heavy hours I used to
   rue   553
The endless sleep of this new-born Adon',
This stranger ay I pitied. For upon
A dreary morning once I fled away
Into the breezy clouds, to weep and pray
For this my love: for vexing Mars had
   teased
Me even to tears: thence, when a little
   eased,
Down-looking, vacant, through a hazy wood,
I saw this youth as he despairing stood: 561
Those same dark curls blown vagrant in
   the wind;
Those same full fringed lids a constant
   blind
Over his sullen eyes: I saw him throw
Himself on wither'd leaves, even as though

Death had come sudden; for no jot he
    moved,
Yet mutter'd wildly. I could hear he loved
Some fair immortal, and that his embrace
Had zoned her through the night. There
    is no trace
Of this in heaven: I have mark'd each
    cheek,   570
And find it is the vainest thing to seek;
And that of all things 't is kept secretest.
Endymion! one day thou wilt be blest:
So still obey the guiding hand that fends
Thee safely through these wonders for
    sweet ends.
'T is a concealment needful in extreme;
And if I guess'd not so, the sunny beam
Thou shouldst mount up with me. Now
    adieu!
Here must we leave thee.' — At these
    words upflew
The impatient doves, uprose the floating
    car,   580
Up went the hum celestial. High afar
The Latmian saw them minish into naught;
And, when all were clear vanish'd, still he
    caught
A vivid lightning from that dreadful bow.
When all was darken'd, with Ætnean throe
The earth closed — gave a solitary moan —
And left him once again in twilight lone.

He did not rave, he did not stare aghast,
For all those visions were o'ergone, and
    past,
And he in loneliness: he felt assured   590
Of happy times, when all he had endured
Would seem a feather to the mighty prize.
So, with unusual gladness, on he hies
Through caves, and palaces of mottled
    ore,
Gold dome, and crystal wall, and turquois
    floor,
Black polish'd porticos of awful shade,
And, at the last, a diamond balustrade,
Leading afar past wild magnificence,
Spiral through ruggedest loopholes, and
    thence
Stretching across a void, then guiding o'er

Enormous chasms, where, all foam and
    roar,   601
Streams subterranean tease their granite
    beds;
Then heighten'd just above the silvery heads
Of a thousand fountains, so that he could
    dash
The waters with his spear; but at the
    splash,
Done heedlessly, those spouting columns
    rose
Sudden a poplar's height, and 'gan to en-
    close
His diamond path with fretwork, streaming
    round
Alive, and dazzling cool, and with a sound,
Haply, like dolphin tumults, when sweet
    shells   610
Welcome the float of Thetis. Long he
    dwells
On this delight; for, every minute's space,
The streams with changed magic interlace:
Sometimes like delicatest lattices,
Cover'd with crystal vines; then weeping
    trees,
Moving about as in a gentle wind,
Which, in a wink, to watery gauze refined,
Pour'd into shapes of curtain'd canopies,
Spangled, and rich with liquid broideries
Of flowers, peacocks, swans, and naiads
    fair.   620
Swifter than lightning went these wonders
    rare;
And then the water, into stubborn streams
Collecting, mimick'd the wrought oaken
    beams,
Pillars, and frieze, and high fantastic roof,
Of those dusk places in times far aloof
Cathedrals call'd. He bade a loth fare-
    well
To these founts Protean, passing gulf, and
    dell,
And torrent, and ten thousand jutting
    shapes,
Half seen through deepest gloom, and
    griesly gapes,
Blackening on every side, and overhead   630
A vaulted dome like Heaven's, far bespread

With starlight gems: aye, all so huge and
    strange,
The solitary felt a hurried change
Working within him into something
    dreary, —
Ver'd like a morning eagle, lost, and weary,
And purblind amid foggy, midnight wolds.
But he revives at once: for who beholds
New sudden things, nor casts his mental
    slough?
Forth from a rugged arch, in the dusk be-
    low,   639
Came mother Cybele! alone — alone —
In sombre chariot; dark foldings thrown
About her majesty, and front death-pale,
With turrets crown'd. Four maned lions
    hale
The sluggish wheels; solemn their toothed
    maws,
Their surly eyes brow-hidden, heavy paws
Uplifted drowsily, and nervy tails
Cowering their tawny brushes. Silent sails
This shadowy queen athwart, and faints
    away
In another gloomy arch.

                    Wherefore delay,
Young traveller, in such a mournful place?
Art thou wayworn, or canst not further
    trace   651
The diamond path? And does it indeed
    end
Abrupt in middle air? Yet earthward
    bend
Thy forehead, and to Jupiter cloud-borne
Call ardently! He was indeed wayworn;
Abrupt, in middle air, his way was lost;
To cloud-borne Jove he bowed, and there
    crost
Towards him a large eagle, 'twixt whose
    wings,
Without one impious word, himself he
    flings,
Committed to the darkness and the gloom:
Down, down, uncertain to what pleasant
    doom,   661
Swift as a fathoming plummet down he
    fell

Through unknown things; till exhaled as-
    phodel,
And rose, with spicy fannings interbreathed,
Came swelling forth where little caves were
    wreathed
So thick with leaves and mosses, that they
    seem'd
Large honeycombs of green, and freshly
    teem'd
With airs delicious. In the greenest nook
The eagle landed him, and farewell took.

    It was a jasmine bower, all bestrown   670
With golden moss. His every sense had
    grown
Ethereal for pleasure; 'bove his head
Flew a delight half-graspable; his tread
Was Hesperean; to his capable ears
Silence was music from the holy spheres;
A dewy luxury was in his eyes;
The little flowers felt his pleasant sighs
And stirr'd them faintly. Verdant cave
    and cell
He wander'd through, oft wondering at
    such swell
Of sudden exaltation: but, 'Alas!'   680
Said he, 'will all this gush of feeling pass
Away in solitude? And must they wane,
Like melodies upon a sandy plain,
Without an echo? Then shall I be left
So sad, so melancholy, so bereft!
Yet still I feel immortal! O my love,
My breath of life, where art thou? High
    above,
Dancing before the morning gates of
    heaven?
Or keeping watch among those starry seven,
Old Atlas' children? Art a maid of the
    waters,   690
One of shell-winding Triton's bright-hair'd
    daughters?
Or art, impossible! a nymph of Dian's,
Weaving a coronal of tender scions
For very idleness? Where'er thou art,
Methinks it now is at my will to start
Into thine arms; to scare Aurora's train,
And snatch thee from the morning; o'er
    the main

To scud like a wild bird, and take thee off
From thy sea-foamy cradle; or to doff
Thy shepherd vest, and woo thee 'mid
  fresh leaves.   700
No, no, too eagerly my soul deceives
Its powerless self: I know this cannot be.
O let me then by some sweet dreaming
  flee
To her entrancements: hither sleep awhile !
Hither most gentle sleep ! and soothing foil
For some few hours the coming solitude.'

  Thus spake he, and that moment felt
    endued
With power to dream deliciously; so wound
Through a dim passage, searching till he
  found
The smoothest mossy bed and deepest,
  where   710
He threw himself, and just into the air
Stretching his indolent arms, he took, O
  bliss !
A naked waist: 'Fair Cupid, whence is
  this ?'
A well-known voice sigh'd, 'Sweetest,
  here am I !'
At which soft ravishment, with doting cry
They trembled to each other. — Helicon !
O fountain'd hill ! Old Homer's Helicon !
That thou wouldst spout a little streamlet
  o'er
These sorry pages; then the verse would
  soar
And sing above this gentle pair, like lark
Over his nested young: but all is dark 721
Around thine aged top, and thy clear fount
Exhales in mists to heaven. Aye, the count
Of mighty Poets is made up; the scroll
Is folded by the Muses; the bright roll
Is in Apollo's hand: our dazed eyes
Have seen a new tinge in the western skies:
The world has done its duty. Yet, oh yet,
Although the sun of poesy is set,
These lovers did embrace, and we must
  weep   730
That there is no old power left to steep
A quill immortal in their joyous tears.
Long time in silence did their anxious fears

Question that thus it was; long time they
  lay
Fondling and kissing every doubt away;
Long time ere soft caressing sobs began
To mellow into words, and then there ran
Two bubbling springs of talk from their
  sweet lips.
'O known Unknown ! from whom my be-
  ing sips   739
Such darling essence, wherefore may I not
Be ever in these arms ? in this sweet spot
Pillow my chin for ever ? ever press
These toying hands and kiss their smooth
  excess ?
Why not for ever and for ever feel
That breath about my eyes ? Ah, thou wilt
  steal
Away from me again, indeed, indeed —
Thou wilt be gone away, and wilt not heed
My lonely madness. Speak, delicious fair
Is — is it to be so ? No ! Who will dare
To pluck thee from me ? And, of thine
  own will,   750
Full well I feel thou wouldst not leave me.
  Still
Let me entwine thee surer, surer — now
How can we part ? Elysium ! Who art
  thou ?
Who, that thou canst not be for ever here,
Or lift me with thee to some starry sphere ?
Enchantress ! tell me by this soft embrace,
By the most soft completion of thy face,
Those lips, O slippery blisses, twinkling
  eyes,
And by these tenderest, milky sovereign-
  ties —
These tenderest, and by the nectar-wine,
The passion' ——— 'O doved Ida the di-
  vine !   761
Endymion ! dearest ! Ah, unhappy me !
His soul will 'scape us — O felicity !
How he does love me ! His poor temples
  beat
To the very tune of love — how sweet,
  sweet, sweet.
Revive, dear youth, or I shall faint and
  die;
Revive, or these soft hours will hurry by

In tranced dullness; speak, and let that
    spell
Affright this lethargy ! I cannot quell
Its heavy pressure, and will press at least
My lips to thine, that they may richly
    feast   771
Until we taste the life of love again.
What ! dost thou move ? dost kiss ? O
    bliss ! O pain !
I love thee, youth, more than I can con-
    ceive;
And so long absence from thee doth be-
    reave
My soul of any rest: yet must I hence:
Yet, can I not to starry eminence
Uplift thee; nor for very shame can own
Myself to thee. Ah, dearest, do not groan
Or thou wilt force me from this secrecy, 780
And I must blush in heaven. O that I
Had done it already ; that the dreadful
    smiles
At my lost brightness, my impassion'd
    wiles,
Had waned from Olympus' solemn height,
And from all serious Gods; that our de-
    light
Was quite forgotten, save of us alone !
And wherefore so ashamed ? 'T is but to
    atone
For endless pleasure, by some coward
    blushes:
Yet must I be a coward ! — Honour rushes
Too palpable before me — the sad look 790
Of Jove — Minerva's start — no bosom
    shook
With awe of purity — no Cupid pinion
In reverence veiled — my crystalline do-
    minion
Half lost, and all old hymns made nul-
    lity !
But what is this to love? O I could fly
With thee into the ken of heavenly pow-
    ers,
So thou wouldst thus, for many sequent
    hours,
Press me so sweetly. Now I swear at
    once
That I am wise, that Pallas is a dunce —

Perhaps her love like mine is but un-
    known —   800
O I do think that I have been alone
In chastity: yes, Pallas has been sighing,
While every eve saw me my hair uptying
With fingers cool as aspen leaves. Sweet
    love,
I was as vague as solitary dove,
Nor knew that nests were built. Now a
    soft kiss —
Aye, by that kiss, I vow an endless bliss,
An immortality of passion 's thine:
Ere long I will exalt thee to the shine
Of heaven ambrosial; and we will shade 810
Ourselves whole summers by a river glade;
And I will tell thee stories of the sky,
And breathe thee whispers of its minstrelsy.
My happy love will overwing all bounds !
O let me melt into thee; let the sounds
Of our close voices marry at their birth;
Let us entwine hoveringly — O dearth
Of human words ! roughness of mortal
    speech !
Lispings empyrean will I sometime teach
Thine honey'd tongue — lute-breathings,
    which I gasp   .   820
To have thee understand, now while I
    clasp
Thee thus, and weep for fondness — I am
    pain'd,
Endymion: woe ! woe ! is grief contain'd
In the very deeps of pleasure, my sole
    life ? ' —
Hereat, with many sobs, her gentle strife
Melted into a languor. He return'd
Entranced vows and tears.

                Ye who have yearn'd
With too much passion, will here stay and
    pity,
For the mere sake of truth; as 't is a ditty
Not of these days, but long ago 't was told
By a cavern wind unto a forest old;   831
And then the forest told it in a dream
To a sleeping lake, whose cool and level
    gleam
A poet caught as he was journeying
To Phœbus' shrine; and in it he did fling

His weary limbs, bathing an hour's space,
And after, straight in that inspired place
He sang the story up into the air,
Giving it universal freedom. There
Has it been ever sounding for those ears 840
Whose tips are glowing hot. The legend
    cheers
Yon sentinel stars; and he who listens
    to it
Must surely be self - doom'd or he will
    rue it:
For quenchless burnings come upon the
    heart,
Made fiercer by a fear lest any part
Should be engulfed in the eddying wind.
As much as here is penn'd doth always
    find
A resting-place, thus much comes clear and
    plain;
Anon the strange voice is upon the wane —
And 't is but echoed from departing sound,
That the fair visitant at last unwound 851
Her gentle limbs, and left the youth
    asleep. —
Thus the tradition of the gusty deep.

Now turn we to our former chroni-
    clers. —
Endymion awoke, that grief of hers
Sweet paining on his ear: he sickly guess'd
How lone he was once more, and sadly
    press'd
His empty arms together, hung his head,
And most forlorn upon that widow'd bed
Sat silently. Love's madness he had
    known: 860
Often with more than tortured lion's groan
Moanings had burst from him; but now
    that rage
Had pass'd away: no longer did he wage
A rough-voiced war against the dooming
    stars.
No, he had felt too much for such harsh
    jars:
The lyre of his soul Æolian tuned
Forgot all violence, and but communed
With melancholy thought : O he had
    swoon'd

Drunken from pleasure's nipple; and his
    love
Henceforth was dove-like. — Loth was he
    to move   870
From the imprinted couch, and when he
    did,
'T was with slow, languid paces, and face
    hid
In muffling hands. So temper'd, out he
    stray'd
Half seeing visions that might have dis-
    may'd
Alecto's serpents; ravishments more keen
Than Hermes' pipe, when anxious he did
    lean
Over eclipsing eyes: and at the last
It was a sounding grotto, vaulted, vast,
O'erstudded with a thousand, thousand
    pearls,
And crimson-mouthed shells with stubborn
    curls,   880
Of every shape and size, even to the bulk
In which whales harbour close, to brood
    and sulk
Against an endless storm. Moreover too,
Fish-semblances, of green and azure hue,
Ready to snort their streams. In this cool
    wonder
Endymion sat down, and 'gan to ponder
On all his life: his youth, up to the day
When 'mid acclaim, and feasts, and gar-
    lands gay,
He stept upon his shepherd throne: the look
Of his white palace in wild forest nook, 890
And all the revels he had lorded there:
Each tender maiden whom he once thought
    fair,
With every friend and fellow-woodlander —
Pass'd like a dream before him. Then the
    spur
Of the old bards to mighty deeds: his plans
To nurse the golden age 'mong shepherd
    clans:
That wondrous night: the great Pan-festi-
    val:
His sister's sorrow; and his wanderings all,
Until into the earth's deep maw he rush'd:
Then all its buried magic, till it flush'd 900

High with excessive love. 'And now,'
thought he,
'How long must I remain in jeopardy
Of blank amazements that amaze no more?
Now I have tasted her sweet soul to the
core,
All other depths are shallow: essences,
Once spiritual, are like muddy lees,
Meant but to fertilize my earthly root,
And make my branches lift a golden fruit
Into the bloom of heaven: other light,
Though it be quick and sharp enough to
blight ·   910
The Olympian eagle's vision, is dark,
Dark as the parentage of chaos. Hark!
My silent thoughts are echoing from these
shells;
Or they are but the ghosts, the dying swells
Of noises far away? — list!' — Hereupon
He kept an anxious ear. The humming
tone
Came louder, and behold, there as he lay,
On either side outgush'd, with misty spray,
A copious spring; and both together dash'd
Swift, mad, fantastic round the rocks, and
lash'd   920
Among the conchs and shells of the lofty
grot,
Leaving a trickling dew. At last they
shot
Down from the ceiling's height, pouring a
noise
As of some breathless racers whose hopes
poise
Upon the last few steps, and with spent
force
Along the ground they took a winding
course.
Endymion follow'd — for it seem'd that
one
Ever pursued, the other strove to shun —
Follow'd their languid mazes, till well nigh
He had left thinking of the mystery, — 930
And was now rapt in tender hoverings
Over the vanish'd bliss. Ah! what is it
sings
His dream away? What melodies are
these?

They sound as through the whispering of
trees,
Not native in such barren vaults. Give
ear!

'O Arethusa, peerless nymph! why fear
Such tenderness as mine? Great Dian,
why,
Why didst thou hear her prayer? O that I
Were rippling round her dainty fairness
now,   939
Circling about her waist, and striving how
To entice her to a dive! then stealing in
Between her luscious lips and eyelids thin.
O that her shining hair was in the sun,
And I distilling from it thence to run
In amorous rillets down her shrinking form!
To linger on her lily shoulders, warm
Between her kissing breasts, and every
charm
Touch raptured! — see how painfully I
flow:
Fair maid, be pitiful to my great woe.
Stay, stay thy weary course, and let me
lead,   950
A happy wooer, to the flowery mead
Where all that beauty snared me.' —
'Cruel god,
Desist! or my offended mistress' nod
Will stagnate all thy fountains: — tease me
not
With siren words — Ah, have I really got
Such power to madden thee? And is it
true —
Away, away, or I shall dearly rue
My very thoughts: in mercy then away,
Kindest Alpheus, for should I obey   959
My own dear will, 't would be a deadly
bane.'
'O, Oread-Queen! would that thou hadst a
pain
Like this of mine, then would I fearless
turn
And be a criminal.' 'Alas, I burn,
I shudder — gentle river, get thee hence.
Alpheus! thou enchanter! every sense
Of mine was once made perfect in these
woods.

Fresh breezes, bowery lawns, and innocent
    floods,
Ripe fruits, and lonely couch, contentment
    gave;
But ever since I heedlessly did lave
In thy deceitful stream, a panting glow 970
Grew strong within me: wherefore serve
    me so,
And call it love ?   Alas ! 't was cruelty.
Not once more did I close my happy eye
Amid the thrush's song.   Away ! avaunt !
O 't was a cruel thing.' — ' Now thou dost
    taunt
So softly, Arethusa, that I think
If thou wast playing on my shady brink,
Thou wouldst bathe once again.   Innocent
    maid !
Stifle thine heart no more; — nor be afraid
Of angry powers: there are deities   980
Will shade us with their wings.   Those
    fitful sighs
'T is almost death to hear: O let me pour
A dewy balm upon them ! — fear no more,
Sweet Arethusa ! Dian's self must feel
Sometimes these very pangs.   Dear maiden,
    steal
Blushing into my soul, and let us fly
These dreary caverns for the open sky.
I will delight thee all my winding course,
From the green sea up to my hidden source
About Arcadian forests; and will show 990
The channels where my coolest waters flow
Through mossy rocks; where 'mid exuber-
    ant green,
I roam in pleasant darkness, more unseen
Than Saturn in his exile; where I brim
Round flowery islands, and take thence a
    skim
Of mealy sweets, which myriads of bees
Buzz from their honey'd wings: and thou
    shouldst please
Thyself to choose the richest, where we
    might
Be incense-pillow'd every summer night.
Doff all sad fears, thou white deliciousness,
And let us be thus comforted; unless 1001
Thou couldst rejoice to see my hopeless
    stream

Hurry distracted from Sol's temperate
    beam,
And pour to death along some hungry
    sands.' —
' What can I do, Alpheus ?   Dian stands
Severe before me: persecuting fate !
Unhappy Arethusa ! thou wast late
A huntress free in' —   At this, sudden
    fell
Those two sad streams adown a fearful
    dell.
The Latmian listen'd, but he heard no
    more,   .   1010
Save echo, faint repeating o'er and o'er
The name of Arethusa.   On the verge
Of that dark gulf he wept, and said: ' I
    urge
Thee, gentle Goddess of my pilgrimage,
By our eternal hopes, to soothe, to assuage,
If thou art powerful, these lovers' pains;
And make them happy in some happy
    plains.'

He turn'd — there was a whelming sound
    — he stept,
There was a cooler light; and so he kept
Towards it by a sandy path, and lo !   1020
More suddenly than doth a moment go,
The visions of the earth were gone and
    fled —
He saw the giant sea above his head.

BOOK III

THERE are who lord it o'er their fellow-
    men
With most prevailing tinsel: who unpen
Their baaing vanities, to browse away
The comfortable green and juicy hay
From human pastures; or, O torturing
    fact !
Who, through an idiot blink, will see un-
    pack'd
Fire-branded foxes to sear up and singe
Our gold and ripe-ear'd hopes.   With not
    one tinge
Of sanctuary splendour, not a sight

Able to face an owl's, they still are dight
By the blear-eyed nations in empurpled
    vesta,   11
And crowns, and turbans. With unladen
    breasts,
Save of blown self-applause, they proudly
    mount
To their spirit's perch, their being's high
    account,
Their tiptop nothings, their dull skies, their
    thrones —
Amid the fierce intoxicating tones
Of trumpets, shoutings, and belabour'd
    drums,
And sudden cannon. Ah! how all this
    hums,
In wakeful ears, like uproar past and
    gone —
Like thunder-clouds that spake to Baby-
    lon,   20
And set those old Chaldeans to their
    tasks. —
Are then regalities all gilded masks ?
No, there are throned seats unscalable
But by a patient wing, a constant spell,
Or by ethereal things that, unconfined,
Can make a ladder of the eternal wind,
And poise about in cloudy thunder-tents
To watch the abysm-birth of elements.
Aye, 'bove the withering of old-lipp'd Fate
A thousand Powers keep religious state, 30
In water, fiery realm, and airy bourne;
And, silent as a consecrated urn,
Hold spherey sessions for a season due.
Yet few of these far majesties, ah, few !
Have bared their operations to this globe —
Few, who with gorgeous pageantry enrobe
Our piece of heaven — whose benevolence
Shakes hand with our own Ceres; every
    sense
Filling with spiritual sweets to plenitude,
As bees gorge full their cells. And, by
    the feud   40
'Twixt Nothing and Creation, I here swear,
Eterne Apollo ! that thy Sister fair
Is of all these the gentlier-mightiest.
When thy gold breath is misting in the
    west,

She unobserved steals unto her throne,
And there she sits most meek and most
    alone;
As if she had not pomp subservient;
As if thine eye, high Poet ! was not bent
Towards her with the Muses in thine heart;
As if the minist'ring stars kept not apart,
Waiting for silver-footed messages.   51
O Moon ! the oldest shades 'mong oldest
    trees
Feel palpitations when thou lookest in:
O Moon ! old boughs lisp forth a holier din
The while they feel thine airy fellowship.
Thou dost bless everywhere, with silver lip
Kissing dead things to life. The sleeping
    kine,
Couch'd in thy brightness, dream of fields
    divine:
Innumerable mountains rise, and rise,
Ambitious for the hallowing of thine eyes;
And yet thy benediction passeth not   61
One obscure hiding-place, one little spot
Where pleasure may be sent: the nested
    wren
Has thy fair face within its tranquil ken,
And from beneath a sheltering ivy leaf
Takes glimpses of thee; thou art a relief
To the poor patient oyster, where it sleeps
Within its pearly house. — The mighty
    deeps,
The monstrous sea is thine — the myriad
    sea !
O Moon ! far-spooming Ocean bows to
    thee,   70
And Tellus feels his forehead's cumbrous
    load.

    Cynthia ! where art thou now ? What
    far abode
Of green or silvery bower doth enshrine
Such utmost beauty ? Alas, thou dost pine
For one as sorrowful: thy cheek is pale
For one whose cheek is pale: thou dost be-
    wail
His tears, who weeps for thee. Where dost
    thou sigh ?
Ah ! surely that light peeps from Vesper's
    eye,

Or what a thing is love ! 'T is She, but lo!
How changed, how full of ache, how gone
    in woe !   80
She dies at the thinnest cloud; her loveli-
    ness
Is wan on Neptune's blue: yet there 's a
    stress
Of love-spangles, just off yon cape of trees,
Dancing upon the waves, as if to please
The curly foam with amorous influence.
O, not so idle: for down-glancing thence,
She fathoms eddies, and runs wild about
O'erwhelming water-courses; scaring out
The thorny sharks from hiding-holes, and
    fright'ning
Their savage eyes with unaccustom'd light-
    ning.   90
Where will the splendour be content to
    reach ?
O love ! how potent hast thou been to
    teach
Strange journeyings !   Wherever beauty
    dwells,
In gulf or aerie, mountains or deep dells,
In light, in gloom, in star or blazing sun,
Thou pointest out the way, and straight 't is
    won.
Amid his toil thou gavest Leander breath;
Thou leddest Orpheus through the gleams
    of death;
Thou madest Pluto bear thin element;
And now, O winged Chieftain ! thou hast
    sent   100
A moonbeam to the deep, deep water-
    world,
To find Endymion.

                On gold sand impearl'd
With lily shells, and pebbles milky white,
Poor Cynthia greeted him, and soothed her
    light
Against his pallid face: he felt the charm
To breathlessness, and suddenly a warm
Of his heart's blood: 't was very sweet; he
    stay'd
His wandering steps, and half-entranced
    laid
His head upon a tuft of straggling weeds,

To taste the gentle moon, and freshening
    beads,   110
Lash'd from the crystal roof by fishes'
    tails.
And so he kept, until the rosy veils
Mantling the east, by Aurora's peering
    hand
Were lifted from the water's breast, and
    fann'd
Into sweet air; and sober'd morning came
Meekly through billows: — when like taper-
    flame
Left sudden by a dallying breath of air,
He rose in silence, and once more 'gan fare
Along his fated way.

                  Far had he roam'd,
With nothing save the hollow vast, that
    foam'd   120
Above, around, and at his feet; save things
More dead than Morpheus' imaginings:
Old rusted anchors, helmets, breastplates
    large
Of gone sea-warriors; brazen beaks and
    targe;
Rudders that for a hundred years had lost
The sway of human hand; gold vase em-
    boss'd
With long-forgotten story, and wherein
No reveller had ever dipp'd a chin
But those of Saturn's vintage; mouldering
    scrolls,
Writ in the tongue of heaven, by those
    souls   130
Who first were on the earth; and sculptures
    rude
In ponderous stone, developing the mood
Of ancient Nox; — then skeletons of man,
Of beast, behemoth, and leviathan,
And elephant, and eagle, and huge jaw
Of nameless monster.   A cold leaden awe
These secrets struck into him; and unless
Dian had chased away that heaviness,
He might have died: but now, with cheered
    feel,
He onward kept; wooing these thoughts to
    steal   140
About the labyrinth in his soul of love.

'What is there in thee, Moon! that
thou shouldst move
My heart so potently? When yet a child
I oft have dried my tears when thou hast
smiled.
Thou seem'dst my sister: hand in hand we
went
From eve to morn across the firmament.
No apples would I gather from the tree,
Till thou hadst cool'd their cheeks de-
liciously:
No tumbling water ever spake romance,
But when my eyes with thine thereon could
dance: 150
No woods were green enough, no bower
divine,
Until thou liftedst up thine eyelids fine:
In sowing-time ne'er would I dibble take,
Or drop a seed, till thou wast wide awake;
And, in the summer tide of blossoming,
No one but thee hath heard me blithely sing
And mesh my dewy flowers all the night.
No melody was like a passing spright
If it went not to solemnize thy reign.
Yes, in my boyhood, every joy and pain 160
By thee were fashion'd to the self-same end;
And as I grew in years, still didst thou
blend
With all my ardours; thou wast the deep
glen;
Thou wast the mountain-top — the sage's
pen —
The poet's harp — the voice of friends —
the sun;
Thou wast the river — thou wast glory
won;
Thou wast my clarion's blast — thou wast
my steed —
My goblet full of wine — my topmost
deed: —
Thou wast the charm of women, lovely
Moon!
O what a wild and harmonized tune 170
My spirit struck from all the beautiful!
On some bright essence could I lean, and
lull
Myself to immortality: I prest
Nature's soft pillow in a wakeful rest.

But gentle Orb! there came a nearer bliss —
My strange love came — Felicity's abyss!
She came, and thou didst fade, and fade
away —
Yet not entirely; no, thy starry sway
Has been an under-passion to this hour.
Now I begin to feel thine orby power 180
Is coming fresh upon me: O be kind,
Keep back thine influence, and do not blind
My sovereign vision. — Dearest love, for-
give
That I can think away from thee and live! —
Pardon me, airy planet, that I prize
One thought beyond thine argent luxuries!
How far beyond!' At this a surprised
start
Frosted the springing verdure of his heart;
For as he lifted up his eyes to swear
How his own goddess was past all things
fair, 190
He saw far in the concave green of the sea
An old man sitting calm and peacefully.
Upon a weeded rock this old man sat,
And his white hair was awful, and a mat
Of weeds were cold beneath his cold thin
feet;
And, ample as the largest winding-sheet,
A cloak of blue wrapp'd up his aged bones,
O'erwrought with symbols by the deepest
groans
Of ambitious magic: every ocean-form
Was woven in with black distinctness;
storm, 200
And calm, and whispering, and hideous roar
Quicksand, and whirlpool, and deserted
shore
Were emblem'd in the woof; with every
shape
That skims, or dives, or sleeps, 'twixt cape
and cape.
The gulphing whale was like a dot in the
spell,
Yet look upon it, and 't would size and
swell
To its huge self; and the minutest fish
Would pass the very hardest gazer's wish,
And show his little eye's anatomy.
Then there was pictured the regality 210

Of Neptune; and the sea-nymphs round
    his state,
In beauteous vassalage, look up and wait.
Beside this old man lay a pearly wand,
And in his lap a book, the which he conn'd
So steadfastly, that the new denizen
Had time to keep him in amazed ken,
To mark these shadowings, and stand in
    awe.

The old man raised his hoary head and
    saw
The wilder'd stranger — seeming not to
    see,
His features were so lifeless. Suddenly 220
He woke as from a trance; his snow-white
    brows
Went arching up, and like two magic
    ploughs
Furrow'd deep wrinkles in his forehead
    large,
Which kept as fixedly as rocky marge,
Till round his wither'd lips had gone a
    smile.
Then up he rose, like one whose tedious toil
Had watch'd for years in forlorn hermitage,
Who had not from mid-life to utmost age
Eased in one accent his o'erburden'd soul,
Even to the trees. He rose: he grasp'd
    his stole,   230
With convulsed clenches waving it abroad,
And in a voice of solemn joy, that awed
Echo into oblivion, he said: —

'Thou art the man!   Now shall I lay
    my head
In peace upon my watery pillow: now
Sleep will come smoothly to my weary
    brow.
O Jove! I shall be young again, be young!
O shell-borne Neptune, I am pierced and
    stung
With new-born life! What shall I do?
    Where go,
When I have cast this serpent-skin of
    woe? —   240
I'll swim to the sirens, and one moment
    listen

Their melodies, and see their long hair
    glisten;
Anon upon that giant's arm I'll be,
That writhes about the roots of Sicily:
To northern seas I'll in a twinkling sail,
And mount upon the snortings of a whale
To some black cloud; thence down I'll
    madly sweep
On forked lightning, to the deepest deep,
Where through some sucking pool I will
    be hurl'd
With rapture to the other side of the
    world!   250
O, I am full of gladness! Sisters three,
I bow full-hearted to your old decree!
Yes, every god be thank'd, and power be-
    nign,
For I no more shall wither, droop, and pine.
Thou art the man!' Endymion started
    back
Dismay'd; and, like a wretch from whom
    the rack
Tortures hot breath, and speech of agony,
Mutter'd: 'What lonely death am I to die
In this cold region? Will he let me freeze,
And float my brittle limbs o'er polar seas?
Or will he touch me with his searing hand,
And leave a black memorial on the sand?
Or tear me piecemeal with a bony saw, 263
And keep me as a chosen food to draw
His magian fish through hated fire and
    flame?
O misery of hell! resistless, tame,
Am I to be burnt up? No, I will shout,
Until the gods through heaven's blue look
    out! —
O, Tartarus! but some few days agone
Her soft arms were entwining me, and on
Her voice I hung like fruit among green
    leaves: 271
Her lips were all my own, and — ah, ripe
    sheaves
Of happiness! ye on the stubble droop,
But never may be garner'd. I must stoop
My head, and kiss death's foot. Love!
    love, farewell!
Is there no hope from thee? This horrid
    spell

Would melt at thy sweet breath. — By
   Dian's hind
Feeding from her white fingers, on the
   wind
I see thy streaming hair! and now, by
   Pan,
I care not for this old mysterious man!' 280

He spake, and walking to that aged form,
Look'd high defiance. Lo! his heart 'gan
   warm
With pity, for the gray-hair'd creature
   wept.
Had he then wrong'd a heart where sorrow
   kept?
Had he, though blindly contumelious,
   brought
Rheum to kind eyes, a sting to human
   thought,
Convulsion to a mouth of many years?
He had in truth; and he was ripe for tears.
The penitent shower fell, as down he knelt
Before that care-worn sage, who trembling
   felt   290
About his large dark locks, and faltering
   spake:

'Arise, good youth, for sacred Phœbus'
   sake!
I know thine inmost bosom, and I feel
A very brother's yearning for thee steal
Into mine own: for why? thou openest
The prison gates that have so long opprest
My weary watching. Though thou know'st
   it not,
Thou art commission'd to this fated spot
For great enfranchisement. O weep no
   more!
I am a friend to love, to loves of yore: 300
Aye, hadst thou never loved an unknown
   power,
I had been grieving at this joyous hour.
But even now most miserable old,
I saw thee, and my blood no longer cold
Gave mighty pulses: in this tottering case
Grew a new heart, which at this moment
   plays
As dancingly as thine. Be not afraid,

For thou shalt hear this secret all display'd,
Now as we speed towards our joyous task.'

So saying, this young soul in age's
   mask   310
Went forward with the Carian side by side:
Resuming quickly thus; while ocean's tide
Hung swollen at their backs, and jewell'd
   sands
Took silently their foot-prints.

        'My soul stands
Now past the midway from mortality,
And so I can prepare without a sigh
To tell thee briefly all my joy and pain.
I was a fisher once, upon this main,
And my boat danced in every creek and bay;
Rough billows were my home by night and
   day, —   320
The sea-gulls not more constant; for I had
No housing from the storm and tempests
   mad,
But hollow rocks, — and they were palaces
Of silent happiness, of slumberous ease:
Long years of misery have told me so.
Aye, thus it was one thousand years ago.
One thousand years! — Is it then possible
To look so plainly through them? to dispel
A thousand years with backward glance
   sublime?
To breathe away as 't were all scummy
   slime   330
From off a crystal pool, to see its deep,
And one's own image from the bottom
   peep?
Yes: now I am no longer wretched thrall,
My long captivity and moanings all
Are but a slime, a thin-pervading scum,
The which I breathe away, and thronging
   come
Like things of yesterday my youthful plea-
   sures:

'I touch'd no lute, I sang not, trod no
   measures:
I was a lonely youth on desert shores.
My sports were lonely, 'mid continuous
   roars,   340

And craggy isles, and sea-mew's plaintive
   cry
Plaining discrepant between sea and sky.
Dolphins were still my playmates; shapes
   unseen
Would let me feel their scales of gold and
   green,
Nor be my desolation; and, full oft,
When a dread waterspout had rear'd aloft
Its hungry hugeness, seeming ready ripe
To burst with hoarsest thunderings, and
   wipe
My life away like a vast sponge of fate, 349
Some friendly monster, pitying my sad
   state,
Has dived to its foundations, gulf'd it down,
And left me tossing safely. But the crown
Of all my life was utmost quietude:
More did I love to lie in cavern rude,
Keeping in wait whole days for Neptune's
   voice,
And if it came at last, hark, and rejoice !
There blush'd no summer eve but I would
   steer
My skiff along green shelving coasts, to hear
The shepherd's pipe come clear from aery
   steep,
Mingled with ceaseless bleatings of his
   sheep: 360
And never was a day of summer shine,
But I beheld its birth upon the brine:
For I would watch all night to see unfold
Heaven's gates, and Æthon snort his morn-
   ing gold
Wide o'er the swelling streams: and con-
   stantly
At brim of day-tide, on some grassy lea,
My nets would be spread out, and I at rest.
The poor folk of the sea-country I blest
With daily boon of fish most delicate:
They knew not whence this bounty, and
   elate   370
Would strew sweet flowers on a sterile
   beach.

   ' Why was I not contented ?   Wherefore
      reach
At things which, but for thee, O Latmian !

Had been my dreary death ? Fool ! I began
To feel distemper'd longings: to desire
The utmost privilege that ocean's sire
Could grant in benediction : to be free
Of all his kingdom.   Long in misery
I wasted, ere in one extremest fit   379
I plunged for life or death.   To interknit
One's senses with so dense a breathing stuff
Might seem a work of pain; so not enough
Can I admire how crystal-smooth it felt,
And buoyant round my limbs.   At first I
   dwelt
Whole days and days in sheer astonishment;
Forgetful utterly of self-intent;
Moving but with the mighty ebb and flow.
Then, like a new-fledged bird that first doth
   show
His spreaded feathers to the morrow chill,
I tried in fear the pinions of my will.   390
'T was freedom ! and at once I visited
The ceaseless wonders of this ocean-bed.
No need to tell thee of them, for I see
That thou hast been a witness — it must be
For these I know thou canst not feel a
   drouth,
By the melancholy corners of that mouth.
So I will in my story straightway pass
To more immediate matter. Woe, alas !
That love should be my bane ! Ah, Scylla
   fair !
Why did poor Glaucus ever — ever dare 400
To sue thee to his heart ? Kind stranger-
   youth !
I loved her to the very white of truth,
And she would not conceive it.   Timid
   thing !
She fled me swift as sea-bird on the wing,
Round every isle, and point, and promon-
   tory,
From where large Hercules wound up his
   story
Far as Egyptian Nile. My passion grew
The more, the more I saw her dainty hue
Gleam delicately through the azure clear:
Until 't was too fierce agony to bear;   410
And in that agony, across my grief
It flash'd, that Circe might find some re-
   lief —

Cruel enchantress! So above the water
I rear'd my head, and look'd for Phœbus'
   daughter.
Æœa's isle was wondering at the moon:—
It seem'd to whirl around me, and a swoon
Left me dead-drifting to that fatal power.

   'When I awoke, 't was in a twilight
     bower;
Just when the light of morn, with hum of
   bees,
Stole through its verdurous matting of
   fresh trees.   420
How sweet, and sweeter! for I heard a
   lyre,
And over it a sighing voice expire.
It ceased — I caught light footsteps; and
   anon
The fairest face that morn e'er look'd upon
Push'd through a screen of roses. Starry
   Jove!
With tears, and smiles, and honey-words
   she wove
A net whose thraldom was more bliss than
   all
The range of flower'd Elysium. Thus did
   fall
The dew of her rich speech: "Ah! art
   awake?
O let me hear thee speak, for Cupid's
   sake!   430
I am so oppress'd with joy! Why, I have
   shed
An urn of tears, as though thou wert cold
   dead;
And now I find thee living, I will pour
From these devoted eyes their silver store,
Until exhausted of the latest drop,
So it will pleasure thee, and force thee
   stop
Here, that I too may live: but if beyond
Such cool and sorrowful offerings, thou art
   fond
Of soothing warmth, of dalliance supreme;
If thou art ripe to taste a long love-dream;
If smiles, if dimples, tongues for ardour
   mute,   441
Hang in thy vision like a tempting fruit,

O let me pluck it for thee!" Thus she
   link'd
Her charming syllables, till indistinct
Their music came to my o'er-sweeten'd
   soul;
And then she hover'd over me, and stole
So near, that if no nearer it had been
This furrow'd visage thou hadst never seen.

   'Young man of Latmos! thus particu-
     lar
Am I, that thou may'st plainly see how
   far   450
This fierce temptation went: and thou
   may'st not
Exclaim, How, then, was Scylla quite forgot?

   'Who could resist? Who in this uni-
     verse?
She did so breathe ambrosia; so immerse
My fine existence in a golden clime.
She took me like a child of suckling time,
And cradled me in roses. Thus con-
   demn'd,
The current of my former life was stemm'd,
And to this arbitrary queen of sense
I bow'd a tranced vassal: nor would thence
Have moved, even though Amphion's harp
   had woo'd   461
Me back to Scylla o'er the billows rude.
For as Apollo each eve doth devise
A new apparelling for western skies;
So every eve, nay, every spendthrift hour
Shed balmy consciousness within that
   bower.
And I was free of haunts umbrageous;
Could wander in the mazy forest-house
Of squirrels, foxes shy, and antler'd deer,
And birds from coverts innermost and
   drear   470
Warbling for very joy mellifluous sor-
   row —
To me new-born delights!

              'Now let me borrow,
For moments few, a temperament as stern
As Pluto's sceptre, that my words not burn

These uttering lips, while I in calm speech
   tell
How specious heaven was changed to real
   hell.

  'One morn she left me sleeping: half
    awake
I sought for her smooth arms and lips, to
   slake
My greedy thirst with nectarous camel-
   draughts;
But she was gone. Whereat the barbed
   shafts   480
Of disappointment stuck in me so sore,
That out I ran and search'd the forest o'er.
Wandering about in pine and cedar gloom
Damp awe assail'd me; for there 'gan to
   boom
A sound of moan, an agony of sound,
Sepulchral from the distance all around.
Then came a conquering earth-thunder, and
   rumbled
That fierce complain to silence: while I
   stumbled
Down a precipitous path, as if impell'd.
I came to a dark valley. — Groanings
   swell'd   490
Poisonous about my ears, and louder grew,
The nearer I approach'd a flame's gaunt
   blue,
That glared before me through a thorny
   brake.
This fire, like the eye of gordian snake,
Bewitch'd me towards; and I soon was
   near
A sight too fearful for the feel of fear:
In thicket hid I cursed the haggard scene —
The banquet of my arms, my arbour queen,
Seated upon an uptorn forest root;
And all around her shapes, wizard and
   brute,   500
Laughing, and wailing, grovelling, serpent-
   ing,
Showing tooth, tusk, and venom-bag, and
   sting !
O such deformities ! old Charon's self,
Should he give up awhile his penny pelf,
And take a dream 'mong rushes Stygian,

It could not be so fantasied. Fierce, wan,
And tyrannizing was the lady's look,
As over them a gnarled staff she shook.
Ofttimes upon the sudden she laugh'd out,
And from a basket emptied to the rout· 510
Clusters of grapes, the which they raven'd
   quick
And roar'd for more; with many a hungry
   lick
About their shaggy jaws. Avenging, slow,
Anon she took a branch of mistletoe,
And emptied on 't a black dull-gurgling
   phial:
Groan'd one and all, as if some piercing
   trial
Was sharpening for their pitiable bones.
She lifted up the charm: appealing groans
From their poor breasts went sueing to her
   ear
In vain; remorseless as an infant's bier 520
She whisk'd against their eyes the sooty
   oil.
Whereat was heard a noise of painful toil,
Increasing gradual to a tempest rage,
Shrieks, yells, and groans of torture-pil-
   grimage;
Until their grieved bodies 'gan to bloat
And puff from the tail's end to stifled
   throat:
Then was appalling silence: then a sight
More wildering than all that hoarse af-
   fright;
For the whole herd, as by a whirlwind
   writhen,
Went through the dismal air like one huge
   Python   530
Antagonizing Boreas, — and so vanish'd.
Yet there was not a breath of wind: she
   banish'd
These phantoms with a nod. Lo ! from the
   dark
Came waggish fauns, and nymphs, and
   satyrs stark,
With dancing and loud revelry, — and went
Swifter than centaurs after rapine bent. —
Sighing an elephant appear'd and bow'd
Before the fierce witch, speaking thus aloud
In human accent: " Potent goddess ! chief

Of pains resistless! make my being brief,
Or let me from this heavy prison fly: 541
Or give me to the air, or let me die!
I sue not for my happy crown again;
I sue not for my phalanx on the plain;
I sue not for my lone, my widow'd wife:
I sue not for my ruddy drops of life,
My children fair, my lovely girls and boys!
I will forget them; I will pass these joys;
Ask nought so heavenward, so too — too
    high:
Only I pray, as fairest boon, to die, 550
Or be deliver'd from this cumbrous flesh,
From this gross, detestable, filthy mesh,
And merely given to the cold bleak air.
Have mercy, Goddess! Circe, feel my
    prayer!"

'That curst magician's name fell icy numb
Upon my wild conjecturing: truth had
    come
Naked and sabre-like against my heart.
I saw a fury whetting a death-dart;
And my slain spirit, overwrought with
    fright,
Fainted away in that dark lair of night. 560
Think, my deliverer, how desolate
My waking must have been! disgust, and
    hate,
And terrors manifold divided me
A spoil amongst them. I prepared to flee
Into the dungeon core of that wild wood:
I fled three days — when lo! before me
    stood
Glaring the angry witch. O Dis, even now,
A clammy dew is beading on my brow,
At mere remembering her pale laugh, and
    curse.
"Ha! ha! Sir Dainty! there must be a
    nurse 570
Made of rose-leaves and thistle-down, ex-
    press,
To cradle thee my sweet, and lull thee:
    yes,
I am too flinty-hard for thy nice touch:
My tenderest squeeze is but a giant's clutch.
So, fairy-thing, it shall have lullabies
Unheard of yet; and it shall still its cries

Upon some breast more lily-feminine.
Oh, no — it shall not pine, and pine, and
    pine
More than one pretty, trifling thousand
    years;
And then 't were pity, but fate's gentle
    shears 580
Cut short its immortality. Sea-flirt!
Young dove of the waters! truly I 'll not
    hurt
One hair of thine: see how I weep and sigh,
That our heart-broken parting is so nigh.
And must we part? Ah, yes, it must be so.
Yet ere thou leavest me in utter woe,
Let me sob over thee my last adieus,
And speak a blessing: Mark me! thou hast
    thews
Immortal, for thou art of heavenly race:
But such a love is mine, that here I chase
Eternally away from thee all bloom 591
Of youth, and destine thee towards a tomb.
Hence shalt thou quickly to the watery
    vast;
And there, ere many days be overpast,
Disabled age shall seize thee; and even
    then
Thou shalt not go the way of aged men;
But live and wither, cripple and still breathe
Ten hundred years: which gone, I then be-
    queath
Thy fragile bones to unknown burial.
Adieu, sweet love, adieu!" — As shot stars
    fall, 600
She fled ere I could groan for mercy.
    Stung
And poisoned was my spirit: despair sung
A war-song of defiance 'gainst all hell.
A hand was at my shoulder to compel
My sullen steps; another 'fore my eyes
Moved on with pointed finger. In this
    guise
Enforced, at the last by ocean's foam
I found me; by my fresh, my native home.
Its tempering coolness, to my life akin,
Came salutary as I waded in; 610
And, with a blind voluptuous rage, I gave
Battle to the swollen billow-ridge, and
    drave

Large froth before me, while there yet
    remain'd
Hale strength, nor from my bones all mar-
    row drain'd.

'Young lover, I must weep — such hell-
    ish spite
With dry cheek who can tell?   While
    thus my might
Proving upon this element, dismay'd,
Upon a dead thing's face my hand I laid;
I look'd — 't was Scylla!   Cursed, cursed
    Circe!
O vulture-witch, hast never heard of mercy?
Could not thy harshest vengeance be con-
    tent,   621
But thou must nip this tender innocent
Because I loved her? — Cold, O cold in-
    deed
Were her fair limbs, and like a common
    weed
The sea-swell took her hair.   Dead as she
    was
I clung about her waist, nor ceased to pass
Fleet as an arrow through unfathom'd
    brine,
Until there shone a fabric crystalline,
Ribb'd and inlaid with coral, pebble, and
    pearl.
Headlong I darted; at one eager swirl 630
Gain'd its bright portal, enter'd, and be-
    hold!
'T was vast, and desolate, and icy-cold;
And all around —   But wherefore this to
    thee
Who in few minutes more thyself shalt
    see? —
I left poor Scylla in a niche and fled.
My fever'd parchings up, my scathing
    dread
Met palsy half way: soon these limbs be-
    came
Gaunt, wither'd, sapless, feeble, cramp'd,
    and lame.

'Now let me pass a cruel, cruel space,
Without one hope, without one faintest
    trace   640

Of mitigation, or redeeming bubble
Of colour'd phantasy: for I fear 't would
    trouble
Thy brain to loss of reason: and next tell
How a restoring chance came down to quell
One half of the witch in me.

               'On a day,
Sitting upon a rock above the spray,
I saw grow up from the horizon's brink
A gallant vessel: soon she seem'd to sink
Away from me again, as though her course
Had been resumed in spite of hindering
    force —   650
So vanish'd: and not long, before arose
Dark clouds, and muttering of winds mo-
    rose.
Old Æolus would stifle his mad spleen,
But could not; therefore, all the billows
    green
Toss'd up the silver spume against the
    clouds.
The tempest came: I saw that vessel's
    shrouds
In perilous bustle; while upon the deck
Stood trembling creatures.   I beheld the
    wreck;
The final gulfing; the poor struggling souls;
I heard their cries amid loud thunder-
    rolls.   660
O they had all been saved but crazed eld
Annull'd my vigorous cravings; and thus
    quell'd
And curb'd, think on 't, O Latmian! did I
    sit
Writhing with pity, and a cursing fit
Against that hell-born Circe.   The crew
    had gone,
By one and one, to pale oblivion;
And I was gazing on the surges prone,
With many a scalding tear, and many a
    groan,
When at my feet emerged an old man's
    hand,
Grasping this scroll, and this same slender
    wand.   670
I knelt with pain — reach'd out my hand
    — had grasp'd

These treasures — touch'd the knuckles —
they unclasp'd —
I caught a finger: but the downward weight
O'erpower'd me — it sank.   Then 'gan
abate
The storm, and through chill aguish gloom
outburst
The comfortable sun.   I was athirst
To search the book, and in the warming
air
Parted its dripping leaves with eager care.
Strange matters did it treat of, and drew
on
My soul page after page, till well nigh
won   680
Into forgetfulness; when, stupefied,
I read these words, and read again, and
tried
My eyes against the heavens, and read
again.
O what a load of misery and pain
Each Atlas-line bore off ! — a shine of hope
Came gold around me, cheering me to
cope
Strenuous with hellish tyranny.   Attend !
For thou hast brought their promise to an
end.'

In the wide sea there lives a forlorn wretch,
Doom'd with enfeebled carcase to outstretch 690
His loath'd existence through ten centuries,
And then to die alone.   Who can devise
A total opposition ?   No one.   So
One million times ocean must ebb and flow,
And he oppressed.   Yet he shall not die,
These things accomplish'd : — If he utterly
Scans all the depths of magic, and expounds
The meanings of all motions, shapes, and
sounds ;
If he explores all forms and substances
Straight homeward to their symbol-essences ;
He shall not die.   Moreover, and in chief, 701
He must pursue this task of joy and grief
Most piously ; — all lovers tempest-tost,
And in the savage overwhelming lost,
He shall deposit side by side, until
Time's creeping shall the dreary space fulfil :
Which done, and all these labours ripened,

A youth, by heavenly power loved and led,
Shall stand before him ; whom he shall direct
How to consummate all.   The youth elect 710
Must do the thing, or both will be de-
stroy'd. —

'Then,' cried the young Endymion, over-
joy'd,
'We are twin brothers in this destiny !
Say, I entreat thee, what achievement high
Is, in this restless world, for me reserved.
What ! if from thee my wandering feet
had swerved,
Had we both perish'd ?' — 'Look !' the
sage replied,
'Dost thou not mark a gleaming through
the tide,
Of divers brilliances ? 't is the edifice
I told thee of, where lovely Scylla lies; 720
And where I have enshrined piously
All lovers, whom fell storms have doom'd
to die
Throughout my bondage.'   Thus discours-
ing, on
They went till unobscured the porches
shone;
Which hurryingly they gain'd, and enter'd
straight.
Sure never since king Neptune held his
state
Was seen such wonder underneath the
stars.
Turn to some level plain where haughty
Mars
Has legion'd all his battle; and behold
How every soldier, with firm foot, doth
hold   730
His even breast: see, many steeled squares,
And rigid ranks of iron — whence who
dares
One step ?   Imagine further, line by line,
These warrior thousands on the field su-
pine : —
So in that crystal place, in silent rows,
Poor lovers lay at rest from joys and
woes. —
The stranger from the mountains, breath-
less, traced

Such thousands of shut eyes in order
placed;
Such ranges of white feet, and patient lips
All ruddy, — for here death no blossom
nips.   740
He mark'd their brows and foreheads; saw
their hair
Put sleekly on one side with nicest care;
And each one's gentle wrists, with rever-
ence,
Put cross-wise to its heart.

               ' Let us commence,'
Whisper'd the guide, stuttering with joy,
' even now.'
He spake, and, trembling like an aspen-
bough,
Began to tear his scroll in pieces small,
Uttering the while some mumblings fu-
neral.
He tore it into pieces small as snow
That drifts unfeather'd when bleak north-
erns blow;   750
And having done it, took his dark blue
cloak
And bound it round Endymion: then struck
His wand against the empty air times
nine. —
' What more there is to do, young man, is
thine:
But first a little patience; first undo
This tangled thread, and wind it to a clue.
Ah, gentle ! 't is as weak as spider's skein;
And shouldst thou break it — What, is it
done so clean ?
A power overshadows thee ! Oh, brave !
The spite of hell is tumbling to its grave.
Here is a shell; 't is pearly blank to me, 761
Nor mark'd with any sign or charactery —
Canst thou read aught ? O read for pity's
sake !
Olympus ! we are safe ! Now, Carian,
break
This wand against yon lyre on the pedes-
tal.'

   'T was done: and straight with sudden
swell and fall

Sweet music breathed her soul away, and
sigh'd
A lullaby to silence. — ' Youth ! now strew
These minced leaves on me, and passing
through
Those files of dead, scatter the same
around,   770
And thou wilt see the issue.' — 'Mid the
sound
Of flutes and viols, ravishing his heart,
Endymion from Glaucus stood apart,
And scatter'd in his face some fragments
light.
How lightning-swift the change ! a youth-
ful wight
Smiling beneath a coral diadem,
Out-sparkling sudden like an upturn'd gem,
Appear'd, and, stepping to a beauteous
corse,
Kneel'd down beside it, and with tenderest
force
Press'd its cold hand, and wept, — and
Scylla sigh'd !   780
Endymion, with quick hand, the charm ap-
plied —
The nymph arose: he left them to their joy,
And onward went upon his high employ,
Showering those powerful fragments on
the dead.
And, as he pass'd, each lifted up its head,
As doth a flower at Apollo's touch.
Death felt it to his inwards: 't was too
much:
Death fell a-weeping in his charnel-house.
The Latmian persevered along, and thus
All were reanimated. There arose   790
A noise of harmony, pulses and throes
Of gladness in the air — while many, who
Had died in mutual arms devout and true,
Sprang to each other madly; and the rest
Felt a high certainty of being blest.
They gazed upon Endymion. Enchant-
ment
Grew drunken, and would have its head
and bent.
Delicious symphonies, like airy flowers,
Budded, and swell'd, and, full-blown, shed
full showers

Of light, soft, unseen leaves of sounds
    divine. 800
The two deliverers tasted a pure wine
Of happiness, from fairy press oozed out.
Speechless they eyed each other, and about
The fair assembly wandered to and fro,
Distracted with the richest overflow
Of joy that ever pour'd from heaven.

                —— ' Away ! '
Shouted the new born god; 'Follow, and
    pay
Our piety to Neptunus supreme ! ' —
Then Scylla, blushing sweetly from her
    dream,
They led on first, bent to her meek sur-
    prise, 810
Through portal columns of a giant size
Into the vaulted, boundless emerald.
Joyous all follow'd, as the leader call'd,
Down marble steps; pouring as easily
As hour-glass sand — and fast, as you
    might see
Swallows obeying the south summer's call,
Or swans upon a gentle waterfall.

    Thus went that beautiful multitude, nor
    far,
Ere from among some rocks of glittering
    spar, 819
Just within ken, they saw descending thick
Another multitude. Whereat more quick
Moved either host. On a wide sand they
    met,
And of those numbers every eye was wet;
For each their old love found. A mur-
    muring rose,
Like what was never heard in all the
    throes
Of wind and waters: 'tis past human wit
To tell; 't is dizziness to think of it.

    This mighty consummation made, the
    host
Moved on for many a league; and gain'd
    and lost
Huge sea-marks; vanward swelling in
    array, 830

And from the rear diminishing away, —
Till a faint dawn surprised them. Glaucus
    cried,
' Behold ! behold, the palace of his pride !
God Neptune's palaces.' With noise in-
    creased,
They shoulder'd on towards that brighten-
    ing east.
At every onward step proud domes arose
In prospect, — diamond gleams and golden
    glows
Of amber 'gainst their faces levelling.
Joyous, and many as the leaves in spring,
Still onward; still the splendour gradual
    swell'd. 840
Rich opal domes were seen, on high upheld
By jasper pillars, letting through their
    shafts
A blush of coral. Copious wonder-draughts
Each gazer drank; and deeper drank more
    near:
For what poor mortals fragment up, as
    mere
As marble was there lavish, to the vast
Of one fair palace, that far, far surpass'd,
Even for common bulk, those olden three,
Memphis, and Babylon, and Nineveh.

    As large, as bright, as colour'd as the
    bow 850
Of Iris, when unfading it doth show
Beyond a silvery shower, was the arch
Through which this Paphian army took its
    march,
Into the outer courts of Neptune's state :
Whence could be seen, direct, a golden
    gate,
To which the leaders sped; but not half
    raught
Ere it burst open swift as fairy thought,
And made those dazzled thousands veil
    their eyes
Like callow eagles at the first sunrise.
Soon with an eagle nativeness their gaze 860
Ripe from hue-golden swoons took all the
    blaze,
And then, behold ! large Neptune on his
    throne

Of emerald deep: yet not exalt alone;
At his right hand stood winged Love, and on
His left sat smiling Beauty's paragon.

Far as the mariner on highest mast
Can see all round upon the calmed vast,
So wide was Neptune's hall: and as the blue
Doth vault the waters, so the waters drew
Their doming curtains, high, magnificent, 870
Awed from the throne aloof; — and when
    storm rent
Disclosed the thunder-gloomings in Jove's
    air;
But soothed as now, flash'd sudden every-
    where,
Noiseless, sub-marine cloudlets, glittering
Death to a human eye: for there did spring
From natural west, and east, and south, and
    north,
A light as of four sunsets, blazing forth
A gold-green zenith 'bove the Sea-God's
    head.
Of lucid depth the floor, and far outspread
As breezeless lake, on which the slim
    canoe   880
Of feather'd Indian darts about, as through
The delicatest air: air verily,
But for the portraiture of clouds and sky:
This palace floor breath-air, — but for the
    amaze
Of deep-seen wonders motionless, — and
    blaze
Of the dome pomp, reflected in extremes,
Globing a golden sphere.

                    They stood in dreams
Till Triton blew his horn. The palace rang;
The Nereids danced; the Sirens faintly
    sang;
And the great Sea-King bow'd his dripping
    head.   890
Then Love took wing, and from his pinions
    shed
On all the multitude a nectarous dew.
The ooze-born Goddess beckoned and drew
Fair Scylla and her guides to conference;
And when they reach'd the throned emi-
    nence

She kiss'd the sea-nymph's cheek, — who
    sat her down
A-toying with the doves. Then, — 'Mighty
    crown
And sceptre of this kingdom!' Venus
    said,
'Thy vows were on a time to Nais paid:
Behold!' — Two copious tear-drops instant
    fell   900
From the God's large eyes; he smiled de-
    lectable,
And over Glaucus held his blessing hands. —
'Endymion! Ah! still wandering in the
    bands
Of love? Now this is cruel. Since the
    hour
I met thee in earth's bosom, all my power
Have I put forth to serve thee. What, not
    yet
Escaped from dull mortality's harsh net?
A little patience, youth! 't will not be long,
Or I am skilless quite: an idle tongue,
A humid eye, and steps luxurious,   910
Where these are new and strange, are
    ominous.
Aye, I have seen these signs in one of
    heaven,
When others were all blind; and were I
    given
To utter secrets, haply I might say
Some pleasant words: — but Love will have
    his day.
So wait awhile expectant. Pr'ythee soon,
Even in the passing of thine honey-moon,
Visit thou my Cytherea: thou wilt find
Cupid well-natured, my Adonis kind;
And pray persuade with thee — Ah, I have
    done,   920
All blisses be upon thee, my sweet son!' —
Thus the fair goddess: while Endymion
Knelt to receive those accents halcyon.

Meantime a glorious revelry began
Before the Water-Monarch. Nectar ran
In courteous fountains to all cups out-
    reach'd;
And plunder'd vines, teeming exhaustless,
    pleach'd

New growth about each shell and pendent
    lyre;
The which, in disentangling for their fire,
Pull'd down fresh foliage and coverture   930
For dainty toying. Cupid, empire-sure,
Flutter'd and laugh'd, and oft-times through
    the throng
Made a delighted way. Then dance, and
    song,
And garlanding, grew wild; and pleasure
    reign'd.
In harmless tendril they each other chain'd,
And strove who should be smother'd deep-
    est in
Fresh crush of leaves.

                   O 't is a very sin
For one so weak to venture his poor verse
In such a place as this. O do not curse,   939
High Muses! let him hurry to the ending.

   All suddenly were silent. A soft blend-
    ing
Of dulcet instruments came charmingly;
And then a hymn.

              'King of the stormy sea!
Brother of Jove, and co-inheritor
Of elements! Eternally before
Thee the waves awful bow. Fast, stubborn
    rock,
At thy fear'd trident shrinking, doth unlock
Its deep foundations, hissing into foam.
All mountain-rivers, lost in the wide home
Of thy capacious bosom, ever flow.   950
Thou frownest, and old Æolus thy foe
Skulks to his cavern, 'mid the gruff com-
    plaint
Of all his rebel tempests. Dark clouds
    faint
When, from thy diadem, a silver gleam
Slants over blue dominion. Thy bright
    team
Gulfs in the morning light, and scuds along
To bring thee nearer to that golden song
Apollo singeth, while his chariot
Waits at the doors of heaven. Thou art
    not

For scenes like this: an empire stern hast
    thou;   960
And it hath furrow'd that large front: yet
    now,
As newly come of heaven, dost thou sit
To blend and interknit
Subdued majesty with this glad time.
O shell-borne King sublime!
We lay our hearts before thee evermore —
We sing, and we adore!

   'Breathe softly, flutes;
Be tender of your strings, ye soothing
    lutes;
Nor be the trumpet heard! O vain, O
    vain;   970
Not flowers budding in an April rain,
Nor breath of sleeping dove, nor river's
    flow, —
No, nor the Æolian twang of Love's own
    bow,
Can mingle music fit for the soft ear
Of goddess Cytherea!
Yet deign, white Queen of Beauty, thy fair
    eyes
On our soul's sacrifice.

   'Bright-winged Child!
Who has another care when thou hast
    smiled?
Unfortunates on earth, we see at last   980
All death-shadows, and glooms that over-
    cast
Our spirits, fann'd away by thy light pin-
    ions.
O sweetest essence! sweetest of all min-
    ions!
God of warm pulses, and dishevell'd hair,
And panting bosoms bare!
Dear unseen light in darkness! eclipser
Of light in light! delicious poisoner!
Thy venom'd goblet will we quaff until
We fill — we fill!   989
And by thy Mother's lips —— '

                Was heard no more
For clamour, when the golden palace door
Open'd again, and from without, in shone

A new magnificence. On easy throne
Smooth-moving came Oceanus the old,
To take a latest glimpse at his sheepfold,
Before he went into his quiet cave
To muse for ever — Then a lucid wave,
Scoop'd from its trembling sisters of mid-
    sea,
Afloat, and pillowing up the majesty
Of Doris, and the Ægean seer, her spouse —
Next, on a dolphin, clad in laurel boughs,
Theban Amphion leaning on his lute: 1000
His fingers went across it — All were mute
To gaze on Amphitrite, queen of pearls,
And Thetis pearly too. —

                 The palace whirls
Around giddy Endymion; seeing he
Was there far strayed from mortality.
He could not bear it — shut his eyes in
    vain;
Imagination gave a dizzier pain.
'O I shall die! sweet Venus, be my stay!
Where is my lovely mistress? Well-
    away!   1011
I die — I hear her voice — I feel my
    wing —'
At Neptune's feet he sank. A sudden
    ring
Of Nereids were about him, in kind strife
To usher back his spirit into life:
But still he slept. At last they interwove
Their cradling arms, and purposed to con-
    vey
Towards a crystal bower far away.

  Lo! while slow carried through the pity-
    ing crowd,
To his inward senses these words spake
    aloud;   1020
Written in starlight on the dark above:
' *Dearest Endymion! my entire love!*
How have I dwelt in fear of fate; 'tis
    done —
Immortal bliss for me too hast thou won.
Arise then! for the hen-dove shall not
    hatch
Her ready eggs, before I'll kissing snatch
Thee into endless heaven. Awake! awake!'

The youth at once arose: a placid lake
Came quiet to his eyes; and forest green,
Cooler than all the wonders he had seen,
Lull'd with its simple song his fluttering
    breast.   1031
How happy once again in grassy nest!

BOOK IV

Muse of my native land! loftiest Muse!
O first-born on the mountains! by the
    hues
Of heaven on the spiritual air begot:
Long didst thou sit alone in northern grot,
While yet our England was a wolfish den;
Before our forests heard the talk of men;
Before the first of Druids was a child; —
Long didst thou sit amid our regions wild,
Rapt in a deep prophetic solitude.
There came an eastern voice of solemn
    mood: —   10
Yet wast thou patient. Then sang forth
    the Nine,
Apollo's garland: — yet didst thou divine
Such home-bred glory, that they cried in
    vain,
'Come hither, Sister of the Island!' Plain
Spake fair Ausonia; and once more she
    spake
A higher summons: — still didst thou be-
    take
Thee to thy native hopes. O thou hast
    won
A full accomplishment! The thing is
    done,
Which undone, these our latter days had
    risen
On barren souls. Great Muse, thou know'st
    what prison   20
Of flesh and bone, curbs, and confines, and
    frets
Our spirits' wings: despondency besets
Our pillows; and the fresh to-morrow morn
Seems to give forth its light in very scorn
Of our dull, uninspired, snail-paced lives.
Long have I said, how happy he who
    shrives

To thee! But then I thought on poets
    gone,
And could not pray:— nor can I now — so
    on
I move to the end in lowliness of heart. —

'Ah, woe is me! that I should fondly
    part   30
From my dear native land! Ah, foolish
    maid!
Glad was the hour, when, with thee, myri-
    ads bade
Adieu to Ganges and their pleasant fields!
To one so friendless the clear freshet
    yields
A bitter coolness; the ripe grape is sour:
Yet I would have, great gods! but one
    short hour
Of native air — let me but die at home.'

Endymion to heaven's airy dome
Was offering up a hecatomb of vows,
When these words reach'd him. Where-
    upon he bows   40
His head through thorny-green entangle-
    ment
Of underwood, and to the sound is bent,
Anxious as hind towards her hidden fawn.

'Is no one near to help me? No fair
    dawn
Of life from charitable voice? No sweet
    saying
To set my dull and sadden'd spirit playing?
No hand to toy with mine? No lips so
    sweet
That I may worship them? No eyelids
    meet
To twinkle on my bosom? No one dies
Before me, till from these enslaving eyes 50
Redemption sparkles! — I am sad and
    lost.'

Thou, Carian lord, hadst better have been
    tost
Into a whirlpool. Vanish into air,
Warm mountaineer! for canst thou only
    bear

A woman's sigh alone and in distress?
See not her charms! Is Phœbe passion-
    less?
Phœbe is fairer far — O gaze no more:—
Yet if thou wilt behold all beauty's store,
Behold her panting in the forest grass!
Do not those curls of glossy jet surpass 60
For tenderness the arms so idly lain
Amongst them? Feelest not a kindred
    pain,
To see such lovely eyes in swimming search
After some warm delight, that seems to
    perch
Dovelike in the dim cell lying beyond
Their upper lids? — Hist!

        'O for Hermes' wand,
To touch this flower into human shape!
That woodland Hyacinthus could escape
From his green prison, and here kneeling
    down
Call me his queen, his second life's fair
    crown!   70
Ah me, how I could love! — My soul doth
    melt
For the unhappy youth — Love! I have
    felt
So faint a kindness, such a meek surrender
To what my own full thoughts had made
    too tender,
That but for tears my life had fled away!
Ye deaf and senseless minutes of the day,
And thou, old forest, hold ye this for true,
There is no lightning, no authentic dew
But in the eye of love: there 's not a sound,
Melodious howsoever, can confound 80
The heavens and earth in one to such a
    death
As doth the voice of love: there 's not a
    breath
Will mingle kindly with the meadow air,
Till it has panted round, and stolen a share
Of passion from the heart!' —

          Upon a bough
He leant, wretched. He surely cannot now
Thirst for another love: O impious,
That he can even dream upon it thus! —

Thought he, 'Why am I not as are the
    dead,
Since to a woe like this I have been led 90
Through the dark earth, and through the
    wondrous sea?
Goddess! I love thee not the less: from
    thee
By Juno's smile I turn not — no, no, no —
While the great waters are at ebb and
    flow. —
I have a triple soul! O fond pretence —
For both, for both my love is so immense,
I feel my heart is cut for them in twain.'

    And so he groan'd, as one by beauty
    slain.
The lady's heart beat quick, and he could
    see
Her gentle bosom heave tumultuously. 100
He sprang from his green covert: there
    she lay,
Sweet as a musk-rose upon new-made hay;
With all her limbs on tremble, and her
    eyes
Shut softly up alive. To speak he tries:
'Fair damsel, pity me! forgive that I
Thus violate thy bower's sanctity!
O pardon me, for I am full of grief —
Grief born of thee, young angel! fairest
    thief!
Who stolen hast away the wings where-
    with
I was to top the heavens. Dear maid, sith
Thou art my executioner, and I feel 111
Loving and hatred, misery and weal,
Will in a few short hours be nothing to me,
And all my story that much passion slew
    me;
Do smile upon the evening of my days;
And, for my tortured brain begins to craze,
Be thou my nurse; and let me understand
How dying I shall kiss that lily hand. —
Dost weep for me? Then should I be con-
    tent.
Scowl on, ye fates! until the firmament 120
Outblackens Erebus, and the full-cavern'd
    earth
Crumbles into itself. By the cloud-girth

Of Jove, those tears have given me a thirst
To meet oblivion.' — As her heart would
    burst
The maiden sobb'd awhile, and then re-
    plied:
'Why must such desolation betide
As that thou speakest of? Are not these
    green nooks
Empty of all misfortune? Do the brooks
Utter a gorgon voice? Does yonder
    thrush,
Schooling its half-fledged little ones to
    brush 130
About the dewy forest, whisper tales? —
Speak not of grief, young stranger, or cold
    snails
Will slime the rose to-night. Though if
    thou wilt,
Methinks 't would be a guilt — a very
    guilt —
Not to companion thee, and sigh away
The light — the dusk — the dark — till
    break of day!'
'Dear lady,' said Endymion, ''t is past:
I love thee! and my days can never last.
That I may pass in patience still speak:
Let me have music dying, and I seek 140
No more delight — I bid adieu to all.
Didst thou not after other climates call,
And murmur about Indian streams?' —
    Then she,
Sitting beneath the midmost forest tree,
For pity sang this roundelay ——

    'O Sorrow,
      Why dost borrow
The natural hue of health, from vermeil
    lips? —
      To give maiden blushes
      To the white rose bushes? 150
Or is 't thy dewy hand the daisy tips?

    'O Sorrow,
      Why dost borrow
The lustrous passion from a falcon-eye? —
      To give the glowworm light?
      Or, on a moonless night,
To tinge, on siren shores, the salt sea-spry?

'O Sorrow,
  Why dost borrow
The mellow ditties from a mourning
    tongue ? —   160
    To give at evening pale
    Unto the nightingale,
That thou mayst listen the cold dews
    among ?

  'O Sorrow,
  Why dost borrow
Heart's lightness from the merriment of
    May ? —
    A lover would not tread
    A cowslip on the head,
Though he should dance from eve till peep
    of day —
    Nor any drooping flower   170
    Held sacred for thy bower,
Wherever he may sport himself and play.

  'To Sorrow,
  I bade good morrow,
And thought to leave her far away behind;
    But cheerly, cheerly,
    She loves me dearly;
She is so constant to me, and so kind:
    I would deceive her,
    And so leave her,   180
But ah ! she is so constant and so kind.

'Beneath my palm-trees, by the river side,
I sat a-weeping: in the whole world wide
There was no one to ask me why I wept, —
    And so I kept
Brimming the water-lily cups with tears
    Cold as my fears.

'Beneath my palm-trees, by the river side,
I sat a-weeping: what enamour'd bride,
Cheated by shadowy wooer from the clouds,
    But hides and shrouds   191
Beneath dark palm-trees by a river side ?

'And as I sat, over the light blue hills
There came a noise of revellers: the rills
Into the wide stream came of purple hue —
    'T was Bacchus and his crew !

The earnest trumpet spake, and silver
    thrills
From kissing cymbals made a merry din —
    'T was Bacchus and his kin !
Like to a moving vintage down they came,
Crown'd with green leaves, and faces all
    on flame;   201
All madly dancing through the pleasant
    valley,
    To scare thee, Melancholy !
O then, O then, thou wast a simple name !
And I forgot thee, as the berried holly
By shepherds is forgotten, when, in June,
Tall chestnuts keep away the sun and
    moon: —
    I rush'd into the folly !

'Within his car, aloft, young Bacchus stood,
Trifling his ivy-dart, in dancing mood, 210
    With sidelong laughing;
And little rills of crimson wine imbrued
His plump white arms, and shoulders,
    enough white
    For Venus' pearly bite;
And near him rode Silenus on his ass,
Pelted with flowers as he on did pass
    Tipsily quaffing.

'Whence came ye, merry Damsels ! whence
    came ye !
So many, and so many, and such glee ?
Why have ye left your bowers desolate, 220
    Your lutes, and gentler fate ? —
" We follow Bacchus ! Bacchus on the wing,
    A conquering !
Bacchus, young Bacchus ! good or ill be-
    tide,
We dance before him thorough kingdoms
    wide: —
Come hither, lady fair, and joined be
    To our wild minstrelsy ! "

'Whence came ye, jolly Satyrs ! whence
    came ye,
So many, and so many, and such glee ?
Why have ye left your forest haunts, why
    left   230
    Your nuts in oak-tree cleft ? —

"For wine, for wine we left our kernel tree;
For wine we left our heath, and yellow
  brooms,
  And cold mushrooms;
For wine we follow Bacchus through the
  earth;
Great god of breathless cups and chirping
  mirth ! —
Come hither, lady fair, and joined be
  To our mad minstrelsy !"

'Over wide streams and mountains great
  we went,
And, save when Bacchus kept his ivy tent,
Onward the tiger and the leopard pants, 241
  With Asian elephants:
Onward these myriads — with song and
  dance,
With zebras striped, and sleek Arabians'
  prance,
Web-footed alligators, crocodiles,
Bearing upon their scaly backs, in files,
Plump infant laughers mimicking the coil
Of seamen, and stout galley-rowers' toil:
With toying oars and silken sails they glide,
  Nor care for wind and tide. 250

'Mounted on panthers' furs and lions'
  manes,
From rear to van they scour about the
  plains;
A three days' journey in a moment done:
And always, at the rising of the sun,
About the wilds they hunt with spear and
  horn,
  On spleenful unicorn.

'I saw Osirian Egypt kneel adown
  Before the vine-wreath crown !
I saw parch'd Abyssinia rouse and sing
  To the silver cymbals' ring ! 260
I saw the whelming vintage hotly pierce
  Old Tartary the fierce !
The Kings of Inde their jewel-sceptres vail,
And from their treasures scatter pearled
  hail;
Great Brahma from his mystic heaven
  groans,

And all his priesthood moans;
Before young Bacchus' eye-wink turning
  pale. —
Into these regions came I following him,
Sick-hearted, weary — so I took a whim
To stray away into these forests drear 270
  Alone, without a peer:
And I have told thee all thou mayest hear.

  'Young Stranger !
  I 've been a ranger
In search of pleasure throughout every
  clime:
  Alas, 't is not for me !
  Bewitch'd I sure must be,
To lose in grieving all my maiden prime.

  'Come then, Sorrow !
  Sweetest Sorrow ! 280
Like an own babe I nurse thee on my
  breast:
  I thought to leave thee
  And deceive thee,
But now of all the world I love thee best.

  'There is not one,
  No, no, not one
But thee to comfort a poor lonely maid;
  Thou art her mother,
  And her brother,
Her playmate, and her wooer in the
  shade.' 290

O what a sigh she gave in finishing,
And look, quite dead to every worldly
  thing !
Endymion could not speak, but gazed on
  her:
And listened to the wind that now did stir
About the crisped oaks full drearily,
Yet with as sweet a softness as might be
Remember'd from its velvet summer song.
At last he said: 'Poor lady, how thus long
Have I been able to endure that voice ? 299
Fair Melody ! kind Siren ! I 've no choice;
I must be thy sad servant evermore:
I cannot choose but kneel here and adore.
Alas, I must not think — by Phœbe, no !

Let me not think, soft Angel! shall it be
   so?
Say, beautifullest, shall I never think?
O thou couldst foster me beyond the brink
Of recollection! make my watchful care
Close up its bloodshot eyes, nor see de-
   spair!
Do gently murder half my soul, and I
Shall feel the other half so utterly!— 310
I'm giddy at that cheek so fair and smooth;
O let it blush so ever! let it soothe
My madness! let it mantle rosy-warm
With the tinge of love, panting in safe
   alarm.—
This cannot be thy hand, and yet it is;
And this is sure thine other softling — this
Thine own fair bosom, and I am so near!
Wilt fall asleep? O let me sip that tear!
And whisper one sweet word that I may
   know
This is this world — sweet dewy blossom!'
   — Woe! 320
Woe! woe to that Endymion! Where is
he?—
Even these words went echoing dismally
Through the wide forest — a most fearful
   tone,
Like one repenting in his latest moan;
And while it died away a shade pass'd by,
As of a thundercloud. When arrows fly
Through the thick branches, poor ring-
   doves sleek forth
Their timid necks and tremble; so these
   both 328
Leant to each other trembling, and sat so
Waiting for some destruction — when lo!
Fleet-feather'd Mercury appear'd sublime
Beyond the tall tree tops; and in less time
Than shoots the slanted hail-storm, down
   he dropt
Towards the ground; but rested not, nor
   stopt
One moment from his home: only the
   sward
He with his wand light touch'd, and hea-
   venward
Swifter than sight was gone — even be-
   fore

The teeming earth a sudden witness bore
Of his swift magic. Diving swans appear
Above the crystal circlings white and
   clear; 340
And catch the cheated eye in wild surprise,
How they can dive in sight and unseen
   rise —
So from the turf outsprang two steeds jet-
   black,
Each with large dark blue wings upon his
   back.
The youth of Caria placed the lovely dame
On one, and felt himself in spleen to tame
The other's fierceness. Through the air
   they flew,
High as the eagles. Like two drops of
   dew
Exhaled to Phœbus' lips, away they are
   gone, 349
Far from the earth away — unseen, alone,
Among cool clouds and winds, but that the
   free,
The buoyant life of song can floating be
Above their heads, and follow them untired.
Muse of my native land, am I inspired?
This is the giddy air, and I must spread
Wide pinions to keep here; nor do I dread
Or height, or depth, or width, or any
   chance
Precipitous: I have beneath my glance
Those towering horses and their mournful
   freight. 359
Could I thus sail, and see, and thus await
Fearless for power of thought, without
   thine aid?—
   There is a sleepy dusk, an odorous shade
From some approaching wonder, and be-
   hold
Those winged steeds, with snorting nostrils
   bold
Snuff at its faint extreme, and seem to
   tire,
Dying to embers from their native fire!

   There curl'd a purple mist around them;
   soon,
It seem'd as when around the pale new
   moon

Sad Zephyr droops the clouds like weeping
   willow:
'T was Sleep slow journeying with head on
   pillow   370
For the first time, since he came nigh dead-
   born
From the old womb of night, his cave for-
   lorn
Had he left more forlorn; for the first
   time,
He felt aloof the day and morning's
   prime —
Because into his depth Cimmerian
There came a dream, showing how a young
   man,
Ere a lean bat could plump its wintery
   skin,
Would at high Jove's empyreal footstool
   win
An immortality, and how espouse
Jove's daughter, and be reckon'd of his
   house.   380
Now was he slumbering towards heaven's
   gate,
That he might at the threshold one hour
   wait
To hear the marriage melodies, and then
Sink downward to his dusky cave again.
His litter of smooth semilucent mist,
Diversely tinged with rose and amethyst,
Puzzled those eyes that for the centre
   sought;
And scarcely for one moment could be
   caught
His sluggish form reposing motionless.
Those two on winged steeds, with all the
   stress   390
Of vision search'd for him, as one would
   look
Athwart the sallows of a river nook
To catch a glance at silver-throated eels, —
Or from old Skiddaw's top, when fog con-
   ceals
His rugged forehead in a mantle pale,
With an eye-guess towards some pleasant
   vale
Descry a favourite hamlet faint and far.

These raven horses, though they foster'd
   are
Of earth's splenetic fire, dully drop
Their full-vein'd ears, nostrils blood wide,
   and stop;   400
Upon the spiritless mist have they out-
   spread
Their ample feathers, are in slumber
   dead, —
And on those pinions, level in mid air,
Endymion sleepeth and the lady fair.
Slowly they sail, slowly as icy isle
Upon a calm sea drifting: and meanwhile
The mournful wanderer dreams. Behold !
   he walks
On heaven's pavement; brotherly he talks
To divine powers: from his hand full fain
Juno's proud birds are pecking pearly
   grain: 410
He tries the nerve of Phœbus' golden bow,
And asketh where the golden apples grow:
Upon his arm he braces Pallas' shield,
And strives in vain to unsettle and wield
A Jovian thunderbolt: arch Hebe brings
A full-brimm'd goblet, dances lightly, sings
And tantalizes long; at last he drinks,
And lost in pleasure, at her feet he sinks,
Touching with dazzled lips her starlight
   hand.
He blows a bugle, — an ethereal band   420
Are visible above: the Seasons four, —
Green-kirtled Spring, flush Summer, golden
   store
In Autumn's sickle, Winter frosty hoar,
Join dance with shadowy Hours; while still
   the blast,
In swells unmitigated, still doth last
To sway their floating morris. 'Whose is
   this ?
Whose bugle ?' he inquires: they smile —
   'O Dis !
Why is this mortal here ? Dost thou not
   know
Its mistress' lips ?   Not thou ? — 'T is
   Dian's: lo !   429
She rises crescented !' He looks, 't is she,
His very goddess: good-bye earth, and sea,

And air, and pains, and care, and suffering;
Good-bye to all but love! Then doth he
    spring
Towards her, and awakes — and, strange,
    o'erhead,
Of those same fragrant exhalations bred,
Beheld awake his very dream: the gods
Stood smiling; merry Hebe laughs and
    nods;
And Phœbe bends towards him crescented.
O state perplexing! On the pinion bed,
Too well awake, he feels the panting side 440
Of his delicious lady. He who died
For soaring too audacious in the sun,
When that same treacherous wax began to
    run,
Felt not more tongue-tied than Endymion.
His heart leapt up as to its rightful throne,
To that fair-shadow'd passion pulsed its
    way —
Ah, what perplexity! Ah, well a day!
So fond, so beauteous was his bed-fellow,
He could not help but kiss her: then he
    grew
Awhile forgetful of all beauty save   450
Young Phœbe's, golden-hair'd; and so 'gan
    crave
Forgiveness: yet he turn'd once more to look
At the sweet sleeper, — all his soul was
    shook, —
She press'd his hand in slumber; so once
    more
He could not help but kiss her and adore.
At this the shadow wept, melting away.
The Latmian started up: 'Bright goddess,
    stay!
Search my most hidden breast! By truth's
    own tongue,
I have no dædale heart; why is it wrung 459
To desperation? Is there nought for me,
Upon the bourne of bliss, but misery?'

These words awoke the stranger of dark
    tresses:
Her dawning love-look rapt Endymion
    blesses
With 'haviour soft. Sleep yawn'd from
    underneath.

'Thou swan of Ganges, let us no more
    breathe
This murky phantasm! thou contented
    seem'st
Pillow'd in lovely idleness, nor dream'st
What horrors may discomfort thee and
    me.
Ah, shouldst thou die from my heart-
    treachery! —   469
Yet did she merely weep — her gentle soul
Hath no revenge in it: as it is whole
In tenderness, would I were whole in love!
Can I prize thee, fair maid, all price above,
Even when I feel as true as innocence?
I do, I do. — What is this soul then?
    Whence
Came it? It does not seem my own, and I
Have no self-passion or identity.
Some fearful end must be: where, where
    is it?
By Nemesis, I see my spirit flit   479
Alone about the dark — Forgive me, sweet:
Shall we away?' He roused the steeds;
    they beat
Their wings chivalrous into the clear air,
Leaving old Sleep within his vapoury lair.

The good-night blush of eve was waning
    slow,
And Vesper, risen star, began to throe
In the dusk heavens silvery, when they
Thus sprang direct towards the Galaxy.
Nor did speed hinder converse soft and
    strange —
Eternal oaths and vows they interchange,
In such wise, in such temper, so aloof 490
Up in the winds, beneath a starry roof,
So witless of their doom, that verily
'T is well nigh past man's search their hearts
    to see;
Whether they wept, or laugh'd, or grieved
    or toy'd —
Most like with joy gone mad, with sorrow
    cloy'd.

Full facing their swift flight, from ebon
    streak,
The moon put forth a little diamond peak,

No bigger than an unobserved star,
Or tiny point of fairy scimetar;
Bright signal that she only stoop'd to tie   500
Her silver sandals, ere deliciously
She bow'd into the heavens her timid head.
Slowly she rose, as though she would have
    fled,
While to his lady meek the Carian turn'd,
To mark if her dark eyes had yet discern'd
This beauty in its birth — Despair! despair!
He saw her body fading gaunt and spare
In the cold moonshine. Straight he seized
    her wrist;
It melted from his grasp; her hand he
    kiss'd,
And, horror! kiss'd his own — he was
    alone.   510
Her steed a little higher soar'd, and then
Dropt hawk-wise to the earth.

                              There lies a den,
Beyond the seeming confines of the space
Made for the soul to wander in and trace
Its own existence, of remotest glooms.
Dark regions are around it, where the
    tombs
Of buried griefs the spirit sees, but scarce
One hour doth linger weeping, for the
    pierce
Of new-born woe it feels more inly smart:
And in these regions many a venom'd
    dart   520
At random flies; they are the proper home
Of every ill: the man is yet to come
Who hath not journey'd in this native hell.
But few have ever felt how calm and well
Sleep may be had in that deep den of all.
There anguish does not sting, nor pleasure
    pall;
Woe-hurricanes beat ever at the gate,
Yet all is still within and desolate.
Beset with painful gusts, within ye hear   529
No sound so loud as when on curtain'd bier
The death-watch tick is stifled. Enter none
Who strive therefore: on the sudden it is
    won.
Just when the sufferer begins to burn,
Then it is free to him; and from an urn,

Still fed by melting ice, he takes a
    draught —
Young Semele such richness never quaff'd
In her maternal longing. Happy gloom!
Dark Paradise! where pale becomes the
    bloom
Of health by due; where silence dreariest
Is most articulate; where hopes infest;   540
Where those eyes are the brightest far that
    keep
Their lids shut longest in a dreamless sleep.
O happy spirit-home! O wondrous soul!
Pregnant with such a den to save the whole
In thine own depth. Hail, gentle Carian!
For, never since thy griefs and woes began,
Hast thou felt so content: a grievous feud
Hath led thee to this Cave of Quietude.
Aye, his lull'd soul was there, although up-
    borne
With dangerous speed: and so he did not
    mourn   550
Because he knew not whither he was going.
So happy was he, not the aerial blowing
Of trumpets at clear parley from the east
Could rouse from that fine relish, that high
    feast.
They stung the feather'd horse; with fierce
    alarm
He flapp'd towards the sound. Alas, no
    charm
Could lift Endymion's head, or he had
    view'd
A skyey mask, a pinion'd multitude, —
And silvery was its passing: voices sweet
Warbling the while as if to lull and greet
The wanderer in his path. Thus warbled
    they,   561
While past the vision went in bright array.

'Who, who from Dian's feast would be
    away?
For all the golden bowers of the day
Are empty left? Who, who away would
    be
From Cynthia's wedding and festivity?
Not Hesperus: lo! upon his silver wings
He leans away for highest heaven and sings,
Snapping his lucid fingers merrily! —

Ah, Zephyrus! art here, and Flora too! 570
Ye tender bibbers of the rain and dew,
Young playmates of the rose and daffodil,
Be careful, ere ye enter in, to fill
    Your baskets high
With fennel green, and balm, and golden
    pines,
Savory, latter-mint, and columbines,
Cool parsley, basil sweet, and sunny thyme;
Yea, every flower and leaf of every clime,
All gather'd in the dewy morning: hie
    Away! fly, fly!— 580
Crystalline brother of the belt of heaven,
Aquarius! to whom king Jove has given
Two liquid pulse streams 'stead of feath-
    er'd wings,
Two fanlike fountains, — thine illuminings
    For Dian play:
Dissolve the frozen purity of air;
Let thy white shoulders silvery and bare
Show cold through watery pinions; make
    more bright
The Star-Queen's crescent on her marriage
    night:
    Haste, haste away!— 590
Castor has tamed the planet Lion, see!
And of the Bear has Pollux mastery:
A third is in the race! who is the third,
Speeding away swift as the eagle bird?
    The ramping Centaur!
The Lion's mane 's on end: the Bear how
    fierce!
The Centaur's arrow ready seems to pierce
Some enemy: far forth his bow is bent
Into the blue of heaven. He 'll be shent,
    Pale unrelentor, 600
When he shall hear the wedding lutes
    a-playing. —
Andromeda! sweet woman! why delaying
So timidly among the stars: come hither!
Join this bright throng, and nimbly follow
    whither
    They all are going.
Danae's Son, before Jove newly bow'd,
Has wept for thee, calling to Jove aloud.
Thee, gentle lady, did he disenthrall:
Ye shall for ever live and love, for all
    Thy tears are flowing. — 610
By Daphne's fright, behold Apollo!'—

          More
Endymion heard not: down his steed him
    bore,
Prone to the green head of a misty hill.

His first touch of the earth went nigh to
    kill.
'Alas!' said he, 'were I but always borne
Through dangerous winds, had but my
    footsteps worn
A path in hell, for ever would I bless
Horrors which nourish an uneasiness
For my own sullen conquering: to him
Who lives beyond earth's boundary, grief
    is dim, 620
Sorrow is but a shadow: now I see
The grass; I feel the solid ground — Ah,
    me!
It is thy voice — divinest! Where?—
    who? who
Left thee so quiet on this bed of dew?
Behold upon this happy earth we are;
Let us ay love each other; let us fare
On forest-fruits, and never, never go
Among the abodes of mortals here below,
Or be by phantoms duped. O destiny!
Into a labyrinth now my soul would fly, 630
But with thy beauty will I deaden it.
Where didst thou melt to? By thee will
    I sit
For ever: let our fate stop here — a kid
I on this spot will offer: Pan will bid
Us live in peace, in love and peace among
His forest wildernesses. I have clung
To nothing, loved a nothing, nothing seen
Or felt but a great dream! Oh, I have
    been
Presumptuous against love, against the
    sky,
Against all elements, against the tie 640
Of mortals each to each, against the blooms
Of flowers, rush of rivers, and the tombs
Of heroes gone! Against his proper glory
Has my own soul conspired: so my story
Will I to children utter, and repent.
There never lived a mortal man, who bent
His appetite beyond his natural sphere,
But starved and died. My sweetest Indian,
    here,

104   ENDYMION

Here will I kneel, for thou redeemed hast
My life from too thin breathing: gone and
    past   650
Are cloudy phantasms.   Caverns lone,
    farewell!
And air of visions, and the monstrous swell
Of visionary seas! No, never more
Shall airy voices cheat me to the shore
Of tangled wonder, breathless and aghast.
Adieu, my daintiest Dream! although so
    vast
My love is still for thee. The hour may
    come
When we shall meet in pure elysium.
On earth I may not love thee; and there-
    fore
Doves will I offer up, and sweetest store 660
All through the teeming year: so thou wilt
    shine
On me, and on this damsel fair of mine,
And bless our simple lives. My Indian
    bliss!
My river-lily bud! one human kiss!
One sigh of real breath — one gentle
    squeeze,
Warm as a dove's nest among summer
    trees,
And warm with dew at ooze from living
    blood!
Whither didst melt? Ah, what of that! —
    all good
We 'll talk about — no more of dreaming.
    — Now,
Where shall our dwelling be?   Under the
    brow   670
Of some steep mossy hill, where ivy dun
Would hide us up, although spring leaves
    were none;
And where dark yew trees, as we rustle
    through
Will drop their scarlet berry cups of dew?
O thou wouldst joy to live in such a place;
Dusk for our loves, yet light enough to
    grace
Those gentle limbs on mossy bed reclined:
For by one step the blue sky shouldst thou
    find,
And by another, in deep dell below,

See, through the trees, a little river go 680
All in its mid-day gold and glimmering.
Honey from out the gnarled hive I 'll bring,
And apples, wan with sweetness, gather
    thee, —
Cresses that grow where no man may them
    see,
And sorrel untorn by the dew-claw'd stag:
Pipes will I fashion of the syrinx flag,
That thou mayst always know whither I
    roam,
When it shall please thee in our quiet
    home
To listen and think of love. Still let me
    speak;
Still let me dive into the joy I seek, — 690
For yet the past doth prison me. The
    rill,
Thou haply mayst delight in, will I fill
With fairy fishes from the mountain tarn,
And thou shalt feed them from the squir-
    rel's barn.
Its bottom will I strew with amber shells,
And pebbles blue from deep enchanted
    wells.
Its sides I 'll plant with dew-sweet eglan-
    tine,
And honeysuckles full of clear bee-wine.
I will entice this crystal rill to trace
Love's silver name upon the meadow's
    face.   700
I 'll kneel to Vesta, for a flame of fire;
And to god Phœbus, for a golden lyre;
To Empress Dian, for a hunting-spear;
To Vesper, for a taper silver-clear,
That I may see thy beauty through the
    night;
To Flora, and a nightingale shall light
Tame on thy finger; to the River-gods,
And they shall bring thee taper fishing-
    rods
Of gold, and lines of Naiads' long bright
    tress.
Heaven shield thee for thine utter loveli-
    ness!   710
Thy mossy footstool shall the altar be
'Fore which I 'll bend, bending, dear love,
    to thee:

Those lips shall be my Delphos, and shall
  speak
Laws to my footsteps, colour to my cheek,
Trembling or steadfastness to this same
  voice,
And of three sweetest pleasurings the
  choice:
And that affectionate light, those diamond
  things,
Those eyes, those passions, those supreme
  pearl springs,
Shall be my grief, or twinkle me to plea-
  sure.
Say, is not bliss within our perfect seiz-
  ure ?   720
O that I could not doubt ! '

                          The mountaineer
Thus strove by fancies vain and crude to
  clear
His brier'd path to some tranquillity.
It gave bright gladness to his lady's eye,
And yet the tears she wept were tears of
  sorrow;
Answering thus, just as the golden mor-
  row
Beam'd upward from the valleys of the
  east:
' O that the flutter of his heart had ceased,
Or the sweet name of love had pass'd
  away.
Young feather'd tyrant ! by a swift de-
  cay   730
Wilt thou devote this body to the earth:
And I do think that at my very birth
I lisp'd thy blooming titles inwardly;
For at the first, first dawn and thought of
  thee,
With uplift hands I blest the stars of hea-
  ven.
Art thou not cruel ?   Ever have I striven
To think thee kind, but ah, it will not do !
When yet a child, I heard that kisses drew
Favour from thee, and so I gave and gave
To the void air, bidding them find out
  love: 740
But when I came to feel how far above
All fancy, pride, and fickle maidenhood,

All earthly pleasure, all imagined good,
Was the warm tremble of a devout kiss, —
Even then, that moment, at the thought of
  this,
Fainting I fell into a bed of flowers,
And languish'd there three days. Ye
  milder powers,
Am I not cruelly wrong'd ?   Believe, be-
  lieve
Me, dear Endymion, were I to weave
With my own fancies garlands of sweet
  life,   750
Thou shouldst be one of all. Ah, bitter
  strife !
I may not be thy love: I am forbidden —
Indeed I am — thwarted, affrighted, chid-
  den,
By things I tremble at, and gorgon wrath.
Twice hast thou ask'd whither I went:
  henceforth
Ask me no more ! I may not utter it,
Nor may I be thy love. We might com-
  mit
Ourselves at once to vengeance; we might
  die;
We might embrace and die: voluptuous
  thought !
Enlarge not to my hunger, or I 'm caught
In trammels of perverse deliciousness.   761
No, no, that shall not be: thee will I bless,
And bid a long adieu.'

                          The Carian
No word return'd: both lovelorn, silent,
  wan,
Into the valleys green together went.
Far wandering, they were perforce con-
  tent
To sit beneath a fair lone beechen tree;
Nor at each other gazed, but heavily
Pored on its hazel cirque of shedded leaves.

  Endymion ! unhappy ! it nigh grieves 770
Me to behold thee thus in last extreme:
Enskied ere this, but truly that I deem
Truth the best music in a first-born song.
Thy lute-voiced brother will I sing ere
  long,

And thou shalt aid — hast thou not aided
    me ?
Yes, moonlight Emperor ! felicity
Has been thy meed for many thousand
    years;
Yet often have I, on the brink of tears,
Mourn'd as if yet thou wert a forester; —
Forgetting the old tale.

              He did not stir
His eyes from the dead leaves, or one small
    pulse   781
Of joy he might have felt. The spirit culls
Unfaded amaranth, when wild it strays
Through the old garden-ground of boyish
    days.
A little onward ran the very stream
By which he took his first soft poppy
    dream;
And on the very bark 'gainst which he
    leant
A crescent he had carved, and round it
    spent
His skill in little stars. The teeming tree
Had swollen and green'd the pious charac-
    tery,   790
But not ta'en out. Why, there was not a
    slope
Up which he had not fear'd the antelope;
And not a tree, beneath whose rooty shade
He had not with his tamed leopards play'd;
Nor could an arrow light, or javelin,
Fly in the air where his had never been —
And yet he knew it not.

              O treachery !
Why does his lady smile, pleasing her eye
With all his sorrowing ? He sees her not.
But who so stares on him ? His sister
    sure !   800
Peona of the woods ! — Can she endure —
Impossible — how dearly they embrace !
His lady smiles; delight is in her face;
It is no treachery.

            'Dear brother mine !
Endymion, weep not so ! Why shouldst
    thou pine

When all great Latmos so exalt will be ?
Thank the great gods, and look not bit-
    terly;
And speak not one pale word, and sigh no
    more.
Sure I will not believe thou hast such store
Of grief, to last thee to my kiss again. 810
Thou surely canst not bear a mind in pain,
Come hand in hand with one so beauti-
    ful.
Be happy both of you ! for I will pull
The flowers of autumn for your coronals.
Pan's holy priest for young Endymion calls;
And when he is restored, thou, fairest
    dame,
Shalt be our queen. Now, is it not a shame
To see ye thus, — not very, very sad ?
Perhaps ye are too happy to be glad:
O feel as if it were a common day;   820
Free-voiced as one who never was away.
No tongue shall ask, Whence come ye ? but
    ye shall
Be gods of your own rest imperial.
Not even I, for one whole month, will pry
Into the hours that have pass'd us by,
Since in my arbour I did sing to thee.
O Hermes ! on this very night will be
A hymning up to Cynthia, queen of light;
For the soothsayers old saw yesternight
Good visions in the air, — whence will be-
    fall,   830
As say these sages, health perpetual
To shepherds and their flocks; and further-
    more,
In Dian's face they read the gentle lore:
Therefore for her these vesper-carols are.
Our friends will all be there from nigh and
    far.
Many upon thy death have ditties made;
And many, even now, their foreheads shade
With cypress, on a day of sacrifice.
New singing for our maids shalt thou devise,
And pluck the sorrow from our huntsmen's
    brows.   840
Tell me, my lady-queen, how to espouse
This wayward brother to his rightful joys!
His eyes are on thee bent, as thou didst
    poise

His fate most goddess-like. Help me, I
    pray,
To lure — Endymion, dear brother, say
What ails thee ? ' He could bear no more,
    and so
Bent his soul fiercely like a spiritual bow,
And twang'd it inwardly, and calmly said:
'I would have thee my only friend, sweet
    maid !
My only visitor ! not ignorant though, 850
That those deceptions which for pleasure
    go
'Mong men, are pleasures real as real may
    be:
But there are higher ones I may not see,
If impiously an earthly realm I take.
Since I saw thee, I have been wide awake
Night after night, and day by day, until
Of the empyrean I have drunk my fill.
Let it content thee, Sister, seeing me
More happy than betides mortality.
A hermit young, I 'll live in mossy cave, 860
Where thou alone shalt come to me, and
    lave
Thy spirit in the wonders I shall tell.
Through me the shepherd realm shall pro-
    sper well;
For to thy tongue will I all health confide.
And, for my sake, let this young maid abide
With thee as a dear sister. Thou alone,
Peona, mayst return to me. I own
This may sound strangely: but when, dear-
    est girl,
Thou seest it for my happiness, no pearl
Will trespass down those cheeks. Compan-
    ion fair ! 870
Wilt be content to dwell with her, to share
This sister's love with me ? ' Like one re-
    sign'd
And bent by circumstance, and thereby
    blind
In self-commitment, thus that meek un-
    known:
'Aye, but a buzzing by my ears has flown,
Of jubilee to Dian: — truth I heard !
Well then, I see there is no little bird,
Tender soever, but is Jove's own care.
Long have I sought for rest, and, unaware,

Behold I find it ! so exalted too ! 880
So after my own heart ! I knew, I knew
There was a place untenanted in it;
In that same void white Chastity shall sit,
And monitor me nightly to lone slumber.
With sanest lips I vow me to the number
Of Dian's sisterhood; and, kind lady,
With thy good help, this very night shall
    see
My future days to her fane consecrate.'

    As feels a dreamer what doth most cre-
    ate
His own particular fright, so these three
    felt: 890
Or like one who, in after ages, knelt
To Lucifer or Baal, when he 'd pine
After a little sleep: or when in mine
Far under-ground, a sleeper meets his
    friends
Who know him not. Each diligently bends
Towards common thoughts and things for
    very fear;
Striving their ghastly malady to cheer,
By thinking it a thing of yes and no,
That housewives talk of. But the spirit-
    blow
Was struck, and all were dreamers. At
    the last 900
Endymion said: ' Are not our fates all
    cast ?
Why stand we here ? Adieu, ye tender
    pair !
Adieu ! ' Whereat those maidens, with
    wild stare,
Walk'd dizzily away. Pained and hot
His eyes went after them, until they got
Near to a cypress grove, whose deadly
    maw,
In one swift moment, would what then he
    saw
Engulf for ever. 'Stay,' he cried, 'ah,
    stay !
Turn, damsels ! hist ! one word I have to
    say:
Sweet Indian, I would see thee once again.
It is a thing I dote on: so I 'd fain, 911
Peona, ye should hand in hand repair,

Into those holy groves that silent are
Behind great Dian's temple. I 'll be yon,
At Vesper's earliest twinkle — they are
    gone —
But once, once, once again — ' At this he
    press'd
His hands against his face, and then did
    rest
His head upon a mossy hillock green,   .
And so remain'd as he a corpse had been
All the long day; save when he scantly
    lifted   920
His eyes abroad, to see how shadows shifted
With the slow move of time, — sluggish
    and weary
Until the poplar tops, in journey dreary,
Had reach'd the river's brim.   Then up he
    rose,
And, slowly as that very river flows,
Walk'd towards the temple grove with this
    lament:
' Why such a golden eve ?   The breeze is
    sent
Careful and soft, that not a leaf may fall
Before the serene father of them all
Bows down his summer head below the
    west.   930
Now am I of breath, speech, and speed
    possest,
But at the setting I must bid adieu
To her for the last time.   Night will·strew
On the damp grass myriads of lingering
    leaves,
And with them shall I die; nor much it
    grieves
To die, when summer dies on the cold
    sward.
Why, I have been a butterfly, a lord
Of flowers, garlands, love-knots, silly po-
    sies,
Groves, meadows, melodies, and arbour-
    roses;   939
My kingdom 's at its death, and just it is
That I should die with it: so in all this
We miscall grief, bale, sorrow, heart-break,
    woe,
What is there to plain of ?   By Titan's foe
I am but rightly served.'   So saying, he

Tripp'd lightly on, in sort of deathful· glee;
Laughing at the clear stream and setting
    sun,
As though they jests had been: nor had he
    done
His laugh at nature's holy countenance,
Until that grove appear'd, as if perchance,
And then his tongue with sober seemlihed
Gave utterance as he enter'd: ' Ha !' I
    said,   951
' King of the butterflies; but by this gloom,
And by old Rhadamanthus' tongue of doom,
This dusk religion, pomp of solitude,
And the Promethean clay by thief endued,
By old Saturnus' forelock, by his head
Shook with eternal palsy, I did wed
Myself to things of light from infancy;
And thus to be cast out, thus lorn to die,
Is sure enough to make a mortal man   960
Grow impious.'   So he inwardly began
On things for which no wording can be
    found;
Deeper and deeper sinking, until drown'd
Beyond the reach of music: for the choir
Of Cynthia he heard not, though rough
    brier
Nor muffling thicket interposed to dull
The vesper hymn, far swollen, soft and full,
Through the dark pillars of those sylvan
    aisles.
He saw not the two maidens, nor their
    smiles,
Wan as primroses gather'd at midnight 970
By chilly-finger'd spring. ' Unhappy wight !
Endymion !' said Peona, ' we are here !
What wouldst thou ere we all are laid on
    bier ? '
Then he embraced her, and his lady's hand
Press'd, saying: ' Sister, I would have com-
    mand,
If it were heaven's will, on our sad fate.'
At which that dark-eyed stranger stood
    elate
And said, in a new voice, but sweet as love,
To Endymion's amaze: ' By Cupid's dove,
And so thou shalt ! and by the lily truth
Of my own breast thou shalt, beloved
    youth ! '   981

And as she spake, into her face there
    came
Light, as reflected from a silver flame:
Her long black hair swell'd ampler, in dis-
    play
Full golden; in her eyes a brighter day
Dawn'd blue, and full of love. Aye, he
    beheld
Phœbe, his passion! joyous she upheld
Her lucid bow, continuing thus: " Drear,
    drear
Has our delaying been; but foolish fear
Withheld me first; and then decrees of
    fate;   990
And then 't was fit that from this mortal
    state

Thou shouldst, my love, by some unlook'd-
    for change
Be spiritualized. Peona, we shall range
These forests, and to thee they safe shall be
As was thy cradle; hither shalt thou flee
To meet us many a time.' Next Cynthia
    bright
Peona kiss'd, and bless'd with fair good
    night:
Her brother kiss'd her too, and knelt adown
Before his goddess, in a blissful swoon. 999
She gave her fair hands to him, and behold,
Before three swiftest kisses he had told,
They vanish'd far away! — Peona went
Home through the gloomy wood in won-
    derment.

THE POEMS OF 1818–1819

The most pregnant year of Keats's genius was that which dates roughly from the spring of 1818 to the spring of 1819, as one may readily see who scans the titles of the poems included in this division. The group here given, beginning with *Isabella* and closing with *Lamia*, includes, besides those poems and *The Eve of St. Agnes*, the great Odes, *Fancy*, and some of the notable Sonnets. The division, besides being a convenient one, seems almost logical and not merely chronological.

ISABELLA, OR THE POT OF BASIL

A STORY FROM BOCCACCIO

Keats and Reynolds projected a volume of metrical tales translated from or based on Boccaccio. Apparently, Keats began *Isabella*, which was to be one of his contributions, some time before he went to Teignmouth, where he finished *Endymion*. At any rate, from that place April 27, 1818, he wrote to Reynolds, who was then quite ill: 'I have written for my folio Shakespeare, in which there are the first few stanzas of my *Pot of Basil*. I have the rest here finished, and will copy the whole out fairly shortly, and George will bring it you — The compliment is paid by us to Boccace, whether we publish or no: so there is content in this world — *mine* is short — you must be deliberate about yours; you must not think of it till many months after you are quite well: then put your passion to it, and I shall be bound up with you in the shadows of Mind, as we are in our matters of human life.' Keats did not wait for Reynolds, but published his *Isabella* in the volume entitled *Lamia, Isabella, The Eve of St. Agnes, and other Poems* issued in the summer of 1820.

I

FAIR Isabel, poor simple Isabel!
  Lorenzo, a young palmer in Love's eye!
They could not in the self-same mansion dwell
  Without some stir of heart, some malady;

They could not sit at meals but feel how well
  It soothed each to be the other by;
They could not, sure, beneath the same roof sleep
  But to each other dream, and nightly weep.

II

With every morn their love grew tenderer,
  With every eve deeper and tenderer still;
He might not in house, field, or garden stir,
  But her full shape would all his seeing fill;
And his continual voice was pleasanter
  To her, than noise of trees or hidden rill;
Her lute-string gave an echo of his name,
She spoilt her half-done broidery with the same.

III

He knew whose gentle hand was at the latch,
  Before the door had given her to his eyes;
And from her chamber-window he would catch
  Her beauty farther than the falcon spies;
And constant as her vespers would he watch,
  Because her face was turn'd to the same skies;
And with sick longing all the night outwear,
To hear her morning-step upon the stair.

IV

A whole long month of May in this sad
      plight
  Made their cheeks paler by the break of
      June:
'To-morrow will I bow to my delight,
  To-morrow will I ask my lady's boon.' —
'O may I never see another night,
  Lorenzo, if thy lips breathe not love's
      tune.' —
So spake they to their pillows; but, alas,
Honeyless days and days did he let pass;

V

Until sweet Isabella's untouch'd cheek
  Fell sick within the rose's just domain,
Fell thin as a young mother's, who doth
      seek
  By every lull to cool her infant's pain:
'How ill she is!' said he, 'I may not
      speak,
  And yet I will, and tell my love all plain:
If looks speak love-laws, I will drink her
      tears,
  And at the least 't will startle off her
      cares.'

VI

So said he one fair morning, and all day
  His heart beat awfully against his side;
And to his heart he inwardly did pray
  For power to speak; but still the ruddy
      tide
Stifled his voice, and pulsed resolve away —
  Fever'd his high conceit of such a bride,
Yet brought him to the meekness of a
      child:
Alas! when passion is both meek and wild!

VII

So once more he had waked and anguished
  A dreary night of love and misery,
If Isabel's quick eye had not been wed
  To every symbol on his forehead high:
She saw it waxing very pale and dead,
  And straight all flush'd; so, lisped ten-
      derly,

'Lorenzo!' — here she ceased her timid
      quest,
But in her tone and look he read the rest.

VIII

'O Isabella, I can half perceive
  That I may speak my grief into thine ear;
If thou didst ever any thing believe,
  Believe how I love thee, believe how
      near
My soul is to its doom: I would not grieve
  Thy hand by unwelcome pressing, would
      not fear
Thine eyes by gazing; but I cannot live
Another night, and not my passion shrive.

IX

'Love! thou art leading me from wintry
      cold,
  Lady! thou leadest me to summer clime,
And I must taste the blossoms that unfold
  In its ripe warmth this gracious morning
      time.'
So said, his erewhile timid lips grew bold,
  And poesied with hers in dewy rhyme:
Great bliss was with them, and great hap-
      piness
Grew, like a lusty flower in June's caress.

X

Parting they seem'd to tread upon the air,
  Twin roses by the zephyr blown apart
Only to meet again more close, and share
  The inward fragrance of each other's
      heart.
She, to her chamber gone, a ditty fair
  Sang, of delicious love and honey'd dart;
He with light steps went up a western hill,
And bade the sun farewell, and joy'd his
      fill.

XI

All close they met again, before the dusk
  Had taken from the stars its pleasant
      veil,
All close they met, all eves, before the dusk
  Had taken from the stars its pleasant
      veil,

Close in a bower of hyacinth and musk,
  Unknown of any, free from whispering
    tale.
Ah! better had it been for ever so,
Than idle ears should pleasure in their
  woe.

XII

Were they unhappy then? — It cannot
  be —
  Too many tears for lovers have been
    shed,
Too many sighs give we to them in fee,
Too much of pity after they are dead,
Too many doleful stories do we see,
  Whose matter in bright gold were best
    be read;
Except in such a page where Theseus'
  spouse
Over the pathless waves towards him bows.

XIII

But, for the general award of love,
  The little sweet doth kill much bitter-
    ness;
Though Dido silent is in under-grove,
  And Isabella's was a great distress,
Though young Lorenzo in warm Indian
  clove
  Was not embalm'd, this truth is not the
    less —
Even bees, the little almsmen of spring-
  bowers,
Know there is richest juice in poison-
  flowers.

XIV

With her two brothers this fair lady dwelt,
  Enriched from ancestral merchandise,
And for them many a weary hand did swelt
  In torched mines and noisy factories,
And many once proud-quiver'd loins did
  melt
  In blood from stinging whip; — with
    hollow eyes
Many all day in dazzling river stood,
To take the rich-ored driftings of the flood.

XV

For them the Ceylon diver held his breath,
  And went all naked to the hungry shark;
For them his ears gush'd blood; for them
  in death
  The seal on the cold ice with piteous
    bark
Lay full of darts; for them alone did
  seethe
  A thousand men in troubles wide and
    dark:
Half-ignorant, they turn'd an easy wheel,
That set sharp racks at work, to pinch and
  peel.

XVI

Why were they proud?   Because their
  marble founts
  Gush'd with more pride than do a
    wretch's tears? —
Why were they proud?   Because fair
  orange-mounts
  Were of more soft ascent than lazar
    stairs? —
Why were they proud?   Because red-
  lined accounts
  Were richer than the songs of Grecian
    years? —
Why were they proud? again we ask
  aloud,
Why in the name of Glory were they
  proud?

XVII

Yet were these Florentines as self-retired
  In hungry pride and gainful cowardice,
As two close Hebrews in that land inspired,
  Paled in and vineyarded from beggar-
    spies;
The hawks of ship-mast forests — the un-
  tired
  And pannier'd mules for ducats and old
    lies —
Quick cat's-paws on the generous stray-
  away, —
Great wits in Spanish, Tuscan, and Malay.

XVIII

How was it these same ledger-men could spy
Fair Isabella in her downy nest?
How could they find out in Lorenzo's eye
A straying from his toil? Hot Egypt's pest
Into their vision covetous and sly!
How could these money-bags see east and west? —
Yet so they did — and every dealer fair
Must see behind, as doth the hunted hare.

XIX

O eloquent and famed Boccaccio!
Of thee we now should ask forgiving boon,
And of thy spicy myrtles as they blow,
And of thy roses amorous of the moon,
And of thy lilies, that do paler grow
Now they can no more hear thy ghittern's tune,
For venturing syllables that ill beseem
The quiet glooms of such a piteous theme.

XX

Grant thou a pardon here, and then the tale
Shall move on soberly, as it is meet;
There is no other crime, no mad assail
To make old prose in modern rhyme more sweet:
But it is done — succeed the verse or fail —
To honour thee, and thy gone spirit greet;
To stead thee as a verse in English tongue,
An echo of thee in the north-wind sung.

XXI

These brethren having found by many signs
What love Lorenzo for their sister had,
And how she loved him too, each unconfines
His bitter thoughts to other, well-nigh mad
That he, the servant of their trade designs,
Should in their sister's love be blithe and glad,
When 't was their plan to coax her by degrees
To some high noble and his olive-trees.

XXII

And many a jealous conference had they,
And many times they bit their lips alone,
Before they fix'd upon a surest way
To make the youngster for his crime atone;
And at the last, these men of cruel clay
Cut Mercy with a sharp knife to the bone;
For they resolved in some forest dim
To kill Lorenzo, and there bury him.

XXIII

So on a pleasant morning, as he leant
Into the sunrise, o'er the balustrade
Of the garden-terrace, towards him they bent
Their footing through the dews; and to him said,
'You seem there in the quiet of content,
Lorenzo, and we are most loth to invade
Calm speculation; but if you are wise,
Bestride your steed while cold is in the skies.

XXIV

'To-day we purpose, aye, this hour we mount
To spur three leagues towards the Apennine;
Come down, we pray thee, ere the hot sun count
His dewy rosary on the eglantine.'
Lorenzo, courteously as he was wont,
Bow'd a fair greeting to these serpents' whine;
And went in haste, to get in readiness,
With belt, and spur, and bracing huntsman's dress.

XXV

And as he to the court-yard pass'd along,
Each third step did he pause, and listen'd oft
If he could hear his lady's matin-song,
Or the light whisper of her footstep soft;

And as he thus over his passion hung,
  He heard a laugh full musical aloft;
When, looking up, he saw her features
    bright
Smile through an in-door lattice, all delight.

XXVI

'Love, Isabel!' said he, 'I was in pain
  Lest I should miss to bid thee a good
    morrow:
Ah! what if I should lose thee, when so
    fain
I am to stifle all the heavy sorrow
Of a poor three hours' absence? but we 'll
    gain
  Out of the amorous dark what day doth
    borrow.
Good bye! I 'll soon be back.' — 'Good
    bye!' said she: —
And as he went she chanted merrily.

XXVII

So the two brothers and their murder'd
    man
  Rode past fair Florence, to where Arno's
    stream
Gurgles through straighten'd banks, and
    still doth fan
  Itself with dancing bulrush, and the
    bream
Keeps head against the freshets.   Sick and
    wan
The brothers' faces in the ford did seem,
Lorenzo's flush with love. — They pass'd the
    water
Into a forest quiet for the slaughter.

XXVIII

There was Lorenzo slain and buried in,
  There in that forest did his great love
    cease;
Ah! when a soul doth thus its freedom
    win,
It aches in loneliness — is ill at peace
As the break-covert bloodhounds of such
    sin:
  They dipp'd their swords in the water,
    and did tease

Their horses homeward, with convulsed
    spur,
Each richer by his being a murderer.

XXIX

They told their sister how, with sudden
    speed,
  Lorenzo had ta'en ship for foreign lands,
Because of some great urgency and need
  In their affairs, requiring trusty hands.
Poor Girl! put on thy stifling widow's weed,
  And 'scape at once from Hope's accursed
    bands;
To-day thou wilt not see him, nor to-morrow,
And the next day will be a day of sorrow.

XXX

She weeps alone for pleasures not to be;
  Sorely she wept until the night came on,
And then, instead of love, O misery!
  She brooded o'er the luxury alone:
His image in the dusk she seem'd to see,
  And to the silence made a gentle moan,
Spreading her perfect arms upon the air,
And on her couch low murmuring,
    'Where?   O where?'

XXXI

But Selfishness, Love's cousin, held not long
  Its fiery vigil in her single breast;
She fretted for the golden hour, and hung
  Upon the time with feverish unrest —
Not long — for soon into her heart a throng
  Of higher occupants, a richer zest,
Came tragic; passion not to be subdued,
And sorrow for her love in travels rude.

XXXII

In the mid days of autumn, on their eves
  The breath of Winter comes from far
    away,
And the sick west continually bereaves
  Of some gold tinge, and plays a rounde-
    lay
Of death among the bushes and the leaves,
  To make all bare before he dares to stray
From his north cavern.   So sweet Isabel
By gradual decay from beauty fell,

XXXIII

Because Lorenzo came not. Oftentimes
　She ask'd her brothers, with an eye all
　　pale,
Striving to be itself, what dungeon climes
　Could keep him off so long ?　They spake
　　a tale
Time after time, to quiet her.　　Their
　　crimes
　Came on them, like a smoke from Hin-
　　nom's vale;
And every night in dreams they groan'd
　aloud,
To see their sister in her snowy shroud.

XXXIV

And she had died in drowsy ignorance,
　But for a thing more deadly dark than
　　all;
It came like a fierce potion, drunk by
　chance,
　Which saves a sick man from the feath-
　　er'd pall
For some few gasping moments; like a
　lance,
　Waking an Indian from his cloudy hall
With cruel pierce, and bringing him again
Sense of the gnawing fire at heart and
　brain.

XXXV

It was a vision. — In the drowsy gloom,
　The dull of midnight, at her couch's foot
Lorenzo stood, and wept: the forest tomb
　Had marr'd his glossy hair which once
　　could shoot
Lustre into the sun, and put cold doom
　Upon his lips, and taken the soft lute
From his lorn voice, and past his loamed
　ears
Had made a miry channel for his tears.

XXXVI

Strange sound it was, when the pale shadow
　spake;
　For there was striving, in its piteous
　　tongue,

To speak as when on earth it was awake,
　And Isabella on its music hung:
Languor there was in it, and tremulous
　shake,
　As in a palsied Druid's harp unstrung;
And through it moan'd a ghostly under-
　song,
Like hoarse night-gusts sepulchral briars
　among.

XXXVII

Its eyes, though wild, were still all dewy
　bright
　With love, and kept all phantom fear
　　aloof
From the poor girl by magic of their light,
　The while it did unthread the horrid
　　woof
Of the late darken'd time, — the murder-
　ous spite
　Of pride and avarice, — the dark pine
　　roof
In the forest, — and the sodden turfed
　dell,
Where, without any word, from stabs he
　fell.

XXXVIII

Saying moreover, ' Isabel, my sweet !
　Red whortleberries droop above my
　　head,
And a large flint-stone weighs upon my
　feet;
　Around me beeches and high chestnuts
　　shed
Their leaves and prickly nuts; a sheepfold
　bleat
　Comes from beyond the river to my bed:
Go, shed one tear upon my heather-bloom,
And it shall comfort me within the tomb.

XXXIX

' I am a shadow now, alas ! alas !
　Upon the skirts of human nature dwell-
　　ing
Alone: I chant alone the holy mass,
　While little sounds of life are round me
　　knelling,

And glossy bees at noon do fieldward pass,
    And many a chapel bell the hour is tell-
        ing,
Paining me through: those sounds grow
    strange to me,
And thou art distant in Humanity.

XL

'I know what was, I feel full well what is,
    And I should rage, if spirits could go
        mad;
Though I forget the taste of earthly bliss,
    That paleness warms my grave, as
        though I had
A Seraph chosen from the bright abyss
    To be my spouse: thy paleness makes
    me glad;
Thy beauty grows upon me, and I feel
A greater love through all my essence
    steal.'

XLI

The Spirit mourn'd 'Adieu!' — dissolved,
    and left
    The atom darkness in a slow turmoil;
As when of healthful midnight sleep be-
    reft,
    Thinking on rugged hours and fruitless
    toil,
We put our eyes into a pillowy cleft,
    And see the spangly gloom froth up and
    boil:
It made sad Isabella's eyelids ache,
And in the dawn she started up awake

XLII

'Ha! ha!' said she, 'I knew not this hard
    life,
    I thought the worst was simple misery;
I thought some Fate with pleasure or with
    strife
    Portion'd us — happy days, or else to
    die;
But there is crime — a brother's bloody
    knife!
    Sweet Spirit, thou hast school'd my in-
    fancy:
I 'll visit thee for this, and kiss thine eyes,
And greet thee morn and even in the skies.'

XLIII

When the full morning came, she had de-
    vised
    How she might secret to the forest hie;
How she might find the clay, so dearly
    prized,
    And sing to it one latest lullaby;
How her short absence might be unsur-
    mised,
    While she the inmost of the dream would
    try.
Resolved, she took with her an aged nurse,
And went into that dismal forest-hearse.

XLIV

See, as they creep along the river side,
    How she doth whisper to that aged
    Dame,
And, after looking round the champaign
    wide,
    Shows her a knife. — 'What feverous
    hectic flame
Burns in thee, child? — what good can
    thee betide,
    That thou shouldst smile again?' —
    The evening came,
And they had found Lorenzo's earthy bed;
The flint was there, the berries at his head.

XLV

Who hath not loiter'd in a green church-
    yard,
    And let his spirit, like a demon-mole,
Work through the clayey soil and gravel
    hard,
    To see skull, coffin'd bones, and funeral
    stole;
Pitying each form that hungry Death hath
    marr'd,
    And filling it once more with human soul?
Ah! this is holiday to what was felt
When Isabella by Lorenzo knelt.

XLVI

She gazed into the fresh-thrown mould, as
    though
    One glance did fully all its secrets tell;

Clearly she saw, as other eyes would know
  Pale limbs at bottom of a crystal well;
Upon the murderous spot she seem'd to
    grow,
  Like to a native lily of the dell:
Then with her knife, all sudden, she began
To dig more fervently than misers can.

XLVII

Soon she turn'd up a soiled glove, whereon
  Her silk had play'd in purple phanta-
    sies:
She kiss'd it with a lip more chill than
    stone,
  And put it in her bosom, where it dries
And freezes utterly unto the bone
  Those dainties made to still an infant's
    cries;
Then 'gan she work again; nor stay'd her
    care,
But to throw back at times her veiling hair.

XLVIII

That old nurse stood beside her wonder-
    ing,
  Until her heart felt pity to the core
At sight of such a dismal labouring,
  And so she kneeled, with her locks all
    hoar,
And put her lean hands to the horrid
    thing:
  Three hours they labour'd at this travail
    sore:
At last they felt the kernel of the grave,
And Isabella did not stamp and rave.

XLIX

Ah! wherefore all this wormy circum-
    stance?
  Why linger at the yawning tomb so
    long?
O for the gentleness of old Romance,
  The simple plaining of a minstrel's song!
Fair reader, at the old tale take a glance,
  For here, in truth, it doth not well be-
    long
To speak: — O turn thee to the very tale,
And taste the music of that vision pale.

L

With duller steel than the Perséan sword
  They cut away no formless monster's
    head,
But one, whose gentleness did well accord
  With death, as life. The ancient harps
    have said,
Love never dies, but lives, immortal Lord:
  If Love impersonate was ever dead,
Pale Isabella kiss'd it, and low moan'd.
'T was love; cold, — dead indeed, but not
    dethron'd.

LI

In anxious secrecy they took it home,
  And then the prize was all for Isabel:
She calm'd its wild hair with a golden
    comb,
  And all around each eye's sepulchral cell
Pointed each fringed lash; the smeared
    loam
  With tears, as chilly as a dripping well,
She drench'd away: and still she comb'd,
    and kept
Sighing all day — and still she kiss'd and
    wept.

LII

Then in a silken scarf, — sweet with the
    dews
  Of precious flowers pluck'd in Araby,
And divine liquids come with odorous ooze
  Through the cold serpent-pipe refresh-
    fully, —
She wrapp'd it up; and for its tomb did
    choose
  A garden-pot, wherein she laid it by,
And cover'd it with mould, and o'er it set
Sweet Basil, which her tears kept ever wet.

LIII

And she forgot the stars, the moon, and
    sun,
  And she forgot the blue above the trees,
And she forgot the dells where waters
    run,
  And she forgot the chilly autumn breeze;

She had no knowledge when the day was
    done,
    And the new morn she saw not: but in
    peace
Hung over her sweet Basil evermore,
And moisten'd it with tears unto the core.

LIV

And so she ever fed it with thin tears,
    Whence thick, and green, and beautiful
    it grew,
So that it smelt more balmy than its peers
Of Basil-tufts in Florence; for it drew
Nurture besides, and life, from human
    fears,
    From the fast mouldering head there
    shut from view:
So that the jewel, safely casketed,
Came forth, and in perfumed leafits spread.

LV

O Melancholy, linger here awhile!
 O Music, Music, breathe despondingly!
O Echo, Echo, from some sombre isle,
    Unknown, Lethean, sigh to us — O sigh!
Spirits in grief, lift up your heads, and
    smile;
    Lift up your heads, sweet Spirits, heavily,
And make a pale light in your cypress
    glooms,
Tinting with silver wan your marble tombs.

LVI

Moan hither, all ye syllables of woe,
    From the deep throat of sad Melpomene!
Through bronzed lyre in tragic order go,
    And touch the strings into a mystery;
Sound mournfully upon the winds and low;
    For simple Isabel is soon to be
Among the dead: She withers, like a palm
Cut by an Indian for its juicy balm.

LVII

O leave the palm to wither by itself;
    Let not quick Winter chill its dying
    hour! —
It may not be — those Baälites of pelf,
    Her brethren, noted the continual shower

From her dead eyes; and many a curious
    elf,
    Among her kindred, wonder'd that such
    dower
Of youth and beauty should be thrown aside
By one mark'd out to be a Noble's bride.

LVIII

And, furthermore, her brethren wonder'd
    much
    Why she sat drooping by the Basil green,
And why it flourish'd, as by magic touch;
    Greatly they wonder'd what the thing
    might mean:
They could not surely give belief, that such
    A very nothing would have power to
    wean
Her from her own fair youth, and pleasures
    gay,
And even remembrance of her love's delay.

LIX

Therefore they watch'd a time when they
    might sift
    This hidden whim; and long they watch'd
    in vain;
For seldom did she go to chapel-shrift,
    And seldom felt she any hunger-pain:
And when she left, she hurried back, as
    swift
As bird on wing to breast its eggs again:
And, patient as a hen-bird, sat her there
Beside her Basil, weeping through her hair.

LX

Yet they contrived to steal the Basil-pot,
    And to examine it in secret place:
The thing was vile with green and livid
    spot,
And yet they knew it was Lorenzo's face:
The guerdon of their murder they had got,
    And so left Florence in a moment's space,
Never to turn again. — Away they went,
With blood upon their heads, to banishment.

LXI

O Melancholy, turn thine eyes away!
    O Music, Music, breathe despondingly!

O Echo, Echo, on some other day,
From isles Lethean, sigh to us — O
    sigh !
Spirits of grief, sing not your ' Well-a-
    way ! '
For Isabel, sweet Isabel, will die;
Will die a death too lone and incomplete,
Now they have ta'en away her Basil sweet.

LXII

Piteous she look'd on dead and senseless
    things,
    Asking for her lost Basil amorously:
And with melodious chuckle in the strings
    Of her lorn voice, she oftentimes would
    cry
After the Pilgrim in his wanderings,
    To ask him where her Basil was; and why
'Twas hid from her: 'For cruel 't is,' said
    she,
'To steal my Basil-pot away from me.'

LXIII

And so she pined, and so she died forlorn,
    Imploring for her Basil to the last.
No heart was there in Florence but did
    mourn
    In pity of her love, so overcast.
And a sad ditty of this story born
    From mouth to mouth through all the
    country pass'd :
Still is the burthen sung — 'O cruelty,
To steal my Basil-pot away from me !'

TO HOMER

The date 1818 was affixed to this by Lord
Houghton in *Life, Letters and Literary Re-
mains*, where it was first published, and is found
she where it occurs in the Dilke manuscripts.
In a letter to Reynolds, dated April 27, 1818,
Keats writes eagerly of his desire to study
Greek.

Standing aloof in giant ignorance,
    Of thee I hear and of the Cyclades,
    As one who sits ashore and longs perchance
To visit dolphin-coral in deep seas.

So thou wast blind ! — but then the veil
    was rent,
    For Jove uncurtain'd Heaven to let thee
    live,
And Neptune made for thee a spumy tent,
    And Pan made sing for thee his forest-
    hive;
Ay on the shores of darkness there is
    light,
    And precipices show untrodden green;
There is a budding morrow in midnight;
    There is a triple sight in blindness
    keen:
Such seeing hadst thou, as it once befell
To Dian, Queen of Earth, and Heaven,
    and Hell.

FRAGMENT OF AN ODE TO MAIA

Copied in a letter to Reynolds, dated May 3,
1818, in which Keats says: 'With respect to
the affections and Poetry you must know by a
sympathy my thoughts that way, and I dare
say these few lines will be but a ratification: I
wrote them on May day — and intend to finish
the ode all in good time; ' a purpose apparently never accomplished.

MOTHER of Hermes! and still youthful
    Maia !
    May I sing to thee
As thou wast hymned on the shores of
    Baiae ?
    Or may I woo thee
In earlier Sicilian ? or thy smiles
Seek as they once were sought, in Grecian
    isles,
By bards who died content on pleasant
    sward,
    Leaving great verse unto a little clan ?
O, give me their old vigour, and unheard
    Save of the quiet Primrose, and the span
    Of heaven and few ears,
Rounded by thee, my song should die away
    Content as theirs,
Rich in the simple worship of a day.

SONG

First published in *Life, Letters and Literary Remains*, and there dated 1818.

I

Hush, hush! tread softly! hush, hush, my
   dear!
All the house is asleep, but we know very
   well
That the jealous, the jealous old bald-pate
   may hear,
  Tho' you 've padded his night-cap — O
    sweet Isabel!
  Tho' your feet are more light than a
    Faery's feet,
  Who dances on bubbles where brook-
    lets meet, —
Hush, hush! soft tiptoe! hush, hush, my
   dear!
For less than a nothing the jealous can
   hear.

II

No leaf doth tremble, no ripple is there
  On the river, — all 's still, and the night's
   sleepy eye
Closes up, and forgets all its Lethean
   care,
  Charm'd to death by the drone of the
    humming May-fly;
  And the Moon, whether prudish or
    complaisant,
  Has fled to her bower, well knowing I
    want
No light in the dusk, no torch in the gloom,
But my Isabel's eyes, and her lips pulp'd
   with bloom.

III

Lift the latch! ah gently! ah tenderly —
   sweet!
We are dead if that latchet gives one
   little clink!
Well done — now those lips, and a flowery
   seat —
  The old man may sleep, and the planets
   may wink;

The shut rose shall dream of our loves
   and awake
Full-blown, and such warmth for the
   morning take,
The stock-dove shall hatch her soft brace
   and shall coo,
While I kiss to the melody, aching all
   through.

VERSES WRITTEN DURING A TOUR IN SCOTLAND

Keats saw his brother George and wife set sail from Liverpool at the end of June, 1818, and then set forth with his friend Charles Armitage Brown on a walking tour through Wordsworth's country and into Scotland. The verses included in this section were all sent in letters, chiefly to his brother Tom. He did not include any in the volume which he published in 1820, and they first saw the light when Lord Houghton included them in the *Life, Letters and Literary Remains*. The more off-hand and familiar verses written at this time are given in the Appendix.

I

ON VISITING THE TOMB OF BURNS

Written at Dumfries on the evening of July 1, 1818. 'Burns's tomb,' writes Keats, ' is in the Churchyard corner, not very much to my taste, though on a scale large enough to show they wanted to honour him. This Sonnet I have written in a strange mood, half asleep. I know not how it is, the Clouds, the Sky, the Houses, all seem anti-Grecian and anti-Charlemagnish.'

THE Town, the churchyard, and the setting
   sun,
  The Clouds, the trees, the rounded hills
   all seem,
  Though beautiful, cold — strange — as
   in a dream,
I dreamed long ago, now new begun.
The short-lived, paly Summer is but won
  From Winter's ague, for one hour's
   gleam;
  Though sapphire-warm, their Stars do
   never beam:

All is cold Beauty; pain is never done:
For who has mind to relish, Minos-wise,
　The Real of Beauty, free from that dead
　　hue
Sickly imagination and sick pride
Cast wan upon it ! Burns ! with honour
　due
　I oft have honour'd thee. Great
　shadow, hide
Thy face; I sin against thy native skies.

II

TO AILSA ROCK

The tourists crossed to Ireland for a short
trip, and after returning to Scotland, made
their way into Ayrshire, entering it a little
beyond Cairn. Their walk led them into
a long wooded glen. ' At the end,' writes
Keats, July 10, 1818, ' we had a gradual ascent
and got among the tops of the mountains
whence in a little time I descried in the Sea
Ailsa Rock, 940 feet high — it was 15 Miles
distant and seemed close upon us. The effect
of Ailsa with the peculiar perspective of the
Sea in connection with the ground we stood on,
and the misty rain then falling gave me a complete Idea of a deluge. Ailsa struck me very
suddenly — really I was a little alarmed.'

HEARKEN, thou craggy ocean pyramid !
　Give answer from thy voice, the sea-
　　fowls' screams !
　When were thy shoulders mantled in
　　huge streams ?
When, from the sun, was thy broad fore-
　head hid ?
How long is 't since the mighty power bid
　Thee heave to airy sleep from fathom
　　dreams ?
　Sleep in the lap of thunder or sunbeams,
Or when gray clouds are thy cold coverlid.
Thou answer'st not; for thou art dead
　asleep;
　Thy life is but two dead eternities —
The last in air, the former in the deep;
　First with the whales, last with the eagle-
　　skies —

Drown'd wast thou till an earthquake made
　thee steep,
Another cannot wake thy giant size.

III

WRITTEN IN THE COTTAGE WHERE BURNS WAS BORN

From Kingswell's, July 13, 1818, Keats
wrote of his experience in visiting Burns's
birthplace : ' The approach to it [Ayr] is extremely fine — quite outwent my expectations
— richly meadowed, wooded, heathed and rivuleted — with a grand Sea view terminated
by the black Mountains of the isle of Annan.
As soon as I saw them so nearby I said to myself, " How is it they did not beckon Burns
to some grand attempt at Epic ? " The bonny
Doon is the sweetest river I ever saw — overhung with fine trees as far as we could see
— We stood some time on the Brig across it,
over which Tam o' Shanter fled — we took a
pinch of snuff on the Keystone — then we
proceeded to the " auld Kirk Alloway." As
we were looking at it a Farmer pointed the
spots where Mungo's Mither hang'd hersel'
and " drunken Charlie brake 's neck's bane."
Then we proceeded to the Cottage he was born
in — there was a board to that effect by the
door side — it had the same effect as the same
sort of memorial at Stratford on Avon. We
drank some Toddy to Burns's memory with an
old Man who knew Burns — damn him and
damn his anecdotes — he was a great bore —
it was impossible for a Southron to understand
above 5 words in a hundred. — There was
something good in his description of Burns's
melancholy the last time he saw him. I was
determined to write a sonnet in the Cottage —
I did — but it was so bad I cannot venture it
here.' He wrote in the same strain to Reynolds, saying, ' I wrote a sonnet for the mere
sake of writing some lines under the Roof —
they are so bad I cannot transcribe them. . . .
I cannot write about scenery and visitings —
Fancy is indeed less than a present palpable
reality, but it is greater than remembrance.
. . . One song of Burns's is of more worth to
you than all I could think for a whole year in
his native country.'

THIS mortal body of a thousand days
  Now fills, O Burns, a space in thine own
      room,
Where thou didst dream alone on budded
      bays,
  Happy and thoughtless of thy day of
      doom !
My pulse is warm with thine old Barley-
      bree,
  My head is light with pledging a great
      soul,
My eyes are wandering, and I cannot see,
  Fancy is dead and drunken at its goal;
Yet can I stamp my foot upon thy floor,
  Yet can I ope thy window-sash to find
The meadow thou hast tramped o'er and
      o'er, —
  Yet can I think of thee till thought is
      blind, —
Yet can I gulp a bumper to thy name, —
O smile among the shades, for this is fame !

IV

AT FINGAL'S CAVE

The verses which follow were first printed
in *Life, Letters and Literary Remains*. They
occur in a letter to Tom Keats from Oban,
July 26, 1818, and were preceded by this description : ' I am puzzled how to give you an
Idea of Staffa. It can only be represented by
a first-rate drawing. One may compare the
surface of the Island to a roof — this roof is
supported by grand pillars of basalt standing
together as thick as honeycombs. The finest
thing is Fingal's cave — it is entirely a hollowing out of Basalt Pillars. Suppose now the
Giants who rebelled against Jove had taken a
whole Mass of black Columns and bound them
together like bunches of matches — and then
with immense axes had made a cavern in the
body of these columns — Of course the roof
and floor must be composed of the broken ends
of the Columns — such is Fingal's cave, except
that the Sea has done the work of excavations,
and is continually dashing there — so that we
walk along the sides of the cave on the pillars
which are left as if for convenient stairs. The
roof is arched somewhat gothic-wise, and the
length of some of the entire side-pillars is fifty
feet. About the island you might seat an
army of men each on a pillar. The length of
the Cave is 120 feet, and from its extremity
the view into the sea, through the large arch
at the entrance — the colour of the column is
a sort of black with a lurking gloom of purple
therein. For solemnity and grandeur it far
surpasses the finest Cathedral. At the extremity of the Cave there is a small perforation into another Cave, at which the waters
meeting and buffeting each other there is sometimes produced a report as of a cannon heard as
far as Iona, which must be 12 miles. As we
approached in the boat, there was such a fine
swell of the sea that the pillars appeared rising
immediately out of the crystal. But it is impossible to describe it.'

Not Aladdin magian
Ever such a work began;
Not the wizard of the Dee
Ever such a dream could see;
Not St. John, in Patmos' isle,
In the passion of his toil,
When he saw the churches seven,
Golden aisled, built up in heaven,
Gazed at such a rugged wonder,
As I stood its roofing under.
Lo ! I saw one sleeping there,
On the marble cold and bare;
While the surges wash'd his feet,
And his garments white did beat
Drench'd about the sombre rocks;
On his neck his well-grown locks,
Lifted dry above the main,
Were upon the curl again.
' What is this ? and what art thou ? '
Whisper'd I, and touch'd his brow;
' What art thou ? and what is this ? '
Whisper'd I, and strove to kiss
The spirit's hand, to wake his eyes;
Up he started in a trice:
' I am Lycidas,' said he,
' Famed in funeral minstrelsy !
This was architectured thus
By the great Oceanus ! —
Here his mighty waters play

Hollow organs all the day;
Here, by turns, his dolphins all,
. Finny palmers, great and small,
Come to pay devotion due, —
Each a mouth of pearls must strew !
Many a mortal of these days
Dares to pass our sacred ways;
Dares to touch, audaciously,
This cathedral of the sea !
I have been the pontiff-priest,
Where the waters never rest,
Where a fledgy sea-bird choir
Soars for ever !   Holy fire
I have hid from mortal man;
Proteus is my Sacristan !
But the dulled eye of mortal
Hath pass'd beyond the rocky portal;
So for ever will I leave
Such a taint, and soon unweave
All the magic of the place.'
So saying, with a Spirit's glance
He dived !

V

WRITTEN UPON THE TOP OF BEN NEVIS

Enclosed in a letter to Tom Keats from
Letter Findlay, August 3, 1818.

READ me a lesson, Muse, and speak it loud
Upon the top of Nevis, blind in mist !
I look into the chasms, and a shroud
    Vaporous doth hide them, — just so
        much I wist
Mankind do know of hell; I look o'erhead,
    And there is sullen mist, — even so much
Mankind can tell of heaven; mist is spread
    Before the earth, beneath me, — even
        such,
Even so vague is man's sight of himself !
    Here are the craggy stones beneath my
        feet, —
Thus much I know that, a poor witless elf,
    I tread on them, — that all my eye doth
        meet
Is mist and crag, not only on this height,
But in the world of thought and mental
        might !

TRANSLATION FROM A SONNET OF RONSARD

Published in *Life, Letters and Literary Re-mains* in a letter to Reynolds, of which the probable date is September 22, 1818; in a letter to Charles Wentworth Dilke September 21, 1818, Keats quotes the last line with the remark : 'You have passed your Romance, and I never gave in to it, or else I think this line a feast for one of your Lovers.'   The text of the sonnet will be found in the Appendix.

NATURE withheld Cassandra in the skies,
    For more adornment, a full thousand
        years;
She took their cream of Beauty's fairest
        dyes,
    And shaped and tinted her above all
        Peers:
Meanwhile Love kept her dearly with his
        wings,
    And underneath their shadow fill'd her
        eyes
With such a richness that the cloudy Kings
Of high Olympus utter'd slavish sighs.
When from the Heavens I saw her first
        descend,
    My heart took fire, and only burning
        pains,
They were my pleasures — they my Life's
        sad end;
    Love pour'd her beauty into my warm
        veins.

.   .   .   .

TO A LADY SEEN FOR A FEW MOMENTS AT VAUXHALL

First published in *Hood's Magazine* for April 1844, and afterward included in *Life, Letters and Literary Remains*.   No date is given, and the poem is placed here from a fancied asso-ciation with the lady whom Keats saw at Hast-ings and who started the train of thought in his letter to his brother and sister, October 25, 1818.

TIME's sea hath been five years at its slow
  ebb,
  Long hours have to and fro let creep the
    sand,
Since I was tangled in thy beauty's web,
  And snared by the ungloving of thine
    hand.
And yet I never look on midnight sky,
  But I behold thine eyes' well-memoried
    light;
I cannot look upon the rose's dye,
  But to thy cheek my soul doth take its
    flight ;
I cannot look on any budding flower,
  But my fond ear, in fancy at thy lips
And hearkening for a love-sound, doth de-
    vour
  Its sweets in the wrong sense: — Thou
    dost eclipse
Every delight with sweet remembering,
And grief unto my darling joys dost bring.

FANCY

Keats enclosed these lines, as lately written,
in a letter to George and Georgiana Keats,
January 2, 1819. He included the poem in the
1820 volume. Mr. John Knowles Paine has
published a cantata for soprano solo, chorus,
and orchestra, entitled *The Realm of Fancy*,
using these lines for his book.

EVER let the Fancy roam,
Pleasure never is at home:
At a touch sweet Pleasure melteth,
Like to bubbles when rain pelteth;
Then let winged Fancy wander
Through the thought still spread beyond
    her:
Open wide the mind's cage-door,
She 'll dart forth, and cloudward soar.
O sweet Fancy ! let her loose;
Summer's joys are spoilt by use,   10
And the enjoying of the Spring
Fades as does its blossoming;
Autumn's red-lipp'd fruitage too,
Blushing through the mist and dew,
Cloys with tasting : What do then ?

Sit thee by the ingle, when
The sear faggot blazes bright,
Spirit of a winter's night;
When the soundless earth is muffled,
And the caked snow is shuffled   20
From the ploughboy's heavy shoon;
When the Night doth meet the Noon
In a dark conspiracy
To banish Even from her sky.
Sit thee there, and send abroad,
With a mind self-overawed,
Fancy, high-commission'd: — send her !
She has vassals to attend her:
She will bring, in spite of frost,
Beauties that the earth hath lost;   30
She will bring thee, all together,
All delights of summer weather;
All the buds and bells of May,
From dewy sward or thorny spray;
All the heaped Autumn's wealth,
With a still, mysterious stealth:
She will mix these pleasures up
Like three fit wines in a cup,
And thou shalt quaff it: — thou shalt hear
Distant harvest-carols clear;   40
Rustle of the reaped corn;
Sweet birds antheming the morn:
And, in the same moment — hark !
'T is the early April lark,
Or the rooks, with busy caw,
Foraging for sticks and straw.
Thou shalt, at one glance, behold
The daisy and the marigold;
White-plumed lilies, and the first
Hedge-grown primrose that hath burst ;   50
Shaded hyacinth, alway
Sapphire queen of the mid-May;
And every leaf, and every flower
Pearled with the self-same shower.
Thou shalt see the field-mouse peep
Meagre from its celled sleep;
And the snake all winter-thin
Cast on sunny bank its skin;
Freckled nest-eggs thou shalt see
Hatching in the hawthorn-tree,   60
When the hen-bird's wing doth rest
Quiet on her mossy nest;

Then the hurry and alarm
When the bee-hive casts its swarm;
Acorns ripe down-pattering
While the autumn breezes sing.

Oh, sweet Fancy ! let her loose;
Every thing is spoilt by use;
Where 's the cheek that doth not fade,
Too much gazed at ?   Where 's the maid 70
Whose lip mature is ever new ?
Where 's the eye, however blue,
Doth not weary ?   Where 's the face
One would meet in every place ?
Where 's the voice, however soft,
One would hear so very oft ?
At a touch sweet Pleasure melteth
Like to bubbles when rain pelteth.
Let, then, winged Fancy find
Thee a mistress to thy mind: 80
Dulcet-eyed as Ceres' daughter
Ere the God of Torment taught her
How to frown and how to chide;
With a waist and with a side
White as Hebe's, when her zone
Slipt its golden clasp, and down
Fell her kirtle to her feet,
While she held the goblet sweet,
And Jove grew languid. — Break the mesh
Of the Fancy's silken leash;   90
Quickly break her prison-string,
And such joys as these she 'll bring. —
Let the winged Fancy roam,
Pleasure never is at home.

ODE

Written on the blank page before Beaumont
and Fletcher's tragi-comedy, The Fair Maid of
the Inn, and addressed thus to these bards in
particular. Sent in a letter to George and Georgiana Keats, January 2, 1819.   It is included
in the 1820 volume.

Bards of Passion and of Mirth,
Ye have left your souls on earth !
Have ye souls in heaven too,
Double-lived in regions new ?
Yes, and those of heaven commune

With the spheres of sun and moon;
With the noise of fountains wond'rous
And the parle of voices thund'rous
With the whisper of heaven's trees
And one another, in soft ease   10
Seated on Elysian lawns
Browsed by none but Dian's fawns;
Underneath large blue-bells tented,
Where the daisies are rose-scented,
And the rose herself has got
Perfume which on earth is not;
Where the nightingale doth sing
Not a senseless, tranced thing,
But divine melodious truth;
Philosophic numbers smooth;   20
Tales and golden histories
Of heaven and its mysteries.

Thus ye live on high, and then
On the earth ye live again;
And the souls ye left behind you
Teach us, here, the way to find you,
Where your other souls are joying,
Never slumber'd, never cloying.
Here, your earth-born souls still speak
To mortals, of their little week;   30
Of their sorrows and delights;
Of their passions and their spites;
Of their glory and their shame;
What doth strengthen and what maim.
Thus ye teach us, every day,
Wisdom, though fled far away.

Bards of Passion and of Mirth,
Ye have left your souls on earth !
Ye have souls in heaven too,
Double-lived in regions new !   40

SONG

' There is just room, I see, in this page to
copy a little thing I wrote off to some Music
as it was playing.'   Keats to George and
Georgiana Keats, January 2, 1819.

I had a dove and the sweet dove died;
   And I have thought it died of grieving:

O, what could it grieve for ? Its feet
    were tied,
  With a silken thread of my own hand's
    weaving;
Sweet little red feet ! why should you
    die —
Why should you leave me, sweet bird !
    why ?
You lived alone in the forest-tree,
Why, pretty thing ! would you not live
    with me ?
I kiss'd you oft and gave you white peas;
Why not live sweetly, as in the green
    trees ?

ODE ON MELANCHOLY

Published in *Lamia, Isabella, the Eve of St.
Agnes and other Poems*, 1820. There is no
date affixed to it, but if it takes its color at
all from Keats's own experience, it might not
be amiss to refer it to the early part of 1819,
when he had come under the influence of his
passion for Fanny Brawne. In a letter to
Haydon, written between January 7 and 14,
1819, Keats says : ' I have been writing a little
now and then lately : but nothing to speak of
— being discontented and as it were moulting.
Yet I do not think I shall ever come to the
rope or the pistol. For after a day or two's
melancholy, although I smoke more and more
my own insufficiency — I see by little and little more of what is to be done, and how it is
to be done, should I ever be able to do it.'
Lord Houghton, in the Aldine edition of
1876, makes the following prefatory note :
' A singular instance of Keats's delicate perception occurred in the composition of this
Ode. In the original manuscript he had intended to represent the vulgar conception of
Melancholy with gloom and horror, in contrast
with the emotion that incites to —

    " glut thy sorrow on a morning rose
Or on the rainbow of the salt sand-wave,
Or on the wealth of globed peonies ; "

and which essentially

    " lives in Beauty — Beauty that must die,
And Joy, whose hand is ever at his lips
Bidding adieu."

The first stanza, therefore, was the following :
as grim a passage as Blake or Fuseli could
have dreamed and painted : —

" Though you should build a bark of dead men's bones,
    And rear a platform gibbet for a mast,
Stitch shrouds together for a sail, with groans
    To fill it out, blood-stained and aghast ;
Although your rudder be a dragon's tail
    Long sever'd, yet still hard with agony,
      Your cordage large uprootings from the skull
Of bald Medusa, certes you would fail
    To find the Melancholy — whether she
      Dreameth in any isle of Lethe dull."

But no sooner was this written, than the poet
became conscious that the coarseness of the
contrast would destroy the general effect of
luxurious tenderness which it was the object
of the poem to produce, and he confined the
gross notion of Melancholy to less violent images, and let the ode at once begin, — '

I

No, no ! go not to Lethe, neither twist
  Wolf's-bane, tight-rooted, for its poison-
    ous wine;
Nor suffer thy pale forehead to be kiss'd
  By nightshade, ruby grape of Proserpine;
Make not your rosary of yew-berries,
  Nor let the beetle, or the death-moth be
    Your mournful Psyche, nor the downy
    owl
A partner in your sorrow's mysteries;
  For shade to shade will come too drows-
    ily,
    And drown the wakeful anguish of the
    soul.

II

But when the melancholy fit shall fall
  Sudden from heaven like a weeping
    cloud,
That fosters the droop-headed flowers all,
  And hides the green hills in an April
    shroud;
Then glut thy sorrow on a morning rose,
  Or on the rainbow of the salt-sand wave,
    Or on the wealth of globed peonies;
Or if thy mistress some rich anger shows,
  Emprison her soft hand, and let her rave,
    And feed deep, deep upon her peerless
    eyes.

III

She dwells with Beauty — Beauty that
    must die ;
And Joy, whose hand is ever at his lips
Bidding adieu ; and aching Pleasure nigh,
    Turning to poison while the bee-mouth
    sips :
Aye, in the very temple of Delight
    Veil'd Melancholy has her sovran shrine,
      Though seen of none save him whose
      strenuous tongue
    Can burst Joy's grape against his palate
    fine ;
His soul shall taste the sadness of her
    might,
    And be among her cloudy trophies
    hung.

THE EVE OF ST. AGNES

Begun early in 1819. In a letter to George
and Georgiana Keats, dated February 14, 1819,
Keats says : 'I was nearly a fortnight at Mr.
John Snook's and a few days at old Mr. Dilke's
(Chichester in Hampshire). Nothing worth
speaking of happened at either place. I took
down some thin paper and wrote on it a little
poem called St. Agnes's Eve.' The poem
underwent a great deal of revision, and was not
in final form before September ; it was published in the 1820 volume.

I

St. Agnes' Eve — Ah, bitter chill it
    was !
The owl, for all his feathers, was a-cold ;
The hare limp'd trembling through the
    frozen grass,
And silent was the flock in woolly fold :
Numb were the Beadsman's fingers, while
    he told
His rosary, and while his frosted breath,
Like pious incense from a censer old,
Seem'd taking flight for heaven, without
    a death,
Past the sweet Virgin's picture, while his
    prayer he saith.

II

His prayer he saith, this patient, holy
    man ;
Then takes his lamp, and riseth from his
    knees,
And back returneth, meagre, barefoot,
    wan,
Along the chapel aisle by slow degrees :
The sculptured dead, on each side, seem
    to freeze,
Emprison'd in black, purgatorial rails :
Knights, ladies, praying in dumb orat'ries,
He passeth by ; and his weak spirit fails
To think how they may ache in icy hoods
    and mails.

III

Northward he turneth through a little
    door,
And scarce three steps, ere Music's
    golden tongue
Flatter'd to tears this aged man and
    poor ;
But no — already had his death-bell rung ;
The joys of all his life were said and
    sung :
His was harsh penance on St. Agnes'
    Eve :
Another way he went, and soon among
Rough ashes sat he for his soul's re-
    prieve,
And all night kept awake, for sinners' sake
    to grieve.

IV

That ancient Beadsman heard the pre-
    lude soft ;
And so it chanced, for many a door was
    wide,
From hurry to and fro. Soon, up aloft,
The silver, snarling trumpets 'gan to
    chide :
The level chambers, ready with their
    pride,
Were glowing to receive a thousand
    guests :
The carved angels, ever eager-eyed,

Stared, where upon their heads the cornice rests,
With hair blown back, and wings put crosswise on their breasts.

V

At length burst in the argent revelry,
With plume, tiara, and all rich array,
Numerous as shadows haunting fairily
The brain, new-stuff'd, in youth, with triumphs gay
Of old romance. These let us wish away,
And turn, sole-thoughted, to one Lady there,
Whose heart had brooded, all that wintry day,
On love, and wing'd St. Agnes' saintly care,
As she had heard old dames full many times declare.

VI

They told her how, upon St. Agnes' Eve,
Young virgins might have visions of delight,
And soft adorings from their loves receive
Upon the honey'd middle of the night,
If ceremonies due they did aright;
As, supperless to bed they must retire,
And couch supine their beauties, lily white;
Nor look behind, nor sideways, but require
Of Heaven with upward eyes for all that they desire.

VII

Full of this whim was thoughtful Madeline:
The music, yearning like a God in pain,
She scarcely heard: her maiden eyes divine,
Fix'd on the floor, saw many a sweeping train
Pass by — she heeded not at all: in vain
Came many a tiptoe, amorous cavalier,
And back retired; not cool'd by high disdain,
But she saw not: her heart was otherwhere;
She sigh'd for Agnes' dreams, the sweetest of the year.

VIII

She danced along with vague, regardless eyes,
Anxious her lips, her breathing quick and short:
The hallow'd hour was near at hand: she sighs
Amid the timbrels, and the throng'd resort
Of whisperers in anger, or in sport;
'Mid looks of love, defiance, hate, and scorn,
Hoodwink'd with faery fancy; all amort,
Save to St. Agnes and her lambs unshorn,
And all the bliss to be before to-morrow morn.

IX

So, purposing each moment to retire,
She linger'd still. Meantime, across the moors,
Had come young Porphyro, with heart on fire
For Madeline. Beside the portal doors,
Buttress'd from moonlight, stands he, and implores
All saints to give him sight of Madeline,
But for one moment in the tedious hours,
That he might gaze and worship all unseen;
Perchance speak, kneel, touch, kiss — in sooth such things have been.

X

He ventures in: let no buzz'd whisper tell:
All eyes be muffled, or a hundred swords
Will storm his heart, Love's fev'rous citadel:
For him, those chambers held barbarian hordes,

Hyena foemen, and hot-blooded lords,
Whose very dogs would execrations howl
Against his lineage: not one breast af-
fords
Him any mercy, in that mansion foul,
Save one old beldame, weak in body and in
soul.

XI

Ah, happy chance! the aged creature
came,
Shuffling along with ivory-headed wand,
To where he stood, hid from the torch's
flame,
Behind a broad hall-pillar, far beyond
The sound of merriment and chorus
bland:
He startled her; but soon she knew his
face,
And grasp'd his fingers in her palsied
hand,
Saying, 'Mercy, Porphyro! hie thee
from this place;
They are all here to-night, the whole
bloodthirsty race!

XII

Get hence! get hence! there's dwarf-
ish Hildebrand;
He had a fever late, and in the fit
He cursed thee and thine, both house and
land:
Then there's that old Lord Maurice, not
a whit
More tame for his gray hairs — Alas me!
flit!
Flit like a ghost away.' — 'Ah, Gossip
dear,
We're safe enough; here in this arm-
chair sit,
And tell me how' — 'Good Saints! not
here, not here;
Follow me, child, or else these stones will
be thy bier.'

XIII

He follow'd through a lowly arched way,
Brushing the cobwebs with his lofty
plume;

And as she mutter'd 'Well-a — well-a-
day!'
He found him in a little moonlight room,
Pale, latticed, chill, and silent as a tomb.
'Now tell me where is Madeline,' said
he,
'O tell me, Angela, by the holy loom
Which none but secret sisterhood may
see,
When they St. Agnes' wool are weaving
piously.'

XIV

'St. Agnes! Ah! it is St. Agnes' Eve —
Yet men will murder upon holy days:
Thou must hold water in a witch's sieve,
And be liege-lord of all the Elves and
Fays,
To venture so: it fills me with amaze
To see thee, Porphyro! — St. Agnes'
Eve!
God's help! my lady fair the conjuror
plays
This very night: good angels her de-
ceive!
But let me laugh awhile, I've mickle time
to grieve.'

XV

Feebly she laugheth in the languid moon,
While Porphyro upon her face doth look,
Like puzzled urchin on an aged crone
Who keepeth closed a wond'rous riddle-
book,
As spectacled she sits in chimney nook.
But soon his eyes grew brilliant, when she
told
His lady's purpose; and he scarce could
brook
Tears, at the thought of those enchant-
ments cold,
And Madeline asleep in lap of legends old.

XVI

Sudden a thought came like a full-blown
rose,
Flushing his brow, and in his pained
heart

Made purple riot: then doth he propose
A stratagem, that makes the beldame
   start:
' A cruel man and impious thou art:
Sweet lady, let her pray, and sleep, and
   dream
Alone with her good angels, far apart
From wicked men like thee. Go, go ! I
   deem
Thou canst not surely be the same that thou
   didst seem.'

XVII

' I will not harm her, by all saints I
   swear,'
Quoth Porphyro: ' O may I ne'er find
   grace
When my weak voice shall whisper its
   last prayer,
If one of her soft ringlets I displace,
Or look with ruffian passion in her face:
Good Angela, believe me by these tears;
Or I will, even in a moment's space,
Awake, with horrid shout, my foemen's
   ears,
And beard them, though they be more
   fang'd than wolves and bears.'

XVIII

' Ah ! why wilt thou affright a feeble
   soul ?
A poor, weak, palsy-stricken, church-yard
   thing,
Whose passing-bell may ere the midnight
   toll ;
Whose prayers for thee, each morn and
   evening,
Were never miss'd.'   Thus plaining, doth
   she bring
A gentler speech from burning Porphyro;
So woful, and of such deep sorrowing,
That Angela gives promise she will do
Whatever he shall wish, betide her weal or
   woe.

XIX

Which was, to lead him, in close secrecy,
Even to Madeline's chamber, and there
   hide

Him in a closet, of such privacy
That he might see her beauty unespied,
And win perhaps that night a peerless
   bride,
While legion'd fairies paced the coverlet,
And pale enchantment held her sleepy-
   eyed.
Never on such a night have lovers met,
Since Merlin paid his Demon all the mon-
   strous debt.

XX

' It shall be as thou wishest,' said the
   Dame:
' All cates and dainties shall be stored
   there
Quickly on this feast-night: by the tam-
   bour frame
Her own lute thou wilt see: no time to
   spare,
For I am slow and feeble, and scarce
   dare
On such a catering trust my dizzy head.
Wait here, my child, with patience;
   kneel in prayer
The while: Ah ! thou must needs the
   lady wed,
Or may I never leave my grave among
   the dead.'

XXI

So saying she hobbled off with busy fear.
The lover's endless minutes slowly pass'd;
The Dame return'd, and whisper'd in
   his ear
To follow her; with aged eyes aghast
From fright of dim espial. Safe at last,
Through many a dusky gallery, they gain
The maiden's chamber, silken, hush'd
   and chaste;
Where Porphyro took covert, pleased
   amain.
His poor guide hurried back with agues in
   her brain.

XXII

Her falt'ring hand upon the balustrade,
Old Angela was feeling for the stair,

When Madeline, St. Agnes' charmed
　　maid,
Rose, like a mission'd spirit, unaware:
With silver taper's light, and pious care,
She turn'd, and down the aged gossip led
To a safe level matting.　Now prepare,
Young Porphyro, for gazing on that bed;
She comes, she comes again, like ring-dove
　　fray'd and fled.

XXIII

Out went the taper as she hurried in;
Its little smoke, in pallid moonshine,
　　died:
She closed the door, she panted, all akin
To spirits of the air, and visions wide:
No uttered syllable, or, woe betide!
But to her heart, her heart was voluble,
Paining with eloquence her balmy side;
As though a tongueless nightingale
　　should swell
Her throat in vain, and die, heart-stifled in
　　her dell.

XXIV

A casement high and triple arch'd there
　　was,
All garlanded with carven imag'ries
Of fruits, and flowers, and bunches of
　　knot-grass,
And diamonded with panes of quaint de-
　　vice,
Innumerable of stains and splendid
　　dyes,
As are the tiger-moth's deep-damask'd
　　wings;
And in the midst, 'mong thousand herald-
　　ries,
And twilight saints, and dim emblazon-
　　ings,
A shielded scutcheon blush'd with blood of
　　queens and kings.

XXV

Full on this casement shone the wintry
　　moon,
And threw warm gules on Madeline's
　　fair breast,

As down she knelt for heaven's grace
　　and boon;
Rose-bloom fell on her hands, together
　　prest,
And on her silver cross soft amethyst,
And on her hair a glory, like a saint:
She seem'd a splendid angel, newly drest,
Save wings, for heaven:—Porphyro grew
　　faint;
She knelt, so pure a thing, so free from
　　mortal taint.

XXVI

Anon his heart revives: her vespers
　　done,
Of all its wreathed pearls her hair she
　　frees;
Unclasps her warmed, jewels one by
　　one;
Loosens her fragrant bodice; by degrees
Her rich attire creeps rustling to her
　　knees:
Half-hidden, like a mermaid in sea-weed,
Pensive awhile she dreams awake, and
　　sees,
In fancy, fair St. Agnes in her bed,
But dares not look behind, or all the charm
　　is fled.

XXVII

Soon, trembling in her soft and chilly
　　nest,
In sort of wakeful swoon, perplex'd she
　　lay,
Until the poppied warmth of sleep op-
　　press'd
Her soothed limbs, and soul fatigued
　　away;
Flown, like a thought, until the morrow-
　　day;
Blissfully haven'd both from joy and
　　pain;
Clasp'd like a missal where swart Pay-
　　nims pray;
Blinded alike from sunshine and from
　　rain,
As though a rose should shut, and be a bud
　　again.

XXVIII

Stol'n to this paradise, and so entranced,
Porphyro gazed upon her empty dress,
And listen'd to her breathing, if it
    chanced
To wake into a slumberous tenderness;
Which when he heard, that minute did
    he bless,
And breathed himself: then from the
    closet crept,
Noiseless as fear in a wide wilderness,
And over the hush'd carpet, silent,
    stept,
And 'tween the curtains peep'd, where, lo !
    — how fast she slept.

XXIX

Then by the bed-side, where the faded
    moon
Made a dim, silver twilight, soft he set
A table, and, half anguish'd, threw
    thereon
A cloth of woven crimson, gold, and
    jet: —
O for some drowsy Morphean amulet !
The boisterous, midnight, festive clarion,
The kettle-drum, and far-heard clarionet,
Affray his ears, though but in dying
    tone: —
The hall-door shuts again, and all the noise
    is gone.

XXX

And still she slept an azure-lidded sleep,
In blanched linen, smooth, and laven-
    der'd,
While he from forth the closet brought
    a heap
Of candied apple, quince, and plum, and
    gourd;
With jellies soother than the creamy
    curd,
And lucent syrops, tinct with cinnamon;
Manna and dates, in argosy transferr'd
From Fez; and spiced dainties, every
    one,
From silken Samarcand to cedar'd Leba-
    non.

XXXI

These delicates he heap'd with glowing
    hand
On golden dishes and in baskets bright
Of wreathed silver: sumptuous they
    stand
In the retired quiet of the night,
Filling the chilly room with perfume
    light. —
'And now, my love, my seraph fair,
    awake !
Thou art my heaven, and I thine ere-
    mite:
Open thine eyes, for meek St. Agnes'
    sake,
Or I shall drowse beside thee, so my soul
    doth ache.'

XXXII

Thus whispering, his warm, unnerved
    arm
Sank in her pillow. Shaded was her
    dream
By the dusk curtains: — 't was a mid-
    night charm
Impossible to melt as iced stream:
The lustrous salvers in the moonlight
    gleam;
Broad golden fringe upon the carpet
    lies:
It seem'd he never, never could redeem
From such a steadfast spell his lady's
    eyes;
So mused awhile, entoil'd in woofed phan-
    tasies.

XXXIII

Awakening up, he took her hollow
    lute, —
Tumultuous, — and, in chords that ten-
    derest be,
He play'd an ancient ditty, long since
    mute,
In Provence call'd 'La belle dame sans
    mercy:'
Close to her ear touching the melody; —
Wherewith disturb'd, she utter'd a soft
    moan:

He ceased — she panted quick — and
   suddenly
Her blue affrayed eyes wide open shone:
Upon his knees he sank, pale as smooth-
   sculptured stone.

XXXIV

Her eyes were open, but she still beheld,
Now wide awake, the vision of her sleep:
There was a painful change, that nigh
   expell'd
The blisses of her dream so pure and
   deep
At which fair Madeline began to weep,
And moan forth witless words with
   many a sigh;
While still her gaze on Porphyro would
   keep;
Who knelt, with joined hands and piteous
   eye,
Fearing to move or speak, she look'd so
   dreamingly.

XXXV

'Ah, Porphyro!' said she, 'but even now
Thy voice was at sweet tremble in mine
   ear,
Made tuneable with every sweetest vow;
And those sad eyes were spiritual and
   clear:
How changed thou art! how pallid, chill,
   and drear!
Give me that voice again, my Porphyro,
Those looks immortal, those complain-
   ings dear!
Oh leave me not in this eternal woe,
For if thou diest, my Love, I know not
   where to go.'

XXXVI

Beyond a mortal man impassion'd far
At these voluptuous accents, he arose,
Ethereal, flush'd, and like a throbbing
   star
Seen mid the sapphire heaven's deep re-
   pose;
Into her dream he melted, as the rose
Blendeth its odour with the violet, —

Solution sweet: meantime the frost-wind
   blows
Like Love's alarum pattering the sharp
   sleet
Against the window-panes; St. Agnes' moon
   hath set.

XXXVII

'T is dark: quick pattereth the flaw-
   blown sleet:
'This is no dream, my bride, my Made-
   line!'
'T is dark: the iced gusts still rave and
   beat:
'No dream, alas! alas! and woe is mine!
Porphyro will leave me here to fade and
   pine. —
Cruel! what traitor could thee hither
   bring?
I curse not, for my heart is lost in thine,
Though thou forsakest a deceived
   thing; —
A dove forlorn and lost with sick unpruned
   wing.'

XXXVIII

'My Madeline! sweet dreamer! lovely
   bride!
Say, may I be for aye thy vassal blest?
Thy beauty's shield, heart-shaped and
   vermeil dyed?
Ah, silver shrine, here will I take my
   rest
After so many hours of toil and quest,
A famish'd pilgrim, — saved by miracle.
Though I have found, I will not rob thy
   nest
Saving of thy sweet self; if thou think'st
   well
To trust, fair Madeline, to no rude infidel.

XXXIX

'Hark! 't is an elfin storm from faery
   land,
Of haggard seeming, but a boon indeed:
Arise — arise! the morning is at hand: —
The bloated wassailers will never heed: —
Let us away, my love, with happy speed;

There are no ears to hear, or eyes to
  see, —
Drown'd all in Rhenish and the sleepy
  mead:
Awake ! arise ! my love, and fearless be,
For o'er the southern moors I have a home
  for thee.'

XL

She hurried at his words, beset with
  fears,
For there were sleeping dragons all
  around,
At glaring watch, perhaps, with ready
  spears —
Down the wide stairs a darkling way they
  found. —
In all the house was heard no human
  sound.
A chain-droop'd lamp was flickering by
  each door;
The arras, rich with horseman, hawk,
  and hound,
Flutter'd in the besieging wind's uproar;
And the long carpets rose along the gusty
  floor.

XLI

They glide, like phantoms, into the wide
  hall;
Like phantoms to the iron porch they
  glide,
Where lay the Porter, in uneasy sprawl,
With a huge empty flagon by his side:
The wakeful bloodhound rose, and shook
  his hide,
But his sagacious eye an inmate owns:
By one, and one, the bolts full easy
  slide: —
The chains lie silent on the footworn
  stones; —
The key turns, and the door upon its hinges
  groans.

XLII

And they are gone: aye, ages long ago
These lovers fled away into the storm.

That night the Baron dreamt of many a
  woe,
And all his warrior-guests, with shade
  and form
Of witch, and demon, and large coffin-
  worm,
Were long be-nightmared. Angela the
  old
Died palsy-twitch'd, with meagre face
  deform;
The Beadsman, after thousand aves told,
For aye unsought-for slept among his ashes
  cold.

ODE ON A GRECIAN URN

Lemprière's classical dictionary made Keats
acquainted with the names and attributes of the
inhabitants of the heavens in the ancient world,
and the Shakesperean Chapman introduced
him to Homer, but his acquaintance with the
subtlest spirit of Greece was by a more direct
means. Keats did not read Greek, and he had
no scholar's knowledge of Greek art, but he
had the poetic divination which scholars sometimes fail to possess, and when he strolled into
the British Museum and saw the Elgin marbles,
the greatest remains in continuous series of perhaps the greatest of Greek sculptures, he saw
them as an artist of kindred spirit with their
makers. He saw them also with the complex
emotion of a modern, and read into them his
own thoughts. The result is most surely read
in his longer poem of *Hyperion*, but the spirit
evoked found its finest expression in this ode.
  The ode appears to have been composed in
the spring of 1819 and first published in January, 1820, in *Annals of the Fine Arts*. There are
then about four years in time between the sonnet, 'On first looking into Chapman's Homer,'
and this ode ; if the former suggests a Balboa,
this suggests a Magellan who has traversed the
Pacific. It is not needful to find any single
piece of ancient sculpture as a model for the
poem, although there is at Holland House,
where Keats might have seen it, an urn with
just such a scene of pastoral sacrifice as is described in the fourth stanza. The ode was
included by Keats in *Lamia, Isabella, The Eve
of St. Agnes and other Poems*. ,

I

THOU still unravish'd bride of quietness,
  Thou foster-child of Silence and slow
    Time,
Sylvan historian, who canst thus express
  A flowery tale more sweetly than our
    rhyme:
What leaf-fringed legend haunts about thy
    shape
  Of deities or mortals, or of both,
    In Tempe or the dales of Arcady?
  What men or gods are these? what
    maidens loth?
What mad pursuit? What struggle to es-
    cape?
    What pipes and timbrels? What wild
      ecstasy?   10

II

Heard melodies are sweet, but those un-
    heard
  Are sweeter; therefore, ye soft pipes,
    play on;
Not to the sensual ear, but, more endear'd
Pipe to the spirit ditties of no tone:
Fair youth, beneath the trees, thou canst
    not leave
  Thy song, nor ever can those trees be
    bare;
    Bold Lover, never, never canst thou
      kiss,
Though winning near the goal — yet, do
    not grieve;
  She cannot fade, though thou hast not
    thy bliss,   19
    For ever wilt thou love, and she be fair!

III

Ah, happy, happy boughs! that cannot
    shed
  Your leaves, nor ever bid the Spring
    adieu;
And, happy melodist, unwearied,
  For ever piping songs for ever new;
More happy love! more happy, happy
    love!
  For ever warm and still to be enjoy'd,
    For ever panting, and for ever young;

All breathing human passion far above,
  That leaves a heart high-sorrowful and
    cloy'd,
    A burning forehead, and a parching
      tongue.   30

IV

Who are these coming to the sacrifice?
  To what green altar, O mysterious priest,
Lead'st thou that heifer lowing at the skies,
  And all her silken flanks with garlands
    drest?
What little town by river or sea shore,
  Or mountain-built with peaceful citadel,
    Is emptied of this folk, this pious
      morn?
And, little town, thy streets for evermore
  Will silent be; and not a soul to tell
    Why thou art desolate, can e'er re-
      turn.   40

V

O Attic shape! Fair attitude! with brede *a*
  Of marble men and maidens overwrought, *b*
With forest branches and the trodden weed; *a*
  Thou, silent form, dost tease us out of *b*
    thought
As doth eternity: Cold Pastoral!   *e*
  When old age shall this generation waste, *c*
    Thou shalt remain, in midst of other *e*
      woe
  Than ours, a friend to man, to whom *d*
    thou say'st,
'Beauty is truth, truth beauty,' — that is *e*
    all
  Ye know on earth, and all ye need to *e*
    know.   50

ODE ON INDOLENCE

'They toil not, neither do they spin.'

Published in *Life, Letters and Literary Remains*. In a letter to George and Georgiana
Keats, dated March 19, 1819, Keats uses language which shows this poem to have been
just then in his mind : ' This morning I am in a
sort of temper, indolent and supremely careless

— I long after a stanza or two of Thomson's Castle of Indolence — my passions are all asleep, from my having slumbered till nearly eleven, and weakened the animal fibre all over me, to a delightful sensation, about three degrees on this side of faintness. If I had teeth of pearl and the breath of lilies I should call it languor, but as I am I must call it laziness. In this state of effeminacy the fibres of the brain are relaxed in common with the rest of the body, and to such a happy degree that pleasure has no show of enticement and pain no unbearable power. Neither Poetry, nor Ambition, nor Love have any alertness of countenance as they pass by me; they seem rather like figures on a Greek vase — a man and two women whom no one but myself could distinguish in their disguisement. This is the only happiness, and is a rare instance of the advantage of the body overpowering the Mind.'

I

ONE morn before me were three figures seen,
    With bowed necks, and joined hands, side-faced;
And one behind the other stepp'd serene,
    In placid sandals, and in white robes graced;
They pass'd, like figures on a marble urn,
    When shifted round to see the other side;
        They came again; as when the urn once more
Is shifted round, the first seen shades return;
    And they were strange to me, as may betide
        With vases, to one deep in Phidian lore.

II

How is it, Shadows! that I knew ye not?
    How came ye muffled in so hush a mask?
Was it a silent deep–disguised plot
    To steal away, and leave without a task
My idle days? Ripe was the drowsy hour;

The blissful cloud of summer-indolence
    Benumb'd my eyes; my pulse grew less and less;
Pain had no sting, and pleasure's wreath no flower:
    O, why did ye not melt, and leave my sense
        Unhaunted quite of all but — nothingness?

III

A third time pass'd they by, and, passing, turn'd
    Each one the face a moment whiles to me;
Then faded, and to follow them I burn'd
    And ached for wings, because I knew the three;
The first was a fair Maid, and Love her name;
    The second was Ambition, pale of cheek,
        And ever watchful with fatigued eye;
The last, whom I love more, the more of blame
    Is heap'd upon her, maiden most unmeek, —
        I knew to be my demon Poesy.

IV

They faded, and, forsooth! I wanted wings:
    O folly! What is Love? and where is it?
And for that poor Ambition! it springs
    From a man's little heart's short fever-fit;
For Poesy! — no, — she has not a joy, —
    At least for me, — so sweet as drowsy noons,
        And evenings steep'd in honied indolence;
O, for an age so shelter'd from annoy,
    That I may never know how change the moons,
        Or hear the voice of busy commonsense!

V

And once more came they by; — alas!
wherefore?
My sleep had been embroider'd with dim
dreams;
My soul had been a lawn besprinkled
o'er
With flowers, and stirring shades, and
baffled beams:
The morn was clouded, but no shower fell,
Tho' in her lids hung the sweet tears of
May;
The open casement press'd a new-
leaved vine,
Let in the budding warmth and throstle's
lay;
O Shadows! 't was a time to bid farewell!
Upon your skirts had fallen no tears
of mine.

VI

So, ye three Ghosts, adieu! Ye cannot
raise
My head cool - bedded in the flowery
grass;
For I would not be dieted with praise,
A pet-lamb in a sentimental farce!
Fade softly from my eyes and be once
more
In masque-like figures on the dreamy
urn;
Farewell! I yet have visions for the
night,
And for the day faint visions there is store;
Vanish, ye Phantoms! from my idle
spright,
Into the clouds, and nevermore return!

SONNET

Published in *Life, Letters and Literary Remains*. In a letter to his brother George and
wife, Keats writes March 19, 1819: 'I am
ever afraid that your anxiety for me will lead
you to fear for the violence of my temperament continually smothered down: for that
reason I did not intend to have sent you the
following sonnet — but look over the two last
pages [of his letter] and ask yourselves whether
I have not that in me which will bear the buffets of the world. It will be the best comment
on my sonnet; it will show you that it was
written with no Agony but that of ignorance;
with no thirst of anything but Knowledge
when pushed to the point, though the first
steps to it were through my human passions, —
they went away and I wrote with my Mind
— and perhaps I must confess a little bit of my
heart.'

WHY did I laugh to-night? No voice will
tell;
No God, no Demon of severe response,
Deigns to reply from Heaven or from Hell:
Then to my human heart I turn at once.
Heart! Thou and I are here sad and alone;
I say, why did I laugh? O mortal pain!
O Darkness! Darkness! ever must I moan,
To question Heaven and Hell and Heart
in vain.
Why did I laugh? I know this Being's
lease,
My fancy to its utmost blisses spreads;
Yet would I on this very midnight cease,
And the world's gaudy ensigns see in
shreds;
Verse, Fame, and Beauty are intense
indeed,
But Death intenser — Death is Life's high
meed.

ODE TO FANNY

First published in *Life, Letters and Literary
Remains*, and there undated.

PHYSICIAN Nature! let my spirit blood!
O ease my heart of verse and let me rest;
Throw me upon thy Tripod, till the flood
Of stifling numbers ebbs from my full
breast.
A theme! a theme! great Nature!
give a theme;
Let me begin my dream.
I come — I see thee, as thou standest there;
Beckon me not into the wintry air.

Ah! dearest love, sweet home of all my
    fears,
  And hopes, and joys, and panting mis-
    eries, —
To-night, if I may guess, thy beauty wears
    A smile of such delight,
    As brilliant and as bright,
  As when with ravished, aching, vassal
    eyes,
    Lost in soft amaze,
    I gaze, I gaze !

Who now, with greedy looks, eats up my
    feast ?
  What stare outfaces now my silver moon !
Ah ! keep that hand unravished at the least ;
    Let, let the amorous burn —
    But, pr'ythee, do not turn
  The current of your heart from me so
    soon.
    O ! save, in charity,
    The quickest pulse for me.

Save it for me, sweet love ! though music
    breathe
  Voluptuous visions into the warm air,
Though swimming through the dance's dan-
    gerous wreath;
    Be like an April day,
    Smiling and cold and gay,
  A temperate lily, temperate as fair;
    Then, Heaven ! there will be
    A warmer June for me.

Why, this — you'll say, my Fanny ! is not
    true:
  Put your soft hand upon your snowy side,
Where the heart beats: confess — 't is
    nothing new —
    Must not a woman be
    A feather on the sea,
  Sway'd to and fro by every wind and
    tide ?
    Of as uncertain speed
    As blow-ball from the mead ?

I know it — and to know it is despair
  To one who loves you as I love, sweet
    Fanny !

Whose heart goes fluttering for you every-
    where,
  Nor, when away you roam,
  Dare keep its wretched home :
Love, love alone, has pains severe and
    many :
  Then, loveliest ! keep me free
  From torturing jealousy.

Ah ! if you prize my subdued soul above
  The poor, the fading, brief pride of an
    hour;
Let none profane my Holy See of love,
    Or with a rude hand break
    The sacramental cake:
  Let none else touch the just new-budded
    flower;
    If not — may my eyes close,
    Love ! on their last repose.

A DREAM, AFTER READING DANTE'S EPISODE OF PAOLO AND FRANCESCA

To George and Georgiana Keats, April 18 or
19, 1819, Keats writes: 'The fifth canto of
Dante pleases me more and more — it is that
one in which he meets with Paolo and Francesca. I had passed many days in rather a
low state of mind, and in the midst of them I
dreamt of being in that region of Hell. The
dream was one of the most delightful enjoyments I ever had in my life. I floated about
the whirling atmosphere, as it is described, with
a beautiful figure, to whose lips mine were
joined as it seemed for an age — and in the
midst of all this cold and darkness I was warm
— even flowery tree-tops sprung up, and we
rested on them, sometimes with the lightness
of a cloud, till the wind blew us away again.
I tried a sonnet upon it — there are fourteen
lines, but nothing of what I felt in it — O that
I could dream it every night.' Keats afterwards printed the sonnet in The Indicator for
June 28, 1820.

As Hermes once took to his feathers light,
  When lulled Argus, baffled, swoon'd and
    slept
So on a Delphic reed, my idle spright

So play'd, so charm'd, so conquer'd, so
    bereft
The dragon-world of all its hundred eyes;
    And, seeing it asleep, so fled away —
Not to pure Ida with its snow-cold skies,
    Nor unto Tempe where Jove grieved a
    day;
But to that second circle of sad hell,
    Where 'mid the gust, the whirlwind, and
    the flaw
Of rain and hail-stones, lovers need not tell
    Their sorrows. Pale were the sweet lips
    I saw,
Pale were the lips I kiss'd, and fair the form
I floated with, about that melancholy storm.

LA BELLE DAME SANS MERCI

Sent in a letter to George and Georgiana
Keats, April 28, 1819, and printed by Leigh
Hunt in *The Indicator*, May 10, 1820. Hunt
says the poem was suggested by that title at
the head of a translation from Alan Chartier
at the end of Chaucer's works.

I

Ah, what can ail thee, wretched wight,
    Alone and palely loitering?
The sedge is wither'd from the lake,
    And no birds sing.

II

Ah, what can ail thee, wretched wight,
    So haggard and so woe-begone?
The squirrel's granary is full,
    And the harvest 's done.

III

I see a lily on thy brow,
    With anguish moist and fever dew;
And on thy cheek a fading rose
    Fast withereth too.

IV

I met a lady in the meads,
    Full beautiful — a faery's child;
Her hair was long, her foot was light,
    And her eyes were wild.

V

I set her on my pacing steed,
    And nothing else saw all day long,
For sideways would she lean, and sing
    A faery's song.

VI

I made a garland for her head,
    And bracelets too, and fragrant zone;
She look'd at me as she did love,
    And made sweet moan.

VII

She found me roots of relish sweet,
    And honey wild, and manna dew;
And sure in language strange she said —
    'I love thee true.'

VIII

She took me to her elfin grot,
    And there she gazed, and sighed deep,
And there I shut her wild wild eyes
    So kiss'd to sleep.

IX

And there we slumber'd on the moss,
    And there I dream'd — Ah! woe betide!
The latest dream I ever dream'd
    On the cold hill side.

X

I saw pale kings, and princes too,
    Pale warriors, death-pale were they all;
They cried — 'La Belle Dame sans Merci
    Hath thee in thrall!'

XI

I saw their starved lips in the gloam,
    With horrid warning gaped wide,
And I awoke, and found me here
    On the cold hill side.

XII

And this is why I sojourn here,
    Alone and palely loitering,
Though the sedge is wither'd from the
    lake,
    And no birds sing.

CHORUS OF FAIRIES

Inclosed in a letter to George and Georgiana
Keats, April 28, 1819, and printed in *Life,
Letters and Literary Remains.*

FIRE, AIR, EARTH, AND WATER
SALAMANDER, ZEPHYR, DUSKETHA, AND
BREAMA

SALAMANDER

Happy, happy glowing fire !

ZEPHYR

Fragrant air ! delicious light !

DUSKETHA

Let me to my glooms retire !

BREAMA

I to green-weed rivers bright !

SALAMANDER

Happy, happy glowing fire !
Dazzling bowers of soft retire,
Ever let my nourish'd wing,
Like a bat's, still wandering,
Faintly fan your fiery spaces,
Spirit sole in deadly places.   10
In unhaunted roar and blaze,
Open eyes that never daze,
Let me see the myriad shapes
Of men, and beasts, and fish, and apes,
Portray'd in many a fiery den,
And wrought by spumy bitumen.
On the deep intenser roof,
Arched every way, aloof,
Let me breathe upon my skies,
And anger their live tapestries;   20
Free from cold, and every care,
Of chilly rain, and shivering air.

ZEPHYR

Spright of Fire ! away ! away !
Or your very roundelay
Will sear my plumage newly budded
From its quilled sheath, and studded
With the self-same dews that fell
On the May-grown Asphodel.
Spright of Fire — away ! away !

BREAMA

Spright of Fire — away ! away !   30
Zephyr, blue-eyed Faery, turn,
And see my cool sedge-shaded urn,
Where it rests its mossy brim
'Mid water-mint and cresses dim;
And the flowers, in sweet troubles,
Lift their eyes above the bubbles,
Like our Queen, when she would please
To sleep, and Oberon will tease.
Love me, blue-eyed Faery ! true,
Soothly I am sick for you.   40

ZEPHYR

Gentle Breama ! by the first
Violet young nature nurst,
I will bathe myself with thee,
So you sometime follow me
To my home, far, far, in west,
Far beyond the search and quest
Of the golden-browed sun.
Come with me, o'er tops of trees,
To my fragrant palaces,
Where they ever floating are   50
Beneath the cherish of a star
Call'd Vesper, who with silver veil
Ever hides his brilliance pale,
Ever gently-drowsed doth keep
Twilight for the Fays to sleep.
Fear not that your watery hair
Will thirst in drouthy ringlets there;
Clouds of stored summer rains
Thou shalt taste, before the stains
Of the mountain soil they take,   60
And too unlucent for thee make.
I love thee, crystal Faery, true !
Sooth I am as sick for you !

SALAMANDER

Out, ye aguish Faeries, out !
Chilly lovers, what a rout
Keep ye with your frozen breath,
Colder than the mortal death.
Adder-eyed Dusketha, speak,
Shall we leave them, and go seek
In the earth's wide entrails old   70
Couches warm as theirs is cold ?
O for a fiery gloom and thee,

Dusketha, so enchantingly
Freckle-wing'd and lizard-sided !

DUSKETHA

By thee, Spright, will I be guided !
I care not for cold or heat;
Frost and flame, or sparks, or sleet,
To my essence are the same; —
But I honour more the flame.
Spright of fire, I follow thee   80
Wheresoever it may be;
To the torrid spouts and fountains,
Underneath earth-quaked mountains;
Or, at thy supreme desire,
Touch the very pulse of fire
With my bare unlidded eyes.

SALAMANDER

Sweet Dusketha ! paradise !
Off, ye icy Spirits, fly !
Frosty creatures of the sky !

DUSKETHA

Breathe upon them, fiery Spright !   90

ZEPHYR, BREAMA (*to each other*)

Away ! away to our delight !

SALAMANDER

Go, feed on icicles, while we
Bedded in tongued flames will be.

DUSKETHA

Lead me to these fev'rous glooms,
Spright of Fire !

BREAMA

                Me to the blooms,
Blue eyed Zephyr of those flowers
Far in the west where the May-cloud lowers:
  And the beams of still Vesper, where
    winds are all whist,
  Are shed thro' the rain and the milder
    mist,
And twilight your floating bowers.   100

FAERY SONGS

These two songs are given in *Life, Letters
and Literary Remains*, but without date. It

seems not inapt to place them near the *Song of
Four Fairies.*

I

SHED no tear !   O shed no tear !
The flower will bloom another year.
Weep no more !   O weep no more !
Young buds sleep in the root's white core.
Dry your eyes !   O dry your eyes,
For I was taught in Paradise
To ease my breast of melodies —
                Shed no tear.

Overhead ! look overhead
'Mong the blossoms white and red —
Look up, look up — I flutter now
On this flush pomegranate bough.
See me ! 't is this silvery bill
Ever cures the good man's ill.
Shed no tear !   O shed no tear !
The flower will bloom another year.
Adieu, Adieu — I fly, adieu,
I vanish in the heaven's blue —
                Adieu, Adieu !

II

Ah ! woe is me ! poor silver-wing !
  That I must chant thy lady's dirge,
And death to this fair haunt of spring,
  Of melody, and streams of flowery
    verge, —
      Poor silver-wing ! ah ! woe is me !
      That I must see
These blossoms snow upon thy lady's pall !
  Go, pretty page ! and in her ear
  Whisper that the hour is near !
  Softly tell her not to fear
Such calm favonian burial !
  Go, pretty page ! and soothly tell, —
  The blossoms hang by a melting spell,
And fall they must, ere a star wink thrice
      Upon her closed eyes,
That now in vain are weeping their last
    tears,
  At sweet life leaving, and those arbours
    green, —
Rich dowry from the Spirit of the
    Spheres, —
      Alas ! poor Queen !

ON FAME

'You cannot eat your cake and have it too.' — *Proverb*.

Sent with the next two to George and Georgiana Keats, April 30, 1819, and printed in *Life, Letters and Literary Remains*.

How fever'd is that man, who cannot look
　Upon his mortal days with temperate blood,
Who vexes all the leaves of his life's book,
　And robs his fair name of its maidenhood:
It is as if the rose should pluck herself,
　Or the ripe plum finger its misty bloom;
As if a Naiad, like a meddling elf,
　Should darken her pure grot with muddy gloom.
But the rose leaves herself upon the brier,
　For winds to kiss and grateful bees to feed,
And the ripe plum still wears its dim attire,
　　The undisturbed lake has crystal space:
　Why then should man, teasing the world for grace,
　Spoil his salvation for a fierce miscreed?

ANOTHER ON FAME

Fame, like a wayward girl, will still be coy
　To those who woo her with too slavish knees,
But makes surrender to some thoughtless boy,
　And dotes the more upon a heart at ease;
She is a Gipsy, — will not speak to those
　Who have not learnt to be content without her;
A Jilt, whose ear was never whisper'd close,
　Who thinks they scandal her who talk about her;
A very Gipsy is she, Nilus-born,
　Sister-in-law to jealous Potiphar;
Ye lovesick Bards! repay her scorn for scorn;

Ye Artists lovelorn! madmen that ye are!
Make your best bow to her and bid adieu,
Then, if she likes it, she will follow you.

TO SLEEP

O soft embalmer of the still midnight,
　Shutting, with careful fingers and benign,
Our gloom-pleased eyes, embower'd from the light,
　Enshaded in forgetfulness divine:
O soothest Sleep! if so it please thee, close,
　In midst of this thine hymn, my willing eyes,
Or wait the amen, ere thy poppy throws
　Around my bed its dewy charities;
　Then save me, or the passed day will shine
Upon my pillow, breeding many woes;
　Save me from curious conscience, that still lords
Its strength for darkness, burrowing like a mole;
　Turn the key deftly in the oiled wards,
And seal the hushed casket of my soul.

ODE TO PSYCHE

'The following poem — the last I have written — is the first and only one with which I have taken even moderate pains. I have, for the most part, dashed off my lines in a hurry. This I have done leisurely — I think it reads the more richly for it, and will I hope encourage me to write other things in even a more peaceable and healthy spirit. You must recollect that Psyche was not embodied as a goddess before the time of Apuleius the Platonist, who lived after the Augustan age, and consequently the Goddess was never worshipped or sacrificed to with any of the ancient fervour — and perhaps never thought of in the old religion — I am more orthodox than to let a heathen Goddess be so neglected.' Keats to his Brother and Sister, April 30, 1819. He afterward included the poem in his volume, *Lamia, Isabella, The Eve of St. Agnes and other Poems*, 1820.

I

O Goddess! hear these tuneless numbers, wrung
  By sweet enforcement and remembrance dear,
And pardon that thy secrets should be sung
  Even into thine own soft-conched ear:
Surely I dreamt to-day, or did I see
  The winged Psyche with awaken'd eyes?
I wander'd in a forest thoughtlessly,
  And, on the sudden, fainting with surprise,
Saw two fair creatures, couched side by side
  In deepest grass, beneath the whisp'ring roof   10
  Of leaves and trembled blossoms, where there ran
     A brooklet, scarce espied:

II

'Mid hush'd, cool-rooted flowers fragrant-eyed,
Blue, silver-white, and budded Tyrian,
They lay calm-breathing on the bedded grass;
  Their arms embraced, and their pinions too;
  Their lips touch'd not, but had not bade adieu,
As if disjoined by soft-handed slumber,
And ready still past kisses to outnumber
At tender eye-dawn of aurorean love: 20
     The winged boy I knew;
  But who wast thou, O happy, happy dove?
     His Psyche true!

III

O latest-born and loveliest vision far
  Of all Olympus' faded hierarchy!
Fairer than Phœbe's sapphire-region'd star,
  Or Vesper, amorous glow-worm of the sky;
Fairer than these, though temple thou hast none,
     Nor altar heap'd with flowers;
  Nor virgin-choir to make delicious moan
     Upon the midnight hours;   31

No voice, no lute, no pipe, no incense sweet
  From chain-swung censer teeming;
No shrine, no grove, no oracle, no heat
  Of pale-mouth'd prophet dreaming.

IV

O brightest! though too late for antique vows,
  Too, too late for the fond believing lyre,
When holy were the haunted forest boughs,
  Holy the air, the water, and the fire;
Yet even in these days so far retired   40
  From happy pieties, thy lucent fans,
  Fluttering among the faint Olympians,
I see, and sing, by my own eyes inspired.
So let me be thy choir, and make a moan
     Upon the midnight hours;
Thy voice, thy lute, thy pipe, thy incense sweet
  From swinged censer teeming;
Thy shrine, thy grove, thy oracle, thy heat
  Of pale-mouth'd prophet dreaming.

V

Yes, I will be thy priest, and build a fane
  In some untrodden region of my mind,
Where branched thoughts, new-grown with pleasant pain,   52
  Instead of pines shall murmur in the wind:
Far, far around shall those dark-cluster'd trees
  Fledge the wild-ridged mountains steep by steep;
And there by zephyrs, streams, and birds, and bees,
  The moss-lain Dryads shall be lulled to sleep;
And in the midst of this wide quietness
A rosy sanctuary will I dress
With the wreath'd trellis of a working brain,   60
  With buds, and bells, and stars without a name,
With all the gardener Fancy e'er could feign,
  Who breeding flowers, will never breed the same:

And there shall be for thee all soft delight
    That shadowy thought can win,
A bright torch, and a casement ope at
    night,
        To let the warm Love in !

SONNET

In copying his ' Ode to Psyche,' Keats added the flourish ' Here endethe ye Ode to Psyche,' and went on ' Incipit altera soneta.' ' I have been endeavouring,' he writes, ' to discover a better Sonnet Stanza than we have. The legitimate does not suit the language over well from the pouncing rhymes — the other kind appears too elegiac — and the couplet at the end of it has seldom a pleasing effect — I do not pretend to have succeeded — it will explain itself.' The sonnet was printed in *Life, Letters and Literary Remains*.

If by dull rhymes our English must be
    chain'd,
    And, like Andromeda, the Sonnet sweet
Fetter'd, in spite of pained loveliness;
    Let us find out, if we must be constrain'd,
    Sandals more interwoven and complete
To fit the naked foot of poesy;
    Let us inspect the lyre, and weigh the
        stress
Of every chord, and see what may be
        gain'd
By ear industrious, and attention meet;
Misers of sound and syllable, no less
Than Midas of his coinage, let us be
    Jealous of dead leaves in the bay-wreath
        crown:
So, if we may not let the Muse be free,
    She will be bound with garlands of her
        own.

ODE TO A NIGHTINGALE

First published in the July, 1819, *Annals of the Fine Arts* and included in the 1820 volume. It was composed in May, 1819. In the Aldine edition of 1876 Lord Houghton prefixes this note: ' In the spring of 1819 a nightingale built her nest next Mr. Bevan's house. Keats took great pleasure in her song, and one morning took his chair from the breakfast table to the grass plot under a plum tree, where he remained between two and three hours. He then reached the house with some scraps of paper in his hand, which he soon put together in the form of this Ode.' Haydon in a letter to Miss Mitford says : ' The death of his brother [in December, 1818] wounded him deeply, and it appeared to me from that hour he began to droop. He wrote his exquisite ' Ode to the Nightingale' at this time, and as we were one evening walking in the Kilburn meadows he repeated it to me, before he put it to paper, in a low, tremulous undertone which affected me extremely.' It may well be that Tom Keats was in the poet's mind when he wrote line 26.

I

My heart aches, and a drowsy numbness
    pains
    My sense, as though of hemlock I had
        drunk,
Or emptied some dull opiate to the drains
    One minute past, and Lethe-wards had
        sunk:
'T is not through envy of thy happy lot,
    But being too happy in thine happiness, —
        That thou, light-winged Dryad of the
        trees,
            In some melodious plot
Of beechen green, and shadows number-
        less,
        Singest of summer in full-throated
        ease.   10

II

O for a draught of vintage ! that hath been
    Cool'd a long age in the deep-delved
        earth,
Tasting of Flora and the country-green,
    Dance, and Provençal song, and sun-
        burnt mirth !
O for a beaker full of the warm South,
    Full of the true, the blushful Hippo-
        crene,
        With beaded bubbles winking at the
        brim,
        And purple-stained mouth ;

That I might drink, and leave the world
  unseen,
  And with thee fade away into the forest dim: 20

with felicity ...instead of joy, grief sorrow

III

Fade far away, dissolve, and quite forget
  What thou among the leaves hast never
  known,
The weariness, the fever, and the fret
  Here, where men sit and hear each other
  groan;
Where palsy shakes a few, sad, last gray
  hairs,
  Where youth grows pale, and spectre-
  thin, and dies;
  Where but to think is to be full of
  sorrow
    And leaden-eyed despairs,
  Where Beauty cannot keep her lustrous
  eyes,
    Or new Love pine at them beyond to-
    morrow. 30

IV

Away! away! for I will fly to thee,
  Not charioted by Bacchus and his pards,
But on the viewless wings of Poesy,
  Though the dull brain perplexes and re-
  tards:
Already with thee! tender is the night,
  And haply the Queen-Moon is on her
  throne,
    Cluster'd around by all her starry
    Fays;
    But here there is no light,
  Save what from heaven is with the breezes
  blown
    Through verdurous glooms and wind-
    ing mossy ways. 40

V

I cannot see what flowers are at my feet,
  Nor what soft incense hangs upon the
  boughs,
But, in embalmed darkness, guess each
  sweet

senses & imagination ...

Wherewith the seasonable month endows
The grass, the thicket, and the fruit-tree
  wild;
  White hawthorn, and the pastoral eglantine;
    Fast fading violets cover'd up in
    leaves;
      And mid-May's eldest child,
  The coming musk-rose, full of dewy
  wine,
    The murmurous haunt of flies on sum-
    mer eves. 50

VI

Darkling I listen; and, for many a time
  I have been half in love with easeful
  Death,
Call'd him soft names in many a mused
  rhyme,
  To take into the air my quiet breath;
Now more than ever seems it rich to die,
  To cease upon the midnight with no
  pain,
    While thou art pouring forth thy soul
    abroad
      In such an ecstasy!
  Still wouldst thou sing, and I have ears
  in vain —
    To thy high requiem become a sod. 60

VII

Thou wast not born for death, immortal
  Bird!
  No hungry generations tread thee down;
The voice I hear this passing night was
  heard
  In ancient days by emperor and clown:
Perhaps the self-same song that found a
  path
  Through the sad heart of Ruth, when,
  sick for home,
    She stood in tears amid the alien corn;
      The same that oft-times hath
  Charm'd magic casements, opening on
  the foam
    Of perilous seas, in faery lands for-
    lorn. 70

VIII

Forlorn ! the very word is like a bell
  To toll me back from thee to my sole
    self !
Adieu ! the fancy cannot cheat so well
  As she is famed to do, deceiving elf.
Adieu ! adieu ! thy plaintive anthem fades
  Past the near meadows, over the still
    stream,
      Up the hill-side; and now 't is buried
        deep
        In the next valley-glades:
  Was it a vision, or a waking dream ?
    Fled is that music: — do I wake or
      sleep ?   80

LAMIA

In the early summer of 1819 Keats felt the
pressure of want of money and determined to
go into the country, where he could live cheaply,
and devote himself to writing. He went accordingly to Shanklin, Isle of Wight, and wrote
thence to Reynolds, July 12, 'I have finished
the Act [the first of *Otho the Great*], and in the
interval of beginning the 2nd have proceeded
pretty well with *Lamia*, finishing the first part
which consists of about 400 lines. I have
great hope of success [in this enterprise of
maintenance], because I make use of my judgment more deliberately than I have yet done.'
He continued to work at *Lamia* in connection
with the tragedy, completing it in August at
Winchester. It formed the leading poem in the
volume *Lamia, Isabella, the Eve of St. Agnes
and other Poems*, published in 1820. Keats's
own judgment of it is in his words: 'I am certain there is that sort of fire in it which must
take hold of people in some way — give them
either pleasant or unpleasant association.' He
found the germ of the story in Burton's *Anatomy of Melancholy*, where it is credited to Phi-
lostratus. The passage will be found in the
Notes. Lord Houghton says, on the authority
of Brown, that Keats wrote the poem after
much study of Dryden's versification.

PART I

UPON a time, before the faery broods
Drove Nymph and Satyr from the prosperous woods,

Before King Oberon's bright diadem,
Sceptre, and mantle, clasp'd with dewy gem.
Frighted away the Dryads and the Fauns
From rushes green, and brakes, and cow-
  slipp'd lawns,
The ever-smitten Hermes empty left
His golden throne, bent warm on amorous
  theft;
From high Olympus had he stolen light,
On this side of Jove's clouds, to escape the
  sight   10
Of his great summoner, and made retreat
Into a forest on the shores of Crete.
For somewhere in that sacred island dwelt
A nymph, to whom all hoofed Satyrs knelt;
At whose white feet the languid Tritons
  poured
Pearls, while on land they wither'd and
  adored.
Fast by the springs where she to bathe was
  wont,
And in those meads where sometimes she
  might haunt,
Were strewn rich gifts, unknown to any
  Muse,
Though Fancy's casket were unlock'd to
  choose.   20
Ah, what a world of love was at her feet !
So Hermes thought, and a celestial heat
Burnt from his winged heels to either ear,
That from a whiteness, as the lily clear,
Blush'd into roses 'mid his golden hair,
Fallen in jealous curls about his shoulders
  bare.

      From vale to vale, from wood to wood,
        he flew,
Breathing upon the flowers his passion new,
And wound with many a river to its head,
To find where this sweet nymph prepared
  her secret bed: 30
In vain; the sweet nymph might nowhere
  be found,
And so he rested, on the lonely ground,
Pensive, and full of painful jealousies
Of the Wood-Gods, and even the very trees
There as he stood, he heard a mournful
  voice,

Such as once heard, in gentle heart, de-
  stroys
All pain but pity: thus the lone voice spake:
'When from this wreathed tomb shall I
  awake!
When move in a sweet body fit for life,
And love, and pleasure, and the ruddy
  strife
Of hearts and lips! Ah, miserable me!'   40
The God, dove-footed, glided silently
Round bush and tree, soft-brushing, in his
  speed,
The taller grasses and full-flowering weed,
Until he found a palpitating snake,
Bright, and cirque-couchant in a dusky
  brake.

  She was a gordian shape of dazzling hue,
Vermilion - spotted, golden, green, and
  blue;
Striped like a zebra, freckled like a pard,
Eyed like a peacock, and all crimson barr'd;
And full of silver moons, that, as she
  breathed,   51
Dissolved, or brighter shone, or inter-
  wreathed
Their lustres with the gloomier tapes-
  tries —
So rainbow-sided, touch'd with miseries,
She seem'd, at once, some penanced lady
  elf,
Some demon's mistress, or the demon's
  self.
Upon her crest she wore a wannish fire
Sprinkled with stars, like Ariadne's tiar:
Her head was serpent, but ah, bitter-sweet!
She had a woman's mouth with all its
  pearls complete: 60
And for her eyes — what could such eyes
  do there
But weep, and weep, that they were born
  so fair?
As Proserpine still weeps for her Sicilian
  air.
Her throat was serpent, but the words she
  spake
Came, as through bubbling honey, for
  Love's sake,

And thus; while Hermes on his pinions lay,
Like a stoop'd falcon ere he takes his prey:

  'Fair Hermes! crown'd with feathers,
    fluttering light,
I had a splendid dream of thee last night:
I saw thee sitting, on a throne of gold,   70
Among the Gods, upon Olympus old,
The only sad one; for thou didst not hear
The soft, lute - finger'd Muses chanting
  clear,
Nor even Apollo when he sang alone,
Deaf to his throbbing throat's long, long
  . melodious moan.
I dreamt I saw thee, robed in purple flakes,
Break amorous through the clouds, as
  morning breaks,
And, swiftly as a bright Phœbean dart,
Strike for the Cretan isle; and here thou
  art!
Too gentle Hermes, hast thou found the
  maid?'   80
Whereat the star of Lethe not delay'd
His rosy eloquence, and thus inquired:
'Thou smooth-lipp'd serpent, surely high-
  inspired!
Thou beauteous wreath, with melancholy
  eyes,
Possess whatever bliss thou canst devise,
Telling me only where my nymph is fled, —
Where she doth breathe!' 'Bright planet,
  thou hast said,'
Return'd the snake, 'but seal with oaths,
  fair God!'
'I swear,' said Hermes, 'by my serpent rod,
And by thine eyes, and by thy starry
  crown!'   90
Light flew his earnest words, among the
  blossoms blown.
Then thus again the brilliance feminine:
'Too frail of heart! for this lost nymph of
  thine,
Free as the air, invisibly, she strays
About these thornless wilds; her pleasant
  days
She tastes unseen; unseen her nimble
  feet
Leave traces in the grass and flowers sweet;

From weary tendrils, and bow'd branches
   green,
She plucks the fruit unseen, she bathes un-
   seen:
And by my power is her beauty veil'd 100
To keep it unaffronted, unassail'd
By the love-glances of unlovely eyes,
Of Satyrs, Fauns, and blear'd Silenus' sighs.
Pale grew her immortality, for woe
Of all these lovers, and she grieved so
I took compassion on her, bade her steep
Her hair in weïrd syrops, that would keep
Her loveliness invisible, yet free
To wander as she loves, in liberty.
Thou shalt behold her, Hermes, thou alone,
If thou wilt, as thou swearest, grant my
   boon!'   111
Then, once again, the charmed God began
An oath, and through the serpent's ears it
   ran
Warm, tremulous, devout, psalterian.
Ravish'd she lifted her Circean head,
Blush'd a live damask, and swift-lisping
   said,
'I was a woman, let me have once more
A woman's shape, and charming as before.
I love a youth of Corinth — O the bliss!
Give me my woman's form, and place me
   where he is.   . 120
Stoop, Hermes, let me breathe upon thy
   brow,
And thou shalt see thy sweet nymph even
   now.'
The God on half-shut feathers sank serene,
She breathed upon his eyes, and swift was
   seen
Of both the guarded nymph near-smiling
   on the green.
It was no dream; or say a dream it was,
Real are the dreams of Gods, and smoothly
   pass
Their pleasures in a long immortal dream.
One warm, flush'd moment, hovering, it
   might seem
Dash'd by the wood-nymph's beauty, so he
·   burn'd;   130
Then, lighting on the printless verdure,
   turn'd

To the swoon'd serpent, and with languid
   arm,
Delicate, put to proof the lithe Caducean
   charm.
So done, upon the nymph his eyes he bent
Full of adoring tears and blandishment,
And towards her stept: she, like a moon in
   wane,
Faded before him, cower'd, nor could re-
   strain
Her fearful sobs, self-folding like a flower
That faints into itself at evening hour:
But the God fostering her chilled hand, 140
She felt the warmth, her eyelids open'd
   bland,
And, like new flowers at morning song of
   bees,
Bloom'd, and gave up her honey to the
   lees.
Into the green-recessed woods they flew;
Nor grew they pale, as mortal lovers do.

Left to herself, the serpent now began
To change; her elfin blood in madness ran,
Her mouth foam'd, and the grass, there-
   with besprent,
Wither'd at dew so sweet and virulent;
Her eyes in torture fix'd, and anguish
   drear,   150
Hot, glazed, and wide, with lid-lashes all
   sear,
Flash'd phosphor and sharp sparks, without
   one cooling tear.
The colours all inflamed throughout her
   train,
She writhed about, convulsed with scarlet
   pain:
A deep volcanian yellow took the place
Of all her milder-mooned body's grace;
And, as the lava ravishes the mead,
Spoilt all her silver mail, and golden brede:
Made gloom of all her frecklings, streaks
   and bars,
Eclipsed her crescents, and lick'd up her
   stars: 160
So that, in moments few, she was undrest
Of all her sapphires, greens, and amethyst,
And rubious-argent: of all these bereft,

Nothing but pain and ugliness were left.
Still shone her crown; that vanish'd, also
    she
Melted and disappear'd as suddenly;
And in the air, her new voice luting soft,
Cried, 'Lycius! gentle Lycius!' — Borne
    aloft
With the bright mists about the mountains
    hoar
These words dissolved: Crete's forests
    heard no more.   170

    Whither fled Lamia, now a lady bright,
A full-born beauty new and exquisite?
She fled into that valley they pass o'er
Who go to Corinth from Cenchreas' shore:
And rested at the foot of those wild hills,
The rugged founts of the Persean rills,
And of that other ridge whose barren back
Stretches, with all its mist and cloudy
    rack,
South-westward to Cleone. There she
    stood   179
About a young bird's flutter from a wood,
Fair, on a sloping green of mossy tread,
By a clear pool, wherein she passioned
To see herself escaped from so sore ills,
While her robes flaunted with the daffo-
    dils.

    Ah, happy Lycius! — for she was a maid
More beautiful than ever twisted braid,
Or sigh'd, or blush'd, or on spring-flowered
    lea
Spread a green kirtle to the minstrelsy:
A virgin purest lipp'd, yet in the lore
Of love deep learned to the red heart's
    core: 190
Not one hour old, yet of sciential brain
To unperplex bliss from its neighbour
    pain;
Define their pettish limits, and estrange
Their points of contact, and swift counter-
    change;
Intrigue with the specious chaos, and dis-
    part
Its most ambiguous atoms with sure art;
As though in Cupid's college she had spent

Sweet days a lovely graduate, still unshent,
And kept his rosy terms in idle languish-
    ment.

    Why this fair creature chose so fairily
By the wayside to linger, we shall see;   201
But first 't is fit to tell how she could muse
And dream, when in the serpent prison-
    house,
Of all she list, strange or magnificent:
How, ever, where she will'd, her spirit
    went;
Whether to faint Elysium, or where
Down through tress-lifting waves the Ne-
    reids fair
Wind into Thetis' bower by many a pearly
    stair;
Or where God Bacchus drains his cups
    divine,
Stretch'd out, at ease, beneath a glutinous
    pine;   210
Or where in Pluto's gardens palatine
Mulciber's columns gleam in far piazzian
    line.
And sometimes into cities she would send
Her dream, with feast and rioting to blend;
And once, while among mortals dreaming
    thus,
She saw the young Corinthian Lycius
Charioting foremost in the envious race,
Like a young Jove with calm uneager
    face,
And fell into a swooning love of him.   219
Now on the moth-time of that evening dim
He would return that way, as well she
    knew,
To Corinth from the shore; for freshly
    blew
The eastern soft wind, and his galley now
Grated the quay-stones with her brazen
    prow
In port Cenchreas, from Egina isle
Fresh anchor'd; whither he had been awhile
To sacrifice to Jove, whose temple there
Waits with high marble doors for blood
    and incense rare.
Jove heard his vows, and better'd his de-
    sire;

For by some freakful chance he made re-
          tire   230
From his companions, and set forth to
          walk,
Perhaps grown wearied of their Corinth
          talk:
Over the solitary hills he fared,
Thoughtless at first, but ere eve's star ap-
          pear'd
His phantasy was lost, where reason fades,
In the calm'd twilight of Platonic shades.
Lamia beheld him coming, near, more
          near —
Close to her passing, in indifference drear,
His silent sandals swept the mossy green;
So neighbour'd to him, and yet so unseen 240
She stood: he pass'd, shut up in mysteries,
His mind wrapp'd like his mantle, while
          her eyes
Follow'd his steps, and her neck regal
          white
Turn'd — syllabling thus, 'Ah, Lycius
          bright!
And will you leave me on the hills alone ?
Lycius, look back! and be some pity shown.'
He did; not with cold wonder fearingly,
But Orpheus-like at an Eurydice;
For so delicious were the words she sung,
It seem'd he had loved them a whole sum-
          mer long: 250
And soon his eyes had drunk her beauty
          up,
Leaving no drop in the bewildering cup,
And still the cup was full, — while he,
          afraid
Lest she should vanish ere his lips had paid
Due adoration, thus began to adore;
Her soft look growing coy, she saw his
          chain so sure:
'Leave thee alone!   Look back!   Ah, God-
          dess, see
Whether my eyes can ever turn from thee !
For pity do not this sad heart belie —
Even as thou vanishest so I shall die.   260
Stay ! though a Naiad of the rivers, stay !
To thy far wishes will thy streams obey:
Stay ! though the greenest woods be thy
          domain,

Alone they can drink up the morning rain:
Though a descended Pleiad, will not one
Of thine harmonious sisters keep in tune
Thy spheres, and as thy silver proxy shine ?
So sweetly to these ravish'd ears of mine
Came thy sweet greeting, that if thou
          shouldst fade,
Thy memory will waste me to a shade: —
For pity do not melt !' — ' If I should
          stay,'   271
Said Lamia, 'here, upon this floor of clay,
And pain my steps upon these flowers too
          rough,
What canst thou say or do of charm enough
To dull the nice remembrance of my home ?
Thou canst not ask me with thee here to
          roam
Over these hills and vales, where no joy
          is, —
Empty of immortality and bliss !
Thou art a scholar, Lycius, and must know
That finer spirits cannot breathe below   280
In human climes, and live: Alas ! poor
          youth,
What taste of purer air hast thou to soothe
My essence ?   What serener palaces,
Where I may all my many senses please,
And by mysterious sleights a hundred thirsts
          appease ?
It cannot be — Adieu !'   So said, she rose
Tiptoe with white arms spread.   He, sick
          to lose
The amorous promise of her lone complain,
Swoon'd murmuring of love, and pale with
          pain.
The cruel lady, without any show   290
Of sorrow for her tender favourite's woe,
But rather, if her eyes could brighter be,
With brighter eyes and slow amenity,
Put her new lips to his, and gave afresh
The life she had so tangled in her mesh:
And as he from one trance was wakening
Into another, she began to sing,
Happy in beauty, life, and love, and every
          thing,
A song of love, too sweet for earthly lyres,
While, like held breath, the stars drew in
          their panting fires.   300

And then she whisper'd in such trembling
tone,
As those who, safe together met alone
For the first time through many anguish'd
days,
Use other speech than looks; bidding him
raise
His drooping head, and clear his soul of
doubt,
For that she was a woman, and without
Any more subtle fluid in her veins
Than throbbing blood, and that the self-
same pains
Inhabited her frail-strung heart as his.
And next she wonder'd how his eyes could
miss   310
Her face so long in Corinth, where, she
said,
She dwelt but half retired, and there had
led
Days happy as the gold coin could invent
Without the aid of love; yet in content
Till she saw him, as once she pass'd him by,
Where 'gainst a column he leant thought-
fully
At Venus' temple porch, 'mid baskets
heap'd
Of amorous herbs and flowers, newly reap'd
Late on that eve, as 't was the night before
The Adonian feast; whereof she saw no
more,   320
But wept alone those days, for why should
she adore?
Lycius from death awoke into amaze,
To see her still, and singing so sweet lays;
Then from amaze into delight he fell
To hear her whisper woman's lore so well;
And every word she spake enticed him on
To unperplex'd delight and pleasure known.
Let the mad poets say whate'er they please
Of the sweets of Fairies, Peris, Goddesses,
There is not such a treat among them
all,   330
Haunters of cavern, lake, and waterfall,
As a real woman, lineal indeed
From Pyrrha's pebbles or old Adam's seed.
Thus gentle Lamia judged, and judged
aright,

That Lycius could not love in half a fright,
So threw the goddess off, and won his heart
More pleasantly by playing woman's part,
With no more awe than what her beauty
gave,
That, while it smote, still guaranteed to
save.
Lycius to all made eloquent reply,   340
Marrying to every word a twin-born sigh:
And last, pointing to Corinth, ask'd her
sweet,
If 't was too far that night for her soft
feet.
The way was short, for Lamia's eagerness
Made, by a spell, the triple league decrease
To a few paces; not at all surmised
By blinded Lycius, so in her comprised:
They pass'd the city gates, he knew not how,
So noiseless, and he never thought to know.

As men talk in a dream, so Corinth all, 350
Throughout her palaces imperial,
And all her populous streets and temples
lewd,
Mutter'd, like tempest in the distance
brew'd,
To the wide-spreaded night above her
towers.
Men, women, rich and poor, in the cool
hours,
Shuffled their sandals o'er the pavement
white,
Companion'd or alone; while many a light
Flared, here and there, from wealthy festi-
vals,
And threw their moving shadows on the
walls,
Or found them cluster'd in the cornieed
shade   360
Of some arch'd temple door, or dusky
colonnade.

Muffling his face, of greeting friends in
fear,
Her fingers he press'd hard, as one came
near
With curl'd gray beard, sharp eyes, and
smooth bald crown,

Slow-stepp'd, and robed in philosophic
    gown:
Lycius shrank closer, as they met and
    past,
Into his mantle, adding wings to haste,
While hurried Lamia trembled: 'Ah,' said
    he,
'Why do you shudder, love, so ruefully?
Why does your tender palm dissolve in
    dew?'—   370
'I'm wearied,' said fair Lamia: 'tell me
    who
Is that old man?   I cannot bring to mind
His features:—Lycius! wherefore did you
    blind
Yourself from his quick eyes?'   Lycius
    replied,
''T is Apollonius sage, my trusty guide
And good instructor; but to-night he seems
The ghost of folly haunting my sweet
    dreams.'

    While yet he spake they had arrived
        before
A pillar'd porch, with lofty portal door,
Where hung a silver lamp, whose phosphor
    glow   380
Reflected in the slabbed steps below,
Mild as a star in water; for so new
And so unsullied was the marble hue,
So through the crystal polish, liquid fine,
Ran the dark veins, that none but feet
    divine
Could e'er have touch'd there.   Sounds
    Æolian
Breathed from the hinges, as the ample
    span
Of the wide doors disclosed a place un-
    known
Some time to any, but those two alone,
And a few Persian mutes, who that same
    year   390
Were seen about the markets: none knew
    where
They could inhabit; the most curious
Were foil'd, who watch'd to trace them to
    their house:
. And but the flitter-winged verse must tell,

For truth's sake, what woe afterwards
    befell,
'T would humour many a heart to leave
    them thus,
Shut from the busy world of more incredu-
    lous.

PART II

LOVE in a hut, with water and a crust,
Is — Love, forgive us! — cinders, ashes,
    dust;
Love in a palace is perhaps at last
More grievous torment than a hermit's
    fast:—
That is a doubtful tale from faery land,
Hard for the non-elect to understand.
Had Lycius lived to hand his story down,
He might have given the moral a fresh
    frown,
Or clench'd it quite: but too short was
    their bliss
To breed distrust and hate, that make the
    soft voice hiss.   10
Besides, there, nightly, with terrific glare,
Love, jealous grown of so complete a pair,
Hover'd and buzz'd his wings, with fearful
    roar,
Above the lintel of their chamber door,
And down the passage cast a glow upon
    the floor.

    For all this came a ruin: side by side
They were enthroned, in the even tide,
Upon a couch, near to a curtaining
Whose airy texture, from a golden string,
Floated into the room, and let appear   20
Unveil'd the summer heaven, blue and
    clear,
Betwixt two marble shafts:— there they
    reposed,
Where use had made it sweet, with eyelids
    closed,
Saving a tithe which love still open kept,
That they might see each other while they
    almost slept;
When from the slope side of a suburb
    hill,

Deafening the swallow's twitter, came a
  thrill
Of trumpets — Lycius started — the sounds
  fled,
But left a thought, a buzzing in his head.
For the first time, since first he harbour'd
  in   30
That purple-lined palace of sweet sin,
His spirit pass'd beyond its golden bourn
Into the noisy world almost forsworn.
The lady, ever watchful, penetrant,
Saw this with pain, so arguing a want
Of something more, more than her empery
Of joys; and she began to moan and sigh
Because he mused beyond her, knowing well
That but a moment's thought is passion's
  passing bell.
'Why do you sigh, fair creature?' whis-
  per'd he: 40
'Why do you think?' return'd she ten-
  derly:
'You have deserted me; — where am I
  now?
Not in your heart while care weighs on
  your brow:
No, no, you have dismiss'd me; and I go
From your breast houseless: aye, it must be
  so.'
He answer'd, bending to her open eyes,
Where he was mirror'd small in paradise,
'My silver planet, both of eve and morn!
Why will you plead yourself so sad forlorn,
While I am striving how to fill my heart   50
With deeper crimson, and a double smart?
How to entangle, trammel up and snare
Your soul in mine, and labyrinth you
  there,
Like the bid scent in an unbudded rose?
Aye, a sweet kiss — you see your mighty
  woes.
My thoughts! shall I unveil them? Lis-
  ten then!
What mortal hath a prize, that other men
May be confounded and abash'd withal,
  but lets it sometimes pace abroad majes-
  tical,
  and triumph, as in thee I should rejoice 60
  amid the hoarse alarm of Corinth's voice.

Let my foes choke, and my friends shout
  afar,
While through the thronged streets your
  bridal car
Wheels round its dazzling spokes.' — The
  lady's cheek
Trembled; she nothing said, but, pale and
  meek,
Arose and knelt before him, wept a rain
Of sorrows at his words; at last with
  pain
Beseeching him, the while his hand she
  wrung,
To change his purpose. He thereat was
  stung,
Perverse, with stronger fancy to reclaim 70
Her wild and timid nature to his aim;
Besides, for all his love, in self despite,
Against his better self, he took delight
Luxurious in her sorrows, soft and new.
His passion, cruel grown, took on a hue
Fierce and sanguineous as 't was possible
In one whose brow had no dark veins to
  swell.
Fine was the mitigated fury, like
Apollo's presence when in act to strike
The serpent — Ha! the serpent! certes,
  she   80
Was none. She burnt, she loved the
  tyranny,
And, all subdued, consented to the hour
When to the bridal he should lead his par-
  amour.
Whispering in midnight silence, said the
  youth,
'Sure some sweet name thou hast, though,
  by my truth,
I have not ask'd it, ever thinking thee
Not mortal, but of heavenly progeny,
As still I do. Hast any mortal name,
Fit appellation for this dazzling frame?
Or friends or kinsfolk on the citied earth,
To share our marriage feast and nuptial
  mirth?'   91
'I have no friends,' said Lamia, 'no, not
  one;
My presence in wide Corinth hardly known:
My parents' bones are in their dusty urns

Sepulchred, where no kindled incense
    burns,
Seeing all their luckless race are dead,
    save me,
And I neglect the holy rite for thee.
Even as you list invite your many guests;
But if, as now it seems, your vision rests
With any pleasure on me, do not bid   100
Old Apollonius — from him keep me hid.'
Lycius, perplex'd at words so blind and
    blank,
Made close inquiry; from whose touch she
    shrank,
Feigning a sleep; and he to the dull shade
Of deep sleep in a moment was betray'd.

    It was the custom then to bring away
The bride from home at blushing shut of
    day,
Veil'd, in a chariot, heralded along
By strewn flowers, torches, and a marriage
    song,
With other pageants: but this fair un-
    known   110
Had not a friend.   So being left alone,
(Lycius was gone to summon all his kin,)
And knowing surely she could never win
His foolish heart from its mad pompous-
    ness,
She set herself, high-thoughted, how to
    dress
The misery in fit magnificence.
She did so, but 't is doubtful how and
    whence
Came, and who were her subtle servitors.
About the halls, and to and from the doors,
There was a noise of wings, till in short
    space   120
The glowing banquet-room shone with
    wide-arched grace.
A haunting music, sole perhaps and lone
Supportress of the faery-roof, made moan
Throughout, as fearful the whole charm
    might fade.
Fresh carved cedar, mimicking a glade
Of palm and plantain, met from either side,
High in the midst, in honour of the bride:
Two palms and then two plantains, and so on,

From either side their stems branch'd one
    to one
All down the aisled place; and beneath all
There ran a stream of lamps straight on
    from wall to wall.   131
So canopied, lay an untasted feast
Teeming with odours.   Lamia, regal drest,
Silently paced about, and as she went,
In pale contented sort of discontent,
Mission'd her viewless servants to enrich
The fretted splendour of each nook and
    niche.
Between the tree-stems, marbled plain at
    first,
Came jasper panels; then, anon, there burst
Forth creeping imagery of slighter trees, 140
And with the larger wove in small intrica-
    cies.
Approving all, she faded at self-will,
And shut the chamber up, close, hush'd
    and still,
Complete and ready for the revels rude,
When dreadful guests would come to spoil
    her solitude.

    The day appear'd, and all the gossip
    rout.
O senseless Lycius!   Madman! wherefore
    flout
The silent-blessing fate, warm cloister'd
    hours,
And show to common eyes these secret
    bowers?
The herd approach'd; each guest, with busy
    brain,   150
Arriving at the portal, gazed amain,
And enter'd marvelling: for they knew the
    street,
Remember'd it from childhood all complete
Without a gap, yet ne'er before had seen
That royal porch, that high-built fair de-
    mesne;
So in they hurried all, mazed, curious and
    keen:
Save one, who look'd thereon with eye se-
    vere,
And with calm-planted steps walk'd in aus-
    tere:

'T was Apollonius: something too he
    laugh'd,
As though some knotty problem, that had
    daft   160
His patient thought, had now begun to
    thaw,
And solve and melt: — 't was just as he
    foresaw.

He met within the murmurous vestibule
His young disciple. ' 'T is no common rule,
Lycius,' said he, 'for uninvited guest
To force himself upon you, and infest
With an unbidden presence the bright
    throng
Of younger friends; yet must I do this
    wrong,
And you forgive me.' Lycius blush'd, and
    led
The old man through the inner doors broad-
    spread;   170
With reconciling words and courteous mien
Turning into sweet milk the sophist's
    spleen.

Of wealthy lustre was the banquet-room,
Fill'd with pervading brilliance and per-
    fume:
Before each lucid panel fuming stood
A censer fed with myrrh and spiced wood,
Each by a sacred tripod held aloft,
Whose slender feet wide-swerved upon the
    soft
Wool - woofed carpets: fifty wreaths of
    smoke
From fifty censers their light voyage took
To the high roof, still mimick'd as they
    rose   181
Along the mirror'd walls by twin-clouds
    odorous.
Twelve sphered tables, by silk seats in-
    spher'd,
High as the level of a man's breast rear'd
On libbard's paws, upheld the heavy gold
Of cups and goblets, and the store thrice told
Of Ceres' horn, and, in huge vessels, wine
Came from the gloomy tun with merry
    shine.

Thus loaded with a feast the tables stood,
Each shrining in the midst the image of a
    God.   190

When in an antechamber every guest
Had felt the cold full sponge to pleasure
    press'd,
By ministering slaves, upon his hands and
    feet,
And fragrant oils with ceremony meet
Pour'd on his hair, they all moved to the
    feast
In white robes, and themselves in order
    placed
Around the silken couches, wondering
Whence all this mighty cost and blaze of
    wealth could spring.

Soft went the music the soft air along,
While fluent Greek a vowel'd under-song
Kept up among the guests, discoursing
    low   201
At first, for scarcely was the wine at flow;
But when the happy vintage touch'd their
    brains,
Louder they talk, and louder come the
    strains
Of powerful instruments: — the gorgeous
    dyes,
The space, the splendour of the draperies,
The roof of awful richness, nectarous cheer,
Beautiful slaves, and Lamia's self, appear,
Now, when the wine has done its rosy
    deed,
And every soul from human trammels
    freed,   210
No more so strange; for merry wine, sweet
    wine,
Will make Elysian shades not too fair, too
    divine.
Soon was God Bacchus at meridian height;
Flush'd were their cheeks, and bright eyes
    double bright:
Garlands of every green, and every scent
From vales deflower'd, or forest - trees
    branch-rent,
In baskets of bright osier'd gold were
    brought

High as the handles heap'd, to suit the thought
Of every guest: that each, as he did please,
Might fancy-fit his brows, silk-pillow'd at his ease.   220

What wreath for Lamia? What for Lycius?
What for the sage, old Apollonius?
Upon her aching forehead be there hung
The leaves of willow and of adder's tongue;
And for the youth, quick, let us strip for him
The thyrsus, that his watching eyes may swim
Into forgetfulness; and, for the sage,
Let spear-grass and the spiteful thistle wage
War on his temples.   Do not all charms fly
At the mere touch of cold philosophy?   230
There was an awful rainbow once in heaven:
We know her woof, her texture; she is given
In the dull catalogue of common things.
Philosophy will clip an Angel's wings,
Conquer all mysteries by rule and line,
Empty the haunted air, and gnomed mine —
Unweave a rainbow, as it erewhile made
The tender-person'd Lamia melt into a shade.

By her glad Lycius sitting, in chief place,
Scarce saw in all the room another face,   240
Till, checking his love trance, a cup he took
Full brimm'd, and opposite sent forth a look
'Cross the broad table, to beseech a glance
From his old teacher's wrinkled countenance,
And pledge him.   The bald-head philosopher
Had fix'd his eye, without a twinkle or stir,
Full on the alarmed beauty of the bride,
Brow-beating her fair form, and troubling her sweet pride.

Lycius then press'd her hand, with devout touch,
As pale it lay upon the rosy couch: 250
'T was icy, and the cold ran through his veins;
Then sudden it grew hot, and all the pains
Of an unnatural heat shot to his heart.
'Lamia, what means this? Wherefore dost thou start?
Know'st thou that man?' Poor Lamia answer'd not.
He gazed into her eyes, and not a jot
Own'd they the lovelorn piteous appeal:
More, more he gazed: his human senses reel:
Some hungry spell that loveliness absorbs:
There was no recognition in those orbs.   260
'Lamia!' he cried — and no soft-toned reply.
The many heard, and the loud revelry
Grew hush: the stately music no more breathes:
The myrtle sicken'd in a thousand wreaths.
By faint degrees, voice, lute, and pleasure ceased;
A deadly silence step by step increased,
Until it seem'd a horrid presence there,
And not a man but felt the terror in his hair.
'Lamia!' he shriek'd; and nothing but the shriek
With its sad echo did the silence break.   270
'Begone, foul dream!' he cried, gazing again
In the bride's face, where now no azure vein
Wander'd on fair-spaced temples; no soft bloom
Misted the cheek; no passion to illume
The deep-recessed vision: — all was blight;
Lamia, no longer fair, there sat a deadly white.
'Shut, shut those juggling eyes, thou ruthless man!
Turn them aside, wretch! or the righteous ban
Of all the Gods, whose dreadful images
Here represent their shadowy presences,

May pierce them on the sudden with the
    thorn   281
Of painful blindness; leaving thee for-
    lorn,
In trembling dotage to the feeblest fright
Of conscience, for their long-offended
    might,
For all thine impious proud-heart sophis-
    tries,
Unlawful magic, and enticing lies.
Corinthians! look upon that gray-beard
    wretch!
Mark how, possess'd, his lashless eyelids
    stretch
Around his demon eyes! Corinthians, see!
My sweet bride withers at their potency.' 290
'Fool!' said the sophist, in an under-tone
Gruff with contempt; which a death-nigh-
    ing moan
From Lycius answer'd, as heart-struck and
    lost,
He sank supine beside the aching ghost.
'Fool! Fool!' repeated he, while his eyes
    still

Relented not, nor moved; 'from every ill
Of life have I preserved thee to this day,
And shall I see thee made a serpent's
    prey?'
Then Lamia breathed death breath; the
    sophist's eye,
Like a sharp spear, went through her ut-
    terly,   300
Keen, cruel, perceant, stinging: she, as
    well
As her weak hand could any meaning tell,
Motion'd him to be silent; vainly so,
He look'd and look'd again a level — No!
'A serpent!' echoed he; no sooner said,
Than with a frightful scream she vanished:
And Lycius' arms were empty of delight,
As were his limbs of life, from that same
    night.
On the high couch he lay! — his friends
    came round —
Supported him — no pulse or breath they
    found,   310
And, in its marriage robe, the heavy body
    wound.

DRAMAS

OTHO THE GREAT

A TRAGEDY IN FIVE ACTS

When Keats went to the Isle of Wight in the early summer of 1819, it was with the determination to make his literary powers yield him a support, and the theatre, which he knew well, offered the surest means, in his judgment, for an immediate return. There was, indeed, something of a literary revival of the drama at this time, and Keats had often discussed with his friends the merits of plays then before the public, and especially the character of Kean's acting. They were rather skeptical of Keats's ability to produce a successful play, and their doubts had some good basis, if we may judge from the account which Charles Armitage Brown gives of Keats's mode of composition. Lord Houghton quotes the following from a manuscript by Brown, who was Keats's companion at Shanklin: 'At Shanklin he undertook a difficult task: I engaged to furnish him with the title, characters and dramatic conduct of a tragedy, and he was to enwrap it in poetry. The progress of this work was curious, for while I sat opposite to him, he caught my description of each scene entire, with the characters to be brought forward, the events, and everything connected with it. Thus he went on, scene after scene, never knowing nor enquiring into the scene which was to follow, until four acts were completed. It was then he required to know at once all the events that were to occupy the fifth act; I explained them to him, but, after a patient hearing and some thought, he insisted that many incidents in it were too humorous, or, as he termed them, too melodramatic. He wrote the fifth act in accordance with his own views, and so contented was I with his poetry that at the time, and for a long time after, I thought he was in the right.'

Keats himself says little of the tragedy, except as a piece of work solely designed for pro-

fit. 'Brown and I,' he writes to John Taylor, his publisher, 'have together been engaged (this I should wish to remain secret) on a Tragedy which I have just finished and from which we hope to share moderate profits. . . . I feel every confidence that, if I choose, I may be a popular writer. That I will never be; but for all that I will get a livelihood.' He wrote shortly after to the same friend: 'Brown likes the tragedy very much. But he is not a fit judge of it, as I have only acted as midwife to his plot; and of course he will be fond of his child.' The money to be got from the tragedy was uppermost in his mind when he wrote to his brother George, who shared his pecuniary difficulties: 'We are certainly in a very low estate — I say we, for I am in such a situation, that were it not for the assistance of Brown and Taylor, I must be as badly off as a man can be. I could not raise any sum by the promise of any poem, no, not by the mortgage of my intellect. We must wait a little while. I really have hopes of success. I have finished a tragedy, which if it succeeds will enable me to sell what I may have in manuscript to a good advantage. I have passed my time in reading, writing, and fretting — the last I intend to give up, and stick to the other two. They are the only chances of benefit to us. . . . Take matters as coolly as you can; and confidently expecting help from England, act as if no help were nigh. Mine, I am sure, is a tolerable tragedy; it would have been a bank to me, if just as I had finished it, I had not heard of Kean's resolution to go to America. That was the worst news I could have had. There is no actor can do the principal character besides Kean. At Covent Garden there is a great chance of its being damn'd. Were it to succeed even there it would lift me out of the mire; I mean the mire of a bad reputation which is continually rising against me. My name with the literary fashionables is vulgar. I am a weaver-boy to them. A tragedy would lift me out of this mess, and mess it is as far as regards our pockets.'

Keats continued to pin his faith on Kean. ' The report seems now,' he writes to the same, September 27, ' more in favour of Kean's stopping in England. If he should I have confident hopes of our tragedy. If he invokes the hot-blooded character of Ludolph, — and he is the only actor that can do it, — he will add to his own fame and improve my fortune.' Keats waited with slowly ebbing hopes. Elliston read it, but wished to put it off till another season. ' Perhaps,' Keats writes in December, ' we may give it another furbish, and try it at Covent Garden. 'T would do one's heart good to see Macready in Ludolph.' But the play never was acted at either Drury Lane or Covent Garden.

OTHO THE GREAT

DRAMATIS PERSONÆ

OTHO THE GREAT, *Emperor of Germany.*
LUDOLPH, *his Son.*
CONRAD, *Duke of Franconia.*
ALBERT, *a Knight, favoured by Otho.*
SIGIFRED, *an Officer, friend of Ludolph.*
THEODORE, } *Officers.*
GONFRED, }
ETHELBERT, *an Abbot.*
GERSA, *Prince of Hungary.*
An Hungarian Captain.
Physician.
Page.
Nobles, Knights, Attendants, and Soldiers.
ERMINIA, *Niece of Otho.*
AURANTHE, *Conrad's Sister.*
Ladies and Attendants.
SCENE. — *The Castle of Friedburg, its vicinity, and the Hungarian Camp.*
TIME. — *One Day.*

ACT I

SCENE I. — *An Apartment in the Castle*

Enter CONRAD.

Conrad. So, I am safe emerged from these broils !
Amid the wreck of thousands I am whole;
For every crime I have a laurel-wreath,
For every lie a lordship. Nor yet has
My ship of fortune furl'd her silken sails, —
Let her glide on ! This danger'd neck is saved,
By dexterous policy, from the rebel's axe;
And of my ducal palace not one stone
Is bruised by the Hungarian petards.
Toil hard, ye slaves, and from the miser-earth   10
Bring forth once more my bullion, treasured deep,
With all my jewel'd salvers, silver and gold,
And precious goblets that make rich the wine.
But why do I stand babbling to myself ?
Where is Auranthe ? I have news for her
Shall —

Enter AURANTHE.

Auranthe. Conrad ! what tidings ? Good, if I may guess
From your alert eyes and high-lifted brows.
What tidings of the battle ? Albert ? Ludolph ? Otho ?
Conrad. You guess aright. And, sister, slurring o'er
Our by-gone quarrels, I confess my heart
Is beating with a child's anxiety,   21
To make our golden fortune known to you.
Auranthe. So serious ?
Conrad.   Yes, so serious, that before
I utter even the shadow of a hint
Concerning what will make that sin-worn cheek
Blush joyous blood through every lineament,
You must make here a solemn vow to me.
Auranthe. I pr'ythee, Conrad, do not overact
The hypocrite. What vow would you impose ?
Conrad. Trust me for once. That you may be assured   30
'T is not confiding to a broken reed,
A poor court-bankrupt, outwitted and lost,

Revolve these facts in your acutest mood,
In such a mood as now you listen to me: —
A few days since, I was an open rebel, —
Against the Emperor, had suborn'd his
    son, —
Drawn off his nobles to revolt, — and
    shown
Contented fools causes for discontent,
Fresh hatched in my ambition's eagle-nest;
So thrived I as a rebel, — and, behold !   40
Now I am Otho's favourite, his dear friend,
His right hand, his brave Conrad.
    Auranthe.   I confess
You have intrigued with these unsteady
    times
To admiration; but to be a favourite —
    Conrad. I saw my moment. The Hun-
        garians,
Collected silently in holes and corners,
Appear'd, a sudden host, in the open day.
I should have perish'd in our empire's
    wreck,
But, calling interest loyalty, swore faith
To most believing Otho; and so help'd   50
His blood-stain'd ensigns to the victory
In yesterday's hard fight, that it has turn'd
The edge of his sharp wrath to eager kind-
    ness.
    Auranthe. So far yourself. But what is
        this to me
More than that I am glad ? I gratulate
    you.
    Conrad. Yes, sister, but it does regard
        you greatly,
Nearly, momentously, — aye, painfully !
Make me this vow —
    Auranthe.   Concerning whom or what ?
    Conrad. Albert !
    Auranthe. I would inquire somewhat of
        him:
You had a letter from me touching him ? 60
No treason 'gainst his head in deed or
    word !
Surely you spared him at my earnest
    prayer ?
Give me the letter — it should not ex-
    ist !

    Conrad. At one pernicious charge of the
        enemy,
I, for a moment-whiles, was prisoner ta'en
And rifled, — stuff ! the horses' hoofs have
    minced it !
    Auranthe. He is alive ?
    Conrad.   He is ! but here make oath
To alienate him from your scheming brain,
Divorce him from your solitary thoughts,
And cloud him in such utter banishment, 70
That when his person meets again your
    eye,
Your vision shall quite lose its memory,
And wander past him as through vacancy.
    Auranthe. I 'll not be perjured.
    Conrad.   No, nor great, nor mighty;
You would not wear a crown, or rule a
    kingdom.
To you it is indifferent.
    Auranthe.   What means this ?
    Conrad. You 'll not be perjured ! Go to
        Albert then,
That camp-mushroom — dishonour of our
    house.
Go, page his dusty heels upon a march,
Furbish his jingling baldric while he sleeps,
And share his mouldy ration in a siege. 81
Yet stay, — perhaps a charm may call you
    back,
And make the widening circlets of your
    eyes
Sparkle with healthy fevers. — The Em-
    peror
Hath given consent that you should marry
    Ludolph !
    Auranthe. Can it be, brother ? For a
        golden crown
With a queen's awful lips I doubly thank
    you !
This is to wake in Paradise ! Farewell
Thou clod of yesterday — 't was not my-
    self !
Not till this moment did I ever feel   90
My spirit's faculties ! I 'll flatter you
For this, and be you ever proud of it;
Thou, Jove-like, struck'dst thy forehead,
And from the teeming marrow of thy brain

I spring complete Minerva! but the
     prince —
His highness Ludolph — where is he?
     Conrad.   I know not:
When, lackying my counsel at a beck,
The rebel lords, on bended knees, received
The Emperor's pardon, Ludolph kept aloof,
Sole, in a stiff, fool-hardy, sulky pride; 100
Yet, for all this, I never saw a father
In such a sickly longing for his son.
We shall soon see him, for the Emperor
He will be here this morning.
     Auranthe.   That I heard
Among the midnight rumours from the
     camp.
     Conrad. You give up Albert to me?
     Auranthe.   Harm him not!
E'en for his highness Ludolph's sceptry
     hand,
I would not Albert suffer any wrong.
     Conrad. Have I not laboured, plotted —?
     Auranthe.   See you spare him:
Nor be pathetic, my kind benefactor! 110
On all the many bounties of your hand, —
'T was for yourself you laboured — not for
     me!
Do you not count, when I am queen, to
     take
Advantage of your chance discoveries
Of my poor secrets, and so hold a rod
Over my life?
     Conrad. Let not this slave — this vil-
     lain —
Be cause of feud between us. See! he
     comes!
Look, woman, look, your Albert is quite
     safe!
In haste it seems. Now shall I be in the
     way,
And wish'd with silent curses in my grave,
Or side by side with' whelmed mariners. 121

         Enter ALBERT.

     Albert. Fair on your graces fall this
     early morrow!
So it is like to do without my prayers,
For your right noble names, like favourite
     tunes,

Have fallen full frequent from our Em-
     peror's lips,
High commented with smiles.
     Auranthe.   Noble Albert!
     Conrad (aside). Noble!
     Auranthe. Such salutation argues a glad
     heart
In our prosperity. We thank you, sir.
     Albert.   Lady!
O, would to Heaven your poor servant
Could do you better service than mere
     words!   130
But I have other greeting than mine own,
From no less man than Otho, who has sent
This ring as pledge of dearest amity;
'T is chosen I hear from Hymen's jewelry,
And you will prize it, lady, I doubt not,
Beyond all pleasures past, and all to come.
To you great duke —
     Conrad.   To me! What of me, ha?
     Albert. What pleased your grace to say?
     Conrad.   Your message, sir!
     Albert. You mean not this to me?
     Conrad.   Sister, this way;
For there shall be no ' gentle Alberts' now,
                       [*Aside.*
No 'sweet Auranthes!'   141
        [*Exeunt* CONRAD *and* AURANTHE.
     Albert (solus). The duke is out of temper;
     if he knows
More than a brother of his sister ought,
I should not quarrel with his peevishness.
Auranthe — Heaven preserve her always
     fair! —
Is in the heady, proud, ambitious vein;
I bicker not with her, — bid her farewell!
She has taken flight from me, then let her
     soar, —
He is a fool who stands at pining gaze!
But for poor Ludolph, he is food for sor-
     row: 150
No leveling bluster of my licensed thoughts,
No military swagger of my mind,
Can smother from myself the wrong I 've
     done him, —
Without design indeed, — yet it is so, —
And opiate for the conscience have I none!
                       [*Exit.*

SCENE II. — *The Court-yard of the Castle*

Martial Music. Enter, from the outer gate, OTHO, *Nobles, Knights, and Attendants. The Soldiers halt at the gate, with Banners in sight.*

Otho. Where is my noble Herald ?

Enter CONRAD, *from the Castle, attended by two Knights and Servants.* ALBERT *following.*

      Well, hast told
Auranthe our intent imperial ?
Lest our rent banners, too o' the sudden shown,
Should fright her silken casements, and dismay
Her household to our lack of entertainment.
A victory !
 Conrad. God save illustrious Otho !
 Otho. Aye, Conrad, it will pluck out all gray hairs;
It is the best physician for the spleen;
The courtliest inviter to a feast;
The subtlest excuser of small faults; 10
And a nice judge in the age and smack of wine.

Enter from the Castle, AURANTHE, *followed by Pages, holding up her robes, and a train of Women. She kneels.*

Hail my sweet hostess ! I do thank the stars,
Or my good soldiers, or their ladies' eyes,
That, after such a merry battle fought,
I can, all safe in body and in soul,
Kiss your fair hand and lady fortune's too.
My ring ! now, on my life, it doth rejoice
These lips to feel 't on this soft ivory !
Keep it, my brightest daughter; it may prove
The little prologue to a line of kings. 20
I strove against thee and my hot-blood son,
Dull blockhead that I was to be so blind,
But now my sight is clear; forgive me, lady.

Auranthe. My lord, I was a vassal to your frown,
And now your favour makes me but more humble;
In wintry winds the simple snow is safe,
But fadeth at the greeting of the sun:
Unto thine anger I might well have spoken,
Taking on me a woman's privilege,
But this so sudden kindness makes me dumb. 30
 Otho. What need of this ? Enough, if you will be
A potent tutoress to my wayward boy.
And teach him, what it seems his nurse could not,
To say, for once, I thank you ! Sigifred !
 Albert. He has not yet returned, my gracious liege.
 Otho. What then ! No tidings of my friendly Arab ?
 Conrad. None, mighty Otho.
  [*To one of his Knights who goes out.*
     Send forth instantly
An hundred horsemen from my honoured gates,
To scour the plains and search the cottages.
Cry a reward, to him who shall first bring
News of that vanished Arabian, 41
A full-heap'd helmet of the purest gold.
 Otho. More thanks, good Conrad; for, except my son's,
There is no face I rather would behold
Than that same quick-eyed pagan's. By the saints,
This coming night of banquets must not light
Her dazzling torches; nor the music breathe
Smooth, without clashing cymbal, tones of peace
And in-door melodies; nor the ruddy wine
Ebb spouting to the lees; if I pledge not, 50
In my first cup, that Arab !
 Albert.   Mighty Monarch,
I wonder not this stranger's victor-deeds
So hang upon your spirit. Twice in the fight

It was my chance to meet his olive brow,
Triumphant in the enemy's shatter'd
   rhomb;
And, to say truth, in any Christian arm
I never saw such prowess.
   Otho.   Did you ever?
O, 't is a noble boy! — tut! — what do I
   say?
I mean a triple Saladin, whose eyes,
When in the glorious scuffle they met
   mine,   60
Seem'd to say — ' Sleep, old man, in safety
   sleep;
I am the victory!'
   Conrad.   Pity he's not here.
   Otho. And my son too, pity he is not
here.
Lady Auranthe, I would not make you
   blush,
But can you give a guess where Ludolph
   is?
Know you not of him?
   Auranthe. Indeed, my liege, no secret —
   Otho. Nay, nay, without more words,
   dost know of him?
   Auranthe. I would I were so over-fortu-
   nate,
Both for his sake and mine, and to make
   glad
A father's ears with tidings of his son.   70
   Otho. I see 't is like to be a tedious day.
Were Theodore and Gonfred and the rest
Sent forth with my commands?
   Albert.   Aye, my lord.
   Otho. And no news! No news! 'Faith!
   't is very strange
He thus avoids us. Lady, is 't not strange?
Will he be truant to you too? It is a
   shame.
   Conrad. Will 't please your highness en-
   ter, and accept,
The unworthy welcome of your servant's
   house?
Leaving your cares to one whose diligence
May in few hours make pleasures of them
   all.   80
   Otho. Not so tedious, Conrad. No, no,
   no, —

I must see Ludolph or the — What's that
   shout?
   Voices without. Huzza! huzza! Long live
   the Emperor!
   Other voices. Fall back! Away there!
   Otho.   Say what noise is that?

ALBERT *advancing from the back of the
Stage, whither he had hastened on hearing
the cheers of the soldiery.*

   Albert. It is young Gersa, the Hungarian
   prince,
Pick'd like a red stag from the fallow herd
Of prisoners. Poor prince, forlorn he steps,
Slow, and demure, and proud in his de-
   spair.
If I may judge by his so tragic bearing,   89
His eye not downcast, and his folded arm,
He doth this moment wish himself asleep
Among his fallen captains on yon plains.

   Enter GERSA, *in chains, and guarded.*

   Otho. Well said, Sir Albert.
   Gersa.   Not a word of greeting,
No welcome to a princely visitor,
Most mighty Otho? Will not my great
   host
Vouchsafe a syllable, before he bids
His gentlemen conduct me with all care
To some securest lodging — cold perhaps!
   Otho. What mood is this? Hath fortune
   touch'd thy brain?
   Gersa. O kings and princes of this fev'-
   rous world,   100
What abject things, what mockeries must
   ye be,
What nerveless minions of safe palaces!
When here, a monarch, whose proud foot
   is used
To fallen princes' necks, as to his stirrup,
Must needs exclaim that I am mad for-
   sooth,
Because I cannot flatter with bent knees
My conqueror!
   Otho.   Gersa, I think you wrong me:
I think I have a better fame abroad.
   Gersa. I pr'ythee mock me not with gen-
   tle speech,   109

But, as a favour, bid me from thy presence;
Let me no longer be the wondering food
Of all these eyes; pr'ythee command me
　　hence!
　　Otho. Do not mistake me, Gersa. That
　　you may not,
Come, fair Auranthe, try if your soft hands
Can manage those hard rivets to set free
So brave a prince and soldier.
　　Auranthe (sets him free). Welcome task!
　　Gersa. I am wound up in deep astonish-
　　ment!
Thank you, fair lady. Otho! emperor!
You rob me of myself; my dignity
Is now your infant; I am a weak child.　120
　　Otho. Give me your hand, and let this
　　kindly grasp
Live in our memories.
　　Gersa. 　　　　　　In mine it will.
I blush to think of my unchasten'd tongue;
But I was haunted by the monstrous ghost
Of all our slain battalions. Sire, reflect,
And pardon you will grant, that, at this
　　hour,
The bruised remnants of our stricken camp
Are huddling undistinguish'd my dear
　　friends,
With common thousands, into shallow
　　graves.
　　Otho. Enough, most noble Gersa. You
　　are free　　　　　　　　　　　　　130
To cheer the brave remainder of your host
By your own healing presence, and that
　　too,
Not as their leader merely, but their king;
For, as I hear, the wily enemy,
Who eased the crownet from your infant
　　brows,
Bloody Taraxa, is among the dead.
　　Gersa. Then I retire, so generous Otho
　　please,
Bearing with me a weight of benefits
Too heavy to be borne.
　　Otho. 　　　　　　It is not so;
Still understand me, King of Hungary,　140
Nor judge my open purposes awry.
Though I did hold you high in my esteem
For your self's sake, I do not personate

The stage-play emperor to entrap applause,
To set the silly sort o' the world agape,
And make the politic smile; no, I have
　　heard
How in the Council you condemn'd this
　　war,
Urging the perfidy of broken faith, —
For that I am your friend.
　　Gersa. 　　　　　　If ever, sire,　150
You are my enemy, I dare here swear
'T will not be Gersa's fault. Otho, fare-
　　well!
　　Otho. Will you return, Prince, to our
　　banqueting?
　　Gersa. As to my father's board I will
　　return.
　　Otho. Conrad, with all due ceremony,
　　give
The prince a regal escort to his camp;
Albert, go thou and bear him company.
Gersa, farewell!
　　Gersa. 　　　　All happiness attend you!
　　Otho. Return with what good speed you
　　may; for soon
We must consult upon our terms of peace.
　　[*Exeunt* GERSA *and* ALBERT *with others.*
And thus a marble column do I build　160
To prop my empire's dome. Conrad, in
　　thee
I have another steadfast one, to uphold
The portals of my state; and, for my own
Pre-eminence and safety, I will strive
To keep thy strength upon its pedestal.
For, without thee, this day I might have
　　been
A show-monster about the streets of Prague,
In chains, as just now stood that noble
　　prince:
And then to me no mercy had been shown,
For when the conquer'd lion is once dun-
　　geon'd,　　　　　　　　　　　　　170
Who lets him forth again? or dares to
　　give
An old lion sugar-cakes of mild reprieve?
Not to thine ear alone I make confession,
But to all here, as, by experience,
I know how the great basement of all
　　power

Is frankness, and a true tongue to the
world;
And how intriguing secrecy is proof
Of fear and weakness, and a hollow state.
Conrad, I owe thee much.
    Conrad.   To kiss that hand,
My emperor, is ample recompense,   180
For a mere act of duty.
    Otho.   Thou art wrong;
For what can any man on earth do more ?
We will make trial of your house's wel-
    come,
My bright Auranthe !
    Conrad.   How is Friedburg honoured !

    Enter ETHELBERT *and six Monks.*

    Ethelbert. The benison of heaven on your
    head,
Imperial Otho !
    Otho.   Who stays me ? Speak ! Quick !
    Ethelbert. Pause but one moment, mighty
    conqueror !
Upon the threshold of this house of joy.
    Otho. Pray, do not prose, good Ethelbert,
    but speak
What is your purpose.
    Ethelbert. The restoration of some cap-
    tive maids,   190
Devoted to Heaven's pious ministries,
Who, driven forth from their religious
    cells,
And kept in thraldom by our enemy,
When late this province was a lawless spoil,
Still weep amid the wild Hungarian camp,
Though hemm'd around by thy victorious
    arms.
    Otho. Demand the holy sisterhood in our
    name
From Gersa's tents.   Farewell, old Ethel-
    bert.
    Ethelbert. The saints will bless you for
    this pious care.
    Otho. Daughter, your hand; Ludolph's
    would fit it best.   200
    Conrad. Ho ! let the music sound !
[*Music.* ETHELBERT *raises his hands, as in
benediction of* OTHO. *Exeunt severally.
The scene closes on them.*

    SCENE III. — *The Country, with the
    Castle in the distance*

    Enter LUDOLPH *and* SIGIFRED.

    Ludolph. You have my secret; let it not
    be breathed.
    Sigifred. Still give me leave to wonder
    that the Prince
Ludolph and the swift Arab are the same;
Still to rejoice that 't was a German
    arm
Death doing in a turban'd masquerade.
    Ludolph. The emperor must not know it,
    Sigifred.
    Sigifred. I pr'ythee, why ? What hap-
    pier hour of time
Could thy pleased star point down upon
    from heaven
With silver index, bidding thee make
    peace ?
    Ludolph. Still it must not be known, good
    Sigifred;   10
The star may point oblique.
    Sigifred.   If Otho knew
His son to be that unknown Mussulman,
After whose spurring heels he sent me
    forth,
With one of his well - pleased Olympian
    oaths,
The charters of man's greatness, at this
    hour
He would be watching round the castle
    walls,
And, like an anxious warder, strain his
    sight
For the first glimpse of such a son re-
    turn'd —
Ludolph, that blast of the Hungarians,
That Saracenic meteor of the fight,   20
That silent fury, whose fell scimitar
Kept danger all aloof from Otho's head,
And left him space for wonder.
    Ludolph.   Say no more.
Not as a swordsman would I pardon claim,
But as a son. The bronzed centurion,
Long toil'd in foreign wars, and whose high
    deeds
Are shaded in a forest of tall spears,

Known only to his troop, hath greater plea
Of favour with my sire than I can have.
   Sigifred. My lord, forgive me that I cannot see   30
How this proud temper with clear reason squares.
What made you then, with such an anxious love,
Hover around that life, whose bitter days
You vext with bad revolt? Was 't opium,
Or the mad-fumed wine? Nay, do not frown,
I rather would grieve with you than upbraid.
   Ludolph. I do believe you. No, 't was not to make
A father his son's debtor, or to heal
His deep heart-sickness for a rebel child.
'T was done in memory of my boyish days,   41
Poor cancel for his kindness to my youth,
For all his calming of my childish griefs,
And all his smiles upon my merriment.
No, not a thousand foughten fields could sponge
Those days paternal from my memory,
Though now upon my head he heaps disgrace.
   Sigifred. My prince, you think too harshly —
   Ludolph.   Can I so?
Hath he not gall'd my spirit to the quick?
And with a sullen rigour obstinate   49
Pour'd out a phial of wrath upon my faults?
Hunted me as the Tartar does the boar,
Driven me to the very edge o' the world,
And almost put a price upon my head?
   Sigifred. Remember how he spared the rebel lords.
   Ludolph. Yes, yes, I know he hath a noble nature
That cannot trample on the fallen. But his
Is not the only proud heart in his realm.
He hath wrong'd me, and I have done him wrong;
He hath loved me, and I have shown him kindness;
We should be almost equal.

   Sigifred.   Yet, for all this,
I would you had appear'd among those lords,   61
And ta'en his favour.
   Ludolph.   Ha! till now I thought
My friend had held poor Ludolph's honour dear.
What! would you have me sue before his throne
And kiss the courtier's missal, its silk steps?
Or hug the golden housings of his steed,
Amid a camp, whose steeled swarms I dared
But yesterday? And, at the trumpet sound,
Bow like some unknown mercenary's flag
And lick the soiled grass? No, no, my friend,   70
I would not, I, be pardon'd in the heap,
And bless indemnity with all that scum,—
Those men I mean, who on my shoulders propp'd
Their weak rebellion, winning me with lies,
And pitying forsooth my many wrongs;
Poor self-deceived wretches, who must think
Each one himself a king in embryo,
Because some dozen vassals cried — my lord!
Cowards, who never knew their little hearts,
Till flurried danger held the mirror up,   80
And then they own'd themselves without a blush,
Curling, like spaniels, round my father's feet.
Such things deserted me and are forgiven,
While I, less guilty, am an outcast still,
And will be, for I love such fair disgrace.
   Sigifred. I know the clear truth; so would Otho see,
For he is just and noble. Fain would I
Be pleader for you —
   Ludolph.   He 'll hear none of it;
You know his temper, hot, proud, obstinate;
Endanger not yourself so uselessly.   90
I will encounter his thwart spleen myself,

To-day, at the Duke Conrad's, where he
    keeps
His crowded state after the victory,
There will I be, a most unwelcome guest,
And parley with him, as a son should do,
Who doubly loathes a father's tyranny;
Tell him how feeble is that tyranny;
How the relationship of father and son
Is no more valid than a silken leash
Where lions tug adverse, if love grow not
From interchanged love through many
    years.   101
Aye, and those turreted Franconian walls,
Like to a jealous casket, hold my pearl —
My fair Auranthe ! Yes, I will be there.
    Sigifred. Be not so rash; wait till his
        wrath shall pass,
Until his royal spirit softly ebbs
Self-influenced; then, in his morning dreams
He will forgive thee, and awake in grief
To have not thy good morrow.
    Ludolph.   Yes, to-day
I must be there, while her young pulses
    beat   110
Among the new - plumed minions of the
    war.
Have you seen her of late ? No ? Au-
    ranthe,
Franconia's fair sister, 't is I mean.
She should be paler for my troublous
    days —
And there it is — my father's iron lips
Have sworn divorcement 'twixt me and my
    right.
    Sigifred (aside). Auranthe ! I had hoped
        this whim had pass'd.
    Ludolph. And, Sigifred, with all his love
        of justice,
When will he take that grandchild in his
    arms,
That, by my love I swear, shall soon be
    his ?   120
This reconcilement is impossible,
For see — but who are these ?
    Sigifred.   They are messengers
From our great emperor; to you, I doubt
    not,
For couriers are abroad to seek you out.

Enter THEODORE *and* GONFRED.

    Theodore. Seeing so many vigilant eyes
        explore
The province to invite your highness back
To your high dignities, we are too happy.
    Gonfred. We have eloquence to colour
        justly
The emperor's anxious wishes.
    Ludolph.   Go. I follow you.
        [*Exeunt* THEODORE *and* GONFRED.
I play the prude: it is but venturing —
Why should he be so earnest ? Come, my
    friend,   131
Let us to Friedburg castle.

                        ACT II

SCENE I. — *An antechamber in the Castle*

            Enter LUDOLPH *and* SIGIFRED.

    Ludolph. No more advices, no more cau-
        tioning;
I leave it all to fate — to any thing !
I cannot square my conduct to time, place,
Or circumstance; to me 't is all a mist !
    Sigifred. I say no more.
    Ludolph.   It seems I am to wait
Here in the anteroom; — that may be a
    trifle.
You see now how I dance attendance here,
Without that tyrant temper, you so blame,
Snapping the rein. You have medicined
    me
With good advices; and I here remain,   10
In this most honourable anteroom,
Your patient scholar.
    Sigifred.   Do not wrong me, Prince.
By Heavens, I 'd rather kiss Duke Conrad's
    slipper,
When in the morning he doth yawn with
    pride,
Than see you humbled but a half-degree !
Truth is, the Emperor would fain dismiss
The Nobles ere he sees you.

    Enter GONFRED *from the Council-room.*

    Ludolph.   Well, sir ! what ?

Gonfred. Great honour to the Prince !
The Emperor,
Hearing that his brave son had reappeared,
Instant dismiss'd the Council from his
sight, 20
As Jove fans off the clouds. Even now
they pass. [*Exit.*

*Enter the Nobles from the Council-room.
They cross the Stage, bowing with respect
to* LUDOLPH, *he frowning on them.* CON-
RAD *follows.* *Exeunt Nobles.*

Ludolph. Not the discoloured poisons of
a fen,
Which he, who breathes, feels warning of
his death,
Could taste so nauseous to the bodily sense,
As these prodigious sycophants disgust
The soul's fine palate.
Conrad. Princely Ludolph, hail !
Welcome, thou younger sceptre to the
realm !
Strength to thy virgin crownet's golden
buds,
That they, against the winter of thy sire,
May burst, and swell, and flourish round
thy brows, 30
Maturing to a weighty diadem !
Yet be that hour far off; and may he live,
Who waits for thee, as the chapp'd earth
for rain.
Set my life's star ! I have lived long
enough,
Since under my glad roof, propitiously,
Father and son each other re-possess.
Ludolph. Fine wording, Duke ! but words
could never yet
Forestall the fates; have you not learnt that
yet ?
Let me look well: your features are the
same;
Your gait the same; your hair of the same
shade; 40
As one I knew some passed weeks ago,
Who sung far different notes into mine
ears.
I have mine own particular comments on 't;
You have your own, perhaps.

Conrad. My gracious Prince,
All men may err. In truth I was deceived
In your great father's nature, as you were.
Had I known that of him I have since
known,
And what you soon will learn, I would have
turn'd
My sword to my own throat, rather than
held
Its threatening edge against a good King's
quiet: 50
Or with one word fever'd you, gentle
Prince,
Who seem'd to me, as rugged times then
went,
Indeed too much oppress'd. May I be
bold
To tell the Emperor you will haste to him ?
Ludolph. Your Dukedom's privilege will
grant so much.
[*Exit* CONRAD.
He 's very close to Otho, a tight leech !
Your hand — I go ! Ha ! here the thunder
comes
Sullen against the wind ! If in two angry
brows
My safety lies, then Sigifred, I 'm safe.

Enter OTHO *and* CONRAD.

Otho. Will you make Titan play the
lackey-page 60
To chattering pigmies ? I would have you
know
That such neglect of our high Majesty
Annuls all feel of kindred. What is son, —
Or friend — or brother — or all ties of
blood, —
When the whole kingdom, centred in our-
self,
Is rudely slighted ? Who am I to wait ?
By Peter's chair ! I have upon my tongue
A word to fright the proudest spirit
here ! —
Death ! — and slow tortures to the hardy
fool,
Who dares take such large charter from
our smiles ! 70
Conrad, we would be private ! Sigifred !

Off! And none pass this way on pain of
death!

[*Exeunt* Conrad *and* Sigifred.

Ludolph. This was but half expected, my
good sire,
Yet I am grieved at it, to the full height,
As though my hopes of favour had been
whole.

Otho. How you indulge yourself! What
can you hope for?

Ludolph. Nothing, my liege, I have to
hope for nothing.
I come to greet you as a loving son,
And then depart, if I may be so free,
Seeing that blood of yours in my warm
veins   80
Has not yet mitigated into milk.

Otho. What would you, sir?

Ludolph.   A lenient banishment;
So please you let me unmolested pass
This Conrad's gates, to the wide air again.
I want no more. A rebel wants no more.

Otho. And shall I let a rebel loose again
To muster kites and eagles 'gainst my
head?
No, obstinate boy, you shall be kept caged
up,
Served with harsh food, with scum for
Sunday-drink.

Ludolph. Indeed!

Otho. And chains too heavy for your life:
I'll choose a jailer, whose swart monstrous
face   90
Shall be a hell to look upon, and she —

Ludolph.   Ha!

Otho. Shall be your fair Auranthe.

Ludolph.   Amaze! Amaze!

Otho. To-day you marry her.

Ludolph.   This is a sharp jest!

Otho. No. None at all. When have I
said a lie?

Ludolph. If I sleep not, I am a waking
wretch.

Otho. Not a word more. Let me embrace my child.

Ludolph. I dare not. 'T would pollute
so good a father!
O heavy crime! that your son's blinded eyes

Could not see all his parent's love aright,
As now I see it. Be not kind to me — 100
Punish me not with favour.

Otho.   Are you sure,
Ludolph, you have no saving plea in store?

Ludolph. My father, none!

Otho.   Then you astonish me.

Ludolph. No, I have no plea. Disobedi-
ence,
Rebellion, obstinacy, blasphemy,
Are all my counsellors. If they can make
My crooked deeds show good and plausible,
Then grant me loving pardon, but not else,
Good Gods! not else, in any way, my liege!

Otho. You are a most perplexing, noble
boy.   111

Ludolph. You not less a perplexing noble
father.

Otho. Well, you shall have free passport
through the gates.
Farewell!

Ludolph. Farewell! and by these tears
believe,
And still remember, I repent in pain
All my misdeeds!

Otho.   Ludolph, I will! I will!
But, Ludolph, ere you go, I would inquire
If you, in all your wandering, ever met
A certain Arab haunting in these parts.

Ludolph. No, my good lord, I cannot say
I did.   120

Otho. Make not your father blind before
his time;
Nor let these arms paternal hunger more
For an embrace, to dull the appetite
Of my great love for thee, my supreme
child!
Come close, and let me breathe into thine
ear.
I knew you through disguise. You are the
Arab!
You can't deny it.   [*Embracing him.*

Ludolph.   Happiest of days!

Otho. We'll make it so.

Ludolph.   'Stead of one fatted calf
Ten hecatombs shall bellow out their last,
Smote 'twixt the horns by the death-stun-
ning mace   130

Of Mars, and all the soldiery shall feast
Nobly as Nimrod's masons, when the towers
Of Nineveh new kiss'd the parted clouds!
  Otho. Large as a God speak out, where all is thine.
  Ludolph. Ay, father, but the fire in my sad breast
Is quench'd with inward tears! I must rejoice
For you, whose wings so shadow over me
In tender victory, but for myself
I still must mourn. The fair Auranthe mine!   139
Too great a boon! I pr'ythee let me ask
What more than I know of could so have changed
Your purpose touching her.
  Otho.   At a word, this:
In no deed did you give me more offence
Than your rejection of Erminia.
To my appalling, I saw too good proof
Of your keen-eyed suspicion, — she is naught!
  Ludolph. You are convinced?
  Otho.   Ay, spite of her sweet looks.
O, that my brother's daughter should so fall!
Her fame has pass'd into the grosser lips
Of soldiers in their cups.
  Ludolph.   'T is very sad.
  Otho. No more of her. Auranthe — Ludolph, come!   151
This marriage be the bond of endless peace!
                           [Exeunt.

SCENE II. — *The entrance of* GERSA'S *Tent in the Hungarian Camp*

Enter ERMINIA.

  Erminia. Where! where! where shall I find a messenger?
A trusty soul? A good man in the camp?
Shall I go myself? Monstrous wickedness!
O cursed Conrad! devilish Auranthe!
Here is proof palpable as the bright sun!
O for a voice to reach the Emperor's ears!
              [Shouts in the camp.

Enter an HUNGARIAN CAPTAIN.

  Captain. Fair prisoner, you hear those joyous shouts?
The king — aye, now our king, — but still your slave,
Young Gersa, from a short captivity
Has just return'd. He bids me say, bright dame,   10
That even the homage of his ranged chiefs
Cures not his keen impatience to behold
Such beauty once again. What ails you, lady?
  Erminia. Say, is not that a German, yonder? There!
  Captain. Methinks by his stout bearing he should be —
Yes — it is Albert; a brave German knight,
And much in the Emperor's favour.
  Erminia.   I would fain
Inquire of friends and kinsfolk; how they fared
In these rough times. Brave soldier, as you pass
To royal Gersa with my humble thanks,   20
Will you send yonder knight to me?
  Captain.   I will.   *[Exit.*
  Erminia. Yes, he was ever known to be a man
Frank, open, generous; Albert I may trust.
O proof! proof! proof! Albert's an honest man;
Not Ethelbert the monk, if he were here,
Would I hold more trustworthy. Now!

Enter ALBERT.

  Albert.   Good Gods!
Lady Erminia! are you prisoner
In this beleaguer'd camp? Or are you here
Of your own will? You pleased to send for me.
By Venus, 't is a pity I knew not   30
Your plight before, and, by her Son, I swear
To do you every service you can ask.
What would the fairest — ?
  Erminia.   Albert, will you swear?
  Albert. I have. Well?

Erminia. Albert, you have fame to lose.
If men, in court and camp, lie not outright,
You should be, from a thousand, chosen
    forth
To do an honest deed. Shall I confide — ?
  Albert. Aye, any thing to me, fair crea-
    ture. Do ;
Dictate my task. Sweet woman, —
  Erminia.   Truce with that.
You understand me not ; and, in your
    speech,   40
I see how far the slander is abroad.
Without proof could you think me inno-
    cent ?
  Albert. Lady, I should rejoice to know
    you so.
  Erminia. If you have any pity for a
    maid,
Suffering a daily death from evil tongues;
Any compassion for that Emperor's niece,
Who, for your bright sword and clear hon-
    esty,
Lifted you from the crowd of common men
Into the lap of honour; — save me, knight !
  Albert. How ? Make it clear; if it be
    possible,   50
I by the banner of Saint Maurice swear
To right you.
  Erminia. Possible ! — Easy. O my
    heart !
This letter 's not so soil'd but you may
    read it ; —
Possible ! There — that letter ! Read —
    read it.   [*Gives him a letter.*

ALBERT (*reading*).

'To the Duke Conrad. — Forget the
threat you made at parting, and I will forget to send the Emperor letters and papers
of yours I have become possessed of. His
life is no trifle to me; his death you shall
find none to yourself.' (*Speaks to himself.*)
Tis me — my life that 's pleaded for !
(*Reads.*) 'He, for his own sake, will be
dumb as the grave. Erminia has my shame
fix'd upon her, sure as a wen. We are
safe.

          'AURANTHE.'

A she-devil ! A dragon ! I her imp !
Fire of Hell ! Auranthe — lewd demon !
Where got you this ? Where ? When ?
  Erminia. I found it in the tent, among
    some spoils
Which, being noble, fell to Gersa's lot.   70
Come in, and see.
           [*They go in and return.*
  Albert.   Villainy ! Villainy !
Conrad's sword, his corslet, and his helm,
And his letter. Caitiff, he shall feel —
  Erminia. I see you are thunderstruck.
    Haste, haste away !
  Albert. O, I am tortured by this villainy.
  Erminia. You needs must be. Carry it
    swift to Otho;
Tell him, moreover, I am prisoner
Here in this camp, where all the sisterhood,
Forced from their quiet cells, are parcel'd
    out
For slaves among these Huns. Away !
    Away !   80
  Albert. I am gone.
  Erminia. Swift be your steed ! Within
    this hour
The Emperor will see it.
  Albert.   Ere I sleep:
That I can swear.   [*Hurries out.*
  Gersa (*without*). Brave captains ! thanks.
    Enough
Of loyal homage now !

        Enter GERSA.

  Erminia.   Hail, royal Hun !
  Gersa. What means this, fair one ? Why
    in such alarm ?
Who was it hurried by me so distract ?
It seem'd you were in deep discourse to-
    gether;
Your doctrine has not been so harsh to
    him
As to my poor deserts. Come, come, be
    plain.
I am no jealous fool to kill you both,   90
Or, for such trifles, rob th' adorned world
Of such a beauteous vestal.
  Erminia.   I grieve, my Lord,
To hear you condescend to ribald-phrase.

Gersa. This is too much ! Hearken, my
    lady pure !
Erminia. Silence ! and hear the magic of
    a name —
Erminia ! I am she, — the Emperor's
    niece !
Praised be the Heavens, I now dare own
    myself !
Gersa. Erminia ! Indeed ! I 've heard
    of her.
Pr'ythee, fair lady, what chance brought
    you here ?   99
Erminia. Ask your own soldiers.
Gersa.   And you dare own your name.
For loveliness you may — and for the rest
My vein is not censorious.
Erminia.   Alas ! poor me !
'T is false indeed.
Gersa.   Indeed you are too fair:
The swan, soft leaning on her fledgy breast,
When to the stream she launches, looks
    not back
With such a tender grace; nor are her wings
So white as your soul is, if that but be
Twin picture to your face, Erminia !
To-day, for the first day, I am a king,   109
Yet would I give my unworn crown away
To know you spotless.
Erminia.   Trust me one day more,
Generously, without more certain guaran-
    tee,
Than this poor face you deign to praise so
    much;
After that, say and do whate'er you please.
If I have any knowledge of you, sir,
I think, nay I am sure, you will grieve
    much
To hear my story.   O be gentle to me,
For I am sick and faint with many wrongs,
Tired out, and weary-worn with contume-
    lies.   119
Gersa. Poor lady !

Enter ETHELBERT.

Erminia. Gentle Prince, 't is false indeed.
Good morrow, holy father ! I have had
Your prayers, though I look'd for you in
    vain.

Ethelbert. Blessings upon you, daughter !
    Sure you look
Too cheerful for these foul pernicious days.
Young man, you heard this virgin say 't was
    false, —
'T is false, I say.   What ! can you not
    employ
Your temper elsewhere, 'mong those burly
    tents,
But you must taunt this dove, for she hath
    lost
The Eagle Otho to beat off assault ?
Fie ! Fie ! But I will be her guard my-
    self,   130
I' the Emperor's name.   I here demand
Herself, and all her sisterhood.   She false !
  Gersa. Peace ! peace, old man ! I can-
    not think she is.
Ethelbert. Whom I have known from her
    first infancy,
Baptized her in the bosom of the Church,
Watch'd her, as anxious husbandmen the
    grain,
From the first shoot till the unripe mid-
    May,
Then to the tender ear of her June days,
Which, lifting sweet abroad its timid green,
Is blighted by the touch of calumny;   140
You cannot credit such a monstrous tale.
  Gersa. I cannot.   Take her.   Fair Er-
    minia,
I follow you to Friedburg, — is 't not so ?
  Erminia. Ay, so we purpose.
  Ethelbert.   Daughter, do you so ?
How 's this ?   I marvel !   Yet you look
    not mad.
  Erminia. I have good news to tell you,
    Ethelbert.
  Gersa. Ho ! ho, there !   Guards !
Your blessing, father !   Sweet Erminia,
Believe me, I am well nigh sure —
  Erminia.   Farewell
Short time will show.   [*Enter Chiefs.*
                Yes, father Ethelbert,
I have news precious as we pass along.   151
  Ethelbert. Dear daughter, you shall guide
    me.
  Erminia. To no ill.

Gersa. Command an escort to the Fried-
    burg lines.   [*Exeunt Chiefs.*
Pray let me lead. Fair lady, forget not
Gersa, how he believed you innocent.
I follow you to Friedburg with all speed.
                     [*Exeunt.*

ACT III

SCENE I. — *The Country*

Enter ALBERT.

Albert. O that the earth were empty, as
    when Cain
Had no perplexity to hide his head !
Or that the sword of some brave enemy
Had put a sudden stop to my hot breath,
And hurl'd me down the illimitable gulf
Of times past, unremember'd ! Better so
Than thus fast-limed in a cursed snare,
The white limbs of a wanton. This the end
Of an aspiring life ! My boyhood past
In feud with wolves and bears, when no
    eye saw   10
The solitary warfare, fought for love
Of honour 'mid the growling wilderness.
My sturdier youth, maturing to the sword,
Won by the syren-trumpets, and the ring
Of shields upon the pavement, when bright
    mail'd
Henry the Fowler pass'd the streets of
    Prague.
Was 't to this end I louted and became
The menial of Mars, and held a spear
Sway'd by command, as corn is by the
    wind ?
Is it for this, I now am lifted up   20
By Europe's throned Emperor, to see
My honour be my executioner, —
My love of fame, my prided honesty
Put to the torture for confessional ?
Then the damn'd crime of blurting to the
    world
A woman's secret ! — Though a fiend she
    be,
Too tender of my ignominious life;
But then to wrong the generous Emperor
In such a searching point, were to give up

My soul for foot-ball at Hell's holiday !   30
I must confess, — and cut my throat, — to-
    day ?
To-morrow ? Ho ! some wine !

Enter SIGIFRED.

Sigifred.   A fine humour —
Albert. Who goes there ? Count Sigi-
    fred ? Ha ! ha !
Sigifred. What, man, do you mistake the
    hollow sky
For a throng'd tavern, — and these stubbed
    trees
For old serge hangings, — me, your humble
    friend,
For a poor waiter ? Why, man, how you
    stare !
What gipsies have you been carousing
    with ?
No, no more wine; methinks you 've had
    enough.   39
Albert. You well may laugh and banter.
    What a fool
An injury may make of a staid man !
You shall know all anon.
Sigifred.   Some tavern brawl ?
Albert. 'T was with some people out of
    common reach;
Revenge is difficult.
Sigifred.   I am your friend;
We meet again to-day, and can confer
Upon it. For the present I 'm in haste.
Albert. Whither ?
Sigifred. To fetch King Gersa to the
    feast.
The Emperor on this marriage is so hot,
Pray Heaven it end not in apoplexy !
The very porters, as I pass'd the doors,   50
Heard his loud laugh, and answer'd in full
    choir.
I marvel, Albert, you delay so long
From these bright revelries; go, show your-
    self,
You may be made a duke.
Albert.   Ay, very like:
Pray, what day has his Highness fix'd
    upon ?
Sigifred. For what ?

Albert. The marriage. What else can I
    mean?

Sigifred. To-day. O, I forgot, you could
    not know;

The news is scarce a minute old with me.

Albert. Married to-day! To-day! You
    did not say so?

Sigifred. Now, while I speak to you,
    their comely heads   60

Are bow'd before the mitre.

Albert.   O! monstrous!

Sigifred. What is this?

Albert.   Nothing, Sigifred. Farewell!

We 'll meet upon our subject. Farewell,
    count!   [*Exit.*

Sigifred. Is this clear-headed Albert?
    He brain-turn'd!

'T is as portentous as a meteor.   [*Exit.*

SCENE II. — *An Apartment in the Castle*

Enter as from the Marriage, OTHO, LU-
DOLPH, AURANTHE, CONRAD, *Nobles,
Knights, Ladies, etc. Music.*

Otho. Now Ludolph! Now, Auranthe!
    Daughter fair!

What can I find to grace your nuptial
    day

More than my love, and these wide realms
    in fee?

Ludolph. I have too much.

Auranthe.   And I, my liege, by far.

Ludolph. Auranthe! I have! O, my
    bride, my love!

Not all the gaze upon us can restrain

My eyes, too long poor exiles from thy
    face,

From adoration, and my foolish tongue

From uttering soft responses to the love

I see in thy mute beauty beaming forth! 10

Fair creature, bless me with a single word!

All mine!

Auranthe. Spare, spare me, my Lord; I
    swoon else.

Ludolph. Soft beauty! by to-morrow I
    should die,

Wert thou not mine.

                [*They talk apart.*

1st Lady. How deep she has bewitch'd
    him!

1st Knight. Ask you for her recipe for
    love philtres.

2d Lady. They hold the Emperor in ad-
    miration.

Otho. If ever king was happy, that am I!

What are the cities 'yond the Alps to
    me,

The provinces about the Danube's mouth,

The promise of fair sail beyond the Rhone;

Or routing out of Hyperborean hordes, 21

To these fair children, stars of a new age?

Unless perchance I might rejoice to win

This little ball of earth, and chuck it them

To play with!

Auranthe. Nay, my Lord, I do not know.

Ludolph. Let me not famish.

Otho (to Conrad).   Good Franconia,

You heard what oath I sware, as the sun
    rose,

That unless Heaven would send me back
    my son,

My Arab, — no soft music should enrich

The cool wine, kiss'd off with a soldier's
    smack;   30

Now all my empire, barter'd for one feast,

Seems poverty.

Conrad.   Upon the neighbour-plain

The heralds have prepared a royal lists;

Your knights, found war-proof in the bloody
    field,

Speed to the game.

Otho.   Well, Ludolph, what say you?

Ludolph. My lord!

Otho.   A tourney?

Conrad.   Or, if 't please you best —

Ludolph. I want no more!

1st Lady.   He soars!

2d Lady.   Past all reason.

Ludolph. Though heaven's choir

Should in a vast circumference descend 39

And sing for my delight, I 'd stop my ears!

Though bright Apollo's car stood burning
    here,

And he put out an arm to bid me mount,

His touch an immortality, not I!

This earth, this palace, this room, Auranthe!

Otho. This is a little painful; just too much.

Conrad, if he flames longer in this wise,
I shall believe in wizard-woven loves
And old romances; but I 'll break the spell.
Ludolph!

  Conrad. He 'll be calm, anon.

  Ludolph.   You call'd!
Yes, yes, yes, I offend. You must forgive
    me: 50
Not being quite recover'd from the stun
Of your large bounties. A tourney, is it
    not?

              [*A senet heard faintly.*

  Conrad. The trumpets reach us.

  Ethelbert (*without*). On your peril, sirs,
Detain us!

  1st Voice (*without*). Let not the abbot
    pass.

  2d Voice (*without*). No,
On your lives!

  1st Voice (*without*). Holy father, you
    must not.

  Ethelbert (*without*). Otho!

  Otho.   Who calls on Otho?

  Ethelbert (*without*).   Ethelbert!

  Otho. Let him come in.

Enter ETHELBERT *leading in* ERMINIA.

                  Thou cursed abbot, why
Hast brought pollution to our holy rites?
Hast thou no fear of hangman, or the fag-
    got?

  Ludolph. What portent — what strange
    prodigy is this?   60

  Conrad. Away!

  Ethelbert.   You, Duke?

  Erminia. Albert has surely fail'd me!
Look at the Emperor's brow upon me
    bent!

  Ethelbert. A sad delay!

  Conrad.   Away, thou guilty thing!

  Ethelbert. You again, Duke? Justice,
    most noble Otho!

  You — go to your sister there and plot
    again,

A quick plot, swift as thought to save your
    heads;

For lo! the toils are spread around your
    den,

The world is all agape to see dragg'd forth
Two ugly monsters.

  Ludolph. What means he, my lord?

  Conrad. I cannot guess.

  Ethelbert.   Best ask your lady sister,
Whether the riddle puzzles her beyond   71
The power of utterance.

  Conrad.   Foul barbarian, cease;
The Princess faints!

  Ludolph. Stab him! O, sweetest wife!

              [*Attendants bear off* AURANTHE.

  Erminia. Alas!

  Ethelbert.   Your wife!

  Ludolph. Ay, Satan! does that yerk ye?

  Ethelbert. Wife! so soon!

  Ludolph.   Ay, wife! Oh, impudence!
Thou bitter mischief! Venomous bad
    priest!
How dar'st thou lift those beetle brows at
    me?
Me — the prince Ludolph, in this presence
    here,   78
Upon my marriage day, and scandalize
My joys with such opprobrious surprise?
Wife! Why dost linger on that syllable,
As if it were some demon's name pro-
    nounced
To summon harmful lightning, and make
    yawn
The sleepy thunder? Hast no sense of
    fear?
No ounce of man in thy mortality?
Tremble! for, at my nod, the sharpen'd axe
Will make thy bold tongue quiver to the
    roots,
Those gray lids wink, and thou not know
    it, monk!

  Ethelbert. O, poor deceived Prince! I
    pity thee!   89
Great Otho! I claim justice —

  Ludolph.   Thou shalt have 't!
Thine arms from forth a pulpit of hot fire
Shall sprawl distracted! O that that dull
    cowl
Were some most sensitive portion of thy
    life,

That I might give it to my hounds to tear !
Thy girdle some fine zealous-pained nerve
To girth my saddle ! And those devil's
    beads
Each one a life, that I might, every day,
Crush one with Vulcan's hammer !
    Otho.   Peace, my son ;
You far outstrip my spleen in this affair.
Let us be calm, and hear the abbot's plea
For this intrusion.
    Ludolph.   I am silent, sire.
    Otho. Conrad, see all depart not wanted
        here.   102
            [*Exeunt Knights, Ladies, etc.*
Ludolph, be calm. Ethelbert, peace awhile.
This mystery demands an audience
Of a just judge, and that will Otho be.
    Ludolph. Why has he time to breathe
        another word ?
    Otho. Ludolph, old Ethelbert, be sure,
        comes not
To beard us for no cause; he 's not the
    man
To cry himself up an ambassador
Without credentials.
    Ludolph.   I 'll chain up myself.
    Otho. Old abbot, stand here forth. Lady
        Erminia,   111
Sit. And now, abbot ! what have you to
    say ?
Our ear is open. First we here denounce
Hard penalties against thee, if 't be found
The cause for which you have disturb'd us
    here,
Making our bright hours muddy, be a thing
Of little moment.
    Ethelbert.   See this innocent !
Otho ! thou father of the people call'd,
Is her life nothing ? Her fair honour no-
    thing ?
Her tears from matins until even-song   120
Nothing ? Her burst heart nothing ? Em-
    peror !
Is this your gentle niece — the simplest
    flower
Of the world's herbal — this fair lily
    blanch'd
Still with the dews of piety, this meek lady

Here sitting like an angel newly-shent,
Who veils its snowy wings and grows all
    pale, —
Is she nothing ?
    Otho. What more to the purpose, abbot ?
    Ludolph. Whither is he winding ?
    Conrad.   No clue yet !
    Ethelbert. You have heard, my Liege, and
        so, no doubt, all here,   129
Foul, poisonous, malignant whisperings;
Nay open speech, rude mockery grown
    common,
Against the spotless nature and clear fame
Of the princess Erminia, your niece.
I have intruded here thus suddenly,
Because I hold those base weeds, with tight
    hand,
Which now disfigure her fair growing stem,
Waiting but for your sign to pull them up
By the dark roots, and leave her palpable,
To all men's sight, a lady innocent.
The ignominy of that whisper'd tale   140
About a midnight gallant, seen to climb
A window to her chamber neighbour'd
    near,
I will from her turn off, and put the load
On the right shoulders; on that wretch's
    head,
Who, by close stratagems, did save her-
    self,
Chiefly by shifting to this lady's room
A rope-ladder for false witness.
    Ludolph.   Most atrocious !
    Otho. Ethelbert, proceed.
    Ethelbert.   With sad lips I shall:
For, in the healing of one wound, I fear
To make a greater. His young highness
    here   150
To-day was married.
    Ludolph.   Good.
    Ethelbert.   Would it were good !
Yet why do I delay to spread abroad
The names of those two vipers, from whose
    jaw
A deadly breath went forth to taint and
    blast
This guileless lady ?
    Otho.   Abbot, speak their names.

Ethelbert. A minute first.   It cannot be
       — but may
I ask, great judge, if you to-day have put
A letter by unread ?
   Otho.   Does 't end in this ?
Conrad. Out with their names !
Ethelbert.   Bold sinner, say you so ?
Ludolph. Out, hideous monk !
Otho.   Confess, or by the wheel —
Ethelbert. My evidence cannot be far
       away;   161
And, though it never come, be on my head
The crime of passing an attaint upon
The slanderers of this virgin.
   Ludolph.   Speak aloud !
   Ethelbert. Auranthe, and her brother
       there.
   Conrad.   Amaze !
Ludolph. Throw them from the win-
       dows !
Otho. Do what you will !
Ludolph.   What shall I do with them ?
Something of quick dispatch, for should she
       hear,
My soft Auranthe, her sweet mercy would
Prevail against my fury.   Damned priest !
What swift death wilt thou die ? As to the
       lady,   171
I touch her not.
   Ethelbert.   Illustrious Otho, stay !
An ample store of misery thou hast,
Choke not the granary of thy noble mind
With more bad bitter grain, too difficult
A cud for the repentance of a man
Gray-growing.   To thee only I appeal,
Not to thy noble son, whose yeasting youth
Will clear itself, and crystal turn again.
A young man's heart, by Heaven's bless-
       ing, is   180
A wide world, where a thousand new-born
       hopes
Empurple fresh the melancholy blood :
But an old man's is narrow, tenantless
Of hopes, and stuff'd with many memories,
Which, being pleasant, ease the heavy
       pulse —
Painful, clog up and stagnate.   Weigh this
       matter

Even as a miser balances his coin;
And, in the name of mercy, give command
That your knight Albert be brought here
       before you.   189
He will expound this riddle; he will show
A noon-day proof of bad Auranthe's guilt.
   Otho. Let Albert straight be summon'd.
                    [*Exit one of the Nobles.*
   Ludolph.   Impossible !
I cannot doubt — I will not — no — to
       doubt
Is to be ashes ! — wither'd up to death !
   Otho. My gentle Ludolph, harbour not a
       fear;
You do yourself much wrong.
   Ludolph.   O, wretched dolt !
Now, when my foot is almost on thy neck,
Wilt thou infuriate me ? Proof ! Thou fool !
Why wilt thou tease impossibility   199
With such a thick-skull'd persevering suit ?
Fanatic obstinacy !   Prodigy !
Monster of folly ! Ghost of a turn'd
       brain !
You puzzle me, — you haunt me, — when I
       dream
Of you my brain will split ! Bold sor-
       cerer !
Juggler ! May I come near you ? On my
       soul
I know not whether to pity, curse, or
       laugh.

   Enter ALBERT, *and the Nobleman.*

Here, Albert, this old phantom wants a
       proof !
Give him his proof ! A camel's load of
       proofs !
   Otho. Albert, I speak to you as a man
Whose words once utter'd pass like current
       gold;   210
And therefore fit to calmly put a close
To this brief tempest. Do you stand pos-
       sess'd
Of any proof against the honourableness
Of Lady Auranthe, our new-spoused daugh-
       ter ?
   Albert. You chill me with astonishment.
       How 's this ?

My liege, what proof should I have 'gainst
    a fame
Impossible of slur?
                        [OTHO *rises*.
Erminia.   O wickedness!
Ethelbert. Deluded monarch, 't is a cruel
    lie.   218
Otho. Peace, rebel-priest!
Conrad.   Insult beyond credence!
Erminia. Almost a dream!
Ludolph.   We have awaked from!
A foolish dream that from my brow hath
    wrung
A wrathful dew. O folly! why did I
So act the lion with this silly gnat?
Let them depart. Lady Erminia!
I ever grieved for you, as who did not?
But now you have, with such a brazen
    front,
So most maliciously, so madly striven
To dazzle the soft moon, when tenderest
    clouds
Should be unloop'd around to curtain her;
I leave you to the desert of the world   230
Almost with pleasure. Let them be set
    free
For me! I take no personal revenge
More than against a nightmare, which a
    man
Forgets in the new dawn. [*Exit* LUDOLPH.
    Otho. Still in extremes! No, they must
        not be loose.
Ethelbert. Albert, I must suspect thee of
    a crime
So fiendish —
    Otho. Fear'st thou not my fury, monk?
Conrad, be they in your safe custody
Till we determine some fit punishment. 240
It is so mad a deed, I must reflect
And question them in private; for per-
    haps,
By patient scrutiny, we may discover
Whether they merit death, or should be
    placed
In care of the physicians.
    [*Exeunt* OTHO *and* *Nobles*, ALBERT
    following.

Conrad. My guards, ho!
    Erminia. Albert, wilt thou follow there?
Wilt thou creep dastardly behind his back,
And shrink away from a weak woman's
    eye?
Turn, thou court - Janus! thou forgett'st
    thyself;
Here is the duke, waiting with open
    arms,
            Enter Guards.
To thank thee; here congratulate each
    other;   250
Wring hands; embrace; and swear how
    lucky 't was
That I, by happy chance, hit the right
    man
Of all the world to trust in.
Albert.   Trust! to me!
Conrad (*aside*). He is the sole one in this
    mystery.
Erminia. Well, I give up, and save my
    prayers for Heaven!
You, who could do this deed, would ne'er
    relent,
Though, at my words, the hollow prison-
    vaults
Would groan for pity.
Conrad.   Manacle them both!
Ethelbert. I know it — it must be — I
    see it all!   259
Albert, thou art the minion!
Erminia.   Ah! too plain —
Conrad. Silence! Gag up their mouths!
    I cannot bear
More of this brawling. That the Emperor
Had placed you in some other custody!
Bring them away.
                [*Exeunt all but* ALBERT.
    Albert. Though my name perish from
        the book of honour,
Almost before the recent ink is dry,
And be no more remember'd after death,
Than any drummer's in the muster-roll;
Yet shall I season high my sudden fall 269
With triumph o'er that evil-witted duke!
He shall feel what it is to have the hand
Of a man drowning, on his hateful throat.

Enter GERSA *and* SIGIFRED.

Gersa. What discord is at ferment in
this house ?

Sigifred. We are without conjecture; not
a soul
We met could answer any certainty.

Gersa. Young Ludolph, like a fiery arrow, shot
By us.

Sigifred. The Emperor, with cross'd
arms, in thought.

Gersa. In one room music, in another
sadness,
Perplexity every where !

Albert.   A trifle more !
Follow ; your presences will much avail 280
To tune our jarred spirits. I 'll explain.
                            [*Exeunt.*

ACT IV

SCENE I. — AURANTHE'S *Apartment*

AURANTHE *and* CONRAD *discovered.*

Conrad. Well, well, I know what ugly
jeopardy
We are caged in; you need not pester that
Into my ears. Pr'ythee, let me be spared
A foolish tongue, that I may bethink me
Of remedies with some deliberation.
You cannot doubt but 't is in Albert's
power
To crush or save us ?

Auranthe.   No, I cannot doubt.
He has, assure yourself, by some strange
means,
My secret; which I ever hid from him, 9
Knowing his mawkish honesty.

Conrad.   Cursed slave !

Auranthe. Ay, I could almost curse him
now myself.
Wretched impediment ! Evil genius !
A glue upon my wings, that cannot spread,
When they should span the provinces ! A
snake,
A scorpion, sprawling on the first gold
step,
Conducting to the throne, high canopied.

Conrad. You would not hear my counsel,
when his life
Might have been trodden out, all sure and
hush'd;
Now the dull animal forsooth must be
Intreated, managed ! When can you con-
trive   20
The interview he demands ?

Auranthe.   As speedily
It must be done as my bribed woman can
Unseen conduct him to me; but I fear
'T will be impossible, while the broad day
Comes through the panes with persecuting
glare.
Methinks, if 't now were night I could in-
trigue
With darkness, bring the stars to second me,
And settle all this trouble.

Conrad.   Nonsense ! Child !
See him immediately; why not now ?

Auranthe. Do you forget that even the
senseless door-posts   30
Are on the watch and gape through all the
house ?
How many whisperers there are about,
Hungry for evidence to ruin me:
Men I have spurn'd, and women I have
taunted ?
Besides, the foolish prince sends, minute
whiles,
His pages — so they tell me — to inquire
After my health, intreating, if I please,
To see me.

Conrad. Well, suppose this Albert here;
What is your power with him ?

Auranthe.   He should be
My echo, my taught parrot ! but I fear 40
He will be cur enough to bark at me;
Have his own say; read me some silly creed
'Bout shame and pity.

Conrad.   What will you do then ?

Auranthe. What I shall do, I know not;
what I would
Cannot be done; for see, this chamber-
floor
Will not yield to the pick-axe and the
spade, —
Here is no quiet depth of hollow ground.

Conrad. Sister, you have grown sensible
    and wise,
Seconding, ere I speak it, what is now,   49
I hope, resolved between us.
    Auranthe.   Say, what is 't ?
    Conrad. You need not be his sexton too;
    a man
May carry that with him shall make him
    die
Elsewhere, — give that to him; pretend
    the while
You will to-morrow succumb to his wishes,
Be what they may, and send him from the
    Castle
On some fool's errand: let his latest groan
Frighten the wolves !
    Auranthe.   Alas ! he must not die !
    Conrad. Would you were both hearsed
    up in stifling lead !
Detested —
    Auranthe. Conrad, hold ! I would not
    bear   59
The little thunder of your fretful tongue,
Tho' I alone were taken in these toils,
And you could free me; but remember,
    sir,
You live alone in my security:
So keep your wits at work, for your own
    sake,
Not mine, and be more mannerly.
    Conrad.   Thou wasp !
If my domains were emptied of these folk,
And I had thee to starve —
    Auranthe.   O, marvellous !
But Conrad, now be gone; the Host is
    look'd for;
Cringe to the Emperor, entertain the Lords,
And, do ye mind, above all things, pro-
    claim   70
My sickness, with a brother's sadden'd eye,
Condoling with Prince Ludolph. In fit
    time
Return to me.
    Conrad. I leave you to your thoughts.
                           [*Exit.*
    Auranthe (*sola*). Down, down, proud
    temper ! down, Auranthe's pride !
Why do I anger him when I should kneel ?

Conrad ! Albert ! help ! help ! What can
    I do ?
O wretched woman ! lost, wreck'd, swal-
    low'd up,
Accursed, blasted ! O, thou golden Crown,
Orbing along the serene firmament   79
Of a wide empire, like a glowing moon;
And thou, bright sceptre ! lustrous in my
    eyes, —
There — as the fabled fair Hesperian tree,
Bearing a fruit more precious ! graceful
    thing,   '
Delicate, godlike, magic ! must I leave
Thee to melt in the visionary air,
Ere, by one grasp, this common hand is
    made
Imperial ? I do not know the time
When I have wept for sorrow; but me-
    thinks   88
I could now sit upon the ground, and shed
Tears, tears of misery ! O, the heavy day !
How shall I bear my life till Albert comes ?
Ludolph ! Erminia ! Proofs ! O heavy
    day !
Bring me some mourning weeds, that I
    may 'tire
Myself, as fits one wailing her own death:
Cut off these curls, and brand this lily
    hand,
And throw these jewels from my loathing
    sight, —
Fetch me a missal, and a string of beads, —
A cup of bitter'd water, and a crust, —
I will confess, O holy Abbot ! — How !   99
What is this ? Auranthe ! thou fool, dolt,
Whimpering idiot ! up ! up ! and quell !
I am safe ! Coward ! why am I in fear ?
Albert ! he cannot stickle, chew the cud
In such a fine extreme, — impossible !
Who knocks ?
    [*Goes to the door, listens, and opens it.*

          Enter ALBERT.

Albert, I have been waiting for you here
With such an aching heart, such swooning
    throbs
On my poor brain, such cruel — cruel sor-
    row,

That I should claim your pity! Art not
    well?   109
  Albert. Yes, lady, well.
  Auranthe.   You look not so, alas!
But pale, as if you brought some heavy
    news.
  Albert. You know full well what makes
    me look so pale.
  Auranthe. No! Do I? Surely I am
    still to learn
Some horror; all I know, this present, is
I am near hustled to a dangerous gulf,
Which you can save me from, — and there-
    fore safe,
So trusting in thy love; that should not
    make
Thee pale, my Albert.
  Albert.   It doth make me freeze.
  Auranthe. Why should it, love?
  Albert.   You should not ask me that,
But make your own heart monitor, and save
Me the great pain of telling. You must
    know.   121
  Auranthe. Something has vext you, Al-
    bert. There are times
When simplest things put on a sombre
    cast;
A melancholy mood will haunt a man,
Until most easy matters take the shape
Of unachievable tasks; small rivulets
Then seem impassable.
  Albert.   Do not cheat yourself
With hope that gloss of words, or suppliant
    action,
Or tears, or ravings, or self-threaten'd
    death,   129
Can alter my resolve.
  Auranthe.   You make me tremble;
Not so much at your threats, as at your
    voice,
Untuned, and harsh, and barren of all love.
  Albert. You suffocate me! Stop this
    devil's parley,
And listen to me; know me once for all.
  Auranthe. I thought I did. Alas! I
    am deceived.
  Albert. No, you are not deceived. You
    took me for

A man detesting all inhuman crime;
And therefore kept from me your demon's
    plot
Against Erminia. Silent? Be so still;
For ever! Speak no more; but hear my
    words,   140
Thy fate. Your safety I have bought to-
    day
By blazoning a lie, which in the dawn
I 'll expiate with truth.
  Auranthe.   O cruel traitor!
  Albert. For I would not set eyes upon
    thy shame;
I would not see thee dragg'd to death by
    the hair,
Penanced, and taunted on a scaffolding!
To-night, upon the skirts of the blind wood
That blackens northward of these horrid
    towers,
I wait for you with horses. Choose your
    fate.   149
Farewell!
  Auranthe. Albert, you jest; I 'm sure
    you must.
You, an ambitious Soldier! I, a Queen,
One who could say, — here, rule these Pro-
    vinces!
Take tribute from those cities for thyself!
Empty these armouries, these treasuries,
Muster thy warlike thousands at a nod!
Go! Conquer Italy!
  Albert.   Auranthe, you have made
The whole world chaff to me. Your doom
    is fix'd.
  Auranthe. Out, villain! dastard!
  Albert.   Look there to the door!
Who is it?
  Auranthe. Conrad, traitor!
  Albert.   Let him in.

       Enter CONRAD.

Do not affect amazement, hypocrite, 160
At seeing me in this chamber.
  Conrad.   Auranthe?
  Albert. Talk not with eyes, but speak
    your curses out
Against me, who would sooner crush and
    grind

A brace of toads, than league with them
    t' oppress
An innocent lady, gull an Emperor,
More generous to me than autumn sun
To ripening harvests.
    Auranthe.   No more insult, sir !
    Albert. Ay, clutch your scabbard; but,
    for prudence sake,
Draw not the sword; 't would make an up-
    roar, Duke,
You would not hear the end of. At night-
    fall   170
Your lady sister, if I guess aright,
Will leave this busy castle. You had best
Take farewell too of worldly vanities.
    Conrad. Vassal !
    Albert.   To-morrow, when the Emperor
    sends
For loving Conrad, see you fawn on him.
Good even !
    Auranthe. You 'll be seen !
    Albert.   See the coast clear then.
    Auranthe (as he goes). Remorseless Al-
    bert ! Cruel, cruel wretch !
                  [She lets him out.
    Conrad. So, we must lick the dust ?
    Auranthe.   I follow him.
    Conrad. How ? Where ? The plan of
    your escape ?
    Auranthe.   He waits
For me with horses by the forest-side, 180
Northward.
    Conrad. Good, good ! he dies. You go,
    say you ?
    Auranthe. Perforce.
    Conrad. Be speedy, darkness! Till that
    comes,
Fiends keep you company !   *[Exit.*
    Auranthe.   And you ! And you !
And all men ! Vanish !
        [Retires to an inner apartment.

SCENE II. — *An Apartment in the Castle*

    Enter LUDOLPH *and a Page.*

    Page. Still very sick, my lord; but now
    I went,
Knowing my duty to so good a Prince;

And there her women, in a mournful throng,
Stood in the passage whispering; if any
Moved, 't was with careful steps, and hush'd
    as death:
They bade me stop.
    Ludolph.   Good fellow, once again
Make soft inquiry; pr'ythee, be not stay'd
By any hindrance, but with gentlest force
Break through her weeping servants, till
    thou com'st
E'en to her chamber door, and there, fair
    boy —   10
If with thy mother's milk thou hast suck'd
    in
Any divine eloquence — woo her ears
With plaints for me, more tender than the
    voice
Of dying Echo, echoed.
    Page.   Kindest master !
To know thee sad thus, will unloose my
    tongue
In mournful syllables. Let but my words
    reach
Her ears, and she shall take them coupled
    with
Moans from my heart, and sighs not coun-
    terfeit.
May I speed better !   *[Exit Page.*
    Ludolph (solus). 'Auranthe ! My Life !
Long have I loved thee, yet till now not
    loved: 20
Remembering, as I do, hard-hearted times
When I had heard e'en of thy death per-
    haps,
And thoughtless, suffer'd thee to pass alone
Into Elysium ! — now I follow thee
A substance or a shadow, wheresoe'er
Thou leadest me, — whether thy white feet
    press,
With pleasant weight, the amorous-aching
    earth,
Or thro' the air thou pioneerest me,
A shade ! Yet sadly I predestinate !
O unbenignest Love, why wilt thou let   30
Darkness steal out upon the sleepy world
So wearily; as if night's chariot-wheels
Were clogg'd in some thick cloud ? O,
    changeful Love,

Let not her steeds with drowsy-footed pace
Pass the high stars, before sweet embas-
    sage
Comes from the pillow'd beauty of that
    fair
Completion of all delicate Nature's wit!
Pout her faint lips anew with rubious
    health;
And, with thine infant fingers, lift the
    fringe
Of her sick eyelids; that those eyes may
    glow   40
With wooing light upon me, ere the Morn
Peers with disrelish, gray, barren, and
    cold!

     Enter GERSA *and Courtiers.*

Otho calls me his Lion — should I blush
To be so tamed? so —
   Gersa.   Do me the courtesy,
Gentlemen, to pass on.
   1st Knight.   We are your servants.
                       [*Exeunt Courtiers.*
   Ludolph. It seems then, Sir, you have
    found out the man
You would confer with; — me?
   Gersa.   If I break not
Too much upon your thoughtful mood, I
    will
Claim a brief while your patience.
   Ludolph.   For what cause
Soe'er, I shall be honour'd.
   Gersa.   I not less.
   Ludolph. What may it be? No trifle
    can take place   51
Of such deliberate prologue, serious 'hav-
    iour.
But, be it what it may, I cannot fail
To listen with no common interest;
For though so new your presence is to
    me,
I have a soldier's friendship for your fame.
Please you explain.
   Gersa.   As thus: — for, pardon me,
I cannot in plain terms grossly assault
A noble nature; and would faintly sketch
What your quick apprehension will fill up;
So finely I esteem you.

   Ludolph.   I attend.   61
   Gersa. Your generous father, most illus-
    trious Otho,
Sits in the banquet-room among his chiefs;
His wine is bitter, for you are not there;
His eyes are fix'd still on the open doors,
And ev'ry passer in he frowns upon,
Seeing no Ludolph comes.
   Ludolph.   I do neglect —
   Gersa. And for your absence may I guess
    the cause?
   Ludolph. Stay there! No — guess?
    More princely you must be   69
Than to make guesses at me. 'T is enough.
I 'm sorry I can hear no more.
   Gersa.   And I
As grieved to force it on you so abrupt;
Yet, one day, you must know a grief, whose
    sting
Will sharpen more the longer 't is con-
    ceal'd.
   Ludolph. Say it at once, sir! dead —
    dead — is she dead?
   Gersa. Mine is a cruel task: she is not
    dead,
And would, for your sake, she were inno-
    cent —
   Ludolph. Thou liest! Thou amazest me
    beyond
All scope of thought, convulsest my heart's
    blood   79
To deadly churning! Gersa, you are young,
As I am; let me observe you, face to face:
Not gray-brow'd like the poisonous Ethel-
    bert,
No rheumed eyes, no furrowing of age,
No wrinkles, where all vices nestle in
Like crannied vermin — no! but fresh and
    young,
And hopeful featured. Ha! by Heaven
    you weep
Tears, human tears! Do you repent you
    then
Of a cursed torturer's office? Why shouldst
    join —
Tell me, the league of devils? Confess —
    confess —
The Lie!

Gersa. Lie !— but begone all ceremo-
nious points   90
Of honour battailous ! I could not turn
My wrath against thee for the orbed world.
   Ludolph. Your wrath, weak boy ? Trem-
ble at mine, unless
Retraction follow close upon the heels
Of that late stounding insult ! Why has
my sword
Not done already a sheer judgment on
thee ?
Despair, or eat thy words ! Why, thou
wast nigh
Whimpering away my reason! Hark ye,
Sir,
It is no secret, that Erminia,
Erminia, Sir, was hidden in your tent; 100
O bless'd asylum ! Comfortable home !
Begone ! I pity thee; thou art a gull,
Erminia's last new puppet !
   Gersa.   Furious fire !
Thou mak'st me boil as hot as thou canst
flame !
And in thy teeth I give thee back the lie !
Thou liest ! Thou, Auranthe's fool ! A
wittol —
   Ludolph. Look ! look at this bright
sword:
There is no part of it, to the very hilt,
But shall indulge itself about thine heart !
Draw ! but remember thou must cower thy
plumes,   110
As yesterday the Arab made thee stoop —
   Gersa. Patience ! Not here; I would
not spill thy blood
Here, underneath this roof where Otho
breathes, —
Thy father, — almost mine.
   Ludolph.   O faltering coward !

Re-enter PAGE.

Stay, stay; here is one I have half a word
with.
Well — What ails thee, child ?
   Page.   My lord !
   Ludolph.   Good fellow !
   Page. They are fled !
   Ludolph.   They ! Who ?

   Page.   When anxiously
I hasten'd back, your grieving messenger,
I found the stairs all dark, the lamps ex-
tinct,
And not a foot or whisper to be heard. 120
I thought her dead, and on the lowest step
Sat listening; when presently came by
Two muffled up, — one sighing heavily,
The other cursing low, whose voice I knew
For the Duke Conrad's. Close I follow'd
them
Thro' the dark ways they chose to the open
air;
And, as I follow'd, heard my lady speak.
   Ludolph. Thy life answers the truth !
   Page.   The chamber 's empty !
   Ludolph. As I will be of mercy ! So, at
last,   129
This nail is in my temples !
   Gersa.   Be calm in this.
   Ludolph. I am.
   Gersa. And Albert too has disappear'd;
Ere I met you, I sought him every where;
You would not hearken.
   Ludolph.   Which way went they, boy ?
   Gersa. I 'll hunt with you.
   Ludolph.   No, no, no. My senses are
Still whole. I have survived. My arm is
strong —
My appetite sharp — for revenge ! I 'll no
sharer
In my feast; my injury is all my own,
And so is my revenge, my lawful chat-
tels !
Terrier, ferret them out ! Burn — burn
the witch !
Trace me their footsteps ! Away ! 140
                         [*Exeunt.*

ACT V

SCENE I. — *A part of the Forest*

Enter CONRAD *and* AURANTHE.

   Auranthe. Go no further; not a step
more. Thou art
A master-plague in the midst of miseries.
Go, — I fear thee ! I tremble every limb,

Who never shook before. There 's moody death
In thy resolved looks ! Yes, I could kneel
To pray thee far away ! Conrad, go !
go ! —
There ! yonder underneath the boughs I see
Our horses !

Conrad. Ay, and the man.

Auranthe.   Yes, he is there.
Go, go, — no blood ! no blood ! — go, gentle Conrad !

Conrad. Farewell !

Auranthe. Farewell ! For this Heaven
pardon you !   10
      [*Exit* AURANTHE.

Conrad. If he survive one hour, then may I die
In unimagined tortures, or breathe through
A long life in the foulest sink o' the world !
He dies ! 'T is well she do not advertise
The caitiff of the cold steel at his back.
      [*Exit* CONRAD.

Enter LUDOLPH *and Page.*

Ludolph. Miss'd the way, boy ? Say not that on your peril !

Page. Indeed, indeed I cannot trace them further.

Ludolph. Must I stop here ? Here solitary die ?
Stifled beneath the thick oppressive shade
Of these dull boughs, — this oven of dark thickets, —   20
Silent, — without revenge ? — pshaw ! —
bitter end, —
A bitter death, — a suffocating death, —
A gnawing — silent — deadly, quiet death !
Escaped ? — fled ? — vanish'd ? melted into air ?
She 's gone ! I cannot clutch her ! no revenge !
A muffled death, ensnared in horrid silence !
Suck'd to my grave amid a dreamy calm !
O, where is that illustrious noise of war,
To smother up this sound of labouring breath,   29
This rustle of the trees !
      [AURANTHE *shrieks at a distance.*

Page.   My lord, a noise !
This way — hark !

Ludolph. Yes, yes ! A hope ! A music !
A glorious clamour ! How I live again !
      [*Exeunt.*

SCENE II. — *Another part of the Forest*

Enter ALBERT (*wounded*).

Albert. O ! for enough life to support me on
To Otho's feet !

Enter LUDOLPH.

Ludolph.   Thrice villanous, stay there !
Tell me where that detested woman is,
Or this is through thee !

Albert.   My good Prince, with me
The sword has done its worst; not without worst
Done to another, — Conrad has it home —
I see you know it all —

Ludolph.   Where is his sister ?

Enter AURANTHE.

Auranthe. Albert !

Ludolph. Ha ! There ! there ! — He is the paramour ! —
There — hug him — dying ! O, thou innocence,
Shrine him and comfort him at his last gasp,   10
Kiss down his eyelids ! Was he not thy love ?
Wilt thou forsake him at his latest hour ?
Keep fearful and aloof from his last gaze,
His most uneasy moments, when cold death
Stands with the door ajar to let him in ?

Albert. O that that door with hollow slam would close
Upon me sudden, for I cannot meet,
In all the unknown chambers of the dead,
Such horrors —

Ludolph. Auranthe ! what can he mean ?
What horrors ? Is it not a joyous time ?
Am I not married to a paragon   21
'Of personal beauty and untainted soul ?'
A blushing fair-eyed purity ? A sylph,

Whose snowy timid hand has never sinn'd
Beyond a flower pluck'd, white as itself?
Albert, you do insult my bride — your mis-
    tress —
To talk of horrors on our wedding-night!
    Albert. Alas! poor Prince, I would you
        knew my heart!
'T is not so guilty —
    Ludolph.   Hear, he pleads not guilty!
You are not? or, if so, what matters it?
You have escaped me, free as the dusk
    air,   31
Hid in the forest, safe from my revenge;
I cannot catch you! You should laugh at
    me,
Poor cheated Ludolph! Make the forest
    hiss
With jeers at me! You tremble; faint at
    once,
You will come to again. O cockatrice,
I have you! Whither wander those fair
    eyes
To entice the Devil to your help, that he
May change you to a spider, so to crawl
Into some cranny to escape my wrath?   40
    Albert. Sometimes the counsel of a dy-
        ing man
Doth operate quietly when his breath is
    gone:
Disjoin those hands — part — part — do
    not destroy
Each other — forget her! — Our miseries
Are equal shared, and mercy is —
    Ludolph.   A boon
When one can compass it. Auranthe, try
Your oratory; your breath is not so hitch'd.
Ay, stare for help!
                [ALBERT *groans and dies.*
                There goes a spotted soul
Howling in vain along the hollow night!
Hear him! He calls you — sweet Auran-
    the, come!   50
    Auranthe. Kill me!
    Ludolph. No! What, upon our mar-
        riage-night!
The earth would shudder at so foul a deed!
A fair bride! A sweet bride! An inno-
    cent bride!

No! we must revel it, as 't is in use
In times of delicate brilliant ceremony:
Come, let me lead you to our halls again!
Nay, linger not; make no resistance,
    sweet; —
Will you? Ah, wretch, thou canst not, for
    I have
The strength of twenty lions 'gainst a
    lamb!
Now — one adieu for Albert! — Come
    away!   60
                [*Exeunt.*

SCENE III. — *An inner Court of the
        Castle*

Enter SIGIFRED, GONFRED, *and* THEODORE,
        meeting.

    1st Knight. Was ever such a night?
    Sigifred.   What horrors more?
Things unbelieved one hour, so strange
        they are,
The next hour stamps with credit.
    1st Knight.   Your last news?
    Gonfred. After the Page's story of the
        death
Of Albert and Duke Conrad?
    Sigifred.   And the return
Of Ludolph with the Princess.
    Gonfred.   No more, save
Prince Gersa's freeing Abbot Ethelbert,
And the sweet lady, fair Erminia,
From prison.
    1st Knight. Where are they now? Hast
        yet heard?
    Gonfred. With the sad Emperor they
        are closeted;   10
I saw the three pass slowly up the stairs,
The lady weeping, the old Abbot cowl'd.
    Sigifred. What next?
    1st Knight.   I ache to think on 't.
    Gonfred.   'T is with fate.
    1st Knight. One while these proud towers
        are hush'd as death.
    Gonfred. The next our poor Prince fills
        the arched rooms
With ghastly ravings.
    Sigifred.   I do fear his brain.

Gonfred. I will see more.   Bear you so
 stout a heart?
     [*Exeunt into the Castle.*

SCENE IV. — *A Cabinet, opening towards
    a terrace*

OTHO, ERMINIA, ETHELBERT, *and a Physician, discovered.*

Otho. O, my poor boy!   My son!   My
 son!   My Ludolph!
Have ye no comfort for me, ye physicians
Of the weak body and soul?
 Ethelbert.   'T is not in medicine,
Either of heaven or earth, to cure, unless
Fit time be chosen to administer.
 Otho. A kind forbearance, holy Abbot.
 Come,
Erminia; here, sit by me, gentle girl;
Give me thy hand; hast thou forgiven me?
 Erminia. Would I were with the saints
  to pray for you!
 Otho. Why will ye keep me from my
  darling child?   10
 Physician. Forgive me, but he must not
  see thy face.
 Otho. Is then a father's countenance a
  Gorgon?
Hath it not comfort in it?   Would it not
Console my poor boy, cheer him, help his
 spirits?
Let me embrace him; let me speak to him;
I will!   Who hinders me?   Who's Em-
 peror?
 Physician. You may not, Sire; 't would
  overwhelm him quite,
He is so full of grief and passionate wrath;
Too heavy a sigh would kill him, or do
 worse.
He must be saved by fine contrivances;   20
And, most especially, we must keep clear
Out of his sight a father whom he loves;
His heart is full, it can contain no more,
And do its ruddy office.
 Ethelbert.   Sage advice;
We must endeavour how to ease and slacken
The tight-wound energies of his despair,
Not make them tenser.

 Otho.   Enough!   I hear, I hear;
Yet you were about to advise more, — I
 listen.
 Ethelbert. This learned doctor will agree
  with me,
That not in the smallest point should he be
  thwarted,   30
Or gainsaid by one word; his very mo-
 tions,
Nods, becks, and hints, should be obey'd
 with care,
Even on the moment; so his troubled mind
May cure itself.
 Physician.   There are no other means.
 Otho. Open the door; let's hear if all is
  quiet.
 Physician. Beseech you, Sire, forbear.
 Erminia.   Do, do.
 Otho.   I command!
Open it straight; — hush! — quiet! — my
 lost boy!
My miserable child!
 Ludolph (*indistinctly without*).   Fill, fill
  my goblet, — here's a health!
 Erminia.   O, close the door!
 Otho. Let, let me hear his voice; this
  cannot last: 39
And fain would I catch up his dying words,
Though my own knell they be!   This can-
 not last!
O let me catch his voice — for lo!   I hear
This silence whisper me that he is dead!
It is so!   Gersa?

    Enter GERSA.

 Physician. Say, how fares the prince?
 Gersa. More calm; his features are less
  wild and flush'd;
Once he complain'd of weariness.
 Physician.   Indeed!
'T is good, — 't is good; let him but fall
 asleep,
That saves him.
 Otho.   Gersa, watch him like a child;
Ward him from harm, — and bring me
 better news!
 Physician. Humour him to the height.
  I fear to go;   50

For should he catch a glimpse of my dull
    garb,
It might affright him, fill him with suspi-
    cion
That we believe him sick, which must not
    be.
    Gersa. I will invent what soothing means
        I can.
                    [*Exit* GERSA.
    Physician. This should cheer up your
        Highness; weariness
Is a good symptom, and most favourable;
It gives me pleasant hopes. Please you,
    walk forth
Upon the terrace; the refreshing air
Will blow one half of your sad doubts
    away.   [*Exeunt.*

SCENE V. — *A Banqueting Hall, bril-
liantly illuminated, and set forth with
all costly magnificence, with supper-
tables laden with services of gold and
silver. A door in the back scene, guarded
by two Soldiers. Lords, Ladies, Knights,
Gentlemen, etc., whispering sadly, and
ranging themselves; part entering and
part discovered.*

    1st Knight. Grievously are we tantalized,
        one and all;
Sway'd here and there, commanded to and
    fro,
As though we were the shadows of a sleep,
And link'd to a dreaming fancy. What do
    we here?
    Gonfred. I am no seer; you know we
        must obey
The prince from A to Z, though it should
    be
To set the place in flames. I pray, hast
    heard
Where the most wicked Princess is?
    1st Knight.   There, sir,
In the next room; have you remark'd those
    two   9
Stout soldiers posted at the door?
    Gonfred.   For what?
                        [*They whisper.*
    1st Lady. How ghast a train!

    2d Lady. Sure this should be some splen-
        did burial.
    1st Lady. What fearful whispering! See,
        see, — Gersa there!

            Enter GERSA.

    Gersa. Put on your brightest looks;
        smile if you can;
Behave as all were happy; keep your eyes
From the least watch upon him; if he
    speaks
To any one, answer collectedly,
Without surprise, his questions, howe'er
    strange.
Do this to the utmost — though, alas! with
    me
The remedy grows hopeless! Here he
    comes, —   20
Observe what I have said — show no sur-
    prise.

Enter LUDOLPH, *followed by* SIGIFRED *and
            Page.*

    Ludolph. A splendid company! rare
        beauties here!
I should have Orphean lips, and Plato's
    fancy,
Amphion's utterance, toned with his lyre,
Or the deep key of Jove's sonorous mouth,
To give fit salutation. Methought I heard,
As I came in, some whispers — what of
    that?
'Tis natural men should whisper; at the
    kiss
Of Psyche given by Love, there was a
    buzz
Among the gods! — and silence is as natu-
    ral.   30
These draperies are fine, and, being a
    mortal,
I should desire no better; yet, in truth,
There must be some superior costliness,
Some wider-domed high magnificence!
I would have, as a mortal I may not,
Hangings of heaven's clouds, purple and
    gold,
Slung from the spheres; gauzes of silver
    mist,

Loop'd up with cords of twisted wreathed
    light,
And tassel'd round with weeping meteors!
These pendent lamps and chandeliers are
    bright   40
As earthly fires from dull dross can be
    cleansed;
Yet could my eyes drink up intenser beams
Undazzled — this is darkness — when I
    close
These lids, I see far fiercer brilliances, —
Skies full of splendid moons, and shooting
    stars,
And spouting exhalations, diamond fires,
And panting fountains quivering with deep
    glows!
Yes — this is dark — is it not dark?
    Sigifred.   My Lord,
'T is late; the lights of festival are ever   49
Quench'd in the morn.
    Ludolph.   'T is not to-morrow then?
    Sigifred. 'T is early dawn.
    Gersa.   Indeed full time we slept;
Say you so, Prince?
    Ludolph.   I say I quarrel'd with you;
We did not tilt each other — that 's a
    blessing, —
Good gods! no innocent blood upon my
    head!
    Sigifred. Retire, Gersa!
    Ludolph.   There should be three more
    here:
For two of them, they stay away perhaps,
Being gloomy-minded, haters of fair rev-
    els, —
They know their own thoughts best.
                     As for the third,
Deep blue eyes, semi-shaded in white lids,
Finish'd with lashes fine for more soft
    shade,   60
Completed by her twin-arch'd ebon-brows;
White temples, of exactest elegance,
Of even mould, felicitous and smooth;
Cheeks fashion'd tenderly on either side,
So perfect, so divine, that our poor eyes
Are dazzled with the sweet proportioning,
And wonder that 't is so — the magic
    chance!

Her nostrils, small, fragrant, fairy-delicate;
Her lips — I swear no human bones e'er
    wore
So taking a disguise; — you shall behold
    her!   70
We 'll have her presently; ay, you shall see
    her,
And wonder at her, friends, she is so fair;
She is the world's chief jewel, and, by
    heaven,
She 's mine by right of marriage! — she is
    mine!
Patience, good people, in fit time I send
A summoner, — she will obey my call,
Being a wife most mild and dutiful.
First I would hear what music is prepared
To herald and receive her; let me hear!
    Sigifred. Bid the musicians soothe him
    tenderly.   80
                [*A soft strain of Music.*
    Ludolph. Ye have none better? No, I
    am content;
'T is a rich sobbing melody, with reliefs
Full and majestic; it is well enough,
And will be sweeter, when you see her pace
Sweeping into this presence, glistened o'er
With emptied caskets, and her train upheld
By ladies, habited in robes of lawn,
Sprinkled with golden crescents, others
    bright
In silks, with spangles shower'd, and bow'd
    to   89
By Duchesses and pearled Margravines!
Sad, that the fairest creature of the earth —
I pray you mind me not — 't is sad, I say,
That the extremest beauty of the world
Should so entrench herself away from me,
Behind a barrier of engender'd guilt!
    2d Lady. Ah! what a moan!
    1st Knight.   Most piteous indeed!
    Ludolph. She shall be brought before this
    company,
And then — then —
    1st Lady. He muses.
    Gersa.   O, Fortune, where will this
    end?
    Sigifred. I guess his purpose! Indeed
    he must not have

That pestilence brought in, — that cannot
be,   100
There we must stop him.
  Gersa.   I am lost! Hush, hush!
He is about to rave again.
  Ludolph. A barrier of guilt! I was the
fool,
She was the cheater! Who 's the cheater
now,
And who the fool? The entrapp'd, the
caged fool,
The bird-limed raven? She shall croak to
death
Secure! Methinks I have her in my fist,
To crush her with my heel! Wait, wait!
I marvel
My father keeps away. Good friend — ah!
Sigifred!
Do bring him to me, — and Erminia   110
I fain would see before I sleep — and Eth-
elbert,
That he may bless me, as I know he will,
Though I have cursed him.
  Sigifred.   Rather suffer me
To lead you to them.
  Ludolph.   No, excuse me, — no!
The day is not quite done. Go, bring them
hither.   [*Exit* SIGIFRED.
Certes, a father's smile should, like sun
light,
Slant on my sheafed harvest of ripe bliss.
Besides, I thirst to pledge my lovely bride
In a deep goblet: let me see — what wine?
The strong Iberian juice, or mellow Greek?
Or pale Calabrian? Or the Tuscan grape?
Or of old Ætna's pulpy wine-presses,   122
Black stain'd with the fat vintage, as it
were
The purple slaughter-house, where Bac-
chus' self
Prick'd his own swollen veins? Where is
my page?
  Page. Here, here!
  Ludolph. Be ready to obey me; anon
thou shalt
Bear a soft message for me; for the hour
Draws near when I must make a winding
up

Of bridal mysteries — a fine-spun ven-
geance!
Carve it on my tomb, that, when I rest
beneath,   130
Men shall confess this Prince was gull'd
and cheated,
But from the ashes of disgrace he rose
More than a fiery phœnix, and did burn
His ignominy up in purging fires!
Did I not send, Sir, but a moment past,
For my Father?
  Gersa.   You did.
  Ludolph.   Perhaps 't would be
Much better he came not.
  Gersa.   He enters now!

Enter OTHO, ERMINIA, ETHELBERT, SIGI-
FRED, *and Physician.*

  Ludolph. O thou good man, against whose
sacred head
I was a mad conspirator, chiefly too,   139
For the sake of my fair newly wedded wife,
Now to be punish'd, do not look so sad!
Those charitable eyes will thaw my heart,
Those tears will wash away a just resolve,
A verdict ten times sworn! Awake —
awake —
Put on a judge's brow, and use a tongue
Made iron-stern by habit! Thou shalt see
A deed to be applauded, 'scribed in gold!
Join a loud voice to mine, and so denounce
What I alone will execute
  Otho.   Dear son,
What is it? By your father's love, I sue
That it be nothing merciless!
  Ludolph.   To that demon?
Not so! No! She is in temple-stall   152
Being garnish'd for the sacrifice, and I,
The Priest of Justice, will immolate her
Upon the altar of wrath! She stings me
through! —
Even as the worm doth feed upon the nut,
So she, a scorpion, preys upon my brain!
I feel her gnawing here! Let her but
vanish,
Then, father, I will lead your legions forth,
Compact in steeled squares, and speared
files,   160

And bid our trumpets speak a fell rebuke
To nations drows'd in peace !
  Otho.　　　　　　　To-morrow, son,
Be your word law; forget to-day —
  Ludolph.　　　　　　　I will
When I have finish'd it ! Now, — now,
  I 'm pight, pʲⁱᵗʰᵗᵉ
Tight-footed for the deed !
  Erminia.　　　　　　Alas ! Alas !
  Ludolph. What angel's voice is that ?
    Erminia !
Ah ! gentlest creature, whose sweet inno-
    cence
Was almost murder'd; I am penitent;
Wilt thou forgive me ?　And thou, holy
  man,
Good Ethelbert, shall I die in peace with
  you ?　　　　　　　　　170
  Erminia. Die, my lord !
  Ludolph.　　　　I feel it possible.
  Otho.　　　　　　　　Physician ?
  Physician. I fear me he is past my skill.
  Otho.　　　　　　　　Not so !
  Ludolph. I see it — I see it — I have
  been wandering !
Half mad — not right here — I forget my
  purpose.
Bestir — bestir — Auranthe ! Ha ! ha ! ha !
Youngster ! Page ! go bid them drag her
  to me !
Obey !　This shall finish it !
             [*Draws a dagger.*
  Otho.　　　　Oh, my son ! my son !

  Sigifred. This must not be — stop there !
  Ludolph.　　　　　　Am I obey'd ?
A little talk with her — no harm — haste !
  haste !　　　　　　　[*Exit Page.*
Set her before me — never fear I can strike.
  Several Voices. My Lord ! My Lord !
  Gersa.　　　　　　　Good Prince !
  Ludolph. Why do ye trouble me ? out
  — out — away !　　.　　182
There she is ! take that ! and that ! no, no —
That 's not well done. — Where is she ?

*The doors open. Enter Page. Several wo-
men are seen grouped about* AURANTHE *in
the inner-room.*

  Page. Alas !　My Lord, my Lord ! they
  cannot move her !
Her arms are stiff, — her fingers clench'd
  and cold !
  Ludolph. She 's dead !
        [*Staggers and falls into their arms.*
  Ethelbert. Take away the dagger.
  Gersa.　　　　　　　Softly; so !
  Otho.　　Thank God for that !
  Sigifred.　　It could not harm him now.
  Gersa. No ! — brief be his anguish !
  Ludolph. She 's gone !　I am content —
  Nobles, good night !　　•　　190
We are all weary — faint — set ope the
  doors —
I will to bed ! — To-morrow —
                    [*Dies.*
      The Curtain falls.

KING STEPHEN

A DRAMATIC FRAGMENT

Lord Houghton, when reprinting this piece in the Aldine edition of 1876, appends the following note from the MSS. of Charles Armitage Brown: 'As soon as Keats had finished *Otho the Great* I pointed out to him a subject for an English historical tragedy in the reign of Stephen, beginning with his defeat by the Empress Maud and ending with the death of his son Eustace. He was struck with the variety of events and characters which must necessarily be introduced, and I offered to give, as before, their dramatic conduct. "The play must open," I began, "with the field of battle, when Stephen's forces are retreating." — "Stop," he cried, "I have been too long in leading strings; I will do all this myself." He immediately set about it, and wrote two or three scenes.'

ACT I

SCENE I. — *Field of Battle*

Alarum. Enter King STEPHEN, *Knights, and Soldiers.*

Stephen. If shame can on a soldier's vein-swoll'n front
Spread deeper crimson than the battle's toil,
Blush in your casing helmets! for see, see!
Yonder my chivalry, my pride of war,
Wrench'd with an iron hand from firm array,
Are routed loose about the plashy meads,
Of honour forfeit. O, that my known voice
Could reach your dastard ears, and fright you more!
Fly, cowards, fly! Glocester is at your backs!
Throw your slack bridles o'er the flurried manes,
Ply well the rowell with faint trembling heels,   10
Scampering to death at last!
  1st Knight.   The enemy
Bears his flaunt standard close upon their rear.

2d Knight. Sure of a bloody prey, seeing the fens
Will swamp them girth-deep.
  Stephen.   Over head and ears,
No matter! 'T is a gallant enemy;
How like a comet he goes streaming on.
But we must plague him in the flank, — hey, friends?
We are well breathed, — follow!

Enter Earl BALDWIN *and Soldiers, as defeated.*

Stephen.   De Redvers!
What is the monstrous bugbear that can fright   20
Baldwin?
  Baldwin. No scare-crow, but the fortunate star
Of boisterous Chester, whose fell truncheon now
Points level to the goal of victory.
This way he comes, and if you would maintain ·
Your person unaffronted by vile odds,
Take horse, my Lord.
  Stephen.   And which way spur for life?
Now I thank Heaven I am in the toils,
That soldiers may bear witness how my arm

Can burst the meshes.   Not the eagle more
Loves to beat up against a tyrannous blast,
Than I to meet the torrent of my foes.   31
This is a brag, — be 't so, — but if I fall,
Carve it upon my 'scutcheon'd sepulchre.
On, fellow soldiers !   Earl of Redvers,
    back !
Not twenty Earls of Chester shall brow-
    beat
The diadem.   [*Exeunt.   Alarum.*

SCENE II. — *Another part of the Field*

Trumpets sounding a Victory.   Enter
GLOCESTER, *Knights, and Forces.*

Glocester. Now may we lift our bruised
    visors up,
And take the flattering freshness of the
    air,
While the wide din of battle dies away
Into times past, yet to be echoed sure
In the silent pages of our chroniclers.
    1*st* Knight. Will Stephen's death be
    mark'd there, my good Lord,
Or that we gave him lodging in yon towers ?
    Glocester. Fain would I know the great
    usurper's fate.

Enter two Captains severally.

1*st* Captain. My Lord !
2*d* Captain.   Most noble Earl !
1*st* Captain. The King —
2*d* Captain.   The Empress greets —
Glocester. What of the King ?
1*st* Captain. He sole and lone maintains
A hopeless bustle 'mid our swarming arms,
And with a nimble savageness attacks,   13
Escapes, makes fiercer onset, then anew
Eludes death, giving death to most that
    dare
Trespass within the circuit of his sword !
He must by this have fallen.   Baldwin is
    taken;
And for the Duke of Bretagne, like a stag
He flies, for the Welsh beagles to hunt
    down.
God save the Empress !

Glocester.   Now our dreaded Queen:
What message from her Highness ?
2*d* Captain.   Royal Maud
From the throng'd towers of Lincoln hath
    look'd down,   22
Like Pallas from the walls of Ilion,
And seen her enemies havock'd at her feet.
She greets most noble Glocester from her
    heart,
Entreating him, his captains, and brave
    knights,
To grace a banquet.   The high city gates
Are envious which shall see your triumph
    pass;
The streets are full of music.

Enter 2d Knight.

Glocester.   Whence come you ?
2*d* Knight. From Stephen, my good
    Prince, — Stephen ! Stephen !   30
Glocester. Why do you make such echo-
    ing of his name ?
2*d* Knight. Because I think, my lord, he
    is no man,
But a fierce demon, 'nointed safe from
    wounds,
And misbaptized with a Christian name.
    Glocester. A mighty soldier ! — Does he
    still hold out ?
2*d* Knight. He shames our victory.   His
    valour still
Keeps elbow-room amid our eager swords,
And holds our bladed falchions all aloof —
His gleaming battle-axe being slaughter-
    sick,
Smote on the morion of a Flemish knight,
Broke short in his hand; upon the which
    he flung   41
The heft away with such a vengeful force,
It paunch'd the Earl of Chester's horse,
    who then
Spleen-hearted came in full career at him.
    Glocester. Did no one take him at a van-
    tage then ?
2*d* Knight. Three then with tiger leap
    upon him flew,
Whom, with his sword swift-drawn and
    nimbly held,

He stung away again, and stood to breathe,
Smiling.   Anon upon him rush'd once more
A throng of foes, and in this renew'd strife,
My sword met his and snapp'd off at the
    hilt.   51
  Glocester. Come, lead me to this man —
    and let us move
In silence, not insulting his sad doom
With clamorous trumpets.   To the Em-
    press bear
My salutation as befits the time.
              [*Exeunt* GLOCESTER *and Forces.*

SCENE III. — *The Field of Battle*

Enter STEPHEN *unarmed.*

  Stephen. Another sword !   And what if
    I could seize
One from Bellona's gleaming armoury,
Or choose the fairest of her sheafed spears !
Where are my enemies ?   Here, close at
    hand,
Here come the testy brood.   O, for a
    sword !
I 'm faint — a biting sword !   A noble
    sword !
A hedge-stake — or a ponderous stone to
    hurl
With brawny vengeance, like the labourer
    Cain.
Come on !   Farewell my kingdom, and all
    hail
Thou superb, plumed, and helmeted re-
    nown,   10
All hail — I would not truck this brilliant
    day
To rule in Pylos with a Nestor's beard —
Come on !

Enter DE KAIMS *and Knights, etc.*

  De Kaims. Is 't madness or a hunger
    after death
That makes thee thus unarm'd throw
    taunts at us ? —
Yield, Stephen, or my sword's point dips in
The gloomy current of a traitor's heart.
  Stephen. Do it, De Kaims, I will not
    budge an inch.

  De Kaims. Yes, of thy madness thou
    shalt take the meed.
  Stephen. Darest thou ?
  De Kaims. How dare, against a man dis-
    arm'd ?
  Stephen. What weapons has the lion but
    himself ?   20
Come not near me, De Kaims, for by the
    price
Of all the glory I have won this day,
Being a king, I will not yield alive
To any but the second man of the realm,
Robert of Glocester.
  De Kaims.   Thou shalt vail to me.
  Stephen. Shall I, when I have sworn
    against it, sir ?
Thou think'st it brave to take a breathing
    king,
That, on a court-day bow'd to haughty
    Maud,
The awed presence-chamber may be bold
To whisper, there 's the man who took
    alive   30
Stephen — me — prisoner.   Certes, De
    Kaims,
The ambition is a noble one.
  De Kaims.   'T is true,
And, Stephen, I must compass it.
  Stephen.   No, no,
Do not tempt me to throttle you on the
    gorge,
Or with my gauntlet crush your hollow
    breast,
Just when your knighthood is grown ripe
    and full
For lordship.
  A Soldier. Is an honest yeoman's spear
Of no use at a need ?   Take that.
  Stephen.   Ah, dastard !
  De Kaims. What, you are vulnerable !
    my prisoner !
  Stephen. No, not yet.   I disclaim it, and
    demand   40
Death as a sovereign right unto a king
Who 'sdains to yield to any but his peer,
If not in title, yet in noble deeds,
The Earl of Glocester.   Stab to the hilt,
    De Kaims,

For I will never by mean hands be led
From this so famous field.   Do you hear !
    Be quick !
Trumpets.   Enter the Earl of CHESTER *and*
    Knights.

SCENE IV.—*A Presence Chamber.   Queen*
MAUD *in a Chair of State, the Earls*
of GLOCESTER *and* CHESTER, *Lords,*
Attendants

Maud. Glocester, no more: I will behold
    that Boulogne:
Set him before me.   Not for the poor sake
Of regal pomp and a vain-glorious hour,
As thou with wary speech, yet near enough,
Hast hinted.
    Glocester. Faithful counsel have I given;
If wary, for your Highness' benefit.
    Maud. The Heavens forbid that I should
        not think so,
For by thy valour have I won this realm,
Which by thy wisdom I will ever keep.
To sage advisers let me ever bend   10
A meek attentive ear, so that they treat
Of the wide kingdom's rule and govern-
    ment,
Not trenching on our actions personal.
Advised, not school'd, I would be; and
    henceforth
Spoken to in clear, plain, and open terms,
Not side-ways sermon'd at.
    Glocester.   Then in plain terms,
Once more for the fallen king—
    Maud.   Your pardon, Brother,
I would no more of that; for, as I said,
'T is not for worldly pomp I wish to see
The rebel, but as dooming judge to give   20
A sentence something worthy of his guilt.
    Glocester. If 't must be so, I 'll bring him
        to your presence.
                    [*Exit* GLOCESTER.
    Maud. A meaner summoner might do as
        well—
My Lord of Chester, is 't true what I
    hear
Of Stephen of Boulogne, our prisoner,
That he, as a fit penance for his crimes,

Eats wholesome, sweet, and palatable food
Off Glocester's golden dishes — drinks pure
    wine,
Lodges soft ?
    Chester. More than that, my gracious
        Queen,
Has anger'd me.   The noble Earl, me-
        thinks,   30
Full soldier as he is, and without peer
In counsel, dreams too much among his
    books.
It may read well, but sure 't is out of date
To play the Alexander with Darius.
    Maud. Truth !   I think so.   By Heavens
        it shall not last !
    Chester. It would amaze your Highness
        now to mark
How Glocester overstrains his courtesy
To that crime-loving rebel, that Boulogne —
    Maud. That ingrate !
    Chester.   For whose vast ingratitude
To our late sovereign lord, your noble sire,
The generous Earl condoles in his mishaps,
And with a sort of lackeying friendliness,
Talks off the mighty frowning from his
        brow,   43
Woos him to hold a duet in a smile,
Or, if it please him, play an hour at chess —
    Maud. A perjured slave !
    Chester.   And for his perjury,
Glocester has fit rewards — nay, I believe,
He sets his bustling household's wits at
        work
For flatteries to ease this Stephen's hours,
And make a heaven of his purgatory;   50
Adorning bondage with the pleasant gloss
Of feasts and music, and all idle shows
Of indoor pageantry; while syren whispers,
Predestined for his ear, 'scape as half-
        check'd
From lips the courtliest and the rubiest,
Of all the realm, admiring of his deeds.
    Maud. A frost upon his summer !
    Chester.   A queen's nod
Can make his June December.   Here he
    comes.

THE EVE OF ST. MARK

A FRAGMENT

In a letter to George and Georgiana Keats, dated February 14, 1819, Keats says that he means to send them in the next packet 'The Pot of Basil,' 'St. Agnes' Eve,' and 'if I should have finished it a little thing called "The Eve of St. Mark."' He does not refer to the poem again directly, until writing from Winchester to the same, September 20, when he says: 'The great beauty of poetry is that it makes everything in every place interesting. The palatine Vienna and the abbotine Winchester are equally interesting. Some time since I began a poem called "The Eve of St. Mark," quite in the spirit of town quietude. I think I will give you the sensation of walking about an old country town in a coolish evening. I know not whether I shall ever finish it. I will give it as far as I have gone.' The poem appears never to have been finished, and was published in this fragmentary form in *Life, Letters and Literary Remains*.

Mr. Forman gives an interesting extract from a letter written him by Mr. Rossetti, which throws a possible light on the origin of the poem. He had been reading Keats's letters to Fanny Brawne, and writes: 'I should think it very conceivable — nay, I will say *to myself* highly probable and almost certain, — that the "Poem which I have in my head" referred to by Keats at page 106 was none other than the fragmentary "Eve of St. Mark." By the light of the extract, . . . I judge that the heroine — remorseful after trifling with a sick and now absent lover — might make her way to the minster-porch to learn his fate by the spell, and perhaps see his figure enter but not return.' The extract from Keats's letter is as follows: 'If my health would bear it, I could write a Poem which I have in my head, which would be a consolation for people in such a situation as mine. I would show some one in Love as I am, with a person living in such Liberty as you do.'

UPON a Sabbath-day it fell;
Twice holy was the Sabbath-bell,
That call'd the folk to evening prayer;
The city streets were clean and fair
From wholesome drench of April rains;
And, on the western window panes,
The chilly sunset faintly told
Of unmatured green valleys cold,
Of the green thorny bloomless hedge,
Of rivers new with spring-tide sedge,   10
Of primroses by shelter'd rills,
And daisies on the aguish hills.
Twice holy was the Sabbath-bell:
The silent streets were crowded well
With staid and pious companies,
Warm from their fireside orat'ries;
And moving, with demurest air,
To even-song, and vesper prayer.

Each arched porch, and entry low,
Was fill'd with patient folk and slow,   20
With whispers hush, and shuffling feet,
While play'd the organ loud and sweet.

The bells had ceased, the prayers begun,
And Bertha had not yet half done
A curious volume, patch'd and torn,
That all day long, from earliest morn,
Had taken captive her two eyes,
Among its golden broideries;
Perplex'd her with a thousand things, —
The stars of Heaven, and angels' wings,   30
Martyrs in a fiery blaze,
Azure saints and silver rays,
Moses' breastplate, and the seven
Candlesticks John saw in Heaven,
The winged Lion of Saint Mark,

renantal Ark,
ny mysteries,
id golden mice.

a maiden fair,
th' old Minster-square;   40
eside she could see,
  rich antiquity,
Bishop's garden-wall;
mores and elm-trees tall,
  the forest had outstript,
  north-wind ever nipt,
  by the mighty pile.
e, and read awhile,
ad 'gainst the window-pane.
ried, and then again,   50
isk eve left her dark
gend of St. Mark.
d lawn-frill, fine and thin,
p her soft warm chin,
: neck and swimming eyes,
with saintly imag'ries.

om, and silent all,
id then the still foot-fall
rning homewards late,
oing minster-gate.   60
ous daws, that all the day
tops and towers play,
  had gone to rest,
ncient belfry-nest,
p they fall betimes,
d the drowsy chimes.

it, all was gloom,
  in the homely room:
t, poor cheated soul !
  lamp from the dismal coal;   70
ard, with bright drooping hair
ook, full against the glare.
, in uneasy guise,
ut, a giant size,
eam and old oak chair,
  cage, and panel-square;

And the warm angled winter-screen,
On which were many monsters seen,
Call'd doves of Siam, Lima mice,
And legless birds of Paradise,   80
Macaw, and tender Avadavat,
And silken-furr'd Angora cat.
Untired she read, her shadow still
Glower'd about, as it would fill
The room with wildest forms and shades,
As though some ghostly queen of spades
Had come to mock behind her back,
And dance, and ruffle her garments black.
Untired she read the legend page,
Of holy Mark, from youth to age,   90
On land, on sea, in pagan chains,
Rejoicing for his many pains.
Sometimes the learned eremite,
With golden star, or dagger bright,
Referr'd to pious poesies
Written in smallest crow-quill size
Beneath the text; and thus the rhyme
Was parcell'd out from time to time:
——— ' Als writith he of swevenis,
Men han beforne they wake in bliss,   100
Whanne that hir friendes thinke him bound
In crimped shroude farre under grounde;
And how a litling child mote be
A saint er its nativitie,
Gif that the modre (God her blesse !)
Kepen in solitarinesse,
And kissen devoute the holy croce,
Of Goddes love, and Sathan's force, —
He writith; and thinges many mo
Of swiche thinges I may not show.   110
Bot I must tellen verilie
Somdel of Sainte Cicilie,
And chieflie what he auctorethe
Of Sainte Markis life and dethe: '

At length her constant eyelids come
Upon the fervent martyrdom;
Then lastly to his holy shrine,
Exalt amid the tapers' shine
At Venice, —

HYPERION

A FRAGMENT

The first mention of *Hyperion* in Keats's letters occurs in that written on Christmas day, 1818, to his brother and sister in America, in which he says: 'I think you knew before you left England that my next subject would be "the fall of Hyperion." I went on a little with it last night, but it will take some time to get into the vein again. I will not give you any extracts because I wish the whole to make an impression.' He speaks of it a week later as 'scarce begun.' Again, February 14, 1819, he writes to the same: 'I have not gone on with *Hyperion* — for to tell the truth I have not been in great cue for writing lately — I must wait for the spring to rouse me up a little.' In August he told Bailey that he had been writing parts of *Hyperion*, but it is quite plain that he did little continuous work on it, but was drawn off by his tales and tragedy. From Winchester, September 22, 1819, he writes to Reynolds: 'I have given up *Hyperion* — there were too many Miltonic inversions in it — Miltonic verse cannot be written but in an artful, or, rather, artist's humour. I wish to give myself up to other sensations. English ought to be kept up. It may be interesting to you to pick out some lines from *Hyperion*, and put a mark × to the false beauty proceeding from art, and one ‖ to the true voice of feeling. Upon my soul 't was imagination — I cannot make the distinction — every now and then there is a Miltonic intonation — but I cannot make the division properly.' From the silence regarding the poem in his after letters, it would appear that he left it at this stage.

That Keats designed a large epic in *Hyperion*, which was to be in ten books, is plain, but it is also tolerably clear that he abandoned his purpose, for he did not actually forbid the publication of the fragment, though it is doubtful if the whole reason for his action is given in the *Publishers' Advertisement* to the 1820 volume, containing the poem. 'If any apology be thought necessary,' it is there said, 'for the

appearance of the unfinished poem of *Hyperion*, the publishers beg to state that they alone are responsible, as it was printed at their particular request, and contrary to the wish of the author. The poem was intended to have been of equal length with *Endymion*, but the reception given to that work discouraged the author from proceeding.'

Keats's friend Woodhouse, in his interleaved and annotated copy of *Endymion*, says of *Hyperion*: 'The poem if completed would have treated of the dethronement of Hyperion, the former God of the Sun, by Apollo, — and incidentally of those of Oceanus by Neptune, of Saturn by Jupiter, etc., and of the war of the Giants for Saturn's reëstablishment, with other events, of which we have but very dark hints in the mythological poets of Greece and Rome.'

It is not impossible that besides the inertia produced by diminution of physical powers, another reason existed for Keats's failure to complete his poem. In the two full books which we have, he had stated so fully and explicitly the underlying thought in his interpretation of the myth that his interest in any delineation of a hopeless struggle might well have been unequal to the task. The speeches successively of Oceanus and Clymene which so enraged Enceladus were the masculine and feminine confessions that as their own supremacy over the antecedent chaos had been due to the law which made order expel disorder, so the supremacy of the new race of gods over them was due to the still further law

'That first in beauty should be first in might.'

Nay, more, the vision they have is not of a restoration of the old order, but of the defeat of the new by some still more distant evolution.

'Another race may drive
Our conquerors to mourn as we do now.'

Of the relation of this poem to *Hyperion, a Vision*, see the Appendix, where the other fragment is printed.

BOOK I

DEEP in the shady sadness of a vale
Far sunken from the healthy breath of
morn,
Far from the fiery noon, and eve's one
star,
Sat gray-hair'd Saturn, quiet as a stone,
Still as the silence round about his lair;
Forest on forest hung about his head
Like cloud on cloud. No stir of air was
there,
Not so much life as on a summer's day
Robs not one light seed from the feather'd
grass,
But where the dead leaf fell, there did it
rest. 10
A stream went voiceless by, still deadened
more
By reason of his fallen divinity
Spreading a shade: the Naiad 'mid her
reeds
Press'd her cold finger closer to her lips.

Along the margin-sand large foot-marks
went,
No further than to where his feet had
stray'd,
And slept there since. Upon the sodden
ground
His old right hand lay nerveless, listless,
dead,
Unsceptred; and his realmless eyes were
closed ;
While his bow'd head seem'd list'ning to
the Earth, 20
His ancient mother, for some comfort yet.

It seem'd no force could wake him from
his place;
But there came one, who with a kindred
hand
Touch'd his wide shoulders, after bending
low
With reverence, though to one who knew
it not.
She was a Goddess of the infant world;
By her in stature the tall Amazon
Had stood a pigmy's height: she would
have ta'en
Achilles by the hair and bent his neck;
Or with a finger stay'd Ixion's wheel. 30
Her face was large as that of Memphian
sphinx,
Pedestal'd haply in a palace-court,
When sages look'd to Egypt for their lore.
But oh ! how unlike marble was that face;
How beautiful, if sorrow had not made
Sorrow more beautiful than Beauty's self.
There was a listening fear in her regard,
As if calamity had but begun;
As if the vanward clouds of evil days 39
Had spent their malice, and the sullen rear
Was with its stored thunder labouring up.
One hand she press'd upon that aching
spot
Where beats the human heart, as if just
there,
Though an immortal, she felt cruel pain:
The other upon Saturn's bended neck
She laid, and to the level of his ear
Leaning with parted lips, some words she
spake
In solemn tenour and deep organ tone:
Some mourning words, which in our feeble
tongue
Would come in these like accents; O how
frail 50
To that large utterance of the early Gods !
'Saturn, look up ! — though wherefore,
poor old King ?
I have no comfort for thee, no not one:
I cannot say, " O wherefore sleepest thou ? "
For heaven is parted from thee, and the
earth
Knows thee not, thus afflicted, for a God;
And ocean too, with all its solemn noise,
Has from thy sceptre pass'd; and all the
air
Is emptied of thine hoary majesty.
Thy thunder, conscious of the new com-
mand, 60
Rumbles reluctant o'er our fallen house;
And thy sharp lightning in unpractised
hands
Scorches and burns our once serene domain.

O aching time ! O moments big as years !
All as ye pass swell out the monstrous
　　truth,
And press it so upon our weary griefs
That unbelief has not a space to breathe.
Saturn, sleep on: — O thoughtless, why
　　did I
Thus violate thy slumbrous solitude ?
Why should I ope thy melancholy eyes ?　70
Saturn, sleep on ! while at thy feet I
　　weep.'

　　As when, upon a tranced summer-night,
Those green - robed senators of mighty
　　woods,
Tall oaks, branch-charmed by the earnest
　　stars,
Dream, and so dream all night without a
　　stir,
Save from one gradual solitary gust
Which comes upon the silence, and dies off,
As if the ebbing air had but one wave:
So came these words and went; the while
　　in tears
She touch'd her fair large forehead to the
　　ground,　　　　　　　　　　　　　　80
Just where her falling hair might be out-
　　spread
A soft and silken mat for Saturn's feet.
One moon, with alteration slow, had shed
Her silver seasons four upon the night,
And still these two were postured motion-
　　less,
Like natural sculpture in cathedral cavern;
The frozen God still couchant on the earth,
And the sad Goddess weeping at his feet:
Until at length old Saturn lifted up　　89
His faded eyes, and saw his kingdom gone,
And all the gloom and sorrow of the place,
And that fair kneeling Goddess; and then
　　spake,
As with a palsied tongue, and while his
　　beard
Shook horrid with such aspen-malady:
' O tender spouse of gold Hyperion,
Thea, I feel thee ere I see thy face;
Look up, and let me see our doom in it;
Look up, and tell me if this feeble shape

Is Saturn's; tell me, if thou hear'st the
　　voice
Of Saturn; tell me, if this wrinkling brow,
Naked and bare of its great diadem,　101
Peers like the front of Saturn. Who had
　　power
To make me desolate ? whence came the
　　strength ?
How was it nurtured to such bursting forth,
While Fate seem'd strangled in my nervous
　　grasp ?
But it is so; and I am smother'd up,
And buried from all godlike exercise
Of influence benign on planets pale,
Of admonitions to the winds and seas,　109
Of peaceful sway above man's harvesting,
And all those acts which Deity supreme
Doth ease its heart of love in. — I am gone
Away from my own bosom: I have left
My strong identity, my real self,
Somewhere between the throne, and where
　　I sit
Here on this spot of earth. Search, Thea,
　　search !
Open thine eyes eterne, and sphere them
　　round
Upon all space: space starr'd, and lorn of
　　light;
Space region'd with life-air, and barren
　　void;
Spaces of fire, and all the yawn of hell.　120
Search, Thea, search ! and tell me if thou
　　seest
A certain shape or shadow, making way
With wings or chariot fierce to repossess
A heaven he lost erewhile: it must — it
　　must
Be of ripe progress — Saturn must be King.
Yes, there must be a golden victory;
There must be Gods thrown down, and
　　trumpets blown
Of triumph calm, and hymns of festival
Upon the gold clouds metropolitan,
Voices of soft proclaim, and silver stir　130
Of strings in hollow shells; and there shall
　　be
Beautiful things made new, for the sur-
　　prise

Of the sky-children; I will give command:
Thea! Thea! Thea! where is Saturn?'

This passion lifted him upon his feet,
And made his hands to struggle in the air,
His Druid locks to shake and ooze with
    sweat,
His eyes to fever out, his voice to cease.
He stood, and heard not Thea's sobbing
    deep;   139
A little time, and then again he snatch'd
Utterance thus: — 'But cannot I create?
Cannot I form? Cannot I fashion forth
Another world, another universe,
To overbear and crumble this to nought?
Where is another chaos? Where?' — That
    word
Found way unto Olympus, and made quake
The rebel three. — Thea was startled up,
And in her bearing was a sort of hope,
As thus she quick-voiced spake, yet full of
    awe.

'This cheers our fallen house: come to
    our friends,   150
O Saturn! come away, and give them
    heart;
I know the covert, for thence came I
    hither.'
Thus brief; then with beseeching eyes she
    went
With backward footing through the shade
    a space:
He follow'd, and she turn'd to lead the
    way
Through aged boughs, that yielded like the
    mist
Which eagles cleave upmounting from
    their nest.

Meanwhile in other realms big tears
    were shed,
More sorrow like to this, and such like
    woe,
Too huge for mortal tongue or pen of
    scribe: 160
The Titans fierce, self - hid, or prison-
    bound,

Groan'd for the old allegiance once more,
And listen'd in sharp pain for Saturn's
    voice.
But one of the whole mammoth-brood still
    kept
His sov'reignty, and rule, and majesty;
Blazing Hyperion on his orbed fire
Still sat, still snuff'd the incense, teeming
    up
From man to the sun's God; yet unsecure:
For as among us mortals omens drear
Fright and perplex, so also shudder'd he,
Not at dog's howl, or gloom-bird's hated
    screech,   171
Or the familiar visiting of one
Upon the first toll of his passing-bell,
Or prophesyings of the midnight lamp;
But horrors, portion'd to a giant nerve,
Oft made Hyperion ache. His palace
    bright
Bastion'd with pyramids of glowing gold,
And touch'd with shade of bronzed obe-
    lisks,
Glared a blood-red through all its thousand
    courts,
Arches, and domes, and fiery galleries; 180
And all its curtains of Aurorian clouds
Flush'd angerly: while sometimes eagles'
    wings,
Unseen before by Gods or wondering men,
Darken'd the place; and neighing steeds
    were heard,
Not heard before by Gods or wondering
    men.
Also, when he would taste the spicy
    wreaths
Of incense, breathed aloft from sacred hills,
Instead of sweets, his ample palate took
Savour of poisonous brass and metal sick:
And so, when harbour'd in the sleepy west,
After the full completion of fair day, 191
For rest divine upon exalted couch
And slumber in the arms of melody,
He paced away the pleasant hours of ease
With stride colossal, on from hall to hall;
While far within each aisle and deep re-
    cess,
His winged minions in close clusters stood,

Amazed and full of fear; like anxious men
Who on wide plains gather in panting
    troops,
When earthquakes jar their battlements
    and towers.   200
Even now, while Saturn, roused from icy
    trance,
Went step for step with Thea through the
    woods,
Hyperion, leaving twilight in the rear,
Came slope upon the threshold of the west;
Then, as was wont, his palace-door flew ope
In smoothest silence, save what solemn
    tubes,
Blown by the serious Zephyrs, gave of
    sweet
And wandering sounds, slow-breathed melo-
    dies;
And like a rose in vermeil tint and shape,
In fragrance soft, and coolness to the eye, 210
That inlet to severe magnificence
Stood full blown, for the God to enter in.

He enter'd, but he enter'd full of wrath;
His flaming robes stream'd out beyond his
    heels,
And gave a roar, as if of earthly fire,
That scared away the meek ethereal Hours
And made their dove-wings tremble. On
    he flared,
From stately nave to nave, from vault to
    vault,
Through bowers of fragrant and enwreathed
    light,
And diamond - paved lustrous long ar-
    cades,   220
Until he reach'd the great main cupola;
There standing fierce beneath, he stampt
    his foot,
And from the basements deep to the high
    towers
Jarr'd his own golden region; and before
The quavering thunder thereupon had
    ceased,
His voice leapt out, despite of godlike
    curb,
To this result: 'O dreams of day and
    night !

O monstrous forms ! O effigies of pain !
O spectres busy in a cold, cold gloom !
O lank-ear'd Phantoms of black-weeded
    pools !   230
Why do I know ye ? why have I seen ye ?
    why
Is my eternal essence thus distraught
To see and to behold these horrors new ?
Saturn is fallen, am I too to fall ?
Am I to leave this haven of my rest,
This cradle of my glory, this soft clime,
This calm luxuriance of blissful light,
These crystalline pavilions, and pure fanes,
Of all my lucent empire ? It is left
Deserted, void, nor any haunt of mine. 240
The blaze, the splendour, and the symme-
    try,
I cannot see — but darkness, death and
    darkness.
Even here, into my centre of repose,
The shady visions come to domineer,
Insult, and blind, and stifle up my pomp. —
Fall ! — No, by Tellus and her briny robes !
Over the fiery frontier of my realms
I will advance a terrible right arm
Shall scare that infant thunderer, rebel
    Jove,
And bid old Saturn take his throne again.'
He spake, and ceased, the while a heavier
    threat   251
Held struggle with his throat, but came
    not forth;
For as in theatres of crowded men
Hubbub increases more they call out
    ' Hush ! '
So at Hyperion's words the Phantoms pale
Bestirr'd themselves, thrice horrible and
    cold;
And from the mirror'd level where he stood
A mist arose, as from a scummy marsh.
At this, through all his bulk an agony
Crept gradual, from the feet unto the
    crown,   260
Like a lithe serpent vast and muscular
Making slow way, with head and neck con-
    vulsed
From over-strained might. Released, he
    fled

To the eastern gates, and full six dewy
    hours
Before the dawn in season due should
    blush, .
He breathed fierce breath against the sleepy
    portals,
Clear'd them of heavy vapours, burst them
    wide
Suddenly on the ocean's chilly streams.
The planet orb of fire, whereon he rode
Each day from east to west the heavens
    through,   270
Spun round in sable curtaining of clouds;
Not therefore veiled quite, blindfold, and
    hid,
But ever and anon the glancing spheres,
Circles, and arcs, and broad-belting colure,
Glow'd through, and wrought upon the
    muffling dark
Sweet-shaped lightnings from the nadir
    deep
Up to the zenith, — hieroglyphics old,
Which sages and keen-eyed astrologers
Then living on the earth, with labouring
    thought
Won from the gaze of many centuries: 280
Now lost, save what we find on remnants
    huge
Of stone, or marble swart; their import
    gone,
Their wisdom long since fled. — Two wings
    this orb
Possess'd for glory, two fair argent wings,
Ever exalted at the God's approach:
And now, from forth the gloom their
    plumes immense
Rose, one by one, till all outspreaded were;
While still the dazzling globe maintain'd
    eclipse,
Awaiting for Hyperion's command.
Fain would he have commanded, fain took
    throne   290
And bid the day begin, if but for change.
He might not: — No, though a primeval
    God:
The sacred seasons might not be disturb'd.
Therefore the operations of the dawn
Stay'd in their birth, even as here 't is told.

Those silver wings expanded sisterly,
Eager to sail their orb; the porches wide
Open'd upon the dusk demesnes of night;
And the bright Titan, phrenzied with new
    woes,   299
Unused to bend, by hard compulsion bent
His spirit to the sorrow of the time;
And all along a dismal rack of clouds,
Upon the boundaries of day and night,
He stretch'd himself in grief and radiance
    faint.
There as he lay, the Heaven with its stars
Look'd down on him with pity, and the
    voice
Of Cœlus, from the universal space,
Thus whisper'd low and solemn in his ear:
' O brightest of my children dear, earth-born
And sky-engendered, Son of Mysteries 310
All unrevealed even to the powers
Which met at thy creating; at whose joys
And palpitations sweet, and pleasures soft,
I, Cœlus, wonder, how they came and
    whence;
And at the fruits thereof what shapes they
    be,
Distinct, and visible; symbols divine,
Manifestations of that beauteous life
Diffused unseen throughout eternal space:
Of these new-form'd art thou, oh brightest
    child !
Of these, thy brethren and the God-
    desses !   320
There is sad feud among ye, and rebellion
Of son against his sire. I saw him fall,
I saw my first-born tumbled from his
    throne !
To me his arms were spread, to me his
    voice
Found way from forth the thunders round
    his head !
Pale wox I, and in vapours hid my face.
Art thou, too, near such doom ? vague fear
    there is:
For I have seen my sons most unlike Gods.
Divine ye were created, and divine
In sad demeanour, solemn, undisturb'd, 330
Unruffled, like high Gods, ye lived and
    ruled:

Now I ~~behold in~~ you fear, hope, and
~~wrath;~~
~~Actions of rage and~~ passion; even as
I ~~see them, in the~~ mortal world beneath,
~~In men who~~ die. — This is the grief, O
Son !
~~Sad sign~~ of ruin, sudden dismay, and fall !
~~Yet~~ do thou strive; as thou art capable,
As thou canst move about, an evident
God;
And canst oppose to each malignant hour
Ethereal presence: — I am but a voice; 340
My life is but the life of winds and tides,
No more than winds and tides can I
avail: —
But thou canst. — Be thou therefore in the
van
Of circumstance; yea, seize the arrow's
barb
Before the tense string murmur. — To the
earth !
For there thou wilt find Saturn, and his
woes.
Meantime I will keep watch on thy bright
sun,
And of thy seasons be a careful nurse.' —
Ere half this region-whisper had come
down,
Hyperion arose, and on the stars   350
Lifted his curved lids, and kept them wide
Until it ceased; and still he kept them
wide:
And still they were the same bright, pa-
tient stars.
Then with a slow incline of his broad
breast,
Like to a diver in the pearly seas,
Forward he stoop'd over the airy shore,
And plunged all noiseless into the deep
night.

BOOK II

Just at the self-same beat of Time's wide
wings
Hyperion slid into the rustled air,
And Saturn gain'd with Thea that sad
place

Where Cybele and the bruised Titans
mourn'd.
It was a den where no insulting light
Could glimmer on their tears; where their
own groans
They felt, but heard not, for the solid roar
Of thunderous waterfalls and torrents
hoarse,
Pouring a constant bulk, uncertain where.
Crag jutting forth to crag, and rocks that
seem'd   10
Ever as if just rising from a sleep,
Forehead to forehead held their monstrous
horns;
And thus in thousand hugest phantasies
Made a fit roofing to this nest of woe.
Instead of thrones, hard flint they sat upon,
Couches of rugged stone, and slaty ridge
Stubborn'd with iron.   All were not assem-
bled:
Some chain'd in torture, and some wander-
ing.
Cœus, and Gyges, and Briareüs,
Typhon, and Dolor, and Porphyrion,   20
With many more, the brawniest in assault,
Were pent in regions of laborious breath;
Dungeon'd in opaque element to keep
Their clenched teeth still clench'd, and all
their limbs
Lock'd up like veins of metal, crampt and
screw'd;
Without a motion, save of their big hearts
Heaving in pain, and horribly convulsed
With sanguine, feverous, boiling gurge of
pulse.
Mnemosyne was straying in the world;
Far from her moon had Phœbe wandered; 30
And many else were free to roam abroad,
But for the main, here found they covert
drear.
Scarce images of life, one here, one there,
Lay vast and edgeways; like a dismal
cirque
Of Druid stones, upon a forlorn moor,
When the chill rain begins at shut of eve,
In dull November, and their chancel vault,
The Heaven itself, is blinded throughout
night.

Each one kept shroud, nor to his neighbour
  gave
Or word, or look, or action of despair.   40
Creüs was one; his ponderous iron mace
Lay by him, and a shatter'd rib of rock
Told of his rage, ere he thus sank and
  pined.
Iapetus another; in his grasp,
A serpent's plashy neck; its barbed tongue
Squeezed from the gorge, and all its un-
  curl'd length
Dead; and because the creature could not
  spit
Its poison in the eyes of conquering Jove.
Next Cottus: prone he lay, chin uppermost,
As though in pain: for still upon the flint 50
He ground severe his skull, with open
  mouth
And eyes at horrid working. Nearest him
Asia, born of most enormous Caf,
Who cost her mother Tellus keener pangs,
Though feminine, than any of her sons:
More thought than woe was in her dusky
  face,
For she was prophesying of her glory;
And in her wide imagination stood
Palm-shaded temples, and high rival fanes,
By Oxus or in Ganges' sacred isles.   60
Even as Hope upon her anchor leans,
So leant she, not so fair, upon a tusk
Shed from the broadest of her elephants.
Above her, on a crag's uneasy shelve,
Upon his elbow raised, all prostrate else,
Shadow'd Enceladus; once tame and mild
As grazing ox unworried in the meads;
Now tiger-passion'd, lion-thoughted, wroth,
He meditated, plotted, and even now
Was hurling mountains in that second
  war,   70
Not long delay'd, that scared the younger
  Gods
To hide themselves in forms of beast and
  bird.
Not far hence Atlas; and beside him prone
Phorcus, the sire of Gorgons. Neighbour'd
  close
Oceanus, and Tethys, in whose lap
Sobb'd Clymene among her tangled hair.

In midst of all lay Themis, at the feet
Of Ops the queen all clouded round from
  sight;
No shape distinguishable, more than when
Thick night confounds the pine-tops with
  the clouds: 80
And many else whose names may not be
  told.
For when the Muse's wings are air-ward
  spread,
Who shall delay her flight? And she
  must chant
Of Saturn, and his guide, who now had
  climb'd
With damp and slippery footing from a
  depth
More horrid still. Above a sombre cliff
Their heads appear'd, and up their stature
  grew
Till on the level height their steps found
  ease:
Then Thea spread abroad her trembling
  arms
Upon the precincts of this nest of pain,   90
And sidelong fix'd her eye on Saturn's
  face:
There saw she direst strife; the supreme
  God
At war with all the frailty of grief,
Of rage, of fear, anxiety, revenge,
Remorse, spleen, hope, but most of all de-
  spair.
Against these plagues he strove in vain:
  for Fate
Had pour'd a mortal oil upon his head,
A disanointing poison: so that Thea,
Affrighted, kept her still, and let him pass
First onwards in, among the fallen tribe. 100

As with us mortal men, the laden heart
Is persecuted more, and fever'd more,
When it is nighing to the mournful house
Where other hearts are sick of the same
  bruise;
So Saturn, as he walk'd into the midst,
Felt faint, and would have sunk among the
  rest,
But that he met Enceladus's eye,

Whose mightiness, and awe of him, at
　　once
Came like an inspiration; and he shouted,
'Titans, behold your God!' at which some
　　groan'd;　　　　　　　　　　　　110
Some started on their feet; some also
　　shouted;
Some wept, some wail'd — all bow'd with
　　reverence;
And Ops, uplifting her black folded veil,
Show'd her pale cheeks, and all her fore-
　　head wan,
Her eyebrows thin and jet, and hollow
　　eyes.
There is a roaring in the bleak-grown
　　pines
When Winter lifts his voice; there is a
　　noise
Among immortals when a God gives sign,
With hushing finger, how he means to
　　load
His tongue with the full weight of utter-
　　less thought,　　　　　　　　　120
With thunder, and with music, and with
　　pomp:
Such noise is like the roar of bleak-grown
　　pines;
Which, when it ceases in this mountain'd
　　world,
No other sound succeeds; but ceasing here,
Among these fallen, Saturn's voice there-
　　from
Grew up like organ, that begins anew
Its strain, when other harmonies, stopt
　　short,
Leave the dinn'd air vibrating silverly.
Thus grew it up: — 'Not in my own sad
　　breast,
Which is its own great judge and searcher
　　out,　　　　　　　　　　　　130
Can I find reason why ye should be thus:
Not in the legends of the first of days,
Studied from that old spirit-leaved book
Which starry Uranus with finger bright
Saved from the shores of darkness, when
　　the waves
Low-ebb'd still hid it up in shallow
　　gloom; —

And the which book ye know I ever kept
For my firm-based footstool: — Ah, in-
　　firm!
Not there, nor in sign, symbol, or portent
Of element, earth, water, air, and fire, —
At war, at peace, or inter-quarrelling　　141
One against one, or two, or three, or all
Each several one against the other three,
As fire with air loud warring when rain-
　　floods
Drown both, and press them both against
　　earth's face,
Where, finding sulphur, a quadruple wrath
Unhinges the poor world; — not in that
　　strife,
Wherefrom I take strange lore, and read
　　it deep,
Can I find reason why ye should be thus:
No, nowhere can unriddle, though I search,
And pore on Nature's universal scroll　151
Even to swooning, why ye, Divinities,
The first-born of all shaped and palpable
　　Gods,
Should cower beneath what, in comparison,
Is untremendous might. Yet ye are here,
O'erwhelm'd, and spurn'd, and batter'd, ye
　　are here!
O Titans, shall I say "Arise!" — Ye
　　groan:
Shall I say "Crouch!" — Ye groan.
　　What can I then?
O Heaven wide! O unseen parent dear!
What can I? Tell me, all ye brethren
　　Gods,　　　　　　　　　　　　160
How we can war, how engine our great
　　wrath!
O speak your counsel now, for Saturn's ear
Is all a-hunger'd. Thou, Oceanus,
Ponderest high and deep; and in thy face
I see, astonied, that severe content
Which comes of thought and musing: give
　　us help!'

　　So ended Saturn; and the God of the
　　Sea,
Sophist and sage, from no Athenian grove,
But cogitation in his watery shades,
Arose, with locks not oozy, and began,　170

In murmurs, which his first-endeavouring
tongue
Caught infant-like from the far-foamed
sands.
'O ye, whom wrath consumes! who, pas-
sion-stung,
Writhe at defeat, and nurse your agonies!
Shut up your senses, stifle up your ears,
My voice is not a bellows unto ire.
Yet listen, ye who will, whilst I bring
proof
How ye, perforce, must be content to stoop;
And in the proof much comfort will I give,
If ye will take that comfort in its truth. 180
We fall by course of Nature's law, not
force
Of thunder, or of Jove. Great Saturn, thou
Hast sifted well the atom-universe;
But for this reason, that thou art the King,
And only blind from sheer supremacy,
One avenue was shaded from thine eyes,
Through which I wander'd to eternal truth.
And first, as thou wast not the first of pow-
ers,
So art thou not the last; it cannot be;
Thou art not the beginning nor the end. 190
From chaos and parental darkness came
Light, the first fruits of that intestine
broil,
That sullen ferment, which for wondrous
ends
Was ripening in itself. The ripe hour
came,
And with it light, and light engendering
Upon its own producer, forthwith touch'd
The whole enormous matter into life.
Upon that very hour, our parentage,
The Heavens and the Earth, were manifest:
Then thou first-born, and we the giant-
race,   200
Found ourselves ruling new and beauteous
realms.
Now comes the pain of truth, to whom 't is
pain;
O folly! for to bear all naked truths,
And to envisage circumstance, all calm,
That is the top of sovereignty. Mark
well!

As Heaven and Earth are fairer, fairer far
Than Chaos and blank Darkness, though
once chiefs;
And as we show beyond that Heaven and
Earth
In form and shape compact and beautiful,
In will, in action free, companionship, 210
And thousand other signs of purer life;
So on our heels a fresh perfection treads,
A power more strong in beauty, born of us
And fated to excel us, as we pass
In glory that old Darkness: nor are we
Thereby more conquer'd, than by us the
rule
Of shapeless Chaos. Say, doth the dull
soil
Quarrel with the proud forests it hath fed,
And feedeth still, more comely than itself?
Can it deny the chiefdom of green groves?
Or shall the tree be envious of the dove 221
Because it cooeth, and hath snowy wings
To wander wherewithal and find its joys?
We are such forest-trees, and our fair
boughs
Have bred forth, not pale solitary doves,
But eagles golden-feather'd, who do tower
Above us in their beauty, and must reign
In right thereof; for 't is the eternal law
That first in beauty should be first in
might: 229
Yes, by that law, another race may drive
Our conquerors to mourn as we do now.
Have ye beheld the young God of the Seas,
My dispossessor? Have ye seen his face?
Have ye beheld his chariot, foam'd along
By noble winged creatures he hath made?
I saw him on the calmed waters scud,
With such a glow of beauty in his eyes,
That it enforced me to bid sad farewell
To all my empire; farewell sad I took,
And hither came, to see how dolorous fate
Had wrought upon ye; and how I might
best   241
Give consolation in this woe extreme.
Receive the truth, and let it be your balm.'

Whether through poz'd conviction, or
disdain,

They guarded silence, when Oceanus
Left murmuring, what deepest thought can
   tell ?
But so it was, none answer'd for a space,
Save one whom none regarded, Clymene:
And yet she answer'd not, only complain'd,
With hectic lips, and eyes up - looking
   mild,   250
Thus wording timidly among the fierce:
' O Father, I am here the simplest voice,
And all my knowledge is that joy is gone,
And this thing woe crept in among our
   hearts,
There to remain for ever, as I fear:
I would not bode of evil, if I thought
So weak a creature could turn off the help
Which by just right should come of mighty
   Gods;
Yet let me tell my sorrow, let me tell
Of what I heard, and how it made me
   weep,   260
And know that we had parted from all
   hope.
I stood upon a shore, a pleasant shore,
Where a sweet clime was breathed from a
   land
Of fragrance, quietness, and trees, and
   flowers.
Full of calm joy it was, as I of grief;
Too full of joy and soft delicious warmth;
So that I felt a movement in my heart
To chide, and to reproach that solitude
With songs of misery, music of our woes;
And sat me down, and took a mouthed
   shell   270
And murmur'd into it, and made melody —
O melody no more ! for while I sang,
And with poor skill let pass into the breeze
The dull shell's echo, from a bowery strand
Just opposite, an island of the sea,
There came enchantment with the shifting
   wind,
That did both drown and keep alive my
   ears.
I threw my shell away upon the sand,
And a wave fill'd it, as my sense was fill'd
With that new blissful golden melody. 280
A living death was in each gush of sounds,

Each family of rapturous hurried notes,
That fell, one after one, yet all at once,
Like pearl beads dropping sudden from
   their string:
And then another, then another strain,
Each like a dove leaving its olive perch,
With music wing'd instead of silent plumes,
To hover round my head, and make me
   sick
Of joy and grief at once. Grief overcame,
And I was stopping up my frantic ears, 290
When, past all hindrance of my trembling
   hands,
A voice came sweeter, sweeter than all
   tune,
And still it cried, " Apollo ! young Apollo !
The morning-bright Apollo ! young Apol-
   lo ! "
I fled, it follow'd me, and cried, " Apollo ! "
O Father, and O Brethren, had ye felt
Those pains of mine; O Saturn, hadst thou
   felt,
Ye would not call this too indulged tongue
Presumptuous, in thus venturing to be
   heard.'

So far her voice flow'd on, like timorous
   brook   300
That, lingering along a pebbled coast,
Doth fear to meet the sea: but sea it met,
And shudder'd; for the overwhelming
   voice
Of huge Enceladus swallow'd it in wrath:
The ponderous syllables, like sullen waves
In the half-glutted hollows of reef-rocks,
Came booming thus, while still upon his
   arm
He lean'd; not rising, from supreme con-
   tempt.
' Or shall we listen to the over-wise,
Or to the over-foolish giant, Gods ? 310
Not thunderbolt on thunderbolt, till all
That rebel Jove's whole armoury were
   spent,
Not world on world upon these shoulders
   piled,
Could agonize me more than baby-words
In midst of this dethronement horrible.

Speak! roar! shout! yell! ye sleepy Ti-
tans all.
Do ye forget the blows, the buffets vile?
Are ye not smitten by a youngling arm?
Dost thou forget, sham Monarch of the
Waves,
Thy scalding in the seas? What! have I
roused   320
Your spleens with so few simple words as
these?
O joy! for now I see ye are not lost:
O joy! for now I see a thousand eyes
Wide-glaring for revenge.' — As this he
said,
He lifted up his stature vast, and stood,
Still without intermission speaking thus:
'Now ye are flames, I 'll tell you how to
burn,
And purge the ether of our enemies;
How to feed fierce the crooked stings of fire,
And singe away the swollen clouds of
Jove,   330
Stifling that puny essence in its tent.
O let him feel the evil he hath done;
For though I scorn Oceanus's lore,
Much pain have I for more than loss of
realms:
The days of peace and slumberous calm
are fled;
Those days, all innocent of scathing war,
When all the fair Existences of heaven
Came open-eyed to guess what we would
speak: —
That was before our brows were taught to
frown,
Before our lips knew else but solemn
sounds;   340
That was before we knew the winged
thing,
Victory, might be lost, or might be won,
And be ye mindful that Hyperion,
Our brightest brother, still is undis-
graced —
Hyperion, lo! his radiance is here!'

All eyes were on Enceladus's face,
And they beheld, while still Hyperion's
name

Flew from his lips up to the vaulted rocks,
A pallid gleam across his features stern:
Not savage, for he saw full many a God
Wroth as himself. He look'd upon them
all,   351
And in each face he saw a gleam of light,
But splendider in Saturn's, whose hoar
locks
Shone like the bubbling foam about a keel
When the prow sweeps into a midnight
cove.
In pale and silver silence they remain'd,
Till suddenly a splendour, like the morn,
Pervaded all the beetling gloomy steeps,
All the sad spaces of oblivion,
And every gulf, and every chasm old,   360
And every height, and every sullen depth,
Voiceless, or hoarse with loud tormented
streams:
And all the everlasting cataracts,
And all the headlong torrents far and near,
Mantled before in darkness and huge
shade,
Now saw the light and made it terrible.
It was Hyperion: — a granite peak
His bright feet touch'd, and there he stay'd
to view
The misery his brilliance had betray'd
To the most hateful seeing of itself.   370
Golden his hair of short Numidian curl,
Regal his shape majestic, a vast shade
In midst of his own brightness, like the
bulk
Of Memnon's image at the set of sun
To one who travels from the dusking
East:
Sighs, too, as mournful as that Memnon's
harp,
He utter'd, while his hands contemplative
He press'd together, and in silence stood.
Despondence seized again the fallen Gods
At sight of the dejected King of Day,   380
And many hid their faces from the light:
But fierce Enceladus sent forth his eyes
Among the brotherhood; and, at their
glare,
Uprose Iäpetus, and Creüs too,
And Phorcus, sea-born, and together strode

To where he tower'd on his eminence.
There those four shouted forth old Saturn's
name;
Hyperion from the peak loud answered
'Saturn!'
Saturn sat near the Mother of the Gods,
In whose face was no joy, though all the
Gods   390
Gave from their hollow throats the name
of 'Saturn!'

BOOK III

Thus in alternate uproar and sad peace,
Amazed were those Titans utterly.
O leave them, Muse! O leave them to
their woes;
For thou art weak to sing such tumults
dire:
A solitary sorrow best befits
Thy lips, and antheming a lonely grief.
Leave them, O Muse! for thou anon wilt
find
Many a fallen old Divinity
Wandering in vain about bewildered shores.
Meantime touch piously the Delphic harp,
And not a wind of heaven but will
breathe   11
In aid soft warble from the Dorian flute;
For lo! 't is for the Father of all verse.
Flush every thing that hath a vermeil hue,
Let the rose glow intense and warm the air,
And let the clouds of even and of morn
Float in voluptuous fleeces o'er the hills;
Let the red wine within the goblet boil,
Cold as a bubbling well; let faint-lipp'd
shells,
On sands or in great deeps, vermilion turn
Through all their labyrinths; and let the
maid   21
Blush keenly, as with some warm kiss sur-
prised.
Chief isle of the embowered Cyclades,
Rejoice, O Delos, with thine olives green,
And poplars, and lawn-shading palms, and
beech,
In which the Zephyr breathes the loudest
song,

And hazels thick, dark-stemm'd beneath
the shade:
Apollo is once more the golden theme!
Where was he, when the Giant of the Sun
Stood bright, amid the sorrow of his peers?
Together had he left his mother fair   31
And his twin-sister sleeping in their bower,
And in the morning twilight wandered
forth
Beside the osiers of a rivulet,
Full ankle-deep in lilies of the vale.
The nightingale had ceased, and a few
stars
Were lingering in the heavens, while the
thrush
Began calm-throated. Throughout all the
isle
There was no covert, no retired cave
Unhaunted by the murmurous noise of
waves,   40
Though scarcely heard in many a green re-
cess.
He listen'd, and he wept, and his bright
tears
Went trickling down the golden bow he
held.
Thus with half-shut suffused eyes he stood,
While from beneath some cumbrous boughs
hard by
With solemn step an awful Goddess came,
And there was purport in her looks for
him,
Which he with eager guess began to read
Perplex'd, the while melodiously he said:
'How cam'st thou over the unfooted sea?
Or hath that antique mien and robed
form   51
Moved in these vales invisible till now?
Sure I have heard those vestments sweep-
ing o'er
The fallen leaves, when I have sat alone
In cool mid-forest. Surely I have traced
The rustle of those ample skirts about
These grassy solitudes, and seen the flow-
ers
Lift up their heads, and still the whisper
pass'd.
Goddess! I have beheld those eyes before,

And their eternal calm, and all that face,
Or I have dream'd.' — 'Yes,' said the su-
preme shape,   61
'Thou hast dream'd of me; and awaking
up
Didst find a lyre all golden by thy side,
Whose strings touch'd by thy fingers, all
the vast
Unwearied ear of the whole universe
Listen'd in pain and pleasure at the birth
Of such new tuneful wonder. Is 't not
strange
That thou shouldst weep, so gifted? Tell
me, youth,
What sorrow thou canst feel; for I am sad
When thou dost shed a tear: explain thy
griefs   70
To one who in this lonely isle hath been
The watcher of thy sleep and hours of life,
From the young day when first thy infant
hand
Pluck'd witless the weak flowers, till thine
arm
Could bend that bow heroic to all times.
Show thy heart's secret to an ancient
Power
Who hath forsaken old and sacred thrones
For prophecies of thee, and for the sake
Of loveliness new-born.' — Apollo then,
With sudden scrutiny and gloomless eyes,
Thus answer'd, while his white melodious
throat   81
Throbb'd with the syllables: — 'Mnemo-
syne!
Thy name is on my tongue, I know not
how;
Why should I tell thee what thou so well
seest?
Why should I strive to show what from
thy lips
Would come no mystery? For me, dark,
dark,
And painful vile oblivion seals my eyes:
I strive to search wherefore I am so sad,
Until a melancholy numbs my limbs;
And then upon the grass I sit, and moan, 90
Like one who once had wings. — O why
should I

Feel cursed and thwarted, when the liege-
less air
Yields to my step aspirant? why should I
Spurn the green turf as hateful to my
feet?
Goddess benign, point forth some unknown
thing:
Are there not other regions than this isle?
What are the stars? There is the sun, the
sun!
And the most patient brilliance of the
moon!
And stars by thousands! Point me out
the way
To any one particular beauteous star, 100
And I will flit into it with my lyre,
And make its silvery splendour pant with
bliss.
I have heard the cloudy thunder: Where
is power?
Whose hand, whose essence, what divinity
Makes this alarum in the elements,
While I here idle listen on the shores
In fearless yet in aching ignorance?
O tell me, lonely Goddess, by thy harp,
That waileth every morn and eventide,
Tell me why thus I rave, about these
groves!   110
Mute thou remainest — Mute! yet I can
read
A wondrous lesson in thy silent face:
Knowledge enormous makes a God of me.
Names, deeds, gray legends, dire events,
rebellions,
Majesties, sovran voices, agonies,
Creations and destroyings, all at once
Pour into the wide hollows of my brain,
And deify me, as if some blithe wine
Or bright elixir peerless I had drunk, 119
And so become immortal.' — Thus the God,
While his enkindled eyes, with level glance
Beneath his white soft temples, steadfast
kept
Trembling with light upon Mnemosyne.
Soon wild commotions shook him, and made
flush
All the immortal fairness of his limbs:
Most like the struggle at the gate of death;

Or liker still to one who should take leave
Of pale immortal death, and with a pang
As hot as death's is chill, with fierce con-
    vulse
Die into life: so young Apollo anguish'd: 130
His very hair, his golden tresses famed
Kept undulation round his eager neck.

During the pain Mnemosyne upheld
Her arms as one who prophesied. — At
    length
Apollo shriek'd; — and lo! from all his
    limbs
Celestial   .   .   .   .
.   .   .   .

TO AUTUMN

In a letter to Reynolds, written from Winchester, September 22, 1819, Keats jots down these sentences: ' How beautiful the season is now — How fine the air. A temperate sharpness about it. Really, without joking, chaste weather — Dian skies — I never liked stubble-fields so much as now — Aye, better than the chilly green of the spring. Somehow, a stubble-field looks warm in the same way that some pictures look warm. This struck me so much in my Sunday's walk that I composed upon it.' These autumn days in Winchester were the last of happy health for Keats. The poem was included in the 1820 volume.

I

SEASON of mists and mellow fruitfulness,
  Close bosom-friend of the maturing sun;
Conspiring with him how to load and bless
    With fruit the vines that round the
        thatch-eaves run;
To bend with apples the moss'd cottage-
        trees,
  And fill all fruit with ripeness to the
        core;
    To swell the gourd, and plump the
        hazel shells
  With a sweet kernel; to set budding
        more,
And still more, later flowers for the bees,
Until they think warm days will never
        cease,
    For Summer has o'er-brimm'd their
        clammy cells.

II

Who hath not seen thee oft amid thy store?
  Sometimes whoever seeks abroad may
        find
Thee sitting careless on a granary floor,
  Thy hair soft-lifted by the winnowing
        wind;
Or on a half-reap'd furrow sound asleep,
  Drowsed with the fume of poppies, while
        thy hook

Spares the next swath and all its
        twined flowers:
And sometimes like a gleaner thou dost keep
  Steady thy laden head across a brook;
Or by a cider-press, with patient look,
    Thou watchest the last oozings, hours
        by hours.

III

Where are the songs of Spring? Ay,
        where are they?
  Think not of them, thou hast thy music
        too, —
While barred clouds bloom the soft-dying
        day,
  And touch the stubble-plains with rosy
        hue;
Then in a wailful choir the small gnats
        mourn
  Among the river sallows, borne aloft
    Or sinking as the light wind lives or
        dies;
And full-grown lambs loud bleat from
        hilly bourn;
  Hedge-crickets sing; and now with treble,
        soft
The redbreast whistles from a garden-
        croft,
  And gathering swallows twitter in the
        skies.

213

VERSES TO FANNY BRAWNE

Although these are not the only poems which owe their origin to Keats's consuming passion, they are grouped here because, apparently written in the same period, they stand as a painful witness to the ebbing tide of Keats's life.

SONNET

The date 1819 is appended to this sonnet in *Life, Letters and Literary Remains.* Mr. Forman connects it with a letter written to Fanny Brawne, October 11, 1819.

THE day is gone, and all its sweets are gone !
   Sweet voice, sweet lips, soft hand, and softer breast,
Warm breath, light whisper, tender semi-tone,
   Bright eyes, accomplish'd shape, and lang'rous waist !
Faded the flower and all its budded charms,
   Faded the sight of beauty from my eyes,
Faded the shape of beauty from my arms,
   Faded the voice, warmth, whiteness, paradise !
Vanish'd unseasonably at shut of eve,
   When the dusk holiday — or holinight —
Of fragrant-curtain'd love begins to weave
   The woof of darkness thick, for hid delight:
But, as I 've read love's missal through to-day,
He 'll let me sleep, seeing I fast and pray.

LINES TO FANNY

First published in *Life, Letters and Literary Remains,* and there dated October, 1819; their exact date seems to be indicated by a passage in a letter to Fanny Brawne, written October 13, 1819, intimating some work, and breaking out into: 'I cannot proceed with any degree of content. I must write you a line or two and see if that will assist in dismissing you from my mind for ever so short a time.'

WHAT can I do to drive away
Remembrance from my eyes? for they
   have seen,
Aye, an hour ago, my brilliant Queen !
Touch has a memory. O say, love, say,
What can I do to kill it and be free
In my old liberty ?
When every fair one that I saw was fair,
Enough to catch me in but half a snare,
Not keep me there:
When, howe'er poor or particolour'd things,
My muse had wings,
And ever ready was to take her course
Whither I bent her force,
Unintellectual, yet divine to me; —
Divine, I say ! — What sea-bird o'er the
   sea
Is a philosopher the while he goes
Winging along where the great water
   throes ?

  How shall I do
  To get anew
Those moulted feathers, and so mount once
   more
  Above, above
  The reach of fluttering Love,
And make him cower lowly while I soar ?
Shall I gulp wine? No, that is vulgarism,
  A heresy and schism,
  Foisted into the canon law of love; —
No, — wine is only sweet to happy men;
  More dismal cares
  Seize on me unawares, —
Where shall I learn to get my peace again ?
To banish thoughts of that most hateful
   land,

Dungeoner of my friends, that wicked
    strand
Where they were wreck'd and live a
    wrecked life;
That monstrous region, whose dull rivers
    pour,
Ever from their sordid urns unto the shore,
Unown'd of any weedy-haired gods;
Whose winds, all zephyrless, hold scour-
    ging rods,
Iced in the great lakes, to afflict mankind;
Whose rank-grown forests, frosted, black,
    and blind,
Would fright a Dryad; whose harsh herb-
    aged meads
Make lean and lank the starved ox while
    he feeds;
There bad flowers have no scent, birds no
    sweet song,
And great unerring Nature once seems
    wrong.

O, for some sunny spell
To dissipate the shadows of this hell !
Say they are gone, — with the new dawn-
    ing light
Steps forth my lady bright !
O, let me once more rest
My soul upon that dazzling breast !
Let once again these aching arms be placed,
The tender gaolers of thy waist !
And let me feel that warm breath here and
    there

To spread a rapture in my very hair, —
O, the sweetness of the pain !
Give me those lips again !
Enough ! Enough ! it is enough for me
To dream of thee !

TO FANNY

With the date 1819 in *Life, Letters and Literary Remains.*

I CRY your mercy — pity — love — aye,
    love !
Merciful love that tantalizes not,
One-thoughted, never-wandering, guileless
    love,
    Unmask'd, and being seen — without a
      blot !
O ! let me have thee whole, — all — all —
    be mine !
    That shape, that fairness, that sweet mi-
      nor zest
Of love, your kiss, — those hands, those
    eyes divine,
    That warm, white, lucent, million-plea-
      sured breast, —
Yourself — your soul — in pity give me
    all,
    Withhold no atom's atom, or I die,
Or living on perhaps, your wretched thrall,
    Forget, in the mist of idle misery,
Life's purposes — the palate of my mind
Losing its gust, and my ambition blind !

THE CAP AND BELLS

OR, THE JEALOUSIES

A Faery Tale. Unfinished

In a letter to John Taylor, his publisher, written from Hampstead, November 17, 1819, Keats, who was then in his most restless mood, writes impulsively: 'I have come to a determination not to publish anything I have now ready written; but, for all that, to publish a poem before long, and that I hope to make a fine one. As the marvellous is the most enticing, and the surest guarantee of harmonious numbers, I have been endeavouring to persuade myself to untether Fancy, and to let her manage for herself. I and myself cannot agree about this at all. Wonders are no wonders to me. I am more at home amongst men and women. I would rather read Chaucer than Ariosto. The little dramatic skill I may as yet have, however badly it might show in a drama, would, I think, be sufficient for a poem. I wish to diffuse the colouring of "St. Agnes' Eve" throughout a poem in which character and sentiment would be the figures to such drapery. Two or three such poems, if God should spare me, written in the course of the next six years, would be a famous Gradus ad Parnassum altissimum — I mean they would nerve me up to the writing of a few fine plays — my greatest ambition, when I do feel ambitious. I am sorry to say that is very seldom.'

Lord Houghton quotes from Keats's friend, Charles Armitage Brown: 'This Poem was written subject to ·future amendments and omissions; it was begun without a plot, and without any presented laws for the supernatural machinery.' Keats apparently designed publishing the poem with the signature 'Lucy Vaughan Lloyd,' and it can only be taken as one of his feverish attempts at using his intellectual powers for self-maintenance, when he was discouraged at the prospect of commercial success with his genuine poetry. Hunt published some of the stanzas in *The Indicator* August 23, 1820, as written by 'a very good poetess Lucy V—— L——' and Lord Houghton included the whole in *Life, Letters and Literary Remains.*

I

In midmost Ind, beside Hydaspes cool,
There stood, or hover'd, tremulous in the
    air,
A faery city, 'neath the potent rule
Of Emperor Elfinan; famed ev'rywhere
For love of mortal women, maidens fair,
Whose lips were solid, whose soft hands
    were made
Of a fit mould and beauty, ripe and rare,
To pamper his slight wooing, warm yet
    staid:
He loved girls smooth as shades, but hated
    a mere shade.

II

This was a crime forbidden by the law;
And all the priesthood of his city wept,
For ruin and dismay they well foresaw,
If impious prince no bound or limit kept,
And faery Zendervester overstept;
They wept, he sinn'd, and still he would
    sin on,
They dreamt of sin, and he sinn'd while
    they slept;
In vain the pulpit thunder'd at the
    throne,
Caricature was vain, and vain the tart lam-
    poon.

III

Which seeing, his high court of parliament
Laid a remonstrance at his Highness'
feet,
Praying his royal senses to content
Themselves with what in faery land was
sweet,
Befitting best that shade with shade
should meet:
Whereat, to calm their fears, he pro-
mised soon
From mortal tempters all to make re-
treat —
Ay, even on the first of the new moon,
An immaterial wife to espouse as heaven's
boon.

IV

Meantime he sent a fluttering embassy
To Pigmio, of Imaus sovereign,
To half beg, and half demand, respect-
fully,
The hand of his fair daughter Bella-
naine;
An audience had, and speeching done,
they gain
Their point, and bring the weeping bride
away;
Whom, with but one attendant, safely
lain
Upon their wings, they bore in bright
array,
While little harps were touch'd by many a
lyric fay.

V

As in old pictures tender cherubim
A child's soul thro' the sapphired canvas
bear,
So, thro' a real heaven, on they swim
With the sweet princess on her plumaged
lair,
Speed giving to the winds her lustrous
hair;
And so she journey'd, sleeping or awake,
Save when, for healthful exercise and
air,
She chose to 'promener à l'aile,' or take
A pigeon's somerset, for sport or change's
sake.

VI

'Dear Princess, do not whisper me so
loud,'
Quoth Corallina, nurse and confidant,
'Do not you see there, lurking in a cloud,
Close at your back, that sly old Crafti-
cant?
He hears a whisper plainer than a rant:
Dry up your tears, and do not look so
blue;
He's Elfinan's great state-spy militant,
He's running, lying, flying footman,
too —
Dear mistress, let him have no handle
against you!

VII

'Show him a mouse's tail, and he will
guess,
With metaphysic swiftness, at the mouse;
Show him a garden, and with speed no
less,
He'll surmise sagely of a dwelling-
house,
And plot, in the same minute, how to
chouse
The owner out of it; show him a — '
'Peace!
Peace! nor contrive thy mistress' ire to
rouse!'
Return'd the princess, 'my tongue shall
not cease
Till from this hated match I get a free
release.

VIII

'Ah, beauteous mortal!' 'Hush!' quoth
Coralline,
'Really you must not talk of him indeed.'
'You hush!' replied the mistress, with
a shine
Of anger in her eyes, enough to breed
In stouter hearts than nurse's fear and
dread:

'T was not the glance itself made nursey
    flinch,
But of its threat she took the utmost
    heed;
Not liking in her heart an hour-long
    pinch,
Or a sharp needle run into her back an
    inch.

IX

So she was silenced, and fair Bellanaine,
Writhing her little body with ennui,
Continued to lament and to complain,
That Fate, cross-purposing, should let
    her be
Ravish'd away far from her dear coun-
    tree;
That all her feelings should be set at
    nought,
In trumping up this match so hastily,
With lowland blood; and lowland blood
    she thought
Poison, as every stanch true-born Imaian
    ought.

X

Sorely she grieved, and wetted three or
    four
White Provence rose-leaves with her
    faery tears,
But not for this cause; — alas! she had
    more
Bad reasons for her sorrow, as appears
In the famed memoirs of a thousand
    years,
Written by Crafticant, and published
By Parpaglion and Co., (those sly com-
    peers
Who raked up ev'ry fact against the
    dead,)
In Scarab Street, Panthea, at the Jubal's
    Head.

XI

Where, after a long hypercritic howl
Against the vicious manners of the
    age,

He goes on to expose, with heart and
    soul,
What vice in this or that year was the
    rage,
Backbiting all the world in every page;
With special strictures on the horrid
    crime,
(Section'd and subsection'd with learn-
    ing sage,)
Of faeries stooping on their wings sub-
    lime
To kiss a mortal's lips, when such were in
    their prime.

XII

Turn to the copious index, you will find
Somewhere in the column, headed let-
    ter B,
The name of Bellanaine, if you 're not
    blind;
Then pray refer to the text, and you
    will see
An article made up of calumny
Against this highland princess, rating
    her
For giving way, so over fashionably,
To this new-fangled vice, which seems a
    burr
Stuck in his moral throat, no coughing e'er
    could stir.

XIII

There he says plainly that she loved a
    man !
That she around him flutter'd, flirted,
    toy'd,
Before her marriage with great Elfi-
    nan;
That after marriage too, she never joy'd
In husband's company, but still employ'd
Her wits to 'scape away to Angle-land;
Where lived the youth, who worried and
    annoy'd
Her tender heart, and its warm ardours
    fann'd
To such a dreadful blaze, her side would
    scorch her hand.

XIV

But let us leave this idle tittle-tattle
To waiting - maids, and bed - room co-
    teries,
Nor till fit time against her fame wage
    battle.
Poor Elfinan is very ill at ease,
Let us resume his subject if you please:
For it may comfort and console him
    much,
To rhyme and syllable his miseries;
Poor Elfinan ! whose cruel fate was
    such,
He sat and cursed a bride he knew he
    could not touch.

XV

Soon as (according to his promises)
The bridal embassy had taken wing,
And vanish'd, bird-like, o'er the suburb
    trees,
The emperor, empierced with the sharp
    sting
Of love, retired, vex'd and murmuring
Like any drone shut from the fair bee-
    queen,
Into his cabinet, and there did fling
His limbs upon the sofa, full of spleen,
And damn'd his House of Commons, in
    complete chagrin.

XVI

'I'll trounce some of the members,' cried
    the Prince,
'I'll put a mark against some rebel
    names,
I'll make the Opposition-benches wince,
I'll show them very soon, to all their
    shames,
What 't is to smother up a Prince's
    flames;
That ministers should join in it, I own,
Surprises me ! — they too at these high
    games !
Am I an Emperor ? Do I wear a crown ?
Imperial Elfinan, go hang thyself or drown !

XVII

'I'll trounce 'em ! — there's the square-
    cut chancellor,
His son shall never touch that bishopric;
And for the nephew of old Palfior,
I'll show him that his speeches made me
    sick,
And give the colonelcy to Phalaric;
The tiptoe marquis, moral and gallant,
Shall lodge in shabby taverns upon tick;
And for the Speaker's second cousin's
    aunt,
She sha'n't be maid of honour, — by heaven
    that she sha'n't !

XVIII

'I'll shirk the Duke of A.; I'll cut his
    brother;
I'll give no garter to his eldest son;
I won't speak to his sister or his mother !
The Viscount B. shall live at cut-and-
    run;
But how in the world can I contrive to
    stun
That fellow's voice, which plagues me
    worse than any,
That stubborn fool, that impudent state-
    dun,
Who sets down ev'ry sovereign as a
    zany, —
That vulgar commoner, Esquire Bianco-
    pany ?

XIX

'Monstrous affair ! Pshaw ! pah ! what
    ugly minx
Will they fetch from Imaus for my
    bride ?
Alas ! my wearied heart within me
    sinks,
To think that I must be so near allied
To a cold dullard fay, — ah, woe betide !
Ah, fairest of all human loveliness !
Sweet Bertha ! what crime can it be to
    glide
About the fragrant plaitings of thy dress,
Or kiss thine eye, or count thy locks, tress
    after tress ?'

XX

So said, one minute's while his eyes remain'd
Half lidded, piteous, languid, innocent;
But, in a wink, their splendour they regain'd,
Sparkling revenge with amorous fury
   blent.
Love thwarted in bad temper oft has
   vent:
He rose, he stampt his foot, he. rang the
   bell,
And order'd some death-warrants to be
   sent
For signature: — somewhere the tempest fell,
As many a poor fellow does not live to
   tell.

XXI

'At the same time, Eban,' — (this was
   his page,
A fay of colour, slave from top to toe,
Sent as a present, while yet under age,
From the Viceroy of Zanguebar, — wise,
   slow,
His speech, his only words were 'yes'
   and 'no,'
But swift of look, and foot, and wing
   was he,) —
'At the same time, Eban, this instant
   go
To Hum the soothsayer, whose name I
   see
Among the fresh arrivals in our empery.

XXII

'Bring Hum to me! But stay — here
   take my ring,
The pledge of favour, that he not sus-
   pect
Any foul play, or awkward murdering,
Tho' I have bowstrung many of his sect;
Throw in a hint, that if he should neg-
   lect
One hour, the next shall see him in my
   grasp,
And the next after that shall see him
   neck'd,

Or swallow'd by my hunger-starved
   asp, —
And mention ('t is as well) the torture of
   the wasp.'

XXIII

These orders given, the Prince, in half a
   pet,
Let o'er the silk his propping elbow
   slide,
Caught up his little legs, and, in a fret,
Fell on the sofa on his royal side.
The slave retreated backwards, humble-
   eyed,
And with a slave-like silence closed the
   door,
And to old Hum thro' street and alley
   hied;
He 'knew the city,' as we say, of yore,
And for short cuts and turns, was nobody
   knew more.

XXIV

It was the time when wholesale dealers
   close
Their shutters with a moody sense of
   wealth,
But retail dealers, diligent, let loose
The gas (objected to on score of health),
Convey'd in little solder'd pipes by
   stealth,
And make it flare in many a brilliant
   form,
That all the powers of darkness it re-
   pell'th,
Which to the oil-trade doth great scaith
   and harm,
And supersedeth quite the use of the glow-
   worm.

XXV

Eban, untempted by the pastry-cooks,
(Of pastry he got store within the pal-
   ace,)
With hasty steps, wrapp'd cloak, and
   solemn looks,
Incognito upon his errand sallies,
His smelling-bottle ready for the allies;

He pass'd the hurdy-gurdies with dis-
    dain,
Vowing he 'd have them sent on board
    the galleys;
Just as he made his vow, it 'gan to rain,
Therefore he call'd a coach, and bade it
    drive amain.

XXVI

' I 'll pull the string,' said he, and further
    said,
' Polluted Jarvey ! Ah, thou filthy hack !
Whose springs of life are all dried up
    and dead,
Whose linsey-woolsey lining hangs all
    slack,
Whose rug is straw, whose wholeness is
    a crack ;
And evermore thy steps go clatter-clit-
    ter;
Whose glass once up can never be got
    back,
Who prov'st, with jolting arguments and
    bitter,
That 't is of modern use to travel in a
    litter.

XXVII

' Thou inconvenience ! thou hungry crop
For all corn ! thou snail-creeper to and
    fro,
Who while thou goest ever seem'st to
    stop,
And fiddle-faddle standest while you go;
I' the morning, freighted with a weight
    of woe,
Unto some lazar-house thou journeyest,
And in the evening tak'st a double row
Of dowdies, for some dance or party
    drest,
Besides the goods meanwhile thou movest
    east and west.

XXVIII

' By thy ungallant bearing and sad mien,
An inch appears the utmost thou couldst
    budge :
Yet at the slightest nod, or hint, or sign,

Round to the curb-stone patient dost
    thou trudge,
School'd in a beckon, learned in a nudge,
A dull-eyed Argus watching for a fare;
Quiet and plodding thou dost bear no
    grudge
To whisking tilburies, or phaetons rare,
Curricles, or mail-coaches, swift beyond
    compare.'

XXIX

Philosophizing thus, he pull'd the check,
And bade the coachman wheel to such a
    street,
Who turning much his body, more his
    neck,
Louted full low, and hoarsely did him
    greet :
' Certes, Monsieur were best take to his
    feet,
Seeing his servant can no farther drive
For press of coaches, that to-night here
    meet,
Many as bees about a straw-capp'd hive,
When first for April honey into faint flow-
    ers they dive.'

XXX

Eban then paid his fare, and tiptoe went
To Hum's hotel; and, as he on did pass
With head inclined, each dusky linea-
    ment
Show'd in the pearl-paved street as in a
    glass;
His purple vest, that ever peeping was
Rich from the fluttering crimson of his
    cloak,
His silvery trowsers, and his silken sash
Tied in a burnish'd knot, their semblance
    took
Upon the mirror'd walls, wherever he
    might look.

XXXI

He smiled at self, and, smiling, show'd
    his teeth,
And seeing his white teeth, he smiled the
    more;

Lifted his eyebrows, spurn'd the path be-
neath,
Show'd teeth again, and smiled as hereto-
fore,
Until he knock'd at the magician's door;
Where, till the porter answer'd, might
be seen,
In the clear panel more he could adore, —
His turban wreathed of gold, and white,
and green,
Mustachios, ear-ring, nose-ring, and his sa-
bre keen.

XXXII

'Does not your master give a rout to-
night?'
Quoth the dark page; 'Oh, no!' return'd
the Swiss,
'Next door but one to us, upon the right,
The *Magazin des Modes* now open is
Against the Emperor's wedding; — and,
sir, this
My master finds a monstrous horrid bore;
As he retired, an hour ago iwis,
With his best beard and brimstone, to
explore
And cast a quiet figure in his second floor.

XXXIII

'Gad! he 's obliged to stick to business!
For chalk, I hear, stands at a pretty
price;
And as for aqua vitæ — there 's a mess!
The *dentes sapientiæ* of mice
Our barber tells me too are on the rise, —
Tinder 's a lighter article, — nitre pure
Goes off like lightning, — grains of Para-
dise
At an enormous figure! — stars not
sure! —
Zodiac will not move without a slight dou-
ceur!

XXXIV

'Venus won't stir a peg without a fee,
And master is too partial *entre nous*
To —' 'Hush — hush!' cried Eban,
'sure that is he

Coming down stairs, — by St. Bartholo-
mew!
As backwards as he can, — is 't something new?
Or is 't his custom, in the name of fun?'
'He always comes down backward, with
one shoe' —
Return'd the porter — 'off, and one shoe
on,
Like, saving shoe for sock or stocking, my
man John!'

XXXV

It was indeed the great Magician,
Feeling, with careful toe, for every stair,
And retrograding careful as he can,
Backwards and downwards from his own
two pair:
'Salpietro!' exclaimed Hum, 'is the dog
there?
He 's always in my way upon the mat!'
'He 's in the kitchen, or the Lord knows
where,' —
Replied the Swiss, — 'the nasty, yelping
brat!'
'Don't beat him!' return'd Hum, and on
the floor came pat.

XXXVI

Then facing right about, he saw the
Page,
And said: 'Don't tell me what you want,
Eban;
The Emperor is now in a huge rage, —
'T is nine to one he 'll give you the rattan!
Let us away!' Away together ran
The plain-dress'd sage and spangled
blackamoor,
Nor rested till they stood to cool, and fan,
And breathe themselves at th' Emperor's
chamber door,
When Eban thought he heard a soft impe-
rial snore.

XXXVII

'I thought you guess'd, foretold, or prophesied,
That 's Majesty was in a raving fit?'

'He dreams,' said Hum, ' or I have ever
     lied,
That he is tearing you, sir, bit by bit.'
'He's not asleep, and you have little
     wit,'
Replied the Page, 'that little buzzing
     noise,
Whate'er your palmistry may make of
     it,
Comes from a plaything of the Em-
     peror's choice,
From a Man-Tiger-Organ, prettiest of his
     toys.'

XXXVIII

Eban then usher'd in the learned Seer:
Elfinan's back was turn'd, but, ne'erthe-
     less,
Both, prostrate on the carpet, ear by
     ear,
Crept silently, and waited in distress,
Knowing the Emperor's moody bitter-
     ness;
Eban especially, who on the floor 'gan
Tremble and quake to death, — he feared
     less
A dose of senna-tea, or nightmare Gor-
     gon,
Than the Emperor when he play'd on his
     Man-Tiger-Organ.

XXXIX

They kiss'd nine times the carpet's vel-
     vet face
Of glossy silk, soft, smooth, and meadow-
     green,
Where the close eye in deep rich fur
     might trace
A silver tissue, scantly to be seen,
As daisies lurk'd in June-grass, buds in
     green;
Sudden the music ceased, sudden the
     hand
Of majesty, by dint of passion keen,
Doubled into a common fist, went grand,
And knock'd down three cut glasses, and
     his best ink-stand.

XL

Then turning round, he saw those trem-
     bling two:
'Eban,' said he, 'as slaves should taste
     the fruits
Of diligence, I shall remember you
To-morrow, or next day, as time suits,
In a finger conversation with my mutes, —
Begone ! — for you, Chaldean ! here re-
     main !
Fear not, quake not, and as good wine
     recruits
A conjurer's spirits, what cup will you
     drain ?
Sherry in silver, hock in gold, or glass'd
     champagne ? '

XLI

'Commander of the Faithful !' answer'd
     Hum,
  In preference to these, I 'll merely taste
A thimble-full of old Jamaica rum.'
'A simple boon !' said Elfinan, 'thou
     may'st
Have Nantz, with which my morning-
     coffee 's laced.'[1]
'I 'll have a glass of Nantz, then,' — said
     the Seer, —
'Made racy — (sure my boldness is mis-
     placed !) —
With the third part — (yet that is drink-
     ing dear !) —
Of the least drop of *crème de citron* crystal
     clear.'

XLII

'I pledge you, Hum ! and pledge my
     dearest love,
My Bertha !' 'Bertha ! Bertha !' cried
     the sage,
'I know a many Berthas !' 'Mine 's
     above
All Berthas !' sighed the Emperor. ' I
     engage,'
Said Hum, 'in duty, and in vassalage,

[1] ' Mr. Nisby is of opinion that laced coffee is bad for
the head.' — *Spectator.*

To mention all the Berthas in the
 earth; —
There's Bertha Watson, — and Miss
 Bertha Page, —
This famed for languid eyes, and that for
 mirth, —
There's Bertha Blount of York, — and
 Bertha Knox of Perth.'

XLIII

'You seem to know' — 'I do know,'
 answer'd Hum,
'Your Majesty's in love with some fine
 girl
Named Bertha; but her surname will not
 come,
Without a little conjuring.' ''T is Pearl,
'T is Bertha Pearl! What makes my
 brains so whirl?
And she is softer, fairer than her name!'
'Where does she live?' ask'd Hum.
 'Her fair locks curl
So brightly, they put all our fays to
 shame! —
Live? — O! at Canterbury, with her old
 grand dame.'

XLIV

'Good! good!' cried Hum, 'I've known
 her from a child!
She is a changeling of my management;
She was born at midnight in an Indian
 wild;
Her mother's screams with the striped
 tiger's blent,
While the torch-bearing slaves a halloo
 sent
Into the jungles; and her palanquin,
Rested amid the desert's dreariment,
Shook with her agony, till fair were seen
The little Bertha's eyes ope on the stars
 serene.'

XLV

'I can't say,' said the monarch, ' that
 may be
Just as it happen'd, true or else a bam!
Drink up your brandy, and sit down by
 me,

Feel, feel my pulse, how much in love I
 am;
And if your science is not all a sham,
Tell me some means to get the lady
 here.'
'Upon my honour!' said the son of
 Cham,[1]
'She is my dainty changeling, near and
 dear,
Although her story sounds at first a little
 queer.'

XLVI

'Convey her to me, Hum, or by my
 crown,
My sceptre, and my cross-surmounted
 globe,
I'll knock you—' 'Does your majesty
 mean — *down?*
No, no, you never could my feelings
 probe
To such a depth!' The Emperor took
 his robe,
And wept upon its purple palatine,
While Hum continued, shamming half
 a sob, —
'In Canterbury doth your lady shine?
But let me cool your brandy with a little
 wine.'

XLVII

Whereat a narrow Flemish glass he
 took,
That since belong'd to Admiral De Witt,
Admired it with a connoisseuring look,
And with the ripest claret crowned it,
And, ere the lively head could burst and
 flit,
He turn'd it quickly, nimbly upside
 down,
His mouth being held conveniently fit
To catch the treasure: 'Best in all the
 town!'
He said, smack'd his moist lips, and gave a
 pleasant frown.

---

[1] Cham is said to have been the inventor of magic.
Lucy learnt this from Bayle's Dictionary, and had
copied a long Latin note from that work.

XLVIII

'Ah! good my Prince, weep not!' And
then again
He fill'd a bumper. 'Great Sire, do not
weep!
Your pulse is shocking, but I'll ease
your pain.'
'Fetch me that Ottoman, and prithee
keep
Your voice low,' said the Emperor, 'and
steep
Some lady's-fingers nice in Candy wine;
And prithee, Hum, behind the screen do
peep
For the rose-water vase, magician mine!
And sponge my forehead — so my love doth
make me pine.'

XLIX

'Ah, cursed Bellanaine!' 'Don't think
of her,'
Rejoin'd the Mago, 'but on Bertha muse;
For, by my choicest best barometer,
You shall not throttled be in marriage
noose;
I've said it, sire; you only have to choose
Bertha or Bellanaine.' So saying, he
drew
From the left pocket of his threadbare
hose,
A sampler hoarded slyly, good as new;
Holding it by his thumb and finger full in
view.

L

'Sire, this is Bertha Pearl's neat handy-
work,
Her name, see here, Midsummer, ninety-
one' —
Elfinan snatch'd it with a sudden jerk,
And wept as if he never would have
done,
Honouring with royal tears the poor
homespun;
Whereon were broider'd tigers with black
eyes,
And long-tailed pheasants, and a rising
sun,

Plenty of posies, great stags, butterflies
Bigger than stags — a moon — with other
mysteries.

LI

The monarch handled o'er and o'er again
These day-school hieroglyphics with a
sigh;
Somewhat in sadness, but pleased in the
main,
Till this oracular couplet met his eye
Astounded — Cupid, I do thee defy!
It was too much. He shrunk back in
his chair,
Grew pale as death, and fainted — very
nigh!
'Pho! nonsense!' exclaim'd Hum, 'now
don't despair:
She does not mean it really. Cheer up,
hearty — there!

LII

'And listen to my words. You say you
won't,
On any terms, marry Miss Bellanaine;
It goes against your conscience — good!
well, don't.
You say, you love a mortal. I would
fain
Persuade your honour's highness to re-
frain
From peccadilloes. But, Sire, as I say,
What good would that do? And, to be
more plain,
You would do me a mischief some odd
day,
Cut off my ears and hands, or head too, by
my fay!

LIII

'Besides, manners forbid that I should
pass any
Vile strictures on the conduct of a prince
Who should indulge his genius, if he has
any,
Not, like a subject, foolish matter mince.
Now I think on't, perhaps I could con-
vince

LIX

'What shall I do with that same book?'
'Why merely
Lay it on Bertha's table, close beside
Her work-box, and 't will help your pur-
pose dearly;
I say no more.' 'Or good or ill betide,
Through the wide air to Kent this morn
I glide!'
Exclaim'd the Emperor, 'When I return,
Ask what you will, — I 'll give you my
new bride!
And take some more wine, Hum; — O,
Heavens! I burn
To be upon the wing! Now, now, that
minx I spurn!'

LX

'Leave her to me,' rejoin'd the magian:
'But how shall I account, illustrious fay!
For thine imperial absence? Pho! I
can
Say you are very sick, and bar the way
To your so loving courtiers for one day;
If either of their two Archbishops' graces
Should talk of extreme unction, I shall
say
You do not like cold pig with Latin
phrases,
Which never should be used but in alarm-
ing cases.'

LXI

'Open the window, Hum; I 'm ready
now!'
'Zooks!' exclaim'd Hum, as up the sash
he drew,
'Behold, your Majesty, upon the brow
Of yonder hill, what crowds of people!'
'Whew!
The monster 's always after something
new,'
Return'd his Highness, 'they are piping
hot
To see my pigsney Bellanaine. Hum!
do
Tighten my belt a little, — so, so, — not
Too tight, — the book! — my wand! — so,
nothing is forgot.'

LXII

'Wounds! how they shout!' said Hum,
'and there, — see, see,
Th' ambassador 's return'd from Pigmio!
The morning 's very fine, — uncommonly!
See, past the skirts of yon white cloud
they go,
Tinging it with soft crimsons! Now
below
The sable-pointed heads of firs and pines
They dip, move on, and with them moves
a glow
Along the forest side! Now amber lines
Reach the hill top, and now throughout the
valley shines.'

LXIII

'Why, Hum, you 're getting quite poeti-
cal!
Those *nows* you managed in a special
style.'
'If ever you have leisure, Sire, you shall
See scraps of mine will make it worth
your while,
Tit-bits for Phœbus! — yes, you well
may smile.
Hark! hark! the bells!' 'A little
further yet,
Good Hum, and let me view this mighty
coil.'
Then the great Emperor full graceful set
His elbow for a prop, and snuff'd his
mignonette.

LXIV

The morn is full of holiday: loud bells
With rival clamors ring from every spire;
Cunningly-station'd music dies and swells
In echoing places; when the winds re-
spire,
Light flags stream out like gauzy tongues
of fire;
A metropolitan murmur, lifeful, warm,
Comes from the northern suburbs; rich
attire
Freckles with red and gold the moving
swarm;
While here and there clear trumpets blow
a keen alarm.

LXV

And now the fairy escort was seen clear,
Like the old pageant of Aurora's train,
Above a pearl-built minster, hovering
    near;
First wily Crafticant, the chamberlain,
Balanced upon his gray-grown pinions
    twain,
His slender wand officially reveal'd;
Then black gnomes scattering sixpences
    like rain;
Then pages three and three; and next,
    slave-held,
The Imaian 'scutcheon bright, — one mouse
    in argent field.

LXVI

Gentlemen pensioners next; and after
    them,
A troop of winged Janizaries flew;
Then slaves, as presents bearing many a
    gem;
Then twelve physicians fluttering two
    and two;
And next a chaplain in a cassock new;
Then Lords in waiting; then (what head
    not reels
For pleasure?) — the fair Princess in
    full view,
Borne upon wings, — and very pleased
    she feels
To have such splendour dance attendance
    at her heels.

LXVII

For there was more magnificence behind:
She waved her handkerchief. ' Ah, very
    grand ! '
Cried Elfinan, and closed the window-
    blind;
' And, Hum, we must not shilly-shally
    stand, —
Adieu ! adieu ! I 'm off for Angle-land !
I say, old Hocus, have you such a thing
About you, — feel your pockets, I com-
    mand, —
I want, this instant, an invisible ring, —
Thank you, old mummy ! — now securely I
    take wing.'

LXVIII

Then Elfinan swift vaulted from the floor,
And lighted graceful on the window-sill;
Under one arm the magic book he bore,
The other he could wave about at will;
Pale was his face, he still look'd very ill:
He bow'd at Bellanaine, and said —
    ' Poor Bell !
Farewell ! farewell ! and if for ever ! still
For ever fare thee well ! ' — and then he
    fell
A laughing ! — snapp'd his fingers ! —
    shame it is to tell !

LXIX

' By 'r Lady ! he is gone ! ' cries Hum,
    ' and I, —
(I own it), — have made too free with
    his wine;
Old Crafticant will smoke me. By-the-
    bye !
This room is full of jewels as a mine, —
Dear valuable creatures, how ye shine !
Some time to-day I must contrive a
    minute,
If Mercury propitiously incline,
To examine his scrutoire, and see what 's
    in it,
For of superfluous diamonds I as well may
    thin it.

LXX

' The Emperor 's horrid bad; yes, that 's
    my cue ! '
Some histories say that this was Hum's
    last speech;
That, being fuddled, he went reeling
    through
The corridor, and scarce upright could
    reach
The stair-head; that being glutted as a
    leech,
And used, as we ourselves have just now
    said,
To manage stairs reversely, like a peach
Too ripe, he fell, being puzzled in his
    head
With liquor and the staircase: verdict —
    found stone dead.

LXXI

This, as a falsehood, Crafticanto treats;
And as his style is of strange elegance,
Gentle and tender, full of soft conceits,
(Much like our Boswell's,) we will take a
glance
At his sweet prose, and, if we can, make
dance
His woven periods into careless rhyme;
O, little faery Pegasus ! rear — prance —
Trot round the quarto — ordinary time !
March, little Pegasus, with pawing hoof
sublime !

LXXII

' Well, let us see, — *tenth book and chapter
nine,*' —
Thus Crafticant pursues his diary: —
' 'T was twelve o'clock at night, the wea-
ther fine,
Latitude thirty-six; our scouts descry
A flight of starlings making rapidly
Towards Thibet. Mem.: — birds fly in
the night;
From twelve to half-past — wings not fit
to fly
For a thick fog — the Princess sulky
quite:
Call'd for an extra shawl, and gave her
nurse a bite.

LXXIII

' Five minutes before one — brought
down a moth
With my new double-barrel — stew'd
the thighs,
And made a very tolerable broth —
Princess turn'd dainty, to our great surprise,
Alter'd her mind, and thought it very
nice:
Seeing her pleasant, tried her with a
pun,
She frown'd; a monstrous owl across us
flies
About this time, — a sad old figure of
fun;
Bad omen — this new match can't be a
happy one.

LXXIV

' From two to half-past, dusky way we
made,
Above the plains of Gobi, — desert,
bleak;
Beheld afar off, in the hooded shade
Of darkness, a great mountain (strange
to speak),
Spitting, from forth its sulphur-baken
peak,
A fan-shaped burst of blood-red, arrowy
fire,
Turban'd with smoke, which still away
did reek,
Solid and black from that eternal pyre,
Upon the laden winds that scantly could
respire.

LXXV

' Just upon three o'clock, a falling star
Created an alarm among our troop,
Kill'd a man-cook, a page, and broke a
jar,
A tureen, and three dishes, at one swoop,
Then passing by the Princess, singed her
hoop:
Could not conceive what Coralline was at,
She clapp'd her hands three times, and
cried out " Whoop !"
Some strange Imaian custom. A large
bat
Came sudden 'fore my face, and brush'd
against my hat.

LXXVI

' Five minutes thirteen seconds after
three,
Far in the west a mighty fire broke out,
Conjectured, on the instant, it might be
The city of Balk — 't was Balk beyond
all doubt:
A griffin, wheeling here and there about
Kept reconnoitering us — doubled our
guard —
Lighted our torches, and kept up a shout,
Till he sheer'd off — the Princess very
scared —
And many on their marrow-bones for death
prepared.

LXXVII

'At half-past three arose the cheerful
　　moon —
Bivouack'd for four minutes on a cloud —
Where from the earth we heard a lively
　　tune
Of tambourines and pipes, severe and
　　loud,
While on a flowery lawn a brilliant
　　crowd
Cinque-parted danced, some half asleep
　　reposed
Beneath the green-faned cedars, some
　　did shroud
In silken tents, and 'mid light fragrance
　　dozed,
Or on the open turf their soothed eyelids
　　closed.

LXXVIII

'Dropp'd my gold watch and kill'd a
　　kettle-drum —
It went for apoplexy — foolish folks ! —
Left it to pay the piper — a good sum —
(I 've got a conscience, maugre people's
　　jokes,)
To scrape a little favour; 'gan to coax
Her Highness' pug-dog — got a sharp
　　rebuff —
She wish'd a game at whist — made
　　three revokes —
Turn'd from myself, her partner, in a
　　huff;
His Majesty will know her temper time
　　enough.

LXXIX

'She cried for chess — I play'd a game
　　with her —
Castled her king with such a vixen
　　look,
It bodes ill to his Majesty — (refer
To the second chapter of my fortieth
　　book,
And see what hoity-toity airs she took).
At half-past four the morn essay'd to
　　beam —
Saluted, as we pass'd, an early rook, —

The Princess fell asleep, and, in her
　　dream,
Talk'd of one Master Hubert, deep in her
　　esteem.

LXXX

'About this time — making delightful
　　way —
Shed a quill-feather from my larboard
　　wing —
Wish'd, trusted, hoped 't was no sign of
　　decay —
Thank Heaven, I 'm hearty yet ! — 't was
　　no such thing: —
At five the golden light began to spring,
With fiery shudder through the bloomed
　　east;
At six we heard Panthea's churches
　　ring —
The city all his unhived swarms had cast,
To watch our grand approach, and hail us
　　as we pass'd.

LXXXI

'As flowers turn their faces to the sun,
So on our flight with hungry eyes they
　　gaze,
And, as we shaped our course, this, that
　　way run,
With mad-cap pleasure, or hand-clasp'd
　　amaze:
Sweet in the air a mild-toned music plays,
And progresses through its own laby-
　　rinth;
Buds gather'd from the green spring's
　　middle-days,
They scatter'd — daisy, primrose, hya-
　　cinth —
Or round white columns wreathed from
　　capital to plinth.

LXXXII

'Onward we floated o'er the panting
　　streets,
That seem'd throughout with upheld
　　faces paved;
Look where we will, our bird's-eye vision
　　meets

Legions of holiday; bright standards
waved,
And fluttering ensigns emulously craved
Our minute's glance; a busy thunderous
roar,
From square to square, among the buildings raved,
As when the sea, at flow, gluts up once
more
The craggy hollowness of a wild-reefed
shore.

LXXXIII

'And "Bellanaine for ever!" shouted
they!
While that fair Princess, from her
winged chair,
Bow'd low with high demeanour, and, to
pay
Their new-blown loyalty with guerdon
fair,
Still emptied, at meet distance, here and
there,
A plenty horn of jewels. And here I
(Who wish to give the devil her due)
declare
Against that ugly piece of calumny,
Which calls them Highland pebble-stones
not worth a fly.

LXXXIV

'Still "Bellanaine!" they shouted, while
we glide
'Slant to a light Ionic portico,
The city's delicacy, and the pride
Of our Imperial Basilic; a row
Of lords and ladies, on each hand, make
show
Submissive of knee-bent obeisance,
All down the steps; and, as we enter'd, lo!
The strangest sight — the most unlook'd-
for chance —
All things turn'd topsy-turvy in a devil's
dance.

LXXXV

''Stead of his anxious Majesty and court
At the open doors, with wide saluting
eyes,

Congées and scrape-graces of every sort,
And all the smooth routine of gallan-
tries,
Was seen, to our immoderate surprise,
A motley crowd thick gather'd in the
hall,
Lords, scullions, deputy-scullions, with
wild cries
Stunning the vestibule from wall to wall,
Where the Chief Justice on his knees and
hands doth crawl.

LXXXVI

'Counts of the palace, and the state pur-
veyor
Of moth's-down, to make soft the royal
beds,
The Common Council and my fool Lord
Mayor
Marching a-row, each other slipshod
treads;
Powder'd bag-wigs and ruffy-tuffy heads
Of cinder wenches meet and soil each
other;
Toe crush'd with heel ill-natured fighting
breeds,
Frill-rumpling elbows brew up many a
bother,
And fists in the short ribs keep up the yell
and pother.

LXXXVII

'A Poet, mounted on the Court-Clown's
back,
Rode to the Princess swift with spurring
heels,
And close into her face, with rhyming
clack,
Began a Prothalamion;— she reels,
She falls, she faints!— while laughter
peals
Over her woman's weakness. "Where!"
cried I,
"Where is his Majesty?" No person
feels
Inclined to answer; wherefore instantly
I plunged into the crowd to find him or
to die.

LXXXVIII

'Jostling my way I gain'd the stairs, and
    ran
To the first landing, where, incredible !
I met, far gone in liquor, that old man,
That vile impostor Hum, ———'
                        So far so well, —
For we have proved the Mago never fell
Down stairs on Crafticanto's evidence;
And therefore duly shall proceed to tell,
Plain in our own original mood and
    tense,
The sequel of this day, though labour 't is
    immense !

.   .   .   .

THE LAST SONNET

On his way to Italy as his last chance of life,
the vessel which bore Keats had been beating
about the English Channel for a fortnight,
when an opportunity was given for landing for
a brief respite on the Dorsetshire coast. 'The
bright beauty of the day,' says Lord Houghton, Keats's biographer, 'and the scene revived
the poet's drooping heart, and the inspiration
remained with him for some time even after
his return to the ship. It was then that he
composed that sonnet of solemn tenderness.'
The date of the poem would thus be September or October, 1820.

BRIGHT star, would I were steadfast as
    thou art !
    Not in lone splendour hung aloft the
    night,
And watching, with eternal lids apart,
    Like Nature's patient sleepless Eremite,
The moving waters at their priestlike task
    Of pure ablution round earth's human
        shores
Or gazing on the new soft fallen mask
    Of snow upon the mountains and the
        moors:
No — yet still steadfast, still unchangeable,
    Pillow'd upon my fair love's ripening
        breast,
To feel for ever its soft fall and swell,
    Awake for ever in a sweet unrest,
Still, still to hear her tender-taken breath,
And so live ever — or else swoon to death.

SUPPLEMENTARY VERSE

The collection which follows is not intended to be taken exactly as containing the leavings of Keats's genius; there are verses in the previous groups which might be placed here, if the intention was to make a marked division between his well-defined poetry and his experiments and mere scintillations; doubtless, too, on any such principle it would be just to take back into the respectability of larger type some of the lines here included. But it seemed wise to put into a subordinate group the poet's fragmentary and posthumous poems, and those which were plainly the mere playthings of his muse.

I. HYPERION: A VISION

Contributed by Lord Houghton to the third volume of the *Bibliographical and Historical Miscellanies* of the Philobiblion Society, 1856-1857. Lord Houghton afterward included it in a new edition of *The Life and Letters of John Keats*, 1867. He also printed it in the Aldine edition of 1876, where he recorded it as an early version of the poem. But Mr. Colvin quotes from Brown's *MS.:* 'In the evenings [of November and December, 1819] at his own desire, he occupied a separate apartment, and was deeply engaged in remodeling the fragment of *Hyperion* into the form of a Vision.' This attempt may well have added to Keats's reluctance to permit the fragmentary *Hyperion* to appear in the 1820 volume. For a full discussion of the question see the Appendix in *John Keats* by Sidney Colvin.

CANTO 1

FANATICS have their dreams, wherewith they weave
A paradise for a sect; the savage, too,
From forth the loftiest fashion of his sleep
Guesses at heaven; pity these have not
Trac'd upon vellum or wild Indian leaf
The shadows of melodious utterance,
But bare of laurel they live, dream, and die;
For Poesy alone can tell her dreams, —
With the fine spell of words alone can save
Imagination from the sable chain   10
And dumb enchantment. Who alive can say,
'Thou art no Poet — may'st not tell thy dreams'?
Since every man whose soul is not a clod
Hath visions and would speak, if he had loved,
And been well nurtured in his mother tongue.
Whether the dream now purpos'd to rehearse
Be poet's or fanatic's will be known
When this warm scribe, my hand, is in the grave.

Methought I stood where trees of every clime,
Palm, myrtle, oak, and sycamore, and beech,   20
With plantane and spice-blossoms, made a screen,
In neighbourhood of fountains (by the noise
Soft-showering in mine ears), and (by the touch
Of scent) not far from roses. Twining round
I saw an arbour with a drooping roof
Of trellis vines, and bells, and larger blooms,
Like floral censers, swinging light in air;
Before its wreathed doorway, on a mound
Of moss, was spread a feast of summer fruits,
Which, nearer seen, seem'd refuse of a meal   30
By angel tasted or our Mother Eve;
For empty shells were scatter'd on the grass,
And grapestalks but half-bare, and remnants more
Sweet-smelling, whose pure kinds I could not know.
Still was more plenty than the fabled horn
Thrice emptied could pour forth at banqueting,
For Proserpine return'd to her own fields,
Where the white heifers low. And appetite,
More yearning than on earth I ever felt,
Growing within, I ate deliciously, —   40
And, after not long, thirsted; for thereby
Stood a cool vessel of transparent juice
Sipp'd by the wander'd bee, the which I took,
And pledging all the mortals of the world,
And all the dead whose names are in our lips,
Drank. That full draught is parent of my theme.

No Asian poppy nor elixir fine
Of the soon-fading, jealous Caliphat,
No poison gender'd in close monkish cell,
To thin the scarlet conclave of old men,   50
Could so have rapt unwilling life away.
Among the fragrant husks and berries crush'd
Upon the grass, I struggled hard against
The domineering potion, but in vain.
The cloudy swoon came on, and down I sank,
Like a Silenus on an antique vase.
How long I slumber'd 't is a chance to guess.
When sense of life return'd, I started up
As if with wings, but the fair trees were gone,
The mossy mound and arbour were no more: 60
I look'd around upon the curved sides
Of an old sanctuary, with roof august,
Builded so high, it seem'd that filmed clouds
Might spread beneath as o'er the stars of hea-
    ven.
So old the place was, I remember'd none
The like upon the earth: what I had seen
Of grey cathedrals, buttress'd walls, rent tow-
    ers,
The superannuations of sunk realms,
Or Nature's rocks toil'd hard in waves and
    winds,
Seem'd but the faulture of decrepit things 70
To that eternal domed monument.
Upon the marble at my feet there lay
Store of strange vessels and large draperies,
Which needs had been of dyed asbestos wove,
Or in that place the moth could not corrupt,
So white the linen, so, in some, distinct
Ran imageries from a sombre loom.
All in a mingled heap confus'd there lay
Robes, golden tongs, censer and chafing-dish,
Girdles, and chains, and holy jewelries. 80

    Turning from these with awe, once more I
    raised
My eyes to fathom the space every way:
The embossed roof, the silent massy range
Of columns north and south, ending in mist
Of nothing; then to eastward, where black
    gates
Were shut against the sunrise evermore;
Then to the west I look'd, and saw far off
An image, huge of feature as a cloud,
At level of whose feet an altar slept,
To be approach'd on either side by steps 90
And marble balustrade, and patient travail
To count with toil the innumerable degrees.
Toward the altar sober-pac'd I went,
Repressing haste as too unholy there;
And, coming nearer, saw beside the shrine
One ministering; and there arose a flame
When in mid-day the sickening east-wind

Shifts sudden to the south, the small warm
    rain
Melts out the frozen incense from all flowers,
And fills the air with so much pleasant health 100
That even the dying man forgets his shroud;—
Even so that lofty sacrificial fire,
Sending forth Maian incense, spread around
Forgetfulness of everything but bliss,
And clouded all the altar with soft smoke;
From whose white fragrant curtains thus I
    heard
Language pronounc'd: 'If thou canst not as-
    cend
These steps, die on that marble where thou
    art.
Thy flesh, near cousin to the common dust,
Will parch for lack of nutriment; thy bones 110
Will wither in few years, and vanish so
That not the quickest eye could find a grain
Of what thou now art on that pavement cold.
The sands of thy short life are spent this
    hour,
And no hand in the universe can turn.
Thy hourglass, if these gummed leaves be burnt
Ere thou canst mount up these immortal steps.'
I heard, I look'd: two senses both at once,
So fine, so subtle, félt the tyranny
Of that fierce threat and the hard task pro-
    posed. 120
Prodigious seem'd the toil; the leaves were yet
Burning, when suddenly a palsied chill
Struck from the paved level up my limbs,
And was ascending quick to put cold grasp
Upon those streams that pulse beside the throat.
I shriek'd, and the sharp anguish of my shriek
Stung my own ears; I strove hard to escape
The numbness, strove to gain the lowest step.
Slow, heavy, deadly was my pace: the cold
Grew stifling, suffocating at the heart; 130
And when I clasp'd my hands I felt them not.
One minute before death my ic'd foot touch'd
The lowest stair; and, as it touch'd, life seem'd
To pour in at the toes; I mounted up
As once fair angels on a ladder flew
From the green turf to heaven. 'Holy Power,'
Cried I, approaching near the horned shrine,
'What am I that should so be saved from
    death?
What am I that another death come not
To choke my utterance, sacrilegious, here?' 140
Then said the veiled shadow: 'Thou hast felt
What 't is to die and live again before
Thy fated hour; that thou hadst power to do
    so
Is thine own safety; thou hast dated on
Thy doom.' 'High Prophetess,' said I, 'purge
    off,

Benign, if so it please thee, my mind's film.'
'None can usurp this height,' return'd that
   shade,
'But those to whom the miseries of the world
Are misery, and will not let them rest.
All else who find a haven in the world,   150
Where they may thoughtless sleep away their
   days,
If by a chance into this fane they come,
Rot on the pavement where thou rottedst half.'
'Are there not thousands in the world,' said I,
Encourag'd by the sooth voice of the shade,
'Who love their fellows even to the death,
Who feel the giant agony of the world,
And more, like slaves to poor humanity,
Labour for mortal good? I sure should see
Other men here, but I am here alone.'   160
'Those whom thou spakest of are no visiona-
   ries,'
Rejoin'd that voice; 'they are no dreamers
   weak;
They seek no wonder but the human face,
No music but a happy-noted voice:
They come not here, they have no thought to
   come;
And thou art here, for thou art less than they.
What benefit canst thou do, or all thy tribe,
To the great world? Thou art a dreaming
   thing,
A fever of thyself: think of the earth;
What bliss, even in hope, is there for thee?   170
What haven? every creature hath its home,
Every sole man hath days of joy and pain,
Whether his labours be sublime or low —
The pain alone, the joy alone, distinct:
Only the dreamer venoms all his days,
Bearing more woe than all his sins deserve.
Therefore, that happiness be somewhat shared,
Such things as thou art are admitted oft
Into like gardens thou didst pass erewhile,
And suffer'd in these temples: for that cause   180
Thou standest safe beneath this statue's knees.'
'That I am favour'd for unworthiness,
By such propitious parley medicined
In sickness not ignoble, I rejoice,
Aye, and could weep for love of such award.'
So answer'd I, continuing, 'If it please,
Majestic shadow, tell me where I am,
Whose altar this, for whom this incense curls;
What image this whose face I cannot see
For the broad marble knees; and who thou
   art,   190
Of accent feminine so courteous?'

   Then the tall shade, in drooping linen veil'd,
Spoke out, so much more earnest, that her
   breath

Stirr'd the thin folds of gauze that drooping
   hung
About a golden censer from her hand
Pendent; and by her voice I knew she shed
Long-treasured tears. 'This temple, sad and
   lone,
Is all spar'd from the thunder of a war
Foughten long since by giant hierarchy
Against rebellion: this old image here,   200
Whose carved features wrinkled as he fell,
Is Saturn's; I, Moneta, left supreme,
Sole goddess of this desolation.'
I had no words to answer, for my tongue,
Useless, could find about its roofed home
No syllable of a fit majesty
To make rejoinder to Moneta's mourn:
There was a silence, while the altar's blaze
Was fainting for sweet food. I look'd thereon,
And on the paved floor, where nigh were piled
Faggots of cinnamon, and many heaps   211
Of other crisped spicewood: then again
I look'd upon the altar, and its horns
Whiten'd with ashes, and its languorous flame,
And then upon the offerings again;
And so, by turns, till sad Moneta cried:
'The sacrifice is done, but not the less
Will I be kind to thee for thy good will.
My power, which to me is still a curse,
Shall be to thee a wonder; for the scenes   220
Still swooning vivid through my globed brain,
With an electral changing misery,
Thou shalt with these dull mortal eyes behold
Free from all pain, if wonder pain thee not.'
As near as an immortal's sphered words
Could to a mother's soften were these last:
And yet I had a terror of her robes,
And chiefly of the veils that from her brow
Hung pale, and curtain'd her in mysteries,
That made my heart too small to hold its
   blood.   230
This saw that Goddess, and with sacred hand
Parted the veils. Then saw I a wan face,
Not pin'd by human sorrows, but bright-
   blanch'd
By an immortal sickness which kills not;
It works a constant change, which happy death
Can put no end to; deathwards progressing
To no death was that visage; it had past
The lily and the snow; and beyond these
I must not think now, though I saw that face.
But for her eyes I should have fled away;   240
They held me back with a benignant light,
Soft, mitigated by divinest lids
Half-clos'd, and visionless entire they seem'd
Of all external things; they saw me not,
But in blank splendour beam'd, like the mild
   moon,

Who comforts those she sees not, who knows
    not
What eyes are upward cast. As I had found
A grain of gold upon a mountain's side,
And, twing'd with avarice, strain'd out my
    eyes
To search its sullen entrails rich with ore,   250
So, at the view of sad Moneta's brow,
I ask'd to see what things the hollow brow
Behind environ'd : what high tragedy
In the dark secret chambers of her skull
Was acting, that could give so dread a stress
To her cold lips, and fill with such a light
Her planetary eyes, and touch her voice
With such a sorrow ? 'Shade of Memory !'
Cried I, with act adorant at her feet,
'By all the gloom hung round thy fallen
    house,   260
By this last temple, by the golden age,
By great Apollo, thy dear foster-child,
And by thyself, forlorn divinity,
The pale Omega of a wither'd race,
Let me behold, according as thou saidst,
What in thy brain so ferments to and fro !'
No sooner had this conjuration past
My devout lips, than side by side we stood
(Like a stunt bramble by a solemn pine)
Deep in the shady sadness of a vale   270
Far sunken from the healthy breath of morn,
Far from the fiery noon and eve's one star.
Onward I look'd beneath the gloomy boughs,
And saw what first I thought an image huge,
Like to the image pedestall'd so high
In Saturn's temple ; then Moneta's voice
Came brief upon mine ear. 'So Saturn sat
When he had lost his realms ;' whereon there
    grew
A power within me of enormous ken
To see as a god sees, and take the depth   280
Of things as nimbly as the outward eye
Can size and shape pervade. The lofty theme
Of those few words hung vast before my mind
With half-unravell'd web. I sat myself
Upon an eagle's watch, that I might see,
And seeing ne'er forget. No stir of life
Was in this shrouded vale, — not so much air
As in the zoning of a summer's day
Robs not one light seed from the feather'd grass
But where the dead leaf fell there did it rest.
A stream went noiseless by, still deaden'd more   293
By reason of the fallen divinity
Spreading more shade ; the Naiad 'mid her
    reeds
Prest her cold finger closer to her lips.

Along the margin-sand large foot-marks went
No further than to where old Saturn's feet

Had rested, and there slept how long a sleep !
Degraded, cold, upon the sodden ground
His old right hand lay nerveless, listless, dead,
Unsceptred, and his realmless eyes were closed :
While his bowed head seem'd listening to the
    Earth,   301
His ancient mother, for some comfort yet.

    It seem'd no force could wake him from his
    place ;
But there came one who, with a kindred hand,
Touch'd his wide shoulders, after bending low
With reverence, though to one who knew it not.
Then came the griev'd voice Mnemosyne,
And griev'd I hearken'd. 'That divinity
Whom thou saw'st step from yon forlornest
    wood,   309
And with slow pace approach our fallen king,
Is Thea, softest-natured of our brood.'
I mark'd the Goddess, in fair statuary
Surpassing wan Moneta by the head,
And in her sorrow nearer woman's tears.
There was a list'ning fear in her regard,
As if calamity had but begun ;
As if the venom'd cloud of evil days
Had spent their malice, and the sullen rear
Was with its stored thunder labouring up,
One hand she press'd upon that aching spot   320
Where beats the human heart, as if just there,
Though an immortal, she felt cruel pain ;
The other upon Saturn's bended neck
She laid, and to the level of his ear
Leaning, with parted lips some words she spoke
In solemn tenour and deep organ-tone ;
Some mourning words, which in our feeble
    tongue
Would come in this like accenting ; how frail
To that large utterance of the early gods !

    'Saturn, look up ! and for what, poor lost
    king ?   330
I have no comfort for thee ; no, not one ;
I cannot say, wherefore thus sleepest thou ?
For Heaven is parted from thee, and the Earth
Knows thee not, so afflicted, for a god.
The Ocean, too, with all its solemn noise,
Has from thy sceptre pass'd ; and all the air
Is emptied of thy hoary majesty.
Thy thunder, captious at the new command,
Rumbles reluctant o'er our fallen house ;
And thy sharp lightning, in unpractis'd hands,
Scourges and burns our once serene domain.   341

    ' With such remorseless speed still come new
    woes,
That unbelief has not a space to breathe.
Saturn ! sleep on : me thoughtless, why should I

Thus violate thy slumbrous solitude?
Why should I ope thy melancholy eyes?
Saturn! sleep on, while at thy feet I weep.'

As when upon a tranced summer-night
Forests, branch-charmed by the earnest stars,
Dream, and so dream all night without a noise,
Save from one gradual solitary gust   351
Swelling upon the silence, dying off,
As if the ebbing air had but one wave,
So came these words and went; the while in
     tears
She prest her fair large forehead to the earth,
Just where her fallen hair might spread in
     curls,
A soft and silken net for Saturn's feet.
Long, long these two were postured motionless,
Like sculpture builded-up upon the grave
Of their own power. A long awful time   360
I look'd upon them: still they were the same;
The frozen God still bending to the earth,
And the sad Goddess weeping at his feet;
Moneta silent. Without stay or prop
But my own weak mortality, I bore
The load of this eternal quietude,
The unchanging gloom and the three fixed
     shapes
Ponderous upon my senses, a whole moon;
For by my burning brain I measured sure
Her silver seasons shedded on the night,   370
And every day by day methought I grew
More gaunt and ghostly. Oftentimes I pray'd
Intense, that death would take me from the
     vale
And all its burthens; gasping with despair
Of change, hour after hour I curs'd myself,
Until old Saturn rais'd his faded eyes,
And look'd around and saw his kingdom gone,
And all the gloom and sorrow of the place,
And that fair kneeling Goddess at his feet.

As the moist scent of flowers, and grass, and
     leaves   380
Fills forest-dells with a pervading air,
Known to the woodland nostril, so the words
Of Saturn fill'd the mossy glooms around,
Even to the hollows of time-eaten oaks,
And to the windings of the foxes' hole,
With sad, low tones, while thus he spoke, and
     sent
Strange moanings to the solitary Pan.
' Moan, brethren, moan, for we are swallow'd
     up
And buried from all godlike exercise
Of influence benign on planets pale,   390
And peaceful sway upon man's harvesting,   ?
And all those acts which Deity supreme

Doth ease its heart of love in. Moan and wail;
Moan, brethren, moan; for lo, the rebel spheres
Spin round; the stars their ancient courses
     keep;
Clouds still with shadowy moisture haunt the
     earth,   .
Still suck their fill of light from sun and moon;
Still buds the tree, and still the seashores mur-
     mur;
There is no death in all the universe,
No smell of death. — There shall be death.
     Moan, moan;   400
Moan, Cybele, moan; for thy pernicious babes
Have chang'd a god into an aching palsy.
Moan, brethren, moan, for I have no strength
     left;
Weak as the reed, weak, feeble as my voice.
Oh! Oh! the pain, the pain of feebleness;
Moan, moan, for still I thaw; or give me help,
Throw down those imps, and give me victory.
Let me hear other groans, and trumpets blown
Of triumph calm, and hymns of festival,
From the gold peaks of heaven's high-piled
     clouds;   410
Voices of soft proclaim, and silver stir
Of strings in hollow shells; and there shall be
Beautiful things made new, for the surprise
Of the sky-children.' So he feebly ceased,
With such a poor and sickly-sounding pause,
Methought I heard some old man of the earth
Bewailing earthly loss; nor could my eyes
And ears act with that unison of sense
Which marries sweet sound with the grace of
     form,
And dolorous accent from a tragic harp   420
With large limb'd visions. More I scrutinized.
Still fixt he sat beneath the sable trees,
Whose arms spread straggling in wild serpent
     forms,
With leaves all hush'd; his awful presence
     there
(Now all was silent) gave a deadly lie
To what I erewhile heard: only his lips
Trembled amid the white curls of his beard;
They told the truth, though round the snowy
     locks
Hung nobly, as upon the face of heaven
A mid-day fleece of clouds. Thea arose   430
And stretcht her white arm through the hol-
     low dark,
Pointing somewhither: whereat he too rose,
Like a vast giant, seen by men at sea
To grow pale from the waves at dull mid-
     night.
They melted from my sight into the woods;
Ere I could turn, Moneta cried, ' These twain
Are speeding to the families of grief,

Where, rooft in by black rocks, they waste in
    pain
And darkness, for no hope.' And she spake
    on,
As ye may read who can unwearied pass   440
Onward from the antechamber of this dream,
Where, even at the open doors, awhile
I must delay, and glean my memory
Of her high phrase — perhaps no further dare.

CANTO II

' Mortal, that thou may'st understand aright,
I humanize my sayings to thine ear,
Making comparisons of earthly things;
Or thou might'st better listen to the wind,
Whose language is to thee a barren noise,
Though it blows legend-laden thro' the trees.
In melancholy realms big tears are shed,
More sorrow like to this, and such like woe,
Too huge for mortal tongue or pen of scribe.
The Titans fierce, self-hid or prison-bound,   10
Groan for the old allegiance once more,
Listening in their doom for Saturn's voice.
But one of the whole eagle-brood still keeps
His sovereignty, and rule, and majesty:
Blazing Hyperion on his orbed fire
Still sits, still snuffs the incense teeming up
From Man to the Sun's God — yet insecure.
For as upon the earth dire prodigies
Fright and perplex, so also shudders he;
Not at dog's howl or gloom-bird's hated screech,
Or the familiar visiting of one   21
Upon the first toll of his passing bell,
Or prophesyings of the midnight lamp;
But horrors, portioned to a giant nerve,
Make great Hyperion ache. His palace bright,
Bastion'd with pyramids of shining gold,
And touch'd with shade of bronzed obelisks,
Glares a blood-red thro' all the thousand courts,
Arches, and domes, and fiery galleries;
And all its curtains of Aurorian clouds   30
Flash angerly; when he would taste the wreaths
Of incense breath'd aloft from sacred hills,
Instead of sweets, his ample palate takes
Savour of poisonous brass and metals sick;
Wherefore when harbour'd in the sleepy West,
After the full completion of fair day,
For rest divine upon exalted couch,
And slumber in the arms of melody,
He paces through the pleasant hours of ease,
With strides colossal, on from hall to hall,   40
While far within each aisle and deep recess
His winged minions in close clusters stand
Amaz'd, and full of fear; like anxious men,
Who on a wide plain gather in sad troops,

When earthquakes jar their battlements and
    towers.
Even now where Saturn, rous'd from icy trance,
Goes step for step with Thea from yon woods,
Hyperion, leaving twilight in the rear,
Is sloping to the threshold of the West.
Thither we tend.' Now in clear light I stood,
Reliev'd from the dusk vale. Mnemosyne   51
Was sitting on a square-edg'd polish'd stone,
That in its lucid depths reflected pure
Her priestess' garments. My quick eyes ran on
From stately nave to nave, from vault to vault,
Through bow'rs of fragrant and enwreathed
    light,
And diamond-paved lustrous long arcades.
Anon rush'd by the bright Hyperion;
His flaming robes stream'd out beyond his heels,
And gave a roar as if of earthy fire,   60
That scar'd away the meek ethereal hours,
And made their dove-wings tremble. On he
    flared.

II. FRAGMENTS

The three fragments that follow are published in *Life, Letters and Literary Remains*,
without date.

I

WHERE 's the Poet? Show him! show him,
Muses nine! that I may know him!
'T is the man who with a man
    Is an equal, be he King,
Or poorest of the beggar-clan,
    Or any other wondrous thing
A man may be 'twixt ape and Plato;
'T is the man who with a bird,
Wren, or Eagle, finds his way to
    All its instincts; he hath heard
The Lion's roaring, and can tell
    What his horny throat expresseth,
And to him the Tiger's yell
    Comes articulate and presseth
On his ear like mother-tongue.

II

MODERN LOVE

AND what is love? It is a doll dress'd up
For idleness to cosset, nurse, and dandle;
A thing of soft misnomers, so divine
That silly youth doth think to make itself
Divine by loving, and so goes on
Yawning and doting a whole summer long,
Till Miss's comb is made a pearl tiara,

And common Wellingtons turn Romeo boots;
Then Cleopatra lives at number seven,
And Antony resides in Brunswick Square.
Fools! if some passions high have warm'd the
world,
If Queens and Soldiers have play'd deep for
hearts,
It is no reason why such agonies
Should be more common than the growth of
weeds.
Fools! make me whole again that weighty
pearl
The Queen of Egypt melted, and I 'll say
That ye may love in spite of beaver hats.

III

FRAGMENT OF 'THE CASTLE BUILDER'

To-NIGHT I 'll have my friar — let me think
About my room — I 'll have it in the pink;
It should be rich and sombre, and the moon,
Just in its mid-life in the midst of June,
Should look thro' four large windows and dis-
play
Clear, but for gold-fish vases in the way,
Their glassy diamonding on Turkish floor;
The tapers keep aside, an hour and more,
To see what else the moon alone can show;
While the night-breeze doth softly let us know
My terrace is well bower'd with oranges.
Upon the floor the dullest spirit sees
A guitar-ribband and a lady's glove
Beside a crumple-leaved tale of love;
A tambour-frame, with Venus sleeping there,
All finish'd but some ringlets of her hair;
A viol, bow-strings torn, cross-wise upon
A glorious folio of Anacreon;
A skull upon a mat of roses lying,
Ink'd purple with a song concerning dying;
An hour-glass on the turn, amid the trails
Of passion-flower; — just in time there sails
A cloud across the moon, — the lights bring
in!
And see what more my phantasy can win.
It is a gorgeous room, but somewhat sad;
The draperies are so, as tho' they had
Been made for Cleopatra's winding-sheet;
And opposite the stedfast eye doth meet
A spacious looking-glass, upon whose face,
In letters raven-sombre, you may trace
Old ' Mene, Mene, Tekel Upharzin.'
Greek busts and statuary have ever been
Held, by the finest spirits, fitter far,
Than vase grotesque and Siamesian jar;
Therefore 't is sure a want of Attic taste

That I should rather love a Gothic waste
Of eyesight on cinque-coloured potter's clay,
Than on the marble fairness of old Greece.
My table-coverlits of Jason's fleece
And black Numidian sheep - wool should be
wrought,
Gold, black, and heavy, from the Lama brought.
My ebon sofas should delicious be
With down from Leda's cygnet progeny.
My pictures all Salvator's, save a few
Of Titian's portraiture, and one, though new,
Of Haydon's in its fresh magnificence.
My wine — O good! 't is here at my desire,
And I must sit to supper with my friar.

. . . .

IV

EXTRACTS FROM AN OPERA

First given in *Life, Letters and Literary Remains*, and there dated 1818. In that case, it is
most likely that the verses formed a portion of
some experiment going on to the autumn after
Keats's return from his northern journey.

O! WERE I one of the Olympian twelve,
Their godships should pass this into a law, —
That when a man doth set himself in toil
After some beauty veiled far away,
Each step he took should make his lady's
hand
More soft, more white, and her fair cheek more
fair;
And for each briar-berry he might eat,
A kiss should bud upon the tree of love,
And pulp and ripen richer every hour,
To melt away upon the traveller's lips.

. . . .

DAISY'S SONG

THE sun, with his great eye,
Sees not so much as I;
And the moon, all silver-proud,
Might as well be in a cloud.

And O the spring — the spring!
I lead the life of a King!
Couch'd in the teeming grass,
I spy each pretty lass.

I look where no one dares,
And I stare where no one stares,
And when the night is nigh,
Lambs bleat my lullaby.

. . . .

FOLLY'S SONG

WHEN wedding fiddles are a-playing,
        Huzza for folly O!
And when maidens go a-Maying,
        Huzza, etc.
When a milk-pail is upset,
        Huzza, etc.
And the clothes left in the wet,
        Huzza, etc.
When the barrel 's set abroach,
        Huzza, etc.
When Kate Eyebrow keeps a coach,
        Huzza, etc.
When the pig is over-roasted,
        Huzza, etc.
And the cheese is over-toasted.
        Huzza, etc.
When Sir Snap is with his lawyer,
        Huzza, etc.
And Miss Chip has kiss'd the sawyer;
        Huzza, etc.

. . . .

OH, I am frighten'd with most hateful thoughts!
Perhaps her voice is not a nightingale's,
Perhaps her teeth are not the fairest pearl;
Her eye-lashes may be, for aught I know,
Not longer than the May-fly's small fan-
    horns;
There may not be one dimple on her hand;
And freckles many; ah! a careless nurse,
In haste to teach the little thing to walk,
May have crumpt up a pair of Dian's legs,
And warpt the ivory of a Juno's neck.

. . . .

SONG

THE stranger lighted from his steed,
    And ere he spake a word,
He seiz'd my lady's lily hand,
    And kiss'd it all unheard.

The stranger walk'd into the hall,
    And ere he spake a word,
He kiss'd my lady's cherry lips,
    And kiss'd 'em all unheard.

The stranger walk'd into the bower, —
    But my lady first did go, —
Ay hand in hand into the bower,
    Where my lord's roses blow.

My lady's maid had a silken scarf,
    And a golden ring had she,

And a kiss from the stranger, as off he went
    Again on his palfrey.

. . . .

ASLEEP! O sleep a little while, white pearl!
And let me kneel, and let me pray to thee,
And let me call Heaven's blessing on thine
    eyes,
And let me breathe into the happy air,
That doth enfold and touch thee all about,
Vows of my slavery, my giving up,
My sudden adoration, my great love!

III. FAMILIAR VERSES

STANZAS TO MISS WYLIE

These verses belong to 1816. It is not impossible that like the valentine on p. 11, they
were written for the use of George Keats.

O COME, Georgiana! the rose is full blown,
The riches of Flora are lavishly strown,
The air is all softness, and crystal the streams;
The West is resplendently clothed in beams.

O come! let us haste to the freshening shades,
The quaintly carv'd seats, and the opening
    glades;
Where the faeries are chanting their evening
    hymns,
And the last sun-beam the sylph lightly swims.

And when thou art weary, I 'll find thee a bed
Of mosses and flowers to pillow thy head:
And there Georgiana I 'll sit at thy feet,
While my story of love I enraptur'd repeat.

So fondly I 'll breathe, and so softly I 'll sigh,
Thou wilt think that some amorous zephyr is
    nigh;
Yet no — as I breathe I will press thy fair knee,
And then thou wilt know that the sigh comes
    from me.

Ah! why, dearest girl, should we lose all these
    blisses?
That mortal 's a fool who such happiness misses:
So smile acquiescence, and give me thy hand,
With love-looking eyes, and with voice sweetly
    bland.

EPISTLE TO JOHN HAMILTON REYNOLDS

'My dear Reynolds,' writes Keats from
Teignmouth, March 25, 1818, 'In hopes of
cheering you through a minute or two, I was

determined, will he, nill he, to send you some
lines, so you will excuse the unconnected subject and careless verse. You know, I am sure,
Claude's Enchanted Castle, and I wish you may
be pleased with my remembrance of it.'

DEAR Reynolds! As last night I lay in bed,
There came before my eyes that wonted thread
Of shapes, and shadows, and remembrances,
That every other minute vex and please:
Things all disjointed come from north and
  south, —
Two Witch's eyes above a Cherub's mouth,
Voltaire with casque and shield and habergeon,
And Alexander with his nightcap on;
Old Socrates a-tying his cravat,
And Hazlitt playing with Miss Edgeworth's
  cat;   10
And Junius Brutus, pretty well so so,
Making the best of 's way towards Soho.

Few are there who escape these visitings, —
Perhaps one or two whose lives have patent
  wings,
And thro' whose curtains peeps no hellish nose,
No wild-boar tushes, and no Mermaid's toes;
But flowers bursting out with lusty pride,
And young Æolian harps personify'd;
Some Titian colours touch'd into real life, —
The sacrifice goes on; the pontiff knife   20
Gleams in the Sun, the milk-white heifer lows,
The pipes go shrilly, the libation flows:
A white sail shows above the green-head cliff,
Moves round the point, and throws her anchor
  stiff;
The mariners join hymn with those on land.

You know the Enchanted Castle, — it doth
  stand
Upon a rock, on the border of a Lake,
Nested in trees, which all do seem to shake
From some old magic-like Urganda's sword.
O Phœbus! that I had thy sacred word   30
To show this Castle, in fair dreaming wise,
Unto my friend, while sick and ill he lies!

You know it well enough, where it doth seem
A mossy place, a Merlin's Hall, a dream;
You know the clear Lake, and the little Isles,
The mountains blue, and cold near neighbour
  rills,
All which elsewhere are but half animate;
There do they look alive to love and hate,
To smiles and frowns; they seem a lifted
  mound
Above some giant, pulsing underground.   40

Part of the building was a chosen See,
Built by a banish'd Santon of Chaldee;
The other part, two thousand years from him,
Was built by Cuthbert de Saint Aldebrim;
Then there 's a little wing, far from the Sun,
Built by a Lapland Witch turn'd maudlin Nun;
And many other juts of aged stone
Founded with many a mason-devil's groan.

The doors all look as if they op'd themselves:
The windows as if latch'd by Fays and Elves, 50
And from them comes a silver flash of light,
As from the westward of a Summer's night;
Or like a beauteous woman's large blue eyes
Gone mad through olden songs and poesies.

See! what is coming from the distance dim!
A golden Galley all in silken trim!
Three rows of oars are lightening, moment
  whiles
Into the verd'rous bosoms of those isles;
Towards the shade, under the Castle wall,
It comes in silence, — now 't is hidden all.   60
The Clarion sounds, and from a Postern-gate
An echo of sweet music doth create
A fear in the poor Herdsman who doth bring
His beasts to trouble the enchanted spring, —
He tells of the sweet music, and the spot,
To all his friends, and they believe him not.

O that our dreamings all, of sleep or wake,
Would all their colours from the sunset take:
From something of material sublime,   69
Rather than shadow our own soul's day-time
In the dark void of night. For in the world
We jostle, — but my flag is not unfurl'd
On the Admiral-staff, — and so philosophise
I dare not yet! O, never will the prize,
High reason, and the love of good and ill,
Be my award! Things cannot to the will
Be settled, but they tease us out of thought;
Or is it imagination brought
Beyond its proper bound, yet still confin'd,   80
Lost in a sort of Purgatory blind,
Cannot refer to any standard law
Of either earth or heaven? It is a flaw
In happiness, to see beyond our bourn. —
It forces us in summer skies to mourn,
It spoils the singing of the Nightingale.

Dear Reynolds! I have a mysterious tale,
And cannot speak it: the first page I read
Upon a Lampit rock of green sea-weed
Among the breakers; 't was a quiet eve,
The rocks were silent, the wide sea did weave
An untumultuous fringe of silver foam   91
Along the flat brown sand; I was at home

And should have been most happy, — but I saw
Too far into the sea, where every maw
The greater on the less feeds evermore. —
But I saw too distinct into the core
Of an eternal fierce destruction,
And so from happiness I far was gone.
Still am I sick of it, and tho' to-day,
I 've gather'd young spring-leaves, and flowers
    gay   100
Of periwinkle and wild strawberry,
Still do I that most fierce destruction see, —
The Shark at savage prey, — the Hawk at
    pounce, —
The gentle Robin, like a Pard or Ounce,
Ravening a worm, — Away, ye horrid moods !
Moods of one's mind ! You know I hate them
    well.
You know I 'd sooner be a clapping Bell
To some Kamschatkan Missionary Church,
Than with these horrid moods be left i' the
    lurch.

A DRAUGHT OF SUNSHINE

Sent in a letter to Reynolds, dated January
31, 1818. 'I cannot write in prose,' says Keats ;
'it is a sunshiny day and I cannot, so here
goes.'

HENCE Burgundy, Claret, and Port,
  Away with old Hock and Madeira,
Too earthly ye are for my sport ;
  There 's a beverage brighter and clearer.
Instead of a pitiful rummer,
My wine overbrims a whole summer ;
  My bowl is the sky,
  And I drink at my eye,
  Till I feel in the brain
  A Delphian pain —
Then follow, my Caius ! then follow :
  On the green of the hill
  We will drink our fill
  Of golden sunshine,
  Till our brains intertwine
With the glory and grace of Apollo !
God of the Meridian,
  And of the East and West,
To thee my soul is flown,
  And my body is earthward press'd. —
It is an awful mission,
A terrible division ;
And leaves a gulf austere
To be fill'd with worldly fear.
Aye, when the soul is fled
To high above our head,
Affrighted do we gaze
After its airy maze,

As doth a mother wild,
When her young infant child
Is in an eagle's claws —
And is not this the cause
Of madness ? — God of Song,
Thou bearest me along
Through sights I scarce can bear :
O let me, let me share
With the hot lyre and thee,
The staid Philosophy.
Temper my lonely hours,
And let me see thy bowers
More unalarm'd !

AT TEIGNMOUTH

Sent as part of a letter to Haydon, written
from Teignmouth, March 21, 1818. 'I have
enjoyed the most delightful walks these three
fine days beautiful enough to make me content
here all the summer could I stay.'

HERE all the summer could I stay,
  For there 's Bishop's teign
  And King's teign
And Coomb at the clear teign head —
  Where close by the stream
  You may have your cream
All spread upon barley bread.

There 's arch Brook
  And there 's larch Brook
Both turning many a mill ;
  And cooling the drouth
  Of the salmon's mouth
And fattening his silver gill.

There is Wild wood,
  A Mild hood
To the sheep on the lea o' the down,
  Where the golden furze
  With its green, thin spurs,
Doth catch at the maiden's gown.

There is Newton marsh
  With its spear grass harsh —
A pleasant summer level
  Where the maidens sweet
  Of the Market Street,
Do meet in the dusk to revel.

There 's the Barton rich
  With dyke and ditch
And hedge for the thrush to live in ;
  And the hollow tree
  For the buzzing bee,
And a bank for the wasp to hive in.

And O, and O
The daisies blow
And the primroses are waken'd,
    And the violets white
    Sit in silver plight,
And the green bud 's as long as the spike end.

    Then who would go
    Into dark Soho,
And chatter with dack'd hair'd critics,
    When he can stay
    For the new-mown hay,
And startle the dappled Prickets?

THE DEVON MAID

Immediately after the preceding, Keats adds: 'I know not if this rhyming fit has done anything — it will be safe with you if worthy to put among my Lyrics. Here 's some doggrel for you,' and these four stanzas follow.

WHERE be ye going, you Devon Maid?
    And what have ye there in the Basket?
Ye tight little fairy just fresh from the dairy,
    Will ye give me some cream if I ask it?

I love your Meads, and I love your flowers,
    And I love your junkets mainly,
But 'hind the door I love kissing more,
    O look not so disdainly.

I love your hills, and I love your dales,
    And I love your flocks a-bleating —
But O, on the heather to lie together,
    With both our hearts a-beating!

I 'll put your Basket all safe in a nook,
    Your shawl I hang up on the willow,
And we will sigh in the daisy's eye
    And kiss on a grass green pillow.

ACROSTIC:

GEORGIANA AUGUSTA KEATS

This is dated 'Foot of Helvellyn, June 27,' 1818, and was sent, as something overlooked, to his brother and sister, September 18, 1819. 'I wrote it in a great hurry which you will see. Indeed I would not copy it if I thought it would ever be seen by any but yourselves.'

GIVE me your patience, sister, while I frame
Exact in capitals your golden name;
Or sue the fair Apollo and he will
Rouse from his heavy slumber and instill

Great love in me for thee and Poesy.
Imagine not that greatest mastery
And kingdom over all the Realms of verse,
Nears more to heaven in aught, than when we
    nurse
And surety give to love and Brotherhood.

Anthropophagi in Othello's mood;
Ulysses storm'd and his enchanted belt
Glow with the Muse, but they are never felt
Unbosom'd so and so eternal made,
Such tender incense in their laurel shade
To all the regent sisters of the Nine
As this poor offering to you, sister mine.

Kind sister! ay, this third name says you are;
Enchanted has it been the Lord knows where;
And may it taste to you like good old wine,
Take you to real happiness and give
Sons, daughters and a home like honied hive.

MEG MERRILIES

Sent in a letter to Fanny Keats, written from Auchencairn, July 2, 1818. 'We are in the midst of Meg Merrilies country of whom I suppose you have heard.' Fanny Keats was a girl of fifteen at this time.

OLD Meg she was a Gipsy,
    And liv'd upon the Moors:
Her bed it was the brown heath turf,
    And her house was out of doors.

Her apples were swart blackberries,
    Her currants pods o' broom;
Her wine was dew of the wild white rose,
    Her book a churchyard tomb.

Her Brothers were the craggy hills,
    Her Sisters larchen trees —
Alone with her great family
    She liv'd as she did please.

No breakfast had she many a morn,
    No dinner many a noon,
And 'stead of supper she would stare
    Full hard against the Moon.

But every morn of woodbine fresh
    She made her garlanding,
And every night the dark glen Yew
    She wove, and she would sing.

And with her fingers old and brown
    She plaited Mats o' Rushes,

And gave them to the Cottagers
She met among the Bushes,

Old Meg was brave as Margaret Queen
And tall as Amazon :
An old red blanket cloak she wore ;
A chip hat had she on.
God rest her aged bones somewhere —
She died full long agone !

A SONG ABOUT MYSELF

'I have so many interruptions,' writes Keats
to his sister Fanny from Kircudbright, July 2,
1818, 'that I cannot manage to fill a Letter
in one day — since I scribbled the song [Meg
Merrilies] we have walked through a beautiful
country to Kircudbright — at which place I
will write you a song about myself.'

THERE was a naughty Boy,
A naughty boy was he,
He would not stop at home,
He could not quiet be —
He took
In his Knapsack
A Book
Full of vowels ;
And a shirt
With some towels —
A slight cap
For night cap —
A hair brush,
Comb ditto,
New Stockings,
For old ones
Would split O !
This Knapsack,
Tight at 's back,
He rivetted close
And follow'd his Nose
To the North,
To the North,
And follow'd his nose
To the North.

There was a naughty boy
And a naughty boy was he,
For nothing would he do
But scribble poetry —
He took
An inkstand
In his hand,
And a Pen
Big as ten
In the other,

And away
In a Pother
He ran
To the mountains,
And fountains
And ghostes,
And Postes,
And witches,
And ditches,
And wrote
In his coat,
When the weather
Was cool,
Fear of gout,
And without
When the weather
Was Warm —
Och the charm
When we choose
To follow one's nose
To the north,
To the north,
To follow one's nose
To the north.

There was a naughty boy
And a naughty boy was he,
He kept little fishes
In washing tubs three
In spite
Of the might
Of the Maid,
Nor afraid
Of his Granny — good —
He often would,
Hurly burly,
Get up early,
And go
By hook or crook
To the brook,
And bring home
Miller's thumb,
Tittlebat
Not over fat,
Minnows small
As the stall
Of a glove,
Not above
The size
Of a nice
Little Baby's
Little fingers —
O, he made,
'T was his trade,
Of Fish a pretty Kettle
A Kettle —
A Kettle

Of Fish, a pretty Kettle,
  A Kettle!

There was a naughty Boy,
  And a naughty Boy was he,
He ran away to Scotland
  The people for to see —
    Then he found
    That the ground
    Was as hard,
    That a yard
    Was as long,
    That a song
    Was as merry,
    That a cherry
    Was as red —
    That lead
    Was as weighty,
    That fourscore
    Was as eighty,
    That a door
    Was as wooden
    As in England —
  So he stood in his shoes
    And he wonder'd,
    He wonder'd,
  He stood in his shoes
    And he wonder'd.

TO THOMAS KEATS

BELANTREE (for Ballantrae) July 10 [1818.]

AH! ken ye what I met the day
  Out oure the Mountains
A coming down by craggies gray
  An mossie fountains —
Ah goud-hair'd Marie yeve I pray
  Ane minute's guessing —
For that I met upon the way
  Is past expressing.
As I stood where a rocky brig
  A torrent crosses
I spied upon a misty rig
  A troup o' Horses —
And as they trotted down the glen
  I sped to meet them
To see if I might know the Men
  To stop and greet them.
First Willie on his sleek mare came
  At canting gallop
His long hair rustled like a flame
  On board a shallop,
Then came his brother Rab and then
  Young Peggy's Mither
And Peggy too — adown the glen
  They went togither —

I saw her wrappit in her hood
  Frae wind and raining —
Her cheek was flush wi' timid blood
  Twixt growth and waning —
She turn'd her dazed eyes full oft
  For there her Brithers
Came riding with her Bridegroom soft
  And mony ithers.
Young Tam came up and eyed me quick
  With reddened cheek —
Braw Tom was daffed like a chick —
  He couldna speak —
Ah, Marie, they are all gane hame
  Through blustering weather
An' every heart is full on flame
  An' light as feather.
Ah! Marie, they are all gone hame
  Frae happy wadding,
Whilst I — Ah is it not a shame?
  Sad tears am shedding.

THE GADFLY

Inclosed in a letter to Tom Keats, July 17,
1818.

ALL gentle folks who owe a grudge
  To any living thing
Open your ears and stay your t(r)udge
  Whilst I in dudgeon sing.

The Gadfly he hath stung me sore —
  O may he ne'er sting you!
But we have many a horrid bore, —
  He may sting black and blue.

Has any here an old gray Mare
  With three legs all her store,
O put it to her Buttocks bare
  And straight she 'll run on four.

Has any here a Lawyer suit
  Of 1743,
Take Lawyer's nose and put it to 't
  And you the end will see.

Is there a Man in Parliament
  Dum(b)founder'd in his speech,
O let his neighbour make a rent
  And put one in his breech.

O Lowther how much better thou
  Hadst figur'd t' other day
When to the folks thou mad'st a bow
  And hadst no more to say.

If lucky Gadfly had but ta'en
  His seat . . .

And put thee to a little pain
  To save thee from a worse.

Better than Southey it had been,
  Better than Mr. D——
Better than Wordsworth, too, I ween,
  Better than Mr. V——.

Forgive me, pray, good people all,
  For deviating so—
In spirit sure I had a call—
  And now I on will go.

Has any here a daughter fair
  Too fond of reading novels,
Too apt to fall in love with care
  And charming Mister Lovels,

O put a Gadfly to that thing
  She keeps so white and pert—
I mean the finger for the ring,
  And it will breed a wort.

Has any here a pious spouse
  Who seven times a day
Scolds as King David pray'd, to chouse
  And have her holy way—

O let a Gadfly's little sting
  Persuade her sacred tongue
That noises are a common thing,
  But that her bell has rung.

And as this is the summum bo-
  num of all conquering,
I leave 'withouten wordes mo'
  The Gadfly's little sting.

ON HEARING THE BAG-PIPE AND SEEING
'THE STRANGER' PLAYED AT INVERARY

'On entering Inverary,' Keats writes to his
brother Tom, July 18, 1818, 'we saw a Play
Bill. Brown was knocked up from new shoes
— so I went to the Barn alone where I saw the
Stranger accompanied by a Bag-pipe. There
they went on about interesting creaters and
human nater till the Curtain fell and then
came the Bag-pipe. When Mrs. Haller fainted
down went the Curtain and out came the Bag-
pipe — at the heartrending, shoemending reconciliation the Piper blew amain. I never read
or saw this play before; not the Bag-pipe nor
the wretched players themselves were little in .

comparison with it — thank heaven it has been
scoffed at lately almost to a fashion.'

OF late two dainties were before me plac'd
  Sweet, holy, pure, sacred and innocent,
  From the ninth sphere to me benignly sent
That Gods might know my own particular
  taste:
First the soft Bag-pipe mourn'd with zealous
  haste,
  The Stranger next with head on bosom bent
  Sigh'd; rueful again the piteous Bag-pipe
  went,
Again the Stranger sighings fresh did waste.
O Bag-pipe, thou didst steal my heart away—
  O Stranger, thou my nerves from Pipe didst
  charm—
O Bag-pipe thou didst re-assert thy sway—
  Again thou, Stranger, gav'st me fresh alarm—
Alas! I could not choose. Ah! my poor heart
Mum chance art thou with both oblig'd to part.

LINES WRITTEN IN THE HIGHLANDS AFTER
A VISIT TO BURNS'S COUNTRY

In a letter to Benjamin Bailey from the
Island of Mull, July 22, 1818.

THERE is a charm in footing slow across a silent
  plain,
Where patriot battle has been fought, where
  glory had the gain;
There is a pleasure on the heath where Druids
  old have been,
Where mantles gray have rustled by and swept
  the nettles green;
There is Joy in every spot made known by
  times of old,
New to the feet, although each tale a hundred
  times be told;
There is a deeper Joy than all, more solemn in
  the heart,
More parching to the tongue than all, of more
  divine a smart,
When weary steps forget themselves upon a
  pleasant turf,
Upon hot sand, or flinty road, or sea-shore iron
  scurf,
Toward the Castle or the Cot, where long ago
  was born
One who was great through mortal days, and
  died of fame unshorn.
Light heather-bells may tremble then, but they
  are far away;
Wood-lark may sing from sandy fern, — the
  Sun may hear his Lay;

Runnels may kiss the grass on shelves and shal-
    lows clear,
But their low voices are not heard, though
    come on travels drear ;
Blood-red the sun may set behind black moun-
    tain peaks ;
Blue tides may sluice and drench their time in
    Caves and weedy creeks ;
Eagles may seem to sleep wing-wide upon the
    Air ;
Ring-doves may fly convuls'd across to some
    high-cedar'd lair ;
But the forgotten eye is still fast lidded to the
    ground,
As Palmer's, that with weariness, mid-desert
    shrine hath found.

    At such a time the soul 's a child, in child-
    hood is the brain ;
Forgotten is the worldly heart — alone, it beats
    in vain. —
Aye, if a Madman could have leave to pass a
    healthful day
To tell his forehead's swoon and faint when
    first began dècay,
He might make tremble many a one whose spirit
    had gone forth
To find a Bard's low cradle-place about the
    silent North.
Scanty the hour and few the steps beyond the
    bourn of Care,
Beyond the sweet and bitter world, — beyond
    it unaware !
Scanty the hour and few the steps, because a
    longer stay
Would bar return, and make a man forget his
    mortal way :
O horrible ! to lose the sight of well remem-
    ber'd face,
Of Brother's eyes, of Sister's brow — constant
    to every place ;
Filling the Air, as on we move, with Portrai-
    ture intense ;
More warm than those heroic tints that pain a
    Painter's sense,
When shapes of old come striding by, and vis-
    ages of old,
Locks shining black, hair scanty gray, and pas-
    sions manifold.
No, no, that horror cannot be, for at the cable's
    length
Man feels the gentle anchor pull and gladdens
    in its strength : -
One hour, half-idiot, he stands by mossy water-
    fall,
But in the very next he reads his soul's Memo-
    rial : —

He reads it on the mountain's height, where
    chance he may sit down
Upon rough marble diadem — that hill's eter-
    nal Crown.
Yet be his Anchor e'er so fast, room is there
    for a prayer
That man may never lose his Mind on Moun-
    tains black and bare ;
That he may stray league after league some
    great birthplace to find
And keep his vision clear from speck, his in-
    ward sight unblind.

MRS. CAMERON AND BEN NEVIS

In his letter to Tom Keats, August 3, 1818,
which contains the sonnet written on Ben Nevis, Keats concludes a lively account of the
ascent they made with this bit of nonsense : —

After all there was one Mrs. Cameron of 50
years of age and the fattest woman in all Inverness-shire who got up this Mountain some
few years ago — true she had her servants —
but then she had herself. She ought to have
hired Sisyphus, — " Up the high hill he heaves
a huge round — Mrs. Cameron." 'T is said a
little conversation took place between the
mountain and the Lady. After taking a glass
of Whisky as she was tolerably seated at ease
she thus began —

MRS. C.

UPON my life Sir Nevis I am piqued
That I have so far panted tugg'd and reek'd
To do an honor to your old bald pate
And now am sitting on you just to bait,
Without your paying me one compliment.
Alas, 't is so with all, when our intent
Is plain, and in the eye of all Mankind
We fair ones show a preference, too blind !
You Gentle man immediately turn tail —
O let me then my hapless fate bewail !
Ungrateful Baldpate have I not disdain'd
The pleasant Valleys — have I not madbrain'd
Deserted all my Pickles and preserves
My China closet too — with wretched Nerves
To boot — say, wretched ingrate, have I not
Left my soft cushion chair and caudle pot ?
'T is true I had no corns — no ! thank the
    fates
My Shoemaker was always Mr. Bates.
And if not Mr. Bates why I 'm not old !
Still dumb ungrateful Nevis — still so cold !

Here the Lady took some more whisky and was putting even more to her lips when she dashed it to the Ground, for the Mountain began to grumble — which continued for a few minutes before he thus began —

BEN NEVIS.

What whining bit of tongue and Mouth thus dares
Disturb my slumber of a thousand years?
Even so long my sleep has been secure —
And to be so awak'd I 'll not endure.
Oh pain — for since the Eagle's earliest scream
I 've had a damn'd confounded ugly dream,
A Nightmare sure. What! Madam, was it you?
It cannot be! My old eyes are not true!
Red-Crag, my Spectacles! Now let me see!
Good Heavens! Lady, how the gemini
Did you get here? O, I shall split my sides!
I shall earthquake —

MRS. C.

Sweet Nevis do not quake, for though I love
Your honest Countenance all things above,
Truly I should not like to be convey'd
So far into your Bosom — gentle Maid
Loves not too rough a treatment, gentle Sir —
Pray thee be calm and do not quake nor stir
No, not a Stone, or I shall go in fits —

BEN NEVIS.

I must — I shall — I meet not such tit bits —
I meet not such sweet creatures every day —
By my old nightcap night and day
I must have one sweet Buss — I must and shall!
Red Crag! — What! Madam, can you then repent
Of all the toil and vigour you have spent
To see Ben Nevis and to touch his nose?
Red Crag I say! O I must have them close!
Red Crag, there lies beneath my farthest toe
A vein of Sulphur — go, dear Red Crag, go —
And rub your flinty back against it — budge!
Dear Madam, I must kiss you, faith I must!
I must embrace you with my dearest gust!
Block-head, d' ye hear! — Block-head, I 'll make her feel.
There lies beneath my east leg's northern heel
A cave of young earth dragons; — well my boy
Go thither quick and so complete my joy.
Take you a bundle of the largest pines,
And when the sun on fiercest Phosphor shines,
Fire them and ram them in the Dragon's nest,
Then will the dragons fry and fizz their best

Until ten thousand now no bigger than
Poor Alligators — poor things of one span —
Will each one swell to twice ten times the size
Of northern whale — then for the tender prize —
The moment then — for then will Red Crag rub
His flinty back — and I shall kiss and snub
And press my dainty morsel to my breast.
Block-head make haste!
         O Muses, weep the rest —
The Lady fainted and he thought her dead;
So pulled the clouds again about his head
And went to sleep again; soon she was rous'd
By her affrighted servants — next day, hous'd
Safe on the lowly ground she bless'd her fate
That fainting fit was not delayed too late.

But what surprised me above all is how the lady got down again. I felt it horribly. 'T was the most vile descent — shook me all to pieces.

SHARING EVE'S · APPLE

Printed by Mr. Forman and assigned to 1818. Mr. Forman does not give his authority, save to say that the verses have been handed about in manuscript.

O BLUSH not so! O blush not so!
  Or I shall think you knowing;
And if you smile the blushing while,
  Then maidenheads are going.

There 's a blush for won't, and a blush for shan't,
  And a blush for having done it:
There 's a blush for thought and a blush for nought,
  And a blush for just begun it.

O sigh not so! O sigh not so!
  For it sounds of Eve's sweet pippin;
By these loosen'd lips you have tasted the pips
  And fought in an amorous nipping.

Will you play once more at nice-cut-core,
  For it only will last our youth out,
And we have the prime of the kissing time,
  We have not one sweet tooth out.

There 's a sigh for yes, and a sigh for no,
  And a sigh for I can't bear it!
O what can be done, shall we stay or run?
  O cut the sweet apple and share it!

A PROPHECY:

TO GEORGE KEATS IN AMERICA

In a letter to his brother and his wife, October 24, 1818, Keats says: 'If I had a prayer to make for any great good, next to Tom's recovery, it should be that one of your children should be the first American Poet. I have a great mind to make a prophecy, and they say prophecies work on their own fulfilment.'

'T is the witching time of night,
Orbed is the moon and bright,
And the Stars they glisten, glisten,
Seeming with bright eyes to listen.
For what listen they?
For a song and for a charm,
See they glisten in alarm,
And the Moon is waxing warm
To hear what I shall say.
Moon! keep wide thy golden ears —
Hearken, Stars! and hearken, Spheres! —
Hearken, thou eternal Sky!
I sing an infant's Lullaby,
O pretty lullaby!
Listen, listen, listen, listen,
Glisten, glisten, glisten, glisten,
And hear my Lullaby!
Though the Rushes, that will make
Its cradle, still are in the lake —
Though the linen that will be
Its swathe, is on the cotton tree —
Though the woollen that will keep
It warm, is on the silly sheep —
Listen, Starlight, listen, listen,
Glisten, glisten, glisten, glisten,
And hear my lullaby!
Child, I see thee! Child, I 've found thee
Midst of the quiet all around thee!
Child, I see thee! Child, I spy thee!
And thy mother sweet is nigh thee!
Child, I know thee! Child no more,
But a Poet evermore!
See, see, the Lyre, the Lyre,
In a flame of fire,
Upon the little cradle's top
Flaring, flaring, flaring,
Past the eyesight's bearing.
Awake it from its sleep,
And see if it can keep
Its eyes upon the blaze —
Amaze, amaze!
It stares, it stares, it stares,
It dares what no one dares!
It lifts its little hand into the flame

Unharm'd, and on the strings
Paddles a little tune, and sings,
With dumb endeavour sweetly —
Bard art thou completely!
    Little child
    O' th' western wild,
Bard art thou completely!
Sweetly with dumb endeavour.
A Poet now or never,
    Little child
    O' th' western wild,
A Poet now or never!

A LITTLE EXTEMPORE

Inclosed in a letter to George and Georgiana Keats, written April 15, 1819.

WHEN they were come into the Faery's Court
They rang — no one at home — all gone to sport
And dance and kiss and love as faeries do
For Faries be as humans lovers true.
Amid the woods they were so lone and wild,
Where even the Robin feels himself exil'd,
And where the very brooks, as if afraid,
Hurry along to some less magic shade.
'No one at home!' the fretful Princess cry'd;
'And all for nothing such a dreary ride,
And all for nothing my new diamond cross;
No one to see my Persian feathers toss,
No one to see my Ape, my Dwarf, my Fool,
Or how I pace my Otaheitan mule.
Ape, Dwarf, and Fool, why stand you gaping
    there,
Burst the door open, quick — or I declare
I 'll switch you soundly and in pieces tear.'
The Dwarf began to tremble, and the Ape
Star'd at the Fool, the Fool was all agape,
The Princess grasp'd her switch, but just in
    time
The dwarf with piteous face began to rhyme.
'O mighty Princess, did you ne'er hear tell
What your poor servants know but too too
    well?
Know you the three great crimes in Faeryland?
The first, alas! poor Dwarf, I understand,
I made a whipstock of a faery's wand;
The next is snoring in their company;
The next, the last, the direst of the three,
Is making free when they are not at home.
I was a Prince — a baby prince — my doom,
You see, I made a whipstock of a wand,
My top has henceforth slept in faery land.
He was a Prince, the Fool, a grown-up Prince,
But he has never been a King's son since
He fell a snoring at a faery Ball.

Yon poor Ape was a Prince, and he poor thing
Picklock'd a faery's boudoir — now no king
But ape — so pray your highness stay awhile,
'T is sooth indeed, we know it to our sorrow —
Persist and you may be an ape to-morrow.'
While the Dwarf spake, the Princess, all for
    spite,
Peel'd the brown hazel twig to lily white,
Clench'd her small teeth, and held her lips
    apart,
Try'd to look unconcern'd with beating heart.
They saw her highness had made up her mind,
A-quavering like the reeds before the wind —
And they had had it, but O happy chance!
The Ape for very fear began to dance
And grinn'd as all his ugliness did ache —
She staid her vixen fingers for his sake,
He was so very ugly: then she took
Her pocket-mirror and began to look
First at herself and then at him, and then
She smil'd at her own beauteous face again.
Yet for all this — for all her pretty face —
She took it in her head to see the place.
Women gain little from experience
Either in Lovers, husbands, or expense.
The more their beauty the more fortune too —
Beauty before the wide world never knew —
So each fair reasons — tho' it oft miscarries.
She thought *her* pretty face would please the
    fairies.
' My darling Ape, I wont whip you to-day,
Give me the Picklock sirrah and go play.'
They all three wept but counsel was as vain
As crying cup biddy to drops of rain.
Yet lingering by did the sad Ape forth draw
The Picklock from the Pocket in his Jaw.
The Princess took it, and dismounting straight
Tripp'd in blue silver'd slippers to the gate
And touch'd the wards, the Door full courteous
Opened — she enter'd with her servants three.
Again it clos'd and there was nothing seen
But the Mule grazing on the herbage green.
                End of Canto XII.

CANTO THE XIII

The Mule no sooner saw himself alone
Than he prick'd up his Ears — and said ' well
    done;
At least unhappy Prince I may be free —
No more a Princess shall side-saddle me.
O King of Otaheite — tho' a Mule,
" Aye, every inch a King " — tho' " Fortune's
    Fool,"
Well done — for by what Mr. Dwarfy said
I would not give a sixpence for her head.'
Even as he spake he trotted in high glee
To the knotty side of an old Pollard tree,

And rubb'd his sides against the mossed bark
Till his Girths burst and left him naked stark
Except his Bridle — how get rid of that
Buckled and tied with many a twist and plait.
At last it struck him to pretend to sleep,
And then the thievish Monkeys down would
    creep
And filch the unpleasant trammels quite away.
No sooner thought of than adown he lay,
Shamm'd a good snore — the Monkey-men de-
    scended
And whom they thought to injure they be-
    friended.
They hung his Bridle on a topmost bough
And off he went run, trot, or anyhow —

SPENSERIAN STANZAS ON CHARLES ARMI-
TAGE BROWN

Inclosed in a letter to George and Georgiana Keats, April 16 or 17, 1819: ' Brown this
morning is writing some Spenserian stanzas
against Mrs., Miss Brawne and me; so I shall
amuse myself with him a little: in the manner
of Spenser.'

HE is to weet a melancholy Carle:
Thin in the waist, with bushy head of hair,
As hath the seeded thistle when in parle
It holds the Zephyr, ere it sendeth fair
Its light balloons into the summer air;
There to his beard had not begun to bloom,
No brush had touch'd his chin, or razor
    sheer;
No care had touched his cheek with mortal
    doom,
But new he was, and bright, as scarf from Per-
    sian loom.

Ne cared he for wine, or half-and-half;
Ne cared he for fish, or flesh, or fowl;
And sauces held he worthless as the chaff;
He 's deigned the swineherd at the wassail
    bowl;
Ne with lewd ribbalds sat he cheek by jowl;
Ne with sly Lemans in the scorner's chair;
But after water-brooks this Pilgrim's soul
Panted, and all his food was woodland air;
Though he would oft-times feast on gilliflowers
    rare.

The slang of cities in no wise he knew;
Tipping the wink to him was heathen Greek;
He sipp'd no ' olden Tom,' or ' ruin blue,'
Or Nantz, or cherry-brandy, drunk full meek

By many a Damsel hoarse, and rouge of
    cheek ;
Nor did he know each aged Watchman's
    beat,
Nor in obscured purlieus would he seek
For curled Jewesses, with ankles neat,
Who, as they walk abroad, make tinkling with
    their feet.

'TWO OR THREE POSIES'

At the close of a letter, April 17, 1819, to
his sister Fanny, Keats writes : 'Mr. and Mrs.
Dilke are coming to dine with us to-day [at
Wentworth Place]. They will enjoy the
country after Westminster. O there is nothing
like fine weather, and health, and Books, and a
fine country, and a contented Mind, and diligent habit of reading and thinking, and an
amulet against the ennui — and, please heaven, a little claret wine cool out of a cellar a
mile deep — with a few or a good many ratafia
cakes — a rocky basin to bathe in, a strawberry
bed to say your prayers to Flora in, a pad nag
to go you ten miles or so ; two or three sensible people to chat with ; two or three spiteful
folks to spar with ; two or three odd fishes to
laugh at and two or three numskulls to argue
with — instead of using dumb bells on a rainy
day.'

Two or three Posies
With two or three simples —
Two or three Noses
With two or three pimples —
Two or three wise men
And two or three ninny's —
Two or three purses
And two or three guineas —
Two or three raps
At two or three doors —
Two or three naps
Of two or three hours —
Two or three Cats
And two or three mice —
Two or three sprats
At a very great price —
Two or three sandies
And two or three tabbies —
Two or three dandies
And two Mrs.   mum !
Two or three Smiles
And two or three frowns —
Two or three Miles
To two or three towns —

Two or three pegs
For two or three bonnets —
Two or three dove eggs
To hatch into sonnets —

A PARTY OF LOVERS

'Somewhere in the *Spectator* is related an
account of a man inviting a party of stutterers
and squinters to his table. It would please me
more to scrape together a party of lovers —
not to dinner but to tea. There would be no
fighting as among knights of old.' Keats to
George and Georgiana Keats, September 17,
1819. The play on names seems to indicate
some trifling reference to Keats's publishers of
Taylor and Hessey.

PENSIVE they sit, and roll their languid eyes,
Nibble their toast, and cool their tea with sighs,
Or else forget the purpose of the night,
Forget their tea — forget their appetite.
See with cross'd arms they sit — ah ! happy
    crew,
The fire is going out and no one rings
For coals, and therefore no coals Betty brings.
A fly is in the milk-pot – must he die
    By a humane society ?
No, no ; there Mr. Werter takes his spoon,
Inserts it, dips the handle, and lo ! soon
The little straggler, sav'd from perils dark,
Across the teaboard draws a long wet mark.

Arise ! take snuffers by the handle,
There 's a large cauliflower in each candle.
A winding-sheet, ah me ! I must away
To No. 7, just beyond the circus gay.
' Alas, my friend ! your coat sits very well ;
Where may your Taylor live ? ' 'I may not
    tell.
O pardon me — I 'm absent now and then.
Where *might* my Taylor live ? I say again
I cannot tell, let me no more be teaz'd —
He lives in Wapping, *might* live where he
    pleas'd.'

TO GEORGE KEATS

WRITTEN IN SICKNESS

This is from a transcript by George Keats,
and dated 1819 ; but Keats's letters do not disclose any sickness during that year which
would be likely to call forth the lines, and the
date is probably 1820, if indeed we are author-

ized to refer this poem to John Keats. It is
not impossible that it was written by Tom
Keats in 1818.

BROTHER belov'd if health shall smile again,
  Upon this wasted form and fever'd cheek:
  If e'er returning vigour bid these weak
And languid limbs their gladsome strength re-
    gain,
Well may thy brow the placid glow retain
  Of sweet content and thy pleas'd eye may
    speak
  The conscious self applause, but should I seek
To utter what this heart can feel, — Ah! vain
Were the attempt! Yet kindest friends while
    o'er
  My couch ye bend, and watch with tenderness
The being whom your cares could e'en restore,
  From the cold grasp of Death, say can you
    guess
  The feelings which these lips can ne'er ex-
    · press?
Feelings, deep fix'd in grateful memory's store.

ON OXFORD

Charles Armitage Brown, writing to Henry
Snook from Hampstead 24 March, 1820, says:
'Tom shall have one of his [Keats's] bits of
comic verses, — I met with them only yesterday, but they have been written long ago, —
it is a song on the City of Oxford.'
  The verses were also copied by Keats in a
letter to Reynolds, given below on p. 269, as a
satirical criticism of Wordsworth.

    THE Gothic looks solemn,
      The plain Doric column
  Supports an old Bishop and Crozier;
      The mouldering arch,
      Shaded o'er by a larch,
  Stands next door to Wilson the Hosier.

Vice, — that is, by turns, —
  O'er pale faces mourns
The black tassell'd trencher and common hat;
  The charity boy sings,
  The Steeple-bell rings
And as for the Chancellor — *dominat.*

    There are plenty of trees,
      And plenty of ease,
  And plenty of fat deer for Parsons;
      And when it is venison,
      Short is the benison, —
  Then each on a leg or thigh fastens.

TO A CAT

  These verses were addressed by Keats to a
cat belonging to Mrs. Reynolds of Little Britain, the mother of his friend John Hamilton
Reynolds. Mrs. Reynolds gave the verses to
her son-in-law, Tom Hood, who published them
in his *Comic Annual* for 1830.

CAT! who has[t] pass'd thy grand clima[c]-
    teric,
  How many mice and rats hast in thy days
  Destroy'd? — How many tit-bits stolen?
    Gaze
With those bright languid segments green, and
    prick
Those velvet ears — but pr'ythee do not stick
  Thy latent talons in me — and upraise
  Thy gentle mew — and tell me all thy frays
Of fish and mice, and rats and tender chick:
Nay, look not down, nor lick thy dainty wrists
  For all the wheezy asthma, — and for all
  Thy tail's tip is nick'd off — and though the
    fists
Of many a maid has given thee many a maul,
Still is that fur as soft as when the lists
  In youth thou enter'dst on glass-bottled wall.

LETTERS

LETTERS OF JOHN KEATS

1. TO CHARLES COWDEN CLARKE

[London, October 31, 1816.]

MY DAINTIE DAVIE — I will be as punctual as the Bee to the Clover. Very glad am I at the thoughts of seeing so soon this glorious Haydon and all his creation. I pray thee let me know when you go to Ollier's and where he resides — this I forgot to ask you — and tell me also when you will help me waste a sullen day — God 'ield you [1] — J. K.

2. TO THE SAME

[London,] Tuesday [December 17, 1816].

MY DEAR CHARLES — You may now look at Minerva's Ægis with impunity, seeing that my awful Visage [2] did not turn you into a John Doree. You have accordingly a legitimate title to a Copy — I will use my interest to procure it for you. I 'll tell you what — I met Reynolds at Haydon's a few mornings since — he promised to be with me this Evening and Yesterday I had the same promise from Severn and I must put you in mind that on last All hallowmas' day you gave me your word that you would spend this Evening with me — so no putting off. I have done little to Endymion lately [2] — I hope to finish it in one more attack. I believe you I went to Richards's — it was so whoreson a Night that I stopped there all the next day. His Remembrances to you. (Ext. from the common place Book of my Mind — Mem. — Wednesday — Hampstead — call in Warner Street — a sketch of Mr. Hunt.) — I will ever consider you my sincere and affectionate friend — you will not doubt that I am yours.

God bless you — JOHN KEATS.

3. TO JOHN HAMILTON REYNOLDS

[London,] Sunday Evening
[March 2, 1817?].

MY DEAR REYNOLDS — Your kindness [3] affects me so sensibly that I can merely put down a few mono-sentences. Your Criticism only makes me extremely anxious that I should not deceive you.

It 's the finest thing by God as Hazlitt would say. However I hope I may not deceive you. There are some acquaintances of mine who will scratch their Beards and although I have, I hope, some Charity, I wish their Nails may be long. I will be ready at the time you mention in all Happiness.

There is a report that a young Lady of 16 has written the new Tragedy, God bless her — I will know her by Hook or by Crook in less than a week. My Brothers' and my Remembrances to your kind Sisters.

Yours most sincerely
JOHN KEATS.

4. TO THE SAME

[London, March 17, 1817.]

MY DEAR REYNOLDS — My Brothers are anxious that I should go by myself into the country — they have always been extremely fond of me, and now that Haydon has pointed out how necessary it is that I should be alone to improve myself, they give up the temporary pleasure of living with me continually for a great good which I hope will follow. So I shall soon be out of Town. You must soon bring all your present troubles to a close, and so must I, but we must, like the Fox, prepare for a fresh swarm of flies. Banish money — Banish sofas — Banish Wine — Banish Music; but right Jack Health, honest Jack Health, true Jack Health — Banish health and banish all the world. I must . . . myself . . . if I come this evening, I shall horribly commit myself elsewhere. So I will send my excuses to them and Mrs. Dilke by my brothers.

Your sincere friend

JOHN KEATS.

5. TO GEORGE AND THOMAS KEATS

[Southampton,] Tuesday Morn
[April 15, 1817].

MY DEAR BROTHERS — I am safe at Southampton — after having ridden three stages outside and the rest in for it began to be very cold. I did not know the Names of any of the Towns I passed through — all I can tell you is that sometimes I saw dusty Hedges — sometimes Ponds — then nothing — then a little Wood with trees look you like Launce's Sister 'as white as a Lily and as small as a Wand' — then came houses which died away into a few straggling Barns — then came hedge trees aforesaid again. As the Lamplight crept along the following things were discovered — 'long heath broom furze' — Hurdles here and there half a Mile — Park palings when the Windows of a House were always discovered by reflection — One Nymph of Fountain — N. B. Stone — lopped Trees — Cow ruminating — ditto Donkey — Man and Woman going gingerly along — William seeing his Sisters over the Heath — John waiting with a Lanthorn for his Mistress — Barber's Pole — Doctor's Shop — However after having had my fill of these I popped my Head out just as it began to Dawn — N. B. this Tuesday Morn saw the Sun rise — of which I shall say nothing at present. I felt rather lonely this Morning at Breakfast so I went and unbox'd a Shakspeare — ' There 's my Comfort.'[1] I went immediately after Breakfast to Southampton Water where I enquired for the Boat to the Isle of Wight as I intend seeing that place before I settle — it will go at 3, so shall I after having taken a Chop. I know nothing of this place but that it is long — tolerably broad — has bye streets — two or three Churches — a very respectable old Gate with two Lions to guard it. The Men and Women do not materially differ from those I have been in the Habit of seeing. I forgot to say that from dawn till half-past six I went through a most delightful Country — some open Down but for the most part thickly wooded. What surprised me most was an immense quantity of blooming Furze on each side the road cutting a most rural dash. The Southampton water when I saw it just now was no better than a low water Water which did no more than answer my expectations — it will have mended its Manners by 3. From the Wharf are seen the shores on each side stretching to the Isle of Wight. You, Haydon, Reynolds, etc. have been pushing each other out of my Brain by turns. I have conned over every Head in Haydon's Picture — you must warn them not to be afraid should my Ghost visit them on Wednesday — tell Haydon to Kiss his Hand at Betty over the Way for me yea and to spy at her for me. I hope one of you will be competent to take part in a Trio while I am away — you need only aggravate your voices a little and mind not to speak Cues and all — when you have said Rum-ti-ti — you must not be rum any more or else another will take up the ti-ti alone and then he might be taken God shield us for little better than a Titmouse. By the by talking of Titmouse Remember me particularly to all my Friends — give my Love to the Miss Reynoldses and to Fanny who I hope you will soon see. Write to me soon about them all — and you George particularly how you get on with Wilkinson's plan. What could I have done without my Plaid? I don't feel inclined to write any more at present for I feel rather muzzy — you must be content with this fac simile of the rough plan of Aunt Dinah's Counterpane.[4]

Your most affectionate Brother

JOHN KEATS.

Reynolds shall hear from me soon.

6. TO JOHN HAMILTON REYNOLDS

Carisbrooke, April 17th [1817].

MY DEAR REYNOLDS — Ever since I wrote to my Brothers from Southampton I have been in a taking — and at this moment I am about to become settled — for I have unpacked my books, put them into a snug corner, pinned up Haydon, Mary Queen of Scots, and Milton with his daughters in a row. In the passage I found a head of Shakspeare which I had not before seen. It is most likely the same that George spoke so well of, for I like it extremely. Well — this head I have hung over my Books, just above the three in a row, having first discarded a French Ambassador — now this alone is a good morning's work. Yesterday I went to Shanklin, which occasioned a great debate in my mind whether I should live there or at Carisbrooke. Shanklin is a most beautiful place — Sloping wood and meadow ground reach round the Chine, which is a cleft between the Cliffs of the depth of nearly 300 feet at least. This cleft is filled with trees and bushes in the narrow part, and as it widens becomes bare, if it were not for primroses on one side, which spread to the very verge of the Sea, and some fishermen's huts on the other, perched midway in the Balustrades of beautiful green Hedges along their steps down to the sands. But the sea, Jack, the sea — the little waterfall — then the white cliff — then St. Catherine's Hill — 'the sheep in the meadows, the cows in the corn.' Then, why are you at Carisbrooke ? say you. Because, in the first place, I should be at twice the Expense, and three times the inconvenience — next that from here I can see your continent —

from a little hill close by the whole north Angle of the Isle of Wight, with the water between us. In the 3rd place, I see Carisbrooke Castle from my window, and have found several delightful wood-alleys, and copses, and quick freshes. As for primroses — the Island ought to be called Primrose Island — that is, if the nation of Cowslips agree thereto, of which there are divers Clans just beginning to lift up their heads. Another reason of my fixing is, that I am more in reach of the places around me. I intend to walk over the Island east — West — North — South. I have not seen many specimens of Ruins — I don't think however I shall ever see one to surpass Carisbrooke Castle. The trench is overgrown with the smoothest turf, and the Walls with ivy. The Keep within side is one Bower of ivy — a colony of Jackdaws have been there for many years. I dare say I have seen many a descendant of some old cawer who peeped through the Bars at Charles the first, when he was there in Confinement. On the road from Cowes to Newport I saw some extensive Barracks, which disgusted me extremely with the Government for placing such a Nest of Debauchery in so beautiful a place. I asked a man on the Coach about this — and he said that the people had been spoiled. In the room where I slept at Newport, I found this on the Window — 'O Isle spoilt by the milatary ! . . .'

The wind is in a sulky fit, and I feel that it would be no bad thing to be the favourite of some Fairy, who would give one the power of seeing how our Friends got on at a Distance. I should like, of all Loves, a sketch of you and Tom and George in ink which Haydon will do if you tell him how I want them. From want of regular rest I have been rather *narvus* — and the passage in *Lear* — 'Do you not hear the sea ?' — has haunted me intensely.

[Here follows the sonnet 'On the Sea,' p. 37.]

April 15th.

Will you have the goodness to do this? Borrow a Botanical Dictionary — turn to the words Laurel and Prunus, show the explanations to your sisters and Mrs. Dilke and without more ado let them send me the Cups Basket and Books they trifled and put off and off while I was in town. Ask them what they can say for themselves — ask Mrs. Dilke wherefore she does so distress me — let me know how Jane has her health — the Weather is unfavourable for her. Tell George and Tom to write. I'll tell you what — on the 23d was Shakspeare born. Now if I should receive a letter from you and another from my Brothers on that day 't would be a parlous good thing. Whenever you write say a word or two on some Passage in Shakspeare that may have come rather new to you, which must be continually happening, notwithstanding that we read the same Play forty times — for instance, the following from the Tempest never struck me so forcibly as at present,

'Urchins
Shall, for the vast of night that they may work,
All exercise on thee — '

How can I help bringing to your mind the line —

In the dark backward and abysm of time —

I find I cannot exist without Poetry — without eternal Poetry — half the day will not do — the whole of it — I began with a little, but habit has made me a Leviathan. I had become all in a Tremble from not having written anything of late — the Sonnet overleaf did me good. I slept the better last night for it — this Morning, however, I am nearly as bad again. Just now I opened Spenser, and the first Lines I saw were these —

'The noble heart that harbours virtuous thought,
And is with child of glorious great intent,
Can never rest until it forth have brought
Th' eternal brood of glory excellent — '

Let me know particularly about Haydon, ask him to write to me about Hunt, if it be only ten lines — I hope all is well — I shall forthwith begin my Endymion, which I hope I shall have got some way with by the time you come, when we will read our verses in a delightful place I have set my heart upon, near the Castle. Give my Love to your Sisters severally — to George and Tom. Remember me to Rice, Mr. and Mrs. Dilke and all we know.

Your sincere Friend   JOHN KEATS.

Direct J. Keats, Mrs. Cook's, New Village, Carisbrooke.

7. TO LEIGH HUNT

Margate, May 10, 1817.

MY DEAR HUNT — The little gentleman that sometimes lurks in a gossip's bowl, ought to have come in the very likeness of a *roasted* crab, and choaked me outright for not answering your letter ere this: however, you must not suppose that I was in town to receive it: no, it followed me to the Isle of Wight, and I got it just as I was going to pack up for Margate, for reasons which you anon shall hear. On arriving at this treeless affair, I wrote to my brother George to request C. C. C. to do the thing you wot of respecting Rimini; and George tells me he has undertaken it with great pleasure; so I hope there has been an understanding between you for many proofs: C. C. C. is well acquainted with Bensley. Now why did you not send the key of your cupboard, which, I know, was full of papers? We would have locked them all in a trunk, together with those you told me to destroy, which indeed I did not do, for fear of demolishing receipts, there not being a more unpleasant thing in the world (saving a thousand and one others) than to pay a bill twice. Mind you, old Wood's a 'very varmint,' shrouded in covetousness: — and now I am upon a horrid subject — what a horrid one you were upon last Sunday, and well you handled it. The last Examiner was a battering-ram against Christianity, blasphemy, Tertullian, Erasmus, Sir Philip

Sidney; and then the dreadful Petzelians and their expiation by blood; and do Christians shudder at the same thing in a newspaper which they attribute to their God in its most aggravated form? What is to be the end of this? I must mention Hazlitt's Southey.[5] O that he had left out the grey hairs; or that they had been in any other paper not concluding with such a thunderclap! That sentence about making a page of the feeling of a whole life, appears to me like a whale's back in the sea of prose. I ought to have said a word on Shakspeare's Christianity. There are two which I have not looked over with you, touching the thing: the one for, the other against: that in favour is in Measure for Measure, Act II. Scene ii. —

Isab. Alas, alas!
Why, all the souls that were, were forfeit once;
And He that might the 'vantage best have took,
Found out the remedy.

That against is in Twelfth Night, Act III. Scene ii. —

Maria. For there is no Christian that means to be saved by believing rightly, can ever believe such impossible passages of grossness.

Before I come to the Nymphs,[6] I must get through all disagreeables. I went to the Isle of Wight, thought so much about poetry, so long together, that I could not get to sleep at night; and, moreover, I know not how it was, I could not get wholesome food. By this means, in a week or so, I became not over capable in my upper stories, and set off pell-mell for Margate, at least a hundred and fifty miles, because, forsooth, I fancied that I should like my old lodging here, and could contrive to do without trees. Another thing, I was too much in solitude, and consequently was obliged to be in continual burning of thought, as an only resource. However, Tom is with me at present, and we are very comfortable. We intend, though, to get among some trees. How have you got on among them? How are the Nymphs? I suppose they have led

you a fine dance. Where are you now? — in Judea, Cappadocia, or the parts of Libya about Cyrene? Stranger from 'Heaven, Hues, and Prototypes,' I wager you have given several new turns to the old saying, 'Now the maid was fair and pleasant to look on,' as well as made a little variation in 'Once upon a time.' Perhaps, too, you have rather varied, 'Here endeth the first lesson.' Thus I hope you have made a horseshoe business of 'unsuperfluous life,' 'faint bowers,' and fibrous roots. I vow that I have been down in the mouth lately at this work. These last two days, however, I have felt more confident — I have asked myself so often why I should be a poet more than other men, seeing how great a thing it is, — how great things are to be gained by it, what a thing to be in the mouth of Fame, — that at last the idea has grown so monstrously beyond my seeming power of attainment, that the other day I nearly consented with myself to drop into a Phaethon. Yet 't is a disgrace to fail, even in a huge attempt; and at this moment I drive the thought from me. I began my poem about a fortnight since, and have done some every day, except travelling ones. Perhaps I may have done a good deal for the time, but it appears such a pin's point to me, that I will not copy any out. When I consider that so many of these pin-points go to form a bodkin-point (God send I end not my life with a bare bodkin, in its modern sense!), and that it requires a thousand bodkins to make a spear bright enough to throw any light to posterity, I see nothing but continual uphill journeying. Now is there anything more unpleasant (it may come among the thousand and one) than to be so journeying and to miss the goal at last? But I intend to whistle all these cogitations into the sea, where I hope they will breed storms violent enough to block up all exit from Russia. Does Shelley go on telling strange stories of the deaths of kings?[7] Tell him, there are strange stories of the deaths of poets.

Some have died before they were conceived. 'How do you make that out,
Master Vellum?' Does Mrs. S. cut bread
and butter as neatly as ever? Tell her to
procure some fatal scissors, and cut the
thread of life of all to-be-disappointed
poets. Does Mrs. Hunt tear linen as
straight as ever? Tell her to tear from
the book of life all blank leaves. Remember me to them all; to Miss Kent and the
little ones all.

   Your sincere Friend
      JOHN KEATS *alias* JUNKETS.
You shall hear where we move.

8. TO BENJAMIN ROBERT HAYDON

Margate, Saturday Eve [May 10, 1817].
MY DEAR HAYDON,

'Let Fame, that all pant after in their lives,
Live register'd upon our brazen tombs,
And so grace us in the disgrace of death:
When spite of cormorant devouring Time
The endeavour of this present breath may buy
That Honour which shall bate his Scythe's keen
    edge
And make us heirs of all eternity.'
    Love's Labour 's Lost, I. i. 1—7.

To think that I have no right to couple
myself with you in this speech would be
death to me, so I have e'en written it, and
I pray God that our 'brazen tombs' be
nigh neighbours. It cannot be long first ;
the 'endeavour of this present breath' will
soon be over, and yet it is as well to breathe
freely during our sojourn — it is as well
as if you have not been teased with that
Money affair, that bill-pestilence. However, I must think that difficulties nerve
the Spirit of a Man — they make our Prime
Objects a Refuge as well as a Passion. The
Trumpet of Fame is as a tower of Strength,
the ambitious bloweth it and is safe. I suppose, by your telling me not to give way to
forebodings, George has mentioned to you
what I have lately said in my Letters to
him — truth is I have been in such a state
of Mind as to read over my Lines and hate

them. I am one that 'gathers Samphire,
dreadful trade' — the Cliff of Poesy
towers above me — yet when Tom who
meets with some of Pope's Homer in Plu-
tarch's Lives reads some of those to me
they seem like Mice to mine. I read and
write about eight hours a day. There is an
old saying 'well begun is half done' —
't is a bad one. I would use instead, 'Not
begun at all till half done;' so according to
that I have not begun my Poem and consequently (à priori) can say nothing about it.
Thank God ! I do begin arduously where
I leave off, notwithstanding occasional de-
pressions ; and I hope for the support of
a High Power while I climb this little eminence, and especially in my Years of more
momentous Labour. I remember your saying that you had notions of a good Genius
presiding over you. I have of late had the
same thought, for things which I do half at
Random are afterwards confirmed by my
judgment in a dozen features of Propriety.
Is it too daring to fancy Shakspeare this
Presider ? When in the Isle of Wight I met
with a Shakspeare in the Passage of the
House at which I lodged — it comes nearer
to my idea of him than any I have seen —
I was but there a Week, yet the old woman
made me take it with me though I went off
in a hurry. Do you not think this is omi-
nous of good ? I am glad you say every
man of great views is at times tormented
as I am.

         Sunday after [May 11]
   This Morning I received a letter from
George by which it appears that Money
Troubles are to follow us up for some time
to come — perhaps for always — these vexations are a great hindrance to one — they
are not like Envy and detraction stimulants
to further exertion as being immediately
relative and reflected on at the same time
with the prime object — but rather like a
nettle leaf or two in your bed. So now I
revoke my Promise of finishing my Poem
by the Autumn which I should have done
had I gone on as I have done — but I can

not write while my spirit is fevered in a contrary direction and I am now sure of having plenty of it this Summer. At this moment I am in no enviable Situation — I feel that I am not in a Mood to write any to-day; and it appears that the loss of it is the beginning of all sorts of irregularities. I am extremely glad that a time must come when everything will leave not a wrack behind. You tell me never to despair — I wish it was as easy for me to observe the saying — truth is I have a horrid Morbidity of Temperament which has shown itself at intervals — it is I have no doubt the greatest Enemy and stumbling-block I have to fear — I may even say that it is likely to be the cause of my disappointment. However every ill has its share of good — this very bane would at any time enable me to look with an obstinate eye on the Devil Himself — aye to be as proud of being the lowest of the human race as Alfred could be in being of the highest. I feel confident I should have been a rebel angel had the opportunity been mine. I am very sure that you do love me as your very Brother — I have seen it in your continual anxiety for me — and I assure you that your welfare and fame is and will be a chief pleasure to me all my Life. I know no one but you who can be fully sensible of the turmoil and anxiety, the sacrifice of all what is called comfort, the readiness to measure time by what is done and to die in six hours could plans be brought to conclusions — the looking upon the Sun, the Moon, the Stars, the Earth and its contents, as materials to form greater things — that is to say ethereal things — but here I am talking like a Madman, — greater things than our Creator himself made ! !

I wrote to Hunt yesterday — scarcely know what I said in it. I could not talk about Poetry in the way I should have liked for I was not in humor with either his or mine. His self-delusions are very lamentable — they have enticed him into a Situation which I should be less eager after than

that of a galley Slave — what you observe thereon is very true must be in time.

Perhaps it is a self-delusion to say so — but I think I could not be deceived in the manner that Hunt is — may I die to-morrow if I am to be. There is no greater Sin after the seven deadly than to flatter oneself into an idea of being a great Poet — or one of those beings who are privileged to wear out their Lives in the pursuit of Honor — how comfortable a feel it is to feel that such a Crime must bring its heavy Penalty ? That if one be a Self-deluder accounts must be balanced ? I am glad you are hard at Work — 't will now soon be done — I long to see Wordsworth's as well as to have mine in:[8] but I would rather not show my face in Town till the end of the Year — if that will be time enough — if not I shall be disappointed if you do not write for me even when you think best. I never quite despair and I read Shakspeare — indeed I shall I think never read any other Book much. Now this might lead me into a long Confab but I desist. I am very near agreeing with Hazlitt that Shakspeare is enough for us. By the by what a tremendous Southean article his last was — I wish he had left out 'grey hairs.' It was very gratifying to meet your remarks on the manuscript — I was reading Anthony and Cleopatra when I got the Paper and there are several Passages applicable to the events you commentate. You say that he arrived by degrees and not by any single struggle to the height of his ambition — and that his Life had been as common in particulars as other Men's. Shakspeare makes Enobarb say —

> Where 's Antony ?
> *Eros.* — He 's walking in the garden, and spurns
> *The rush that lies* before him ; cries, Fool, Lepidus !

In the same scene we find —

> Let determined things
> To destiny hold unbewailed their way.

Dolabella says of Anthony's Messenger,

An argument that he is pluck'd when hither
He sends so poor a pinion of his wing.

Then again —

Eno. — I see Men's Judgments are
A parcel of their fortunes; and things outward
Do draw the inward quality after them,
To suffer all alike.

The following applies well to Bertrand ¹ —

　　　　　Yet he that can endure
To follow with allegiance a fallen Lord,
Does conquer him that did his Master conquer,
And earns a place i' the story.

But how differently does Buonaparte bear his fate from Anthony!

'T is good, too, that the Duke of Wellington has a good Word or so in the Examiner. A man ought to have the Fame he deserves — and I begin to think that detracting from him as well as from Wordsworth is the same thing. I wish he had a little more taste — and did not in that respect 'deal in Lieutenantry.' You should have heard from me before this — but in the first place I did not like to do so before I had got a little way in the First Book, and in the next as G. told me you were going to write I delayed till I had heard from you. Give my Respects the next time you write to the North and also to John Hunt. Remember me to Reynolds and tell him to write. Ay, and when you send Westward tell your Sister that I mentioned her in this. So now in the name of Shakspeare, Raphael and all our Saints, I commend you to the care of heaven!

Your everlasting Friend JOHN KEATS.

9.　TO MESSRS. TAYLOR AND HESSEY

Margate, May 16, 1817.

MY DEAR SIRS — I am extremely indebted to you for your liberality in the shape of manufactured rag, value £20, and shall immediately proceed to destroy some of the minor heads of that hydra the dun; to conquer which the knight need have no Sword Shield Cuirass, Cuisses Herbadgeon Spear Casque Greaves Paldrons spurs Chevron or any other scaly commodity, but he need only take the Bank-note of Faith and Cash of Salvation, and set out against the monster, invoking the aid of no Archimago or Urganda, but finger me the paper, light as the Sibyl's leaves in Virgil, whereat the fiend skulks off with his tail between his legs. Touch him with this enchanted paper, and he whips you his head away as fast as a snail's horn — but then the horrid propensity he has to put it up again has discouraged many very valiant Knights. He is such a never-ending still-beginning sort of a body — like my landlady of the Bell. I should conjecture that the very spright that 'the green sour ringlets makes Whereof the ewe not bites' had manufactured it of the dew fallen on said sour ringlets. I think I could make a nice little allegorical poem, called 'The Dun,' where we would have the Castle of Carelessness, the drawbridge of credit, Sir Novelty Fashion's expedition against the City of Tailors, etc. etc. I went day by day at my poem for a Month — at the end of which time the other day I found my Brain so over-wrought that I had neither rhyme nor reason in it — so was obliged to give up for a few days. I hope soon to be able to resume my work — I have endeavoured to do so once or twice; but to no purpose. Instead of Poetry, I have a swimming in my head and feel all the effects of a Mental debauch, lowness of Spirits, anxiety to go on without the power to do so, which does not at all tend to my ultimate progression. However tomorrow I will begin my next month. This evening I go to Canterbury, having got tired of Margate. I was not right in my head when I came — At Canterbury I hope the remembrance of Chaucer will set me forward like a Billiard Ball. I am glad to hear of Mr. T.'s health, and of the welfare of the 'In-town-stayers.' And think Reynolds will like his Trip — I have some idea of seeing the Continent some time this summer. In repeating how sensible I am of your kindness, I remain

Y' obed' serv' and friend JOHN KEATS.

I shall be happy to hear any little intelligence in the literary or friendly way when you have time to scribble.

10. TO THE SAME

[London] Tuesday Morn [July 8, 1817].

MY DEAR SIRS — I must endeavour to lose my maidenhead with respect to money Matters as soon as possible — And I will too — So, here goes! A couple of Duns that I thought would be silent till the beginning, at least, of next month (when I am certain to be on my legs, for certain sure), have opened upon me with a cry most 'untuneable;' never did you hear such un-'gallant chiding.' Now you must know, I am not desolate, but have, thank God, 25 good notes in my fob. But then, yon know, I laid them by to write with and would stand at bay a fortnight ere they should grab me. In a month's time I must pay, but it would relieve my mind if I owed you, instead of these Pelican duns.

I am afraid you will say I have 'wound about with circumstance,' when I should have asked plainly — however as I said I am a little maidenish or so, and I feel my virginity come strong upon me, the while I request the loan of a £20 and a £10, which, if you would enclose to me, I would acknowledge and save myself a hot forehead. I am sure you are confident of my responsibility, and in the sense of squareness that is always in me.

Your obliged friend   JOHN KEATS.

11. TO MARIANE AND JANE REYNOLDS [10]

Oxf[ord, September 5, 1817].

MY DEAR FRIENDS — You are I am glad to hear comfortable at Hampton,[11] where I hope you will receive the Biscuits we ate the other night at Little Britain. I hope you found them good. There you are among sands, stones, Pebbles, Beeches, Cliffs, Rocks, Deeps, Shallows, weeds, ships, Boats (at a distance), Carrots, Turnips, sun, moon, and stars and all those sort of things — here am I among Colleges, halls, Stalls, Plenty of Trees, thank God — Plenty of water, thank heaven — Plenty of Books, thank the Muses — Plenty of Snuff, thank Sir Walter Raleigh — Plenty of segars, — Ditto — Plenty of flat country, thank Tellus's rolling-pin. I'm on the sofa — Buonaparte is on the snuff-box — But you are by the seaside — argal, you bathe — you walk — you say 'how beautiful' — find out resemblances between waves and camels — rocks and dancing-masters — fireshovels and telescopes — Dolphins and Madonas — which word, by the way, I must acquaint you was derived from the Syriac, and came down in a way which neither of you I am sorry to say are at all capable of comprehending. But as a time may come when by your occasional converse with me you may arrive at 'something like prophetic strain,' I will unbar the gates of my pride and let my condescension stalk forth like a ghost at the Circus. — The word Ma-don-a, my dear Ladies — or — the word Mad — Ona— so I say! I am not mad — Howsumever when that aged Tamer Kewthon sold a certain camel called Peter to the overseer of the Babel Sky-works, he thus spake, adjusting his cravat round the tip of his chin — 'My dear Ten-story-up-in-air! this here Beast, though I say it as should n't say 't, not only has the power of subsisting 40 days and 40 nights without fire and candle but he can sing. — Here I have in my Pocket a Certificate from Signor Nicolini of the King's Theatre; a Certificate to this effect —— ' I have had dinner since I left that effect upon you, and feel too heavy in mentibus to display all the Profundity of the Polygon — so you had better each of you take a glass of cherry Brandy and drink to the health of Archimedes, who was of so benign a disposition that he never would leave Syracuse in his life — So kept himself out of all Knight-Errantry. — This I know to be a faqt; for it is written in the 45th book of Winkine's treatise on garden-rollers, that he trod on a fishwoman's toe in Liverpool, and never begged her pardon. Now the long and short is this — that is by comparison — for a long day may be a short year — A long Pole may be a very stupid fellow as a man. But let us refresh ourself from this depth of thinking, and turn to some innocent jocularity — the Bow cannot always be bent — nor the gun always loaded, if you ever let it off — and the life of man is like a great Mountain — his breath is like a Shrewsbury cake — he comes into the world like a shoeblack, and goes out of it like a cobbler — he eats like a chimney-sweeper, drinks like a gingerbread baker — and breathes like Achilles — so it being that we are such sublunary creatures, let us endeavour to correct all our bad spelling — all our most delightful abominations, and let us wish health to Mariane and Jane, whoever they be and wherever.

Yours truly   JOHN KEATS.

12. TO FANNY KEATS

Oxford, September 10 [1817].

MY DEAR FANNY — Let us now begin a regular question and answer — a little pro and con; letting it interfere as a pleasant method of my coming at your favorite little wants and enjoyments, that I may meet them in a way befitting a brother.

We have been so little together since you have been able to reflect on things that I know not whether you prefer the History of King Pepin to Bunyan's Pilgrim's Progress — or Cinderella and her glass slipper to Moore's Almanack. However in a few Letters I hope I shall be able to come at that and adapt my scribblings to your Pleasure. You must tell me about all you read if it be only six Pages in a Week and

this transmitted to me every now and then will procure you full sheets of Writing from me pretty frequently. — This I feel as a necessity for we ought to become intimately acquainted, in order that I may not only, as you grow up love you as my only Sister, but confide in you as my dearest friend. When I saw you last I told you of my intention of going to Oxford and 't is now a Week since I disembark'd from his Whip-ship's Coach the Defiance in this place. I am living in Magdalen Hall on a visit to a young Man with whom I have not been long acquainted, but whom I like very much — we lead very industrious lives — he in general Studies and I in proceeding at a pretty good rate with a Poem which I hope you will see early in the next year. — Perhaps you might like to know what I am writing about. I will tell you. Many Years ago there was a young handsome Shepherd who fed his flocks on a Mountain's Side called Latmus — he was a very contempla-tive sort of Person and lived solitary among the trees and Plains little thinking that such a beautiful Creature as the Moon was growing mad in Love with him. — However so it was; and when he was asleep on the Grass she used to come down from heaven and admire him excessively for a long time; and at last could not refrain from carrying him away in her arms to the top of that high Mountain Latmus while he was a dreaming — but I daresay you have read this and all the other beautiful Tales which have come down from the ancient times of that beautiful Greece. If you have not let me know and I will tell you more at large of others quite as delightful. This Oxford I have no doubt is the finest City in the world — it is full of old Gothic buildings — Spires — towers — Quadrangles — Clois-ters — Groves, etc., and is surrounded with more clear streams than ever I saw to-gether. I take a Walk by the Side of one of them every Evening and, thank God, we have not had a drop of rain these many days. I had a long and interesting Letter from George, cross lines by a short one from Tom yesterday dated Paris. They both send their loves to you. Like most Englishmen they feel a mighty preference for everything English — the French Meadows, the trees, the People, the Towns, the Churches, the Books, the everything — although they may be in themselves good: yet when put in comparison with our green Island they all vanish like Swallows in October. They have seen Cathedrals, Manuscripts, Fountains, Pictures, Tragedy, Comedy, — with other things you may by chance meet with in this Country such as Washerwomen, Lamplighters, Turnpikemen, Fishkettles, Dancing Masters, Kettle drums, Sentry Boxes, Rocking Horses, etc. — and, now they have taken them over a set of boxing-gloves.

I· have written to George and requested him, as you wish I should, to write to you. I have been writing very hard lately, even till an utter incapacity came on, and I feel it now about my head: so you must not mind a little out-of-the-way sayings — though by the bye were my brain as clear as a bell I think I should have a little propensity thereto. I shall stop here till I have finished the 3d Book of my Story; which I hope will be accomplish'd in at most three Weeks from to-day — about which time you shall see me. How do you like Miss Taylor's essays in Rhyme [12] — I just look'd into the Book and it appeared to me suitable to you — especially since I remember your liking for those pleasant little things the Original Poems — the essays are the more mature production of the same hand. While I was speaking about France it occurred to me to speak a few Words on their Language — it is perhaps the poorest one ever spoken since the jabbering in the Tower of Babel, and when you come to know that the real use and greatness of a Tongue is to be referred to its Literature — you will be astonished to find how very inferior it is to our native Speech. — I wish the Italian would supersede French in every school throughout the

Country, for that is full of real Poetry and Romance of a kind more fitted for the Pleasure of Ladies than perhaps our own. — It seems that the only end to be gained in acquiring French is the immense accomplishment of speaking it — it is none at all — a most lamentable mistake indeed. Italian indeed would sound most musically from Lips which had began to pronounce it as early as French is crammed down our Mouths, as if we were young Jackdaws at the mercy of an overfeeding Schoolboy. Now Fanny you must write soon — and write all you think about, never mind what — only let me have a good deal of your writing — You need not do it all at once — be two or three or four days about it, and let it be a diary of your little Life. You will preserve all my Letters and I will secure yours — and thus in the course of time we shall each of us have a good Bundle — which, hereafter, when things may have strangely altered and God knows what happened, we may read over together and look with pleasure on times past — that now are to come. Give my Respects to the Ladies — and so my dear Fanny I am ever

Your most affectionate Brother JOHN.

If you direct — Post Office, Oxford — your Letter will be brought to me.

13. TO JANE REYNOLDS

Oxford, Sunday Evg. [September 14, 1817].

MY DEAR JANE — You are such a literal translator, that I shall some day amuse myself with looking over some foreign sentences, and imagining how you would render them into English. This is an age for typical Curiosities; and I would advise you, as a good speculation, to study Hebrew, and astonish the world with a figurative version in our native tongue. The Mountains skipping like rams, and the little hills like lambs, you will leave as far behind as the hare did the tortoise. It must be so or you would never have thought that I really

meant you would like to pro and con about
those Honeycombs — no, I had no such
idea, or, if I had, 't would be only to tease
you a little for love. So now let me put
down in black and white briefly my sentiments thereon. — Imprimis — I sincerely
believe that Imogen is the finest creature,
and that I should have been disappointed
at hearing you prefer Juliet — Item — Yet
I feel such a yearning towards Juliet that I
would rather follow her into Pandemonium
than Imogen into Paradise — heartily wishing myself a Romeo to be worthy of her,
and to hear the Devils quote the old proverb, 'Birds of a feather flock together' —
Amen. —

Now let us turn to the Seashore. Believe
me, my dear Jane, it is a great happiness to
see that you are in this finest part of the
year winning a little enjoyment from the
hard world. In truth, the great Elements
we know of, are no mean comforters: the
open sky sits upon our senses like a sapphire
crown — the Air is our robe of state — the
Earth is our throne, and the Sea a mighty
minstrel playing before it — able, like David's harp, to make such a one as you forget
almost the tempest cares of life. I have
found in the ocean's music, — varying (tho
self-same) more than the passion of Timo-
theus, an enjoyment not to be put into
words; and, 'though inland far I be,' I
now hear the voice most audibly while
pleasing myself in the idea of your sensations.

—— is getting well apace, and if you
have a few trees, and a little harvesting
about you, I'll snap my fingers in Lucifer's
eye. I hope you bathe too — if you do not,
I earnestly recommend it. Bathe thrice a
week, and let us have no more sitting up
next winter. Which is the best of Shakspeare's plays? I mean in what mood and
with what accompaniment do you like the
sea best? It is very fine in the morning,
when the sun,

'Opening on Neptune with fair blessed beams,
Turns into yellow gold his salt sea streams,'

and superb when

'The sun from meridian height
Illumines the depth of the sea,
And the fishes, beginning to sweat,
Cry d—— it! how hot we shall be,'

and gorgeous, when the fair planet hastens

'To his home
Within the Western foam.'

But don't you think there is something
extremely fine after sunset, when there are
a few white clouds about and a few stars
blinking — when the waters are ebbing, and
the horizon a mystery? This state of things
has been so fulfilling to me that I am
anxious to hear whether it is a favourite
with you. So when you and Marianne club
your letter to me put in a word or two
about it. Tell Dilke [13] that it would be
perhaps as well if he left a Pheasant or
Partridge alive here and there to keep up a
supply of game for next season — tell him
to rein in if Possible all the Nimrod of his
disposition, he being a mighty hunter before
the Lord — of the Manor. Tell him to shoot
fair, and not to have at the Poor devils in
a furrow — when they are flying, he may
fire, and nobody will be the wiser.

Give my sincerest respects to Mrs. Dilke,
saying that I have not forgiven myself for
not having got her the little box of medicine I promised, and that, had I remained
at Hampstead I would have made precious
havoc with her house and furniture — drawn
a great harrow over her garden — poisoned
Boxer — eaten her clothes-pegs — fried her
cabbages — fricaseed (how is it spelt?)
her radishes — ragout'd her Onions —
belaboured her beet-root — outstripped her
scarlet-runners — parlez-vous'd with her
french-beans — devoured her mignon or
mignionette — metamorphosed her bell-
handles — splintered her looking-glasses —
bullocked at her cups and saucers — ago-
nised her decanters — put old Phillips to
pickle in the brine-tub — disorganised her
piano — dislocated her candlesticks — emptied her wine-bins in a fit of despair —

turned out her maid to grass — and astonished Brown; whose letter to her on these events I would rather see than the original Copy of the Book of Genesis. Should you see Mr. W. D. remember me to him, and to little Robinson Crusoe, and to Mr. Snook. Poor Bailey, scarcely ever well, has gone to bed, pleased that I am writing to you. To your brother John (whom henceforth I shall consider as mine) and to you, my dear friends, Marianne and Jane, I shall ever feel grateful for having made known to me so real a fellow as Bailey. He delights me in the selfish and (please God) the disinterested part of his disposition. If the old Poets have any pleasure in looking down at the enjoyers of their works, their eyes must bend with a double satisfaction upon him. I sit as at a feast when he is over them, and pray that if, after my death, any of my labours should be worth saving, they may have so 'honest a chronicler' as Bailey. Out of this, his enthusiasm in his own pursuit and for all good things is of an exalted kind — worthy a more healthful frame and an untorn spirit. He must have happy years to come — 'he shall not die by God.'

A letter from John the other day was a chief happiness to me. I made a little mistake when, just now, I talked of being far inland. How can that be when Endymion and I are at the bottom of the sea? whence I hope to bring him in safety before you leave the seaside; and, if I can so contrive it, you shall be greeted by him upon the sea-sands, and he shall tell you all his adventures, which having finished, he shall thus proceed — ' My dear Ladies, favourites of my gentle mistress, however my friend Keats may have teased and vexed you, believe me he loves you not the less — for instance, I am deep in his favour, and yet he has been hauling me through the earth and sea with unrelenting perseverance. I know for all this that he is mighty fond of me, by his contriving me all sorts of pleasures. Nor is this the least, fair ladies, this

one of meeting you on the desert shore, and greeting you in his name. He sends you moreover this little scroll — ' My dear Girls, I send you, per favour of Endymion, the assurance of my esteem for you, and my utmost wishes for your health and pleasure, being ever,

Your affectionate Brother JOHN KEATS.

14. TO JOHN HAMILTON REYNOLDS

Oxford, Sunday Morn [September 21, 1817].

MY DEAR REYNOLDS — So you are determined to be my mortal foe — draw a Sword at me, and I will forgive — Put a Bullet in my Brain, and I will shake it out as a dewdrop from the Lion's Mane — put me on a Gridiron, and I will fry with great complacency — but — oh, horror! to come upon me in the shape of a Dun! Send me bills! as I say to my Tailor, send me Bills and I'll never employ you more. However, needs must, when the devil drives: and for fear of 'before and behind Mr. Honeycomb' I'll proceed. I have not time to elucidate the forms and shapes of the grass and trees; for, rot it! I forgot to bring my mathematical case with me, which unfortunately contained my triangular Prism so that the hues of the grass cannot be dissected for you —

For these last five or six days, we have had regularly a Boat on the Isis, and explored all the streams about, which are more in number than your eye-lashes. We sometimes skim into a Bed of rushes, and there become naturalised river-folks, — there is one particularly nice nest, which we have christened ' Reynolds's Cove,' in which we have read Wordsworth and talked as may be. I think I see you and Hunt meeting in the Pit. — What a very pleasant fellow he is, if he would give up the sovereignty of a Room pro bono. What Evenings we might pass with him, could we have him from Mrs. H. Failings I am always rather rejoiced to find in a man than sorry for;

they bring us to a Level. He has them, but then his makes-up are very good. He agrees with the Northern Poet [14] in this, 'He is not one of those who much delight to season their fireside with personal talk' — I must confess however having a little itch that way, and at this present moment I have a few neighbourly remarks to make. The world, and especially our England, has, within the last thirty years, been vexed and teased by a set of Devils, whom I detest so much that I almost hunger after an Acherontic promotion to a Torturer, purposely for their accommodation. These devils are a set of women, who having taken a snack or Luncheon of Literary scraps, set themselves up for towers of Babel in languages, Sapphos in Poetry, Euclids in Geometry, and everything in nothing. Among such the name of Montague has been preëminent. The thing has made a very uncomfortable impression on me. I had longed for some real feminine Modesty in these things, and was therefore gladdened in the extreme on opening the other day, one of Bailey's Books — a book of poetry written by one beautiful Mrs. Philips, a friend of Jeremy Taylor's, and called 'The Matchless Orinda — ' You must have heard of her, and most likely read her Poetry — I wish you have not, that I may have the pleasure of treating you with a few stanzas — I do it at a venture — You will not regret reading them once more. The following, to her friend Mrs. M. A. at parting, you will judge of.

> I have examin'd and do find,
>   Of all that favour me
> There's none I grieve to leave behind
>   But only, only thee.
> To part with thee I needs must die,
> Could parting sep'rate thee and I.
>
> But neither Chance nor Complement
>   Did element our Love;
> 'T was sacred sympathy was lent
>   Us from the Quire above.
> That Friendship Fortune did create,
> Still fears a wound from Time or Fate.

> Our chang'd and mingled Souls are grown
>   To such acquaintance now,
> That if each would resume their own,
>   Alas! we know not how.
> We have each other so engrost,
> That each is in the Union lost.
>
> And thus we can no Absence know,
>   Nor shall we be confin'd;
> Our active Souls will daily go
>   To learn each others mind.
> Nay, should we never meet to Sense,
> Our Souls would hold Intelligence.
>
> Inspired with a Flame Divine
>   I scorn to court a stay;
> For from that noble Soul of thine
>   I ne're can be away.
> But I shall weep when thou dost grieve;
> Nor can I die whil'st thou dost live.
>
> By my own temper I shall guess
>   At thy felicity,
> And only like my happiness
>   Because it pleaseth thee.
> Our hearts at any time will tell
> If thou, or I, be sick, or well.
>
>   All Honour sure I must pretend,
>   All that is good or great;
>   She that would be *Rosania's* Friend
>   Must be at least compleat.[1]
>   If I have any bravery,
>   'T is cause I have so much of thee.
>
> Thy Leiger Soul in me shall lie,
>   And all thy thoughts reveal;
> Then back again with mine shall flie,
>   And thence to me shall steal.
> Thus still to one another tend;
> Such is the sacred name of *Friend*.
>
> Thus our twin-Souls in one shall grow,
>   And teach the World new Love,
> Redeem the Age and Sex, and show
>   A Flame Fate dares not move:
> And courting Death to be our friend,
> Our Lives together too shall end.
>
> A Dew shall dwell upon our Tomb
>   Of such a quality,
> That fighting Armies, thither come,
>   Shall reconciled be.
> We'll ask no Epitaph, but say
> Orinda and Rosania.

[1] A complete friend. This line sounded very oddly to me at first.

In other of her poems there is a most delicate fancy of the Fletcher kind — which we will con over together. So Haydon is in Town. I had a letter from him yesterday. We will contrive as the winter comes on — but that is neither here nor there. Have you heard from Rice? Has Martin met with the Cumberland Beggar, or been wondering at the old Leech-gatherer? Has he a turn for fossils? that is, is he capable of sinking up to his Middle in a Morass? How is Hazlitt? We were reading his Table [15] last night. I know he thinks himself not estimated by ten people in the world — I wish he knew he is. I am getting on famous with my third Book — have written 800 lines thereof, and hope to finish it next Week. Bailey likes what I have done very much. Believe me, my dear Reynolds, one of my chief layings-up is the pleasure I shall have in showing it to you, I may now say, in a few days. I have heard twice from my Brothers, they are going on very well, and send their Remembrances to you. We expected to have had notices from little-Hampton this morning — we must wait till Tuesday. I am glad of their Days with the Dilkes. You are, I know, very much teased in that precious London, and want all the rest possible; so I shall be contented with as brief a scrawl — a Word or two, till there comes a pat hour.

Send us a few of your stanzas to read in 'Reynolds's Cove.' Give my Love and respects to your Mother, and remember me kindly to all at home.

Yours faithfully   JOHN KEATS.

I have left the doublings for Bailey, who is going to say that he will write to you to-morrow.

15. TO THE SAME

[Oxford, September, 1817.]

. . . .

Wordsworth sometimes, though in a fine way, gives us sentences in the style of school exercises. — For instance,

The lake doth glitter,
Small birds twitter.

Now I think this is an excellent method of giving a very clear description of an interesting place such as Oxford is.

[Here follows the verses on Oxford, given on p. 252.]

16. TO BENJAMIN ROBERT HAYDON

Oxford, September 28 [1817].

MY DEAR HAYDON — I read your letter to the young Man, whose Name is Cripps. He seemed more than ever anxious to avail himself of your offer. I think I told you we asked him to ascertain his Means. He does not possess the Philosopher's stone — nor Fortunatus's purse, nor Gyges's ring — but at Bailey's suggestion, whom I assure you is very capital fellow, we have stummed up a kind of contrivance whereby he will be enabled to do himself the benefits you will lay in his Path. I have a great Idea that he will be a tolerable neat brush. 'T is perhaps the finest thing that will befal him this many a year: for he is just of an age to get grounded in bad habits from which you will pluck him. He brought a copy of Mary Queen of Scots: it appears to me that he has copied the bad style of the painting, as well as coloured the eyeballs yellow like the original. He has also the fault that you pointed out to me in Hazlitt on the constringing and diffusing of substance. However I really believe that he will take fire at the sight of your Picture — and set about things. If he can get ready in time to return to town with me, which will be in a few days — I will bring him to you. You will be glad to hear that within these last three weeks I have written 1000 lines — which are the third Book of my Poem. My Ideas with respect to it I assure you are very low — and I would write the subject thoroughly again — but I am tired of it and think the time would be better spent in writing a new Romance which I have in my eye for next summer — Rome was not built in a Day — and all the good I expect from my employment this

summer is the fruit of Experience which I hope to gather in my next Poem. Bailey's kindest wishes, and my vow of being
        Yours eternally   JOHN KEATS.

17. TO BENJAMIN BAILEY

Hampstead, Wednesday [October 8, 1817].

MY DEAR BAILEY — After a tolerable journey, I went from Coach to Coach as far as Hampstead where I found my Brothers — the next Morning finding myself tolerably well I went to Lamb's Conduit Street and delivered your parcel. Jane and Marianne were greatly improved. Marianne especially, she has no unhealthy plumpness in the face, but she comes me healthy and angular to the chin — I did not see John — I was extremely sorry to hear that poor Rice, after having had capital health during his tour, was very ill. I daresay you have heard from him. From No. 19 I went to Hunt's and Haydon's who live now neighbours. — Shelley was there — I know nothing about anything in this part of the world — every Body seems at Loggerheads. There's Hunt infatuated — there's Haydon's picture in statu quo — There's Hunt walks up and down his painting room criticising every head most unmercifully. There's Horace Smith tired of Hunt. 'The web of our life is of mingled yarn.' Haydon having removed entirely from Marlborough Street, Cripps must direct his letter to Lisson Grove, North Paddington. Yesterday Morning while I was at Brown's, in came Reynolds, he was pretty bobbish, we had a pleasant day — he would walk home at night that cursed cold distance. Mrs. Bentley's children are making a horrid row — whereby I regret I cannot be transported to your Room to write to you. I am quite disgusted with literary men and will never know another except Wordsworth — no not even Byron. Here is an instance of the friendship of such.

Haydon and Hunt have known each other many years — now they live, pour ainsi dire, jealous neighbours — Haydon says to me, Keats, don't show your lines to Hunt on any Account, or he will have done half for you — so it appears Hunt wishes it to be thought. When he met Reynolds in the Theatre, John told him that I was getting on to the completion of 4000 lines — Ah! says Hunt, had it not been for me they would have been 7000! If he will say this to Reynolds, what would he to other people? Haydon received a Letter a little while back on this subject from some Lady — which contains a caution to me, through him, on the subject — now is not all this a most paltry thing to think about? You may see the whole of the case by the following Extract from a Letter I wrote to George in the Spring — 'As to what you say about my being a Poet, I can return no Answer but by saying that the high Idea I have of poetical fame makes me think I see it towering too high above me. At any rate, I have no right to talk until Endymion is finished — it will be a test, a trial of my Powers of Imagination, and chiefly of my invention, which is a rare thing indeed — by which I must make 4000 lines of one bare circumstance, and fill them with poetry: and when I consider that this is a great task, and that when done it will take me but a dozen paces towards the temple of fame — it makes me say — God forbid that I should be without such a task! I have heard Hunt say, and I may be asked — *why endeavour after a long Poem?* To which I should answer, Do not the Lovers of Poetry like to have a little Region to wander in, where they may pick and choose, and in which the images are so numerous that many are forgotten and found new in a second Reading: which may be food for a Week's stroll in the Summer? Do not they like this better than what they can read through before Mrs. Williams comes down stairs? a Morning work at most.

'Besides, a long poem is a test of invention, which I take to be the Polar star of Poetry, as Fancy is the Sails — and Imagination the rudder. Did our great Poets ever write short Pieces? I mean in the shape of Tales — this same invention seems indeed of late years to have been forgotten as a Poetical excellence — But enough of this, I put on no Laurels till I shall have finished Endymion, and I hope Apollo is not angered at my having made a Mockery at him at Hunt's' —

You see, Bailey, how independent my Writing has been. Hunt's dissuasion was of no avail — I refused to visit Shelley that I might have my own unfettered scope; — and after all, I shall have the Reputation of Hunt's élève. His corrections and amputations will by the knowing ones be traced in the Poem. This is, to be sure, the vexation of a day, nor would I say so many words about it to any but those whom I know to have my welfare and reputation at heart. Haydon promised to give directions for those Casts, and you may expect to see them soon, with as many Letters — You will soon hear the dinning of Bells — never mind! you and Gleig [16] will defy the foul fiend — But do not sacrifice your health to Books: do take it kindly and not so voraciously. I am certain if you are your own Physician, your Stomach will resume its proper strength and then what great benefits will follow. — My sister wrote a Letter to me, which I think must be at the post-office — Ax Will to see. My Brother's kindest remembrances to you — we are going to dine at Brown's where I have some hopes of meeting Reynolds. The little Mercury I have taken has corrected the poison and improved my health — though I feel from my employment that I shall never be again secure in Robustness. Would that you were as well as

Your Sincere friend and brother
JOHN KEATS.

18. TO THE SAME

[Hampstead: about November 1, 1817.]

MY DEAR BAILEY — So you have got a Curacy — good, but I suppose you will be obliged to stop among your Oxford favourites during Term time. Never mind. When do you preach your first sermon? — tell me, for I shall propose to the two R.'s [17] to hear it, — so don't look into any of the old corner oaken pews, for fear of being put out by us. Poor Johnny Moultrie can't be there. He is ill, I expect — but that's neither here nor there. All I can say, I wish him as well through it as I am like to be. For this fortnight I have been confined at Hampstead. Saturday evening was my first day in town, when I went to Rice's — as we intend to do every Saturday till we know not when. We hit upon an old gent we had known some few years ago, and had a *veiry pleasante daye*. In this world there is no quiet, — nothing but teasing and snubbing and vexation. My brother Tom looked very unwell yesterday, and I am for shipping him off to Lisbon. Perhaps I ship there with him. I have not seen Mrs. Reynolds since I left you, wherefore my conscience smites me. I think of seeing her tomorrow; have you any message? I hope Gleig came soon after I left. I don't suppose I've written as many lines as you have read volumes, or at least chapters, since I saw you. However, I am in a fair way now to come to a conclusion in at least three weeks, when I assure you I shall be glad to dismount for a month or two; although I'll keep as tight a rein as possible till then, nor suffer myself to sleep. I will copy for you the opening of the Fourth Book, in which you will see from the manner I had not an opportunity of mentioning any poets, for fear of spoiling the effect of the passage by particularising them.

Thus far had I written when I received your last, which made me at the sight of the direction caper for despair; but for one thing I am glad that I have been neglectful, and that is, therefrom I have received a proof of your utmost kindness, which at this present I feel very much, and I wish I had a heart always open to such sensations; but there is no altering a man's nature, and mine must be radically wrong, for it will lie dormant a whole month. This leads me to suppose that there are no men thoroughly wicked, so as never to be self-spiritualised into a kind of sublime misery; but, alas! 't is but for an hour. He is the only Man 'who has kept watch on man's mortality,' who has philanthropy enough to overcome the disposition to an indolent enjoyment of intellect, who is brave enough to volunteer for uncomfortable hours. You remember in Hazlitt's essay on commonplace people he says, 'they read the Edinburgh and Quarterly, and think as they do.' Now, with respect to Wordsworth's 'Gipsy,' I think he is right, and yet I think Hazlitt is right, and yet I think Wordsworth is rightest. If Wordsworth had not been idle, he had not been without his task; nor had the 'Gipsies' — they in the visible world had been as picturesque an object as he in the invisible. The smoke of their fire, their attitudes, their voices, were all in harmony with the evenings. It is a bold thing to say — and I would not say it in print — but it seems to me that if Wordsworth had thought a little deeper at that moment, he would not have written the poem at all. I should judge it to have been written in one of the most comfortable moods of his life — it is a kind of sketchy intellectual landscape, not a search after truth, nor is it fair to attack him on such a subject; for it is with the critic as with the poet; had Hazlitt thought a little deeper, and been in a good temper, he would never have spied out imaginary faults there. The Sunday before last I asked Haydon to dine with me, when I thought of settling all matters with him, in regard to Cripps, and let you know about it. Now, although I engaged him a fortnight before, he sent illness as an excuse. He never will come. I have not been well enough to stand the chance of a wet night, and so have not seen him, nor been able to expurgatorise more masks for you; but I will not speak — your speakers are never doers. Then Reynolds, — every time I see him and mention you, he puts his hand to his head and looks like a son of Niobe's; but he 'll write soon.

Rome, you know, was not built in a day. I shall be able, by a little perseverance, to read your letters off-hand. I am afraid your health will suffer from over study before your examination. I think you might regulate the thing according to your own pleasure, — and I would too. They were talking of your being up at Christmas. Will it be before you have passed? There is nothing, my dear Bailey, I should rejoice at more than to see you comfortable, with a little Peona wife; an affectionate wife, I have a sort of confidence, would do you a great happiness. May that be one of the many blessings I wish you. Let me be but the one-tenth of one to you, and I shall think it great. My brother George's kindest wishes to you. My dear Bailey, I am,

Your affectionate friend JOHN KEATS.

I should not like to be pages in your way; when in a tolerable hungry mood you have no mercy. Your teeth are the Rock Tarpeian down which you capsize epic poems like mad. I would not for forty shillings be Coleridge's Lays in your way. I hope you will soon get through this abominable writing in the schools, and be able to keep the terms with more comfort in the hope of retiring to a comfortable and quiet home out of the way of all Hopkinses and black beetles. When you are settled, I will come and take a peep at your church, your house; try whether I shall have grown too lusty for my chair by the fireside, and take a peep at my earliest bower. A question is the best beacon towards a little speculation. Then ask me after my health and spirits. This question ratifies in my mind what I have said above. Health and spirits can only belong unalloyed to the selfish man — the man who thinks much of his fellows can never be in spirits. You must forgive, although I have only written three hundred lines; they would have been five, but I have been obliged to go to town. Yesterday I called at Lamb's. St. Jane looked very flush when I first looked in, but was much better before I left.

19. TO THE SAME

[Fragment from an outside sheet: postmark London, November 5, 1817.]

. . . I will speak of something else, or my spleen will get higher and higher — and I am a bearer of the two-edged sword. — I hope you will receive an answer from Haydon soon — if not, Pride! Pride! Pride! I have received no more subscription — but shall soon have a full health, Liberty and leisure to give a good part of my time to him. I will certainly be in time for him. We have promised him one year: let that have elapsed, then do as we think proper. If I did not know how impossible it is, I should say — 'do not at this time of disappointments, disturb yourself about others.'

There has been a flaming attack upon Hunt in the Endinburgh Magazine. I never read anything so virulent — accusing him of the greatest Crimes, depreciating his Wife, his Poetry, his Habits, his Company, his Conversation. These Philippics are to come out in numbers — called 'the Cockney School of Poetry.' There has been but one number published — that on Hunt — to which they have prefixed a motto from one Cornelius Webb Poetaster — who unfortunately was of our party occasionally at Hampstead and took it into his head to write the following, — something about 'we 'll talk on Wordsworth, Byron, a theme we never tire on;' and so forth till he comes to Hunt and Keats. In the Motto

they have put Hunt and Keats in large letters — I have no doubt that the second number was intended for me: but have hopes of its non-appearance, from the following Advertisement in last Sunday's Examiner: — 'To Z. — The writer of the Article signed Z., in Blackwood's Edinburgh Magazine for October 1817 is invited to send his address to the printer of the Examiner, in order that Justice may be Executed on the proper person.' I don't mind the thing much — but if he should go to such lengths with me as he has done with Hunt, I must infallibly call him to an Account if he be a human being, and appears in Squares and Theatres, where we might possibly meet — I don't relish his abuse. . . .

20. TO CHARLES WENTWORTH DILKE

[Hampstead, November 1817.]

MY DEAR DILKE — Mrs. Dilke or Mr. Wm. Dilke, whoever of you shall receive this present, have the kindness to send pr. bearer Sibylline Leaves, and your petitioner shall ever pray as in duty bound.

Given under my hand this Wednesday morning of Novr. 1817. JOHN KEATS.

Vivant Rex et Regina — amen.

21. TO BENJAMIN BAILEY

[Burford Bridge, November 22, 1817.]

MY DEAR BAILEY — I will get over the first part of this (*unpaid*) Letter as soon as possible, for it relates to the affairs of poor Cripps. — To a Man of your nature such a Letter as Haydon's must have been extremely cutting — What occasions the greater part of the World's Quarrels? — simply this — two Minds meet, and do not understand each other time enough to prevent any shock or surprise at the conduct of either party — As soon as I had known Haydon three days, I had got enough of his Character not to have been surprised at such a Letter as he has hurt you with. Nor, when I knew it, was it a principle with me to drop his acquaintance; although with you it would have been an imperious feeling. I wish you knew all that I think about Genius and the Heart — and yet I think that you are thoroughly acquainted with my innermost breast in that respect, or you could not have known me even thus long, and still hold me worthy to be your dear Friend. In passing, however, I must say one thing that has pressed upon me lately, and increased my Humility and capability of submission — and that is this truth — Men of Genius are great as certain ethereal Chemicals operating on the Mass of neutral intellect — but they have not any individuality, any determined Character — I would call the top and head of those who have a proper self Men of Power.

But I am running my head into a subject which I am certain I could not do justice to under five Years' study, and 3 vols. octavo — and, moreover, I long to be talking about the Imagination — so my dear Bailey, do not think of this unpleasant affair, if possible do not — I defy any harm to come of it — I defy. I shall write to Cripps this week, and request him to tell me all his goings-on from time to time by Letter wherever I may be. It will go on well — so don't because you have suddenly discovered a Coldness in Haydon suffer yourself to be teased — Do not my dear fellow — O! I wish I was as certain of the end of all your troubles as that of your momentary start about the authenticity of the Imagination. I am certain of nothing but of the holiness of the Heart's affections, and the truth of Imagination. What the Imagination seizes as Beauty must be truth — whether it existed before or not, — for I have the same idea of all our passions as of Love: they are all, in their sublime, creative of essential Beauty. In a Word, you may know my favourite speculation by my first Book, and the little Song[16] I sent in my last, which is a representation from the fancy of the probable mode of operating in these Matters. The Imagination may be compared to Adam's dream, — he awoke and found it truth: — I am more zealous in this affair, because I have never yet been able to perceive how anything can be known for truth by consecutive reasoning — and yet it must be. Can it be that even the greatest Philosopher ever arrived at his Goal without putting aside numerous objections? However it may be, O for a life of Sensations rather than of Thoughts! It is 'a Vision in the form of Youth,' a shadow of reality to come — And this consideration has further convinced me, — for it has come as auxiliary to another favourite speculation of mine, — that we shall enjoy ourselves hereafter by having what we called happiness on Earth repeated in a finer tone — And yet such a fate can only befall those who delight in Sensation, rather than hunger as you do after Truth. Adam's dream will do here, and seems to be a Conviction that Imagination and its empyreal reflection, is the same as human life and its spiritual repetition. But, as I was saying, the Simple imaginative Mind may have its rewards in the repetition of its own silent Working coming continually on the Spirit with a fine Suddenness — to compare great things with small, have you never by being surprised with an old Melody, in a delicious place by a delicious voice, *felt* over again your very speculations and surmises at the time it first operated on your soul? — do you not remember forming to yourself the Singer's face — more beautiful than it was possible, and yet with the elevation of the Moment you did not think so? Even then you were mounted on the Wings of Imagination, so high that the prototype must be hereafter — that delicious face you will see. What a time! I am continually running away from the subject. Sure this cannot be exactly the Case with a complex mind — one that is imaginative, and at the same time careful of its fruits, — who would exist partly on Sensation, partly on thought

— to whom it is necessary that years should bring the philosophic Mind ? Such a one I consider yours, and therefore it is necessary to your eternal happiness that you not only drink this old Wine of Heaven, which I shall call the redigestion of our most ethereal Musings upon Earth, but also increase in knowledge and know all things. I am glad to hear that you are in a fair way for Easter. You will soon get through your unpleasant reading, and then ! — but the world is full of troubles, and I have not much reason to think myself pestered with many.

I think Jane or Marianne has a better opinion of me than I deserve: for, really and truly, I do not think my Brother's illness connected with mine — you know more of the real Cause than they do; nor have I any chance of being rack'd as you have been. You perhaps at one time thought there was such a thing as worldly happiness to be arrived at, at certain periods of time marked out, — you have of necessity from your disposition been thus led away — I scarcely remember counting upon any Happiness — I look not for it if it be not in the present hour, — nothing startles me beyond the moment. The Setting Sun will always set me to rights, or if a Sparrow come before my Window, I take part in its existence and pick about the gravel. The first thing that strikes me on hearing a Misfortune having befallen another is this — ' Well, it cannot be helped: he will have the pleasure of trying the resources of his Spirit ' — and I beg now, my dear Bailey, that hereafter should you observe anything cold in me not to put it to the account of heartlessness, but abstraction — for I assure you I sometimes feel not the influence of a passion or affection during a whole Week — and so long this sometimes continues, I begin to suspect myself, and the genuineness of my feelings at other times — thinking them a few barren Tragedy Tears.

My brother Tom is much improved — he is going to Devonshire — whither I shall follow him. At present, I am just arrived at Dorking — to change the Scene — change the Air, and give me a spur to wind up my Poem, of which there are wanting 500 lines. I should have been here a day sooner, but the Reynoldses persuaded me to stop in Town to meet your friend Christie.[19] There were Rice and Martin — we talked about Ghosts. I will have some Talk with Taylor and let you know, — when please God I come down at Christmas. I will find that Examiner if possible. My best regards to Gleig, my Brothers' to you and Mrs. Bentley.

Your affectionate Friend JOHN KEATS.

I want to say much more to you — a few hints will set me going. Direct Burford Bridge near Dorking.

22. TO JOHN HAMILTON REYNOLDS

[Burford Bridge,] November 22, 1817.

MY DEAR REYNOLDS — There are two things which tease me here — one of them Cripps, and the other that I cannot go with Tom into Devonshire. However, I hope to do my duty to myself in a week or so; and then I 'll try what I can do for my neighbour — now, is not this virtuous ? On returning to Town I 'll damm all Idleness — indeed, in superabundance of employment, I must not be content to run here and there on little two-penny errands, but turn Rakehell, i. e. go a masking, or Bailey will think me just as great a Promise Keeper as *he* thinks you; for myself I do not, and do not remember above one complaint against you for matter o' that. Bailey writes so abominable a hand, to give his Letter a fair reading requires a little time: so I had not seen, when I saw you last, his invitation to Oxford at Christmas. I 'll go with you. You know how poorly Rice was. I do not think it was all corporeal, — bodily pain was not used to keep him silent. I 'll tell you what; he was hurt at what your Sisters said about his joking with your Mother, he was, soothly to sain. It will all blow over. God knows, my dear Reynolds, I should not talk any sorrow to you — you must have enough vexations — so I won't any more. If I ever start a rueful subject in a letter to you — blow me ! Why don't you ? — now I am going to ask you a very silly Question neither you nor anybody else could answer, under a folio, or at least a Pamphlet — you shall judge — why don't you, as I do, look unconcerned at what may be called more particularly Heart-vexations ? They never surprise me — lord ! a man should have the fine point of his soul taken off to become fit for this world.

I like this place very much. There is Hill and Dale and a little River. I went up Box hill this Evening after the Moon — ' you a' seen the Moon ' — came down, and wrote some lines. Whenever I am separated from you, and not engaged in a continued Poem, every letter shall bring you a lyric — but I am too anxious for you to enjoy the whole to send you a particle. One of the three books I have with me is Shakspeare's Poems: I never found so many beauties in the sonnets — they seem to be full of fine things said unintentionally — in the intensity of working out conceits. Is this to be borne ? Hark ye !

' When lofty trees I see barren of leaves,
  Which erst from heat did canopy the head,
And Summer's green all girded up in sheaves,
  Borne on the bier with white and bristly
      head.'

He has left nothing to say about nothing or anything: for look at snails — you know what he says about Snails — you know when he talks about ' cockled Snails ' — well, in one of these sonnets, he says — the chap slips into — no ! I lie ! this is in the Venus and Adonis: the simile brought it to my Mind.

' As the snail, whose tender horns being hit,
  Shrinks back into his shelly cave with pain,
And there all smothered up in shade doth sit,
  Long after fearing to put forth again ;
So at his bloody view her eyes are fled,
Into the deep dark Cabins of her head.'

He overwhelms a genuine Lover of poesy with all manner of abuse, talking about —

> ' a poet's rage
> And stretched metre of an antique song.'

Which, by the bye, will be a capital motto for my poem, won't it ? He speaks too of ' Time's antique pen ' — and ' April's first-born flowers ' — and ' Death's eternal cold.' — By the Whim-King ! I 'll give you a stanza, because it is not material in connection, and when I wrote it I wanted you — to give your vote, pro or con. —

[Here follow lines 581-590, Book IV. of *Endymion*.]

. . . I see there is an advertisement in the *Chronicle* to Poets — he is so over-loaded with poems on the ' late Princess.' I suppose you do not lack — send me a few — lend me thy hand to laugh a little — send me a little pullet-sperm, a few finch-eggs — and remember me to each of our card-playing Club. When you die you will all be turned into Dice, and be put in pawn with the devil: for cards, they crumble up like anything. . . .

I rest Your affectionate friend
                    JOHN KEATS.

Give my love to both houses — hinc atque illinc.

23. TO GEORGE AND THOMAS KEATS

Hampstead, December 22, 1817.

MY DEAR BROTHERS — I must crave your pardon for not having written ere this. . . . I saw Kean return to the public in Richard III., and finely he did it, and, at the request of Reynolds, I went to criticise his *Duke* in Rich⁴· — the critique is in to-day's Champion, which I send you with the Examiner, in which you will find very proper lamentation on the obsoletion of Christmas Gambols and pastimes : but it was mixed up with so much egotism of that drivelling nature that pleasure is entirely lost. Hone the publisher's trial, you must find very amusing, and as Englishmen very encouraging: his *Not Guilty* is a thing, which not to have been, would have dulled still more Liberty's Emblazoning — Lord Ellenborough has been paid in his own coin — Wooler and Hone have done us an essential service. I have had two very pleasant evenings with Dilke yesterday and to-day, and am at this moment just come from him, and feel in the humour to go on with this, begun in the morning, and from which he came to fetch me. I spent Friday evening with Wells [20] and went next morning to see *Death on the Pale horse.* It is a wonderful picture, when West's age is considered; but there is nothing to be intense upon, no women one feels mad to kiss, no face swelling into reality. The excellence of every art is its intensity, capable of making all disagreeables evaporate from their being in close relationship with Beauty and Truth — Examine King Lear, and you will find this exemplified throughout; but in this picture we have unpleasantness without any momentous depth of speculation excited, in which to bury its repulsiveness — The picture is larger than Christ rejected.

I dined with Haydon the Sunday after you left, and had a very pleasant day. I dined too (for I have been out too much lately) with Horace Smith and met his two Brothers with Hill and Kingston and one Du Bois, they only served to convince me how superior humour is to wit, in respect to enjoyment — These men say things which make one start, without making one feel, they are all alike ; their manners are alike ; they all know fashionables ; they have all a mannerism in their very eating and drinking, in their mere handling a Decanter. They talked of Kean and his low company — would I were with that company instead of yours said I to myself! I know such like acquaintance will never do for me and yet I am going to Reynolds, on Wednesday. Brown and Dilke walked with me and back from the Christmas pantomime. I had not a dispute, but a dis-

quisition, with Dilke upon various subjects; several things dove-tailed in my mind, and at once it struck me what quality went to form a Man of Achievement, especially in Literature, and which Shakspeare possessed so enormously — I mean *Negative Capability*, that is, when a man is capable of being in uncertainties, mysteries, doubts, without any irritable reaching after fact and reason. Coleridge, for instance, would let go by a fine isolated verisimilitude caught from the Penetralium of mystery, from being incapable of remaining content with half-knowledge. This pursued through volumes would perhaps take us no further than this, that with a great poet the sense of Beauty overcomes every other consideration, or rather obliterates all consideration.

Shelley's poem [21] is out and there are words about its being objected to, as much as Queen Mab was. Poor Shelley I think he has his Quota of good qualities, in sooth la ! Write soon to your most sincere friend and affectionate Brother

JOHN.

24. TO THE SAME

Featherstone Buildings,
Monday [January 5, 1818].

MY DEAR BROTHERS — I ought to have written before, and you should have had a long letter last week, but I undertook the Champion for Reynolds, who is at Exeter. I wrote two articles, one on the Drury Lane Pantomime, the other on the Covent Garden new Tragedy,[23] which they have not put in; the one they have inserted is so badly punctuated that you perceive I am determined never to write more, without some care in that particular. Wells tells me that you are licking your chops, Tom, in expectation of my book coming out. I am sorry to say I have not begun my corrections yet : to-morrow I set out. I called on Sawrey this morning. He did not seem to be at all put out at anything I said and the inquiries I made with regard to your spitting of blood, and moreover desired me to ask you to send him a correct account of all your sensations and symptoms concerning the palpitation and the spitting and the cough — if you have any. Your last letter gave me a great pleasure, for I think the invalid is in a better spirit there along the Edge; and as for George, I must immediately, now I think of it, correct a little misconception of a part of my last letter. The Misses Reynolds have never said one word against me about you, or by any means endeavoured to lessen you in my estimation. That is not what I referred to; but the manner and thoughts which I knew they internally had towards you, time will show. Wells and Severn dined with me yesterday. We had a very pleasant day. I pitched upon another bottle of claret, we enjoyed ourselves very much; were all very witty and full of Rhymes. We played a concert [23] from 4 o'clock till 10 — drank your healths, the Hunts', and (N.B.) seven Peter Pindars. I said on that day the only good thing I was ever guilty of. We were talking about Stephens and the 1st Gallery. I said I wondered that careful folks would go there, for although it was but a shilling, still you had to pay through the Nose. I saw the Peachey family in a box at Drury one night. I have got such a curious . . . or rather I had such, now I am in my own hand.

I have had a great deal of pleasant time with Rice lately, and am getting initiated into a little band. They call drinking deep dyin' scarlet. They call good wine a pretty tipple, and call getting a child knocking out an apple; stopping at a tavern they call hanging out. Where do you sup? is where do you hang out?

Thursday I promised to dine with Wordsworth, and the weather is so bad that I am undecided, for he lives at Mortimer Street. I had an invitation to meet him at Kingston's, but not liking that place I sent my excuse. What I think of doing to-day is to dine in Mortimer Street (Words[th]), and

sup here in the Feath[s] buildings, as Mr. Wells has invited me. On Saturday, I called on Wordsworth before he went to Kingston's, and was surprised to find him with a stiff collar. I saw his spouse, and I think his daughter. I forget whether I had written my last before my Sunday evening at Haydon's — no, I did not, or I should have told you, Tom, of a young man you met at Paris, at Scott's, . . . Ritchie. I think he is going to Fezan, in Africa; then to proceed if possible like Mungo Park. He was very polite to me, and inquired very particularly after you. Then there was Wordsworth, Lamb, Monkhouse, Landseer, Kingston, and your humble servant. Lamb got tipsy and blew up Kingston — proceeding so far as to take the candle across the room, hold it to his face, and show us what a soft fellow he was.[24] I astonished Kingston at supper with a pertinacity in favour of drinking, keeping my two glasses at work in a knowing way.

I have seen Fanny twice lately — she inquired particularly after you and wants a co-partnership letter from you. She has been unwell, but is improving. I think she will be quick. Mrs. Abbey was saying that the Keatses were ever indolent, that they would ever be so, and that it is born in them. Well, whispered Fanny to me, if it is born with us, how can we help it? She seems very anxious for a letter. As I asked her what I should get for her, she said a 'Medal of the Princess.' [25] I called on Haslam — we dined very snugly together. He sent me a Hare last week, which I sent to Mrs. Dilke. Brown is not come back. I and Dilke are getting capital friends. He is going to take the Champion. He has sent his farce to Covent Garden. I met Bob Harris [26] on the steps at Covent Garden; we had a good deal of curious chat. He came out with his old humble opinion. The Covent Garden pantomime is a very nice one, but they have a middling Harlequin, a bad Pantaloon, a worse Clown, and a shocking Columbine, who is one of the

Miss Dennets. I suppose you will see my critique on the new tragedy in the next week's Champion. It is a shocking bad one. I have not seen Hunt; he was out when I called. Mrs. Hunt looks as well as ever I saw her after her confinement. There is an article in the se'nnight Examiner on Godwin's Mandeville, signed E. K. — I think it Miss Kent's [27] — I will send it. There are fine subscriptions going on for Hone.

You ask me what degrees there are between Scott's novels and those of Smollett. They appear to me to be quite distinct in every particular, more especially in their aims. Scott endeavours to throw so interesting and romantic a colouring into common and low characters as to give them a touch of the sublime. Smollett on the contrary pulls down and levels what with other men would continue romance. The grand parts of Scott are within the reach of more minds than the finest humours in Humphrey Clinker. I forget whether that fine thing of the Serjeant is Fielding or Smollett, but it gives me more pleasure than the whole novel of the Antiquary. You must remember what I mean. Some one says to the Serjeant: 'That's a non-sequitur!' — 'If you come to that,' replies the Serjeant, 'you're another!' —

I see by Wells's letter Mr. Abbey [28] does not overstock you with money. You must write. I have not seen . . . yet, but expect it on Wednesday. I am afraid it is gone. Severn tells me he has an order for some drawings for the Emperor of Russia.

You must get well Tom, and then I shall feel whole and genial as the winter air. Give me as many letters as you like, and write to Sawrey soon. I received a short letter from Bailey about Cripps, and one from Haydon, ditto. Haydon thinks he improved very much. Mrs. Wells desires particularly . . . to Tom and her respects to George, and I desire no better than to be ever your most affectionate Brother

JOHN.

P. S. — I had not opened the Champion before I found both my articles in it.

I was at a dance at Redhall's, and passed a pleasant time enough — drank deep, and won 10/6 at cutting for half guineas. . . . Bailey was there and seemed to enjoy the evening. Rice said he cared less about the hour than any one, and the proof is his dancing — he cares not for time, dancing as if he was deaf. Old Redhall not being used to give parties, had no idea of the quantity of wine that would be drank, and he actually put in readiness on the kitchen stairs eight dozen.

Every one inquires after you, and desires their remembrances to you.

Your Brother JOHN.

25. TO BENJAMIN ROBERT HAYDON

[Hampstead,] Saturday Morn
[January 10, 1818].

MY DEAR HAYDON — I should have seen you ere this, but on account of my sister being in Town: so that when I have sometimes made ten paces towards you, Fanny has called me into the City; and the Christmas Holydays are your only time to see Sisters, that is if they are so situated as mine. I will be with you early next week — to-night it should be, but we have a sort of a Club every Saturday evening — to-morrow, but I have on that day an insuperable engagement. Cripps has been down to me, and appears sensible that a binding to you would be of the greatest advantage to him — if such a thing be done it cannot be before £150 or £200 are secured in subscriptions to him. I will write to Bailey about it, give a Copy of the Subscribers' names to every one I know who is likely to get a £5 for him. I will leave a Copy at Taylor and Hessey's, Rodwell and Martin, and will ask Kingston and Co. to cash up.

Your friendship for me is now getting into its teens — and I feel the past. Also every day older I get — the greater is my idea of your achievements in Art: and I am convinced that there are three things to rejoice at in this Age — The Excursion, Your Pictures, and Hazlitt's depth of Taste.

Yours affectionately   JOHN KEATS.

26. TO JOHN TAYLOR

[Hampstead,] Saturday Morning [January 10, 1818].

MY DEAR TAYLOR — Several things have kept me from you lately: — first you had got into a little hell, which I was not anxious to reconnoitre — secondly, I have made a vow not to call again without my first book: so you may expect to see me in four days. Thirdly, I have been racketing too much, and do not feel over well. I have seen Wordsworth frequently — Dined with him last Monday — Reynolds, I suppose you have seen. Just scribble me thus many lines, to let me know you are in the land of the living, and well. Remember me to the Fleet Street Household — and should you see any from Percy Street, give my kindest regards to them.

Your sincere friend   JOHN KEATS.

27. TO GEORGE AND THOMAS KEATS

[Hampstead,] Tuesday [January 13, 1818].

MY DEAR BROTHERS — I am certain I think of having a letter to-morrow morning for I expected one so much this morning, having been in town two days, at the end of which my expectations began to get up a little. I found two on the table, one from Bailey and one from Haydon, I am quite perplexed in a world of doubts and fancies — there is nothing stable in the world; uproar 's your only music — I don't mean to include Bailey in this and so dismiss him from this with all the opprobrium he deserves — that is in so many words, he is one of the noblest men alive at the present day. In a note to Haydon about a week ago (which I wrote with a full sense of what he had done, and how he had never manifested any little mean drawback in his

value of me) I said if there were three things superior in the modern world, they were 'the Excursion,' 'Haydon's pictures,' and 'Hazlitt's depth of Taste' — so I do believe — Not thus speaking with any poor vanity that works of genius were the first things in this world. No! for that sort of probity and disinterestedness which such men as Bailey possess, does hold and grasp the tiptop of any spiritual honours that can be paid to anything in this world — And moreover having this feeling at this present come over me in its full force, I sat down to write to you with a grateful heart, in that I had not a Brother who did not feel and credit me for a deeper feeling and devotion for his uprightness, than for any marks of genius however splendid. I was speaking about doubts and fancies — I mean there has been a quarrel of a severe nature between Haydon and Reynolds and another ('the Devil rides upon a fiddlestick') between Hunt and Haydon — the first grew from the Sunday on which Haydon invited some friends to meet Wordsworth. Reynolds never went, and never sent any Notice about it, this offended Haydon more than it ought to have done — he wrote a very sharp and high note to Reynolds and then another in palliation — but which Reynolds feels as an aggravation of the first — Considering all things, Haydon's frequent neglect of his Appointments, etc. his notes were bad enough to put Reynolds on the right side of the question — but then Reynolds has no power of sufferance; no idea of having the thing against him; so he answered Haydon in one of the most cutting letters I ever read; exposing to himself all his own weaknesses and going on to an excess, which whether it is just or no, is what I would fain have unsaid, the fact is, they are both in the right and both in the wrong.

The quarrel with Hunt I understand thus far. Mrs. H. was in the habit of borrowing silver of Haydon — the last time she did so, Haydon asked her to return it at a certain time — she did not — Haydon sent for it — Hunt went to expostulate on the indelicacy, etc. — they got to words and parted for ever. All I hope is at some time to bring them together again. — Lawk! Molly there's been such doings — Yesterday evening I made an appointment with Wells to go to a private theatre, and it being in the neighbourhood of Drury Lane, and thinking we might be fatigued with sitting the whole evening in one dirty hole, I got the Drury Lane ticket, and therewith we divided the evening with a spice of Richard III ——

[Later, January 19 or 20.]

Good Lord! I began this letter nearly a week ago, what have I been doing since — I have been — I mean not been — sending last Sunday's paper to you. I believe because it was not near me — for I cannot find it, and my conscience presses heavy on me for not sending it. You would have had one last Thursday, but I was called away, and have been about somewhere ever since. Where? What! Well I rejoice almost that I have not heard from you because no news is good news. I cannot for the world recollect why I was called away, all I know is that there has been a dance at Dilke's, and another at the London Coffee House; to both of which I went. But I must tell you in another letter the circumstances thereof — for though a week should have passed since I wrote on the other side it quite appals me. I can only write in scraps and patches. Brown is returned from Hampstead. Haydon has returned an answer in the same style — they are all dreadfully irritated against each other. On Sunday I saw Hunt and dined with Haydon, met Hazlitt and Bewick there, and took Haslam with me — forgot to speak about Cripps though I broke my engagement to Haslam's on purpose. Mem. — Haslam came to meet me, found me at Breakfast, had the goodness to go with me my way — I have just finished the revision of my first book, and shall take it to Taylor's to-morrow — intend to persevere — Do not let me see many days pass without hearing from you.

Your most affectionate Brother JOHN.

28. TO JOHN TAYLOR

[Hampstead,] Friday 23d [January 1818].

MY DEAR TAYLOR — I have spoken to Haydon about the drawing. He would do it with all his Art and Heart too, if so I will it; however, he has written thus to me; but I must tell you, first, he intends painting a finished Picture from the Poem. Thus he writes — ' When I do anything for your Poem it must be effectual — an honour to both of us: to hurry up a sketch for the season won't do. I think an engraving from your head, from a Chalk drawing of mine, done with all my might, to which I would put my name, would answer Taylor's idea better than the other. Indeed, I am sure of it. This I will do, and this will be effectual, and as I have not done it for any other human being, it will have an effect.'

What think you of this? Let me hear. I shall have my second Book in readiness forthwith.

Yours most sincerely JOHN KEATS.

If Reynolds calls tell him three lines will be acceptable, for I am squat at Hampstead.

29. TO GEORGE AND THOMAS KEATS

[Hampstead,] Friday 23d January [1818].

MY DEAR BROTHERS — I was thinking what hindered me from writing so long, for I have so many things to say to you, and know not where to begin. It shall be upon a thing most interesting to you, my Poem. Well! I have given the first Book to Taylor; he seemed more than satisfied with it, and to my surprise proposed publishing it in Quarto if Haydon would make a drawing of some event therein, for a Frontispiece.

I called on Haydon, he said he would do anything I liked, but said he would rather paint a finished picture, from it, which he seems eager to do; this in a year or two will be a glorious thing for us; and it will be, for Haydon is struck with the 1st Book. I left Haydon and the next day received a letter from him, proposing to make, as he says, with all his might, a finished chalk sketch of my head, to be engraved in the first style and put at the head of my Poem, saying at the same time he had never done the thing for any human being, and that it must have considerable effect as he will put his name to it — I begin to-day to copy my 2nd Book — 'thus far into the bowels of the land' — You shall hear whether it will be Quarto or non Quarto, picture or non picture. Leigh Hunt I showed my 1st Book to —— he allows it not much merit as a whole; says it is unnatural and made ten objections to it in the mere skimming over. He says the conversation is unnatural and too high-flown for Brother and Sister — says it should be simple forgetting do ye mind that they are both overshadowed by a supernatural Power, and of force could not speak like Francesca in the Rimini. He must first prove that Caliban's poetry is unnatural — This with me completely overturns his objections — the fact is he and Shelley are hurt, and perhaps justly, at my not having showed them the affair officiously and from several hints I have had they appear much disposed to dissect and anatomise any trip or slip I may have made. — But who's afraid? Ay! Tom! Demme if I am. I went last Tuesday, an hour too late, to Hazlitt's Lecture on poetry, got there just as they were coming out, when all these pounced upon me. Hazlitt, John Hunt and Son, Wells, Bewick, all the Landseers, Bob Harris, aye and more — the Landseers enquired after you particularly — I know not whether Wordsworth has left town — But Sunday I dined with Hazlitt and Haydon, also that I took Has-

lam with me — I dined with Brown lately. Dilke having taken the Champion Theatricals was obliged to be in town — Fanny has returned to Walthamstow. — Mr. Abbey appeared very glum, the last time I went to see her, and said in an indirect way, that I had no business there — Rice has been ill, but has been mending much lately —

I think a little change has taken place in my intellect lately — I cannot bear to be uninterested or unemployed, I, who for so long a time have been addicted to passiveness. Nothing is finer for the purposes of great productions than a very gradual ripening of the intellectual powers. As an instance of this — observe — I sat down yesterday to read King Lear once again: the thing appeared to demand the prologue of a sonnet, I wrote it, and began to read — (I know you would like to see it.)

[Here follows the Sonnet, for which see p. 40.]

So you see I am getting at it, with a sort of determination and strength, though verily I do not feel it at this moment — this is my fourth letter this morning, and I feel rather tired, and my head rather swimming — so I will leave it open till to-morrow's post. —

I am in the habit of taking my papers to Dilke's and copying there; so I chat and proceed at the same time. I have been there at my work this evening, and the walk over the Heath takes off all sleep, so I will even proceed with you. I left off short in my last just as I began an account of a private theatrical — Well it was of the lowest order, all greasy and oily, insomuch that if they had lived in olden times, when signs were hung over the doors, the only appropriate one for that oily place would have been — a guttered Candle. They played John Bull, The Review, and it was to conclude with Bombastes Furioso — I saw from a Box the first Act of John Bull, then went to Drury and did not return till

it was over — when by Wells's interest we
got behind the scenes — there was not a
yard wide all the way round for actors,
scene-shifters, and interlopers to move in
— for 'Nota Bene' the Green Room was
under the stage, and there was I threatened
over and over again to be turned out by
the oily scene-shifters, there did I hear a
little painted Trollop own, very candidly,
that she had failed in Mary, with a 'damn'd
if she'd play a serious part again, as long
as she lived,' and at the same time she was
habited as the Quaker in the Review. —
There was a quarrel, and a fat good-
natured looking girl in soldiers' clothes
wished she had only been a man for Tom's
sake. One fellow began a song, but an unlucky finger-point from the Gallery sent him
off like a shot. One chap was dressed to
kill for the King in Bombastes, and he
stood at the edge of the scene in the very
sweat of anxiety to show himself, but Alas
the thing was not played. The sweetest
morsel of the night moreover was, that the
musicians began pegging and fagging away
— at an overture — never did you see faces
more in earnest, three times did they play
it over, dropping all kinds of corrections
and still did not the curtain go up. Well
then they went into a country dance, then
into a region they well knew, into the old
boonsome Pothouse, and then to see how
pompous o' the sudden they turned; how
they looked about and chatted; how they
did not care a damn; was a great treat——

I hope I have not tired you by this filling
up of the dash in my last. Constable the
bookseller has offered Reynolds ten guineas
a sheet to write for his Magazine — it is an
Edinburgh one, which Blackwood's started
up in opposition to. Hunt said he was
nearly sure that the 'Cockney School' was
written by Scott [29] so you are right Tom !
— There are no more little bits of news I
can remember at present.

I remain, My dear Brothers, Your very
affectionate Brother   JOHN.

[Hampstead,] Friday Jany 23 [1818].

MY DEAR BAILEY — Twelve days have
pass'd since your last reached me. — What
has gone through the myriads of human
minds since the 12th ? We talk of the immense Number of Books, the Volumes
ranged thousands by thousands — but perhaps more goes through the human intelligence in Twelve days than ever was written.
— *How has that unfortunate family lived
through the twelve ?* One saying of yours I
shall never forget — you may not recollect
it — it being perhaps said when you were
looking on the Surface and seeming of
Humanity alone, without a thought of the
past or the future — or the deeps of good
and evil — you were at that moment
estranged from speculation, and I think
you have arguments ready for the Man
who would utter it to you — this is a formidable preface for a simple thing — merely
you said, ' *Why should woman suffer ?* ' Aye,
why should she ? ' By heavens I'd coin
my very Soul, and drop my Blood for
Drachmas !' These things are, and he,
who feels how incompetent the most skyey
Knight-errantry is to heal this bruised fairness, is like a sensitive leaf on the hot hand
of thought. — Your tearing, my dear
friend, a spiritless and gloomy letter up,
to re-write to me, is what I shall never
forget — it was to me a real thing — Things
have happened lately of great perplexity
— you must have heard of them — Reynolds and Haydon retorting and recrimi-
nating — and parting for ever — the same
thing has happened between Haydon and
Hunt. It is unfortunate — Men should
bear with each other: there lives not the
Man who may not be cut up, aye Lashed to
pieces on his weakest side. The best of
Men have but a portion of good in them —
a kind of spiritual yeast in their frames,
which creates the ferment of existence —
by which a Man is propelled to act, and
strive, and buffet with Circumstance. The

sure way, Bailey, is first to know a Man's faults, and then be passive — if after that he insensibly draws you towards him then you have no power to break the link. Before I felt interested in either Reynolds or Haydon, I was well read in their faults; yet, knowing them, I have been cementing gradually with both. I have an affection for them both, for reasons almost opposite — and to both must I of necessity cling, supported always by the hope that, when a little time, a few years, shall have tried me more fully in their esteem, I may be able to bring them together. The time must come, because they have both hearts: and they will recollect the best parts of each other, when this gust is overblown. — I had a message from you through a letter to Jane — I think, about Cripps — there can be no idea of binding until a sufficient sum is sure for him — and even then the thing should be maturely considered by all his helpers — I shall try my luck upon as many fat purses as I can meet with. — Cripps is improving very fast: I have the greater hopes of him because he is so slow in development. A Man of great executing powers at 20, with a look and a speech almost stupid, is sure to do something.

I have just looked through the Second Side of your Letter — I feel a great content at it. — I was at Hunt's the other day, and he surprised me with a real authenticated lock of *Milton's Hair.* I know you would like what I wrote thereon, so here it is — *as they say of a Sheep in a Nursery Book :* —

[Here follow the lines, printed above, p. 39.]

This I did at Hunt's at his request — perhaps I should have done something better alone and at home. — I have sent my first Book to the press, and this afternoon shall begin preparing the Second — my visit to you will be a great spur to quicken the proceeding. — I have not had your Sermon returned — I long to make it the Subject of a Letter to you — What do they say at Oxford?

I trust you and Gleig pass much fine time together. Remember me to him and Whitehead. My Brother Tom is getting stronger, but his spitting of Blood continues. I sat down to read King Lear yesterday, and felt the greatness of the thing up to the Writing of a Sonnet preparatory thereto — in my next you shall have it. — There were some miserable reports of Rice's health — I went, and lo ! Master Jemmy had been to the play the night before, and was out at the time — he always comes on his legs like a Cat. I have seen a good deal of Wordsworth. Hazlitt is lecturing on Poetry at the Surrey Institution — I shall be there next Tuesday.

Your most affectionate friend
JOHN KEATS.

31. TO JOHN TAYLOR

[Hampstead, January 30, 1818.]
MY DEAR TAYLOR — These lines as they now stand about ' happiness,' having rung in my ears like 'a chime a mending' — See here,

'Behold
Wherein lies happiness, Peona ? fold, etc.'

It appears to me the very contrary of blessed. I hope this will appear to you more eligible.

'Wherein lies Happiness? In that which becks
Our ready minds to fellowship divine,
A fellowship with Essence till we shine
Full alchemised, and free of space — Behold
The clear religion of Heaven — fold, etc.'

You must indulge me by putting this in, for setting aside the badness of the other, such a preface is necessary to the subject. The whole thing must, I think, have appeared to you, who are a consecutive man, as a thing almost of mere words, but I assure you that, when I wrote it, it was a regular stepping of the Imagination towards a truth. My having written that argument will perhaps be of the greatest service to me of anything I ever did. It set before me the gradations of happiness, even

like a kind of pleasure thermometer, and is
my first step towards the chief attempt in
the drama. The playing of different natures
with joy and Sorrow —
Do me this favour, and believe me
Your sincere friend   J. KEATS.
I hope your next work will be of a more
general Interest. I suppose you cogitate a
little about it, now and then.

32. TO JOHN HAMILTON REYNOLDS

Hampstead, Saturday [January 31, 1818].

MY DEAR REYNOLDS — I have parcelled
out this day for Letter Writing — more
resolved thereon because your Letter will
come as a refreshment and will have (sic
parvis etc.) the same effect as a Kiss in
certain situations where people become
over-generous. I have read this first sentence over, and think it savours rather;
however an inward innocence is like a
rested dove, as the old song says. . . .[30]
Now I purposed to write to you a serious
poetical letter, but I find that a maxim I
met with the other day is a just one : 'On
cause mieux quand on ne dit pas causons.'
I was hindered, however, from my first intention by a mere muslin Handkerchief
very neatly pinned — but 'Hence, vain de-
luding,' etc. Yet I cannot write in prose;
it is a sunshiny day and I cannot, so here
goes, —

['Hence Burgundy, Claret, and Port,' printed
above in the Appendix, p. 242.]

My dear Reynolds, you must forgive all
this ranting — but the fact is, I cannot
write sense this Morning — however you
shall have some — I will copy out my last
Sonnet.

['When I have fears that I may cease to be,'
given above, p. 39.]

I must take a turn, and then write to
Teignmouth. Remember me to all, not
excepting yourself.
Your sincere friend   JOHN KEATS.

33. TO THE SAME

Hampstead, Tuesday [February 3, 1818].

MY DEAR REYNOLDS — I thank you for
your dish of Filberts — would I could get
a basket of them by way of dessert every
day for the sum of twopence.[31] Would we
were a sort of ethereal Pigs, and turned
loose to feed upon spiritual Mast and
Acorns — which would be merely being a
squirrel and feeding upon filberts, for what
is a squirrel but an airy pig, or a filbert but
a sort of archangelical acorn? About the
nuts being worth cracking, all I can say is,
that where there are a throng of delightful
Images ready drawn, simplicity is the only
thing. The first is the best on account of
the first line, and the 'arrow, foil'd of its
antler'd food,' and moreover (and this is
the only word or two I find fault with, the
more because I have had so much reason
to shun it as a quicksand) the last has
'tender and true.' We must cut this, and
not be rattlesnaked into any more of the
like. It may be said that we ought to read
our contemporaries, that Wordsworth, etc.
should have their due from us. But, for
the sake of a few fine imaginative or domestic passages, are we to be bullied into
a certain Philosophy engendered in the
whims of an Egotist? Every man has his
speculations, but every man does not brood
and peacock over them till he makes a false
coinage and deceives himself. Many a man
can travel to the very bourne of Heaven,
and yet want confidence to put down his
half-seeing. Sancho will invent a Journey
heavenward as well as anybody. We hate
poetry that has a palpable design upon us,
and, if we do not agree, seems to put its
hand into its breeches pocket. Poetry
should be great and unobtrusive, a thing
which enters into one's soul, and does not
startle it or amaze it with itself — but with
its subject. How beautiful are the retired
flowers ! — how would they lose their
beauty were they to throng into the high-
way, crying out, 'Admire me, I am a

violet ! Dote upon me, I am a primrose !'
Modern poets differ from the Elizabethans
in this: each of the moderns like an Elector
of Hanover governs his petty state and
knows how many straws are swept daily
from the Causeways in all his dominions,
and has a continual itching that all the
Housewives should have their coppers well
scoured: The ancients were Emperors of
vast Provinces, they had only heard of the
remote ones and scarcely cared to visit
them. I will cut all this — I will have no
more of Wordsworth or Hunt in particular — Why should we be of the tribe of
Manasseh, when we can wander with Esau ?
Why should we kick against the Pricks,
when we can walk on Roses ? Why should
we be owls, when we can be eagles ? Why
be teased with ' nice-eyed wagtails,' when
we have in sight ' the Cherub Contemplation ' ? Why with Wordsworth's ' Matthew
with a bough of wilding in his hand,' when
we can have Jacques ' under an oak,' etc. ?
The secret of the Bough of Wilding will
run through your head faster than I can
write it. Old Matthew spoke to him some
years ago on some nothing, and because he
happens in an Evening Walk to imagine
the figure of the old Man, he must stamp
it down in black and white, and it is henceforth sacred. I don't mean to deny Wordsworth's grandeur and Hunt's merit, but I
mean to say we need not be teased with
grandeur and merit when we can have
them uncontaminated and unobtrusive. Let
us have the old Poets and Robin Hood.
Your letter and its sonnets gave me more
pleasure than will the Fourth Book of
Childe Harold and the whole of anybody's
life and opinions. In return for your Dish
of Filberts, I have gathered a few Catkins,
I hope they 'll look pretty.

[To J. H. R. in answer to his Robin Hood
Sonnets. See p. 41.]

I hope you will like them — they are
at least written in the Spirit of Outlawry.
Here are the Mermaid lines,

[See p. 40.]

I will call on you at 4 tomorrow, and we
will trudge together, for it is not the thing
to be a stranger in the Land of Harpsicols.
I hope also to bring you my 2nd Book. In
the hope that these Scribblings will be some
amusement for you this Evening, I remain,
copying on the Hill,
Your sincere friend and Co-scribbler
JOHN KEATS.

34. TO JOHN TAYLOR

Fleet Street, Thursday Morn
[February 5, 1818].
MY DEAR TAYLOR — I have finished
copying my Second Book — but I want it
for one day to overlook it. And moreover
this day I have very particular employ in
the affair of Cripps — so I trespass on your
indulgence, and take advantage of your
good nature. You shall hear from me or
see me soon. I will tell Reynolds of your
engagement to-morrow.
Yours unfeignedly JOHN KEATS.

35. TO GEORGE AND THOMAS KEATS

Hampstead, Saturday Night
[February 14, 1818].
MY DEAR BROTHERS — When once a
man delays a letter beyond the proper time,
he delays it longer, for one or two reasons
— first, because he must begin in a very
common-place style, that is to say, with an
excuse; and secondly things and circumstances become so jumbled in his mind,
that he knows not what, or what not, he has
said in his last — I shall visit you as soon
as I have copied my poem all out, I am
now much beforehand with the printer,
they have done none yet, and I am half
afraid they will let half the season by before the printing. I am determined they
shall not trouble me when I have copied it
all. — Horace Smith has lent me his manuscript called ' Nehemiah Muggs, an ex-
posure of the Methodists ' — perhaps I may
send you a few extracts — Hazlitt's last

Lecture was on Thomson, Cowper, and Crabbe, he praised Thomson and Cowper but he gave Crabbe an unmerciful licking —I think Hunt's article of Fazio — no it was not, but I saw Fazio the first night, it hung rather heavily on me — I am in the high way of being introduced to a squad of people, Peter Pindar, Mrs. Opie, Mrs. Scott — Mr. Robinson a great friend of Coleridge's called on me.[32] Richards tells me that my poems are known in the west country, and that he saw a very clever copy of verses, headed with a Motto from my Sonnet to George — Honours rush so thickly upon me that I shall not be able to bear up against them. What think you — am I to be crowned in the Capitol, am I to be made a Mandarin — No! I am to be invited, Mrs. Hunt tells me, to a party at Ollier's, to keep Shakspeare's birthday — Shakspeare would stare to see me there. The Wednesday before last Shelley, Hunt and I wrote each a Sonnet on the River Nile, some day you shall read them all. I saw a sheet of Endymion, and have all reason to suppose they will soon get it done, there shall be nothing wanting on my part. I have been writing at intervals many songs and Sonnets, and I long to be at Teignmouth, to read them over to you: however I think I had better wait till this Book is of my mind; it will not be long first.

Reynolds has been writing two very capital articles, in the Yellow Dwarf, on popular Preachers — All the talk here is about Dr. Croft the Duke of Devon etc.

Your most affectionate Brother JOHN.

[Hampstead, February 19, 1818.]

MY DEAR REYNOLDS — I had an idea that a Man might pass a very pleasant life in this manner — Let him on a certain day read a certain page of full Poesy or distilled Prose, and let him wander with it, and muse upon it, and reflect from it, and bring home to it, and prophesy upon it,

and dream upon it: until it becomes stale — But when will it do so ? Never — When Man has arrived at a certain ripeness in intellect any one grand and spiritual passage serves him as a starting-post towards all 'the two-and-thirty Palaces.' How happy is such a voyage of conception, what delicious diligent indolence ! A doze upon a sofa does not hinder it, and a nap upon Clover engenders ethereal finger-pointings — the prattle of a child gives it wings, and the converse of middle-age a strength to beat them — a strain of music conducts to 'an odd angle of the Isle,' and when the leaves whisper it puts a girdle round the earth. — Nor will this sparing touch of noble Books be any irreverence to their Writers — for perhaps the honors paid by Man to Man are trifles in comparison to the benefit done by great works to the 'spirit and pulse of good' by their mere passive existence. Memory should not be called Knowledge — Many have original minds who do not think it — they are led away by Custom. Now it appears to me that almost any Man may like the spider spin from his own inwards his own airy Citadel — the points of leaves and twigs on which the spider begins her work are few, and she fills the air with a beautiful circuiting. Man should be content with as few points to tip with the fine Web of his Soul, and weave a tapestry empyrean — full of symbols for his spiritual eye, of softness for his spiritual touch, of space for his wandering, of distinctness for his luxury. But the minds of mortals are so different and bent on such diverse journeys that it may at first appear impossible for any common taste and fellowship to exist between two or three under these suppositions. It is however quite the contrary. Minds would leave each other in contrary directions, traverse each other in numberless points, and at last greet each other at the journey's end. An old man and a child would talk together and the old man be led on his path and the child left thinking. Man should not dispute or assert, but whisper results to his Neighbour, and thus by every germ of spirit sucking the sap from mould ethereal every human might become great, and humanity instead of being a wide heath of furze and briars, with here and there a remote Oak or Pine, would become a grand democracy of forest trees. It has been an old comparison for our urging on — the beehive — however it seems to me that we should rather be the flower than the Bee — for it is a false notion that more is gained by receiving than giving — no, the receiver and the giver are equal in their benefits. The flower, I doubt not, receives a fair guerdon from the Bee — its leaves blush deeper in the next spring — and who shall say between Man and Woman which is the most delighted? Now it is more noble to sit like Jove than to fly like Mercury: — let us not therefore go hurrying about and collecting honey, bee-like, buzzing here and there impatiently from a knowledge of what is to be arrived at. But let us open our leaves like a flower, and be passive and receptive; budding patiently under the eye of Apollo and taking hints from every noble insect that favours us with a visit — Sap will be given us for meat, and dew for drink. I was led into these thoughts, my dear Reynolds, by the beauty of the morning operating on a sense of Idleness. I have not read any Books — the Morning said I was right — I had no idea but of the Morning, and the Thrush said I was right — seeming to say,

[Here follows the sonnet 'What the Thrush said,' p. 43.]

Now I am sensible all this is a mere sophistication (however it may neighbour to any truths), to excuse my own indolence — So I will not deceive myself that Man should be equal with Jove — but think himself very well off as a sort of scullion-Mercury or even a humble-bee. It is no matter whether I am right or wrong either one way or another, if there is sufficient to lift a little time from your shoulders — Your affectionate friend JOHN KEATS.

37. TO GEORGE AND THOMAS KEATS

Hampstead, Saturday [February 21, 1818.]

MY DEAR BROTHERS — I am extremely sorry to have given you so much uneasiness by not writing; however, you know good news is no news or vice versâ. I do not like to write a short letter to you, or you would have had one long before. The weather although boisterous to-day has been very much milder; and I think Devonshire is not the last place to receive a temperate Change. I have been abominably idle since you left, but have just turned over a new leaf, and used as a marker a letter of excuse to an invitation from Horace Smith. The occasion of my writing to-day is the enclosed letter — by Postmark from Miss W[ylie]. Does she expect you in town George? I received a letter the other day from Haydon, in which he says, his Essays on the Elgin Marbles are being translated into Italian, the which he superintends. I did not mention that I had seen the British Gallery, there are some nice things by Stark, and Bathsheba by Wilkie, which is condemned. I could not bear Alston's Uriel.

Reynolds has been very ill for some time, confined to the house, and had leeches applied to his chest; when I saw him on Wednesday he was much the same, and he is in the worst place for amendment, among the strife of women's tongues, in a hot and parch'd room: I wish he would move to Butler's for a short time. The Thrushes and Blackbirds have been singing me into an idea that it was Spring, and almost that leaves were on the trees. So that black clouds and boisterous winds seem to have mustered and collected in full Divan, for the purpose of convincing me to the contrary. Taylor says my poem shall be out in a month, I think he will be out before it. . . .

The thrushes are singing now as if they would speak to the winds, because their big brother Jack, the Spring, was not far off. I am reading Voltaire and Gibbon, although I wrote to Reynolds the other day to prove reading of no use; I have not seen Hunt since, I am a good deal with Dilke and Brown, we are very thick; they are very kind to me, they are well. I don't think I could stop in Hampstead but for their neighbourhood. I hear Hazlitt's lectures regularly, his last was on Gray, Collins, Young, etc., and he gave a very fine piece of discriminating Criticism on Swift, Voltaire, and Rabelais. I was very disappointed at his treatment of Chatterton. I generally meet with many I know there. Lord Byron's 4th Canto is expected out, and I heard somewhere, that Walter Scott has a new Poem in readiness. I am sorry that Wordsworth has left a bad impression wherever he visited in town by his egotism, Vanity, and bigotry. Yet he is a great poet if not a philosopher. I have not yet read Shelley's Poem, I do not suppose you have it yet, at the Teignmouth libraries. These double letters must come rather heavy, I hope you have a moderate portion of cash, but don't fret at all, if you have not — Lord ! I intend to play at cut and run as well as Falstaff, that is to say, before he got so lusty.

I remain praying for your health my dear Brothers

Your affectionate Brother   JOHN.

38. TO JOHN TAYLOR

Hampstead, February 27 [1818].

MY DEAR TAYLOR — Your alteration strikes me as being a great Improvement — And now I will attend to the punctuations you speak of — The comma should be at *soberly*, and in the other passage, the Comma should follow *quiet*. I am extremely indebted to you for this alteration, and also for your after admonitions. It is a sorry thing for me that any one should have to overcome prejudices in reading my verses — that affects me more than any hypercriticism on any particular passage — In Endymion, I have most likely but moved into the go-cart from the leading-strings — In poetry I have a few axioms, and you will see how far I am from their centre.

1st. I think poetry should surprise by a fine excess, and not by singularity; It should strike the reader as a wording of his own highest thoughts, and appear almost a remembrance.

2d. Its touches of beauty should never be half-way, thereby making the reader breathless, instead of content. The rise, the progress, the setting of Imagery should, like the sun, come natural to him, shine over him, and set soberly, although in magnificence, leaving him in the luxury of twilight. But it is easier to think what poetry should be, than to write it — And this leads me to

Another axiom — That if poetry comes not as naturally as the leaves to a tree, it had better not come at all. — However it may be with me, I cannot help looking into new countries with 'O for a Muse of Fire to ascend !' If Endymion serves me as a pioneer, perhaps I ought to be content — I have great reason to be content, for thank God I can read, and perhaps understand Shakspeare to his depths; and I have I am sure many friends, who, if I fail, will attribute any change in my life and temper to humbleness rather than pride — to a cowering under the wings of great poets, rather than to a bitterness that I am not appreciated. I am anxious to get Endymion printed that I may forget it and proceed. I have copied the 3rd Book and begun the 4th. On running my eye over the proofs, I saw one mistake — I will notice it presently, and also any others, if there be any. There should be no comma in 'the raft branch down sweeping from a tall ash-top.' I have besides made one or two alterations, and also altered the thirteenth line p. 32 to make sense of it, as you will see. I will take care the printer shall not trip up my heels. There should be no dash after Dryope, in the line ' Dryope's lone lulling of her child.'

Remember me to Percy Street.

Your sincere and obliged friend

JOHN KEATS.

P. S. — You shall have a short preface in good time.

39. TO MESSRS. TAYLOR AND HESSEY

Hampstead, March [1818?]

MY DEAR SIRS — I am this morning making a general clearance of all lent Books — all — I am afraid I do not return all — I must fog your memories about them — however with many thanks here are the remainder — which I am afraid are not worth so much now as they were six months ago — I mean the fashions may have changed —

Yours truly   JOHN KEATS.

40. TO BENJAMIN BAILEY

Teignmouth, Friday [March 13, 1818].

MY DEAR BAILEY — When a poor devil is drowning, it is said he comes thrice to the surface ere he makes his final sink — if however even at the third rise he can manage to catch hold of a piece of weed or rock he stands a fair chance, as I hope I do now, of being saved. I have sunk twice in our correspondence, have risen twice, and have been too idle, or something worse, to extricate myself. I have sunk the third time, and just now risen again at this two of the Clock P. M., and saved myself from utter perdition by beginning this, all drenched as I am, and fresh from the water. And I would rather endure the present inconvenience of a wet jacket than you should keep a laced one in store for me. Why did I not stop at Oxford in my way? How can you ask such a Question? Why, did

I not promise to do so? Did I not in a letter to you make a promise to do so? Then how can you be so unreasonable as to ask me why I did not? This is the thing — (for I have been rubbing up my Invention — trying several sleights — I first polished a cold, felt it in my fingers, tried it on the table, but could not pocket it: — I tried Chillblains, Rheumatism, Gout, tight boots, — nothing of that sort would do, — so this is, as I was going to say, the thing) — I had a letter from Tom, saying how much better he had got, and thinking he had better stop — I went down to prevent his coming up. Will not this do? turn it which way you like — it is selvaged all round. I have used it, these three last days, to keep out the abominable Devonshire weather — by the by, you may say what you will of Devonshire: the truth is, it is a splashy, rainy, misty, snowy, foggy, haily, floody, muddy, slipshod county. The hills are very beautiful, when you get a sight of 'em — the primroses are out, but then you are in — the Cliffs are of a fine deep colour, but then the Clouds are continually vieing with them — the Women like your London people in a sort of negative way — because the native men are the poorest creatures in England —because Government never have thought it worth while to send a recruiting party among them. When I think of Wordsworth's sonnet 'Vanguard of Liberty ! ye men of Kent !' the degenerated race about me are Pulvis ipecac. simplex — a strong dose. Were I a corsair, I 'd make a descent on the south coast of Devon; if I did not run the chance of having Cowardice imputed to me. As for the men, they 'd run away into the Methodist meeting-houses, and the women would be glad of it. Had England been a large Devonshire, we should not have won the Battle of Waterloo. There are knotted oaks — there are lusty rivulets ? there are meadows such as are not — there are valleys of feminine [?] climate — but there are no thews and

sinews — Moor's Almanack is here a Curiosity — Arms, neck, and shoulders may at
least be seen there, and the ladies read it
as some out-of-the-way Romance. Such a
quelling Power have these thoughts over
me that I fancy the very air of a deterio-
rating quality. I fancy the flowers, all
precocious, have an Acrasian spell about
them — I feel able to beat off the Devonshire waves like soapfroth. I think it well
for the honour of Britain that Julius Cæsar
did not first land in this County. A Devon-
shirer standing on his native hills is not a
distinct object — he does not show against
the light — a wolf or two would dispossess
him. I like, I love England. I like its
living men — give me a long brown plain
' for my morning,' [money ?] so I may meet
with some of Edmund Ironside's descendants. Give me a barren mould, so I may
meet with some shadowing of Alfred in the
shape of a Gipsy, a huntsman or a shepherd. Scenery is fine — but human nature
is finer — the sward is richer for the tread
of a real nervous English foot — the Eagle's
nest is finer, for the Mountaineer has looked
into it. Are these facts or prejudices ?
Whatever they be, for them I shall never
be able to relish entirely any Devonshire
scenery — Homer is fine, Achilles is fine,
Diomed is fine, Shakspeare is fine, Hamlet
is fine, Lear is fine, but dwindled Englishmen are not fine. Where too the women
are so passable, and have such English
names, such as Ophelia, Cordelia etc. that
they should have such Paramours or rather
Imparamours — As for them, I cannot in
thought help wishing, as did the cruel
Emperor, that they had but one head, and
I might cut it off to deliver them from any
horrible Courtesy they may do their un-
deserving countrymen. I wonder I meet
with no born monsters — O Devonshire, last
night I thought the moon had dwindled in
heaven ——

I have never had your Sermon from
Wordsworth, but Mr. Dilke lent it me.
You know my ideas about Religion. I do
not think myself more in the right than
other people, and that nothing in this world
is proveable. I wish I could enter into all
your feelings on the subject, merely for one
short 10 minutes, and give you a page or
two to your liking. I am sometimes so
very sceptical as to think Poetry itself a
mere Jack o' Lantern to amuse whoever
may chance to be struck with its brilliance.
As tradesmen say everything is worth what
it will fetch, so probably every mental pursuit takes its reality and worth from the
ardour of the pursuer — being in itself a
Nothing. Ethereal things may at least be
thus real, divided under three heads —
Things real — things semireal — and nothings. Things real, such as existences of
Sun moon and Stars — and passages of
Shakspeare. — Things semireal, such as
love, the clouds etc., which require a greeting of the Spirit to make them wholly exist
— and Nothings, which are made great and
dignified by an ardent pursuit — which, by
the by, stamp the Burgundy mark on the
bottles of our minds, insomuch as they are
able to ' consecrate whate'er they look upon.'
I have written a sonnet here of a somewhat
collateral nature — so don't imagine it an
' apropos des bottes ' —

[The sonnet is that entitled ' The Human
Seasons,' given on p. 44.]

Aye, this may be carried — but what am
I talking of ? — it is an old maxim of mine,
and of course must be well known, that
every point of thought is the Centre of an
intellectual world. The two uppermost
thoughts in a Man's mind are the two poles
of his world — he revolves on them, and
everything is Southward or Northward to
him through their means. — We take but
three steps from feathers to iron. — Now,
my dear fellow, I must once for all tell
you I have not one idea of the truth of any
of my speculations — I shall never be a
reasoner, because I care not to be in the
right, when retired from bickering and in
a proper philosophical temper. So you

must not stare if in any future letter, I endeavour to prove that Apollo, as he had catgut strings to his lyre, used a cat's paw as a pecten — and further from said Pecten's reiterated and continual teasing came the term *hen-pecked*. My Brother Tom desires to be remembered to you; he has just this moment had a spitting of blood, poor fellow — Remember me to Gleig and Whitehead. Your affectionate friend JOHN KEATS.

41. TO JOHN HAMILTON REYNOLDS

Teignmouth, Saturday [March 14, 1818].

DEAR REYNOLDS — I escaped being blown over and blown under and trees and house being toppled on me. — I have since hearing of Brown's accident had an aversion to a dose of parapet, and being also a lover of antiquities I would sooner have a harmless piece of Herculaneum sent me quietly as a present than ever so modern a chimney-pot tumbled on to my head — Being agog to see some Devonshire, I would have taken a walk the first day, but the rain would not let me; and the second, but the rain would not let me; and the third, but the rain forbade it. Ditto 4 — ditto 5 — ditto — so I made up my Mind to stop indoors, and catch a sight flying between the showers: and, behold I saw a pretty valley — pretty cliffs, pretty Brooks, pretty Meadows, pretty trees, both standing as they were created, and blown down as they are uncreated — The green is beautiful, as they say, and pity it is that it is amphibious — *mais!* but alas! the flowers here wait as naturally for the rain twice a day as the Mussels do for the Tide; so we look upon a brook in these parts as you look upon a splash in your Country. There must be something to support this — aye, fog, hail, snow, rain, Mist blanketing up three parts of the year. This Devonshire is like Lydia Languish, very entertaining when it smiles, but cursedly subject to sympathetic moisture. You have the sensation of walking under one great Lamplighter: and you can't go on the other side of the ladder to keep your frock clean, and cosset your superstition. Buy a girdle — put a pebble in your mouth — loosen your braces — for I am going among scenery whence I intend to tip you the Damosel Radcliffe — I 'll cavern you, and grotto you, and waterfall you, and wood you, and water you, and immense-rock you, and tremendous-sound you, and solitude you. I 'll make a lodgment on your glacis by a row of Pines, and storm your covered way with bramble Bushes. I 'll have at you with hip and haw small-shot, and cannonade you with Shingles — I 'll be witty upon salt-fish, and impede your cavalry with clotted cream. But ah Coward! to talk at this rate to a sick man, or, I hope, to one that was sick — for I hope by this you stand on your right foot. If you are not — that 's all, — I intend to cut all sick people if they do not make up their minds to cut Sickness — a fellow to whom I have a complete aversion, and who strange to say is harboured and countenanced in several houses where I visit — he is sitting now quite impudent between me and Tom — He insults me at poor Jem Rice's — and you have seated him before now between us at the Theatre, when I thought he looked with a longing eye at poor Kean. I shall say, once for all, to my friends generally and severally, cut that fellow, or I cut you —

I went to the Theatre here the other night, which I forgot to tell George, and got insulted, which I ought to remember to forget to tell any Body; for I did not fight, and as yet have had no redress — 'Lie thou there, sweetheart!' I wrote to Bailey yesterday, obliged to speak in a high way, and a damme who 's afraid — for I had owed him so long; however, he shall see I will be better in future. Is he in town yet? I have directed to Oxford as the better chance. I have copied my fourth Book, and shall write the Preface soon. I wish it was all done; for I want to forget it and make my mind free for something new — Atkins the Coachman, Bartlett the Surgeon, Simmons the Barber, and the Girls over at the Bonnetshop, say we shall now have a month of seasonable weather — warm, witty, and full of invention — Write to me and tell me that you are well or thereabouts, or by the holy Beaucœur, which I suppose is the Virgin Mary, or the repented Magdalen (beautiful name, that Magdalen), I 'll take to my Wings and fly away to anywhere but old or Nova Scotia — I wish I had a little innocent bit of Metaphysic in my head, to criss-cross the letter: but you know a favourite tune is hardest to be remembered when one wants it most and you, I know, have long ere this taken it for granted that I never have any speculations without associating you in them, where they are of a pleasant nature, and you know enough of me to tell the places where I haunt most, so that if you think for five minutes after having read this, you will find it a long letter, and see written in the Air above you,

Your most affectionate friend
JOHN KEATS.

Remember me to all. Tom's remembrances to you.

42. TO BENJAMIN ROBERT HAYDON

Teignmouth, Saturday Morn [March 21, 1818].

MY DEAR HAYDON — In sooth, I hope you are not too sanguine about that seal [33] — in sooth I hope it is not Brumidgeum — in double sooth I hope it is his — and in triple sooth I hope I shall have an impression. Such a piece of intelligence came doubly welcome to me while in your own County and in your own hand — not but I have blown up the said County for its urinal qualifications — the six first days I was here it did nothing but rain; and at that time having to write to a friend I gave Devonshire a good blowing up — it has been fine for almost three days, and I was coming round a bit; but to-day it rains again — with me the County is yet upon its

good behaviour. I have enjoyed the most delightful Walks these three fine days beautiful enough to make me content here all the summer could I stay.

[Here follow the verses 'At Teignmouth,' given above, p. 242.]

I know not if this rhyming fit has done anything — it will be safe with you if worthy to put among my Lyrics. Here 's some doggrel for you — Perhaps you would like a bit of b——hrell—

['The Devon Maid,' see above, p. 243.]

How does the work go on? I should like to bring out my 'Dentatus' [34] at the time your Epic makes its appearance. I expect to have my Mind soon clear for something new. Tom has been much worse: but is now getting better — his remembrances to you. I think of seeing the Dart and Plymouth — but I don't know. It has as yet been a Mystery to me how and where Wordsworth went. I can't help thinking he has returned to his Shell — with his beautiful Wife and his enchanting Sister. It is a great Pity that People should by associating themselves with the finest things, spoil them. Hunt has damned Hampstead and masks and sonnets and Italian tales. Wordsworth has damned the lakes — Milman has damned the old drama — West has damned —— wholesale. Peacock has damned satire — Ollier has damn'd Music — Hazlitt has damned the Bigoted and the blue-stockinged; how durst the Man? he is your only good damner, and if ever I am damn'd — damn me if I should n't like him to damn me. It will not be long ere I see you, but I thought I would just give you a line out of Devon.

Yours affectionately   JOHN KEATS.
Remember me to all we know.

43. TO MESSRS. TAYLOR AND HESSEY

Teignmouth, Saturday Morn [March 21, 1818].

MY DEAR SIRS — I had no idea of your getting on so fast — I thought of bringing my 4th Book to Town all in good time for you — especially after the late unfortunate chance.

I did not however for my own sake delay finishing the copy which was done a few days after my arrival here. I send it off to-day, and will tell you in a Postscript at what time to send for it from the Bull and Mouth or other Inn. You will find the Preface and dedication and the title Page as I should wish it to stand — for a Romance is a fine thing notwithstanding the circulating Libraries. My respects to Mrs. Hessey and to Percy Street.

Yours very sincerely JOHN KEATS.

P. S. — I have been advised to send it to you — you may expect it on Monday — for I sent it by the Postman to Exeter at the same time with this Letter. Adieu!

44. TO JAMES RICE

Teignmouth, Tuesday [March 24, 1818].

MY DEAR RICE — Being in the midst of your favourite Devon, I should not, by rights, pen one word but it should contain a vast portion of Wit, Wisdom and learning — for I have heard that Milton ere he wrote his answer to Salmasius came into these parts, and for one whole month, rolled himself for three whole hours (per day?), in a certain meadow hard by us — where the mark of his nose at equidistances is still shown. The exhibitor of the said meadow further saith, that, after these rollings, not a nettle sprang up in all the seven acres for seven years, and that from the said time, a new sort of plant was made from the whitethorn, of a thornless nature, very much used by the bucks of the present day to rap their boots withal. This account made me very naturally suppose that the nettles and thorns etherealised by the scholar's rotatory motion, and garnered in his head, thence flew after a process of fermentation against the luckless Salmasius and occasioned his well-known and unhappy end. What a happy thing it would be if

we could settle our thoughts and make our minds up on any matter in five minutes, and remain content — that is, build a sort of mental cottage of feelings, quiet and pleasant — to have a sort of philosophical back-garden, and cheerful holiday-keeping front one — but alas! this never can be: for as the material cottager knows there are such places as France and Italy, and the Andes and burning mountains, so the spiritual Cottager has knowledge of the terra semi-incognita of things unearthly, and cannot for his life keep in the check-rein — or I should stop here quiet and comfortable in my theory of nettles. You will see, however, I am obliged to run wild being attracted by the load-stone concatenation. No sooner had I settled the knotty point of Salmasius, than the Devil put this whim into my head in the likeness of one of Pythagoras's questionings — Did Milton do more good or harm in the world? He wrote, let me inform you (for I have it from a friend, who had it of——,) he wrote Lycidas, Comus, Paradise Lost and other Poems, with much delectable prose — He was moreover an active friend to man all his life, and has been since his death. — Very good — but, my dear Fellow, I must let you know that, as there is ever the same quantity of matter constituting this habitable globe — as the ocean notwithstanding the enormous changes and revolutions taking place in some or other of its demesnes — notwithstanding Waterspouts whirlpools and mighty rivers emptying themselves into it — still is made up of the same bulk, nor ever varies the number of its atoms — and as a certain bulk of water was instituted at the creation — so very likely a certain portion of intellect was spun forth into the thin air, for the brains of man to prey upon it. You will see my drift without any unnecessary parenthesis. That which is contained in the Pacific could not lie in the hollow of the Caspian — that which was in Milton's head could not find room in Charles the Second's — He like a moon attracted intellect to its flow — it has not ebbed yet, but has left the shore-pebbles all bare — I mean all Bucks, Authors of Hengist, and Castlereaghs of the present day; who without Milton's gormandising might have been all wise men — Now forasmuch as I was very predisposed to a country I had heard you speak so highly of, I took particular notice of everything during my journey, and have bought some folio asses' skins for memorandums. I have seen everything but the wind — and that, they say, becomes visible by taking a dose of acorns, or sleeping one night in a hog-trough, with your · tail to the Sow-Sow-West. Some of the little Bar-maids look'd at me as if I knew Jem Rice, — but when I took (cherry?) Brandy they were quite convinced. One asked whether you preserved (?) a secret she gave you on the nail — Another, how many buttons of your coat were buttoned in general. — I told her it used to be four — But since you had become acquainted with one Martin you had reduced it to three, and had been turning this third one in your mind — and would do so with finger and thumb only you had taken to snuff. I have met with a brace or twain of little Long-heads — not a bit o' the German. All in the neatest little dresses, and avoiding all the puddles, but very fond of peppermint drops, laming ducks and ... Well, I can't tell! I hope you are showing poor Reynolds the way to get well. Send me a good account of him, and if I can, I'll send you one of Tom — Oh! for a day and all well!

I went yesterday to Dawlish fair.

Over the Hill and over the Dale,
  And over the Bourne to Dawlish,
Where ginger-bread wives have a scanty sale,
  And ginger-bread nuts are smallish, etc. etc.

Tom's remembrances and mine to you all.

Your sincere friend

JOHN KEATS.

45. TO JOHN HAMILTON REYNOLDS

[Teignmouth, March 25, 1818.]

MY DEAR REYNOLDS — In hopes of cheering you through a Minute or two, I was determined will he nill he to send you some lines, so you will excuse the unconnected subject and careless verse. You know, I am sure, Claude's Enchanted Castle,[35] and I wish you may be pleased with my remembrance of it. The Rain is come on again — I think with me Devonshire stands a very poor chance. I shall damn it up hill and down dale, if it keep up to the average of six fine days in three weeks. Let me have better news of you.

Tom's remembrances to you. Remember us to all.

Your affectionate friend, JOHN KEATS.

[The letter concludes with the lines given on p. 241.]

46. TO BENJAMIN ROBERT HAYDON

Wednesday, [Teignmouth, April 8, 1818].

MY DEAR HAYDON — I am glad you were pleased with my nonsense, and if it so happen that the humour takes me when I have set down to prose to you I will not gainsay it. I should be (God forgive me) ready to swear because I cannot make use of your assistance in going through Devon if I was not in my own Mind determined to visit it thoroughly at some more favourable time of the year. But now Tom (who is getting greatly better) is anxious to be in Town — therefore I put off my threading the County. I purpose within a month to put my knapsack at my back and make a pedestrian tour through the North of England, and part of Scotland — to make a sort of Prologue to the Life I intend to pursue — that is to write, to study and to see all Europe at the lowest expence. I will clamber through the Clouds and exist. I will get such an accumulation of stupendous recollections that as I walk through the suburbs of London I may not see them — I will stand upon Mount Blanc and remember this coming Summer when I intend to straddle Ben Lomond — with my soul! — galligaskins are out of the Question. I am nearer myself to hear your 'Christ' is being tinted into immortality. Believe me Haydon your picture is part of myself — I have ever been too sensible of the labyrinthian path to eminence in Art (judging from Poetry) ever to think I understood the emphasis of painting. The innumerable compositions and decompositions which take place between the intellect and its thousand materials before it arrives at that trembling delicate and snail-horn perception of beauty. I know not your many havens of intenseness — nor ever can know them: but for this I hope not [*sic* nought ?] you achieve is lost upon me: for when a Schoolboy the abstract Idea I had of an heroic painting — was what I cannot describe. I saw it somewhat sideways, large, prominent, round, and colour'd with magnificence — somewhat like the feel I have of Anthony and Cleopatra. Or of Alcibiades leaning on his Crimson Couch in his Galley, his broad shoulders imperceptibly heaving with the Sea. That passage in Shakspeare is finer than this —

'See how the surly Warwick mans the Wall.'

I like your consignment of Corneille — that's the humour of it — they shall be called your Posthumous Works.⁹⁶ I don't understand your bit of Italian. I hope she will awake from her dream and flourish fair — my respects to her. The Hedges by this time are beginning to leaf — Cats are becoming more vociferous — young Ladies who wear Watches are always looking at them. Women about forty-five think the Season very backward — Ladies' Mares have but half an allowance of food. It rains here again, has been doing so for three days — however as I told you I'll take a trial in June, July, or August next year.

I am afraid Wordsworth went rather huffd out of Town — I am sorry for it —

he cannot expect his fireside Divan to be infallible — he cannot expect but that every man of worth is as proud as himself. O that he had not fit with a Warrener — that is dined at Kingston's. I shall be in town in about a fortnight and then we will have a day or so now and then before I set out on my northern expedition — we will have no more abominable Rows — for they leave one in a fearful silence — having settled the Methodists let us be rational — not upon compulsion — no — if it will out let it — but I will not play the Bassoon any more deliberately. Remember me to Hazlitt, and Bewick —

Your affectionate friend, JOHN KEATS.

47. TO JOHN HAMILTON REYNOLDS

Thy. morng., [Teignmouth, April 9, 1818].

MY DEAR REYNOLDS — Since you all agree that the thing [the first preface to *Endymion*] is bad, it must be so — though I am not aware there is anything like Hunt in it (and if there is, it is my natural way, and I have something in common with Hunt). Look it over again, and examine into the motives, the seeds, from which any one sentence sprung — I have not the slightest feel of humility towards the public — or to anything in existence, — but the eternal Being, the Principle of Beauty, and the Memory of great Men. When I am writing for myself for the mere sake of the moment's enjoyment, perhaps nature has its course with me — but a Preface is written to the Public; a thing I cannot help looking upon as an Enemy, and which I cannot address without feelings of Hostility. If I write a Preface in a supple or subdued style, it will not be in character with me as a public speaker — I would be subdued before my friends, and thank them for subduing me — but among Multitudes of Men — I have no feel of stooping, I hate the idea of humility to them.

I never wrote one single Line of Poetry with the least Shadow of public thought.

Forgive me for vexing you and making a Trojan horse of such a Trifle, both with respect to the matter in Question, and myself — but it eases me to tell you — I could not live without the love of my friends — I would jump down Ætna for any great Public good — but I hate a Mawkish Popularity. I cannot be subdued before them — My glory would be to daunt and dazzle the thousand jabberers about Pictures and Books — I see swarms of Porcupines with their Quills erect 'like lime-twigs set to catch my Wingèd Book,' and I would fright them away with a torch. You will say my Preface is not much of a Torch. It would have been too insulting 'to begin from Jove,' and I could not set a golden head upon a thing of clay. If there is any fault in the Preface it is not affectation, but an undersong of disrespect to the Public — if I write another Preface it must be done without a thought of those people — I will think about it. If it should not reach you in four or five days, tell Taylor to publish it without a Preface, and let the Dedication simply stand — 'inscribed to the Memory of Thomas Chatterton.'

I had resolved last night to write to you this morning — I wish it had been about something else — something to greet you towards the close of your long illness. I have had one or two intimations of your going to Hampstead for a space; and I regret to see your confounded Rheumatism keeps you in Little Britain where I am sure the air is too confined. Devonshire continues rainy. As the drops beat against the window, they give me the same sensation as a quart of cold water offered to revive a half-drowned devil — no feel of the clouds dropping fatness; but as if the roots of the earth were rotten, cold, and drenched. I have not been able to go to Kent's cave at Babbicombe — however on one very beautiful day I had a fine Clamber over the rocks all along as far as that place. I shall be in Town in about Ten days — We go by way of Bath on purpose to call

on Bailey. I hope soon to be writing to you about the things of the north, purposing to wayfare all over those parts. I have settled my accoutrements in my own mind, and will go to gorge wonders. However, we'll have some days together before I set out —

I have many reasons for going wonderways: to make my winter chair free from spleen — to enlarge my vision — to escape disquisitions on Poetry and Kingston Criticism; to promote digestion and economise shoe-leather. I'll have leather buttons and belt; and, if Brown holds his mind, over the Hills we go. If my Books will help me to it, then will I take all Europe in turn, and see the Kingdoms of the Earth and the glory of them. Tom is getting better, he hopes you may meet him at the top o' the hill. My Love to your nurses. I am ever

Your affectionate Friend JOHN KEATS.

48. TO THE SAME

[Teignmouth,] Friday [April 10, 1818].

MY DEAR REYNOLDS — I am anxious you should find this Preface tolerable. If there is an affectation in it 't is natural to me. Do let the Printer's Devil cook it, and let me be as 'the casing air.'

You are too good in this Matter — were I in your state, I am certain I should have no thought but of discontent and illness — I might though be taught patience: I had an idea of giving no Preface; however, don't you think this had better go? O, let it — one should not be too timid — of committing faults.

The climate here weighs us down completely; Tom is quite low-spirited. It is impossible to live in a country which is continually under hatches. Who would live in a region of Mists, Game Laws, indemnity Bills, etc., when there is such a place as Italy? It is said this England from its Clime produces a Spleen, able to engender the finest Sentiments, and cover the whole face of the isle with Green — so it ought, I'm sure. — I should still like the Dedication simply, as I said in my last.

I wanted to send you a few songs written in your favorite Devon — it cannot be — Rain! Rain! Rain! I am going this morning to take a facsimile of a Letter of Nelson's, very much to his honour — you will be greatly pleased when you see it — in about a week. What a spite it is one cannot get out — the little way I went yesterday, I found a lane banked on each side with store of Primroses, while the earlier bushes are beginning to leaf.

I shall hear a good account of you soon. Your affectionate Friend JOHN KEATS.

My Love to all and remember me to Taylor.

49. TO JOHN TAYLOR

Teignmouth, Friday [April 24, 1818].

MY DEAR TAYLOR — I think I did wrong to leave to you all the trouble of Endymion — But I could not help it then — another time I shall be more bent to all sorts of troubles and disagreeables. Young men for some time have an idea that such a thing as happiness is to be had, and therefore are extremely impatient under any unpleasant restraining. In time however, of such stuff is the world about them, they know better, and instead of striving from uneasiness, greet it as an habitual sensation, a pannier which is to weigh upon them through life — And in proportion to my disgust at the task is my sense of your kindness and anxiety. The book pleased me much. It is very free from faults: and, although there are one or two words I should wish replaced, I see in many places an improvement greatly to the purpose.

I think those speeches which are related — those parts where the speaker repeats a speech, such as Glaucus's repetition of Circe's words, should have inverted commas to every line. In this there is a little confusion. — If we divide the speeches into

indentical and related; and to the former put merely one inverted Comma at the beginning and another at the end; and to the latter inverted Commas before every line, the book will be better understood at the 1st glance. Look at pages 126, 127, you will find in the 3d line the beginning of a related speech marked thus ' Ah ! art awake —' while, at the same time, in the next page the continuation of the indentical speech is marked in the same manner, ' Young man of Latmos —' You will find on the other side all the parts which should have inverted commas to every line.

I was proposing to travel over the North this summer. There is but one thing to prevent me. — I know nothing — I have read nothing — and I mean to follow Solomon's directions, ' Get learning — get understanding.' I find earlier days are gone by — I find that I can have no enjoyment in the world but continual drinking of knowledge. I find there is no worthy pursuit but the idea of doing some good for the world — Some do it with their Society — some with their wit — some with their benevolence — some with a sort of power of conferring pleasure and good-humour on all they meet — and in a thousand ways, all dutiful to the command of great Nature — there is but one way for me. The road lies through application, study, and thought. — I will pursue it; and for that end, purpose retiring for some years. I have been hovering for some time between an exquisite sense of the luxurious, and a love for philosophy, — were I calculated for the former, I should be glad. But as I am not, I shall turn all my soul to the latter. — My brother Tom is getting better, and I hope I shall see both him and Reynolds better before I retire from the world. I shall see you soon, and have some talk about what Books I shall take with me.

Your very sincere friend JOHN KEATS.

Pray remember me to Hessey Woodhouse and Percy Street.

50. TO JOHN HAMILTON REYNOLDS

Teignmouth, April 27, 1818.

MY DEAR REYNOLDS — It is an awful while since you have heard from me — I hope I may not be punished, when I see you well, and so anxious as you always are for me, with the remembrance of my so seldom writing when you were so horribly confined. The most unhappy hours in our lives are those in which we recollect times past to our own blushing — If we are immortal that must be the Hell. If I must be immortal, I hope it will be after having taken a little of 'that watery labyrinth' in order to forget some of my school-boy days and others since those.

I have heard from George at different times how slowly you were recovering — It is a tedious thing — but all Medical Men will tell you how far a very gradual amendment is preferable; you will be strong after this, never fear. We are here still enveloped in clouds — I lay awake last night listening to the Rain with a sense of being drowned and rotted like a grain of wheat. There is a continual courtesy between the Heavens and the Earth. The heavens rain down their unwelcomeness, and the Earth sends it up again to be returned to-morrow. Tom has taken a fancy to a physician here, Dr. Turton, and I think is getting better — therefore I shall perhaps remain here some Months. I have written to George for some Books — shall learn Greek, and very likely Italian — and in other ways prepare myself to ask Hazlitt in about a year's time the best metaphysical road I can take. For although I take poetry to be Chief, yet there is something else wanting to one who passes his life among Books and thoughts on Books — I long to feast upon old Homer as we have upon Shakspeare, and as I have lately upon Milton. If you understood Greek, and would read me passages, now and then, explaining their meaning, 't would be, from its mistiness, perhaps, a greater luxury than reading the thing one's self. I shall be happy when I can do the same for you. I have written for my folio Shakspeare, in which there are the first few stanzas of my 'Pot of Basil.' I have the rest here finished, and will copy the whole out fair shortly, and George will bring it you — The compliment is paid by us to Boccace, whether we publish or no: so there is content in this world — *mine* is short — you must be deliberate about yours: you must not think of it till many months after you are quite well: — then put your passion to it, and I shall be bound up with you in the shadows of Mind, as we are in our matters of human life. Perhaps a Stanza or two will not be too foreign to your Sickness.

[Here are inserted stanzas xii., xiii., and xxx.]

I heard from Rice this morning — very witty — and have just written to Bailey. Don't you think I am brushing up in the letter way? and being in for it, you shall hear again from me very shortly: — if you will promise not to put hand to paper for me until you can do it with a tolerable ease of health — except it be a line or two. Give my Love to your Mother and Sisters. Remember me to the Butlers — not forgetting Sarah.

Your affectionate Friend JOHN KEATS.

51. TO THE SAME

Teignmouth, May 3d [1818].

MY DEAR REYNOLDS — What I complain of is that I have been in so uneasy a state of Mind as not to be fit to write to an invalid. I cannot write to any length under a disguised feeling. I should have loaded you with an addition of gloom, which I am sure you do not want. I am now thank God in a humour to give you a good groat's worth — for Tom, after a Night without a Wink of sleep, and over-burthened with fever, has got up after a refreshing day-sleep and is better than he has been for a long time; and you I trust have been again round the common without any effect but refreshment. As in the Matter I hope I can say with Sir Andrew 'I have matter enough in my head' in your favour — And now, in the second place, for I reckon that I have finished my Imprimis, I am glad you blow up the weather — all through your letter there is a leaning towards a climate-curse, and you know what a delicate satisfaction there is in having a vexation anathematized: one would think there has been growing up for these last four thousand years, a grand-child Scion of the old forbidden tree, and that some modern Eve had just violated it; and that there was come with double charge

'Notus and Afer, black with thundrous clouds From Serraliona —'

I shall breathe worsted stockings ⁂ sooner than I thought for — Tom wants to be in Town — we will have some such days upon the heath like that of last summer — and why not with the same book? or what say you to a black Letter Chaucer, printed in 1596: aye I've got one huzza! I shall have it bound en gothique — a nice sombre binding — it will go a little way to un-modernise. And also I see no reason, because I have been away this last month, why I should not have a peep at your Spenserian — notwithstanding you speak of your office, in my thought a little too early, for I do not see why a Mind like yours is not capable of harbouring and digesting the whole Mystery of Law as easily as Parson Hugh does pippins, which did not hinder him from his poetic canary. Were I to study physic or rather Medicine again, I feel it would not make the least difference in my Poetry; when the mind is in its infancy a Bias is in reality a Bias, but when we have acquired more strength, a Bias becomes no Bias. Every department of Knowledge we see excellent and calculated towards a great whole — I am so convinced of this that I am glad at not having given away my medical Books, which I shall

again look over to keep alive the little I know thitherwards; and moreover intend through you and Rice to become a sort of pip-civilian. An extensive knowledge is needful to thinking people — it takes away the heat and fever; and helps, by widening speculation, to ease the Burden of the Mystery, a thing which I begin to understand a little, and which weighed upon you in the most gloomy and true sentence in your Letter. The difference of high Sensations with and without knowledge appears to me this: in the latter case we are falling continually ten thousand fathoms deep and being blown up again, without wings, and with all horror of a bare-shouldered Creature — in the former case, our shoulders are fledged, and we go through the same air and space without fear. This is running one's rigs on the score of abstracted benefit — when we come to human Life and the affections, it is impossible to know how a parallel of breast and head can be drawn (you will forgive me for thus privately treading out of my depth, and take it for treading as school-boys tread the water); it is impossible to know how far knowledge will console us for the death of a friend, and the ill 'that flesh is heir to.' With respect to the affections and Poetry you must know by a sympathy my thoughts that way, and I daresay these few lines will be but a ratification: I wrote them on Mayday — and intend to finish the ode all in good time —

'Mother of Hermes! and still youthful Maia!' [See p. 119.]

You may perhaps be anxious to know for fact to what sentence in your Letter I allude. You say, 'I fear there is little chance of anything else in this Life' — you seem by that to have been going through with a more painful and acute zest the same labyrinth that I have — I have come to the same conclusion thus far. My Branchings out therefrom have been numerous: one of them is the consideration of Wordsworth's genius and as a help, in the manner of gold being the meridian Line of worldly wealth, how he differs from Milton. And here I have nothing but surmises, from an uncertainty whether Milton's apparently less anxiety for Humanity proceeds from his seeing further or not than Wordsworth: And whether Wordsworth has in truth epic passion, and martyrs himself to the human heart, the main region of his song. In regard to his genius alone — we find what he says true as far as we have experienced, and we can judge no further but by larger experience — for axioms in philosophy are not axioms until they are proved upon our pulses. We read fine things, but never feel them to the full until we have gone the same steps as the author. — I know this is not plain; you will know exactly my meaning when I say that now I shall relish Hamlet more than I ever have done — Or, better — you are sensible no man can set down Venery as a bestial or joyless thing until he is sick of it, and therefore all philosophising on it would be mere wording. Until we are sick, we understand not; in fine, as Byron says, 'Knowledge is sorrow'; and I go on to say that 'Sorrow is wisdom' — and further for aught we can know for certainty 'Wisdom is folly' — So you see how I have run away from Wordsworth and Milton, and shall still run away from what was in my head, to observe, that some kind of letters are good squares, others handsome ovals, and others some orbicular, others spheroid — and why should not there be another species with two rough edges like a Rattrap? I hope you will find all my long letters of that species, and all will be well; for by merely touching the spring delicately and ethereally, the rough-edged will fly immediately into a proper compactness; and thus you may make a good wholesome loaf, with your own leaven in it, of my fragments — If you cannot find this said flat-trap sufficiently tractable, alas for me, it being an impossibility in grain for my ink

to stain otherwise: If I scribble long letters I must play my vagaries — I must be too heavy, or too light, for whole pages — I must be quaint and free of Tropes and figures — I must play my draughts as I please, and for my advantage and your erudition, crown a white with a black, or a black with a white, and move into black or white, far and near as I please — I must go from Hazlitt to Patmore, and make Wordsworth and Coleman play at leap-frog, or keep one of them down a whole half-holiday at fly-the-garter — ' From Gray to Gay, from Little to Shakspeare.' Also as a long cause requires two or more sittings of the Court, so a long letter will require two or more sittings of the Breech, wherefore I shall resume after dinner —

Have you not seen a Gull, an ore, a Sea-Mew, or anything to bring this Line to a proper length, and also fill up this clear part; that like the Gull I may *dip* * — I hope, not out of sight — and also, like a Gull, I hope to be lucky in a good-sized fish — This crossing a letter is not without its association — for chequer-work leads us naturally to a Milkmaid, a Milkmaid to Hogarth, Hogarth to Shakspeare — Shakspeare to Hazlitt — Hazlitt to Shakspeare — and thus by merely pulling an apron-string we set a pretty peal of Chimes at work — Let them chime on while, with your patience, I will return to Wordsworth — whether or no he has an extended vision or a circumscribed grandeur — whether he is an eagle in his nest or on the wing — And to be more explicit and to show you how tall I stand by the giant, I will put down a simile of human life as far as I now perceive it; that is, to the point to which I say we both have arrived at — Well — I compare human life to a large Mansion of Many apartments, two of which I can only describe, the doors of the rest

* The crossing of the letter, begun at the words 'Have you not,' here *dips* into the original writing.

being as yet shut upon me — The first we step into we call the infant or thoughtless Chamber, in which we remain as long as we do not think — We remain there a long while, and notwithstanding the doors of the second Chamber remain wide open, showing a bright appearance, we care not to hasten to it; but are at length imperceptibly impelled by the awakening of the thinking principle within us — we no sooner get into the second Chamber, which I shall call the Chamber of Maiden-Thought, than we become intoxicated with the light and the atmosphere, we see nothing but pleasant wonders, and think of delaying there for ever in delight: However among the effects this breathing is father of is that tremendous one of sharpening one's vision into the heart and nature of Man — of convincing one's nerves that the world is full of Misery and Heart-break, Pain, Sickness, and oppression — whereby this Chamber of Maiden-Thought becomes gradually darkened, and at the same time, on all sides of it, many doors are set open — but all dark — all leading to dark passages — We see not the balance of good and evil — we are in a mist — we are now in that state — We feel the 'burden of the Mystery.' To this point was Wordsworth come, as far as I can conceive, when he wrote 'Tintern Abbey,' and it seems to me that his Genius is explorative of those dark Passages. Now if we live, and go on thinking, we too shall explore them — He is a genius and superior to us, in so far as he can, more than we, make discoveries and shed a light in them — Here I must think Wordsworth is deeper than Milton, though I think it has depended more upon the general and gregarious advance of intellect, than individual greatness of Mind — From the Paradise Lost and the other Works of Milton, I hope it is not too presuming, even between ourselves, to say, that his philosophy, human and divine, may be tolerably understood by one not much advanced in years. In his time, Englishmen were just

emancipated from a great superstition, and Men had got hold of certain points and resting-places in reasoning which were too newly born to be doubted, and too much opposed by the Mass of Europe not to be thought ethereal and authentically divine — Who could gainsay his ideas on virtue. vice, and Chastity in Comus, just at the time of the dismissal of a hundred disgraces? who would not rest satisfied with his hintings at good and evil in the Paradise Lost, when just free from the Inquisition and burning in Smithfield? The Reformation produced such immediate and great benefits, that Protestantism was considered under the immediate eye of heaven, and its own remaining Dogmas and superstitions then, as it were, regenerated, constituted those resting-places and seeming sure points of Reasoning — from that I have mentioned, Milton, whatever he may have thought in the sequel, appears to have been content with these by his writings — He did not think into the human heart as Wordsworth has done — Yet Milton as a Philosopher had sure as great powers as Wordsworth — What is then to be inferred? O many things — It proves there is really a grand march of intellect, — It proves that a mighty providence subdues the mightiest Minds to the service of the time being, whether it be in human Knowledge or Religion. I have often pitied a tutor who has to hear 'Nom. Musa' so often dinn'd into his ears — I hope you may not have the same pain in this scribbling — I may have read these things before, but I never had even a thus dim perception of them; and moreover I like to say my lesson to one who will endure my tediousness for my own sake — After all there is certainly something real in the world — Moore's present to Hazlitt is real — I like that Moore, and am glad I saw him at the Theatre just before I left Town. Tom has spit a *leetle* blood this afternoon, and that is rather a damper — but I know — the truth is there is something real in the

World. Your third Chamber of Life shall be a lucky and a gentle one — stored with the wine of love — and the Bread of Friendship — When you see George if he should not have received a letter from me tell him he will find one at home most likely — tell Bailey I hope soon to see him — Remember me to all. The leaves have been out here for many a day — I have written to George for the first stanzas of my Isabel — I shall have them soon, and will copy the whole out for you.

Your affectionate Friend JOHN KEATS.

52. TO MRS. JEFFREY

Honiton, [May, 1818].

MY DEAR MRS. JEFFREY — My Brother has borne his Journey thus far remarkably well. I am too sensible of your anxiety for us not to send this by the chaise back for you. Give our goodbyes to Marrian and Fanny. Believe me we shall bear you in Mind and that I shall write soon.

Yours very truly, JOHN KEATS.

53. TO BENJAMIN BAILEY

Hampstead, Thursday [May 28, 1818].

MY DEAR BAILEY — I should have answered your Letter on the Moment, if I could have said yes to your invitation. What hinders me is insuperable: I will tell it at a little length. You know my Brother George has been out of employ for some time: it has weighed very much upon him, and driven him to scheme and turn over things in his Mind. The result has been his resolution to emigrate to the back Settlements of America, become Farmer and work with his own hands, after purchasing 14 hundred acres of the American Government. This for many reasons has met with my entire Consent — and the chief one is this; he is of too independent and liberal a Mind to get on in Trade in this Country, in which a generous Man with a scanty resource must be ruined. I would sooner he should till the ground than bow to a customer. There is no choice with him: he could not bring himself to the latter. I would not consent to his going alone; — no — but that objection is done away with: he will marry before he sets sail a young lady he has known for several years, of a nature liberal and highspirited enough to follow him to the Banks of the Mississippi. He will set off in a month or six weeks, and you will see how I should wish to pass that time with him. — And then I must set out on a journey of my own. Brown and I are going a pedestrian tour through the north of England and Scotland as far as John o' Grot's. I have this morning such a lethargy that I cannot write. The reason of my delaying is oftentimes from this feeling, — I wait for a proper temper. Now you ask for an immediate answer, I do not like to wait even till to-morrow. However, I am now so depressed that I have not an idea to put to paper — my hand feels like lead — and yet it is an unpleasant numbness; it does not take away the pain of Existence. I don't know what to write.

Monday [June 1].

You see how I have delayed; and even now I have but a confused idea of what I should be about. My intellect must be in a degenerating state — it must be — for when I should be writing about — God knows what — I am troubling you with moods of my own mind, or rather body, for mind there is none. I am in that temper that if I were under water I would scarcely kick to come up to the top — I know very well 't is all nonsense — In a short time I hope I shall be in a temper to feel sensibly your mention of my book. In vain have I waited till Monday to have any Interest in that or anything else. I feel no spur at my Brother's going to America, and am almost stony-hearted about his wedding. All this will blow over — All I am sorry for is having to write to you in such a time — but I cannot force my letters in a hotbed. I could not feel comfortable in making sentences for you. I am your debtor — I must ever remain so — nor do I wish to be clear of any Rational debt: there is a comfort in throwing oneself on the charity of one's friends — 'tis like the albatross sleeping on its wings. I will be to you wine in the cellar, and the more modestly, or rather, indolently, I retire into the backward bin, the more Falerne will I be at the drinking. There is one thing I must mention — my Brother talks of sailing in a fortnight — if so I will most probably be with you a week before I set out for Scotland. The middle of your first page should be sufficient to rouse me. What I said is true, and I have dreamt of your mention of it, and my not answering it has weighed on me since. If I come, I will bring your letter, and hear more fully your sentiments ou one or two points. I will call about the Lectures at Taylor's, and at Little Britain, to-morrow. Yesterday I dined with Hazlitt, Barnes, and Wilkie, at Haydon's. The topic was the Duke of Wellington — very amusingly pro-and-con'd. Reynolds has been getting much better; and Rice may begin to crow, for he got a little so-so at a party of his, and was none the worse for it the next morning. I hope I shall soon see you, for we must have many new thoughts and feelings to analyse, and to discover whether a little more knowledge has not made us more ignorant.

Yours affectionately   JOHN KEATS.

54. TO MISSES M. AND S. JEFFREY

Hampstead, June 4th [1818.]

MY DEAR GIRLS — I will not pretend to string a list of excuses together for not having written before — but must at once confess the indolence of my disposition, which makes a letter more formidable to me than a Pilgrimage. I am a fool in delay for the idea of neglect is an everlasting Knapsack which even now I have scarce power to hoist off. By the bye talking of everlasting Knapsacks I intend to make my fortune by them in case of a War (which you must consequently pray for) by contracting with Government for said material to the economy of one branch of the Revenue. At all events a Tax which is taken from the people and shoulder'd upon the Military ought not to be snubb'd at. I promised to send you all the news. Harkee ! The whole city corporation, with a deputation from the Fire Offices are now engaged at the London Coffee house in secret conclave concerning Saint Paul's Cathedral its being washed clean. Many interesting speeches have been demosthenized in said Coffee house as to the Cause of the black appearance of the said Cathedral. One of the veal-thigh Aldermen actually brought up three Witnesses to depose how they beheld the ci-devant fair Marble turn black on the tolling of the great Bell for the amiable and tea-table-lamented Princess — adding moreover that this sort of sympathy in inanimate objects was by no means uncommon for said the Gentleman ' As we were once debating in the Common Hall Mr. Waithman in illustration of some case in point quoted Peter Pindar, at which the head of George the third although in hard marble squinted over the Mayor's seat at the honorable speaker so oddly that he was obliged to sit down.' However I will not tire you about these Affairs for they must be in your Newspapers by this time. You see how badly I have written these last three lines so I will remain here and take a pinch of snuff every five Minutes until my head becomes fit and proper and legitimately inclined to scribble — Oh ! there's nothing like a pinch of snuff except perhaps a few trifles almost beneath a philosopher's dignity, such as a ripe Peach or a Kiss that one takes on a lease of 91 moments — on a baildling lease. Talking of that is the Capt[n] married yet, or rather married Miss Mitchel — is she stony hearted enough to hold out this season ? Has the Doctor given Miss Perryman a little love powder ? — tell him

to do *so*. It really would not be unamusing
to see her languish a little — Oh she must
be quite melting this hot Weather. Are
the little Robins weaned yet? Do they
walk alone? You have had a christening
a top o' the tiles and a Hawk has stood
Godfather and taken the little brood under
the Shadows of its Wings much in the way
of Mother Church — a Cat too has very
tender bowels in such pathetic cases. They
say we are all (that is our set) mad at
Hampstead. There's George took unto
himself a Wife a Week ago and will in a
little time sail for America — and I with a
friend am preparing for a four Months
Walk all over the North — and belike Tom
will not stop here — he has been getting
much better — Lord what a Journey I had
and what a relief at the end of it — I'm
sure I could not have stood it many more
days. Hampstead is now in fine order. I
suppose Teignmouth and the *contagious*
country is now quite remarkable — you
might praise it I dare say in the manner of
a grammatical exercise — *The* trees *are* full
— *the* den *is* crowded — *the* boats *are* sailing — *the* mnsick *is* playing. I wish you
were here a little while — but lauk we
have n't got any female friend in the house.
Tom is taken for a Madman and I being
somewhat stunted am taken for nothing —
We lounge on the Walk opposite as you
might on the Den — I hope the fine season
will keep up your Mother's Spirits — she
was used to be too much down hearted.
No Women ought to be born into the world
for they may not touch the bottle for shame
— now a Man may creep into a bung-hole
— However this is a tale of a tub — however I like to play upon a pipe sitting upon
a puncheon and intend to be so drawn in
the frontispiece to my next book of Pastorals — My Brothers' respects and mine to
your Mother and all our Loves to you.

    Yours very sincerely, JOHN KEATS.

P. S. has many significations — here it
signifies Post Script — on the corner of a

Handkerchef Polly Saunders — Upon a
Garter Pretty Secret — Upon a Band Box
Pink Sattin — At the Theatre Princes Side
— on a Pulpit Parson's Snuffle — and at a
Country Ale House Pail Sider.

55. TO BENJAMIN BAILEY

London [June 10, 1818].

MY DEAR BAILEY — I have been very
much gratified and very much hurt by your
letters in the Oxford Paper: because independent of that unlawful and mortal feeling of pleasure at praise, there is a glory in
enthusiasm; and because the world is malignant enough to chuckle at the most honourable Simplicity. Yes, on my soul, my dear
Bailey, you are too simple for the world —
and that Idea makes me sick of it. How
is it that by extreme opposites we have,
as it were, got discontented nerves? You
have all your life (I think so) believed
everybody. I have suspected everybody.
And, although you have been so deceived,
you make a simple appeal — the world has
something else to do, and I am glad of it —
Were it in my choice, I would reject a
Petrarchal coronation — on account of my
dying day, and because women have cancers.
I should not by rights speak in this tone to
you for it is an incendiary spirit that would
do so. Yet I am not old enough or magnan-
imous enough to annihilate self — and it
would perhaps be paying you an ill compliment. I was in hopes some little time
back to be able to relieve your dulness by
my spirits — to point out things in the
world worth your enjoyment — and now I
am never alone without rejoicing that there
is such a thing as death — without placing
my ultimate in the glory of dying for a
great human purpose. Perhaps if my affairs
were in a different state, I should not have
written the above — you shall judge: I
have two brothers; one is driven, by the
'burden of Society,' to America; the other
with an exquisite love of life, is in a linger-

ing state — My love for my Brothers, from the early loss of our Parents, and even from earlier misfortunes, has grown into an affection 'passing the love of women.' I have been ill-tempered with them — I have vexed them — but the thought of them has always stifled the impression that any woman might otherwise have made upon me. I have a sister too, and may not follow them either to America or to the grave. Life must be undergone, and I certainly derive some consolation from the thought of writing one or two more poems before it ceases.

I have heard some hints of your retiring to Scotland — I shall like to know your feeling on it — it seems rather remote. Perhaps Gleig will have a duty near you. I am not certain whether I shall be able to go any journey, on account of my Brother Tom, and a little indisposition of my own. If I do not you shall see me soon, if *no* on my return or I 'll quarter myself on you next winter. I had known my sister-in-law some time before she was my sister, and was very fond of her. I like her better and better. She is the most disinterested woman I ever knew — that is to say, she goes beyond degree in it. To see an entirely disinterested girl quite happy is the most pleasant and extraordinary thing in the world — It depends upon a thousand circumstances — On my word it is extraordinary. Women must want Imagination, and they may thank God for it; and so may we, that a delicate being can feel happy without any sense of crime. It puzzles me, and I have no sort of logic to comfort me — I shall think it over. I am not at home, and your letter being there I cannot look it over to answer any particular — only I must say I feel that passage of Dante. If I take any book with me it shall be those minute volumes of Carey, for they will go into the aptest corner.

Reynolds is getting, I may say, robust, his illness has been of service to him — like every one just recovered, he is high-spirited

— I hear also good accounts of Rice. With respect to domestic literature, the Edinburgh Magazine, in another blow-up against Hunt, calls me 'the amiable Mister Keats' — and I have more than a laurel from the Quarterly Reviewers for they have smothered me in *Foliage.* I want to read you my ' Pot of Basil ' — if you go to Scotland, I should much like to read it there to you, among the snows of next winter. My Brothers' remembrances to you.

Your affectionate friend JOHN KEATS.

56. TO JOHN TAYLOR

[Hampstead,] Sunday Evening
[June 21, 1818].

MY DEAR TAYLOR — I am sorry I have not had time to call and wish you health till my return — Really I have been hard run these last three days — However, au revoir, God keep us all well! I start to-morrow Morning. My brother Tom will I am afraid be lonely. I can scarce ask a loan of books for him, since I still keep those you lent me a year ago. If I am overweening, you will I know be indulgent. Therefore when you shall write, do send him some you think will be most amusing — he will be careful in returning them. Let him have one of my books bound. I am ashamed to catalogue these messages. There is but one more, which ought to go for nothing as there is a lady concerned. I promised Mrs. Reynolds one of my books bound. As I cannot write in it let the opposite ³⁸ be pasted in 'prythee. Remember me to Percy St. — Tell Hilton that one gratification on my return will be to find him engaged on a history piece to his own content — And tell Dewint I shall become a disputant on the landscape — Bow for me very genteelly to Mrs. D. or she will not admit your diploma. Remember me to Hessey, saying I hope he 'll *Cary* his point. I would not forget Woodhouse. Adieu !

Your sincere friend JOHN o' GROTS.

57. TO THOMAS KEATS

Keswick, June 29th [1818].

MY DEAR TOM — I cannot make my Journal as distinct and actual as I could wish, from having been engaged in writing to George, and therefore I must tell you without circumstance that we proceeded from Ambleside to Rydal, saw the Water-falls there, and called on Wordsworth, who was not at home, nor was any one of his family. I wrote a note and left it on the mantel-piece. Thence on we came to the foot of Helvellyn, where we slept, but could not ascend it for the mist. I must mention that from Rydal we passed Thirls-water, and a fine pass in the Mountains — from Helvellyn we came to Keswick on Derwent Water. The approach to Derwent Water surpassed Windermere — it is richly wooded, and shut in with rich-toned Moun-tains. From Helvellyn to Keswick was eight miles to Breakfast, after which we took a complete circuit of the Lake, going about ten miles, and seeing on our way the Fall of Lowdore. I had an easy climb among the streams, about the fragments of Rocks and should have got I think to the summit, but unfortunately I was damped by slipping one leg into a squashy hole. There is no great body of water, but the accompaniment is delightful; for it oozes out from a cleft in perpendicular Rocks, all fledged with Ash and other beautiful trees. It is a strange thing how they got there. At the south end of the Lake, the Moun-tains of Borrowdale are perhaps as fine as anything we have seen. On our return from this circuit, we ordered dinner, and set forth about a mile and a half on the Penrith road, to see the Druid temple. We had a fag up hill, rather too near dinner-time, which was rendered void by the gratification of seeing those aged stones on a gentle rise in the midst of the Moun-tains, which at that time darkened all around, except at the fresh opening of the Vale of St. John. We went to bed rather fatigued, but not so much so as to hinder us getting up this morning to mount Skid-daw. It promised all along to be fair, and we had fagged and tugged nearly to the top, when, at half-past six, there came a Mist upon us and shut out the view. We did not, however, lose anything by it : we were high enough without mist to see the coast of Scotland — the Irish Sea — the hills beyond Lancaster — and nearly all the large ones of Cumberland and Westmoreland, parti-cularly Helvellyn and Scawfell. It grew colder and colder as we ascended, and we were glad, at about three parts of the way, to taste a little rum which the Guide brought with him, mixed, mind ye, with Mountain water. I took two glasses going and one returning. It is about six miles from where I am writing to the · top — So we have walked ten miles before Breakfast to-day. We went up with two others, very good sort of fellows — All felt, on arising into the cold air, that same elevation which a cold bath gives one — I felt as if I were going to a Tournament.

Wordsworth's house is situated just on the rise of the foot of Mount Rydal; his parlour-window looks directly down Win-andermere; I do not think I told you how fine the Vale of Grasmere is, and how I discovered 'the ancient woman seated on Helm Crag' — We shall proceed immedi-ately to Carlisle, intending to enter Scot-land on the 1st of July viâ —

[Carlisle,] July 1st.

We are this morning at Carlisle. After Skiddaw, we walked to Treby the oldest market town in Cumberland — where we were greatly amused by a country dancing-school holden at the Tun, it was indeed 'no new cotillon fresh from France.' No, they kickit and jumpit with mettle extraordi-nary, and whiskit, and friskit, and toed it, and go'd it, and twirl'd it, and whirl'd it, and stamped it, and sweated it, tattooing the floor like mad. The difference between our country dances and these Scottish figures is about the same as leisurely stirring a cup o' Tea and beating up a batter-pudding. I was extremely gratified to think that, if I had pleasures they knew nothing of, they had also some into which I could not possibly enter. I hope I shall not return without having got the Highland fling. There was as fine a row of boys and girls as you ever saw; some beautiful faces, and one exquisite mouth. I never felt so near the glory of Patriotism, the glory of making by any means a country happier. This is what I like better than scenery. I fear our continued moving from place to place will prevent our becoming learned in village affairs: we are mere creatures of Rivers, Lakes, and Mountains. Our yesterday's journey was from Treby to Wigton, and from Wigton to Carlisle. The Cathedral does not appear very fine — the Castle is very ancient, and of brick. The City is very various — old white-washed narrow streets — broad red-brick ones more modern — I will tell you anon whether the inside of the Cathedral is worth looking at. It is built of sandy red stone or Brick. We have now walked 114 miles, and are merely a little tired in the thighs, and a little blistered. We shall ride 38 miles to Dumfries, when we shall linger awhile about Nithsdale and Galloway. I have written two letters to Liverpool. I found a letter from sister George; very delightful indeed: I shall preserve it in the bottom of my knapsack for you.

[Dumfries, evening of same day, July 1.]
You will see by this sonnet ['On visiting the tomb of Burns.' See p. 120] that I am at Dumfries. We have dined in Scotland. Burns's tomb is in the Churchyard corner, not very much to my taste, though on a scale large enough to show they wanted to honour him. Mrs. Burns lives in this place; most likely we shall see her to-morrow — This Sonnet I have written in a strange mood, half-asleep. I know not how it is, the Clouds, the Sky, the Houses, all

seem anti-Grecian and anti-Charlemagnish. I will endeavour to get rid of my prejudices and tell you fairly about the Scotch.

[Dumfries,] July 2nd.
In Devonshire they say, 'Well, where be ye going?' Here it is, 'How is it wi' yoursel?' A man on the Coach said the horses took a Hellish heap o' drivin'; the same fellow pointed out Burns's Tomb with a deal of life — 'There de ye see it, amang the trees — white, wi' a roond tap?' The first well-dressed Scotchman we had any conversation with, to our surprise confessed himself a Deist. The careful manner of delivering his opinions, not before he had received several encouraging hints from us, was very amusing. Yesterday was an immense Horse-fair at Dumfries, so that we met numbers of men and women on the road, the women nearly all barefoot, with their shoes and clean stockings in hand, ready to put on and look smart in the Towns. There are plenty of wretched cottages whose smoke has no outlet but by the door. We have now begun upon Whisky, called here Whuskey, — very smart stuff it is. Mixed like our liquors, with sugar and water, 't is called toddy; very pretty drink, and much praised by Burns.

58. TO FANNY KEATS

Dumfries, July 2nd [1818].
MY DEAR FANNY — I intended to have written to you from Kirkcudbright, the town I shall be in to-morrow — but I will write now because my Knapsack has worn my coat in the Seams, my coat has gone to the Tailor's and I have but one Coat to my back in these parts. I must tell you how I went to Liverpool with George and our new Sister and the Gentleman my fellow traveller through the Summer and autumn — We had a tolerable journey to Liverpool — which I left the next morning before George was up for Lancaster — Then we

set off from Lancaster on foot with our Knapsacks on, and have walked a Little zig-zag through the mountains and Lakes of Cumberland and Westmoreland — We came from Carlisle yesterday to this place — We are employed in going up Mountains, looking at strange towns, prying into old ruins and eating very hearty breakfasts. Here we are full in the Midst of broad Scotch 'How is it a' wi' yoursel' — the Girls are walking about bare-footed and in the worst cottages the smoke finds its way out of the door. I shall come home full of news for you and for fear I should choak you by too great a dose at once I must make you used to it by a letter or two. We have been taken for travelling Jewellers, Razor sellers and Spectacle vendors because friend Brown wears a pair. The first place we stopped at with our Knapsacks contained one Richard Bradshaw, a notorious tippler. He stood in the shape of a 3 and ballanced himself as well as he could saying with his nose right in Mr. Brown's face 'Do — yo—u sell spect—ta—cles ? ' Mr. Abbey says we are Don Quixotes — tell him we are more generally taken for Pedlars. All I hope is that we may not be taken for excisemen in this whisky country. We are generally up about 5 walking before breakfast and we complete our 20 miles before dinner. — Yesterday we visited Burns's Tomb and this morning the fine Ruins of Lincluden.

[Auchencairn, same day, July 2.]

I had done thus far when my coat came back fortified at all points — so as we lose no time we set forth again through Galloway — all very pleasant and pretty with no fatigue when one is used to it — We are in the midst of Meg Merrilies's country of whom I suppose you have heard.

[Here follow the lines, 'Meg Merrilies,' p. 243.]

If you like these sort of ballads I will now and then scribble one for you — if I send any to Tom I 'll tell him to send them to you.

[Kirkcudbright, evening of same day, July 2.]

I have so many interruptions that I cannot manage to fill a Letter in one day — since I scribbled the song we have walked through a beautiful Country to Kirkcudbright — at which place I will write you a song about myself —

[Here Keats throws off the nonsense lines 'There was a Naughty Boy,' given in the Appendix, p. 244.]

[Newton Stewart, July 4.]

My dear Fanny, I am ashamed of writing you such stuff, nor would I if it were not for being tired after my day's walking, and ready to tumble into bed so fatigued that when I am asleep you might sew my nose to my great toe and trundle me round the town, like a Hoop, without waking me. Then I get so hungry a Ham goes but a very little way and fowls are like Larks to me — A Batch of Bread I make no more ado with than a sheet of parliament ; and I can eat a Bull's head as easily as I used to do Bull's eyes. I take a whole string of Pork Sausages down as easily as a Pen'orth of Lady's fingers. Ah dear I must soon be contented with an acre or two of oaten cake a hogshead of Milk and a Clothes-basket of Eggs morning noon and night when I get among the Highlanders. Before we see them we shall pass into Ireland and have a chat with the Paddies, and look at the Giant's Causeway which you must have heard of — I have not time to tell you particularly for I have to send a Journal to Tom of whom you shall hear all particulars or from me when I return. Since I began this we have walked sixty miles to Newton Stewart at which place I put in this Letter — to-night we sleep at Glenluce — to-morrow at Portpatrick and the next day we shall cross in the passage boat to Ireland. I hope Miss Abbey has quite recovered. Present my Respects to her and to Mr. and Mrs. Abbey. God bless you.

Your affectionate Brother,   JOHN.

Do write me a Letter directed to *Inverness*, Scotland.

59. TO THOMAS KEATS

Auchtercairn [for Auchencairn,]
3rd [for 2d] July 1818.

MY DEAR TOM — We are now in Meg
Merrilies's country, and have this morning
passed through some parts exactly suited
to her. Kirkcudbright County is very
beautiful, very wild, with craggy hills,
somewhat in the Westmoreland fashion.
We have come down from Dumfries to the
sea-coast part of it. The following song
[the Meg Merrilies piece] you will have
from Dilke, but perhaps you would like it
here.

[Newton Stewart,] July 5th [for 4th].

Yesterday was passed in Kirkcudbright,
the country is very rich, very fine, and with
a little of Devon. I am now writing at
Newton Stewart, six miles into Wigtown.
Our landlady of yesterday said very few
southerners passed hereaways. The children jabber away, as if in a foreign language ; the bare - footed girls look very
much in keeping, I mean with the scenery
about them. Brown praises their cleanli-
ness and appearance of comfort, the neatness of their cottages, etc. — it may be —
they are very squat among trees and fern
and heath and broom, on levels slopes and
heights — but I wish they were as snug as
those up the Devonshire valleys. We are
lodged and entertained in great varieties.
We dined yesterday on dirty Bacon, dirtier
eggs, and dirtiest potatoes, with a slice of
salmon — we breakfast this morning in a
nice carpeted room, with sofa, hair-bot-
tomed Chairs, and green-baized Mahogany.
A spring by the road-side is always welcome : we drink water for dinner, diluted
with a Gill of whisky.

[Donaghadee] July 6.

Yesterday morning we set out from
Glenluce, going some distance round to see
some rivers : they were scarcely worth the
while. We went on to Stranraer, in a

burning sun, and had gone about six miles
when the Mail overtook us : we got up,
were at Port Patrick in a jiffey, and I am
writing now in little Ireland. The dialects
on the neighbouring shores of Scotland and
Ireland are much the same, yet I can perceive a great difference in the nations, from
the chamber-maid at this *nate toone* kept by
Mr. Kelly. She is fair, kind, and ready to
laugh, because she is out of the horrible
dominion of the Scotch Kirk. A Scotch
girl stands in terrible awe of the Elders —
poor little Susannahs, they will scarcely
laugh, and their Kirk is greatly to be
damned. These Kirk-men have done Scotland good (Query ?). They have made
men, women ; old men, young men ; old
women, young women ; boys, girls ; and
all infants careful — so that they are
formed into regular Phalanges of savers
and gainers. Such a thrifty army cannot
fail to enrich their Country, and give it a
greater appearance of Comfort, than that
of their poor rash neighbourhood — these
Kirk-men have done Scotland harm ; they
have banished puns, and laughing, and kissing, etc. (except in cases where the very
danger and crime must make it very gust-
ful). I shall make a full stop at kissing,
for after that there should be a better
parenthesis, and go on to remind you of
the fate of Burns — poor unfortunate fellow, his disposition was Southern — how
sad it is when a luxurious imagination is
obliged, in self-defence, to deaden its delicacy in vulgarity, and rot (?) in things
attainable, that it may not have leisure to
go mad after things which are not. No
man, in such matters, will be content with
the experience of others — It is true that
out of suffering there is no dignity, no
greatness, that in the most abstracted
pleasure there is no lasting happiness —
Yet who would not like to discover over
again that Cleopatra was a Gipsy, Helen a
rogue, and Ruth a deep one ? I have not
sufficient reasoning faculty to settle the
doctrine of thrift, as it is consistent with

the dignity of human Society — with the happiness of Cottagers. All I can do is by plump contrasts ; were the fingers made to squeeze a guinea or a white hand ? — were the lips made to hold a pen or a kiss ? and yet in Cities man is shut out from his fellows if he is poor — the cottager must be very dirty, and very wretched, if she be not thrifty — the present state of society demands this, and this convinces me that the world is very young, and in a very ignorant state — We live in a barbarous age — I would sooner be a wild deer, than a girl under the dominion of the Kirk ; and I would sooner be a wild hog, than be the occasion of a poor Creature's penance before those execrable elders.

It is not so far to the Giant's Causeway as we supposed — We thought it 70, and hear it is only 48 miles — So we shall leave one of our knapsacks here at Donaghadee, take our immediate wants, and be back in a week, when we shall proceed to the County of Ayr. In the Packet yesterday we heard some ballads from two old men — One was a Romance which seemed very poor — then there was 'The Battle of the Boyne,' then 'Robin Huid,' as they call him — 'Before the King you shall go, go, go; before the King you shall go.'

[Stranraer,] July 9th.

We stopped very little in Ireland, and that you may not have leisure to marvel at our speedy return to Port Patrick, I will tell you that it is as dear living in Ireland as at the Hummums — thrice the expense of Scotland — it would have cost us £15 before our return ; moreover we found those 48 miles to be Irish ones, which reach to 70 English — so having walked to Belfast one day, and back to Donaghadee the next, we left Ireland with a fair breeze. We slept last night at Port Patrick, when I was gratified by a letter from you. On our walk in Ireland, we had too much opportunity to see the worse than nakedness, the rags, the dirt and misery, of the poor common Irish — A Scotch cottage, though in that sometimes the smoke has no exit but at the door, is a palace to an Irish one. We could observe that impetuosity in Man and Woman — We had the pleasure of finding our way through a Peat-bog, three miles long at least — dreary, flat, dank, black, and spongy — here and there were poor dirty Creatures, and a few strong men cutting or carting Peat — We heard on passing into Belfast through a most wretched suburb, that most disgusting of all noises, worse than the Bagpipes — the laugh of a Monkey — the chatter of women — the scream of a Macaw — I mean the sound of the Shuttle. What a tremendous difficulty is the improvement of such people. I cannot conceive how a mind "*with child*" of philanthropy could grasp at its possibility — with me it is absolute despair —

At a miserable house of entertainment, half-way between Donaghadee and Belfast, were two men sitting at Whisky — one a labourer, and the other I took to be a drunken weaver — the labourer took me to be a Frenchman, and the other hinted at bounty-money ; saying he was ready to take it — On calling for the letters at Port Patrick, the man snapped out " what Regiment ? " On our return from Belfast we met a sedan — the Duchess of Dunghill. It is no laughing matter though. Imagine the worst dog-kennel you ever saw, placed upon two poles from a mouldy fencing — In such a wretched thing sat a squalid old woman, squat like an ape half-starved, from a scarcity of biscuit in its passage from Madagascar to the Cape, with a pipe in her mouth, and looking out with a round-eyed skinny-lidded inanity; with a sort of horizontal idiotic movement of her head — Squat and lean she sat, and puffed out the smoke, while two ragged tattered girls carried her along. What a thing would be a history of her life and sensations ; I shall endeavour when I have thought a little more, to give you my idea of the difference between the Scotch and Irish — The two

Irishmen I mentioned were speaking of their treatment in England, when the weaver said — " Ah you were a civil man, but I was a drinker."

Till further notice you must direct to Inverness.

Your most affectionate Brother

JOHN.

60. TO THE SAME

Belantree [for Ballantrae,] July 10.

MY DEAR TOM — The reason for my writing these lines ['Ah! ken ye what I met the day,' p. 145] was that Brown wanted to impose a Galloway song upon Dilke — but it won't do. The subject I got from meeting a wedding just as we came down into this place — where I am afraid we shall be imprisoned a while by the weather. Yesterday we came 27 Miles from Stranraer — entered Ayrshire a little beyond Cairn, and had our path through a delightful Country. I shall endeavour that you may follow our steps in this walk — it would be uninteresting in a Book of Travels — it can not be interesting but by my having gone through it. When we left Cairn our Road lay half way up the sides of a green mountainous shore, full of clefts of verdure and eternally varying — sometimes up sometimes down, and over little Bridges going across green chasms of moss, rock and trees — winding about everywhere. After two or three Miles of this we turned suddenly into a magnificent glen finely wooded in Parts — seven Miles long — with a Mountain stream winding down the Midst — full of cottages in the most happy situations — the sides of the Hills covered with sheep — the effect of cattle lowing I never had so finely. At the end we had a gradual ascent and got among the tops of the Mountains whence in a little time I descried in the Sea Ailsa Rock 940 feet high — it was 15 Miles distant and seemed close upon us. The effect of Ailsa with the peculiar perspective of the Sea in connection with the ground we stood on, and the misty rain then falling gave me a complete Idea of a deluge. Ailsa struck me very suddenly — really I was a little alarmed.

[Girvan, same day, July 10.]

Thus far had I written before we set out this morning. Now we are at Girvan 13 Miles north of Belantree. Our Walk has been along a more grand shore to-day than yesterday — Ailsa beside us all the way. — From the heights we could see quite at home Cantire and the large Mountains of Arran, one of the Hebrides. We are in comfortable Quarters. The Rain we feared held up bravely and it has been 'fu fine this day.' — To-morrow we shall be at Ayr.

[Kirkoswald, July 11.]

'T is now the 11th of July and we have come 8 Miles to Breakfast to Kirkoswald. I hope the next Kirk will be Kirk Alloway. I have nothing of consequence to say now concerning our journey — so I will speak as far as I can judge on the Irish and Scotch — I know nothing of the higher Classes — yet I have a persuasion that there the Irish are victorious. As to the profanum vulgus I must incline to the Scotch. They never laugh — but they are always comparatively neat and clean. Their constitutions are not so remote and puzzling as the Irish. The Scotchman will never give a decision on any point — he will never commit himself in a sentence which may be referred to as a meridian in his notion of things — so that you do not know him — and yet you may come in nigher neighbourhood to him than to the Irishman who commits himself in so many places that it dazés your head. A Scotchman's motive is more easily discovered than an Irishman's. A Scotchman will go wisely about to deceive you, an Irishman cunningly. An Irishman would bluster out of any discovery to his disadvantage. A Scotchman would retire perhaps without much desire for revenge. An Irishman likes to be thought a gallous fellow. A Scotchman is contented with himself. It seems to me they are both sensible of the Character they hold in England and act accordingly to Englishmen. Thus the Scotchman will become over grave and over decent and the Irishman over-impetuous. I like a Scotchman best because he is less of a bore — I like the Irishman best because he ought to be more comfortable. — The Scotchman has made up his Mind within himself in a sort of snail shell wisdom. The Irishman is full of strongheaded instinct. The Scotchman is farther in Humanity than the Irishman — there he will stick perhaps when the Irishman will be refined beyond him — for the former thinks he cannot be improved — the latter would grasp at it for ever, place but the good plain before him.

Maybole [same day, July 11].

Since breakfast we have come only four Miles to dinner, not merely, for we have examined in the way two Ruins, one of them very fine, called Crossraguel Abbey — there is a winding Staircase to the top of a little Watch Tower.

Kingswells, July 13.

I have been writing to Reynolds — therefore any particulars since Kirkoswald have escaped me — from said Kirk we went to Maybole to dinner — then we set forward to Burness' town Ayr — the approach to it is extremely fine — quite outwent my expectations — richly meadowed, wooded, heathed and rivuleted — with a grand Sea view terminated by the black Mountains of the isle of Arran. As soon as I saw them so nearly I said to myself 'How is it they did not beckon Burns to some grand attempt at Epic?'

The bonny Doon is the sweetest river I ever saw — overhung with fine trees as far as we could see — We stood some time on the Brig across it, over which Tam o' Shanter fled — we took a pinch of snuff on the Key stone — then we proceeded to the 'auld Kirk Alloway.' As we were looking at it a Farmer pointed the spots where Mungo's Mither hang'd hersel' and 'drunken Charlie brake 's neck's bane.' Then we proceeded to the Cottage he was born in — there was a board to that effect by the door side — it had the same effect as the same sort of memorial at Stratford on Avon. We drank some Toddy to Burns's Memory with an old Man who knew Burns — damn him and damn his anecdotes — he was a great bore — it was impossible for a Southron to understand above 5 words in a hundred. — There was something good in his description of Burns's melancholy the last time he saw him. I was determined to write a sonnet in the Cottage — I did — but it was so bad I cannot venture it here.

Next we walked into Ayr Town and before we went to Tea saw the new Brig and the Auld Brig and Wallace tower. Yesterday we dined with a Traveller. We were talking about Kean. He said he had seen him at Glasgow 'in Othello in the Jew, I mean er, er, er, the Jew in Shylock.' He got bother'd completely in vague ideas of the Jew in Othello, Shylock in the Jew, Shylock in Othello, Othello in Shylock, the Jew in Othello, etc. etc. etc. — he left himself in a mess at last. — Still satisfied with himself he went to the Window and gave an abortive whistle of some tune or other — it might have been Handel. There is no end to these Mistakes — he 'll go and tell people how he has seen 'Malvolio in the Countess' — 'Twelfth night in Midsummer night's dream' — Bottom in much ado about Nothing — Viola in Barrymore — Antony in Cleopatra — Falstaff in the mouse Trap. —

[Glasgow,] July 14.

We enter'd Glasgow last Evening under the most oppressive Stare a body could feel. When we had crossed the Bridge Brown look'd back and said its whole population had turned out to wonder at us — we came on till a drunken Man came up to me — I put him off with my Arm — he returned all up in Arms saying aloud that, 'he had seen all foreigners bu-u-ut he never saw the like o' me.' I was obliged to mention the word Officer and Police before he would desist. — The City of Glasgow I take to be a very fine one — I was astonished to hear it was twice the size of Edinburgh. It is built of Stone and has a much more solid appearance than London. We shall see the Cathedral this morning — they have devilled it into ' High Kirk.' I want very much to know the name of the ship George is gone in — also what port he will land in — I know nothing about it. I hope you are leading a quiet Life and gradually improving. Make a long lounge of the whole Summer — by the time the Leaves fall I shall be near you with plenty of confab — there are a thousand things I cannot write. Take care of yourself — I mean in not being vexed or bothered at anything.

God bless you !   JOHN ——.

61. TO JOHN HAMILTON REYNOLDS

Maybole, July 11 [1818].

MY DEAR REYNOLDS — I 'll not run over the Ground we have passed; that would be merely as bad as telling a dream — unless perhaps I do it in the manner of the Laputan printing press — that is I put down Mountains, Rivers Lakes, dells, glens, Rocks, and Clouds, with beautiful enchanting, Gothic picturesque fine, delightful, enchanting, Grand, sublime — a few blisters, etc. — and now you have our journey thus far : where I begin a letter to you because I am approaching Burns's Cottage very fast. We have made continual inquiries from the time we saw his Tomb at Dumfries — his name of course is known all about — his great reputation among the plodding people is, ' that he wrote a good *mony* sensible things.' One of the pleasantest means of annulling self is approaching such a shrine as the Cottage of Burns — we need not think of his misery — that is all gone, bad luck to it — I shall look upon it hereafter with unmixed pleasure,

as I do upon my Stratford-on-Avon day with Bailey. I shall fill this sheet for you in the Bardie's country, going no further than this till I get into the town of Ayr which will be a 9 miles' walk to Tea.

[Kingswells, July 13.]

We were talking on different and indifferent things, when on a sudden we turned a corner upon the immediate Country of Ayr — the Sight was as rich as possible. I had no Conception that the native place of Burns was so beautiful — the idea I had was more desolate, his 'rigs of Barley' seemed always to me but a few strips of Green on a cold hill — O prejudice! it was as rich as Devon — I endeavoured to drink in the Prospect, that I might spin it out to you as the Silkworm makes silk from Mulberry leaves — I cannot recollect it — Besides all the Beauty, there were the Mountains of Arran Isle, black and huge over the Sea. We came down upon everything suddenly — there were in our way the 'bonny Doon,' with the Brig that Tam o' Shanter crossed, Kirk Alloway, Burns's Cottage, and then the Brigs of Ayr. First we stood upon the Bridge across the Doon; surrounded by every Phantasy of green in Tree, Meadow, and Hill, — the stream of the Doon, as a Farmer told us, is covered with trees from head to foot — you know those beautiful heaths so fresh against the weather of a summer's evening — there was one stretching along behind the trees. I wish I knew always the humour my friends would be in at opening a letter of mine, to suit it to them as nearly as possible. I could always find an egg shell for Melancholy, and as for Merriment a Witty humour will turn anything to Account — My head is sometimes in such a whirl in considering the million likings and antipathies of our Moments — that I can get into no settled strain in my Letters. My Wig ! Burns and sentimentality coming across you and Frank Fladgate in the office — O scenery that thou shouldst be crushed between two Puns — As for them I venture the rascalliest in the Scotch Region — I hope Brown does not put them punctually in his journal — If he does I must sit on the cutty-stool all next winter. We went to Kirk Alloway — 'a Prophet is no Prophet in his own Country' — We went to the Cottage and took some Whisky. I wrote a sonnet for the mere sake of writing some lines under the roof — they are so bad I cannot transcribe them — The Man at the Cottage was a great Bore with his Anecdotes — I hate the rascal — his Life consists in fuz, fuzzy, fuzziest — He drinks glasses five for the Quarter and twelve for the hour — he is a mahogany-faced old Jackass who knew Burns — He ought to have been kicked for having spoken to him. He calls himself "a curious old Bitch ".— but he is a flat old dog — I should like to employ Caliph Vathek to kick him. O the flummery of a birthplace! Cant! Cant! Cant! It is enough to give a spirit the guts-ache — Many a true word, they say, is spoken in jest — this may be because his gab hindered my sublimity: the flat dog made me write a flat sonnet. My dear Reynolds — I cannot write about scenery and visitings — Fancy is indeed less than a present palpable reality, but it is greater than remembrance — you would lift your eyes from Homer only to see close before you the real Isle of Tenedos — you would rather read Homer afterwards than remember yourself — One song of Burns's is of more worth to you than all I could think for a whole year in his native country. His Misery is a dead weight upon the nimbleness of one's quill — I tried to forget it — to drink Toddy without any Care — to write a merry sonnet — it won't do — he talked with Bitches — he drank with Blackguards, he was miserable — We can see horribly clear, in the works of such a Man his whole life, as if we were God's spies. — What were his addresses to Jean in the latter part of his life ? I should not speak so to you — yet why not — you are

not in the same case, you are in the right path, and you shall not be deceived. I have spoken to you against Marriage, but it was general — the Prospect in those matters has been to me so blank, that I have not been unwilling to die — I would not now, for I have inducements to Life — I must see my little Nephews in America, and I must see you marry your lovely Wife. My sensations are sometimes deadened for weeks together — but believe me I have more than once yearned for the time of your happiness to come, as much as I could for myself after the lips of Juliet. — From the tenor of my occasional rodomontade in chit-chat, you might have been deceived concerning me in these points — upon my soul, I have been getting more and more close to you, every day, ever since I knew you, and now one of the first pleasures I look to is your happy Marriage — the more, since I have felt the pleasure of loving a sister in Law. I did not think it possible to become so much attached in so short a time — Things like these, and they are real, have made me resolve to have a care of my health — you must be as careful.

The rain has stopped to-day at the end of a dozen Miles, yet we hope to see Loch Lomond the day after to-morrow; — I will piddle out my information, as Rice says, next Winter, at any time when a substitute is wanted for Vingt-un. We bear the fatigue very well — 20 Miles a day in general — A Cloud came over us in getting up Skiddaw — I hope to be more lucky in Ben Lomond — and more lucky still in Ben Nevis. What I think you would enjoy is poking about Ruins — sometimes Abbey, sometimes Castle. The short stay we made in Ireland has left few remembrances — but an old woman in a dog-kennel Sedan with a pipe in her Mouth, is what I can never forget — I wish I may be able to give you an idea of her — Remember me to your Mother and Sisters, and tell your Mother how I hope she will pardon me for having a scrap of paper [30] pasted in the

Book sent to her. I was driven on all sides and had not time to call on Taylor — So Bailey is coming to Cumberland — well, if you 'll let me know where at Inverness, I will call on my return and pass a little time with him — I am glad 't is not Scotland — Tell my friends I do all I can for them, that is, drink their healths in Toddy. Perhaps I may have some lines by and by to send you fresh, on your own Letter — Tom has a few to show you.

Your affectionate friend
JOHN KEATS.

62. TO THOMAS KEATS

Cairn-something [Cairndow], July 17, [1818].

MY DEAR TOM — Here 's Brown going on so that I cannot bring to mind how the two last days have vanished — for example he says The Lady of the Lake went to Rock herself to sleep on Arthur's seat and the Lord of the Isles coming to Press a Piece. . . . I told you last how we were stared at in Glasgow — we are not out of the Crowd yet. Steam Boats on Loch Lomond and Barouches on its sides take a little from the Pleasure of such romantic chaps as Brown and I. The Banks of the Clyde are extremely beautiful — the north end of Loch Lomond grand in excess — the entrance at the lower end to the narrow part from a little distance is precious good — the Evening was beautiful nothing could surpass our fortune in the weather — yet was I worldly enough to wish for a fleet of chivalry Barges with Trumpets and Banners just to die away before me into that blue place among the mountains — I must give you an outline as well as I can.

No' B — the Water was a fine Blue silvered and the Mountains a dark purple, the Sun setting aslant behind them — meantime the head of ben Lomond was covered with a rich Pink Cloud. We did not ascend Ben Lomond — the price being very high and a half a day of rest being quite acceptable. We were up at 4 this morning and have walked to breakfast 15 Miles through two Tremendous Glens — at the end of the first there is a place called rest and be thankful which we took for an Inn — it was nothing but a Stone and so we were cheated into 5 more Miles to Breakfast — I have just been bathing in Loch Fyne a salt water Lake opposite the Windows, — quite pat and fresh but for the cursed Gad flies — damn 'em they have been at me ever since I left the Swan and two necks.[40]

[Keats here objurgates The Gadfly in the lines printed on p. 245.]

[Inverary, July 18.]

Last Evening we came around the End of Loch Fyne to Inverary — the Duke of Argyle's Castle is very modern magnificent and more so from the place it is in — the woods seem old enough to remember two or three changes in the Crags about them — the Lake was beautiful and there was a Band at a distance by the Castle. I must say I enjoyed two or three common tunes — but nothing could stifle the horrors of a solo on the Bag-pipe — I thought the Beast would never have done. — Yet was I doomed to hear another. — On entering Inverary we saw a Play Bill. Brown was knocked up from new shoes — so I went to the Barn alone where I saw the Stranger accompanied by a Bag-pipe. There they went on about interesting creaters and human nater till the Curtain fell and then came the Bag-pipe. When Mrs. Haller fainted down went the Curtain and out came the Bag-pipe — at the heartrending, shoemending reconciliation the Piper blew amain. I never read or saw this play before ; not the Bag-pipe nor the wretched players themselves were little in comparison with it — thank heaven it has been scoffed at lately almost to a fashion —

[The sonnet printed above, p. 246, is here copied.]

I think we are the luckiest fellows in Christendom — Brown could not proceed this morning on account of his feet and lo there is thunder and rain.

[Kilmelford,] July 20th.

For these two days past we have been so badly accommodated more particularly in coarse food that I have not been at all in cue to write. Last night poor Brown with his feet blistered and scarcely able to walk, after a trudge of 20 Miles down the Side of Loch Awe had no supper but Eggs and Oat Cake — we have lost the sight of white bread entirely — Now we have eaten nothing but Eggs all day — about 10 a piece and they had become sickening — To-day we have fared rather better — but no oat Cake wanting — we had a small Chicken and even a good bottle of Port but all together the fare is too coarse — I feel it a little. — Another week will break us in. I forgot to tell you that when we came through Glenside it was early in the morning and we were pleased with the noise of Shepherds, Sheep and dogs in the misty heights close above us — we saw none of them for some time, till two came in

sight creeping among the Crags like Emmets, yet their voices came quite plainly to us — The approach to Loch Awe was very solemn towards nightfall — the first glance was a streak of water deep in the Bases of large black Mountains. — We had come along a complete mountain road, where if one listened there was not a sound but that of Mountain Streams. We walked 20 Miles by the side of Loch Awe — every ten steps creating a new and beautiful picture — sometimes through little wood — there are two islands on the Lake each with a beautiful ruin — one of them rich in ivy. — We are detained this morning by the rain. I will tell you exactly where we are. We are between Loch Craignish and the sea just opposite Long [Luing] Island. Yesterday our walk was of this description — the near Hills were not very lofty but many of them steep, beautifully wooded — the distant Mountains in the Hebrides very grand, the Saltwater Lakes coming up between Crags and Islands full tide and scarcely ruffled — sometimes appearing as one large Lake, sometimes as three distinct ones in different directions. At one point we saw afar off a rocky opening into the main sea. — We have also seen an Eagle or two. They move about without the least motion of Wings when in an indolent fit. — I am for the first time in a country where a foreign Language is spoken — they gabble away Gaelic at a vast rate — numbers of them speak English. There are not many Kilts in Argyleshire — at Fort William they say a Man is not admitted into Society without one — the Ladies there have a horror at the indecency of Breeches. I cannot give you a better idea of Highland Life than by describing the place we are in. The Inn or public is by far the best house in the immediate neighbourhood. It has a white front with tolerable windows — the table I am writing on surprises me as being a nice flapped Mahogany one. . . . You may if you peep see through the floor chinks into the ground rooms. The old Grandmother of the house seems intelligent though not over clean. *N. B.* No snuff being to be had in the village she made us some. The Guid Man is a rough-looking hardy stout Man who I think does not speak so much English as the Guid wife who is very obliging and sensible and moreover though stockingless has a pair of old Shoes — Last night some Whisky Men sat up clattering Gaelic till I am sure one o'Clock to our great annoyance. There is a Gaelic testament on the Drawers in the next room. White and blue China ware has crept all about here — Yesterday there passed a Donkey laden with tin-pots — opposite the Window there are hills in a Mist — a few Ash trees and a mountain stream at a little distance. — They possess a few head of Cattle. — If you had gone round to the back of the House just now — you would have seen more hills in a Mist — some dozen wretched black Cottages scented of peat smoke which finds its way by the door or a hole in the roof — a girl here and there barefoot. There was one little thing driving Cows down a slope like a mad thing. There was another standing at the cowhouse door rather pretty fac'd all up to the ankles in dirt.

[Oban, July 21.]

We have walk'd 15 Miles in a soaking rain to Oban opposite the Isle of Mull which is so near Staffa we had thought to pass to it — but the expense is 7 Guineas and those rather extorted. — Staffa you see is a fashionable place and therefore every one concerned with it either in this town or the Island are what you call up. 'T is like paying sixpence for an apple at the playhouse — this irritated me and Brown was not best pleased — we have therefore resolved to set northward for fort William to-morrow morning. I fed upon a bit of white Bread to-day like a Sparrow — it was very fine — I cannot manage the cursed Oat Cake. Remember me to all and let me hear a good account of you at Inverness — I am sorry Georgy had not those lines. Good-bye.

Your affectionate Brother JOHN ——.

63. TO BENJAMIN BAILEY

Inverary, July 18 [1818].

MY DEAR BAILEY — The only day I have had a chance of seeing you when you were last in London I took every advantage of — some devil led you out of the way — Now I have written to Reynolds to tell me where you will be in Cumberland — so that I cannot miss you. And when I see you, the first thing I shall do will be to read that about Milton and Ceres, and Proserpine — for though I am not going after you to John o' Grot's, it will be but poetical to say so. And here, Bailey, I will say a few words written in a sane and seber mind, a very scarce thing with me, for they may, hereafter, save you a great deal of trouble about me, which you do not deserve, and for which I ought to be bastinadoed. I carry all matters to an extreme — so that when I have any little vexation, it grows in five minutes into a theme for Sophocles. Then, and in that temper, if I write to any friend, I have so little self-possession that I give him matter for grieving at the very time perhaps when I am laughing at a Pun. Your last letter made me blush for the pain I had given you — I know my own disposition so well that I am certain of writing many times hereafter in the same strain to you — now, you know how far to believe in them. You must allow for Imagination. I know I shall not be able to help it.

I am sorry you are grieved at my not continuing my visits to Little Britain — Yet I think I have as far as a Man can do who has Books to read and subjects to think upon — for that reason I have been nowhere else except to Wentworth Place so nigh at hand — moreover I have been too often in a state of health that made it prudent not to hazard the night air. Yet, farther, I will confess to you that I cannot enjoy Society small or numerous — I am certain that our fair friends are glad I should come for the mere sake of my coming; but I am certain I bring with me a vexation they are better without — If I can possibly at any time feel my temper coming upon me I refrain even from a promised visit. I am certain I have not a right feeling towards women — at this moment, I am striving to be just to them, but I cannot — Is it because they fall so far beneath my boyish Imagination? When I was a schoolboy I thought a fair woman a pure Goddess; my mind was a soft nest in which some one of them slept, though she knew it not. I have no right to expect more than their reality — I thought them ethereal above men — I find them perhaps equal — great by comparison is very small. Insult may be inflicted in more ways than by word or action — One who is tender of being insulted does not like to think an insult against another. I do not like to think insults in a lady's company — I commit a crime with her which absence would not have known. Is it not extraordinary? — when among men, I have no evil thoughts, no malice, no spleen — I feel free to speak or to be silent — I can listen, and from every one I can learn — my hands are in my pockets, I am free from all suspicion and comfortable. When I am among women, I have evil thoughts, malice, spleen — I cannot speak, or be silent — I am full of suspicions and therefore listen to nothing — I am in a hurry to be gone. You must be charitable and put all this perversity to my being disappointed since my boyhood. Yet with such feelings I am happier alone among crowds of men, by myself, or with a friend or two. With all this, trust me, I have not the least idea that men of different feelings and inclinations are more short-sighted than myself. I never rejoiced more than at my Brother's marriage, and shall do so at that of any of my friends. I must absolutely get over

this — but how? the only way is to find the root of the evil, and so cure it ' with backward mutters of dissevering power' — that is a difficult thing; for an obstinate Prejudice can seldom be produced but from a gordian complication of feelings, which must take time to unravel, and care to keep unravelled. I could say a good deal about this, but I will leave it, in hopes of better and more worthy dispositions — and also content that I am wronging no one, for after all I do think better of womankind than to suppose they care whether Mister John Keats five feet high likes them or not. You appeared to wish to know my moods on this subject — don't think it a bore my dear fellow, it shall be my Amen. I should not have consented to myself these four months tramping in the highlands, but that I thought it would give me more experience, rub off more prejudice, use to more hardship, identify finer scenes, load me with grander mountains, and strengthen more my reach in Poetry, than would stopping at home among books, even though I should reach Homer. By this time I am comparatively a Mountaineer. I have been among wilds and mountains too much to break out much about their grandeur. I have fed upon oat-cake — not long enough to be very much attached to it. — The first mountains I saw, though not so large as some I have since seen, weighed very solemnly upon me. The effect is wearing away — yet I like them mainly.

[Island of Mull, July 22.]
We have come this Evening with a guide — for without was impossible — into the middle of the Isle of Mull, pursuing our cheap journey to Iona, and perhaps Staffa. We would not follow the common and fashionable mode, from the great Imposition of Expense. We have come over heath and rock, and river and bog, to what in England would be called a horrid place. Yet it belongs to a Shepherd pretty well off perhaps. The family speak not a word

but Gaelic, and we have not yet seen their faces for the smoke, which, after visiting every cranny (not excepting my eyes very much incommoded for writing), finds its way out at the door. I am more comfortable than I could have imagined in such a place, and so is Brown. The people are all very kind — We lost our way a little yesterday; and inquiring at a Cottage, a young woman without a word threw on her cloak and walked a mile in a mizzling rain and splashy way to put us right again.

I could not have had a greater pleasure in these parts than your mention of my sister. She is very much prisoned from me. I am afraid it will be some time before I can take her to many places I wish. I trust we shall see you ere long in Cumberland — At least I hope I shall, before my visit to America, more than once. I intend to pass a whole year there, if I live to the completion of the three next. My sister's welfare, and the hopes of such a stay in America, will make me observe your advice. I shall be prudent and more careful of my health than I have been. I hope you will be about paying your first visit to Town after settling when we come into Cumberland — Cumberland however will be no distance to me after my present journey. I shall spin to you in a Minute. I begin to get rather a contempt of distances. I hope you will have a nice convenient room for a library. Now you are so well in health, do keep it up by never missing your dinner, by not reading hard, and by taking proper exercise. You 'll have a horse, I suppose, so you must make a point of sweating him. You say I must study Dante — well, the only Books I have with me are those 3 little volumes.[41] I read that fine passage you mention a few days ago. Your letter followed me from Hampstead to Port-Patrick, and thence to Glasgow. You must think me by this time a very pretty fellow. One of the pleasantest bouts we have had was our walk to Burns's Cottage, over the Doon, and past Kirk

Alloway. I had determined to write a Sonnet in the Cottage. I did — but lawk! it was so wretched I destroyed it — however in a few days afterwards I wrote some lines cousin-german to the circumstance, which I will transcribe, or rather cross-scribe in the front of this. [Here follow the lines printed on pp. 246, 247.]

Reynolds's illness has made him a new man — he will be stronger than ever — before I left London he was really getting a fat face. Brown keeps on writing volumes of adventures to Dilke. When we get in of an evening and I have perhaps taken my rest on a couple of chairs, he affronts my indolence and Luxury by pulling out of his knapsack 1st his paper — 2ndly his pens and last his ink. Now I would not care if he would change a little. I say now why not Bailey, take out his pens first sometimes — But I might as well tell a hen to hold up her head before she drinks instead of afterwards.

Your affectionate Friend, JOHN KEATS.

64. TO THOMAS KEATS

Dun an cullen, [Derrynaculan ?]
Island of Mull [July 23, 1818].

MY DEAR TOM — Just after my last had gone to the Post, in came one of the Men with whom we endeavoured to agree about going to Staffa — he said what a pity it was we should turn aside and not see the curiosities. So we had a little talk, and finally agreed that he should be our guide across the Isle of Mull. We set out, crossed two ferries — one to the Isle of Kerrara, of little distance ; the other from Kerrara to Mull 9 Miles across — we did it in forty minutes with a fine Breeze. The road through the Island, or rather the track, is the most dreary you can think of — between dreary Mountains, over bog and rock and river with our Breeches tucked up and our Stockings in hand. About 8 o'Clock we arrived at a shepherd's Hut, into which we could scarcely get for the Smoke through a door lower than my Shoulders. We found our way into a little compartment with the rafters and turf-thatch blackened with smoke, the earth floor full of Hills and Dales. We had some white Bread with us, made a good supper, and slept in our Clothes in some Blankets; our Guide snored on another little bed about an Arm's length off. This morning we came about sax Miles to Breakfast, by rather a better path, and we are now in by comparison a Mansion. Our Guide is I think a very obliging fellow — in the way this morning he sang us two Gaelic songs — one made by a Mrs. Brown on her husband's being drowned, the other a jacobin one on Charles Stuart. For some days Brown has been enquiring out his Genealogy here — he thinks his Grandfather came from long Island. He got a parcel of people about him at a Cottage door last Evening, chatted with ane who had been a Miss Brown, and who I think from a likeness, must have been a Relation — he jawed with the old Woman — flattered a young one — kissed a child who was afraid of his Spectacles and finally drank a pint of Milk. They handle his Spectacles as we do a sensitive leaf.

[Oban,] July 26th.

Well — we had a most wretched walk of 37 Miles across the Island of Mull and then we crossed to Iona or Icolmkill — from Icolmkill we took a boat at a bargain to take us to Staffa and land us at the head of Loch Nakgal, [Loch na Keal] whence we should only have to walk half the distance to Oban again and on a better road. All this is well passed and done, with this singular piece of Luck, that there was an interruption in the bad Weather just as we saw Staffa at which it is impossible to land but in a tolerable Calm sea. But I will first mention Icolmkill — I know not whether you have heard much about this Island; I never did before I came nigh it. It is rich in the most interesting Antiquities. Who would expect to find the ruins of a fine Cathedral Church, of Cloisters Col-

leges Monasteries and Nunneries in so remote an Island? The beginning of these things was in the sixth Century, under the superstition of a would-be-Bishop-saint, who landed from Ireland, and chose the spot from its Beauty — for at that time the now treeless place was covered with magnificent Woods. Columba in the Gaelic is Colm, signifying Dove — Kill signifies church, and I is as good as Island — so I-colm-kill means the Island of Saint Columba's Church. Now this Saint Columba became the Dominic of the barbarian Christians of the north and was famed also far south — but more especially was reverenced by the Scots the Picts the Norwegians the Irish. In a course of years perhaps the Island was considered the most holy ground of the north, and the old Kings of the aforementioned nations chose it for their burial-place. We were shown a spot in the Churchyard where they say 61 Kings are buried 48 Scotch from Fergus II. to Macbeth 8 Irish 4 Norwegians and 1 French — they lie in rows compact. Then we were shown other matters of later date, but still very ancient — many tombs of Highland Chieftains — their effigies in complete armour, face upwards, black and moss-covered — Abbots and Bishops of the island always of one of the chief Clans. There were plenty Macleans and Macdonnels; among these latter, the famous Macdonel Lord of the Isles. There have been 300 Crosses in the Island but the Presbyterians destroyed all but two, one of which is a very fine one, and completely covered with a shaggy coarse Moss. The old Schoolmaster, an ignorant little man but reckoned very clever, showed us these things. He is a Maclean, and as much above 4 foot as he is under 4 foot three inches. He stops at one glass of whisky unless you press another and at the second unless you press a third —

I am puzzled how to give you an Idea of Staffa. It can only be represented by a first-rate drawing. One may compare the surface of the Island to a roof — this roof is supported by grand pillars of basalt standing together as thick as honeycombs. The finest thing is Fingal's Cave — it is entirely a hollowing out of Basalt Pillars. Suppose now the Giants who rebelled against Jove had taken a whole Mass of black Columns and bound them together like bunches of matches — and then with immense axes had made a cavern in the body of these columns — Of course the roof and floor must be composed of the broken ends of the Columns — such is Fingal's Cave, except that the Sea has done the work of excavations, and is continually dashing there — so that we walk along the sides of the cave on the pillars which are left as if for convenient stairs. The roof is arched somewhat gothic-wise, and the length of some of the entire side-pillars is fifty feet. About the island you might seat an army of Men each on a pillar. The length of the Cave is 120 feet, and from its extremity the view into the sea, through the large Arch at the entrance — the colour of the columns is a sort of black with a lurking gloom of purple therein. For solemnity and grandeur it far surpasses the finest Cathedral. At the extremity of the Cave there is a small perforation into another cave, at which the waters meeting and buffeting each other there is sometimes produced a report as of a cannon heard as far as Iona, which must be 12 Miles. As we approached in the boat, there was such a fine swell of the sea that the pillars appeared rising immediately out of the crystal. But it is impossible to describe it. [The lines 'At Fingal's Cave,' p. 122, are here given in a variant.]

I am sorry I am so indolent as to write such stuff as this. It can't be helped. The western coast of Scotland is a most strange place — it is composed of rocks, Mountains, mountainous and rocky Islands intersected by lochs — you can go but a short distance anywhere from salt water in the highlands. I have a slight sore throat and think it best to stay a day or two at Oban — then we shall proceed to Fort William and Inverness, where I am anxious to be on account of a Letter from you. Brown in his Letters puts down every little circumstance. I should like to do the same, but I confess myself too indolent, and besides next winter everything will come up in prime order as we verge on such and such things.

Have you heard in any way of George? I should think by this time he must have landed. I in my carelessness never thought of knowing where a letter would find him on the other side — I think Baltimore, but I am afraid of directing it to the wrong place. I shall begin some chequer work for him directly, and it will be ripe for the post by the time I hear from you next after this. I assure you I often long for a seat and a Cup o' tea at Well Walk, especially now that mountains, castles, and Lakes are becoming common to me. Yet I would rather summer it out, for on the whole I am happier than when I have time to be glum — perhaps it may cure me. Immediately on my return I shall begin studying hard, with a peep at the theatre now and then — and depend upon it I shall be very luxurious. With respect to Women I think I shall be able to conquer my passions hereafter better than I have yet done. You will help me to talk of George next winter, and we will go now and then to see Fanny. Let me hear a good account of your health and comfort, telling me truly how you do alone. Remember me to all including Mr. and Mrs. Bentley.

Your most affectionate Brother
JOHN.

65. TO THE SAME

Letter Findlay, August 3 [1818].
Ah mio Ben.

MY DEAR TOM — We have made but poor progress lately, chiefly from bad weather, for my throat is in a fair way of getting quite well, so I have had nothing of consequence to tell you till yesterday when we went up Ben Nevis, the highest Mountain in Great Britain. On that account I will never ascend another in this empire — Skiddaw is nothing to it either in height or in difficulty. It is above 4300 feet from the Sea level, and Fortwilliam stands at the head of a Salt water Lake, consequently we took it completely from that level. I am heartily glad it is done — it is almost like a fly crawling up a wainscoat. Imagine the task of mounting ten Saint Pauls without the convenience of Staircases. We set out about five in the morning with a Guide in the Tartan and Cap, and soon arrived at the foot of the first ascent which we immediately began upon. After much fag and tug and a rest and a glass of whisky apiece we gained the top of the first rise and saw then a tremendous chap above us, which the guide said was still far from the top. After the first Rise our way lay along a heath valley in which there was a Loch — after about a Mile in this Valley we began upon the next ascent, more formidable by far than the last, and kept mounting with short intervals of rest until we got above all vegetation, among nothing but loose Stones which lasted us to the very top. The Guide said we had three Miles of a stony ascent — we gained the first tolerable level after the valley to the height of what in the Valley we had thought the top and saw still above us another huge crag which still the Guide said was not the top — to that we made with an obstinate fag, and having gained it there came on a Mist, so that from that part to the very top we walked in a Mist. The whole immense head of the Mountain is composed of large loose stones — thousands of acres. Before we had got halfway up we passed large patches of snow and near the top there is a chasm some hundred feet deep completely glutted with it. — Talking of chasms they are the finest wonder of the whole — they appear great rents in the very heart of the mountain

though they are not, being at the side of it, but other huge crags arising round it give the appearance to Nevis of a shattered heart or Core in itself. These Chasms are 1500 feet in depth and are the most tremendous places I have ever seen — they turn one giddy if you choose to give way to it. We tumbled in large stones and set the echoes at work in fine style. Sometimes these chasms are tolerably clear, sometimes there is a misty cloud which seems to steam up and sometimes they are entirely smothered with clouds.

After a little time the Mist cleared away but still there were large Clouds about attracted by old Ben to a certain distance so as to form as it appeared large dome curtains which kept sailing about, opening and shutting at intervals here and there and everywhere: so that although we did not see one vast wide extent of prospect all round we saw something perhaps finer — these cloud veils opening with a dissolving motion and showing us the mountainous region beneath as through a loophole — these cloudy loopholes ever varying and discovering fresh prospect east, west, north and south. Then it was misty again, and again it was fair — then puff came a cold breeze of wind and bared a craggy chap we had not yet seen though in close neighbourhood. Every now and then we had overhead blue Sky clear and the sun pretty warm. I do not know whether I can give you an Idea of the prospect from a large Mountain top. You are on a stony plain which of course makes you forget you are on any but low ground — the horizon or rather edges of this plain being above 4000 feet above the Sea hide all the Country immediately beneath you, so that the next object you see all round next to the edges of the flat top are the Summits of Mountains of some distance off. As you move about on all sides you see more or less of the near neighbour country according as the Mountain you stand upon is in different parts steep or rounded — but the most new thing of all is the sudden leap of the eye from the extremity of what appears a plain into so vast a distance. On one part of the top there is a handsome pile of Stones done pointedly by some soldiers of artillery; I clim[b]ed on to them and so got a little higher than old Ben himself. It was not so cold as I expected — yet cold enough for a glass of Whisky now and then. There is not a more fickle thing than the top of a Mountain — what would a Lady give to change her head-dress as often and with as little trouble! — There are a good many red deer upon Ben Nevis — we did not see one — the dog we had with us kept a very sharp look out and really languished for a bit of a worry. I have said nothing yet of our getting on among the loose stones large and small sometimes on two, sometimes on three, sometimes four legs — sometimes two and stick, sometimes three and stick, then four again, then two, then a jump, so that we kept on ringing changes on foot, hand, stick, jump, boggle, stumble, foot, hand, foot (very gingerly), stick again, and then again a game at all fours. After all there was one Mrs. Cameron of 50 years of age and the fattest woman in all Inverness-shire who got up this Mountain some few years ago — true she had her servants — but then she had her self. She ought to have hired Sisyphus, — 'Up the high hill he heaves a huge round — Mrs. Cameron.' 'T is said a little conversation took place between the mountain and the Lady. After taking a glass of Whisky as she was tolerably seated at ease she thus began —

[Here follow the nonsense verses and intercalary sentences, given on pp. 247, 248.]

Over leaf you will find a Sonnet I wrote on the top of Ben Nevis, [see p. 123]. We have just entered Inverness. I have three Letters from you and one from Fanny — and one from Dilke. I would set about crossing this all over for you but I will first write to Fanny and Mrs. Wylie. Then I will begin another to you and not before because I think it better you should have

this as soon as possible. My Sore throat is not quite well and I intend stopping here a few days.

Good-bye till to morrow.

Your most affectionate Brother
JOHN ——.

66. TO MRS. WYLIE

Inverness, August 6 [1818].

MY DEAR MADAM — It was a great regret to me that I should leave all my friends, just at the moment when I might have helped to soften away the time for them. I wanted not to leave my brother Tom, but more especially, believe me, I should like to have remained near you, were it but for an atom of consolation after parting with so dear a daughter. My brother George has ever been more than a brother to me; he has been my greatest friend, and I can never forget the sacrifice you have made for his happiness. As I walk along the Mountains here I am full of these things, and lay in wait, as it were, for the pleasure of seeing you immediately on my return to town. I wish, above all things, to say a word of Comfort to you, but I know not how. It is impossible to prove that black is white; it is impossible to make out that sorrow is joy, or joy is sorrow.

Tom tells me that you called on Mr. Haslam, with a newspaper giving an account of a gentleman in a Fur cap falling over a precipice in Kirkcudbrightshire. If it was me, I did it in a dream, or in some magic interval between the first and second cup of tea; which is nothing extraordinary when we hear that Mahomet, in getting out of Bed, upset a jug of water, and, whilst it was falling, took a fortnight's trip, as it seemed, to Heaven; yet was back in time to save one drop of water being spilt. As for Fur caps, I do not remember one beside my own, except at Carlisle: this was a very good Fur cap I met in High Street, and I daresay was the unfortunate one. I daresay that the fates, seeing but two Fur caps in the north, thought it too extraordinary, and so threw the dies which of them should be drowned. The lot fell upon Jones: I daresay his name was Jones. All I hope is that the gaunt Ladies said not a word about hanging; if they did I shall repent that I was not half-drowned in Kirkcudbright. Stop! let me see!—being half-drowned by falling from a precipice, is a very romantic affair: why should I not take it to myself? How glorious to be introduced in a drawing-room to a Lady who reads Novels, with 'Mr. So-and-so—Miss So-and-so; Miss So-and-so, this is Mr. So-and-so, who fell off a precipice and was half-drowned.' Now I refer to you, whether I should lose so fine an opportunity of making my fortune. No romance lady could resist me—none. Being run under a Waggon—sidelamed in a playhouse, Apoplectic through Brandy—and a thousand other tolerably decent things for badness, would be nothing, but being tumbled over a precipice into the sea—oh! it would make my fortune—especially if you could contrive to hint, from this bulletin's authority, that I was not upset on my own account, but that I dashed into the waves after Jessy of Dumblane, and pulled her out by the hair. But that, alas! she was dead, or she would have made me happy with her hand—however in this you may use your own discretion. But I must leave joking, and seriously aver, that I have been very romantic indeed among these Mountains and Lakes. I have got wet through, day after day—eaten oat-cake, and drank Whisky—walked up to my knees in Bog—got a sore throat—gone to see Icolmkill and Staffa; met with wholesome food just here and there as it happened—went up Ben Nevis, and—N. B., came down again. Sometimes when I am rather tired I lean rather languishingly on a rock, and long for some famous Beauty to get down from her Palfrey in passing, approach me, with—her saddle-bags, and give me—a dozen or two capital roastbeef Sandwiches.

When I come into a large town, you know there is no putting one's Knapsack into one's fob, so the people stare. We have been taken for Spectacle-vendors, Razor-sellers, Jewellers, travelling linen-drapers, Spies, Excisemen, and many things I have no idea of. When I asked for letters at Port Patrick, the man asked what regiment? I have had a peep also at little Ireland. Tell Henry I have not camped quite on the bare Earth yet, but nearly as bad, in walking through Mull, for the Shepherds' huts you can scarcely breathe in, for the Smoke which they seem to endeavour to preserve for smoking on a large scale. Besides riding about 400, we have walked above 600 Miles, and may therefore reckon ourselves as set out.

I assure you, my dear Madam, that one of the greatest pleasures I shall have on my return, will be seeing you, and that I shall ever be

Yours, with the greatest respect and sincerity, JOHN KEATS.

67. TO FANNY KEATS

Hampstead, August 18 [1818].

MY DEAR FANNY—I am afraid you will think me very negligent in not having answered your Letter—I see it is dated June 12. I did not arrive at Inverness till the 8th of this Month so I am very much concerned at your being disappointed so long a time. I did not intend to have returned to London so soon but have a bad sore throat from a cold I caught in the island of Mull: therefore I thought it best to get home as soon as possible, and went on board the Smack from Cromarty. We had a nine days' passage and were landed at London Bridge yesterday. I shall have a good deal to tell you about Scotland—I would begin here but I have a confounded toothache. Tom has not been getting better since I left London and for the last fortnight has been worse than ever—he has been getting a little better for these two or three days. I shall ask Mr. Abbey to let me bring you to Hampstead. If Mr. A. should see this Letter tell him that he still must if he pleases forward the Post Bill to Perth as I have empowered my fellow traveller to receive it. I have a few Scotch pebbles for you from the Island of Icolm-kill — I am afraid they are rather shabby — I did not go near the Mountain of Cairn Gorm. I do not know the Name of George's ship — the Name of the Port he has gone to is Philadelphia whence he will travel to the Settlement across the Country — I will tell you all about this when I see you. The Title of my last Book is Endymion — you shall have one soon. — I would not advise you to play on the Flageolet — however I will get you one if you please. I will speak to Mr. Abbey on what you say concerning school. I am sorry for your poor Canary. You shall have another volume of my first Book. My toothache keeps on so that I cannot write with any pleasure — all I can say now is that your Letter is a very nice one without fault and that you will hear from or see in a few days if his throat will let him,

Your affectionate Brother   JOHN.

68. TO THE SAME

Hampstead, Tuesday [August 25, 1818].

MY DEAR FANNY — I have just written to Mr. Abbey to ask him to let you come and see poor Tom who has lately been much worse. He is better at present — sends his Love to you and wishes much to see you — I hope he will shortly — I have not been able to come to Walthamstow on his account as well as a little Indisposition of my own. I have asked Mr. A. to write me — if he does not mention anything of it to you, I will tell you what reasons he has though I do not think he will make any objection. Write me what you want with a Flageolet and I will get one ready for you by the time you come.

Your affectionate Brother JOHN ——.

69. TO JANE REYNOLDS

Well Walk, September 1st [1818].

MY DEAR JANE — Certainly your kind note would rather refresh than trouble me, and so much the more would your coming if as you say, it could be done without agitating my Brother too much. Receive on your Hearth our deepest thanks for your Solicitude concerning us.

I am glad John is not hurt, but gone safe into Devonshire — I shall be in great expectation of his Letter — but the promise of it in so anxious and friendly a way I prize more than a hundred. I shall be in town to-day on some business with my guardian 'as was' with scarce a hope of being able to call on you. For these two last days Tom has been more cheerful: you shall hear again soon how he will be.

Remember us particularly to your Mother.

Your sincere friend   JOHN KEATS.

70. TO CHARLES WENTWORTH DILKE

[Hampstead, September 21, 1818.]

MY DEAR DILKE — According to the Wentworth place Bulletin you have left Brighton much improved : therefore now a few lines will be more of a pleasure than a bore. I have things to say to you, and would fain begin upon them in this fourth line : but I have a Mind too well regulated to proceed upon anything without due preliminary remarks. — You may perhaps have observed that in the simple process of eating radishes I never begin at the root but constantly dip the little green head in the salt — that in the Game of Whist if I have an ace I constantly play it first. So how can I with any face begin without a dissertation on letter-writing ? Yet when I consider that a sheet of paper contains room only for three pages and a half, how can I do justice to such a pregnant subject ? However, as you have seen the history of the world stamped as it were by a diminishing glass in the form of a chronological Map, so will I 'with retractile claws' draw this into the form of a table — whereby it will occupy merely the remainder of this first page —

Folio — Parsons, Lawyers, Statesmen, Physicians out of place — ut — Eustace — Thornton — out of practice or on their travels.

Foolscap — 1. Superfine — Rich or noble poets — ut Byron. 2. common ut egomet.

Quarto — Projectors, Patentees, Presidents, Potato growers.

Bath — Boarding schools, and suburbans in general.

Gilt edge — Dandies in general, male, female, and literary.

Octavo or tears — All who make use of a lascivious seal.

Duodec. — May be found for the most part on Milliners' and Dressmakers' Parlour tables.

Strip — At the Playhouse-doors, or anywhere.

Slip — Being but a variation.

Snip — So called from its size being disguised by a twist.

I suppose you will have heard that Hazlitt has on foot a prosecution against Blackwood. I dined with him a few days since at Hessey's — there was not a word said about it, though I understand he is excessively vexed. Reynolds, by what I hear, is almost over-happy, and Rice is in town. I have not seen him, nor shall I for some time, as my throat has become worse after getting well, and I am determined to stop at home till I am quite well. I was going to Town to-morrow with Mrs. D. but I thought it best to ask her excuse this morning. I wish I could say Tom was any better. His identity presses upon me so all day that I am obliged to go out — and although I intended to have given some time to study alone, I am obliged to write

and plunge into abstract images to ease myself of his countenance, his voice, and feebleness — so that I live now in a continual fever. It must be poisonous to life, although I feel well. Imagine 'the hateful siege of contraries' — if I think of fame, of poetry, it seems a crime to me, and yet I must do so or suffer. I am sorry to give you pain — I am almost resolved to burn this — but I really have not self-possession and magnanimity enough to manage the thing otherwise — after all it may be a nervousness proceeding from the Mercury.

Bailey I hear is gaining his spirits, and he will yet be what I once thought impossible, a cheerful Man — I think he is not quite so much spoken of in Little Britain. I forgot to ask Mrs. Dilke if she had anything she wanted to say immediately to you. This morning look'd so unpromising that I did not think she would have gone — but I find she has, on sending for some volumes of Gibbon. I was in a little funk yesterday, for I sent in an unseal'd note of sham abuse, until I recollected, from what I heard Charles say, that the servant could neither read nor write — not even to her Mother as Charles observed. I have just had a Letter from Reynolds — he is going on gloriously. The following is a translation of a line of Ronsard —

'Love pour'd her beauty into my warm veins.'

You have passed your Romance, and I never gave in to it, or else I think this line a feast for one of your Lovers. How goes it with Brown?

Your sincere friend   JOHN KEATS.

71. TO JOHN HAMILTON REYNOLDS

[Hampstead, about September 22, 1818.]

MY DEAR REYNOLDS — Believe me I have rather rejoiced at your happiness than fretted at your silence. Indeed I am grieved on your account that I am not at the same time happy — But I conjure you

to think at Present of nothing but pleasure — 'Gather the rose, etc.' — gorge the
honey of life. I pity you as much that it
cannot last for ever, as I do myself now
drinking bitters. Give yourself up to it —
you cannot help it — and I have a Consolation in thinking so. I never was in love —
Yet the voice and shape of a Woman [42] has
haunted me these two days — at such a
time, when the relief, the feverous relief
of Poetry seems a much less crime — This
morning Poetry has conquered — I have
relapsed into those abstractions which are
my only life — I feel escaped from a new
strange and threatening sorrow — And I am
thankful for it — There is an awful warmth
about my heart like a load of Immortality.

Poor Tom — that woman — and Poetry
were ringing changes in my senses — Now
I am in comparison happy — I am sensible
this will distress you — you must forgive
me. Had I known you would have set out
so soon I could have sent you the 'Pot of
Basil' for I had copied it out ready. — Here
is a free translation of a Sonnet of Ronsard [see p. 123], which I think will
please you — I have the loan of his works
— they have great Beauties.

I had not the original by me when I wrote
it, and did not recollect the purport of the
last lines.

I should have seen Rice ere this — but I
am confined by Sawrey's mandate in the
house now, and have as yet only gone out
in fear of the damp night. — You know
what an undangerous matter it is. I shall
soon be quite recovered — Your offer I
shall remember as though it had even now
taken place in fact — I think it cannot be.
Tom is not up yet — I cannot say he is
better. I have not heard from George.
Your affectionate friend JOHN KEATS.

72. TO FANNY KEATS

[Hampstead, October 9, 1818.]

MY DEAR FANNY — Poor Tom is about
the same as when you saw him last ; perhaps weaker — were it not for that I
should have been over to pay you a visit
these fine days. I got to the stage half an
hour before it set out and counted the buns
and tarts in a Pastry-cook's window and
was just beginning with the Jellies. There
was no one in the Coach who had a Mind
to eat me like Mr. Sham-deaf. I shall be
punctual in enquiring about next Thursday —

Your affectionate Brother   JOHN.

73. TO JAMES AUGUSTUS HESSEY

[Hampstead, October 9, 1818.]

MY DEAR HESSEY — You are very good
in sending me the letters from the Chronicle — and I am very bad in not acknowledg-
ing such a kindness sooner — pray forgive
me. It has so chanced that I have had
that paper every day — I have seen to-
day's. I cannot but feel indebted to those
Gentlemen who have taken my part — As
for the rest, I begin to get a little acquainted with my own strength and weakness. — Praise or blame has but a momentary effect on the man whose love of beauty
in the abstract makes him a severe critic
on his own Works. My own domestic
criticism has given me pain without comparison beyond what Blackwood or the
Quarterly could possibly inflict — and also
when I feel I am right, no external praise
can give me such a glow as my own solitary
reperception and ratification of what is
fine. J. S. is perfectly right in regard to
the slip-shod Endymion.[43] That it is so is no
fault of mine. No ! — though it may sound
a little paradoxical. It is as good as I had
power to make it — by myself — Had I
been nervous about its being a perfect piece,
and with that view asked advice, and trembled over every page, it would not have
been written ; for it is not in my nature to
fumble — I will write independently. — I
have written independently *without Judgment*. I may write independently, and
with Judgment, hereafter. The Genius of

Poetry must work out its own salvation in a man : It cannot be matured by law and precept, but by sensation and watchfulness in itself — That which is creative must create itself — In Endymion, I leaped headlong into the sea, and thereby have become better acquainted with the Soundings, the quicksands, and the rocks, than if I had stayed upon the green shore, and piped a silly pipe, and took tea and comfortable advice. I was never afraid of failure ; for I would sooner fail than not be among the greatest — But I am nigh getting into a rant. So, with remembrances to Taylor and Woodhouse etc. I am

Yours very sincerely   JOHN KEATS.

74. TO GEORGE AND GEORGIANA KEATS

[Hampstead, October 13 or 14, 1818.]

MY DEAR GEORGE — There was a part in your Letter which gave me a great deal of pain, that where you lament not receiving Letters from England. I intended to have written immediately on my return from Scotland (which was two Months earlier than I had intended on account of my own as well as Tom's health) but then I was told by Mrs. W. that you had said you would not wish any one to write till we had heard from you. This I thought odd and now I see that it could not have been so ; yet at the time I suffered my unreflecting head to be satisfied, and went on in that sort of abstract careless and restless Life with which you are well acquainted. This sentence should it give you any uneasiness do not let it last for before I finish it will be explained away to your satisfaction —

I am grieved to say I am not sorry you had not Letters at Philadelphia ; you could have had no good news of Tom and I have been withheld on his account from beginning these many days ; I could not bring myself to say the truth, that he is no better but much worse — However it must be told ; and you must my dear Brother and Sister take example from me and bear up against any Calamity for my sake as I do for yours. Our's are ties which independent of their own Sentiment are sent us by providence to prevent the deleterious effects of one great solitary grief. I have Fanny and I have you — three people whose Happiness to me is sacred — and it does annul that selfish sorrow which I should otherwise fall into, living as I do with poor Tom who looks upon me as his only comfort — the tears will come into your Eyes — let them — and embrace each other — thank heaven for what happiness you have, and after thinking a moment or two that you suffer in common with all Mankind hold it not a sin to regain your cheerfulness —

I will relieve you of one uneasiness of overleaf : I returned I said on account of my health — I am now well from a bad sore throat which came of bog trotting in the Island of Mull — of which you shall hear by the copies I shall make from my Scotch Letters —

Your content in each other is a delight to me which I cannot express — the Moon is now shining full and brilliant — she is the same to me in Matter, what you are to me in Spirit. If you were here my dear Sister I could not pronounce the words which I can write to you from a distance : I have a tenderness for you, and an admiration which I feel to be as great and more chaste than I can have for any woman in the world. You will mention Fanny — her character is not formed, her identity does not press upon me as yours does. I hope from the bottom of my heart that I may one day feel as much for her as I do for you — I know not how it is, but I have never made any acquaintance of my own — nearly all through your medium my dear Brother — through you I know not only a Sister but a glorious human being. And now I am talking of those to whom you have made me known I cannot forbear mentioning

Haslam as a most kind and obliging and constant friend. His behaviour to Tom during my absence and since my return has endeared him to me for ever — besides his anxiety about you. To-morrow I shall call on your Mother and exchange information with her. On Tom's account I have not been able to pass so much time with her as I would otherwise have done — I have seen her but twice — once I dined with her and Charles — She was well, in good spirits, and I kept her laughing at my bad jokes. We went to tea at Mrs. Millar's, and in going were particularly struck with the light and shade through the Gate way at the Horse Guards. I intend to write you such Volumes that it will be impossible for me to keep any order or method in what I write : that will come first which is uppermost in my Mind, not that which is uppermost in my heart — besides I should wish to give you a picture of our Lives here whenever by a touch I can do it; even as you must see by the last sentence our walk past Whitehall all in good health and spirits — this I am certain of, because I felt so much pleasure from the simple idea of your playing a game at Cricket. At Mrs. Millar's I saw Henry quite well — there was Miss Keasle — and the good-natured Miss Waldegrave — Mrs. Millar began a long story and you know it is her Daughter's way to help her on as though her tongue were ill of the gout. Mrs. M. certainly tells a story as though she had been taught her Alphabet in Crutched Friars. Dilke has been very unwell; I found him very ailing on my return — he was under Medical care for some time, and then went to the Sea Side whence he has returned well. Poor little Mrs. D. has had another gall-stone attack; she was well ere I returned — she is now at Brighton. Dilke was greatly pleased to hear from you, and will write a letter for me to enclose — He seems greatly desirous of hearing from you of the settlement itself —

[October 14 or 15.]

I came by ship from Inverness, and was nine days at Sea without being sick — a little Qualm now and then put me in mind of you — however as soon as you touch the shore all the horrors of Sickness are soon forgotten, as was the case with a Lady on board who could not hold her head up all the way. We had not been in the Thames an hour before her tongue began to some tune; paying off as it was fit she should all old scores. I was the only Englishman on board. There was a downright Scotchman who hearing that there had been a bad crop of Potatoes in England had brought some triumphant specimens from Scotland — these he exhibited with national pride to all the Lightermen and Watermen from the Nore to the Bridge. I fed upon beef all the way; not being able to eat the thick Porridge which the Ladies managed to manage with large awkward horn spoons into the bargain. Severn has had a narrow escape of his Life from a Typhus fever: he is now gaining strength — Reynolds has returned from a six weeks' enjoyment in Devonshire — he is well, and persuades me to publish my pot of Basil as an answer to the attacks made on me in Blackwood's Magazine and the Quarterly Review. There have been two Letters in my defence in the Chronicle and one in the Examiner, copied from the Alfred Exeter Paper, and written by Reynolds. I do not know who wrote those in the Chronicle. This is a mere matter of the moment — I think I shall be among the English Poets after my death. Even as a Matter of present interest the attempt to crush me in the Quarterly has only brought me more into notice, and it is a common expression among book men ' I wonder the Quarterly should cut its own throat.'

It does me not the least harm in Society to make me appear little and ridiculous: I know when a man is superior to me and give him all due respect — he will be the last to laugh at me and as for the rest I feel that I make an impression upon them which insures me personal respect while I am in sight whatever they may say when my back is turned. Poor Haydon's eyes will not suffer him to proceed with his picture — he has been in the Country — I have seen him but once since my return. I hurry matters together here because I do not know when the Mail sails — I shall enquire to-morrow, and then shall know whether to be particular or general in my letter — You shall have at least two sheets a day till it does sail whether it be three days or a fortnight — and then I will begin a fresh one for the next Month. The Miss Reynoldses are very kind to me, but they have lately displeased me much, and in this way — Now I am coming the Richardson. On my return the first day I called they were in a sort of taking or bustle about a Cousin of theirs who having fallen out with her Grandpapa in a serious manner was invited by Mrs. R. to take Asylum in her house. She is an east indian and ought to be her Grandfather's Heir. At the time I called Mrs. R. was in conference with her up stairs, and the young Ladies were warm in her praises down stairs, calling her genteel, interesting and a thousand other pretty things to which I gave no heed, not being partial to 9 days' wonders — Now all is completely changed — they hate her, and from what I hear she is not without faults — of a real kind: but she has others which are more apt to make women of inferior charms hate her. She is not a Cleopatra, but she is at least a Charmian. She has a rich Eastern look; she has fine eyes and fine manners. When she comes into a room she makes an impression the same as the Beauty of a Leopardess. She is too fine and too conscious of herself to repulse any Man who may address her — from habit she thinks that nothing *particular*. I always find myself more at ease with such a woman; the picture before me always gives me a life and animation which I cannot possibly feel with anything inferior. I am at such times too much occupied in admiring to be awkward or in a tremble. I forget myself entirely because I live in her. You will by this time think I am in love with her; so before I go any further I will tell you I am not — she kept me awake one Night as a tune of Mozart's might do. I speak of the thing as a pastime and an amusement, than which I can feel none deeper than a conversation with an imperial woman, the very 'yes' and 'no' of whose Lips is to me a Banquet. I don't cry to take the moon home with me in my Pocket nor do I fret to leave her behind me. I like her and her like because one has no *sensations* — what we both are is taken for granted. You will suppose I have by this had much talk with her — no such thing — there are the Miss Reynoldses on the look out — They think I don't admire her because I did not stare at her.

They call her a flirt to me — What a want of knowledge! She walks across a room in such a manner that a Man is drawn towards her with a magnetic Power. This they call flirting! they do not know things. They do not know what a Woman is. I believe though she has faults — the same as Charmian and Cleopatra might have had. Yet she is a fine thing speaking in a worldly way: for there are two distinct tempers of mind in which we judge of things — the worldly, theatrical and panto-mimical; and the unearthly, spiritual and ethereal — in the former Buonaparte, Lord Byron and this Charmian hold the first place in our Minds; in the latter, John Howard, Bishop Hooker rocking his child's cradle and you my dear Sister are the conquering feelings. As a Man in the world I love the rich talk of a Charmian; as an eternal Being I love the thought of you. I should like her to ruin me, and I should like you to save me. Do not think, my dear Brother, from this that my Passions

are headlong, or likely to be ever of any pain to you —
'I am free from Men of Pleasure's cares,
By dint of feelings far more deep than theirs.'
This is Lord Byron, and is one of the finest things he has said. I have no town talk for you, as I have not been much among people — as for Politics they are in my opinion only sleepy because they will soon be too wide awake. Perhaps not — for the long and continued Peace of England itself has given us notions of personal safety which are likely to prevent the re-establishment of our national Honesty. There is, of a truth, nothing manly or sterling in any part of the Government. There are many Madmen in the Country I have no doubt, who would like to be beheaded on tower Hill merely for the sake of éclat, there are many Men like Hunt who from a principle of taste would like to see things go on better, there are many like Sir F. Burdett who like to sit at the head of political dinners, — but there are none prepared to suffer in obscurity for their Country — The motives of our worst men are Interest and of our best Vanity. We have no Milton, no Algernon Sidney — Governors in these days lose the title of Man in exchange for that of Diplomat and Minister. We breathe in a sort of Officinal Atmosphere — All the departments of Government have strayed far from Simplicity which is the greatest of Strength there is as much difference in this respect between the present Government and Oliver Cromwell's as there is between the 12 Tables of Rome and the volumes of Civil Law which were digested by Justinian. A Man now entitled Chancellor has the same honour paid to him whether he be a Hog or a Lord Bacon. No sensation is created by Greatness but by the number of Orders a Man has at his Button holes. Notwithstanding the part which the Liberals take in the Cause of Napoleon, I cannot but think he has done more harm to the life of Liberty than any one else

could have done : not that the divine right Gentlemen have done or intend to do any good — no they have taken a Lesson of him, and will do all the further harm he would have done without any of the good. The worst thing he has done is, that he has taught them how to organise their monstrous armies. The Emperor Alexander it is said intends to divide his Empire as did Diocletian — creating two Czars besides himself, and continuing the supreme Monarch of the whole. Should he do this and they for a series of Years keep peaceable among themselves Russia may spread her conquest even to China — I think it a very likely thing that China itself may fall, Turkey certainly will. Meanwhile European north Russia will hold its horns against the rest of Europe, intriguing constantly with France. Dilke, whom you know to be a Godwin perfectibility Man, pleases himself with the idea that America will be the country to take up the human intellect where England leaves off — I differ there with him greatly — A country like the United States, whose greatest Men are Franklins and Washingtons will never do that. They are great Men doubtless, but how are they to be compared to those our countrymen Milton and the two Sidneys? The one is a philosophical Quaker full of mean and thrifty maxims, the other sold the very Charger who had taken him through all his Battles. Those Americans are great, but they are not sublime Man — the humanity of the United States can never reach the sublime. Birkbeck's mind is too much in the American style — you must endeavour to infuse a little Spirit of another sort into the settlement, always with great caution, for thereby you may do your descendants more good than you may imagine. If I had a prayer to make for any great good, next to Tom's recovery, it should be that one of your Children should be the first American Poet. I have a great mind to make a prophecy, and they say prophecies work out their own fulfilment —

[Here are inserted the lines printed above, p. 249.]

[October 16.]

This is Friday, I know not what day of the Month — I will enquire to-morrow, for it is fit you should know the time I am writing. I went to Town yesterday, and calling at Mrs. Millar's was told that your Mother would not be found at home — I met Henry as I turned the corner — I had no leisure to return, so I left the letters with him. He was looking very well. Poor Tom is no better to-night — I am afraid to ask him what Message I shall send from him. And here I could go on complaining of my Misery, but I will keep myself cheerful for your Sakes. With a great deal of trouble I have succeeded in getting Fanny to Hampstead. She has been several times. Mr. Lewis has been very kind to Tom all the summer, there has scarce a day passed but he has visited him, and not one day without bringing or sending some fruit of the nicest kind. He has been very assiduous in his enquiries after you — It would give the old Gentleman a great deal of pleasure if you would send him a Sheet enclosed in the next parcel to me, after you receive this — how long it will be first — Why did I not write to Philadelphia? Really I am sorry for that neglect. I wish to go on writing ad infinitum to you — I wish for interesting matter and a pen as swift as the wind — But the fact is I go so little into the Crowd now that I have nothing fresh and fresh every day to speculate upon except my own Whims and Theories. I have been but once to Haydon's, once to Hunt's, once to Rice's, once to Hessey's. I have not seen Taylor, I have not been to the Theatre. Now if I had been many times to all these and was still in the habit of going I could on my return at night have each day something new to tell you of without any stop — But now I have such a dearth that when I get to the end of this sentence and to the bottom of this page I must wait till I can find something interesting to you before I begin another. After all it is not much matter what it may be about, for the very words from such a distance penned by this hand will be grateful to you — even though I were to copy out the tale of Mother Hubbard or Little Red Riding Hood.

[Later.]

I have been over to Dilke's this evening — there with Brown we have been talking of different and indifferent Matters — of Euclid, of Metaphysics, of the Bible, of Shakspeare, of the horrid System and consequences of the fagging at great schools. I know not yet how large a parcel I can send — I mean by way of Letters — I hope there can be no objection to my dowling up a quire made into a small compass. That is the manner in which I shall write. I shall send you more than Letters — I mean a tale — which I must begin on account of the activity of my Mind; of its inability to remain at rest. It must be prose and not very exciting. I must do this because in the way I am at present situated I have too many interruptions to a train of feeling to be able to write Poetry. So I shall write this Tale, and if I think it worth while get a duplicate made before I send it off to you.

[October 21].

This is a fresh beginning the 21st October. Charles and Henry were with us on Sunday, and they brought me your Letter to your Mother — we agree to get a Packet off to you as soon as possible. I shall dine with your Mother to-morrow, when they have promised to have their Letters ready. I shall send as soon as possible without thinking of the little you may have from me in the first parcel, as I intend; as I said before, to begin another Letter of more regular information. Here I want to communicate so largely in a little time that I am puzzled where to direct my attention. Haslam has promised to let me know from Capper and Hazlewood. For want of something better I shall proceed to give you some extracts from my Scotch Letters — Yet now I think on it why not send you the letters themselves — I have three of them at present — I believe Haydon has two which I will get in time. I dined with your Mother and Henry at Mrs. Millar's on Thursday, when they gave me their Letters. Charles's I have not yet — he has promised to send it. The thought of sending my Scotch Letters has determined me to enclose a few more which I have received and which will give you the best cue to how I am going on, better than you could otherwise know. Your Mother was well, and I was sorry I could not stop later. I called on Hunt yesterday — it has been always my fate to meet Ollier there — On Thursday I walked with Hazlitt as far as Covent Garden: he was going to play Racquets. I think Tom has been rather better these few last days — he has been less nervous. I expect Reynolds to-morrow.

[Later, about October 25.]

Since I wrote thus far I have met with that same Lady again, whom I saw at Hastings and whom I met when we were going to the English Opera. It was in a street which goes from Bedford Row to Lamb's Conduit Street. — I passed her and turned back : she seemed glad of it — glad to see me, and not offended at my passing her before. We walked on towards Islington, where we called on a friend of hers who keeps a Boarding School. She has always been an enigma to me — she has been in a Room with you and Reynolds, and wishes we should be acquainted without any of our common acquaintance knowing it. As we went along, sometimes through shabby, sometimes through decent Streets, I had my guessing at work, not knowing what it would be, and prepared to meet any surprise. First it ended at this House at Islington : on parting from which

I pressed to attend her home. She consented, and then again my thoughts were at work what it might lead to, though now they had received a sort of genteel hint from the Boarding School. Our walk ended in 34 Gloucester Street, Queen Square — not exactly so, for we went up-stairs into her sitting-room, a very tasty sort of place with Books, Pictures, a bronze Statue of Buonaparte, Music, æolian Harp, a Parrot, a Linnet, a Case of choice Liqueurs, etc. etc. She behaved in the kindest manner — made me take home a grouse for Tom's dinner. Asked for my address for the purpose of sending more game. . . . I expect to pass some pleasant hours with her now and then: in which I feel I shall be of service to her in matters of knowledge and taste : if I can I will. . . . She and your George are the only women à peu près de mon age whom I would be content to know for their mind and friendship alone. — I shall in a short time write you as far as I know how I intend to pass my Life — I cannot think of those things now Tom is so unwell and weak. Notwithstanding your Happiness and your recommendation I hope I shall never marry. Though the most beautiful Creature were waiting for me at the end of a Journey or a Walk; though the Carpet were of Silk, the Curtains of the morning Clouds; the chairs and Sofa stuffed with Cygnet's down ; the food Manna, the Wine beyond Claret, the Window opening on Winander mere, I should not feel — or rather my Happiness would not be so fine, as my Solitude is sublime. Then instead of what I have described, there is a sublimity to welcome me home — The roaring of the wind is my wife and the Stars through the window pane are my Children. The mighty abstract Idea I have of Beauty in all things stifles the more divided and minute domestic happiness — an amiable wife and sweet Children I contemplate as a part of that Beauty, but I must have a thousand of those beautiful particles to fill up my heart.

I feel more and more every day, as my imagination strengthens, that I do not live in this world alone but in a thousand worlds — No sooner am I alone than shapes of epic greatness are stationed around me, and serve my Spirit the office which is equivalent to a King's bodyguard — then 'Tragedy with sceptred pall comes sweeping by.' According to my state of mind I am with Achilles shouting in the Trenches, or with Theocritus in the Vales of Sicily. Or I throw my whole being into Troilus, and repeating those lines, 'I wander like a lost Soul upon the stygian Banks staying for waftage,' I melt into the air with a voluptuousness so delicate that I am content to be alone. These things, combined with the opinion I have of the generality of women — who appear to me as children to whom I would rather give a sugar Plum than my time, form a barrier against Matrimony which I rejoice in.

I have written this that you might see I have my share of the highest pleasures, and that though I may choose to pass my days alone I shall be no Solitary. You see there is nothing spleenical in all this. The only thing that can ever affect me personally for more than one short passing day, is any doubt about my powers for poetry — I seldom have any, and I look with hope to the nighing time when I shall have none. I am as happy as a Man can be — that is, in myself I should be happy if Tom was well, and I knew you were passing pleasant days. Then I should be most enviable — with the yearning Passion I have for the beautiful, connected and made one with the ambition of my intellect. Think of my Pleasure in Solitude in comparison of my commerce with the world — there I am a child — there they do not know me, not even my most intimate acquaintance — I give in to their feelings as though I were refraining from irritating a little child. Some think me middling, others silly, others foolish — every one thinks he sees my weak side against my will, when

in truth it is with my will — I am content to be thought all this because I have in my own breast so great a resource. This is one great reason why they like me so ; because they can all show to advantage in a room and eclipse from a certain tact one who is reckoned to be a good Poet. I hope I am not here playing tricks 'to make the angels weep' : I think not : for I have not the least contempt for my species, and though it may sound paradoxical, my greatest elevations of soul leave me every time more humbled — Enough of this — though in your Love for me you will not think it enough.

[Later, October 29 or 31.]

Haslam has been here this morning and has taken all the Letters except this sheet, which I shall send him by the Twopenny, as he will put the Parcel in the Boston post Bag by the advice of Capper and Hazlewood, who assure him of the safety and expedition that way — the Parcel will be forwarded to Warder and thence to you all the same. There will not be a Philadelphia ship for these six weeks — by that time I shall have another Letter to you. Mind you I mark this Letter A. By the time you will receive this you will have I trust passed through the greatest of your fatigues. As it was with your Sea Sickness I shall not hear of them till they are past. Do not set to your occupation with too great an anxiety — take it calmly — and let your health be the prime consideration. I hope you will have a Son, and it is one of my first wishes to have him in my Arms — which I will do please God before he cuts one double tooth. Tom is rather more easy than he has been : but is still so nervous that I cannot speak to him of these Matters — indeed it is the care I have had to keep his Mind aloof from feelings too acute that has made this Letter so short a one — I did not like to write before him a Letter he knew was to reach your hands — I cannot even now ask him for any Message

— his heart speaks to you. Be as happy as you can. Think of me, and for my sake be cheerful.

Believe me, my dear Brother and sister, Your anxious and affectionate Brother

JOHN.

This day is my Birth day.

All our friends have been anxious in their enquiries, and all send their remembrances.

75. TO FANNY KEATS

Hampstead, Friday Morn [October 16, 1818].

MY DEAR FANNY — You must not condemn me for not being punctual to Thursday, for I really did not know whether it would not affect poor Tom too much to see you. You know how it hurt him to part with you the last time. At all events you shall hear from me ; and if Tom keeps pretty well to - morrow, I will see Mr. Abbey the next day, and endeavour to settle that you shall be with us on Tuesday or Wednesday. I have good news from George — He has landed safely with our Sister — they are both in good health — their prospects are good — and they are by this time nighing to their journey's end — you shall hear the particulars soon.

Your affectionate Brother   JOHN.
Tom's love to you.

76. TO THE SAME

[Hampstead, October 26, 1818.]

MY DEAR FANNY — I called on Mr. Abbey in the beginning of last Week : when he seemed averse to letting you come again from having heard that you had been to other places besides Well Walk. I do not mean to say you did wrongly in speaking of it, for there should rightly be no objection to such things: but you know with what People we are obliged in the course of Childhood to associate, whose conduct forces us into duplicity and falsehood to them. To the worst of People we should

be openhearted: but it is as well as things are to be prudent in making any communication to any one, that may throw an impediment in the way of any of the little pleasures you may have. I do not recommend duplicity but prudence with such people. Perhaps I am talking too deeply for you: if you do not now, you will understand what I mean in the course of a few years. I think poor Tom is a little Better: he sends his love to you. I shall call on Mr. Abbey to-morrow : when I hope to settle when to see you again. Mrs. Dilke has been for some time at Brighton — she is expected home in a day or two. She will be pleased I am sure with your present. I will try for permission for you to remain here all Night should Mrs. D. return in time.

Your affectionate Brother   JOHN ——.

77. TO RICHARD WOODHOUSE

[Hampstead, October 27, 1818.]

MY DEAR WOODHOUSE — Your letter gave me great satisfaction, more on account of its friendliness than any relish of that matter in it which is accounted so acceptable to the 'genus irritabile.' The best answer I can give you is in a clerklike manner to make some observations on two principal points which seem to point like indices into the midst of the whole pro and con about genius, and views, and achievements, and ambition, et cætera. — 1st. As to the poetical Character itself (I mean that sort, of which, if I am anything, I am a member ; that sort distinguished from the Wordsworthian, or egotistical Sublime; which is a thing per se, and stands alone,) it is not itself — it has no self — It is everything and nothing. — It has no character — it enjoys light and shade : it lives in gusto, be it foul or fair, high or low, rich or poor, mean or elevated — It has as much delight in conceiving an Iago as an Imogen. What shocks the virtuous philosopher delights the chameleon poet. It does no harm from its relish of the dark side of things, any more than from its taste for the bright one, because they both end in speculation. A poet is the most unpoetical of anything in existence, because he has no Identity — he is continually in for and filling some other body. The Sun, — the Moon, — the Sea, and men and women, who are creatures of impulse, are poetical, and have about them an unchangeable attribute; the poet has none, no identity — he is certainly the most unpoetical of all God's creatures. — If then he has no self, and if I am a poet, where is the wonder that I should say I would write no more? Might I not at that very instant have been cogitating on the Characters of Saturn and Ops? It is a wretched thing to confess; but it is a very fact, that not one word I ever utter can be taken for granted as an opinion growing out of my identical Nature — how can it, when I have no Nature? When I am in a room with people, if I ever am free from speculating on creations of my own brain, then, not myself goes home to myself, but the identity of every one in the room begins to press upon me, so that I am in a very little time annihilated — not only among men; it would be the same in a nursery of Children. I know not whether I make myself wholly understood: I hope enough so to let you see that no dependence is to be placed on what I said that day.

In the 2d place, I will speak of my views, and of the life I purpose to myself. I am ambitious of doing the world some good: if I should be spared, that may be the work of maturer years — in the interval I will assay to reach to as high a summit in poetry as the nerve bestowed upon me will suffer. The faint conceptions I have of poems to come bring the blood frequently into my forehead — All I hope is, that I may not lose all interest in human affairs — that the solitary Indifference I feel for applause, even from the finest spirits, will not blunt any acuteness of vision I may have. I do not think it will.

I feel assured I should write from the mere yearning and fondness I have for the beautiful, even if my night's labours should be burnt every Morning, and no eye ever shine upon them. But even now I am perhaps not speaking from myself, but from some Character in whose soul I now live.

I am sure however that this next sentence is from myself — I feel your anxiety, good opinion, and friendship, in the highest degree, and am

Yours most sincerely   JOHN KEATS.

78. TO FANNY KEATS

[Hampstead, November 5, 1818.]

MY DEAR FANNY — I have seen Mr. Abbey three times about you, and have not been able to get his consent. He says that once more between this and the Holidays will be sufficient. What can I do? I should have been at Walthamstow several times, but I am not able to leave Tom for so long a time as that would take me. Poor Tom has been rather better these 4 last days in consequence of obtaining a little rest a nights. Write to me as often as you can, and believe that I would do anything to give you any pleasure — we must as yet wait patiently.

Your affectionate Brother   JOHN ——.

79. TO JAMES RICE

Well Walk [Hampstead,] Nov'. 24, [1818].

MY DEAR RICE — Your amende Honorable I must call ' un surcroît d'Amitié,' for I am not at all sensible of anything but that you were unfortunately engaged and I was unfortunately in a hurry. I completely understand your feeling in this mistake, and find in it that balance of comfort which remains after regretting your uneasiness. I have long made up my mind to take for granted the genuine-heartedness of my friends, notwithstanding any temporary ambiguousness in their behaviour or their tongues, nothing of which however I had the least scent of this morning. I say completely understand ; for I am everlastingly getting my mind into such-like painful trammels — and am even at this moment suffering under them in the case of a friend of ours. — I will tell you two most unfortunate and parallel slips — it seems downright pre-intention — A friend says to me, ' Keats, I shall go and see Severn this week.' — ' Ah ! (says I) you want him to take your Portrait.' — And again, ' Keats,' says a friend, ' when will you come to town again ? ' — ' I will,' says I, ' let you have the MS. next week.' In both these cases I appeared to attribute an interested motive to each of my friends' questions — the first made him flush, the second made him look angry : — and yet I am innocent in both cases ; my mind leapt over every interval, to what I saw was per se a pleasant subject with him. You see I have no allowances to make — you see how far I am from supposing you could show me any neglect. I very much regret the long time I have been obliged to exile from you : for I have one or two rather pleasant occasions to confer upon with you. What I have heard from George is favourable — I expect a letter from the Settlement itself.

Your sincere friend   JOHN KEATS.
I cannot give any good news of Tom.

80. TO FANNY KEATS

[Hampstead.] Tuesday Morn
[December 1, 1818].

MY DEAR FANNY — Poor Tom has been so bad that I have delayed your visit hither — as it would be so painful to you both. I cannot say he is any better this morning — he is in a very dangerous state — I have scarce any hopes of him.⁴⁴ Keep up your spirits for me my dear Fanny — repose entirely in

Your affectionate Brother   JOHN.

81. TO GEORGE AND GEORGIANA KEATS

[Hampstead, about Dec.ʳ· 18, 1818.]

MY DEAR BROTHER AND SISTER — You will have been prepared before this reaches you for the worst news you could have, nay, if Haslam's letter arrives in proper time, I have a consolation in thinking that the first shock will be past before you receive this. The last days of poor Tom were of the most distressing nature ; but his last moments were not so painful, and his very last was without a pang. I will not enter into any parsonic comments on death — yet the common observations of the commonest people on death are as true as their proverbs. I have scarce a doubt of immortality of some nature or other — neither had Tom. My friends have been exceedingly kind to me every one of them — Brown detained me at his House. I suppose no one could have had their time made smoother than mine has been. During poor Tom's illness I was not able to write and since his death the task of beginning has been a hindrance to me. Within this last Week I have been everywhere — and I will tell you as nearly as possible how all go on. With Dilke and Brown I am quite thick — with Brown indeed I am going to domesticate — that is, we shall keep house together. I shall have the front parlour and he the back one, by which I shall avoid the noise of Bentley's Children — and be the better able to go on with my Studies — which have been greatly interrupted lately, so that I have not the shadow of an idea of a book in my head, and my pen seems to have grown too gouty for sense. How are you going on now ? The goings on of the world makes me dizzy — There you are with Birkbeck — here I am with Brown — sometimes I fancy an immense separation, and sometimes as at present, a direct communication of Spirit with you. That will be one of the grandeurs of immortality — There will be no space, and consequently the only commerce between spirits will be by their intelligence of each other — when they will completely understand each other, while we in this world merely comprehend each other in different degrees — the higher the degree of good so higher is our Love and friendship. I have been so little used to writing lately that I am afraid you will not smoke my meaning so I will give an example — Suppose Brown or Haslam or any one whom I understand in the next degree to what I do you, were in America, they would be so much the farther from me in proportion as their identity was less impressed upon me. Now the reason why I do not feel at the present moment so far from you is that I remember your Ways and Manners and actions ; I know your manner of thinking, your manner of feeling : I know what shape your joy or your sorrow would take ; I know the manner of your walking, standing, sauntering, sitting down, laughing, punning, and every action so truly that you seem near to me. You will remember me in the same manner — and the more when I tell you that I shall read a passage of Shakspeare every Sunday at ten o'Clock — you read one at the same time, and we shall be as near each other as blind bodies can be in the same room.

I saw your Mother the day before yesterday, and intend now frequently to pass half a day with her — she seem'd tolerably well. I called in Henrietta Street and so was speaking with your Mother about Miss Millar — we had a chat about Heiresses — she told me I think of 7 or eight dying Swains. Charles was not at home. I think I have heard a little more talk about Miss Keasle — all I know of her is she had a new sort of shoe on of bright leather like our Knapsacks. Miss Millar gave me one of her confounded pinches. N. B. did not like it. Mrs. Dilke went with me to see Fanny last week, and Haslam went with me last Sunday. She was well — she gets a little plumper and had a little Colour. On Sunday I brought from

her a present of facescreens and a workbag for Mrs. D. — they were really very pretty. From Walthamstow we walked to Bethnal green — where I felt so tired from my long walk that I was obliged to go to Bed at ten. Mr. and Mrs. Keasle were there. Haslam has been excessively kind, and his anxiety about you is great ; I never meet him but we have some chat thereon. He is always doing me some good turn — he gave me this thin paper [45] for the purpose of writing to you. I have been passing an hour this morning with Mr. Lewis — he wants news of you very much. Haydon was here yesterday — he amused us much by speaking of young Hoppner who went with Captain Ross on a voyage of discovery to the Poles. The Ship was sometimes entirely surrounded with vast mountains and crags of ice, and in a few Minutes not a particle was to be seen all round the Horizon. Once they met with so vast a Mass that they gave themselves over for lost ; their last resource was in meeting it with the Bowsprit, which they did, and split it asunder and glided through it as it parted, for a great distance — one Mile and more. Their eyes were so fatigued with the eternal dazzle and whiteness that they lay down on their backs upon deck to relieve their sight on the blue sky. Hoppner describes his dreadful weariness at the continual day — the sun ever moving in a circle round above their heads — so pressing upon him that he could not rid himself of the sensation even in the dark Hold of the Ship. The Esquimaux are described as the most wretched of Beings — they float from their summer to their winter residences and back again like white Bears on the ice floats. They seem never to have washed, and so when their features move the red skin shows beneath the cracking peel of dirt. They had no notion of any inhabitants in the World but themselves. The sailors who had not seen a Star for some time, when they came again southwards on the hailing of the first revision of one, all ran upon deck with feelings of the most joyful nature. Haydon's eyes will not suffer him to proceed with his Picture — his Physician tells him he must remain two months more, inactive. Hunt keeps on in his old way — I am completely tired of it all. He has lately publish'd a Pocket Book called the literary Pocket-Book — full of the most sickening stuff you can imagine. Reynolds is well; he has become an Edinburgh Reviewer. I have not heard from Bailey. Rice I have seen very little of lately — and I am very sorry for it. The Miss R's. are all as usual. Archer above all people called on me one day — he wanted some information by my means, from Hunt and Haydon, concerning some Man they knew. I got him what he wanted, but know none of the whys and wherefores. Poor Kirkman left Wentworth Place one evening about half-past eight and was stopped, beaten and robbed of his Watch in Pond Street. I saw him a few days since; he had not recovered from his bruises. I called on Hazlitt the day I went to Romney Street.— I gave John Hunt extracts from your letters — he has taken no notice. I have seen Lamb lately — Brown and I were taken by Hunt to Novello's — there we were devastated and excruciated with bad and repeated puns — Brown don't want to go again. We went the other evening to see Brutus a new Tragedy by Howard Payne, an American — Kean was excellent — the play was very bad. It is the first time I have been since I went with you to the Lyceum.

Mrs. Brawne who took Brown's house for the Summer, still resides in Hampstead. She is a very nice woman, and her daughter senior [46] is I think beautiful and elegant, graceful, silly, fashionable and strange. We have a little tiff now and then — and she behaves a little better, or I must have sheered off. I find by a sidelong report from your Mother that I am to be invited to Miss Millar's birthday dance. Shall I dance with Miss Waldegrave? Eh! I shall be obliged to shirk a good many there. I shall be the only Dandy there — and indeed I merely comply with the invitation that the party may not be entirely destitute of a specimen of that race. I shall appear in a complete dress of purple, Hat and all — with a list of the beauties I have conquered embroidered round my Calves.

Thursday [December 24].

This morning is so very fine, I should have walked over to Walthamstow if I had thought of it yesterday. What are you doing this morning? Have you a clear hard frost as we have? How do you come on with the gun? Have you shot a Buffalo? Have you met with any Pheasants? My Thoughts are very frequently in a foreign Country — I live more out of England than in it. The Mountains of Tartary are a favourite lounge, if I happen to miss the Alleghany ridge, or have no whim for Savoy. There must be great pleasure in pursuing game — pointing your gun — no, it won't do — now, no — rabbit it — now bang — smoke and feathers — where is it? Shall you be able to get a good pointer or so? Have you seen Mr. Trimmer? He is an acquaintance of Peachey's. Now I am not addressing myself to G. minor, and yet I am — for you are one. Have you some warm furs? By your next Letters I shall expect to hear exactly how you go on — smother nothing — let us have all; fair and foul, all plain. Will the little bairn have made his entrance before you have this? Kiss it for me, and when it can first know a cheese from a Caterpillar show it my picture twice a Week. You will be glad to hear that Gifford's attack upon me has done me service — it has got my Book among several *sets* — Nor must I forget to mention once more what I suppose Haslam has told you, the present of a £25 note I had anonymously sent me. I have many things to tell you — the best way will be to make copies of my correspondence; and I must not forget the Sonnet I received with the Note. Last Week I received the following from Woodhouse whom you must recollect: —

'MY DEAR KEATS — I send enclosed a Letter, which when read take the trouble to return to me. The History of its reaching me is this. My Cousin, Miss Frogley of Hounslow, borrowed my copy of *Endymion* for a specified time. Before she had time to look into it, she and my friend Mr. Hy. Neville of Esher, who was house Surgeon to the late Princess Charlotte, insisted upon having it to read for a day or two, and undertook to make my Cousin's peace with me on account of the extra delay. Neville told me that one of the Misses Porter (of romance Celebrity) had seen it on his table, dipped into it, and expressed a wish to read it. I desired he should keep it as long and lend it to as many as he pleased, provided it was not allowed to slumber on any one's shelf. I learned subsequently from Miss Frogley that these Ladies had requested of Mr. Neville, if he was acquainted with the Author, the Pleasure of an introduction. About a week back the enclosed was transmitted by Mr. Neville to my Cousin, as a species of Apology for keeping her so long without the Book, and she sent it to me, knowing that it would give me Pleasure — I forward it to you for somewhat the same reason, but principally because it gives me the opportunity of naming to you (which it would have been fruitless to do before) the opening there is for an introduction to a class of society from which you may possibly derive advantage, as well as qualification, if you think proper to avail yourself of it. In such a case I should be very happy to further your Wishes. But do just as you please. The whole is entirely *entre nous*. —
        'Yours, etc.,   R. W.'

Well — now this is Miss Porter's Letter to Neville —

'DEAR SIR — As my Mother is sending a Messenger to Esher, I cannot but make the same the bearer of my regrets for not having had the pleasure of seeing you the morning you called at the gate. I had given orders to be denied, I was so very unwell with my still adhesive cold; but had I known it was you I should have taken off the interdict for a few minutes, to say how very much I am delighted with *Endymion*. I had just finished the Poem and have done as you permitted, lent it to Miss Fitzgerald. I regret you are not personally acquainted with the Author, for I should have been happy to have acknowledged to him, through the advantage of your communication, the very rare delight my sister and myself have enjoyed from the first fruits of Genius. I hope the ill-natured Review will not have damaged' (or damped) 'such true Parnassian fire — it ought not, for when Life is granted, etc.'

— and so she goes on. Now I feel more obliged than flattered by this — so obliged that I will not at present give you an extravaganza of a Lady Romancer. I will be introduced to them if it be merely for the pleasure of writing to you about it — I shall certainly see a new race of People. I shall more certainly have no time for them.

Hunt has asked me to meet Tom Moore some day — so you shall hear of him. The Night we went to Novello's there was a complete set to of Mozart and punning. I was so completely tired of it that if I were to follow my own inclinations I should never meet any one of that set again, not even Hunt, who is certainly a pleasant fellow in the main when you are with him — but in reality he is vain, egotistical, and disgusting in matters of taste and in morals. He understands many a beautiful thing; but then, instead of giving other minds credit for the same degree of perception as he himself professes — he begins an explanation in such a curious manner that our taste and self-love is offended continually. Hunt does one harm by making fine things petty, and beautiful things hateful. Through him I am indifferent to Mozart, I care not for white Busts — and many a glorious thing when associated with him becomes a nothing. This distorts one's mind — makes one's thoughts bizarre — perplexes one in the standard of Beauty. Martin is very much irritated against Blackwood for printing some Letters in his Magazine which were Martin's property — he always found excuses for Blackwood till he himself was injured, and now he is enraged. I have been several times thinking whether or not I should send you the Examiners, as Birkbeck no doubt has all the good periodical Publications — I will save them at all events. I must not forget to mention how attentive and useful Mrs. Bentley has been — I am very sorry to leave her — but I must, and I hope she will not be much a loser by it. Bentley is very well — he has just brought me a clothes'-basket of Books. Brown has gone to town to-day to take his Nephews who are on a visit here to see the Lions. I am passing a Quiet day — which I have not done for a long while — and if I do continue so, I feel I must again begin with my poetry — for if I am not in action mind or Body I am in pain — and from that I suffer greatly by going into parties where from the rules of society and a natural pride I am obliged to smother my Spirit and look like an Idiot — because I feel my impulses given way to would too much amaze them. I live under an everlasting restraint — never relieved except when I am composing — so I will write away.

Friday [December 25].

I think you knew before you left England that my next subject would be 'the fall of Hyperion.' I went on a little with it last night, but it will take some time to get into the vein again. I will not give you any extracts because I wish the whole to make an impression. I have however a few Poems which you will like, and I will copy out on the next sheet. I shall dine with Haydon on Sunday, and go over to Walthamstow on Monday if the frost hold. I think also of going into Hampshire this Christmas to Mr. Snook's — they say I shall be very much amused — But I don't know — I think I am in too huge a Mind for study — I must do it — I must wait at home and let those who wish come to see me. I cannot always be (how do you spell it ?) trapsing. Here I must tell you that I have not been able to keep the journal or write the Tale I promised — now I shall be able to do so. I will write to Haslam this

morning to know when the Packet sails, and till it does I will write something every day — After that my journal shall go on like clockwork, and you must not complain of its dulness — for what I wish is to write a quantity to you — knowing well that dulness itself will from me be interesting to you — You may conceive how this not having been done has weighed upon me. I shall be able to judge from your next what sort of information will be of most service or amusement to you. Perhaps as you were fond of giving me sketches of character you may like a little picnic of scandal even across the Atlantic. But now I must speak particularly to you, my dear Sister — for I know you love a little quizzing better than a great bit of apple dumpling. Do you know Uncle Redhall ? He is a little Man with an innocent powdered upright head, he lisps with a protruded under lip — he has two Nieces, each one would weigh three of him — one for height and the other for breadth — he knew Bartolozzi. He gave a supper, and ranged his bottles of wine all up the Kitchen and cellar stairs — quite ignorant of what might be drunk — It might have been a good joke to pour on the sly bottle after bottle into a washing tub, and roar for more — If you were to trip him up it would discompose a Pigtail and bring his under lip nearer to his nose. He never had the good luck to lose a silk Handkerchief in a Crowd, and therefore has only one topic of conversation — Bartolozzi. Shall I give you Miss Brawne ? She is about my height — with a fine style of countenance of the lengthened sort — she wants sentiment in every feature — she manages to make her hair look well — her nostrils are fine — though a little painful — her mouth is bad and good — her Profile is better than her full-face which indeed is not full but pale and thin without showing any bone. Her shape is very graceful and so are her movements — her Arms are good her hands baddish — her feet tolerable. She is not seventeen — but she is ignorant — monstrous in her behaviour, flying out in all directions — calling people such names that I was forced lately to make use of the term *Minx* — this is I think not from any innate vice, but from a penchant she has for acting stylishly — I am however tired of such style and shall decline any more of it. She had a friend to visit her lately — you have known plenty such — her face is raw as if she was standing out in a frost ; her lips raw and seem always ready for a Pullet — she plays the Music without one sensation but the feel of the ivory at her fingers. She is a downright Miss without one set off — We hated her and smoked her and baited her and I think drove her away. Miss B. thinks her a Paragon of fashion, and says she is the only woman she would change persons with. What a stupe — She is superior as a Rose to a Dandelion. When we went to bed Brown observed as he put out the Taper what a very ugly old woman that Miss Robinson would make — at which I must have groaned aloud for I'm sure ten minutes. I have not seen the thing Kingston again — George will describe him to you — I shall insinuate some of these Creatures into a Comedy some day — and perhaps have Hunt among them —

Scene, a little Parlour. *Enter* Hunt — Gattie — Hazlitt — Mrs. Novello — Ollier. *Gattie.* Ha ! Hunt, got into your new house ? Ha ! Mrs. Novello : seen Altam and his Wife ? — *Mrs. N.* Yes (with a grin), it 's Mr. Hunt's, is n't it ? — *Gattie.* Hunt's ? no, ha ! Mr. Ollier, I congratulate you upon the highest compliment I ever heard paid to the Book. Mr. Hazlitt, I hope you are well. — *Hazlitt.* Yes Sir, no Sir. — *Mr. Hunt* (at the Music), 'La Biondina,' etc. Hazlitt did you ever hear this ? — 'La Biondina,' etc. — *Hazlitt.* O no Sir — I never. — *Ollier.* Do, Hunt, give it us over again — divine. — *Gattie.* Divino — Hunt, when does your Pocket-Book come out ? — *Hunt.* 'What is this absorbs me quite ?' O we are spinning on a little, we

shall floridise soon I hope. Such a thing was very much wanting — people think of nothing but money getting — now for me I am rather inclined to the liberal side of things. I am reckoned lax in my Christian principles, etc. etc. etc.

[December 29.]

It is some days since I wrote the last page — and what I have been about since I have no Idea. I dined at Haslam's on Sunday — with Haydon yesterday, and saw Fanny in the morning ; she was well. Just now I took out my poem to go on with it, but the thought of my writing so little to you came upon me and I could not get on — so I have began at random and I have not a word to say — and yet my thoughts are so full of you that I can do nothing else. I shall be confined at Hampstead a few days on account of a sore throat — the first thing I do will be to visit your Mother again. The last time I saw Henry he show'd me his first engraving, which I thought capital. Mr. Lewis called this morning and brought some American Papers — I have not look'd into them — I think we ought to have heard of you before this — I am in daily expectation of Letters — Nil desperandum. Mrs. Abbey wishes to take Fanny from School — I shall strive all I can against that. There has happened a great Misfortune in the Drewe Family — old Drewe has been dead some time ; and lately George Drewe expired in a fit — on which account Reynolds has gone into Devonshire. He dined a few days since at Horace Twisse's with Liston and Charles Kemble. I see very little of him now, as I seldom go to Little Britain because the *Ennui* always seizes me there, and John Reynolds is very dull at home. Nor have I seen Rice. How you are now going on is a Mystery to me — I hope a few days will clear it up.

[December 30.]

I never know the day of the Month. It is very fine here to-day, though I expect a.

Thundercloud, or rather a snow cloud, in less than an hour. I am at present alone at Wentworth Place — Brown being at Chichester and Mr. and Mrs. Dilke making a little stay in Town. I know not what I should do without a sunshiny morning now and then — it clears up one's spirits. Dilke and I frequently have some chat about you. I have now and then some doubt, but he seems to have a great confidence. I think there will soon be perceptible a change in the fashionable slang literature of the day — it seems to me that Reviews have had their day — that the public have been surfeited — there will soon be some new folly to keep the Parlours in talk — What it is I care not. We have seen three literary Kings in our Time — Scott, Byron, and then the Scotch novels. All now appears to be dead — or I may mistake, literary Bodies may still keep up the Bustle which I do not hear. Haydon show'd me a letter he had received from Tripoli — Ritchie was well and in good Spirits, among Camels, Turbans, Palm Trees, and Sands. You may remember I promised to send him an Endymion which I did not — however he has one — you have one. One is in the Wilds of America — the other is on a Camel's back in the plains of Egypt. I am looking into a Book of Dubois's — he has written directions to the Players — one of them is very good. 'In singing never mind the music — observe what time you please. It would be a pretty degradation indeed if you were obliged to confine your genius to the dull regularity of a fiddler — horse hair and cat's guts — no, let him keep *your* time and play *your* tune — *dodge him.*' I will now copy out the Letter and Sonnet I have spoken of. The outside cover was thus directed, 'Messrs. Taylor and Hessey, (Booksellers), No. 93 Fleet Street, London,' and it contained this:

'Messrs. Taylor and Hessey are requested to forward the enclosed letter by some *safe* mode of conveyance to the Author of Endymion, who is not known at Teignmouth: or if they have not his address, they will return the letter by post, directed as below, within a *fortnight,* "Mr. P. Fenbank, P. O., Teignmouth." 9th Novr. 1818.

In this sheet was enclosed the following, with a superscription — 'Mr. John Keats, Teignmouth.' Then came Sonnet to John Keats — which I would not copy for any in the world but you — who know that I scout 'mild light and loveliness' or any such nonsense in myself.

Star of high promise ! — not to this dark age
  Do thy mild light and loveliness belong ;
  For it is blind, intolerant, and wrong ;
Dead to empyreal soarings, and the rage
Of scoffing spirits bitter war doth wage
  With all that bold integrity of song.
  Yet thy clear beam shall shine through ages strong
To ripest times a light and heritage.
And there breathe now who dote upon thy fame,
  Whom thy wild numbers wrap beyond their being,
Who love the freedom of thy lays — their aim
  Above the scope of a dull tribe unseeing —
And there is one whose hand will never scant
From his poor store of fruits all *thou* canst want.
November 1818.   turn over

I turn'd over and found a £25 note. Now this appears to me all very proper — if I had refused it I should have behaved in a very bragadochio dunderheaded manner — and yet the present galls me a little, and I do not know whether I shall not return it if I ever meet with the donor after, whom to no purpose I have written. I have your Miniature on the Table George the great — it's very like — though not quite about the upper lip. I wish we had a better of your little George. I must not forget to tell you that a few days since I went with Dilke a shooting on the heath and shot a Tomtit. There were as many guns abroad as Birds. I intended to have been at Chichester this Wednesday — but on account of this sore throat I wrote him (Brown) my excuse yesterday.

Thursday [December 31].

(I will date when I finish.) — I received a Note from Haslam yesterday — asking if my letter is ready — now this is only the second sheet — notwithstanding all my promises. But you must reflect what hindrances I have had. However on sealing this I shall have nothing to prevent my proceeding in a gradual journal, which will increase in a Month to a considerable size. I will insert any little pieces I may write — though I will not give any extracts from my large poem which is scarce began. I want to hear very much whether Poetry and literature in general has gained or lost interest with you — and what sort of writing is of the highest gust with you now. With what sensation do you read Fielding? — and do not Hogarth's pictures seem an old thing to you? Yet you are very little more removed from general association than I am — recollect that no Man can live but in one society at a time — his enjoyment in the different states of human society must depend upon the Powers of his Mind — that is you can imagine a Roman triumph or an Olympic game as well as I can. We with our bodily eyes see but the fashion and Manners of one country for one age — and then we die. Now to me manners and customs long since passed whether among the Babylonians or the Bactrians are as real, or even more real than those among which I now live — My thoughts have turned lately this way — The more we know the more inadequacy we find in the world to satisfy us — this is an old observation; but I have made up my Mind never to take anything for granted — but even to examine the truth of the commonest proverbs — This however is true. Mrs. Tighe and Beattie once delighted me — now I see through them and can find nothing in them but weakness, and yet how many they still delight! Perhaps a superior being may look upon Shakspeare in the same light — is it possible? No — This same inadequacy is

discovered (forgive me, little George, you know I don't mean to put you in the mess) in Women with few exceptions — the Dress Maker, the blue Stocking, and the most charming sentimentalist differ but in a slight degree and are equally smokeable. But I will go no further — I may be speaking sacrilegiously — and on my word I have thought so little that I have not one opinion upon anything except in matters of taste — I never can feel certain of any truth but from a clear perception of its Beauty — and I find myself very young minded even in that perceptive power — which I hope will increase. A year ago I could not understand in the slightest degree Raphael's cartoons — now I begin to read them a little — And how did I learn to do so? By seeing something done in quite an opposite spirit — I mean a picture of Guido's in which all the Saints, instead of that heroic simplicity and unaffected grandeur which they inherit from Raphael, had each of them both in countenance and gesture all the canting, solemn, melodramatic mawkishness of Mackenzie's father Nicholas. When I was last at Haydon's I looked over a Book of Prints taken from the fresco of the Church at Milan, the name of which I forget — in it are comprised Specimens of the first and second age of art in Italy. I do not think I ever had a greater treat out of Shakspeare. Full of Romance and the most tender feeling — magnificence of draperies beyond any I ever saw, not excepting Raphael's. But Grotesque to a curious pitch — yet still making up a fine whole — even finer to me than more accomplish'd works — as there was left so much room for Imagination. I have not heard one of this last course of Hazlitt's lectures. They were upon 'Wit and Humour,' 'the English comic writers.'

Saturday, Jany. 2nd [1819].

Yesterday Mr. and Mrs. D. and myself dined at Mrs. Brawne's — nothing particular passed. I never intend hereafter to spend any time with Ladies unless they are handsome — you lose time to no purpose. For that reason I shall beg leave to decline going again to Redall's or Butler's or any Squad where a fine feature cannot be mustered among them all — and where all the evening's amusement consists in saying 'your good health, *your* good health, and YOUR good health — and (O I beg your pardon) yours, Miss ——,' and such thing not even dull enough to keep one awake — With respect to amiable speaking I can read — let my eyes be fed or I'll never go out to dinner anywhere. Perhaps you may have heard of the dinner given to Thos. Moore in Dublin, because I have the account here by me in the Philadelphia democratic paper. The most pleasant thing that occurred was the speech Mr. Tom made on his Father's health being drank. I am afraid a great part of my Letters are filled up with promises and what I will do rather than any great deal written — but here I say once for all — that circumstances prevented me from keeping my promise in my last, but now I affirm that as there will be nothing to hinder me I will keep a journal for you. That I have not yet done so you would forgive if you knew how many hours I have been repenting of my neglect. For I have no thought pervading me so constantly and frequently as that of you — my Poem cannot frequently drive it away — you will retard it much more than you could by taking up my time if you were in England. I never forget you except after seeing now and then some beautiful woman — but that is a fever — the thought of you both is a passion with me, but for the most part a calm one. I asked Dilke for a few lines for you — he has promised them — I shall send what I have written to Haslam on Monday Morning — what I can get into another sheet to-morrow I will — There are one or two little poems you might like. I have given up snuff very nearly quite — Dilke has promised to sit with me this evening, I wish he would come this minute

for I want a pinch of snuff very much just now — I have none though in my own snuff box. My sore throat is much better to-day — I think I might venture on a pinch. Here are the Poems — they will explain themselves — as all poems should do without any comment —

[The poem entitled 'Fancy,' pp. 124, 125, is here inserted.]

I did not think this had been so long a Poem. I have another not so long — but as it will more conveniently be copied on the other side I will just put down here some observations on Caleb Williams by Hazlitt — I meant to say St. Leon, for although he has mentioned all the Novels of Godwin very freely I do not quote them, but this only on account of its being a specimen of his usual abrupt manner, and fiery laconicism. He says of St. Leon —

'He is a limb torn off society. In possession of eternal youth and beauty he can feel no love; surrounded, tantalised, and tormented with riches, he can do no good. The faces of Men pass before him as in a speculum; but he is attached to them by no common tie of sympathy or suffering. He is thrown back into himself and his own thoughts. He lives in the solitude of his own breast — without wife or child or friend or Enemy in the world. *This is the solitude of the soul, not of woods or trees or mountains* — but the desert of society — the waste and oblivion of the heart. He is himself alone. His existence is purely intellectual, and is therefore intolerable to one who has felt the rapture of affection, or the anguish of woe.'

As I am about it I might as well give you his character of Godwin as a Romancer: —

'Whoever else is, it is pretty clear that the author of Caleb Williams is not the author of Waverley. Nothing can be more distinct or excellent in their several ways than these two writers. If the one owes almost everything to external observations and traditional character, the other owes everything to internal conception and contemplation of the possible workings of the human Mind. There is little knowledge of the world, little variety, neither an eye for the picturesque nor a talent for the humorous in Caleb Williams, for instance, but you cannot doubt for a moment of the originality of the work and the force of the conception. The impression made upon the reader is the exact measure of the strength of the author's genius. For the effect both in Caleb Williams and St. Leon is entirely made out, not by facts nor dates, by blackletter, or magazine learning, by transcript nor record, but by intense and patient study of the human heart, and by an imagination projecting itself into certain situations, and capable of working up its imaginary feelings to the height of reality.'

This appears to me quite correct — Now I will copy the other Poem — it is on the double immortality of Poets —

['Bards of Passion and of Mirth,' p. 125].

These are specimens of a sort of rondeau which I think I shall become partial to — because you have one idea amplified with greater ease and more delight and freedom than in the sonnet. It is my intention to wait a few years before I publish any minor poems — and then I hope to have a volume of some worth — and which those people will relish who cannot bear the burthen of a long poem. In my journal I intend to copy the poems I write the days they are written — There is just room, I see, in this page to copy a little thing I wrote off to some Music as it was playing —

['I had a dove and the sweet dove died,' p. 125].

Sunday [January 3].

I have been dining with Dilke to-day — He is up to his Ears in Walpole's letters. Mr. Manker is there, and I have come round to see if I can conjure up anything for you. Kirkman came down to see me this morning — his family has been very badly off lately. He told me of a villainous trick of his Uncle William in Newgate Street, who became sole Creditor to his father under pretence of serving him, and put an execution on his own Sister's goods. He went in to the family at Portsmouth; conversed with them, went out and sent in the Sherriff's officer. He tells me too of

abominable behaviour of Archer to Caroline Mathew — Archer has lived nearly at the Mathews these two years; he has been amusing Caroline — and now he has written a Letter to Mrs. M. declining, on pretence of inability to support a wife as he would wish, all thoughts of marriage. What is the worst is Caroline is 27 years old. It is an abominable matter. He has called upon me twice lately — I was out both times. What can it be for? — There is a letter to-day in the Examiner to the Electors of Westminster on Mr. Hobhouse's account. In it there is a good character of Cobbett — I have not the paper by me or I would copy it. I do not think I have mentioned the discovery of an African Kingdom — the account is much the same as the first accounts of Mexico — all magnificence — There is a Book being written about it. I will read it and give you the cream in my next. The romance we have heard upon it runs thus: They have window frames of gold — 100,000 infantry — human sacrifices. The Gentleman who is the Adventurer has his wife with him — she, I am told, is a beautiful little sylphid woman — her husband was to have been sacrificed to their Gods and was led through a Chamber filled with different instruments of torture with privilege to choose what death he would die, without their having a thought of his aversion to such a death, they considering it a supreme distinction. However he was let off, and became a favourite with the King, who at last openly patronised him, though at first on account of the Jealousy of his Ministers he was wont to hold conversations with his Majesty in the dark middle of the night. All this sounds a little Bluebeardish — but I hope it is true. There is another thing I must mention of the momentous kind; — but I must mind my periods in it — Mrs. Dilke has two Cats — a Mother and a Daughter — now the Mother is a tabby and the daughter a black and white like the spotted child. Now it appears to me, for the doors of both houses are opened frequently, so that there is a complete thoroughfare for both Cats (there being no board up to the contrary), they may one and several of them come into my room ad libitum. But no — the Tabby only comes — whether from sympathy for Ann the Maid or me I cannot tell — or whether Brown has left behind him any atmospheric spirit of Maidenhood I cannot tell. The Cat is not an old Maid herself — her daughter is a proof of it — I have questioned her — I have look'd at the lines of her paw — I have felt her pulse — to no purpose. Why should the *old* Cat come to me ? I ask myself — and myself has not a word to answer. It may come to light some day ; if it does you shall hear of it.

Kirkman this morning promised to write a few lines to you and send them to Haslam. I do not think I have anything to say in the Business way. You will let me know what you would wish done with your property in England — what things you would wish sent out — But I am quite in the dark about what you are doing — If I do not hear soon I shall put on my wings and be after you. I will in my next, and after I have seen your next letter, tell you my own particular idea of America. Your next letter will be the key by which I shall open your hearts and see what spaces want filling with any particular information — Whether the affairs of Europe are more or less interesting to you — whether you would like to hear of the Theatres — of the bear Garden — of the Boxers — the Painters, the Lectures — the Dress — The progress of Dandyism — The Progress of Courtship — or the fate of Mary Millar — being a full, true, and très particular account of Miss M.'s ten Suitors — How the first tried the effect of swearing; the second of stammering; the third of whispering; — the fourth of sonnets — the fifth of Spanish leather boots, — the sixth of flattering her body — the seventh of flattering her mind — the eighth of flattering himself — the

ninth stuck to the Mother — the tenth kissed the Chambermaid and told her to tell her Mistress — But he was soon discharged, his reading led him into an error; he could not sport the Sir Lucius to any advantage. And now for this time I bid you good-bye — I have been thinking of these sheets so long that I appear in closing them to take my leave of you — but that is not it — I shall immediately as I send this off begin my journal — when some days I shall write no more than 10 lines and others 10 times as much. Mrs. Dilke is knocking at the wall for Tea is ready — I will tell you what sort of a tea it is and then bid you Good-bye.

[January 4].

This is Monday morning — nothing particular happened yesterday evening, except that when the tray came up Mrs. Dilke and I had a battle with celery stalks — she sends her love to you. I shall close this and send it immediately to Haslam — remaining ever, My dearest brother and sister,

Your most affectionate Brother JOHN.

82. TO RICHARD WOODHOUSE

Wentworth Place, Friday Morn
[December 18, 1818].

MY DEAR WOODHOUSE — I am greatly obliged to you. I must needs feel flattered by making an impression on a set of ladies. I should be content to do so by meretricious romance verse, if they alone, and not men, were to judge. I should like very much to know those ladies — though look here, Woodhouse — I have a new leaf to turn over: I must work; I must read; I must write. I am unable to afford time for new acquaintances. I am scarcely able to do my duty to those I have. Leave the matter to chance. But do not forget to give my remembrances to your cousin.

Yours most sincerely   JOHN KEATS.

83. TO MRS. REYNOLDS

Wentworth Place, Tuesd.
[December 22, 1818].

MY DEAR MRS. REYNOLDS — When I left you yesterday, 't was with the conviction that you thought I had received no previous invitation for Christmas day : the truth is I had, and had accepted it under the conviction that I should be in Hampshire at the time: else believe me I should not have done so, but kept in Mind my old friends. I will not speak of the proportion of pleasure I may receive at different Houses — that never enters my head — you may take for a truth that I would have given up even what I did see to be a greater pleasure, for the sake of old acquaintanceship — time is nothing — two years are as long as twenty.

Yours faithfully   JOHN KEATS.

84. TO BENJAMIN ROBERT HAYDON

Wentworth Place, Tuesday
[December 22, 1818].

MY DEAR HAYDON — Upon my Soul I never felt your going out of the room at all — and believe me I never rhodomontade anywhere but in your Company — my general Life in Society is silence. I feel in myself all the vices of a Poet, irritability, love of effect and admiration — and influenced by such devils I may at times say more ridiculous things than I am aware of — but I will put a stop to that in a manner I have long resolved upon — I will buy a gold ring and put it on my finger — and from that time a Man of superior head shall never have occasion to pity me, or one of inferior Nunskull to chuckle at me. I am certainly more for greatness in a shade than in the open day — I am speaking as a mortal — I should say I value more the privilege of seeing great things in loneliness than the fame of a Prophet. Yet here I am sinning — so I will turn to a thing I have thought on more — I mean your means till your picture be finished:

not only now but for this year and half have I thought of it. Believe me Haydon I have that sort of fire in my heart that would sacrifice everything I have to your service — I speak without any reserve — I know you would do so for me — I open my heart to you in a few words. I will do this sooner than you shall be distressed: but let me be the last stay — Ask the rich lovers of Art first — I 'll tell you why — I have a little money which may enable me to study, and to travel for three or four years. I never expect to get anything by my Books: and moreover I wish to avoid publishing — I admire Human Nature but I do not like *Men*. I should like to compose things honourable to Man — but not fingerable over by *Men*. So I am anxious to exist without troubling the printer's devil or drawing upon Men's or Women's admiration — in which great solitude I hope God will give me strength to rejoice. Try the long purses — but do not sell your drawings or I shall consider it a breach of friendship. I am sorry I was not at home when Salmon [Haydon's servant] called. Do write and let me know all your present whys and wherefores.

Yours most faithfully   JOHN KEATS.

85. TO JOHN TAYLOR

Wentworth Place, [December 24, 1818].

MY DEAR TAYLOR — Can you lend me £30 for a short time ? Ten I want for myself — and twenty for a friend — which will be repaid me by the middle of next month. I shall go to Chichester on Wednesday and perhaps stay a fortnight — I am afraid I shall not be able to dine with you before I return. Remember me to Woodhouse.

Yours sincerely   JOHN KEATS.

86. TO BENJAMIN ROBERT HAYDON

Wentworth Place, [December 27, 1818].

MY DEAR HAYDON — I had an engagement to-day — and it is so fine a morning that I cannot put it off — I will be with you to-morrow — when we will thank the Gods, though you have bad eyes and I am idle.

I regret more than anything the not being able to dine with you to-day. I have had several movements that way — but then I should disappoint one who has been my true friend. I will be with you to-morrow morning and stop all day — we will hate the profane vulgar and make us Wings.

God bless you.   J. KEATS.

87. TO FANNY KEATS

Wentworth Place, Wednesday
[December 30, 1818].

MY DEAR FANNY — I am confined at Hampstead with a sore throat; but I do not expect it will keep me above two or three days. I intended to have been in Town yesterday but feel obliged to be careful a little while. I am in general so careless of these trifles, that they tease me for Months, when a few days' care is all that is necessary. I shall not neglect any chance of an endeavour to let you return to School — nor to procure you a Visit to Mrs. Dilke's which I have great fears about. Write me if you can find time — and also get a few lines ready for George as the Post sails next Wednesday.

Your affectionate Brother JOHN ——.

88. TO BENJAMIN ROBERT HAYDON

Wentworth Place, Monday Aft.
[January 4, 1819].

MY DEAR HAYDON — I have been out this morning, and did not therefore see your note till this minute, or I would have gone to town directly — it is now too late for to-day. I will be in town early to-morrow, and trust I shall be able to lend you assistance noon or night. I was struck with the improvement in the architectural part of your Picture — and, now I think on

it, I cannot help wondering you should have had it so poor, especially after the Solomon. Excuse this dry bones of a note: for though my pen may grow cold, I should be sorry my Life should freeze —

Your affectionate friend JOHN KEATS.

89. TO THE SAME

Wentworth Place,
[between January 7 and 14, 1819].

MY DEAR HAYDON — We are very unlucky — I should have stopped to dine with you, but I knew I should not have been able to leave you in time for my plaguy sore throat; which is getting well.

I shall have a little trouble in procuring the Money and a great ordeal to go through — no trouble indeed to any one else — or ordeal either. I mean I shall have to go to town some thrice, and stand in the Bank an hour or two — to me worse than anything in Dante — I should have less chance with the people around me than Orpheus had with the Stones. I have been writing a little now and then lately: but nothing to speak of — being discontented and as it were moulting. Yet I do not think I shall ever come to the rope or the Pistol, for after a day or two's melancholy, although I smoke more and more my own insufficiency — I see by little and little more of what is to be done, and how it is to be done, should I ever be able to do it. On my soul, there should be some reward for that continual *agonie ennuyeuse*. I was thinking of going into Hampshire for a few days. I have been delaying it longer than I intended. You shall see me soon; and do not be at all anxious, for *this* time I really will do, what I never did before in my life, business in good time, and properly. — With respect to the Bond — it may be a satisfaction to you to let me have it: but as you love me do not let there be any mention of interest, although we are mortal men — and bind ourselves for fear of death.

Yours for ever   JOHN KEATS.

Wentworth Place, [January 1819].

MY DEAR HAYDON — My throat has not suffered me yet to expose myself to the night air : however I have been to town in the day time — have had several interviews with my guardian — have written him rather a plain-spoken Letter — which has had its effect; and he now seems inclined to put no stumbling-block in my way: so that I see a good prospect of performing my promise. What I should have lent you ere this if I could have got it, was belonging to poor Tom — and the difficulty is whether I am to inherit it before my Sister is of age; a period of six years. Should it be so I must incontinently take to Corduroy Trousers. But I am nearly confident 't is all a Bam. I shall see you soon — but do let me have a line to-day or to-morrow concerning your health and spirits.

Your sincere friend   JOHN KEATS.

Wentworth Place, [January 1819].

MY DEAR FANNY — I send this to Walthamstow for fear you should not be at Pancras Lane when I call to-morrow — before going into Hampshire for a few days — I will not be more I assure you — You may think how disappointed I am in not being able to see you more and spend more time with you than I do — but how can it be helped? The thought is a continual vexation to me — and often hinders me from reading and composing — Write to me as often as you can — and believe me,

Your affectionate Brother JOHN ——.

Bedhampton, 24 January 1819.

DEAR DILKE, — This letter is for your Wife, and if you are a Gentleman, you will

* Keats's portion of this letter is printed in Italic, but this does not apply to the italicized

deliver it to her, without reading one word further. *'read thou Squire.* There is a wager depending on this.

MY CHARMING DEAR MRS. DILKE, — It was delightful to receive a letter from you, — but such a letter ! what presumption in me to attempt to answer it ! Where shall I find, in my poor brain, such jibes, such jeers, such flashes of merriment ? Alas ! you will say, as you read me, Alas ! poor Brown ! quite chop fallen ! But that 's not true; my chops have been beautifully plumped out since I came here : my dinners have been good & nourishing & my inside never washed by a red herring broth. Then my mind has been so happy ! I have been smiled on by the fair ones, the Lacy's, the Prices, & the Mullings's, but not by the Richards's ; Old Dicky has not called here during my visit, — I have not seen him; the whole of the family are *shuffling* to carriage folks for acquaintances, *cutting* their old friends, and *dealing* out pride & folly, while we allow they have got the *odd trick,* but dispute their *honours.* I was determined to be beforehand with them, & behaved cavalierly & neglectingly to the family, & passed the girls in Havant with a slight bow. — Keats is much better, owing to a strict forbearance from a third glass of wine. He & I walked from Chicester yesterday, we were here at 3, but the Dinner was finished ; a brace of Muir fowl had been dressed; I ate a piece of the breast cold, & it was not tainted ; I dared not venture further. Mr. Snook was nearly turned sick by being merely asked to take a mouthful. The other brace was so *high,* that the cook declined preparing them for the spit, & they were thrown away. I see your husband declared them to be in excellent order ; I supposed he enjoyed them in a disgusting manner, — sucking the rotten flesh off the bones, & crunching the putrid bones. Did you eat any ? I hope not, for an *ooman* should be delicate

words in the second paragraph designed by Brown to make his joke perfectly clear.

in her food. — O you Jezabel! to sit quietly
in your room, while the thieves were ran-
sacking my house! No doubt poor Ann's
throat was cut; has the Coroner sat on her
yet? — Mrs. Snook says she knows how to
hold a pen very well, & wants no lessons
from me; only think of the vanity of the
ooman! She tells me to make honourable
mention of your letter which she received
at Breakfast time, but how can I do so?
I have not read it; & I'll lay my life it is
not a tenth part so good as mine, — pshaw
on your letter to her! — On Tuesday night
I think you'll see me. In the mean time
I'll not say a word about spasms in the
way of my profession, tho' as your friend
I must profess myself very sorry. Keats
& I are going to call on Mr. Butler &
Mr. Burton this morning, and tomorrow
we shall go to Sanstead to see Mr. Way's
Chapel consecrated by the two Big-wigs
of Gloucester & St. Davids. If that vile
Carver & Gilder does not do me justice,
I'll annoy him all his life with legal
expenses at every quarter, if my rent is
not sent to the day, & that will not be
revenge enough for the trouble & confusion he has put me to. — Mrs. Dilke is
remarkably well for Mrs. Dilke in winter.
— Have you heard anything of John Blag-
den; he is off! want of business has made
him play the fool, — I am sorry — *that
Brown and you are getting so very witty —
my modest feathered Pen frizzles like baby
roast beef at making its entrance among such
tantrum sentences — or rather ten senses.
Brown super or supper sir named the Sleek
has been getting thinner a little by pining opposite Miss Muggins — (Brown says Mullins
but I beg to differ from him) — we sit it out
till ten o' clock — Miss M. has persuaded
Brown to shave his whiskers — he came down
to Breakfast like the sign of the full Moon —
his Profile is quite alter'd. He looks more like
an ooman than I ever could think it possible
— and on putting on Mrs. D.'s calash the deception was complete especially as his voice is*

*trebled by making love in the draught of a
doorway. I too am metamorphosed — a young
ooman here in Bed—hampton has over persuaded me to wear my shirt collar up to my
eyes. Mrs. Snook I catch smoking it every
now and then and I believe Brown does but I
cannot now look sideways. Brown wants to
scribble more so I will finish with a marginal
note — Viz. Remember me to Wentworth
Place and Elm Cottage — not forgetting
Millamant —*
Your's if possible   J. Keats.

This is abominable! I did but go up-
stairs to put on a clean & starched handkerchief, & that overweening rogue read
my letter & scrawled over one of my sheets,
and given him a counterpain, — I wish I
could blank-it all over *and beat him with a*
[*certain rod,* & have a fresh one bolstered
up. *Ah! he may dress me as he likes but he*
shan't tic[kle me pil]low *the feathers,* — *I
would not give a tester for such puns, let
us ope brown* (erratum — a large B — *a
Bumble B.*) *will go no further in the Bedroom*
& not call Mat Snook a relation to Matt-
rass — *This is grown to a conclusion — I had
excellent puns in my head but one bad one
from Brown has quite upset me* but I am
quite set-up for more, but I'm content to
be conqueror.
Your's in love.   Chas. Brown.
N. B. *I beg leaf* (sic) *to withdraw all my
puns — they are all wash, an base uns.*

93. TO FANNY KEATS

Wentworth Place, Feb^y [11, 1819]. Thursday.

My dear Fanny — Your Letter to me
at Bedhampton hurt me very much, —
What objection can there be to your receiving a Letter from me? At Bedhampton I was unwell and did not go out of the
Garden Gate but twice or thrice during
the fortnight I was there — Since I came
back I have been taking care of myself —

I have been obliged to do so, and am now in hopes that by this care I shall get rid of a sore throat which has haunted me at intervals nearly a twelvemonth. I had always a presentiment of not being able to succeed in persuading Mr. Abbey to let you remain longer at School — I am very sorry that he will not consent. I recommend you to keep up all that you know and to learn more by yourself however little. The time will come when you will be more pleased with Life — look forward to that time and, though it may appear a trifle be careful not to let the idle and retired Life you lead fix any awkward habit or behaviour on you — whether you sit or walk endeavour to let it be in a seemly and if possible a graceful manner. We have been very little together: but you have not the less been with me in thought. You have no one in the world besides me who would sacrifice anything for you — I feel myself the only Protector you have. In all your little troubles think of me with the thought that there is at least one person in England who if he could would help you out of them — I live in hopes of being able to make you happy. — I should not perhaps write in this manner, if it were not for the fear of not being able to see you often or long together. I am in hopes Mr. Abbey will not object any more to your receiving a letter now and then from me. How unreasonable ! I want a few more lines from you for George — there are some young Men, acquaintances of a Schoolfellow of mine, going out to Birkbeck's at the latter end of this Month — I am in expectation every day of hearing from George — I begin to fear his last letters miscarried. I shall be in town to-morrow — if you should not be in town, I shall send this little parcel by the Walthamstow Coach — I think you will like Goldsmith — Write me soon —

Your affectionate Brother JOHN ——.

Mrs. Dilke has not been very well — she is gone a walk to town to-day for exercise.

94. TO GEORGE AND GEORGIANA KEATS

Sunday Morn⁵ February 14, [1818].

MY DEAR BROTHER AND SISTER — How is it that we have not heard from you from the Settlement yet ? The letters must surely have miscarried. I am in expectation every day. Peachey wrote me a few days ago, saying some more acquaintances of his were preparing to set out for Birkbeck; therefore I shall take the opportunity of sending you what I can muster in a sheet or two. I am still at Wentworth Place — indeed, I have kept indoors lately, resolved if possible to rid myself of my sore throat ; consequently I have not been to see your Mother since my return from Chichester ; but my absence from her has been a great weight upon me. I say since my return from Chichester — I believe I told you I was going thither. I was nearly a fortnight at Mr. John Snook's and a few days at old Mr. Dilke's. Nothing worth speaking of happened at either place. I took down some thin paper and wrote on it a little poem called St. Agnes's Eve, which you shall have as it is when I have finished the blank part of the rest for you. I went out twice at Chichester to dowager Card parties. I see very little now, and very few persons, being almost tired of men and things. Brown and Dilke are very kind and considerate towards me. The Miss R.'s have been stopping next door lately, but are very dull. Miss Brawne and I have every now and then a chat and a tiff. Brown and Dilke are walking round their garden, hands in pockets, making observations. The literary world I know nothing about. There is a poem from Rogers dead born ; and another satire is expected from Byron, called "Don Giovanni." Yesterday I went to town for the first time for these three weeks. I met people from all parts and of all sets — Mr. Towers, one of the Holts, Mr. Dominie Williams, Mr. Woodhouse, Mrs. Hazlitt and son, Mrs. Webb, and Mrs. Septimus

Brown. Mr. Woodhouse was looking up at a book window in Newgate Street, and, being short-sighted, twisted his muscles into so queer a stage that I stood by in doubt whether it was him or his brother, if he has one, and turning round, saw Mrs. Hazlitt, with that little Nero, her son. Woodhouse, on his features subsiding, proved to be Woodhouse, and not his brother. I have had a little business with Mr. Abbey from time to time ; he has behaved to me with a little Brusquerie : this hurt me a little, especially when I knew him to be the only man in England who dared to say a thing to me I did not approve of without its being resented, or at least noticed — so I wrote him about it, and have made an alteration in my favour — I expect from this to see more of Fanny, who has been quite shut out from me. I see Cobbett has been attacking the Settlement, but I cannot tell what to believe, and shall be all out at elbows till I hear from you. I am invited to Miss Miller's birthday dance on the 19th — I am nearly sure I shall not be able to go. A dance would injure my throat very much. I see very little of Reynolds. Hunt, I hear, is going on very badly — I mean in money matters. I shall not be surprised to hear of the worst. Haydon too, in consequence of his eyes, is out at elbows. I live as prudently as it is possible for me to do. I have not seen Haslam lately. I have not seen Richards for this half year, Rice for three months, or Charles Cowden Clarke for God knows when.

When I last called in Henrietta Street [47] Miss Millar was very unwell, and Miss Waldegrave as staid and self-possessed as usual. Henry was well. There are two new tragedies — one by the apostate Maw, and one by Miss Jane Porter. Next week I am going to stop at Taylor's for a few days, when I will see them both and tell you what they are. Mr. and Mrs. Bentley are well, and all the young carrots. I said nothing of consequence passed at Snooks's

— no more than this — that I like the family very much. Mr. and Mrs. Snooks were very kind. We used to have a little religion and politics together almost every evening, — and sometimes about you. He proposed writing out for me his experience in farming, for me to send to you. If I should have an opportunity of talking to him about it, I will get all I can at all events ; but you may say in your answer to this what value you place upon such information. I have not seen Mr. Lewis lately, for I have shrunk from going up the hill. Mr. Lewis went a few mornings ago to town with Mrs. Brawne. They talked about me, and I heard that Mr. L. said a thing I am not at all contented with. Says he, 'O, he is quite the little poet.' Now this is abominable — You might as well say Buonaparte is quite the little soldier. You see what it is to be under six foot and not a lord. There is a long fuzz to-day in the Examiner about a young man who delighted a young woman with a valentine — I think it must be Ollier's. Brown and I are thinking of passing the summer at Brussels — If we do, we shall go about the first of May. We — i. e. Brown and I — sit opposite one another all day authorizing (N. B., an 's' instead of a 'z' would give a different meaning). He is at present writing a story of an old woman who lived in a forest, and to whom the Devil or one of his aides-de-feu came one night very late and in disguise. The old dame sets before him pudding after pudding — mess after mess — which he devours, and moreover casts his eyes up at a side of Bacon hanging over his head, and at the same time asks if her Cat is a·Rabbit. On going he leaves her three pips of Eve's Apple, and somehow she, having lived a virgin all her life, begins to repent of it, and wished herself beautiful enough to make all the world and even the other world fall in love with her. So it happens, she sets out from her smoky cottage in magnificent apparel. — The first City she enters, every one falls in love with her, from the Prince to the Blacksmith. A young gentleman on his way to the Church to be married leaves his unfortunate Bride and follows this nonsuch — A whole regiment of soldiers are smitten at once and follow her — A whole convent of Monks in Corpus Christi procession join the soldiers. The mayor and corporation follow the same road — Old and young, deaf and dumb, — all but the blind, — are smitten, and form an immense concourse of people, who —— what Brown will do with them I know not. The devil himself falls in love with her, flies away with her to a desert place, in consequence of which she lays an infinite number of eggs — the eggs being hatched from time to time, fill the world with many nuisances, such as John Knox, George Fox, Johanna Southcote, and Gifford.

There have been within a fortnight eight failures of the highest consequence in London. Brown went a few evenings since to Davenport's, and on his coming in he talked about bad news in the city with such a face I began to think of a national bankruptcy. I did not feel much surprised and was rather disappointed. Carlisle, a bookseller on the Hone principle, has been issuing pamphlets from his shop in Fleet Street called the Deist. He was conveyed to Newgate last Thursday ; he intends making his own defence. I was surprised to hear from Taylor the amount of money of the bookseller's last sale. What think you of £25,000 ? He sold 4000 copies of Lord Byron. I am sitting opposite the Shakspeare I brought from the Isle of Wight — and I never look at him but the silk tassels " on it give me as much pleasure as the face of the poet itself.

In my next packet, as this is one by the way, I shall send you the Pot of Basil, St. Agnes Eve, and if I should have finished it, a little thing called the Eve of St. Mark. You see what fine Mother Radcliff names

I have — it is not my fault — I do not search for them. I have not gone on with Hyperion — for to tell the truth I have not been in great cue for writing lately — I must wait for the spring to rouse me up a little. The only time I went out from Bedhampton was to see a chapel consecrated — Brown, I, and John Snook the boy, went in a chaise behind a leaden horse. Brown drove, but the horse did not mind him. This chapel is built by a Mr. Way, a great Jew converter, who in that line has spent one hundred thousand pounds. He maintains a great number of poor Jews — *Of course his communion plate was stolen.* He spoke to the clerk about it — The clerk said he was very sorry, adding, '*I dare shay, your honour, it 's among ush.*'

The chapel is built in Mr. Way's park. The consecration was not amusing. There were numbers of carriages — and his house crammed with clergy — They sanctified the Chapel, and it being a wet day, consecrated the burial-ground through the vestry window. I begin to hate parsons ; they did not make me love them that day when I saw them in their proper colours. A parson is a Lamb in a drawing-room, and a Lion in a vestry. The notions of Society will not permit a parson to give way to his temper in any shape — So he festers in himself — his features get a peculiar, diabolical, self sufficient, iron stupid expression. He is continually acting — his mind is against every man, and every man's mind is against him — He is a hypocrite to the Believer and a coward to the unbeliever — He must be either a knave or an idiot — and there is no man so much to be pitied as an idiot parson. The soldier who is cheated into an Esprit du Corps by a red coat, a band, and colours, for the purpose of nothing, is not half so pitiable as the parson who is led by the nose by the Bench of Bishops and is smothered in absurdities — a poor necessary subaltern of the Church.

Friday, Feby. 18.

The day before yesterday I went to Romney Street — your Mother was not at home — but I have just written her that I shall see her on Wednesday. I call'd on Mr. Lewis this morning — he is very well — and tells me not to be uneasy about Letters, the chances being so arbitrary. He is going on as usual among his favourite democrat papers. We had a chat as usual about Cobbett and the Westminster electors. Dilke has lately been very much harrassed about the manner of educating his son — he at length decided for a public school — and then he did not know what school — he at last has decided for Westminster; and as Charley is to be a day boy, Dilke will remove to Westminster. We lead very quiet lives here — Dilke is at present in Greek histories and antiquities, and talks of nothing but the electors of Westminster and the retreat of the ten - thousand. I never drink now above three glasses of wine — and never any spirits and water. Though by the bye, the other day Woodhouse took me to his coffee house and ordered a Bottle of Claret — now I like Claret, whenever I can have Claret I must drink it, — 't is the only palate affair that I am at all sensual in. Would it not be a good speck to send you some vine roots — could it be done? I 'll enquire — If you could make some wine like Claret to drink on summer evenings in an arbour! For really 't is so fine — it fills one's mouth with a gushing freshness — then goes down cool and feverless — then you do not feel it quarrelling with your liver — no, it is rather a Peacemaker, and lies as quiet as it did in the grape; then it is as fragrant as the Queen Bee, and the more ethereal Part of it mounts into the brain, not assaulting the cerebral apartments like a bully in a bad-house looking for his trull and hurrying from door to door bouncing against the wainstcoat, but rather walks like Aladdin about his own enchanted palace so gently that you do not feel his step. Other wines of a heavy and spirituous nature transform a Man to a Silenus: this makes him a Hermes — and gives a Woman the soul and immortality of Ariadne, for whom Bacchus always kept a good cellar of claret — and even of that he could never persuade her to take above two cups. I said this same claret is the only palate-passion I have — I forgot game — I must plead guilty to the breast of a Partridge, the back of a hare, the backbone of a grouse, the wing and side of a Pheasant and a Woodcock *passim.* Talking of game (I wish I could make it), the Lady whom I met at Hastings and of whom I said something in my last I think has lately made me many presents of game, and enabled me to make as many. She made me take home a Pheasant the other day, which I gave to Mrs. Dilke; on which to-morrow Rice, Reynolds and the Wentworthians will dine next door. The next I intend for your Mother. These moderate sheets of paper are much more pleasant to write upon than those large thin sheets which I hope you by this time have received — though that can't be, now I think of it. I have not said in any Letter yet a word about my affairs — in a word I am in no despair about them — my poem has not at all succeeded; in the course of a year or so I think I shall try the public again — in a selfish point of view I should suffer my pride and my contempt of public opinion to hold me silent — but for yours and Fanny's sake I will pluck up a spirit and try again. I have no doubt of success in a course of years if I persevere — but it must be patience, for the Reviews have enervated and made indolent men's minds — few think for themselves. These Reviews too are getting more and more powerful, especially the Quarterly — they are like a superstition which the more it prostrates the Crowd and the longer it continues the more powerful it becomes just in proportion to their increasing weakness. I was in hopes that when people saw, as they must do now, all the trickery and iniquity of these Plagues they would scout them, but no, they are like the spectators at the Westminster cock-pit — they like the battle and do not care who wins or who loses. Brown is going on this morning with the story of his old woman and the Devil — He makes but slow progress — The fact is it is a Libel on the Devil, and as that person is Brown's Muse, look ye, if he libels his own Muse how can he expect to write ? Either Brown or his Muse must turn tail. Yesterday was Charley Dilke's birthday. Brown and I were invited to tea. During the evening nothing passed worth notice but a little conversation between Mrs. Dilke and Mrs. Brawne. The subject was the Watchman. It was ten o'clock, and Mrs. Brawne, who lived during the summer in Brown's house and now lives in the Road, recognized her old Watchman's voice, and said that he came as far as her now. 'Indeed,' said Mrs. D., 'does he turn the Corner ? ' There have been some letters passed between me and Haslam but I have not seen him lately. The day before yesterday — which I made a day of Business — I called upon him — he was out as usual. Brown has been walking up and down the room a-breeding — now at this moment he is being delivered of a couplet, and I daresay will be as well as can be expected. Gracious — he has twins !

I have a long story to tell you about Bailey — I will say first the circumstances as plainly and as well as I can remember, and then I will make my comment. You know that Bailey was very much cut up about a little Jilt in the country somewhere. I thought he was in a dying state about it when at Oxford with him: little supposing, as I have since heard, that he was at that very time making impatient Love to Marian Reynolds — and guess my astonishment at hearing after this that he had been trying at Miss Martin. So Matters have been — So Matters stood — when he got ordained

and went to a Curacy near Carlisle, where the family of the Gleigs reside. There his susceptible heart was conquered by Miss Gleig — and thereby all his connections in town have been annulled — both male and female. I do not now remember clearly the facts — These however I know — He showed his correspondence with Marian to Gleig, returned all her Letters and asked for his own — he also wrote very abrupt Letters to Mrs. Reynolds. I do not know any more of the Martin affair than I have written above. No doubt his conduct has been very bad. The great thing to be considered is — whether it is want of delicacy and principle or want of knowledge and polite experience. And again weakness — yes, that is it ; and the want of a Wife — yes, that is it; and then Marian made great Bones of him although her Mother and sister have teased her very much about it. Her conduct has been very upright throughout the whole affair — She liked Bailey as a Brother but not as a Husband — especially as he used to woo her with the Bible and Jeremy Taylor under his arm — they walked in no grove but Jeremy Taylor's. Marian's obstinacy is some excuse, but his so quickly taking to Miss Gleig can have no excuse — except that of a Ploughman who wants a wife. The thing which sways me more against him than anything else is Rice's conduct on the occasion; Rice would not make an immature resolve : he was ardent in his friendship for Bailey, he examined the whole for and against minutely; and he has abandoned Bailey entirely. All this I am not supposed by the Reynoldses to have any hint of. It will be a good lesson to the Mother and Daughters — nothing would serve but Bailey. If you mentioned the word Tea-pot some one of them came out with an à propros about Bailey — noble fellow — fine fellow ! was always in their mouths — This may teach them that the man who ridicules romance is the most romantic of Men — that he who abuses women and slights them loves them the most — that he who talks of roasting a Man alive would not do it when it came to the push — and above all, that they are very shallow people who take everything literally. A Man's life of any worth is a continual allegory, and very few eyes can see the Mystery of his life — a life like the scriptures, figurative — which such people can no more make out than they can the Hebrew Bible. Lord Byron cuts a figure but he is not figurative — Shakspeare led a life of Allegory: his works are the comments on it —

March 12, Friday.

I went to town yesterday chiefly for the purpose of seeing some young Men who were to take some Letters for us to you — through the medium of Peachey. I was surprised and disappointed at hearing they had changed their minds, and did not purpose going so far as Birkbeck's. I was much disappointed, for I had counted upon seeing some persons who were to see you — and upon your seeing some who had seen me. I have not only lost this opportunity, but the sail of the Post-Packet to New York or Philadelphia, by which last your Brothers have sent some Letters. The weather in town yesterday was so stifling that I could not remain there though I wanted much to see Kean in Hotspur. I have by me at present Hazlitt's Letter to Gifford — perhaps you would like an extract or two from the high-seasoned parts. It begins thus:

'Sir, you have an ugly trick of saying what is not true of any one you do not like; and it will be the object of this Letter to cure you of it. You say what you please of others; it is time you were told what you are. In doing this give me leave to borrow the familiarity of your style: — for the fidelity of the picture I shall be answerable. You are a little person but a considerable cat's paw; and so far worthy of notice. Your clandestine connection with persons high in office constantly influences your opinions and alone gives importance to them. You are the government critic, a character

nicely differing from that of a government spy — the invisible link which connects literature with the Police.'

Again:

'Your employers, Mr. Gifford, do not pay their hirelings for nothing — for condescending to notice weak and wicked sophistry; for pointing out to contempt what excites no admiration; for cautiously selecting a few specimens of bad taste and bad grammar where nothing else is to be found. They want your invisible pertness, your mercenary malice, your impenetrable dulness, your bare-faced impudence, your pragmatical self-sufficiency, your hypocritical zeal, your pious frauds to stand in the gap of their Prejudices and pretensions to flyblow and taint public opinion, to defeat independent efforts, to apply not the touch of the scorpion but the touch of the Torpedo to youthful hopes, to crawl and leave the slimy track of sophistry and lies over every work that does not dedicate its sweet leaves to some Luminary of the treasury bench, or is not fostered in the hotbed of corruption. This is your office; "this is what is look'd for at your hands, and this you do not baulk" — to sacrifice what little honesty and prostitute what little intellect you possess to any dirty job you are commission'd to execute. "They keep you as an ape does an apple in the corner of his jaw, first mouth'd to be at last swallow'd." You are by appointment literary toadeater to greatness and taster to the court. You have a natural aversion to whatever differs from your own pretensions, and an acquired one for what gives offence to your superiors. Your vanity panders to your interest, and your malice truckles only to your love of Power. If your instructive or premeditated abuse of your enviable trust were found wanting in a single instance; if you were to make a single slip in getting up your select committee of enquiry and green bag report of the state of Letters, your occupation would be gone. You would never after obtain a squeeze of the hand from acquaintance, or a smile from a Punk of quality. The great and powerful whom you call wise and good do not like to have the privacy of their self-love startled by the obtrusive and unmanageable claims of Literature and Philosophy, except through the intervention of people like you, whom, if they have common penetration, they soon find out to be without any superiority of intellect; or if they do not, whom they can despise for their meanness of soul. You "have the office opposite to Saint Peter." You keep a corner in the public mind for foul prejudice and corrupt power to knot and gender in; you volunteer your services to people of quality to ease scruples of mind and qualms of conscience; you lay the flattering unction of venal prose and laurell'd verse to their souls. You persuade them that there is neither purity of morals, nor depth of understanding except in themselves and their hangers-on; and would prevent the unhallow'd names of Liberty and humanity from ever being whispered in ears polite! You, sir, do you not all this? I cry you mercy then: I took you for the Editor of the Quarterly Review.'

This is the sort of feu de joie he keeps up. There is another extract or two — one especially which I will copy to-morrow — for the candles are burnt down and I am using the wax taper — which has a long snuff on it — the fire is at its last click — I am sitting with my back to it with one foot rather askew upon the rug and the other with the heel a little elevated from the carpet — I am writing this on the Maid's Tragedy, which I have read since tea with great pleasure — Besides this volume of Beaumont and Fletcher, there are on the table two volumes of Chaucer and a new work of Tom Moore's, called Tom Cribb's Memorial to Congress — nothing in it. These are trifles — but I require nothing so much of you but that you will give one a like description of yourselves, however it may be when you are writing to me. Could I see the same thing done of any great Man long since dead it would be a great delight: as to know in what position Shakspeare sat when he began 'To be or not to be' — such things become interesting from distance of time or place. I hope you are both now in that sweet sleep which no two beings deserve more than you do — I must fancy so — and please myself in the fancy of speaking a prayer and a blessing over you and your lives — God bless you — I whisper good-night in your ears, and you will dream of me.

March 13, Saturday.

I have written to Fanny this morning and received a note from Haslam. I was to have dined with him to-morrow: he gives me a bad account of his Father, who has not been in Town for five weeks, and is not well enough for company. Haslam is well — and from the prosperous state of some love affair he does not mind the double tides he has to work. I have been a Walk past west end — and was going to call at Mr. Monkhouse's — but I did not, not being in the humour. I know not why Poetry and I have been so distant lately; I must make some advances soon or she will cut me entirely. Hazlitt has this fine Passage in his Letter : Gifford in his Review of Hazlitt's characters of Shakspeare's plays attacks the Coriolanus critique. He says that Hazlitt has slandered Shakspeare in saying that he had a leaning to the arbitrary side of the question. Hazlitt thus defends himself,

'My words are, "Coriolanus is a storehouse of political common-places. The Arguments for and against aristocracy and democracy on the Privileges of the few and the claims of the many, on Liberty and slavery, power and the abuse of it, peace and war, are here very ably handled, with the spirit of a Poet and the acuteness of a Philosopher. Shakspeare himself seems to have had a leaning to the arbitrary side of the question, perhaps from some feeling of contempt for his own origin, and to have spared no occasion of bating the rabble. What he says of them is very true; what he says of their betters is also very true, though he dwells less upon it." I then proceed to account for this by showing how it is that "the cause of the people is but little calculated for a subject for poetry; or that the language of Poetry naturally falls in with the language of power." I affirm, Sir, that Poetry, that the imagination generally speaking, delights in power, in strong excitement, as well as in truth, in good, in right, whereas pure reason and the moral sense approve only of the true and good. I proceed to show that this general love or tendency to immediate excitement or theatrical effect, no matter how produced, gives a Bias to the imagination often consistent with the greatest good, that in Poetry it triumphs over principle, and bribes the passions to make a sacrifice of common humanity. You say that it does not, that there is no such original Sin in Poetry, that it makes no such sacrifice or unworthy compromise between poetical effect and the still small voice of reason. And how do you prove that there is no such principle giving a bias to the imagination and a false colouring to poetry? Why, by asking in reply to the instances where this principle operates, and where no other can with much modesty and simplicity — " But are these the only topics that afford delight in Poetry, etc. ? " No; but these objects do afford delight in poetry, and they afford it in proportion to their strong and often tragical effect, and not in proportion to the good produced, or their desireableness in a moral point of view. Do we read with more pleasure of the ravages of a beast of prey than of the Shepherd's pipe upon the Mountain? No; but we do read with pleasure of the ravages of a beast of prey, and we do so on the principle I have stated, namely, from the sense of power abstracted from the sense of good; and it is the same principle that makes us read with admiration and reconciles us in fact to the triumphant progress of the conquerors and mighty Hunters of mankind, who come to stop the Shepherd's Pipe upon the Mountains and sweep away his listening flock. Do you mean to deny that there is anything imposing to the imagination in power, in grandeur, in outward show, in the accumulation of individual wealth and luxury, at the expense of equal justice and the common weal? Do you deny that there is anything in the " Pride, Pomp, and Circumstances of glorious war, that makes ambition virtue" in the eyes of admiring multitudes? Is this a new theory of the pleasures of the imagination, which says that the pleasures of the imagination do not take rise solely in the calculation of the understanding? Is it a paradox of my creating that " one murder makes a villain, millions a Hero"? or is it not true that here, as in other cases, the enormity of the evil overpowers and makes a convert of the imagination by its very magnitude? You contradict my reasoning because you know nothing of the question, and you think that no one has a right to understand what you do not. My offence against purity in the passage alluded to, " which contains the concentrated venom of my malignity," is that I have admitted that there are tyrants and slaves abroad in the world; and you would hush the matter up and pretend that there is no such thing in order that there may be nothing else. Further, I have explained the cause, the subtle sophistry of the human mind, that tolerates and pampers the evil in order to guard against its approaches; you would conceal the

cause in order to prevent the cure, and to leave the proud flesh about the heart to harden and ossify into one impenetrable mass of selfishness and hypocrisy, that we may not " sympathise in the distresses of suffering virtue " in any case in which they come in competition with the fictitious wants and "imputed weaknesses of the great." You ask, " Are we gratified by the cruelties of Domitian or Nero? " No, not we — they were too petty and cowardly to strike the imagination at a distance; but the Roman senate tolerated them, addressed their perpetrators, exalted them into gods, the fathers of the people, they had pimps and scribblers of all sorts in their pay, their Senecas, etc., till a turbulent rabble, thinking there were no injuries to Society greater than the endurance of unlimited and wanton oppression, put an end to the farce and abated the sin as well as they could. Had you and I lived in those times we should have been what we are now, I "a sour malcontent," and you "a sweet courtier." '

The manner in which this is managed: the force and innate power with which it yeasts and works up itself — the feeling for the costume of society; is in a style of genius. He hath a demon, as he himself says of Lord Byron. We are to have a party this evening. The Davenports from Church Row — I don't think you know anything of them — they have paid me a good deal of attention. I like Davenport himself. The names of the rest are Miss Barnes, Miss Winter with the Children.

[Later, March 17 or 18.]

On Monday we had to dinner Severn and Cawthorn, the Bookseller and printvirtuoso; in the evening Severn went home to paint, and we other three went to the play, to see Sheil's new tragedy ycleped Evadné. In the morning Severn and I took a turn round the Museum — There is a Sphinx there of a giant size, and most voluptuous Egyptian expression, I had not seen it before. The play was bad even in comparison with 1818, the Augustan age of the Drama, 'comme on sait,' as Voltaire says — the whole was made up of a virtuous young woman, an indignant brother, a suspecting lover, a libertine prince, a gratuitous villain, a street in Naples, a Cypress grove, lilies and roses, virtue and vice, a bloody sword, a spangled jacket, one Lady Olivia, one Miss O'Neil alias Evadné, alias Bellamira, alias — Alias — Yea, and I say unto you a greater than Elias — There was Abbot, and talking of Abbot his name puts me in mind of a spelling-book lesson, descriptive of the whole Dramatis personæ — Abbot — Abbess — Actor — Actress — The play is a fine amusement, as a friend of mine once said to me — 'Do what you will,' says he, 'a poor gentleman who wants a guinea, cannot spend his two shillings better than at the playhouse.' The pantomime was excellent, I had seen it before and I enjoyed it again. Your Mother and I had some talk about Miss H.—— Says I, will Henry have that Miss ——, a lath with a boddice, she who has been fine drawn — fit for nothing but to cut up into Cribbage pins, to the tune of B. 2; one who is all muslin ; all feathers and bone ; once in travelling she was made use of as a lynch pin; I hope he will not have her, though it is no uncommon thing to be *smitten with a staff;* though she might be very useful as his walking-stick, his fishing-rod, his toothpik, his hat-stick (she runs so much in his head) — let him turn farmer, she would cut into hurdles ; let him write poetry, she would be his turn-style. Her gown is like a flag on a pole ; she would do for him if he turn freemason ; I hope she will prove a flag of truce ; when she sits languishing with her one foot on a stool, and one elbow on the table, and her head inclined, she looks like the sign of the crooked billet — or the frontispiece to Cinderella, or a tea-paper wood-cut of Mother Shipton at her studies ; she is a make-believe — She is bona *side* a thin young 'oman— But this is mere talk of a fellow-creature ; yet pardie I would not that Henry have her — Non volo ut eam possideat, nam, for, it would be a bam, for it would be a sham —

Don't think I am writing a petition to the Governors of St. Luke — no, that would be in another style. May it please your Worships ; forasmuch as the undersigned has committed, transferred, given up, made over, consigned, and aberrated himself, to the art and mystery of poetry ; forasmuch as he hath cut, rebuffed, affronted, huffed, and shirked, and taken stint at, all other employments, arts, mysteries, and occupations, honest, middling, and dishonest; forasmuch as he hath at sundry times and in divers places, told truth unto the men of this generation, and eke to the women ; moreover, forasmuch as he hath kept a pair of boots that did not fit, and doth not admire Sheil's play, Leigh Hunt, Tom Moore, Bob Southey, and Mr. Rogers; and does admire Wm. Hazlitt ; moreoverer for as more as he liketh half of Wordsworth, and none of Crabbe ; moreover-est for as most as he hath written this page of penmanship — he prayeth your Worships to give him a lodging —Witnessed by Rd. Abbey and Co., cum familiaribus et consanguineis (signed) Count de Cockaigne.

The nothing of the day is a machine called the velocipede. It is a wheel carriage to ride cock-horse upon, sitting astride and pushing it along with the toes, a rudder wheel in hand — they will go seven miles an hour — A handsome gelding will come to eight guineas ; however they will soon be cheaper, unless the army takes to them. I look back upon the last month, I find nothing to write about ; indeed I do not recollect anything particular in it. It's all alike ; we keep on breathing. The only amusement is a little scandal, of however fine a shape, a laugh at a pun — and then after all we wonder how we could enjoy the scandal, or laugh at the pun.

I have been at different times turning it in my head whether I should go to Edinburgh and study for a physician; I am afraid I should not take kindly to it ; I am sure I could not take fees — and yet I should like to do so; it's not worse than writing poems, and hanging them up to be fly-blown on the Review shambles. Everybody is in his own mess. Here is the parson at Hampstead quarrelling with all the world, he is in the wrong by this same token; when the black cloth was put up in the Church for the Queen's mourning, he asked the workmen to hang it the wrong side outwards, that it might be better when taken down, it being his perquisite — Parsons will always keep up their character, but as it is said there are some animals the ancients knew which we do not, let us hope our posterity will miss the black badger with tri-cornered hat; Who knows but some Reviewer of Buffon or Pliny may put an account of the parson in the Appendix; No one will then believe it any more than we believe in the Phœnix. I think we may class the lawyer in the same natural history of Monsters; a green bag will hold as much as a lawn sleeve. The only difference is that one is fustian and the other flimsy; I am not unwilling to read Church history at present and have Milner's in my eye; his is reckonéd a very good one.

[18th September 1819.]

In looking over some of my papers I found the above specimen of my carelessness. It is a sheet you ought to have had long ago — my letter must have appeared very unconnected, but as I number the sheets you must have discovered how the mistake happened. How many things have happened since I wrote it — How have I acted contrary to my resolves. The interval between writing this sheet and the day I put this supplement to it, has been completely filled with generous and most friendly actions of Brown towards me. How frequently I forget to speak of things which I think of and feel most. 'T is very singular, the idea about Buffon above has been taken up by Hunt in the Examiner, in some papers which he calls 'A Preternatural History.'

Friday 19th March.

This morning I have been reading 'the False One.' Shameful to say, I was in bed at ten — I mean this morning. The Blackwood Reviewers have committed themselves in a scandalous heresy — they have been putting up Hogg, the Ettrick Shepherd, against Burns: the senseless villains! The Scotch cannot manage themselves at all, they want imagination, and that is why they are so fond of Hogg, who has a little of it. This morning I am in a sort of temper, indolent and supremely careless — I long after a Stanza or two of Thomson's Castle of Indolence — my passions are all asleep, from my having slumbered till nearly eleven, and weakened the animal fibre all over me, to a delightful sensation, about three degrees on this side of faintness. If I had teeth of pearl and the breath of lilies I should call it languor, but as I am *I must call it laziness. In this state of effeminacy the fibres of the brain are relaxed in common with the rest of the body, and to such a happy degree that pleasure has no show of enticement and pain no unbearable power. Neither Poetry, nor Ambition, nor Love have any alertness of countenance as they pass by me; they seem rather like figures on a Greek vase — a Man and two women whom no one but myself could distinguish in their disguisement. This is the only happiness, and is a rare instance of the advantage of the body overpowering the Mind. I have this moment received a note from Haslam, in which he expects the death of his Father, who has been for some time in a state of insensibility; his mother bears up he says very well — I shall go to town to-morrow to see him. This is the world — thus we cannot expect to give way many hours to pleasure. Circumstances are like Clouds continually gathering and bursting — While we are laughing, the seed of some trouble is put into the wide arable land of events — while we are laughing it sprouts it grows and suddenly bears a poison fruit which we must pluck. Even so we have leisure to reason on the misfortunes of our friends;

* Especially as I have a black eye.

our own touch us too nearly for words. Very few men have ever arrived at a complete disinterestedness of Mind : very few have been influenced by a pure desire of the benefit of others, — in the greater part of the Benefactors to Humanity some meretricious motive has sullied their greatness — some melodramatic scenery has fascinated them. From the manner in which I feel Haslam's misfortune I perceive how far I am from any humble standard of disinterestedness. Yet this feeling ought to be carried to its highest pitch, as there is no fear of its ever injuring society — which it would do, I fear, pushed to an extremity. For in wild nature the Hawk would lose his Breakfast of Robins and the Robin his of Worms — The Lion must starve as well as the swallow. The greater part of Men make their way with the same instinctiveness, the same unwandering eye from their purposes, the same animal eagerness as the Hawk. The Hawk wants a Mate, so does the Man — look at them both, they set about it and procure one in the same manner. They want both a nest and they both set about one in the same manner — they get their food in the same manner. The noble animal Man for his amusement smokes his pipe—the Hawk balances about the Clouds — that is the only difference of their leisures. This it is that makes the Amusement of Life—to a speculative Mind — I go among the Fields and catch a glimpse of a Stoat or a fieldmouse peeping out of the withered grass — the creature hath a purpose, and its eyes are bright with it. I go amongst the buildings of a city and I see a Man hurrying along — to what ? the Creature has a purpose and his eyes are bright with it. But then, as Wordsworth says, 'we have all one human heart——' There is an electric fire in human nature tending to purify — so that among these human creatures there is continually some birth of new heroism. The pity is that we must wonder at it, as we should at finding a pearl in rubbish. I have

no doubt that thousands of people never heard of have had hearts completely disinterested : I can remember but two— Socrates and Jesus — Their histories evince it. What I heard a little time ago, Taylor observe with respect to Socrates, may be said of Jesus — That he was so great a man that though he transmitted no writing of his own to posterity, we have his Mind and his sayings and his greatness handed to us by others. It is to be lamented that the history of the latter was written and revised by Men interested in the pious frauds of Religion. Yet through all this I see his splendour. Even here, though I myself am pursuing the same instinctive course as the veriest human animal you can think of, I am, however young, writing at random, straining at particles of light in the midst of a great darkness, without knowing the bearing of any one assertion, of any one opinion. Yet may I not in this be free from sin ? May there not be superior beings amused with any graceful, though instinctive, attitude my mind may fall into as I am entertained with the alertness of a Stoat or the anxiety of a Deer ? Though a quarrel in the Streets is a thing to be hated, the energies displayed in it are fine ; the commonest Man shows a grace in his quarrel. By a superior Being our reasonings may take the same tone — though erroneous they may be fine. This is the very thing in which consists Poetry, and if so it is not so fine a thing as philosophy — For the same reason that an eagle is not so fine a thing as a truth. Give me this credit — Do you not think I strive — to know myself ? Give me this credit, and you will not think that on my own account I repeat Milton's lines —

'How charming is divine Philosophy,
  Not harsh and crabbed, as dull fools suppose,
  But musical as is Apollo's lute.'

No — not for myself — feeling grateful as I do to have got into a state of mind to relish them properly. Nothing ever becomes real till it is experienced — Even a Proverb is no proverb to you till your Life has illustrated it. I am ever afraid that your anxiety for me will lead you to fear for the violence of my temperament continually smothered down : for that reason I did not intend to have sent you the following sonnet — but look over the two last pages and ask yourselves whether I have not that in me which will bear the buffets of the world. It will be the best comment on my sonnet ; it will show you that it was written with no Agony but that of ignorance ; with no thirst of anything but Knowledge when pushed to the point though the first steps to it were through my human passions — they went away and I wrote with my Mind — and perhaps I must confess a little bit of my heart —

['Why did I laugh to-night? No voice will tell,' p. 137.]

I went to bed and enjoyed an uninterrupted sleep. Sane I went to bed and sane I arose.

[April 15.]

This is the 15th of April — you see what a time it is since I wrote ; all that time I have been day by day expecting Letters from you. I write quite in the dark. In the hopes of a Letter daily I have deferred that I might write in the light. I was in town yesterday, and at Taylor's heard that young Birkbeck had been in Town and was to set forward in six or seven days — so I shall dedicate that time to making up this parcel ready for him. I wish I could hear from you to make me 'whole and general as the casing air.' A few days after the 19th of April, [sic. accurately, March], I received a note from Haslam containing the news of his father's death. The Family has all been well. Haslam has his father's situation. The Framptons have behaved well to him. The day before yesterday I went to a rout at Sawrey's— it was made pleasant by Reynolds being there and our getting into conversation with one of the most beautiful Girls I ever saw — She gave a

remarkable prettiness to all those commonplaces which most women who talk must utter — I liked Mrs. Sawrey very well. The Sunday before last your Brothers were to come by a long invitation — so long that for the time I forgot it when I promised Mrs. Brawne to dine with her on the same day. On recollecting my engagement with your Brothers I immediately excused myself with Mrs Brawne, but she would not hear of it, and insisted on my bringing my friends with me. So we all dined at Mrs. Brawne's. I have been to Mrs. Bentley's this morning, and put all the letters to and from you and poor Tom and me. I found some of the correspondence between him and that degraded Wells and Amena. It is a wretched business ; I do not know the rights of it, but what I do know would, I am sure, affect you so much that I am in two minds whether I will tell you anything about it. And yet I do not see why — for anything, though it be unpleasant, that calls to mind those we still love has a compensation in itself for the pain it occasions — so very likely to-morrow I may set about copying the whole of what I have about it : with no sort of a Richardson self-satisfaction — I hate it to a sickness — and I am afraid more from indolence of mind than anything else. I wonder how people exist with all their worries. I have not been to Westminster but once lately, and that was to see Dilke in his new Lodgings — I think of living somewhere in the neighbourhood myself. Your mother was well by your Brothers' account. I shall see her perhaps to-morrow — yes I shall. We have had the Boys here lately — they make a bit of a racket — I shall not be sorry when they go. I found also this morning, in a note from George to you and my dear sister a lock of your hair which I shall this moment put in the miniature case. A few days ago Hunt dined here and Brown invited Davenport to meet him, Davenport from a sense of weakness thought it incumbent on him to show off —

and pursuant to that never ceased talking and boring all day till I was completely fagged out. Brown grew melancholy — but Hunt perceiving what a complimentary tendency all this had bore it remarkably well — Brown grumbled about it for two or three days. I went with Hunt to Sir John Leicester's gallery ; there I saw Northcote — Hilton — Bewick, and many more of great and Little note. Haydon's picture is of very little progress this year — He talks about finishing it next year. Wordsworth is going to publish a Poem called Peter Bell — what a perverse fellow it is ! Why will he talk about Peter Bells — I was told not to tell — but to you it will not be telling — Reynolds hearing that said Peter Bell was coming out, took it into his head to write a skit upon it called Peter Bell. He did it as soon as thought on, it is to be published this morning, and comes out before the real Peter Bell, with this admirable motto from the 'Bold Stroke for a Wife' ' I am the real Simon Pure.' It would be just as well to trounce Lord Byron in the same manner. I am still at a stand in versifying — I cannot do it yet with any pleasure — I mean, however, to look round on my resources and means, and see what I can do without poetry — To that end I shall live in Westminster — I have no doubt of making by some means a little to help on, or I shall be left in the Lurch — with the burden of a little Pride — However I look in time. The Dilkes like their Lodgings at Westminster tolerably well. I cannot help thinking what a shame it is that poor Dilke should give up his comfortable house and garden for his Son, whom he will certainly ruin with too much care. The boy has nothing in his ears all day but himself and the importance of his education. Dilke has continually in his mouth 'My Boy.' This is what spoils princes : it may have the same effect with Commoners. Mrs. Dilke has been very well lately — But what a shameful thing it is that for that obstinate Boy

Dilke should stifle himself in Town Lodgings and wear out his Life by his continual apprehension of his Boy's fate in Westminster school, with the rest of the Boys and the Masters. Every one has some wear and tear. One would think Dilke ought to be quiet and happy — but no — this one Boy makes his face pale, his society silent and his vigilance jealous — He would I have no doubt quarrel with any one who snubb'd his Boy — With all this he has no notion how to manage him. O what a farce is our greatest cares ! Yet one must be in the pother for the sake of Clothes food and Lodging. There has been a squabble between Kean and Mr. Bucke — There are faults on both sides — on Bucke's the faults are positive to the Question : Kean's fault is a want of genteel knowledge and high Policy. The former writes knavishly foolish, and the other silly bombast. It was about a Tragedy written by said Mr. Bucke which, it appears, Mr. Kean kick'd at — it was so bad — After a little struggle of Mr. Bucke's against Kean, Drury Lane had the Policy to bring it out and Kean the impolicy not to appear in it. It was damn'd. The people in the Pit had a favourite call on the night of 'Buck, Buck, rise up ' and ' Buck, Buck, how many horns do I hold up.' Kotzebue the German Dramatist and traitor to his country was murdered lately by a young student whose name I forget — he stabbed himself immediately after crying out Germany ! Germany ! I was unfortunate to miss Richards the only time I have been for many months to see him.

Shall I treat you with a little extempore ? —

['When they were come into the Faery's Court,' p. 249.]

Brown is gone to bed — and I am tired of rhyming — there is a north wind blowing playing young gooseberry with the trees — I don't care so it helps even with a side wind a Letter to me — for I cannot put faith in any reports I hear of the Settlement ; some are good and some bad. Last Sunday I took a Walk towards Highgate and in the lane that winds by the side of Lord Mansfield's park I met Mr. Green our Demonstrator at Guy's in conversation with Coleridge — I joined them, after enquiring by a look whether it would be agreeable — I walked with him at his alderman-after-dinner pace for near two miles I suppose. In those two Miles he broached a thousand things — let me see if I can give you a list — Nightingales — Poetry — on Poetical Sensation — Metaphysics — Different genera and species of Dreams — Nightmare — a dream accompanied by a sense of touch — single and double touch — a dream related — First and second consciousness — the difference explained between will and Volition — so say metaphysicians from a want of smoking the second consciousness — Monsters — the Kraken — Mermaids — Southey believes in them — Southey's belief too much diluted — a Ghost story — Good morning — I heard his voice as he came towards me — I heard it as he moved away — I had heard it all the interval — if it may be called so. He was civil enough to ask me to call on him at Highgate. Good-night !

[Later, April 16 or 17.]

It looks so much like rain I shall not go to town to-day: but put it off till to-morrow. Brown this morning is writing some Spenserian stanzas against Mrs., Miss Brawne and me ; so I shall amuse myself with him a little : in the manner of Spenser—

[' He is to weet a melancholy Carle,' p. 250.] This character would ensure him a situation in the establishment of patient Griselda. The servant has come for the little Browns this morning — they have been a toothache to me which I shall enjoy the riddance of — Their little voices are like wasps' stings — Sometimes am I all wound with Browns.[49] We had a claret feast some little while ago. There were Dilke, Reynolds, Skinner, Mancur, John Brown,

Martin, Brown and I. We all got a little tipsy — but pleasantly so — I enjoy Claret to a degree.

[Later, April 18 or 19.]

I have been looking over the correspondence of the pretended Amena and Wells this evening — I now see the whole cruel deception. I think Wells must have had an accomplice in it — Amena's letters are in a Man's language and in a Man's hand imitating a woman's. The instigations to this diabolical scheme were vanity, and the love of intrigue. It was no thoughtless hoax — but a cruel deception on a sanguine Temperament, with every show of friendship. I do not think death too bad for the villain. The world would look upon it in a different light should I expose it — they would call it a frolic — so I must be wary — but I consider it my duty to be prudently revengeful. I will hang over his head like a sword by a hair. I will be opium to his vanity — if I cannot injure his interests — He is a rat and he shall have ratsbane to his vanity — I will harm him all I possibly can — I have no doubt I shall be able to do so — Let us leave him to his misery alone, except when we can throw in a little more. The fifth canto of Dante pleases me more and more — it is that one in which he meets with Paolo and Francesca. I had passed many days in rather a low state of mind, and in the midst of them I dreamt of being in that region of Hell. The dream was one of the most delightful enjoyments I ever had in my life. I floated about the whirling atmosphere, as it is described, with a beautiful figure, to whose lips mine were joined as it seemed for an age — and in the midst of all this cold and darkness I was warm — even flowery tree-tops sprung up, and we rested on them, sometimes with the lightness of a cloud, till the wind blew us away again. I tried a sonnet upon it — there are fourteen lines, but nothing of what I felt in it — O that I could dream it every night —

['As Hermes once took to his feathers light,' p. 138.]

I want very very much a little of your wit, my dear Sister — a Letter or two of yours just to bandy back a pun or two across the Atlantic, and send a quibble over the Floridas. Now you have by this time crumpled up your large Bonnet, what do you wear — a cap? do you put your hair in papers of a night? do you pay the Miss Birkbecks a morning visit — have you any tea? or do you milk-and-water with them — What place of Worship do you go to — the Quakers, the Moravians, the Unitarians, or the Methodists? Are there any flowers in bloom you like — any beautiful heaths — any streets full of Corset Makers? What sort of shoes have you to fit those pretty feet of yours? Do you desire Compliments to one another? Do you ride on Horseback? What do you have for breakfast, dinner, and supper? without mentioning lunch and bever [a bite between meals] and wet and snack — and a bit to stay one's stomach? Do you get any Spirits — now you might easily distill some whiskey — and going into the woods, set up a whiskey shop for the Monkeys — Do you and the Miss Birkbecks get groggy on anything — a little so-soish so as to be obliged to be seen home with a Lantern? You may perhaps have a game at puss in the corner — Ladies are warranted to play at this game though they have not whiskers. Have you a fiddle in the Settlement — or at any rate a Jew's harp — which will play in spite of one's teeth — When you have nothing else to do for a whole day I tell you how you may employ it — First get up and when you are dressed, as it would be pretty early with a high wind in the woods, give George a cold Pig with my Compliments. Then you may saunter into the nearest coffee-house, and after taking a dram and a look at the Chronicle — go and frighten the wild boars upon the strength — you may as well bring one home for breakfast, serving up the hoofs garnished

with bristles and a grunt or two to accompany the singing of the kettle — then if George is not up give him a colder Pig always with my Compliments — When you are both set down to breakfast I advise you to eat your full share, but leave off immediately on feeling yourself inclined to anything on the other side of the puffy — avoid that, for it does not become young women —After you have eaten your breakfast keep your eye upon dinner — it is the safest way — You should keep a Hawk's eye over your dinner and keep hovering over it till due time then pounce taking care not to break any plates. While you are hovering with your dinner in prospect you may do a thousand things — put a hedgehog into George's hat — pour a little water into his rifle — soak his boots in a pail of water — cut his jacket round into shreds like a Roman kilt or the back of my grandmother's stays — Sew *off* his buttons —

[Later, April 21 or 22.]

Yesterday I could not write a line I was so fatigued, for the day before I went to town in the morning, called on your Mother, and returned in time for a few friends we had to dinner. These were Taylor, Woodhouse, Reynolds: we began cards at about 9 o'clock, and the night coming on, and continuing dark and rainy, they could not think of returning to town — So we played at Cards till very daylight — and yesterday I was not worth a sixpence. Your Mother was very well but anxious for a Letter. We had half an hour's talk and no more, for I was obliged to be home. Mrs. and Miss Millar were well, and so was Miss Waldegrave. I have asked your Brothers here for next Sunday. When Reynolds was here on Monday he asked me to give Hunt a hint to take notice of his Peter Bell in the Examiner — the best thing I can do is to write a little notice of it myself, which I will do here, and copy out if it should suit my Purpose —

Peter Bell. There have been lately advertised two Books both Peter Bell by name ; what stuff the one was made of might be seen by the motto — 'I am the real Simon Pure.' This false Florimel has hurried from the press and obtruded herself into public notice, while for aught we know the real one may be still wandering about the woods and mountains. Let us hope she may soon appear and make good her right to the magic girdle. The Pamphleteering Archimage, we can perceive, has rather a splenetic love than a downright hatred to real Florimels — if indeed they had been so christened — or had even a pretention to play at bob cherry with Barbara Lewthwaite : but he has a fixed aversion to those three rhyming Graces Alice Fell, Susan Gale and Betty Foy ; and now at length especially to Peter Bell — fit Apollo. It may be seen from one or two Passages in this little skit, that the writer of it has felt the finer parts of Mr. Wordsworth, and perhaps expatiated with his more remote and sublimer muse. This as far as it relates to Peter Bell is unlucky. The more he may love the sad embroidery of the Excursion, the more he will hate the coarse Samplers of Betty Foy and Alice Fell ; and as they come from the same hand, the better will he be able to imitate that which can be imitated, to wit Peter Bell — as far as can be imagined from the obstinate Name. We repeat, it is very unlucky — this real Simon Pure is in parts the very Man — there is a pernicious likeness in the scenery, a 'pestilent humour' in the rhymes, and an inveterate cadence in some of the Stanzas, that must be lamented. If we are one part amused with this we are three parts sorry that an appreciator of Wordsworth should show so much temper at this really provoking name of Peter Bell — !

This will do well enough — I have copied it and enclosed it to Hunt. You will call it a little politic — seeing I keep clear of all parties. I say something for and against both parties — and suit it to the tune of the Examiner — I meant to say I do not unsuit it — and I believe I think what I say, nay I am sure I do — I and my conscience are in luck to-day — which is an excellent thing. The other night I went to the Play with Rice, Reynolds, and Martin — we saw a new dull and half-damn'd opera call'd the 'Heart of Midlothian,' that was on Saturday — I stopt at Taylor's on Sunday with Woodhouse — and passed a quiet sort of pleasant day. I have been very much pleased with the Panorama of the Ship at the North Pole — with the icebergs, the Mountains, the Bears, the Wolves — the seals, the Penguins — and a large whale floating back above water — it is impossible to describe the place —

Wednesday Evening [April 28].

[Here follows the poem for which see p. 139. The eighth stanza reads :

She took me to her elfin grot
  And there she wept and sigh'd full sore,
And there I shut her wild, wild eyes
    With kisses four —]

Why four kisses — you will say — why four, because I wish to restrain the headlong impetuosity of my Muse — she would have fain said 'score' without hurting the rhyme — but we must temper the Imagination, as the Critics say, with Judgment. I was obliged to choose an even number, that both eyes might have fair play, and to speak truly I think two a piece quite sufficient. Suppose I had said seven there would have been three and a half a piece — a very awkward affair, and well got out of on my side —

[Later.]

CHORUS OF FAIRIES. 4 — FIRE, AIR, EARTH, AND WATER — SALAMANDER, ZEPHYR, DUSKETHA, BREAMA.

[Keats here copies the verses given on pp. 140, 141.]

I have been reading lately two very different books, Robertson's America and Voltaire's Siècle de Louis XIV. It is like walking arm and arm between Pizarro and the great-little Monarch. In how lamentable a case do we see the great body of the people in both instances; in the first, where Men might seem to inherit quiet of Mind from unsophisticated senses ; from uncontamination of civilisation, and especially from their being, as it were, estranged from the mutual helps of Society and its mutual injuries — and thereby more immediately under the Protection of Providence — even there they had mortal pains to bear as bad, or even worse than Bailiffs, Debts, and Poverties of civilised Life. The whole appears to resolve into this — that Man is originally a poor forked creature subject to the same mischances as the beasts of the forest, destined to hardships and disquietude of some kind or other. If he improves by degrees his bodily accommodations and comforts — at each stage, at each ascent there are waiting for him a fresh set of annoyances — he is mortal, and there is still a heaven with its Stars above his head. The most interesting question that can come before us is, How far by the persevering endeavours of a seldom appearing Socrates Mankind may be made happy — I can imagine such happiness carried to an extreme, but what must it end in ? — Death — and who could in such a case bear with death ? The whole troubles of life, which are now frittered away in a series of years, would then be accumulated for the last days of a being who instead of hailing its approach would leave this world as Eve left Paradise. But in truth I do not at all believe in this sort of perfectibility — the nature of the world will not admit of it — the inhabitants of the world will correspond to itself. Let the fish Philosophise the ice away from the Rivers in winter time, and they shall be at continual play in the tepid delight of summer. Look at the Poles and at the Sands of Africa, whirlpools and volcanoes — Let men exterminate them and I will say that they may arrive at earthly Happiness. The point at which Man may arrive is as far as the parallel state in inanimate nature, and no further. For instance suppose a rose to have sensation, it blooms on a beautiful morning, it enjoys itself, but then comes a cold wind, a hot sun — it cannot escape it, it cannot destroy its annoyances — they are as native to the world as itself : no more can man be happy in spite, the worldly elements will prey upon his nature. The common cognomen of this world among the misguided and superstitious is 'a vale of tears,' from which we are to be redeemed by a certain arbitrary interposition of God and taken to Heaven — What a little circumscribed straightened notion ! Call the world if you please 'The vale of Soul-making.' Then you will find out the use of the world (I am speaking now in the highest terms for human nature admitting it to be immortal which I will here take for granted for the purpose of showing a thought which has struck me concerning it) I say ' *Soul-making* ' — Soul as distinguished from an Intelligence. There may be intelligences or sparks of the divinity in millions — but they are not Souls till they acquire identities, till each one is personally itself. Intelligences are atoms of perception — they know and they see and they are pure, in short they are God — how then are Souls to be made ? How then are these sparks which are God to have identity given them — so as ever to possess a bliss peculiar to each one's individual existence ? How, but by the medium of a world like this ? This point I sincerely wish to consider because I think it a grander system of salvation than the Christian religion — or rather it is a system of Spirit-creation — This is effected by three grand materials acting the one upon the other for a series of years — These three Materials are the *Intelligence* — the *human heart* (as distinguished from intelligence or Mind), and the *World* or *Elemental space* suited for the proper action of *Mind and Heart* on each other for the purpose of forming the *Soul* or *Intelligence destined to possess the sense of Identity.* I can scarcely express what I but dimly perceive — and yet I think I perceive it — that you may judge the more clearly I will put it in the most homely form possible. I will call the *world* a School instituted for the purpose of teaching little children to read — I will call the *human heart* the *horn Book* used in that School — and I will call the *Child able to read, the Soul* made from that *School* and its *horn book*. Do you not see how necessary a World of Pains and troubles is to school an Intelligence and make it a soul? A Place where the heart must feel and suffer in a thousand diverse ways. Not merely is the Heart a Hornbook, It is the Mind's Bible, it is the Mind's experience, it is the text from which the Mind or Intelligence sucks its identity. As various as the Lives of Men are — so various become their souls, and thus does God make individual beings, Souls, Identical Souls of the sparks of his own essence. This appears to me a faint sketch of a system of Salvation which does not offend our reason and humanity — I am convinced that many difficulties which Christians labour under would vanish before it — there is one which even now strikes me — the salvation of Children. In them the spark or intelligence returns to God without any identity — it having had no time to learn of and be altered by the heart — or seat of the human Passions. It is pretty generally suspected that the Christian scheme has been copied from the ancient Persian and Greek Philosophers. Why may they not have made this simple thing even more simple for common apprehension by introducing Mediators and Personages, in the same manner as in the heathen mythology abstractions are personified? Seriously I think it probable that this system of Soul-making may have been the Parent of all the more palpable and personal schemes of Redemption among the Zoroastrians the Christians and the Hindoos. For as one part of the human species must have their carved Jupiter; so another part must have the palpable and named Mediator and Saviour, their Christ, their Oromanes, and their Vishnu. If what I have said should not be plain enough, as I fear it may not be, I will put you in the place where I began in this series of thoughts — I mean I began by seeing how man was formed by circumstances — and what are circumstances but touchstones of his heart? and what are touchstones but provings of his heart, but fortifiers or alterers of his nature? and what is his altered nature but his Soul? — and what was his Soul before it came into the world and had these provings and alterations and perfectionings? — An intelligence without Identity — and how is this Identity to be made? Through the medium of the Heart? and how is the heart to become this Medium but in a world of Circumstances?

There now I think what with Poetry and Theology, you may thank your stars that my pen is not very long-winded. Yesterday I received two Letters from your Mother and Henry, which I shall send by young Birkbeck with this.

Friday, April 30.

Brown has been here rummaging up some of my old sins — that is to say sonnets. I do not think you remember them, so I will copy them out, as well as two or three lately written. I have just written one on Fame — which Brown is transcribing and he has his book and mine. I must employ myself perhaps in a sonnet on the same subject. — [Here are given the two sonnets on Fame, and the one To Sleep, p. 142.]

The following Poem — the last I have written — is the first and the only one with which I have taken even moderate pains. I have for the most part dash'd off my lines in a hurry. This I have done leisurely — I think it reads the more richly for it, and will I hope encourage me to write other things in even a more peaceable and healthy spirit. You must recollect that Psyche was not embodied as a goddess before the time of Apuleius the Platonist who lived after the Augustan age, and consequently the Goddess was never worshipped or sacrificed to with any of the ancient fervour — and perhaps never thought of in the old religion — I am more orthodox than to let a heathen Goddess be so neglected —

[The Ode to Psyche, p. 142, here follows.]

Here endethe ye Ode to Psyche.

Incipit altera Sonneta

I have been endeavouring to discover a better Sonnet Stanza than we have. The legitimate does not suit the language over well from the pouncing rhymes — the other kind appears too elegiac — and the couplet at the end of it has seldom a pleasing effect — I do not pretend to have succeeded — it will explain itself. [See p. 144.]

[May 3.]
This is the third of May, and everything is in delightful forwardness; the violets are not withered before the peeping of the first rose. You must let me know everything — how parcels go and come, what papers you have, and what newspapers you want, and other things. God bless you, my dear brother and sister.
Your ever affectionate Brother
JOHN KEATS.

95. TO FANNY KEATS

Wentworth Place. Saturday Morn.
[Postmark, February 27, 1819.]
MY DEAR FANNY — I intended to have not failed to do as you requested, and write you as you say once a fortnight. On looking to your letter I find there is no date; and not knowing how long it is since I received it I do not precisely know how great a sinner I am. I am getting quite well, and Mrs. Dilke is getting on pretty well.

You must pay no attention to Mrs. Abbey's unfeeling and ignorant gabble. You can't stop an old woman's crying more than you can a Child's. The old woman is the greatest nuisance because she is too old for the rod. Many people live opposite a Blacksmith's till they cannot hear the hammer. I have been in Town for two or three days and came back last night. I have been a little concerned at not hearing from George — I continue in daily expectation. Keep on reading and play as much on the music and the grassplot as you can. I should like to take possession of those Grassplots for a Month or so; and send Mrs. A. to Town to count coffee berries instead of currant Bunches, for I want you to teach me a few common dancing steps — and I would buy a Watch box to practise them in by myself. I think I had better always pay the postage of these Letters. I shall send you another book the first time I am in Town early enough to book it with one of the morning Walthamstow Coaches. You did not say a word about your Chillblains. Write me directly and let me know about them — Your Letter shall be answered like an echo.
Your affectionate Brother JOHN ——.

96. TO BENJAMIN ROBERT HAYDON

Wentworth Place,
[Postmark, March 8, 1819.]
MY DEAR HAYDON, — You must be wondering where I am and what I am about! I am mostly at Hampstead, and about nothing; being in a sort of qui bono temper, not exactly on the road to an epic poem. Nor must you think I have forgotten you. No, I have about every three days been to Abbey's and to the Law[y]ers. Do let me know how you have been getting on, and in what spirits you are.

You got out gloriously in yesterday's Examiner. What a set of little people we live amongst! I went the other day into an ironmonger's shop — without any change in my sensations — men and tin kettles are much the same in these days — they do not study like children at five and thirty — but they talk like men of twenty. Conversation is not a search after knowledge, but an endeavour at effect.

In this respect two most opposite men, Wordsworth and Hunt, are the same. A friend of mine observed the other day that if Lord Bacon were to make any remark in a party of the present day, the conversation would stop on the sudden. I am convinced of this, and from this I have come to this resolution — never to write for the sake of writing or making a poem, but from running over with any little knowledge or experience which many years of reflection may perhaps give me ; otherwise I will be dumb. What imagination I have I shall enjoy, and greatly, for I have experienced the satisfaction of having great conceptions without the trouble of sonnetteering. I will not spoil my love of gloom by writing an Ode to Darkness !

With respect to my livelihood, I will not write for it, — for I will not run with that most vulgar of all crowds, the literary. Such things I ratify by looking upon myself, and trying myself at lifting mental weights, as it were. I am three and twenty with little knowledge and middling intellect. It is true that in the height of enthusiasm I have been cheated into some fine passages ; but that is not the thing.

I have not been to see you because all my going out has been to town, and that has been a great deal. Write soon.

Yours constantly,   JOHN KEATS.

97. TO FANNY KEATS

Wentworth Place, March 13 [1819].

MY DEAR FANNY — I have been employed lately in writing to George — I do not send him very short letters, but keep on day after day. There were some young Men I think I told you of who were going to the Settlement : they have changed their minds, and I am disappointed in my expectation of sending Letters by them. — I went lately to the only dance I have been to these twelve months or shall go to for twelve months again — it was to our Brother in law's cousin's — She gave a dance for her Birthday and I went for the sake of Mrs. Wylie. I am waiting every day to hear from George — I trust there is no harm in the silence: other people are in the same expectation as we are. On looking at your seal I cannot tell whether it is done or not with a Tassie — it seems to me to be paste. As I went through Leicester Square lately I was going to call and buy you some, but not knowing but you might have some I would not run the chance of buying duplicates. Tell me if you have any or if you would like any — and whether you would rather have motto ones like that with which I seal this letter ; or heads of great Men such as Shakspeare, Milton, etc. — or fancy pieces of Art; such as Fame, Adonis, etc. — those gentry you read of at the end of the English Dictionary. Tell me also if you want any particular Book ; or Pencils, or drawing paper — anything but live stock. Though I will not now be very severe on it, remembering how fond I used to be of Goldfinches, Tomtits, Minnows, Mice, Ticklebacks, Dace, Cock salmons and all the whole tribe of the Bushes and the Brooks: but verily they are better in the Trees and the water — though I must confess even now a partiality for a handsome Globe of gold-fish — then I would have it hold 10 pails of water and be fed continually fresh through a cool pipe with another pipe to let through the floor — well ventilated they would preserve all their beautiful silver and Crimson. Then I would put it before a handsome painted window and shade it all round with myrtles and Japonicas. I should like the window to open onto the Lake of Geneva — and there I'd sit and read all day like the picture of somebody reading. The weather now and then begins to feel like spring; and therefore I have begun my walks on the heath again. Mrs. Dilke is getting better than she has been as she has at length taken a Physician's advice. She ever and anon asks after you and always bids me remember her in my Letters to you. She is going to leave Hampstead for the sake of educating their son Charles at the Westminster School. We (Mr. Brown and I) shall leave in the beginning of May; I do not know what I shall do or where be all the next summer. Mrs. Reynolds has had a sick house; but they are all well now. You see what news I can send you I do — we all live one day like the other as well as you do — the only difference is being sick and well — with the variations of single and double knocks, and the story of a dreadful fire in the Newspapers. I mentioned Mr. Brown's name — yet I do not think I ever said a word about him to you. He is a friend of mine of two years' standing, with whom I walked through Scotland: who has been very kind to me in many things when I most wanted his assistance and with whom I keep house till the first of May — you will know him some day. The name of the young Man who came with me is William Haslam.

Ever your affectionate Brother JOHN.

98. TO THE SAME

[Postmark, Hampstead, March 24, 1819.]

MY DEAR FANNY — It is impossible for me to call on you to-day — for I have particular Business at the other end of the Town this morning, and must be back to Hampstead with all speed to keep a long agreed on appointment. To-morrow I shall see you. Your affectionate Brother
JOHN ——.

99. TO JOSEPH SEVERN

Wentworth Place, Monday Aft.
[March 29? 1819].

MY DEAR SEVERN — Your note gave me some pain, not on my own account, but on

yours. Of course I should never suffer any petty vanity of mine to hinder you in any wise; and therefore I should say 'put the miniature in the exhibition' if only myself was to be hurt. But, will it not hurt you? What good can it do to any future picture. Even a large picture is lost in that canting place — what a drop of water in the ocean is a Miniature. Those who might chance to see it for the most part if they had ever heard of either of us and know what we were and of what years would laugh at the puff of the one and the vanity of the other. I am however in these matters a very bad judge — and would advise you to act in a way that appears to yourself the best for your interest. As your 'Hermia and Helena' is finished send that without the prologue of a Miniature. I shall see you soon, if you do not pay me a visit sooner — there's a Bull for you. Yours ever sincerely
JOHN KEATS.

100. TO BENJAMIN ROBERT HAYDON

Tuesday [April 13, 1819].

MY DEAR HAYDON — When I offered you assistance I thought I had it in my hand; I thought I had nothing to do but to do. The difficulties I met with arose from the alertness and suspicion of Abbey: and especially from the affairs being still in a Lawyer's hand — who has been draining our Property for the last six years of every charge he could make. I cannot do two things at once, and thus this affair has stopped my pursuits in every way — from the first prospect I had of difficulty. I assure you I have harrassed myself ten times more than if I alone had been concerned in so much gain or loss. I have also ever told you the exact particulars as well as and as literally as any hopes or fear could translate them: for it was only by parcels that I found all those petty obstacles which for my own sake should not exist a moment — and yet why not —

for from my own imprudence and neglect all my accounts are entirely in my Guardian's Power. This has taught me a Lesson. Hereafter I will be more correct. I find myself possessed of much less than I thought for and now if I had all on the table all I could do would be to take from it a moderate two years' subsistence and lend you the rest; but I cannot say how soon I could become possessed of it. This would be no sacrifice nor any matter worth thinking of — much less than parting as I have more than once done with little sums which might have gradually formed a library to my taste. These sums amount together to nearly £200, which I have but a chance of ever being repaid or paid at a very distant period. I am humble enough to put this in writing from the sense I have of your struggling situation and the great desire that you should do me the justice to credit me the unostentatious and willing state of my nerves on all such occasions. It has not been my fault. I am doubly hurt at the slightly reproachful tone of your note and at the occasion of it, — for it must be some other disappointment; you seem'd so sure of some important help when I last saw you — now you have maimed me again; I was whole, I had began reading again — when your note came I was engaged in a Book. I dread as much as a Plague the idle fever of two months more without any fruit. I will walk over the first fine day : then see what aspect your affairs have taken, and if they should continue gloomy walk into the City to Abbey and get his consent for I am persuaded that to me alone he will not concede a jot.

101. TO FANNY KEATS

Wentworth Place [April 13, 1819].

MY DEAR FANNY —I have been expecting a Letter from you about what the Parson said to your answers. I have thought also of writing to you often, and I am sorry to confess that my neglect of it has been but a small instance of my idleness of late — which has been growing upon me, so that it will require a great shake to get rid of it. I have written nothing and almost read nothing — but I must turn over a new leaf. One most discouraging thing hinders me — we have no news yet from George — so that I cannot with any confidence continue the Letter I have been preparing for him. Many are in the same state with us and many have heard from the Settlement. They must be well however: and we must consider this silence as good news. I ordered some bulbous roots for you at the Gardener's, and they sent me some, but they were all in bud — and could not be sent — so I put them in our Garden. There are some beautiful heaths now in bloom in Pots — either heaths or some seasonable plants I will send you instead — perhaps some that are not yet in bloom that you may see them come out. To-morrow night I am going to a rout, a thing I am not at all in love with. Mr. Dilke and his Family have left Hampstead — I shall dine with them to-day in Westminster where I think I told you they were going to reside for the sake of sending their son Charles to the Westminster School. I think I mentioned the Death of Mr. Haslam's Father. Yesterday week the two Mr. Wylies dined with me. I hope you have good store of double violets — I think they are the Princesses of flowers, and in a shower of rain, almost as fine as barley sugar drops are to a schoolboy's tongue. I suppose this fine weather the lambs' tails give a frisk or two extraordinary — when a boy would cry huzzah and a Girl O my! a little Lamb frisks its tail. I have not been lately through Leicester Square — the first time I do I will remember your Seals. I have thought it best to live in Town this Summer, chiefly for the sake of books, which cannot be had with any comfort in the Country — besides my Scotch journey gave me a dose of the Picturesque with which I ought to be contented for some time. Westminster is the place I have pitched upon — the City or any place very confined would soon turn me pale and thin — which is to be avoided. You must make up your mind to get stout this summer — indeed I have an idea we shall both be corpulent old folks with tripple chins and stumpy thumbs.

Your affectionate Brother JOHN.

102. TO THE SAME

Wentworth Place, Saturday.
[April 17, 1819?.]

MY DEAR FANNY — If it were but six o'Clock in the morning I would set off to see you to-day : if I should do so now I could not stop long enough for a how d 'ye do — it is so long a walk through Hornsey and Tottenham — and as for Stage Coaching it besides that it is very expensive it is like going into the Boxes by way of the pit. I cannot go out on Sunday — but if on Monday it should promise as fair as to-day I will put on a pair of loose easy palatable boots and me rendre chez vous. I continue increasing my letter [Letter 94] to George to send it by one of Birkbeck's sons who is going out soon — so if you will let me have a few more lines, they will be in time. I am glad you got on so well with Monsͬ. le Curé. Is he a nice clergyman ? — a great deal depends upon a cock'd hat and powder — not gunpowder, lord love us, but lady-meal, violet-smooth, dainty - scented, lilly-white, feather - soft, wigsby - dressing,   coat - collar - spoiling, whisker-reaching, pig-tail-loving, swansdown-puffing, parson-sweetening powder. I shall call in passing at the Tottenham nursery and see if I can find some seasonable plants for you. That is the nearest place — or by our la'kin or lady kin, that is by the virgin Mary's kindred, is there not a twig-manufacturer in Walthamstow ? Mr. and Mrs. Dilke are coming to dine with us to-day. They will enjoy the country after Westminster O there is nothing

like fine weather, and health, and Books, and a fine country, and a contented Mind, and diligent habit of reading and thinking, and an amulet against the ennui — and, please heaven, a little claret wine cool out of a cellar a mile deep — with a few or a good many ratafia cakes — a rocky basin to bathe in, a strawberry bed to say your prayers to Flora in, a pad nag to go you ten miles or so ; two or three sensible people to chat with ; two or three spiteful folks to spar with ; two or three odd fishes to laugh at and two or three numskulls to argue with·— instead of using dumb bells on a rainy day —

[Keats goes on with the same play, dropping into the rhymes 'Two or three Posies' given above, p. 251.]

Good-bye I 've an appointment — can't
    stop pon word — good-bye — now
    don't get up — open the door my-
    self — good-bye — see ye Monday..
                                J. K.

103. TO THE SAME

[Hampstead, May 13, 1819.]

MY DEAR FANNY — I have a letter from George at last — and it contains, considering all things, good news — I have been with it to-day to Mrs. Wylie's, with whom I have left it. I shall have it again as soon as possible and then I will walk over and read it to you. They are quite well and settled tolerably in comfort after a great deal of fatigue and harass. They had the good chance to meet at Louisville with a Schoolfellow of ours. You may expect me within three days. I am writing to-night several notes concerning this to many of my friends. Good night ; God bless you.
                                JOHN KEATS.

104. TO WILLIAM HASLAM

[Postmark, Hampstead, May 13, 1819.]

MY DEAR HASLAM — We have news at last — and tolerably good — they have not.

gone to the Settlement — they are both in good Health — I read the letter to Mrs. Wylie today and requested her after her Sons had read it — they would enclose it to you immediately which was faithfully promised. Send it me like Lightning that I may take it to Walthamstow.

Yours ever and amen,

JOHN KEATS.

105. TO FANNY KEATS

[Hampstead, May 26, 1819.]

MY DEAR FANNY — I have been looking for a fine day to pass at Walthamstow: there has not been one Morning (except Sunday and then I was obliged to stay at home) that I could depend upon. I have I am sorry to say had an accident with the Letter — I sent it to Haslam and he returned it torn into a thousand pieces. So I shall be obliged to tell you all I can remember from Memory. You would have heard from me before this but that I was in continual expectation of a fine Morning — I want also to speak to you concerning myself. Mind I do not purpose to quit England, as George has done ; but I am afraid I shall be forced to take a voyage or two. However we will not think of that for some Months. Should it be a fine morning tomorrow you will see me.

Your affectionate Brother   JOHN ——.

106. TO MISS JEFFREY

C. Brown, Esqre's Wentworth Place,
    Hampstead [Postmark May 31, 1819].

MY DEAR LADY — I was making a day or two ago a general conflagration of all old Letters and Memorandums, which had become of no interest to me — I made, however, like the Barber-inquisitor in Don Quixote some reservations — among the rest your and your Sister's Letters. I assure you you had not entirely vanished from my Mind, or even become shadows in my remembrance : it only needed such a memento as your Letters to bring you back to me. Why have I not written before? Why did I not answer your Honiton Letter? I had no good news for you — every concern of ours, (ours I wish I could say) and still I must say ours — though George is in America and I have no Brother left. Though in the midst of my troubles I had no relation except my young sister — I have had excellent friends. Mr. B. at whose house I now am, invited me, — I have been with him ever since. I could not make up my mind to let you know these things. Nor should I now — but see what a little interest will do — I want you to do me a Favor ; which I will first ask and then tell you the reasons. Enquire in the Villages round Teignmouth if there is any Lodging commodious for its cheapness ; and let me know where it is and what price. I have the choice as it were of two Poisons (yet I ought not to call this a Poison) the one is voyaging to and from India for a few years ; the other is leading a fevrous life alone with Poetry — This latter will suit me best ; for I cannot resolve to give up my Studies.

It strikes me it would not be quite so proper for you to make such inquiries — so give my love to your mother and ask her to do it. Yes, I would rather conquer my indolence and strain my nerves at some grand Poem than to be in a dunder-headed indiaman. Pray let no one in Teignmouth know anything of this. Fanny must by this time have altered her name — perhaps you have also — are you all alive? Give my Compts to Mrs. —— your Sister. I have had good news, (tho' 't is a queerish world in which such things are call'd good) from George — he and his wife are well. I will tell you more soon. Especially don't let the Newfoundland fishermen know it — and especially no one else. I have been always till now almost as careless of the world as a fly — my troubles were all of the Imagination — My Brother George always stood between me and any dealings with the world. Now I find I must buffet it — I must take my stand upon some vantage ground and begin to fight — I must choose between despair and Energy — I choose the latter — though the world has taken on a quakerish look with me, which I once thought was impossible —

'Nothing can bring back the hour
Of splendour in the grass and glory in the flower.'

I once thought this a Melancholist's dream —
But why do I speak to you in this manner? No believe me I do not write for a mere selfish purpose — the manner in which I have written of myself will convince you. I do not do so to Strangers. I have not quite made up my mind. Write me on the receipt of this — and again at your Leisure; between whiles you shall hear from me again —
Your sincere friend   JOHN KEATS.

107. TO THE SAME

Wentworth Place, [Postmark, June 9, 1819].
MY DEAR YOUNG LADY — I am exceedingly obliged by your two letters — Why I did not answer your first immediately was that I have had a little aversion to the South of Devon from the continual remembrance of my Brother Tom. On that account I do not return to my old Lodgings in Hampstead though the people of the house have become friends of mine — This, however, I could think nothing of, it can do no more than keep one's thoughts employed for a day or two. I like your description of Bradley very much and I dare say shall be there in the course of the summer; it would be immediately but that a friend with ill health and to whom I am greatly attached call'd on me yesterday and proposed my spending a month with him at the back of the Isle of Wight. This is just the thing at present — the morrow will take care of itself — I do not like the name of Bishop's Teigntown — I hope the road from Teignmouth to Bradley does not lie that way — Your advice about the Indiaman is a very wise advice, because it just suits me, though you are a little in the wrong concerning its destroying the energies of Mind; on the contrary it would be the finest thing in the world to strengthen them — To be thrown among people who care not for you, with whom you have no sympathies forces the Mind upon its own resources, and leaves it free to make its speculations of the differences of human character and to class them with the calmness of a Botanist. An Indiaman is a little world. One of the great reasons that the English have produced the finest writers in the world is, that the English world has ill treated them during their lives and foster'd them after their deaths. They have in general been trampled aside into the bye paths of life and seen the festerings of Society. They have not been treated like the Raphaels of Italy. And where is the Englishman and Poet who has given a magnificent Entertainment at the christening of one of his Hero's Horses as Boyardo did? He had a Castle in the Apennine. He was a noble Poet of Romance; not a miserable and mighty Poet of the human Heart. The middle age of Shakspeare was all c[l]ouded over; his days were not more happy than Hamlet's who is perhaps more like Shakspeare himself in his common everyday Life than any other of his Characters — Ben Johnson (sic) was a common Soldier and in the Low countries, in the face of two armies, fought a single combat with a french Trooper and slew him — For all this I will not go on board an Indiaman, nor for example's sake run my head into dark alleys: I dare say my discipline is to come, and plenty of it too. I have been very idle lately, very averse to writing; both from the overpowering idea of our dead poets and from abatement of my love of fame. I hope I am a little more of a Philosopher than I

was, consequently a little less of a versifying Pet-lamb. I have put no more in Print or you should have had it. You will judge of my 1819 temper when I tell you that the thing I have most enjoyed this year has been writing an ode to Indolence. Why did you not make your long-haired sister put her great brown hard fist to paper and cross your Letter? Tell her when you write again that I expect chequer work — My friend Mr. Brown is sitting opposite me employed in writing a Life of David. He reads me passages as he writes them stuffing my infidel mouth as though I were a young rook — Infidel Rooks do not provender with Elisha's Ravens. If he goes on as he has begun your new Church had better not proceed, for parsons will be superseeded (*sic*) — and of course the Clerks must follow. Give my love to your Mother with the assurance that I can never forget her anxiety for my Brother Tom. Believe also that I shall ever remember our leave-taking with *you*.

Ever sincerely yours,   JOHN KEATS.

108. TO FANNY KEATS

Wentworth Place [June 9, 1819].

MY DEAR FANNY — I shall be with you next Monday at the farthest. I could not keep my promise of seeing you again in a week because I am in so unsettled a state of mind about what I am to do — I have given up the Idea of the Indiaman; I cannot resolve to give up my favorite studies: so I purpose to retire into the Country and set my Mind at work once more. A Friend of Mine [James Rice] who has an ill state of health called on me yesterday and proposed to spend a little time with him at the back of the Isle of Wight where he said we might live very cheaply. I agreed to his proposal. I have taken a great dislike to Town — I never go there — some one is always calling on me and as we have spare beds they often stop a couple of days. I have written lately to some acquaintances

in Devonshire concerning a cheap Lodging and they have been very kind in letting me know all I wanted. They have described a pleasant place which I think I shall eventually retire to. How came you on with my young Master Yorkshire Man? Did not Mrs. A. sport her Carriage and one? They really surprised me with super civility — how did Mrs. A. manage it? How is the old tadpole gardener and little Master next door? it is to be hop'd they will both die some of these days. Not having been to Town I have not heard whether Mr. A. purposes to retire from business. Do let me know if you have heard anything more about it. If he should not I shall be very disappointed. If any one deserves to be put to his shifts it is that Hodgkinson — as for the other he would live a long time upon his fat and be none the worse for a good long lent. How came miledi to give one Lisbon wine — had she drained the Gooseberry? Truly I cannot delay making another visit — asked to take Lunch, whether I will have ale, wine, take sugar, — objection to green — like cream — thin bread and butter — another cup — agreeable — enough sugar — little more cream — too weak — 12 shillin etc. etc. etc. — Lord I must come again. We are just going to Dinner I must must [*sic*] with this to the Post ——

Your affectionate Brother   JOHN —.

109. TO JAMES ELMES [51]

Wentworth Place, Hampstead
[June 12, 1819].

SIR — I did not see your Note till this Saturday evening, or I should have answered it sooner — However as it happens I have but just received the Book which contains the only copy of the verses in question. I have asked for it repeatedly ever since I promised Mr. Haydon and could not help the delay; which I regret. The verses can be struck out in no time, and will I hope be quite in time. If you think it at all necessary a proof may be forwarded ; but as I shall transcribe it fairly perhaps there may be no need.

I am, Sir, your obed' Serv'

JOHN KEATS.

110. TO FANNY KEATS

Wentworth Place, [June 14, 1819].

MY DEAR FANNY — I cannot be with you to-day for two reasons — 1'y I have my sore-throat coming again to prevent my walking. 2'y I do not happen just at present to be flush of silver so that I might ride. To-morrow I am engaged — but the day after you shall see me. Mr. Brown is waiting for me as we are going to Town together, so good-bye.

Your affectionate Brother JOHN.

111. TO THE SAME

Wentworth Place [June 16, 1819].

MY DEAR FANNY — Still I cannot afford to spend money by Coachhire and still my throat is not well enough to warrant my walking. I went yesterday to ask Mr. Abbey for some money ; but I could not on account of a Letter he showed me from my Aunt's solicitor. You do not understand the business. I trust it will not in the end be detrimental to you. I am going to try the Press once more, and to that end shall retire to live cheaply in the country and compose myself and verses as well as I can. I have very good friends ready to help me — and I am the more bound to be careful of the money they lend me. It will all be well in the course of a year I hope. I am confident of it, so do not let it trouble you at all. Mr. Abbey showed me a Letter he had received from George containing the news of the birth of a Niece for us — and all doing well — he said he would take it to you — so I suppose to-day you will see it. I was preparing to enquire for a situation with an apothecary, but Mr. Brown persuades me to try the press once more ;

so I will with all my industry and ability. Mr. Rice a friend of mine in ill health has proposed retiring to the back of the Isle of Wight — which I hope will be cheap in the summer — I am sure it will in the winter. Thence you shall frequently hear from me in the Letters I will copy those lines I may write which will be most pleasing to you in the confidence you will show them to no one. I have not run quite aground yet I hope, having written this morning to several people to whom I have lent money requesting repayment. I shall henceforth shake off my indolent fits, and among other reformation be more diligent in writing to you, and mind you always answer me. I shall be obliged to go out of town on Saturday and shall have no money till to-morrow, so I am very sorry to think I shall not be able to come to Walthamstow. The Head Mr. Severn did of me is now too dear, but here inclosed is a very capital Profile done by Mr. Brown. I will write again on Monday or Tuesday — Mr. and Mrs. Dilke are well.

Your affectionate Brother JOHN ——.

112. TO BENJAMIN ROBERT HAYDON

Wentworth Place.
Thursday Morning [June 17, 1819].

MY DEAR HAYDON — I know you will not be prepared for this, because your Pocket must needs be very low having been at ebb tide so long : but what can I do ? mine is lower. I was the day before yesterday much in want of Money : but some news I had yesterday has driven me into necessity. I went to Abbey's for some Cash, and he put into my hand a letter from my Aunt's Solicitor containing the pleasant information that she was about to file a Bill in Chancery against us. Now in case of a defeat Abbey will be very undeservedly in the wrong box ; so I could not ask him for any more money, nor can I till the affair is decided; and if it goes against him I must in conscience make over to him what little he may have remaining. My purpose is now to make one more attempt in the Press — if that fail, 'ye hear no more of me' as Chaucer says. Brown has lent me some money for the present. Do borrow or beg somehow what you can for me. Do not suppose I am at all uncomfortable about the matter in any other way than as it forces me to apply to the needy. I could not send you those lines, for I could not get the only copy of them before last Saturday evening. I sent them Mr. Elmes on Monday. I saw Monkhouse on Sunday — he told me you were getting on with the Picture. I would have come over to you to-day, but I am fully employed.

Yours ever sincerely   JOHN KEATS.

113. TO FANNY BRAWNE

Shanklin, Isle of Wight, Thursday,
[Postmark, Newport, July 3, 1819].

MY DEAREST LADY — I am glad I had not an opportunity of sending off a Letter which I wrote for you on Tuesday night — 't was too much like one out of Rousseau's Heloise. I am more reasonable this morning. The morning is the only proper time for me to write to a beautiful Girl whom I love so much: for at night, when the lonely day has closed, and the lonely, silent, unmusical Chamber is waiting to receive me as into a Sepulchre, then believe me my passion gets entirely the sway, then I would not have you see those Rhapsodies which I once thought it impossible I should ever give way to, and which I have often laughed at in another, for fear you should [think me] either too unhappy or perhaps a little mad. I am now at a very pleasant Cottage window, looking onto a beautiful hilly country, with a glimpse of the sea; the morning is very fine. I do not know how elastic my spirit might be, what pleasure I might have in living here and breathing and wandering as free as a stag about this beautiful Coast if the remembrance of you did not weigh so upon me. I have

never known any unalloy'd Happiness for many days together: the death or sickness of some one has always spoilt my hours — and now when none such troubles oppress me, it is you must confess very hard that another sort of pain should haunt me. Ask yourself my love whether you are not very cruel to have so entrammelled me, so destroyed my freedom. Will you confess this in the Letter you must write immediately and do all you can to console me in it — make it rich as a draught of poppies to intoxicate me — write the softest words and kiss them that I may at least touch my lips where yours have been. For myself I know not how to express my devotion to so fair a form: I want a brighter word than bright, a fairer word than fair. I almost wish we were butterflies and liv'd but three summer days — three such days with you I could fill with more delight than fifty common years could ever contain. But however selfish I may feel, I am sure I could never act selfishly: as I told you a day or two before I left Hampstead, I will never return to London if my Fate does not turn up Pam or at least a Court-card. Though I could centre my Happiness in you, I cannot expect to engross your heart so entirely — indeed if I thought you felt as much for me as I do for you at this moment I do not think I could restrain myself from seeing you again tomorrow for the delight of one embrace. But no — I must live upon hope and Chance. In case of the worst that can happen, I shall still love you — but what hatred shall I have for another! Some lines I read the other day are continually ringing a peal in my ears:

To see those eyes I prize above mine own
Dart favors on another —
And those sweet lips (yielding immortal nectar)
Be gently press'd by any but myself —
Think, think Francesca, what a cursed thing
It were beyond expression!

                     J.

Do write immediately. There is no Post from this Place, so you must address Post

Office, Newport, Isle of Wight. I know before night I shall curse myself for having sent you so cold a Letter; yet it is better to do it as much in my senses as possible. Be as kind as the distance will permit to your

J. KEATS.

Present my Compliments to your mother, my love to Margaret and best remembrances to your Brother — if you please so.

114. TO FANNY KEATS

Shanklin, Isle of Wight, Tuesday, July 6, [1819].

MY DEAR FANNY — I have just received another Letter from George — full of as good news as we can expect. I cannot inclose it to you as I could wish because it contains matters of Business to which I must for a Week to come have an immediate reference. I think I told you the purpose for which I retired to this place — to try the fortune of my Pen once more, and indeed I have some confidence in my success: but in every event, believe me my dear sister, I shall be sufficiently comfortable, as, if I cannot lead that life of competence and society I should wish, I have enough knowledge of my gallipots to ensure me an employment and maintenance. The Place I am in now I visited once before and a very pretty place it is were it not for the bad weather. Our window looks over house-tops and Cliffs onto the Sea, so that when the Ships sail past the Cottage chimneys you may take them for weathercocks. We have Hill and Dale, forest and Mead, and plenty of Lobsters. I was on the Portsmouth Coach the Sunday before last in that heavy shower — and I may say I went to Portsmouth by water — I got a little cold, and as it always flies to my throat I am a little out of sorts that way. There were on the Coach with me some common French people but very well behaved — there was a woman amongst them to whom the poor Men in ragged coats were more gallant than ever I saw gentleman to Lady at a Ball. When we got down to walk up hill — one of them pick'd a rose, and on remounting gave it to the woman with 'Ma'mselle voila une belle rose!' I am so hard at work that perhaps I should not have written to you for a day or two if George's Letter had not diverted my attention to the interests and pleasure of those I love — and ever believe that when I do not behave punctually it is from a very necessary occupation, and that my silence is no proof of my not thinking of you, or that I want more than a gentle fillip to bring your image with every claim before me. You have never seen mountains, or I might tell you that the hill at Steephill is I think almost of as much consequence as Mount Rydal on Lake Winander. Bonchurch too is a very delightful Place — as I can see by the Cottages, all romantic — covered with creepers and honeysuckles, with roses and eglantines peeping in at the windows. Fit abodes for the People I guess live in them, romantic old maids fond of novels, or soldiers' widows with a pretty jointure — or any body's widows or aunts or anythings given to Poetry and a Piano-forte — as far as in 'em lies — as people say. If I could play upon the Guitar I might make my fortune with an old song — and get two blessings at once — a Lady's heart and the Rheumatism. But I am almost afraid to peep at those little windows — for a pretty window should show a pretty face, and as the world goes chances are against me. I am living with a very good fellow indeed, a Mr. Rice. — He is unfortunately labouring under a complaint which has for some years been a burthen to him. This is a pain to me. He has a greater tact in speaking to people of the village than I have, and in those matters is a great amusement as well as good friend to me. He bought a ham the other day for says he 'Keats, I don't think a Ham is a wrong thing to have in a house.' Write to me, Shanklin, Isle of Wight, as soon as you can; for a Letter is a great treat to me here — believing me ever,

Your affectionate Brother JOHN ——.

115. TO FANNY BRAWNE

July 8, [1819].

MY SWEET GIRL — Your Letter gave me more delight than any thing in the world but yourself could do; indeed I am almost astonished that any absent one should have that luxurious power over my senses which I feel. Even when I am not thinking of you I receive your influence and a tenderer nature stealing upon me. All my thoughts, my unhappiest days and nights, have I find not at all cured me of my love of Beauty, but made it so intense that I am miserable that you are not with me: or rather breathe in that dull sort of patience that cannot be called Life. I never knew before, what such a love as you have made me feel, was; I did not believe in it; my Fancy was afraid of it, lest it should burn me up. But if you will fully love me, though there may be some fire, 't will not be more than we can bear when moistened and bedewed with Pleasures. You mention 'horrid people' and ask me whether it depend upon them whether I see you again. Do understand me, my love, in this. I have so much of you in my heart that I must turn Mentor when I see a chance of harm befalling you. I would never see any thing but Pleasure in your eyes, love on your lips, and Happiness in your steps. I would wish to see you among those amusements suitable to your inclinations and spirits; so that our loves might be a delight in the midst of Pleasures agreeable enough, rather than a resource from vexations and cares. But I doubt much, in case of the worst, whether I shall be philosopher enough to follow my own Lessons: if I saw my resolution give you a pain I could not. Why may I not speak of your Beauty, since without that I could never have lov'd you? — I cannot conceive any beginning of such

love as I have for you but Beauty. There may be a sort of love for which, without the least sneer at it, I have the highest respect and can admire it in others : but it has not the richness, the bloom, the full form, the enchantment of love after my own heart. So let me speak of your Beauty, though to my own endangering; if you could be so cruel to me as to try elsewhere its Power. You say you are afraid I shall think you do not love me — in saying this you make me ache the more to be near you. I am at the diligent use of my faculties here, I do not pass a day without sprawling some blank verse or tagging some rhymes; and here I must confess, that (since I am on that subject) I love you the more in that I believe you have liked me for my own sake and for nothing else. I have met with women whom I really think would like to be married to a Poem and to be given away by a Novel. I have seen your Comet, and only wish it was a sign that poor Rice would get well whose illness makes him rather a melancholy companion: and the more so as to conquer his feelings and hide them from me, with a forc'd Pun. I kiss'd your writing over in the hope you had indulg'd me by leaving a trace of honey. What was your dream? Tell it me and I will tell you the interpretation thereof.

Ever yours, my love !

JOHN KEATS.

Do not accuse me of delay — we have not here an opportunity of sending letters every day. Write speedily.

116. TO JOHN HAMILTON REYNOLDS

Extract from a letter dated Shanklin, n' Ryde, Isle of Wight, Sunday. July 12 [for 11] 1819.

· · · · · · ·

You will be glad to hear, under my own hand (though Rice says we are like Sauntering Jack and Idle Joe), how diligent I have been, and am being. I have finished the Act, [*Otho the Great, I*] and in the interval of beginning the 2^d have proceeded pretty well with Lamia, finishing the 1st part which consists of about 400 lines. I have great hopes of success, because I make use of my Judgment more deliberately than I have yet done; but in case of failure with the world, I shall find my content. And here (as I know you have my good at heart as much as a Brother), I can only repeat to you what I have said to George — that however I should like to enjoy what the competencies of life procure, I am in no wise dashed at a different prospect. I have spent too many thoughtful days and moralised through too many nights for that, and fruitless would they be indeed, if they did not by degrees make me look upon the affairs of the world with a healthy delibration. I have of late been moulting : not for fresh feathers and wings : they are gone, and in their stead I hope to have a pair of patient sublunary legs. I have altered, not from a Chrysalis into a butterfly, but the contrary ; having two little loopholes, whence I may look out into the stage of the world: and that world on our coming here I almost forgot. The first time I sat down to write, I could scarcely believe in the necessity for so doing. It struck me as a great oddity — Yet the very corn which is now so beautiful, as if it had only took to ripening yesterday, is for the market ; so, why should I be delicate ?

. . . .

117. TO FANNY BRAWNE

Shanklin, Thursday Evening
[July 15, 1819?]

MY LOVE — I have been in so irritable a state of health these two or three last days, that I did not think I should be able to write this week. Not that I was so ill, but so much so as only to be capable of an unhealthy teasing letter. To night I am greatly recovered only to feel the languor I have felt after you touched with ardency.

You say you perhaps might have made me better: you would then have made me worse: now you could quite effect a cure : What fee my sweet Physician would I not give you to do so. Do not call it folly, when I tell you I took your letter last night to bed with me. In the morning I found your name on the sealing wax obliterated. I was startled at the bad omen till I recollected that it must have happened in my dreams, and they you know fall out by contraries. You must have found out by this time I am a little given to bode ill like the raven; it is my misfortune not my fault; it has proceeded from the general tenor of the circumstances of my life, and rendered every event suspicious. However I will no more trouble either you or myself with sad prophecies ; though so far I am pleased at it as it has given me opportunity to love your disinterestedness towards me. I can be a raven no more ; you and pleasure take possession of me at the same moment. I am afraid you have been unwell. If through me illness have touched you (but it must be with a very gentle hand) I must be selfish enough to feel a little glad at it. Will you forgive me this ? I have been reading lately an oriental tale of a very beautiful color [52] — It is of a city of melancholy men, all made so by this circumstance. Through a series of adventures each one of them by turns reach some gardens of Paradise where they meet with a most enchanting Lady; and just as they are going to embrace her, she bids them shut their eyes — they shut them — and on opening their eyes again find themselves descending to the earth in a magic basket. The remembrance of this Lady and their delights lost beyond all recovery render them melancholy ever after. How I applied this to you, my dear ; how I palpitated at it ; how the certainty that you were in the same world with myself, and though as beautiful, not so talismanic as that Lady; how I could not bear you should be so you must believe because I swear it by yourself. I cannot say when I shall get a volume ready. I have three or four stories half done, but as I cannot write for the mere sake of the press, I am obliged to let them progress or lie still as my fancy chooses. By Christmas perhaps they may appear, but I am not yet sure they ever will. 'T will be no matter, for Poems are as common as newspapers and I do not see why it is a greater crime in me than in another to let the verses of an half-fledged brain tumble into the reading-rooms and drawing-room windows. Rice has been better lately than usual: he is not suffering from any neglect of his parents who have for some years been able to appreciate him better than they did in his first youth, and are now devoted to his comfort. Tomorrow I shall, if my health continues to improve during the night, take a look farther about the country, and spy at the parties about here who come hunting after the picturesque like beagles. It is astonishing how they raven down scenery like children do sweetmeats. The wondrous Chine here is a very great Lion: I wish I had as many guineas as there have been spy-glasses in it. I have been. I cannot tell why, in capital spirits this last hour. What reason? When I have to take my candle and retire to a lonely room, without the thought as I fall asleep, of seeing you tomorrow morning? or the next day. or the next — it takes on the appearance of impossibility and eternity — I will say a month — I will say I will see you in a month at most, though no one but yourself should see me ; if it be but for an hour. I should not like to be so near you as London without being continually with you : after having once more kissed you Sweet I would rather be here alone at my task than in the bustle and hateful literary chitchat. Meantime you must write to me — as I will every week — for your letters keep me alive. My sweet Girl I cannot speak my love for you. Good night ! and

     Ever yours   JOHN KEATS.

IIA. TO THE SAME

Sunday Night. [Postmark. July 27, 1819.]

MY SWEET GIRL — I hope you did not blame me much for not obeying your request of a Letter on Saturday : we have had four in our small room playing at cards night and morning leaving me no undisturb'd opportunity to write. Now Rice and Martin are gone I am at liberty. Brown to my sorrow confirms the account you give of your ill health. You cannot conceive how I ache to be with you: how I would die for one hour —— for what is in the world? I say you cannot conceive ; it is impossible you should look with such eyes upon me as I have upon you: it cannot be. Forgive me if I wander a little this evening, for I have been all day employ'd in a very abstract Poem and I am in deep love with you — two things which must excuse me. I have, believe me, not been an age in letting you take possession of me; the very first week I knew you I wrote myself your vassal; but burnt the Letter as the very next time I saw you I thought you manifested some dislike to me. If you should ever feel for Man at the first sight what I did for you, I am lost. Yet I should not quarrel with you, but hate myself if such a thing were to happen — only I should burst if the thing were not as fine as a Man as you are as a Woman. Perhaps I am too vehement, then fancy me on my knees, especially when I mention a part of your Letter which hurt me: you say speaking of Mr. Severn 'but you must be satisfied in knowing that I admired you much more than your friend.' My dear love. I cannot believe there ever was or ever could be any thing to admire in me especially as far as sight goes — I cannot be admired. I am not a thing to be admired. You are. I love you: all I can bring you is a swooning admiration of your Beauty. I hold that place among Men which snub-nos'd brunettes with meeting eyebrows do among women — they are trash to me — unless I should find one among them with a fire in her heart like the one that burns in mine. You absorb me in spite of myself — you alone: for I look not forward with any pleasure to what is call'd being settled in the world; I tremble at domestic cares — yet for you I would meet them, though if it would leave you the happier I would rather die than do so. I have two luxuries to brood over in my walks, your Loveliness and the hour of my death. O that I could have possession of them both in the same minute. I hate the world: it batters too much the wings of my self-will, and would I could take a sweet poison from your lips to send me out of it. From no others would I take it. I am indeed astonish'd to find myself so careless of all charms but yours — remembering as I do the time when even a bit of ribband was a matter of interest with me. What softer words can I find for you after this — what it is I will not read. Nor will I say more here, but in a Postscript answer any thing else you may have mentioned in your Letter in so many words — for I am distracted with a thousand thoughts. I will imagine you Venus tonight and pray, pray, pray to your star like a Heathen.

Your's ever, fair Star, JOHN KEATS.

My seal is mark'd like a family table cloth with my Mother's initial F for Fanny: put between my Father's initials. You will soon hear from me again. My respectful Compliments to your Mother. Tell Margaret I 'll send her a reef of best rocks and tell Sam I will give him my light bay hunter if he will tie the Bishop hand and foot and pack him in a hamper and send him down for me to bathe him for his health with a Necklace of good snubby stones about his Neck.

119. TO CHARLES WENTWORTH DILKE

Shanklin, Saturday Evening [July 31, 1819].

MY DEAR DILKE — I will not make my diligence an excuse for not writing to you sooner — because I consider idleness a much better plea. A Man in the hurry of business of any sort is expected and ought to be expected to look to everything — his mind is in a whirl, and what matters it what whirl? But to require a Letter of a Man lost in idleness is the utmost cruelty ; you cut the thread of his existence, you beat, you pummel him, you sell his goods and chattels, you put him in prison ; you impale him ; you crucify him. If I had not put pen to paper since I saw you this would be to me a vi et armis taking up before the Judge ; but having got over my darling lounging habits a little, it is with scarcely any pain I come to this dating from Shanklin and Dear Dilke. The Isle of Wight is but so so, etc. Rice and I passed rather a dull time of it. I hope he will not repent coming with me. He was unwell, and I was not in very good health : and I am afraid we made each other worse by acting upon each other's spirits. We would grow as melancholy as need be. I confess I cannot bear a sick person in a House, especially alone — it weighs upon me day and night — and more so when perhaps the Case is irretrievable. Indeed I think Rice is in a dangerous state. I have had a Letter from him which speaks favourably of his health at present. Brown and I are pretty well harnessed again to our dog-cart. I mean the Tragedy, which goes on sinkingly. We are thinking of introducing an Elephant, but have not historical reference within reach to determine us as to Otho's Menagerie. When Brown first mentioned this I took it for a joke ; however he brings such plausible reasons, and discourses so eloquently on the dramatic effect that I am giving it a serious consideration. The Art of Poetry is not sufficient for us, and if we get on in that as well as we do in painting, we shall by next winter crush the Reviews and the Royal Academy. Indeed, if Brown would take a little of my advice, he could not fail to be first palette of his day. But .

odd as it may appear, he says plainly that he cannot see any force in my plea of putting skies in the background, and leaving Indian ink out of an ash tree. The other day he was sketching Shanklin Church, and as I saw how the business was going on, I challenged him to a trial of skill — he lent me Pencil and Paper — we keep the Sketches to contend for the Prize at the Gallery. I will not say whose I think best — but really I do not think Brown's done to the top of the Art.

A word or two on the Isle of Wight. I have been no further than Steephill. If I may guess, I should say that there is no finer part in the' Island than from this Place to Steephill. I do not hesitate to say it is fine. Bonchurch is the best. But I have been so many finer walks, with a background of lake and mountain instead of the sea, that I am not much touch'd with it, though I credit it for all the Surprise I should have felt if it had taken my cockney maidenhead. But I may call myself an old Stager in the picturesque, and unless it be something very large and overpowering, I cannot receive any extraordinary relish.

I am sorry to hear that Charles is so much oppress'd at Westminster, though I am sure it will be the finest touchstone for his Metal in the world. His troubles will grow day by day less, as his age and strength increase. The very first Battle he wins will lift him from the Tribe of Manasseh. I do not know how I should feel were I a Father — but I hope I should strive with all my Power not to let the present trouble me. When your Boy shall be twenty, ask him about his childish troubles and he will have no more memory of them than you have of yours. Brown tells me Mrs. Dilke sets off to-day for Chichester. I am glad — I was going to say she had a fine day — but there has been a great Thunder cloud muttering over Hampshire all day — I hope she is now at supper with a good appetite.

So Reynolds's Piece succeeded — that is all well. Papers have with thanks been duly received. We leave this place on the 13th, and will let you know where we may be a few days after — Brown says he will write when the fit comes on him. If you will stand law expenses I'll beat him into one before his time. When I come to town I shall have a little talk with you about Brown and one Jenny Jacobs. Open daylight! he don't care. I am afraid there will be some more feet for little stockings — [*of Keats's making. (I mean the feet.*)] Brown here tried at a piece of Wit but it failed him, as you see, though long a brewing — [*this is a 2ᵈ lie.*] Men should never despair — you see he has tried again and succeeded to a miracle. — He wants to try again, but as I have a right to an inside place in my own Letter — I take possession.

Your sincere friend   JOHN KEATS.

120. TO FANNY BRAWNE

Shanklin, Thursday Night.
[Postmark, Newport, August 9, 1819.]

MY DEAR GIRL — You say you must not have any more such Letters as the last: I'll try that you shall not by running obstinate the other way. Indeed I have not fair play — I am not idle enough for proper downright love-letters — I leave this minute a scene in our Tragedy [Otho the Great] and see you (think it not blasphemy) through the mist of Plots, speeches, counterplots and counterspeeches. The Lover is madder than I am — I am nothing to him — he has a figure like the Statue of Meleager and double distilled fire in his heart. Thank God for my diligence! were it not for that I should be miserable. I encourage it, and strive not to think of you — but when I have succeeded in doing so all day and as far as midnight, you return, as soon as this artificial excitement goes off, more severely from the fever I am left in. Upon my soul

* The bracketed portions are by Brown.

I cannot say what you could like me for. I do not think myself a fright any more than I do Mr. A., Mr. B., and Mr. C. — yet if I were a woman I should not like A. B. C. But enough of this. So you intend to hold me to my promise of seeing you in a short time. I shall keep it with as much sorrow as gladness : for I am not one of the Paladins of old who liv'd upon water grass and smiles for years together. What though would I not give tonight for the gratification of my eyes alone ? This day week we shall move to Winchester ; for I feel the want of a Library. Brown will leave me there to pay a visit to Mr. Snook at Bedhampton : in his absence I will flit to you and back. I will stay very little while, for as I am in a train of writing now I fear to disturb it — let it have its course bad or good — in it I shall try my own strength and the public pulse. At Winchester I shall get your Letters more readily ; and it being a cathedral City I shall have a pleasure always a great one to me when near a Cathedral, of reading them during the service up and down the Aisle.

Friday Morning. — Just as I had written thus far last night, Brown came down in his morning coat and nightcap, saying he had been refresh'd by a good sleep and was very hungry. I left him eating and went to bed, being too tired to enter into any discussions. You would delight very greatly in the walks about here ; the Cliffs, woods, hills, sands, rocks &c. about here. They are however not so fine but I shall give them a hearty good bye to exchange them for my Cathedral. — Yet again I am not so tired of Scenery as to hate Switzerland. We might spend a pleasant year at Berne or Zurich — if it should please Venus to hear my 'Beseech thee to hear us O Goddess.' And if she should hear, God forbid we should what people call, *settle* — turn into a pond, a stagnant Lethe — a vile crescent, row or buildings. Better be imprudent moveables than prudent fix-

tures. Open my Mouth at the Street door like the Lion's head at Venice to receive hateful cards, letters, messages. Go out and wither at tea parties ; freeze at dinners ; bake at dances ; simmer at routs. No my love, trust yourself to me and I will find you nobler amusements, fortune favouring. I fear you will not receive this till Sunday or Monday : as the Irishman would write do not in the meanwhile hate me. I long to be off for Winchester, for I begin to dislike the very door-posts here — the names, the pebbles. You ask after my health, not telling me whether you are better. I am quite well. Your going out is no proof that you are : how is it ? Late hours will do you great harm. What fairing is it ? I was alone for a couple of days while Brown went gadding over the country with his ancient knapsack. Now I like his society as well as any Man's, yet regretted his return — it broke in upon me like a Thunderbolt. I had got in a dream among my Books — really luxuriating in a solitude and silence you alone should have disturb'd.

Your ever affectionate JOHN KEATS.

121. TO BENJAMIN BAILEY

[*Fragment (outside sheet) of a letter addressed to Bailey at St. Andrews.*
Winchester, August 15, 1819].

· · · · · · · · ·

We removed to Winchester for the convenience of a library, and find it an exceeding pleasant town, enriched with a beautiful Cathedral and surrounded by a fresh-looking country. We are in tolerably good and cheap lodgings — Within these two months I have written 1500 lines, most of which, besides many more of prior composition, you will probably see by next winter. I have written 2 tales, one from Boccaccio, called the Pot of Basil, and another called St. Agnes's Eve, on a popular Superstition, and a 3rd called Lamia (half finished). I have also been writing parts of my 'Hyperion,' and completed 4 Acts of a tragedy. It was the opinion of most of my friends that I should never be able to write a scene. I will endeavour to wipe away the prejudice—I sincerely hope you will be pleased when my labours, since we last saw each other, shall reach you. One of my Ambitions is to make as great a revolution in modern dramatic writing as Kean has done in acting. Another to upset the drawling of the blue-stocking literary world—if in the Course of a few years I do these two things, I ought to die content, and my friends should drink a dozen of claret on my tomb. I am convinced more and more every day that (excepting the human friend philosopher), a fine writer is the most genuine being in the world. Shakspeare and the Paradise lost every day become greater wonders to me. I look upon fine phrases like a lover. I was glad to see by a passage of one of Brown's letters, some time ago, from the North that you were in such good spirits. Since that you have been married, and in congratulating you I wish you every continuance of them. Present my respects to Mrs. Bailey. This sounds oddly to me, and I daresay I do it awkwardly enough: but I suppose by this time it is nothing new to you. Brown's remembrances to you. As far as I know, we shall remain at Winchester for a goodish while.

Ever your sincere friend

JOHN KEATS.

122. TO FANNY BRAWNE

Winchester, August 17th.
[Postmark, August 16, 1819.]

MY DEAR GIRL — what shall I say for myself? I have been here four days and not yet written you — 't is true I have had many teasing letters of business to dismiss — and I have been in the Claws, like a serpent in an Eagle's, of the last act of our Tragedy. This is no excuse ; I know it ; I do not presume to offer it. I have no

right either to ask a speedy answer to let me know how lenient you are — I must remain some days in a Mist — I see you through a Mist : as I daresay you do me by this time. Believe in the first Letters I wrote you : I assure you I felt as I wrote — I could not write so now. The thousand images I have had pass through my brain — my uneasy spirits — my unguess'd fate — all spread as a veil between me and you. Remember I have had no idle leisure to brood over you — 't is well perhaps I have not. I could not have endured the throng of jealousies that used to haunt me before I had plunged so deeply into imaginary interests. I would fain, as my sails are set, sail on without an interruption for a Brace of Months longer — I am in complete cue — in the fever ; and shall in these four Months do an immense deal. This Page as my eye skims over it I see is excessively unloverlike and ungallant — I cannot help it — I am no officer in yawning quarters ; no Parson-Romeo. My Mind is heap'd to the full ; stuff'd like a cricket ball — if I strive to fill it more it would burst. I know the generality of women would hate me for this ; that I should have so unsoften'd, so hard a Mind as to forget them ; forget the brightest realities for the dull imaginations of my own Brain. But I conjure you to give it a fair thinking ; and ask yourself whether 't is not better to explain my feelings to you, than write artificial Passion. — Besides, you would see through it. It would be vain to strive to deceive you. 'T is harsh, harsh, I know it. My heart seems now made of iron — I could not write a proper answer to an invitation to Idalia. You are my Judge : my forehead is on the ground. You seem offended at a little simple innocent childish playfulness in my last. I did not seriously mean to say that you were endeavouring to make me keep my promise. I beg your pardon for it. 'T is but *just* your Pride should take the alarm — *seriously*. You say I may do as I please — I do not think

with any conscience I can; my cash resources are for the present stopp'd; I fear
for some time. I spend no money, but it
increases my debts. I have all my life
thought very little of these matters — they
seem not to belong to me. It may be a
proud sentence; but by Heaven I am as
entirely above all matters of interest as the
Sun is above the Earth — and though of
my own money I should be careless; of my
Friends' I must be spare. You see how I
go on — like so many strokes of a hammer.
I cannot help it — I am impell'd, driven
to it. I am not happy enough for silken
Phrases, and silver sentences. I can no
more use soothing words to you than if I
were at this moment engaged in a charge
of Cavalry. Then you will say I should
not write at all. — Should I not? This
Winchester is a fine place: a beautiful
Cathedral and many other ancient buildings in the Environs. The little coffin of
a room at Shanklin is changed for a large
room, where I can promenade at my pleasure — looks out onto a beautiful — blank
side of a house. It is strange I should like
it better than the view of the sea from our
window at Shanklin. I began to hate the
very posts there — the voice of the old
Lady over the way was getting a great
Plague. The Fisherman's face never altered any more than our black teapot —
the knob however was knock'd off to my
little relief. I am getting a great dislike
of the picturesque; and can only relish it
over again by seeing you enjoy it. One of
the pleasantest things I have seen lately
was at Cowes. The Regent in his Yatch
(I think they spell it) was anchored opposite — a beautiful vessel — and all the
Yatchs and boats on the coast were passing
and repassing it; and circuiting and tack-
ing about it in every direction — I never
beheld anything so silent, light, and graceful. — As we pass'd over to Southampton,
there was nearly an accident. There came
by a Boat well mann'd, with two naval
officers at the stern. Our Bow-lines took

the top of their little mast and snapped it
off close by the board. Had the mast been
a little stouter they would have been upset. In so trifling an event I could not
help admiring our seamen — neither officer
nor man in the whole Boat moved a muscle
— they scarcely notic'd it even with words.
Forgive me for this flint-worded Letter,
and believe and see that I cannot think of
you without some sort of energy — though
mal à propos. Even as I leave off it seems
to me that a few more moments' thought
of you would uncrystallize and dissolve me.
I must not give way to it — but turn to my
writing again — if I fail I shall die hard.
O my love, your lips are growing sweet
again to my fancy — I must forget them.
    Ever your affectionate   KEATS.

123. TO JOHN TAYLOR

                    Winchester, Monday morn
                        [August 23, 1819.]
MY DEAR TAYLOR — . . . Brown and
I have together been engaged (this I
should wish to remain secret) on a Tragedy
which I have just finished and from which
we hope to share moderate profits. . . . I
feel every confidence that, if I choose, I
may be a popular writer. That I will
never be; but for all that I will get a livelihood. I equally dislike the favour of the
public with the love of a woman. They
are both a cloying treacle to the wings of
Independence. I shall ever consider them
(People) as debtors to me for verses, not
myself to them for admiration — which I
can do without. I have of late been indulging my spleen by composing a preface AT
them: after all resolving never to write a
preface at all. 'There are so many verses,'
would I have said to them, 'give so much
means for me to buy pleasure with, as a
relief to my hours of labour' — You will
observe at the end of this if you put down
the letter, 'How a solitary life engenders
pride and egotism!' True — I know it

does : but this pride and egotism will enable me to write finer things than anything else could — so I will indulge it. Just so much as I am humbled by the genius above my grasp am I exalted and look with hate and contempt upon the literary world. — A drummer-boy who holds out his hand familiarly to a field Marshal, — that drummer-boy with me is the good word and favour of the public. Who could wish to be among the common-place crowd of the little famous — who are each individually lost in a throng made up of themselves ? Is this worth louting or playing the hypocrite for ? To beg suffrages for a seat on the benches of a myriad-aristocracy in letters ? This is not wise. — I am not 'a wise man — 'T is pride — I will give you a definition of a proud man — He is a man who has neither Vanity nor Wisdom — One filled with hatreds cannot be vain, neither can he be wise. Pardon me for hammering instead of writing. Remember me to Woodhouse Hessey and all in Percy Street. Ever yours sincerely JOHN KEATS.

124. TO JOHN HAMILTON REYNOLDS

Winchester, August 25 [1819].

MY DEAR REYNOLDS — By this post I write to Rice, who will tell you why we have left Shanklin ; and how we like this place. I have indeed scarcely anything else to say, leading so monotonous a life, except I was to give you a history of sensations, and day-nightmares. You would not find me at all unhappy in it, as all my thoughts and feelings which are of the selfish nature, home speculations, every day continue to make me more iron — I am convinced more and more, every day, that fine writing is, next to fine doing, the top thing in the world ; the Paradise Lost becomes a greater wonder. The more I know what my diligence may in time probably effect, the more does my heart distend with Pride and Obstinacy — I feel it in my power to become a popular writer — I feel

it in my power to refuse the poisonous suffrage of a public. My own being which I know to be becomes of more consequence to me than the crowds of Shadows in the shape of men and women that inhabit a kingdom. The soul is a world of itself, and has enough to do in its own home. Those whom I know already, and who have grown as it were a part of myself, I could not do without : but for the rest of mankind, they are as much a dream to me as Milton's Hierarchies. I think if I had a free and healthy and lasting organisation of heart, and lungs as strong as an ox's so as to be able to bear unhurt the shock of extreme thought and sensation without weariness, I could pass my life very nearly alone though it should last eighty years. But I feel my body too weak to support me to the height, I am obliged continually to check myself, and be nothing. It would be vain for me to endeavour after a more reasonable manner of writing to you. I have nothing to speak of but myself, and what can I say but what I feel ? If you should have any reason to regret this state of excitement in me, I will turn the tide of your feelings in the right Channel, by mentioning that it is the only state for the best sort of Poetry — that is all I care for, all I live for. Forgive me for not filling up the whole sheet ; Letters become so irksome to me, that the next time I leave London I shall petition them all to be spared me. To give me credit for constancy, and at the same time waive letter writing will be the highest indulgence I can think of.

Ever your affectionate friend
JOHN KEATS.

125. TO FANNY KEATS

Winchester, August 28 [1819].

MY DEAR FANNY — You must forgive me for suffering so long a space to elapse between the dates of my letters. It is more than a fortnight since I left Shanklin chiefly for the purpose of being near a tolerable

Library, which after all is not to be found in this place. However we like it very much: it is the pleasantest Town I ever was in, and has the most recommendations of any. There is a fine Cathedral which to me is always a source of amusement, part of it built 1400 years ago; and the more modern by a magnificent Man, you may have read of in our History, called William of Wickham. The whole town is beautifully wooded. From the Hill at the eastern extremity you see a prospect of Streets, and old Buildings mixed up with Trees. Then there are the most beautiful streams about I ever saw — full of Trout. There is the Foundation of St. Croix about half a mile in the fields — a charity greatly abused. We have a Collegiate School, a Roman catholic School; a chapel ditto and a Nunnery! and what improves it all is, the fashionable inhabitants are all gone to Southampton. We are quiet — except a fiddle that now and then goes like a gimlet through my Ears — our Landlady's son not being quite a Proficient. I have still been hard at work, having completed a Tragedy I think I spoke of to you. But there I fear all my labour will be thrown away for the present, as I hear Mr. Kean is going to America. For all I can guess I shall remain here till the middle of October — when Mr. Brown will return to his house at Hampstead; whither I shall return with him. I some time since sent the Letter I told you I had received from George to Haslam with a request to let you and Mrs. Wylie see it: he sent it back to me for very insufficient reasons without doing so; and I was so irritated by it that I would not send it travelling about by the post any more: besides the postage is very expensive. I know Mrs. Wylie will think this a great neglect. I am sorry to say my temper gets the better of me — I will not send it again. Some correspondence I have had with Mr. Abbey about George's affairs — and I must confess he has behaved very kindly to me as far as the wording of his Letter went.

Have you heard any further mention of his retiring from Business? I am anxious to hear whether Hodgkinson, whose name I cannot bear to write, will in any likelihood be thrown upon himself. The delightful Weather we have had for two Months is the highest gratification I could receive — no chill'd red noses — no shivering — but fair atmosphere to think in — a clean towel mark'd with the mangle and a basin of clear Water to drench one's face with ten times a day: no need of much exercise — a Mile a day being quite sufficient. My greatest regret is that I have not been well enough to bathe though I have been two Months by the seaside and live now close to delicious bathing — Still I enjoy the Weather — I adore fine Weather as the greatest blessing I can have. Give me Books, fruit, French wine and fine weather and a little music out of doors, played by somebody I do not know — not pay the price of one's time for a jig — but a little chance music: and I can pass a summer very quietly without caring much about Fat Louis, fat Regent or the Duke of Wellington. Why have you not written to me? Because you were in expectation of George's Letter and so waited? Mr. Brown is copying out our Tragedy of Otho the Great in a superb style — better than it deserves — there as I said is labour in vain for the present. I had hoped to give Kean another opportunity to shine. What can we do now? There is not another actor of Tragedy in all London or Europe. The Covent Garden company is execrable. Young is the best among them and he is a ranting coxcombical tasteless Actor — a Disgust, a Nausea — and yet the very best after Kean. What a set of barren asses are actors! I should like now to promenade round your Gardens — apple-tasting — pear-tasting — plum-judging — apricot-nibbling — peach-scrunching — nectarine-sucking and Melon-carving. I also have a great feeling for antiquated cherries full of sugar cracks — and a white currant tree kept for company. I admire lolling on a lawn by a water lilied pond to eat white currants and see gold-fish: and go to the Fair in the Evening if I'm good. There is not hope for that — one is sure to get into some mess before evening. Have these hot days I brag of so much been well or ill for your health? Let me hear soon. Your affectionate Brother JOHN ——.

126. TO JOHN TAYLOR

Winchester, September 1, 1819.

MY DEAR TAYLOR — Brown and I have been employed for these 3 weeks past from time to time in writing to our different friends — a dead silence is our only answer — we wait morning after morning. Tuesday is the day for the Examiner to arrive, this is the 2d Tuesday which has been barren even of a newspaper — Men should be in imitation of spirits 'responsive to each other's note.' Instead of that I pipe and no one hath danced. We have been cursing like Mandeville and Lisle — With this I shall send by the same post a 3d letter to a friend of mine, who though it is of consequence has neither answered right or left. We have been much in want of news from the Theatres, having heard that Kean is going to America — but no — not a word. Why I should come on you with all these complaints I cannot explain to myself, especially as I suspect you must be in the country. Do answer me soon for I really must know something. I must steer myself by the rudder of Information. . . .

Ever yours sincerely   JOHN KEATS.

127. TO THE SAME

Winchester, September 5 [1819].

MY DEAR TAYLOR — This morning I received yours of the 2d, and with it a letter from Hessey enclosing a Bank post Bill of £30, an ample sum I assure you — more I had no thought of. — You should not have delayed so long in Fleet St. — leading an inactive life as you did was breathing poison: you will find the country air do more for you than you expect. But it must be proper country air. You must choose a spot. What sort of a place is Retford? You should have a dry, gravelly, barren, elevated country, open to the currents of air, and such a place is generally furnished with the finest springs — The neighbourhood of a rich enclosed fulsome manured arable land, especially in a valley and almost as bad on a flat, would be almost as bad as the smoke of Fleet Street. — Such a place as this was Shanklin, only open to the south-east, and surrounded by hills in every other direction. From this south-east came the damps of the sea; which, having no egress, the air would for days together take on an unhealthy idiosyncrasy altogether enervating and weakening as a city smoke — I felt it very much. Since I have been here at Winchester I have been improving in health — it is not so confined — and there is on one side of the City a dry chalky down, where the air is worth Sixpence a pint. So if you do not get better at Retford, do not impute it to your own weakness before you have well considered the Nature of the air and soil — especially as Autumn is encroaching — for the Autumn fog over a rich land is like the steam from cabbage water. What makes the great difference between valesmen, flatlandmen and mountaineers? The cultivation of the earth in a great measure — Our health temperament and disposition are taken more (notwithstanding the contradiction of the history of Cain and Abel) from the air we breathe, than is generally imagined. See the difference between a Peasant and a Butcher. — I am convinced a great cause of it is the difference of the air they breathe: the one takes *his* mingled with the fume of slaughter, the other from the dank exhalement from the glebe; the teeming damp that comes up from the plough-furrow is of great effect in taming the fierceness of a strong man — more than his labour — Let him be mowing furz upon a mountain, and at the day's end his thoughts will run upon a . . . axe if he ever had handled one; let him leave the plough, and he will think quietly of his supper. Agriculture is the tamer of men — the steam from the earth is like drinking their Mother's milk — it enervates their nature — this appears a great cause of the imbecility of the Chinese: and if this sort of atmosphere is a mitigation to the energy of a strong man, how much more must it injure a weak one unoccupied unexercised — For what is the cause of so many men maintaining a good state in Cities, but occupation — An idle man, a man who is not sensitively alive to self-interest in a city cannot continue long in good health. This is easily explained — If you were to walk leisurely through an unwholesome path in the fens, with a little horror of them, you would be sure to have your ague. But let Macbeth cross the same path, with the dagger in the air leading him on, and he would never have an ague or anything like it — You should give these things a serious consideration. Notts, I believe, is a flat county — You should be on the slope of one of the dry barren hills in Somersetshire. I am convinced there is as harmful air to be breathed in the country as in town. I am greatly obliged to you for your letter. Perhaps, if you had had strength and spirits enough, you would have felt offended by my offering a note of hand, or rather expressed it. However, I am sure you will give me credit for not in anywise mistrusting you: or imagining that you would take advantage of any power I might give me over me. No — It proceeded from my serious resolve not to be a gratuitous borrower, from a great desire to be correct in money matters, to have in my desk the Chronicles of them to refer to, and know my worldly nonestate: besides in case of my death such documents would be but just, if merely as memorials of the friendly turns I had done to me — Had I known of your illness I should not have written in such fiery phrase in my first let-

ter. I hope that shortly you will be able to bear six times as much. Brown likes the tragedy very much: But he is not a fit judge of it, as I have only acted as midwife to his plot; and of course he will be fond of his child. I do not think I can make you any extracts without spoiling the effect of the whole when you come to read it — I hope you will then not think my labour misspent. Since I finished it, I have finished Lamia, and am now occupied in revising St. Agnes's Eve, and studying Italian. Ariosto I find as diffuse, in parts, as Spenser — I understand completely the difference between them. I will cross the letter with some lines from Lamia. [The lines copied are 122–177.] Brown's kindest remembrances to you — and I am ever your most sincere friend   JOHN KEATS.

This is a good sample of the story. Brown is gone to Chichester a-visiting — I shall be alone here for 3 weeks, expecting accounts of your health.

128. TO FANNY BRAWNE

Fleet Street, Monday Morn.
[Postmark, Lombard Street,
September 14, 1819.]

MY DEAR GIRL — I have been hurried to town by a Letter from my brother George; it is not of the brightest intelligence. Am I mad or not? I came by the Friday night coach and have not yet been to Hampstead. Upon my soul it is not my fault. I cannot resolve to mix any pleasure with my days: they go one like another, undistinguishable. If I were to see you to-day it would destroy the half comfortable sullenness I enjoy at present into downright perplexities. I love you too much to venture to Hampstead, I feel it is not paying a visit, but venturing into a fire. *Que feraije?* as the French novel writers say in fun, and I in earnest: really what can I do? Knowing well that my life must be passed in fatigue and trouble, I have been endeavouring to wean myself from you: for to myself alone what can be much of a misery? As far as they regard myself I can despise all events: but I cannot cease to love you. This morning I scarcely know what I am doing. I am going to Walthamstow. I shall return to Winchester to-morrow; whence you shall hear from me in a few days. I am a Coward, I cannot bear the pain of being happy: 't is out of the question: I must admit no thought of it.

Yours ever affectionately JOHN KEATS.

129. TO GEORGE AND GEORGIANA KEATS

Winchester, September [17, 1819], Friday.

MY DEAR GEORGE — I was closely employed in reading and composition in this place, whither I had come from Shanklin for the convenience of a library, when I received your last dated 24th July. You will have seen by the short letter I wrote from Shanklin how matters stand between us and Mr. Jennings. They had not at all moved, and I knew no way of overcoming the inveterate obstinacy of our affairs. On receiving your last, I immediately took a place in the same night's coach for London. Mr. Abbey behaved extremely well to me, appointed Monday evening at seven to meet me, and observed that he should drink tea at that hour. I gave him the enclosed note and showed him the last leaf of yours to me. He really appeared anxious about it, and promised he would forward your money as quickly as possible. I think I mentioned that Waltou was dead. ... He will apply to Mr. Gliddon the partner, endeavour to get rid of Mr. Jenning's claim, and be expeditious. He has received an answer from my letter to Fry. That is something. We are certainly in a very low estate — I say we, for I am in such a situation, that were it not for the assistance of Brown and Taylor, I must be as badly off as a man can be. I could not raise any sum by the promise of any poem, no, not by the mortgage of my intellect.

We must wait a little while. I really have hopes of success. I have finished a tragedy, which if it succeeds will enable me to sell what I may have in manuscript to a good advantage. I have passed my time in reading, writing, and fretting — the last I intend to give up, and stick to the other two. They are the only chances of benefit to us. Your wants will be a fresh spur to me. I assure you you shall more than share what I can get whilst I am still young. The time may come when age will make me more selfish. I have not been well treated by the world, and yet I have, capitally well. I do not know a person to whom so many purse-strings would fly open as to me, if I could possibly take advantage of them, which I cannot do, for none of the owners of these purses are rich. Your present situation I will not suffer myself to dwell upon. When misfortunes are so real, we are glad enough to escape them and the thought of them. I cannot help thinking Mr. Audubon a dishonest man. Why did he make you believe that he was a man of property? How is it that his circumstances have altered so suddenly? In truth, I do not believe you fit to deal with the world, or at least the American world. But, good God! who can avoid these chances? You have done your best. Take matters as coolly as you can; and confidently expecting help from England, act as if no help were nigh. Mine, I am sure, is a tolerable tragedy; it would have been a bank to me, if just as I had finished it, I had not heard of Kean's resolution to go to America. That was the worst news I could have had. There is no actor can do the principal character besides Kean. At Covent Garden there is a great chance of its being damm'd. Were it to succeed even there it would lift me out of the mire; I mean the mire of a bad reputation which is continually rising against me. My name with the literary fashionables is vulgar. I am a weaver-boy to them. A tragedy would lift me out of this mess, and mess it is as far as regards our pockets. But be not cast down any more than I am; I feel that I can bear real ills better than imaginary ones. Whenever I find myself growing vapourish, I rouse myself, wash, and put on a clean shirt, brush my hair and clothes, tie my shoestrings neatly, and in fact adonise as I were going out. Then, all clean and comfortable, I sit down to write. This I find the greatest relief. Besides I am becoming accustomed to the privations of the pleasures of sense. In the midst of the world I live like a hermit. I have forgot how to lay plans for the enjoyment of any pleasure. I feel I can bear anything, — any misery, even imprisonment, so long as I have neither wife nor child. Perhaps you will say yours are your only comfort; they must be. I returned to Winchester the day before yesterday, and am now here alone, for Brown, some days before I left, went to Bedhampton, and there he will be for the next fortnight. The term of his house will be up in the middle of next month when we shall return to Hampstead. On Sunday, I dined with your mother and Hen and Charles in Henrietta Street. Mrs. and Miss Millar were in the country. Charles had been but a few days returned from Paris. I daresay you will have letters expressing the motives of his journey. Mrs. Wylie and Miss Waldegrave seem as quiet as two mice there alone. I did not show your last. I thought it better not, for better times will certainly come, and why should they be unhappy in the meantime? On Monday morning I went to Walthamstow. Fanny looked better than I had seen her for some time. She complains of not hearing from you, appealing to me as if it were half my fault. I had been so long in retirement that London appeared a very odd place. I could not make out I had so many acquaintances, and it was a whole day before I could feel among men. I had another strange sensation. There was not one house I felt any pleasure to call at. Reynolds was in the coun-

try, and, saving himself, I am prejudiced against all that family. Dilke and his wife and child were in the country. Taylor was at Nottingham. I was out, and everybody was out. I walked about the streets as in a strange land. Rice was the only one at home. I passed some time with him. I know him better since we have lived a month together in the Isle of Wight. He is the most sensible and even wise man I know. He has a few John Bull prejudices, but they improve him. His illness is at times alarming. We are great friends, and there is no one I like to pass a day with better. Martin called in to bid him goodbye before he set out for Dublin. If you would like to hear one of his jokes, here is one which, at the time, we laughed at a good deal: A Miss ——, with three young ladies, one of them Martin's sister, had come a-gadding in the Isle of Wight and took for a few days a cottage opposite ours. We dined with them one day, and as I was saying they had fish. Miss —— said she thought *they tasted of the boat.* 'No' says Martin, very seriously, 'they have n't been kept long enough.' I saw Haslam. He is very much occupied with love and business, being one of Mr. Saunders' executors and lover to a young woman. He showed me her picture by Severn. I think she is, though not very cunning, too cunning for him. Nothing strikes me so forcibly with a sense of the ridiculous as love. A man in love I do think cuts the sorriest figure in the world; queer, when I know a poor fool to be really in pain about it, I could burst out laughing in his face. His pathetic visage becomes irresistible. Not that I take Haslam as a pattern for lovers; he is a very worthy man and a good friend. His love is very amusing. Somewhere in the Spectator is related an account of a man inviting a party of stutterers and squinters to his table. It would please me more to scrape together a party of lovers — not to dinner, but to tea. There would be no fighting as among knights of old.

[Here follow the lines given on p. 251.]
You see, I cannot get on without writing, as boys do at school, a few nonsense verses. I begin them and before I have written six the whim has passed — if there is anything deserving so respectable a name in them. I shall put in a bit of information anywhere, just as it strikes me. Mr. Abbey is to write to me as soon as he can bring matters to bear, and then I am to go to town and tell him the means of forwarding to you through Capper and Hazlewood. I wonder I did not put this before. I shall go on to-morrow ; it is so fine now I must take a bit of a walk.

Saturday [September 18].

With my inconstant disposition it is no wonder that this morning, amid all our bad times and misfortunes, I should feel so alert and well-spirited. At this moment you are perhaps in a very different state of mind. It is because my hopes are ever paramount to my despair. I have been reading over a part of a short poem I have composed lately, called Lamia, and I am certain there is that sort of fire in it that must take hold of people some way. Give them either pleasant or unpleasant sensation — what they want is a sensation of some sort. I wish I could pitch the key of your spirits as high as mine is ; but your organ-loft is beyond the reach of my voice.

I admire the exact admeasurement of my niece in your mother's letter — O ! the little span-long elf. I am not in the least a judge of the proper weight and size of an infant. Never trouble yourselves about that. She is sure to be a fine woman. Let her have only delicate nails both on hands and feet, and both as small as a May-fly's, who will live you his life on a 3 square inch of oak-leaf ; and nails she must have, quite different from the market-women here, who plough into butter and make a quarter pound taste of it. I intend to write a letter to your wife, and there I may say more on this little plump subject — I hope she 's plump. Still harping on my daughter. This Winchester is a place tolerably well suited to me. There is a fine cathedral, a college, a Roman Catholic chapel, a Methodist do., and Independent do. ; and there is not one loom, or anything like manufacturing beyond bread and butter, in the whole city. There are a number of rich Catholics in the place. It is a respectable, ancient, and aristocratic place, and moreover it contains a nunnery. Our set are by no means so hail fellow well met on literary subjects as we were wont to be. Reynolds has turn'd to the law. By the bye, he brought out a little piece at the Lyceum call'd One, Two, Three, Four : by Advertisement. It met with complete success. The meaning of this odd title is explained when I tell you the principal actor is a mimic, who takes off four of our best performers in the course of the farce. Our stage is loaded with mimics. I did not see the piece, being out of town the whole time it was in progress. Dilke is entirely swallowed up in his boy. It is really lamentable to what a pitch he carries a sort of parental mania. I had a letter from him at Shanklin. He went on, a word or two about the Isle of Wight, which is a bit of hobby horse of his, but he soon deviated to his boy. 'I am sitting,' says he, 'at the window expecting my boy from ——.' I suppose I told you somewhere that he lives in Westminster, and his boy goes to school there, where he gets beaten, and every bruise he has, and I daresay deserves, is very bitter to Dilke. The place I am speaking of puts me in mind of a circumstance which occurred lately at Dilke's. I think it very rich and dramatic and quite illustrative of the little quiet fun that he will enjoy sometimes. First I must tell you that their house is at the corner of Great Smith Street, so that some of the windows look into one street, and the back windows look into another around the corner. Dilke had some old people to dinner — I know not who, but there were two old ladies among them. Brown was there — they had known him from a child. Brown is very pleasant with old women, and on that day it seems behaved himself so winningly that they became hand and glove together, and a little complimentary. Brown was obliged to depart early. He bid them good-bye and passed into the passage. No sooner was his back turned than the old women began lauding him. When Brown had reached the street door, and was just going, Dilke threw up the window and called : ' Brown ! Brown ! They say you look younger than ever you did ! ' Brown went on, and had just turned the corner into the other street when Dilke appeared at the back window, crying : ' Brown ! Brown ! By God, they say you're handsome ! ' You see what a many words it requires to give any identity to a thing I could have told you in half a minute.

I have been reading lately Burton's Anatomy of Melancholy, and I think you will be very much amused with a page I here copy for you. I call it a Feu de Joie round the batteries of Fort St. Hyphen-de-Phrase on the birthday of the Digamma. The whole alphabet was drawn up in a phalanx on the corner of an old dictionary, band playing, ' Amo, Amas,' etc.

' Every lover admires his mistress, though she be very deformed of herself, ill-favoured, wrinkled, pimpled, pale, red, yellow, tan'd, tallow-faced, have a swoln juglers platter face, or a thin, lean, chitty face, have clouds in her face, be crooked, dry, bald, goggle-ey'd, bleary'd or with staring eys, she looks like a squis'd cat, holds her head still awry, heavy, dull, hollow-mouthed, Persean hook-nosed, have a sharp Jose nose, a red nose, China flat, great nose, *nare simo patuloque*, a nose like a promontory, gubber-tushed, rotten teeth, black, uneven, brown teeth, beetle browed, a witches beard, her breath stink all over the room, her nose drop winter and summer with a Bavarian poke under her chin, a sharp chin, lave eared, with a long cranes neck, which stands awry too, *pendulis mammis, her dugs like two double jugs*, or else no dugs in the other extream, bloody faln fingers, she have filthy long unpaired nails, scabbed hands or wrists, a tan'd skin, a rotten carkass, crooked back, she stoops, is lame, splea-footed, *as slender in the middle as a cow in the waste*, gowty legs, her ankles hang over her shooes, her feet stink, she breed lice, a mere changeling, a very monster, an aufe imperfect, her whole complexion savours, an harsh voyce, incondite gesture, vile gait, a vast virago, or an ugly tit, a slug, a fat fustilugs, a truss, a long lean rawbone, a skeleton, a sneaker (*si qua latent meliora puta*), and to thy judgment looks like a Mard in a lanthorn, whom thou couldst not fancy for a world, but hatest, loathest, and wouldst have spit in her face, or blow thy nose in her bosome, *remedium amoris* to another man, a dowdy, a slut, a scold, a nasty, rank, rammy, filthy, beastly quean, dishonest peradventure, obscene, base, beggerly, rude, foolish, untaught, peevish, Irus' daughter, Thersite's sister, Grobian's schollar ; if he love her once, he admires her for all this, he takes no notice of any such errors, or imperfections of body or minde.'

There's a dose for you. Fire ! ! I would give my favourite leg to have written this as a speech in a play. With what effect could Matthews pop-gun it at the pit ! This I think will amuse you more than so much poetry. Of that I do not like to copy any, as I am afraid it is too mal à propos for you at present ; and yet I will send you some, for by the time you receive it, things in England may have taken a different turn. When I left Mr. Abbey on Monday evening, I walked up Cheapside, but returned to put some letters in the post, and met him again in Bucklesbury. We walked together through the Poultry as far as the baker's shop he has some concern in — He spoke of it in such a way to me, I thought he wanted me to make an offer to assist him in it. I do believe if I could be a hatter I might be one. He seems anxious about me. He began blowing up Lord Byron while I was sitting with him : ' However, may be the fellow says true now and then,' at which he picked up a magazine, and read some extracts from Don Juan (Lord Byron's last flash poem), and particularly one against literary ambition. I do think I must be well spoken of among sets, for Hodgkinson is more than polite, and the coffee German endeavoured to be very close to me the other night at Covent Garden, where I went at half price before I tumbled into bed. Every one, however distant an acquaintance, behaves in the most conciliating manner to me. You will see I speak of this as a matter of interest. On the next sheet I will give you a little politics.

In every age there has been in England, for two or three centuries, subjects of great popular interest on the carpet, so that however great the uproar, one can scarcely prophecy any material change in the Government, for as loud disturbances have agitated the country many times. All civilized countries become gradually more enlightened, and there should be a continual change for the better. Look at this country at present, and remember it when it was even thought impious to doubt the justice of a trial by combat. From that time there has been a gradual change. Three great changes have been in progress: first for the better, next for the worse, and a third for the better once more. The first was the gradual annihilation of the tyranny of the nobles, when kings found it their interest to conciliate the common people, elevate them, and be just to them. Just when baronial power ceased, and before standing armies were so dangerous, taxes were few, kings were lifted by the people over the heads of their nobles, and those people held a rod over kings. The change for the worse in Europe was again this: the obligation of kings to the multitude began to be forgotten. Custom had made noblemen the humble servants of kings. Then kings turned to the nobles as the adorners of their power, the slaves of it, and from the people as creatures continually endeavouring to check them. Then in every kingdom there was a long struggle of kings to destroy all popular privileges. The English were the only people in Europe who made a grand kick at this. They were slaves to Henry VIII, but were freemen under William III at the time the French were abject slaves under Louis XIV. The example of England, and the liberal writers of France and England, sowed the seed of opposition to this tyranny, and it was swelling in the ground till it burst out in the French Revolution. That has had an unlucky termination. It put a stop to the rapid progress of free sentiments in England, and gave our Court hopes of turning back to the despotism of the eighteenth century. They have made a handle of this event in every way to undermine our freedom. They spread a horrid superstition against all innovation and improvement. The present struggle in England of the people is to destroy this superstition. What has roused them to do it is their distresses. Perhaps, on this account, the present distresses of this nation are a fortunate thing though so horrid in their experience. You will see I mean that the French Revolution put a temporary stop to this third change — the change for the better — Now it is in progress again, and I think it is an effectual one. This is no contest between Whig and Tory, but between right and wrong. There is scarcely a grain of party spirit now in England. Right and wrong considered by each man abstractedly, is the fashion. I know very little of these things. I am convinced, however, that apparently small causes make great alterations. There are little signs whereby we may know how matters are going on. This makes the business of Carlisle the bookseller of great amount in my mind. He has been selling deistical pamphlets, republished Tom Paine, and many other works held in superstitious horror. He even has been selling, for some time, immense numbers of a work called The Deist, which comes out in weekly numbers. For this conduct he, I think, has had about a dozen indictments issued against him, for which he has found bail to the amount of many thousand pounds. After all, they are afraid to prosecute. They are afraid of his defence ; it would be published in all the papers all over the empire. They shudder at this. The trials would light a flame they could not extinguish. Do you not think this of great import ? You will hear by the papers of the proceedings at Manchester, and Hunt's triumphal entry into London.[58] It would take me a whole day and a quire of paper to give you anything like detail. I will merely mention that it is calculated that 30,000 people were in the streets waiting for him. The whole distance from the Angel at Islington to the Crown and Anchor was lined with multitudes.

As I passed Colnaghi's window I saw a profile portrait of Sandt, the destroyer of Kotzebue. His very look must interest every one in his favour. I suppose they have represented him in his college dress. He seems to me like a young Abelard — a fine mouth, cheek bones (and this is no joke) full of sentiment, a fine, unvulgar nose, and plump temples.

On looking over some letters I found the one I wrote, intended for you, from the foot of Helvellyn to Liverpool; but you had sailed, and therefore it was returned to me. It contained, among other nonsense, an acrostic of my sister's name — and a pretty long name it is. I wrote it in a great hurry which you will see. Indeed I would not copy it if I thought it would ever be seen by any but yourselves. [See p. 243.]

I sent you in my first packet some of my Scotch letters. I find I have one kept back, which was written in the most interesting part of our tour, and will copy part of it in the hope you will not find it unamusing. I would give now anything for Richardson's power of making mountains of molehills.

Incipit epistola caledoniensa —

' Dunancullen.'

(I did not know the day of the month, for I find I have not added it. Brown must have been asleep). 'Just after my last had gone to the post ' (before I go any further, I must premise that I would send the identical letter, instead of taking the trouble to copy it ; I do not do so, for it would spoil my notion of the neat manner in which I intend to fold these three genteel sheets. The original is written on coarse paper, and the soft one would ride in the post bag very uneasy. Perhaps there might be a quarrel * . . .

. . . .

I ought to make a large ' ? ' here, but I had better take the opportunity of telling you I have got rid of my haunting sore throat, and conduct myself in a manner not to catch another.

You speak of Lord Byron and me. There is this great difference between us : he describes what he sees — I describe what I imagine. Mine is the hardest task ; now see the immense difference. The Edinburgh Reviewers are afraid to touch upon my poem. They do not know what to make of it ; they do not like to condemn it, and they will not praise it for fear. They are as shy of it as I should be of wearing a Quaker's hat. The fact is, they have no real taste. They dare not compromise their judgments on so puzzling a question. If on my next publication they should praise me, and so lug in Endymion, I will address them in a manner they will not at all relish. The cowardliness of the Edinburgh is more than the abuse of the Quarterly.

* Keats here copies, with slight changes and abridgments, his letter to Tom of July 23, 1818 (see above, p. 320) ending with the lines written after visiting Staffa : as to which he adds, 'I find I must keep memorandums of the verses I send you, for I do not remember whether I have sent the following lines upon Staffa. I hope not; 't would be a horrid bore to you, especially after reading this dull specimen of description. For myself I hate descriptions. I would not send it if it were not mine.'

Monday [September 20].

This day is a grand day for Winchester. They elect the mayor. It was indeed high time the place should have some sort of excitement. There was nothing going on —all asleep. Not an old maid's sedan returning from a card party; and if any old women have got tipsy at christenings, they have not exposed themselves in the street. The first night, though, of our arrival here there was a slight uproar took place at about ten of the clock. We heard distinctly a noise patting down the street, as of a walking-cane of the good old dowager breed; and a little minute after we heard a less voice observe, 'What a noise the ferril made—it must be loose.' Brown wanted to call the constables, but I observed it was only a little breeze, and would soon pass over. The side streets here are excessively maiden-lady-like; the doorsteps always fresh from the flannel. The knockers have a very staid, serious, nay almost awful quietness about them. I never saw so quiet a collection of lions' and rams' heads. The doors most part black, with a little brass handle just above the keyhole, so that you may easily shut yourself out of your own house. He! He! There is none of your Lady Bellaston ringing and rapping here; no thundering Jupiter-footmen, no opera-treble tattoos, but a modest lifting up of the knocker by a set of little wee old fingers that peep through the gray mittens, and a dying fall thereof. The great beauty of poetry is that it makes everything in every place interesting. The palatine Venice and the abbotine Winchester are equally interesting. Some time since I began a poem called 'The Eve of St. Mark,' quite in the spirit of town quietude. I think I will give you the sensation of walking about an old country town in a coolish evening. I know not whether I shall ever finish it; I will give it as far as I have gone. Ut tibi placeat—

[The Eve of St. Mark. See p. 196.]

I hope you will like this for all its carelessness. I must take an opportunity here to observe that though I am writing to you, I am all the while writing at your wife. This explanation will account for my speaking sometimes hoity-toity-ishly, whereas if you were alone, I should sport a little more sober sadness. I am like a squinty gentleman, who, saying soft things to one lady ogles another, or what is as bad, in arguing with a person on his left hand, appeals with his eyes to one on the right. His vision is elastic; he bends it to a certain object, but having a patent spring it flies off. Writing has this disadvantage of speaking—one cannot write a wink, or a nod, or a grin, or a purse of the lips, or a smile—O law! One cannot put one's finger to one's nose, or yerk ye in the ribs, or lay hold of your button in writing; but in all the most lively and titterly parts of my letter you must not fail to imagine me, as the epic poets say, now here, now there; now with one foot pointed at the ceiling, now with another; now with my pen on my ear, now with my elbow in my mouth. O, my friends, you lose the action, and attitude is everything, as Fuseli said when he took up his leg like a musket to shoot a swallow just darting behind his shoulder. And yet does not the word 'mum' go for one's finger beside the nose? I hope it does. I have to make use of the word 'mum' before I tell you that Severn has got a little baby—all his own, let us hope. He told Brown he had given up painting, and had turned modeller. I hope sincerely 't is not a party concern—that no Mr.—— or —— is the real Pinxit and Severn the poor Sculpsit to this work of art. You know he has long studied in the life Academy. 'Haydon—yes,' your wife will say, 'Here is a sum total account of Haydon again. I wonder your brother don't put a monthly bulletin in the Philadelphia papers about him. I won't hear —no. Skip down to the bottom, and there are some more of his verses—skip (lullaby-by) them too.' — 'No, let's go regularly through.' — 'I won't hear a word about Haydon — bless the child, how rioty she is — there, go on there.'

Now, pray go on here, for I have a few words to say about Haydon. Before this chancery threat had cut off every legitimate supply of cash from me, I had a little at my disposal. Haydon being very much in want, I lent him £30 of it. Now in this see-saw game of life, I got nearest to the ground, and this chancery business riveted me there, so that I was sitting in that uneasy position where the seat slants so abominably. I applied to him for payment. He could not. That was no wonder; but Goodman Delver, where was the wonder then? Why marry in this: he did not seem to care much about it, and let me go without my money with almost nonchalance, when he ought to have sold his drawings to supply me. I shall perhaps still be acquainted with him, but for friendship, that is at an end. Brown has been my friend in this. He got him to sign a bond, payable at three months. Haslam has assisted me with the return of part of the money you lent him.

Hunt — 'there,' says your wife, 'there's another of those dull folk! Not a syllable about my friends? Well, Hunt — What about Hunt? You little thing, see how she bites my finger! My! is not this a tooth?' Well when you have done with the tooth, read on. Not a syllable about your friends! Here are some syllables. As far as I could smoke things on the Sunday before last, thus matters stood in Henrietta Street. Henry was a greater blade then ever I remember to have seen him. He had on a very nice coat, a becoming waistcoat, and buff trousers. I think his face has lost a little of the Spanish-brown, but no flesh. He carved some beef exactly to suit my appetite, as if I had been measured for it. As I stood looking out of the window with Charles, after dinner, quizzing the passengers, — at which I am sorry to say he is too apt, — I observed that this young son of a

gun's whiskers had begun to curl and curl, little twists and twists, all down the sides of his face, getting properly thickest on the angles of the visage. He certainly will have a notable pair of whiskers. 'How shiny your gown is in front,' says Charles. 'Why don't you see? 'tis an apron,' says Henry; whereat I scrutinised, and behold your mother had a purple stuff gown on, and over it an apron of the same colour, being the same cloth that was used for the lining. And furthermore to account for the shining, it was the first day of wearing. I guessed as much of the gown — but that is entre nous. Charles likes England better than France. They've got a fat, smiling, fair cook as ever you saw; she is a little lame, but that improves her; it makes her go more swimmingly. When I asked 'Is Mrs. Wylie within?' she gave me such a large five-and-thirty-year-old smile, it made me look round upon the fourth stair — it might have been the fifth; but that's a puzzle. I shall never be able, if I were to set myself a recollecting for a year, to recollect. I think I remember two or three specks in her teeth, but I really can't say exactly. Your mother said something about Miss Keasle — what that was is quite a riddle to me now, whether she had got fatter or thinner, or broader or longer, straiter, or had taken to the zigzags — whether she had taken to or had left off asses' milk. That, by the bye, she ought never to touch. How much better it would be to put her out to nurse with the wise woman of Brentford. I can say no more on so spare a subject. Miss Millar now is a different morsel, if one knew how to divide and subdivide, theme her out into sections and subsections, lay a little on every part of her body as it is divided, in common with all her fellow-creatures, in Moor's Almanack. But, alas, I have not heard a word about her, no cue to begin upon: there was indeed a buzz about her and her mother's being at old Mrs. So and So's, *who was like to die*, as the Jews say.

But I dare say, keeping up their dialect, *she was not like to die.* I must tell you a good thing Reynolds *did.* 'T was the best thing he ever *said.* You know at taking leave of a party at a doorway, sometimes a man dallies and foolishes and gets awkward, and does not know how to make off to advantage. Good-bye — well, good-bye — and yet he does not go; good-bye, and so on, ⸺ well, good bless you — you know what I mean. Now Reynolds was in this predicament, and got out of it in a very witty way. He was leaving us at Hampstead. He delayed, and we were pressing at him, and even said 'be off,' at which he put the tails of his coat between his legs and sneak'd off as nigh like a spaniel as could be. He went with flying colours. This is very clever. I must, being upon the subject, tell you another good thing of him. He began, for the service it might be of to him in the law, to learn French; he had lessons at the cheap rate of 2s. 6d. per fag, and observed to Brown, 'Gad,' says he, 'the man sells his lessons so cheap he must have stolen 'em.' You have heard of Hook, the farce writer. Horace Smith said to one who asked him if he knew Hook, 'Oh yes, Hook and I are very intimate.' There 's a page of wit for you, to put John Bunyan's emblems out of countenance.

Tuesday [September 21].

You see I keep adding a sheet daily till I send the packet off, which I shall not do for a few days, as I am inclined to write a good deal; for there can be nothing so remembrancing and enchaining as a good long letter, be it composed of what it may. From the time you left me our friends say I have altered completely — am not the same person. Perhaps in this letter I am, for in a letter one takes up one's existence from the time we last met. I daresay you have altered also — every man does — our bodies every seven years are completely material'd. Seven years ago it was not this hand that clinched itself against Hammond. We are like the relict garments of a saint — the same and not the same, for the careful monks patch it and patch it till there's not a thread of the original garment left, and still they show it for St. Anthony's shirt. This is the reason why men who have been bosom friends, on being separated for any number of years meet coldly, neither of them knowing why. The fact is they are both altered.

Men who live together have a silent moulding and influencing power over each other. They interassimilate. 'T is an uneasy thought, that in seven years the same hands cannot greet each other again. All this may be obviated by a wilful and dramatic exercise of our minds towards each other. Some think I have lost that poetic ardour and fire 't is said I once had — the fact is, perhaps I have; but, instead of that, I hope I shall substitute a more thoughtful and quiet power. I am more frequently now contented to read and think, but now and then haunted with ambitious thoughts. Quieter in my pulse, improved in my digestion, exerting myself against vexing speculations, scarcely content to write the best verses for the fever they leave behind. I want to compose without this fever. I hope I one day shall. You would scarcely imagine I could live alone so comfortably. 'Kepen in solitarinesse.' I told Anne, the servant here, the other day, to say I was not at home if any one should call. I am not certain how I should endure loneliness and bad weather together. Now the time is beautiful. I take a walk every day for an hour before dinner, and this is generally my walk: I go out the back gate, across one street into the cathedral yard, which is always interesting; there I pass under the trees along a paved path, pass the beautiful front of the cathedral, turn to the left under a stone doorway, — then I am on the other side of the building, — which leaving behind me, I pass on through two college-like squares, seemingly built for the dwelling-place of deans and prebendaries, garnished with grass and shaded with trees; then I pass through one of the old city gates, and then you are in one college street, through which I pass and at the end thereof crossing some meadows, and at last a country alley of gardens, I arrive, that is my worship arrives, at the foundation of St. Cross, which is a very interesting old place, both for its gothic tower and alms square and for the appropriation of its rich rents to a relation of the Bishop of Winchester. Then I pass across St. Cross meadows till you come to the most beautifully clear river — now this is only one mile of my walk. I will spare you the other two till after supper, when they would do you more good. You must avoid going the first mile best after dinner —

[Wednesday, September 22.]

I could almost advise you to put by this nonsense until you are lifted out of your difficulties; but when you come to this part, feel with confidence what I now feel, that though there can be no stop put to troubles we are inheritors of, there can be, and must be, an end to immediate difficulties. Rest in the confidence that I will not omit any exertion to benefit you by some means or other — If I cannot remit you hundreds, I will tens, and if not that, ones. Let the next year be managed by you as well as possible — the next month, I mean, for I trust you will soon receive Abbey's remittance. What he can send you will not be a sufficient capital to ensure you any command in America. What he has of mine I have nearly anticipated by debts, so I would advise you not to sink it, but to live upon it, in hopes of my being able to increase it. To this end I will devote whatever I may gain for a few years to come, at which period I must begin to think of a security of my own comforts, when quiet will become more pleasant to me than the world. Still I would have you doubt my success. 'T is at

present the cast of a die with me. You say, 'These things will be a great torment to me.' I shall not suffer them to be so. I shall only exert myself the more, while the seriousness of their nature will prevent me from nursing up imaginary griefs. I have not had the blue devils once since I received your last. I am advised not to publish till it is seen whether the tragedy will or not succeed. Should it, a few months may see me in the way of acquiring property. Should it not, it will be a drawback, and I shall have to perform a longer literary pilgrimage. You will perceive that it is quite out of my interest to come to America. What could I do there? How could I employ myself out of reach of libraries? You do not mention the name of the gentleman who assists you. 'T is an extraordinary thing. How could you do without that assistance? I will not trust myself with brooding over this. The following is an extract from a letter of Reynolds to me: —

'I am glad to hear you are getting on so well with your writings. I hope you are not neglecting the revision of your poems for the press, from which I expect more than you do.'

The first thought that struck me on reading your last was to mortgage a poem to Murray, but on more consideration, I made my mind not to do so; my reputation is very low; he would not have negotiated my bill of intellect, or given me a very small sum. I should have bound myself down for some time. 'T is best to meet present misfortunes; not for a momentary good to sacrifice great benefits which one's own untrammell'd and free industry may bring one in the end. In all this do never think of me as in any way unhappy: I shall not be so. I have a great pleasure in thinking of my responsibility to you, and shall do myself the greatest luxury if I can succeed in any way so as to be of assistance to you. We shall look back upon these times, even before our eyes are at all dim — I am convinced of it. But be careful of those

Americans. I could almost advise you to come, whenever you have the sum of £500, to England. Those Americans will, I am afraid, still fleece you. If ever you think of such a thing, you must bear in mind the very different state of society here, — the immense difficulties of the times, the great sum required per annum to maintain yourself in any decency. In fact the whole is with Providence. I know not how to advise you but by advising you to advise with yourself. In your next tell me at large your thoughts about America — what chance there is of succeeding there, for it appears to me you have as yet been somehow deceived. I cannot help thinking Mr. Audubon has deceived you. I shall not like the sight of him. I shall endeavour to avoid seeing him. You see how puzzled I am. I have no meridian to fix you to, being the slave of what is to happen. I think I may bid you finally remain in good hopes, and not tease yourself with my changes and variations of mind. If I say nothing decisive in any one particular part of my letter, you may glean the truth from the whole pretty correctly. You may wonder why I had not put your affairs with Abbey in train on receiving your letter before last, to which there will reach you a short answer dated from Shanklin. I did write and speak to Abbey, but to no purpose. Your last, with the enclosed note, has appealed home to him. He will not see the necessity of a thing till he is hit in the mouth. 'T will be effectual.

I am sorry to mix up foolish and serious things together, but in writing so much I am obliged to do so, and I hope sincerely the tenor of your mind will maintain itself better. In the course of a few months I shall be as good an Italian scholar as I am a French one. I am reading Ariosto at present, not managing more than six or eight stanzas at a time. When I have done this language, so as to be able to read it tolerably well, I shall set myself to get complete in Latin, and there my learning

must stop. I do not think of returning upon Greek. I would not go even so far if I were not persuaded of the power the knowledge of any language gives one. The fact is I like to be acquainted with foreign languages. It is, besides, a nice way of filling up intervals, etc. Also the reading of Dante is well worth the while; and in Latin there is a fund of curious literature of the Middle Ages, the works of many great men — Aretino and Sannazaro and Machiavelli. I shall never become attached to a foreign idiom, so as to put it into my writings. The Paradise Lost, though so fine in itself, is a corruption of our language. It should be kept as it is — unique, a curiosity, a beautiful and grand curiosity, the most remarkable production of the world ; a northern dialect accommodating itself to Greek and Latin inversions and intonations. The purest English, I think — or what ought to be purest — is Chatterton's. The language had existed long enough to be entirely uncorrupted of Chaucer's Gallicisms, and still the old words are used. Chatterton's language is entirely northern. I prefer the native music of it to Milton's, cut by feet. I have but lately stood on my guard against Milton. Life to him would be death to me. Miltonic verse cannot be written, but is the verse of art. I wish to devote myself to another verse alone.

Friday [September 24].

I have been obliged to intermit your letter for two days (this being Friday morning), from having had to attend to other correspondence. Brown, who was at Bedhampton, went thence to Chichester, and I am still directing my letters Bedhampton. There arose a misunderstanding about them. I began to suspect my letters had been stopped from curiosity. However, yesterday Brown had four letters from me all in a lump, and the matter is cleared up. Brown complained very much in his letter to me of yesterday of the great alteration the disposition of Dilke has undergone. He thinks of nothing but political justice and his boy. Now, the first political duty a man ought to have a mind to is the happiness of his friends. I wrote Brown a comment on the subject, wherein I explained what I thought of Dilke's character, which resolved itself into this conclusion, that Dilke was a man who cannot feel he has a personal identity unless he has made up his mind about everything. The only means of strengthening one's intellect is to make up one's mind about nothing — to let the mind be a thoroughfare for all thoughts, not a select party. The genus is not scarce in population; all the stubborn arguers you meet with are of the same brood. They never begin upon a subject they have not pre-resolved on. They want to hammer their nail into you, and if you have the point, still they think you wrong. Dilke will never come at a truth as long as he lives, because he is always trying at it. He is a Godwin Methodist.

I must not forget to mention that your mother show'd me the lock of hair — 't is of a very dark colour for so young a creature. Then it is two feet in length. I shall not stand a barley corn higher. That's not fair; one ought to go on growing as well as others. At the end of this sheet I shall stop for the present and send it off. You may expect another letter immediately after it. As I never know the day of the month but by chance, I put here that this is the 24th September.

I would wish you here to stop your ears, for I have a word or two to say to your wife.

MY DEAR SISTER — In the first place I must quarrel with you for sending me such a shabby piece of paper, though that is in some degree made up for by the beautiful impression of the seal. You should like to know what I was doing the first of May. Let me see — I cannot recollect. I have all the Examiners ready to send — they will be a great treat to you when they reach you. I shall pack them up when my business with Abbey has come to a good conclusion, and the remittance is on the road to you. I have dealt round your best wishes like a pack of cards, but being always given to cheat myself, I have turned up ace. You see I am making game of you. I see you are not all happy in that America. England, however, would not be over happy for you if you were here. Perhaps 't would be better to be teased here than there. I must preach patience to you both. No step hasty or injurious to you must be taken. You say let one large sheet be all to me. You will find more than that in different parts of this packet for you. Certainly, I have been caught in rains. A catch in the rain occasioned my last sore throat; but as for red-haired girls, upon my word, I do not recollect ever having seen one. Are you quizzing me or Miss Waldegrave when you talk of promenading? As for pun-making, I wish it was as good a trade as pin-making. There is very little business of that sort going on now. We struck for wages, like the Manchester weavers, but to no purpose. So we are all out of employ. I am more lucky than some, you see, by having an opportunity of exporting a few — getting into a little foreign trade, which is a comfortable thing. I wish one could get change for a pun in silver currency. I would give three and a half any night to get into Drury pit, but they won't ring at all. No more will notes you will say; but notes are different things, though they make together a pun-note as the term goes. If I were your son, I shouldn't mind you, though you rapt me with the scissors. But, Lord! I should be out of favour when the little un be comm'd. You have made an uncle of me, you have, and I don't know what to make of myself. I suppose next there will be a nevey. You say in my last, write directly. I have not received your letter above ten days. The thought of your little girl puts me in mind of a thing I heard a Mr. Lamb say. A child in arms was passing by towards its mother, in the nurse's arms. Lamb took hold of the long clothes, saying: 'Where, God bless me, where does it leave off?'

Saturday [September 25].

If you would prefer a joke or two to anything else, I have two for you, fresh hatched, just ris, as the bakers' wives say by the rolls. The first I played off on Brown; the second I played on myself. Brown, when he left me, 'Keats,' says he, 'my good fellow' (staggering upon his left heel and fetching an irregular pirouette with his right); 'Keats,' says he (depressing his left eyebrow and elevating his right one), though by the way at the moment I did not know which was the right one; 'Keats,' says he (still in the same posture, but furthermore both his hands in his waistcoat pockets and putting out his stomach), 'Keats — my — go-o-ood fell-o-o-ooh,' says he (interlarding his exclamation with certain ventriloquial parentheses), — no, this is all a lie — He was as sober as a judge, when a judge happens to be sober, and said: 'Keats, if any letters come for me, do not forward them, but open them and give me the marrow of them in a few words.' At the time I wrote my first to him no letter had arrived. I thought I would invent one, and as I had not time to manufacture a long one, I dabbed off a short one, and that was the reason of the joke succeeding beyond my expectations. Brown let his house to a Mr. Benjamin — a Jew. Now, the water which furnishes the house is in a tank, sided with a composition of lime, and the lime impregnates the water unpleasantly. Taking advantage of this circumstance, I pretended that Mr. Benjamin had written the following short note —

SIR — By drinking your damn'd tank water I have got the gravel. What reparation can you make to me and my family?
NATHAN BENJAMIN.

By a fortunate hit, I hit upon his right — heathen name — his right pronomen. Brown in consequence, it appears, wrote to the surprised Mr. Benjamin the following —

SIR — I cannot offer you any remuneration until your gravel shall have formed itself into a stone — when I will cut you with pleasure.   C. BROWN.

This of Brown's Mr. Benjamin has answered, insisting on an explanation of this singular circumstance. B. says: 'When I read your letter and his following, I roared; and in came Mr. Snook, who on reading them seem'd likely to burst the hoops of his fat sides.' So the joke has told well.

Now for the one I played on myself. I must first give you the scene and the dramatis personæ. There are an old major and his youngish wife here in the next appartments to me. His bedroom door opens at an angle with my sitting-room door. Yesterday I was reading as demurely as a parish clerk, when I heard a rap at the door. I got up and opened it; no one was to be seen. I listened, and heard some one in the major's room. Not content with this, I went upstairs and down, looked in the cupboards and watch'd. At last I set myself to read again, not quite so demurely, when there came a louder rap. I was determined to find out who it was. I looked out; the staircases were all silent. 'This must be the major's wife,' said I. 'At all events I will see the truth.' So I rapt me at the major's door and went in, to the utter surprise and confusion of the lady, who was in reality there. After a little explanation, which I can no more describe than fly, I made my retreat from her, convinced of my mistake. She is to all appearance a silly body, and is really surprised about it. She must have been, for I have discovered that a little girl in the house was the rapper. I assure you she has nearly made me sneeze. If the lady tells tits, I shall put a very grave and moral face on the matter with the old gentleman, and make his little boy a present of a humming top.

[Monday, September 27.]

MY DEAR GEORGE — This Monday morning, the 27th, I have received your last, dated 12th July. You say you have not heard from England for three months. Then my letter from Shanklin, written, I think, at the end of June, has not reach'd you. You shall not have cause to think I neglect you. I have kept this back a little time in expectation of hearing from Mr. Abbey. You will say I might have remained in town to be Abbey's messenger in these affairs. That I offered him, but he in his answer convinced me that he was anxious to bring the business to an issue. He observed, that by being himself the agent in the whole, people might be more expeditious. You say you have not heard for three months, and yet your letters have the tone of knowing how our affairs are situated, by which I conjecture I acquainted you with them in a letter previous to the Shanklin one. That I may not have done. To be certain, I will here state that it is in consequence of Mrs. Jennings threatening a chancery suit that you have been kept from the receipt of monies, and myself deprived of any help from Abbey. I am glad you say you keep up your spirits. I hope you make a true statement on that score. Still keep them up, for we are all young. I can only repeat here that you shall hear from me again immediately. Notwithstanding this bad intelligence, I have experienced some pleasure in receiving so correctly two letters from you, as it gives me, if I may so say, a distant idea of proximity. This last improves upon my little niece — kiss her for me. Do not fret yourself about the delay of money on account of my immediate opportunity being lost, for in a new country whoever has money must have an opportunity of employing it in many ways. The report runs now more in favour of Kean stopping in England. If he should, I have confident hopes of our tragedy. If he invokes the hot-blooded character of Ludolph, — and he is the only actor that can do it, — he will add to his own fame and improve my fortune. I will give you a half-dozen lines of it before I part as a specimen —

Not as a swordsman would I pardon crave,
But as a son: the bronz'd Centurion,
Long-toil'd in foreign wars, and whose high deeds
Are shaded in a forest of tall spears,
Known only to his troop, hath greater plea
Of favour with my sire than I can have.

Believe me, my dear brother and sister, your affectionate and anxious Brother
JOHN KEATS.

130. TO —— ——

· · · · · · ·

If George succeeds it will be better, certainly, that they should stop in America; if not, why not return? It is better in ill luck to have at least the comfort of one's friends than to be shipwrecked among Americans. But I have good hopes as far as I can judge from what I have heard of George. He should by this time be taught alertness and carefulness. If they should stop in America for five or six years let us hope they may have about three children. Then the eldest will be getting old enough to be society. The very crying will keep their ears employed and their spirits from being melancholy.

· · · · · · ·

131. TO JOHN HAMILTON REYNOLDS

Winchester, September 22, 1819.

MY DEAR REYNOLDS — I was very glad to hear from Woodhouse that you would meet in the country. I hope you will pass some pleasant time together. Which I wish to make pleasanter by a brace of letters, very highly to be estimated, as really I have had very bad luck with this sort of game this season. I 'kepen in solitarinesse,' for Brown has gone a-visiting. I am surprised myself at the pleasure I live alone in. I can give you no news of the place here, or any other idea of it but what I have to this effect written to George. Yesterday I say to him was a grand day for Winchester. They elected a Mayor. It was indeed high time the place should receive some sort of excitement. There was nothing going on : all asleep : not an old maid's sedan returning from a card party : and if any old woman got tipsy at Christenings they did not expose it in the streets. The first night though of our arrival here, there was a slight uproar took place at about 10 o' the Clock. We heard distinctly a noise pattering down the High Street as of a walking cane of the good old Dowager breed ; and a little minute after we heard a less voice observe 'What a noise the ferril made — it must be loose.' Brown wanted to call the constables, but I observed 't was only a little breeze and would soon pass over. — The side streets here are excessively maiden-lady-like : the door-steps always fresh from the flannel. The knockers have a staid serious, nay almost awful quietness about them. I never saw so quiet a collection of Lions' and Rams' heads. The doors are most part black, with a little brass handle just above the keyhole, so that in Winchester a man may very quietly shut himself out of his own house. How beautiful the season is now — How fine the air. A temperate sharpness about it. Really, without joking, chaste weather — Dian skies — I never liked stubble-fields so much as now — Aye better than the chilly green of the Spring. Somehow, a stubble-field looks warm — in the same way that some pictures look warm. This struck me so much in my Sunday's walk that I composed upon it. [The Ode to Autumn, p. 213.]

I hope you are better employed than in gaping after weather. I have been at different times so happy as not to know what weather it was — No I will not copy a parcel of verses. I always somehow associate Chatterton with autumn. He is the purest writer in the English Language. He has no French idiom or particles, like Chaucer — 't is genuine English Idiom in English words. I have given up Hyperion, — there were too many Miltonic inversions in it — Miltonic verse cannot be written but in an artful, or, rather, artist's humour. I wish to give myself up to other sensations. English ought to be kept up. It may be interesting to you to pick out some lines from Hyperion, and put a mark ✕ to the false beauty proceeding from art, and one ‖ to the true voice of feeling. Upon my soul 't was imagination — I cannot make the distinction — Every now and then there is a Miltonic intonation — But I cannot make the division properly. The fact is, I must take a walk : for I am writing a long letter to George : and have been employed at it all the morning. You will ask, have I heard from George. I am sorry to say not the best news — I hope for better. This is the reason, among others, that if I write to you it must be in such a scrap-like way. I have no meridian to date interests from, or measure circumstances — To-night I am all in a mist ; I scarcely know what's what — But you knowing my unsteady and vagarish disposition, will guess that all this turmoil will be settled by to-morrow morning. It strikes me to-night that I have led a very odd sort of life for the two or three last years — Here and there — no anchor — I am glad of it. — If you can get a peep at Babbicombe before you leave the country, do. — I think it the finest place I have seen, or is to be seen, in the South. There is a Cottage there I took warm water at, that made up for the tea. I have lately shirk'd some friends of ours, and I advise you to do the same, I mean the blue-devils — I am never at home to them. You need not fear them while you remain in Devonshire — there will be some of the family waiting for you at the Coach office — but go by another Coach.

I shall beg leave to have a third opinion in the first discussion you have with Woodhouse — just half-way, between both. You know I will not give up my argument — In my walk to-day I stoop'd under a railing that lay across my path, and asked myself 'Why I did not get over.' 'Because,' answered I, 'no one wanted to force you under.' I would give a guinea to be a reasonable man — good sound sense — a says what he thinks and does what he says man — and did not take snuff. They say men near death, however mad they may have been, come to their senses — I hope I shall here in this letter — there is a decent space to be very sensible in — many a good proverb has been in less — nay, I have heard of the statutes at large being changed into the Statutes at Small and printed for a watch paper.

Your sisters, by this time, must have got the Devonshire 'ees' — short ees — you know 'em — they are the prettiest ees in the language. O how I admire the middle-sized delicate Devonshire girls of about fifteen. There was one at an Inn door holding a quartern of brandy — the very thought of her kept me warm a whole stage — and a 16 miler too — ' You 'll pardon me for being jocular.'

Ever your affectionate friend
JOHN KEATS.

132. TO CHARLES WENTWORTH DILKE

Winchester, Wednesday Eve.
[September 22, 1819.]

MY DEAR DILKE — Whatever I take to for the time I cannot leave off in a hurry; letter writing is the go now; I have consumed a quire at least. You must give me credit, now, for a free Letter when it is in reality an interested one, on two points, the one requestive, the other verging to the pros and cons. As I expect they will lead me to seeing and conferring with you in a short time, I shall not enter at all upon a letter I have lately received from George, of not the most comfortable intelligence: but proceed to these two points, which if you can theme out into sections and subsections, for my edification, you will oblige me. This first I shall begin upon, the other will follow like a tail to a Comet. I have written to Brown on the subject, and can but go over the same ground with you in a very short time, it not being more in length than the ordinary paces between the Wickets. It concerns a resolution I have taken to endeavour to acquire something by temporary writing in periodical works. You must agree with me how unwise it is to keep feeding upon hopes, which depending so much on the state of temper and imagination, appear gloomy or bright, near or afar off, just as it happens. Now an act has three parts — to act, to do, and to perform — I mean I should *do* something for my immediate welfare. Even if I am swept away like a spider from a drawing-room, I am determined to spin — homespun anything for sale. Yea, I will traffic. Anything but Mortgage my Brain to Blackwood. I am determined not to lie like a dead lump. If Reynolds had not taken to the law, would he not be earning something? Why cannot I. You may say I want tact — that is easily acquired. You may be up to the slang of a cock pit in three battles. It is fortunate I have not before this been tempted to venture on the common. I should a year or two ago have spoken my mind on every subject with the utmost simplicity. I hope I have learned a little better and am confident I shall be able to cheat as well as any literary Jew of the Market and shine up an article on anything without much knowledge of the subject, aye like an orange. I would willingly have recourse to other means. I cannot; I am fit for nothing but literature. Wait for the issue of this Tragedy? No — there cannot be greater uncertainties east, west, north, and south than concerning dramatic composition. How many months must I wait! Had I not better begin to look about me now? If better events supersede this necessity what harm will be done? I have no trust whatever on Poetry I don't wonder at it — the marvel is to me how people read so much of it. I think you will see the reasonableness of my plan. To forward it I purpose living in cheap Lodging in Town, that I may be in the reach of books and information, of which there is here a plentiful lack. If I can find any place tolerably comfortable I will settle myself and fag till I can afford to buy Pleasure — which if I never can afford I must go without. Talking of Pleasure, this moment I was writing with one hand, and with the other holding to my Mouth a Nectarine — Good God how fine. It went down soft, pulpy, slushy, oozy — all its delicious embonpoint melted down my throat like a large beatified Strawberry. I shall certainly breed. Now I come to my request. Should you like me for a neighbour again? Come, plump it out, I won't blush. I should also be in the neighbourhood of Mrs. Wylie, which I should be glad of, though that of course does not influence me. Therefore will you look about Marsham, or Rodney [Romney?] Street for a couple of rooms for me. Rooms like the gallant's legs in Massinger's time, 'as good as the times allow, Sir.' I have written to-day to Reynolds, and to Woodhouse. Do you know him? He is a Friend of Taylor's at whom Brown has taken one of his funny odd dislikes. I'm sure he's wrong, because Woodhouse likes my Poetry — conclusive. I ask your opinion and yet I must say to you as to him, Brown, that if you have anything to say against it I shall be as obstinate and heady as a Radical. By the Examiner coming in your handwriting you must be in Town. They have put me into spirits. Notwithstanding my aristocratic temper I cannot help being very much pleased with the present public proceedings. I hope sincerely I shall be able to put a Mite of help to the Liberal side of the Question before I die. If you should have left Town again (for your Holidays cannot be up yet) let me know when this is forwarded to you. A most extraordinary mischance has befallen two letters I wrote Brown — one from London whither I was obliged to go on business for George; the other from this place since my return. I can't make it out. I am excessively sorry for it. I shall hear from Brown and from you almost together, for I have sent him a Letter to-day: you must positively agree with me or by the delicate toe nails of the virgin I will not open your Letters. If they are as David says 'suspicious looking letters' I won't open them. If St. John had been half as cunning he might have seen the revelations comfortably in his own room, without giving angels the trouble of breaking open seals. Remember me to Mrs. D. and the Westmonasteranian and believe me Ever your sincere friend JOHN KEATS.

133. TO CHARLES ARMITAGE BROWN

Winchester, September 23, 1819.

. . . . . .

Now I am going to enter on the subject of self. It is quite time I should set myself doing something, and live no longer upon hopes. I have never yet exerted myself. I am getting into an idle-minded, vicious way of life, almost content to live upon others. In no period of my life have I acted with any self-will but in throwing up the apothecary profession. That I do not repent of. Look at Reynolds, if he was not in the law, he would be acquiring by his abilities, something towards his support. My occupation is entirely literary: I will do so, too. I will write, on the liberal side of the question, for whoever will pay me. I have not known yet what it is to be diligent. I purpose living in town in a cheap lodging, and endeavouring, for a beginning, to get the theatricals of some paper. When I can afford to compose deliberate poems, I will. I shall be in expectation of an answer to this. Look on my side of the question. I am convinced I am right. Suppose the tragedy should succeed, — there will be no harm done. And here I will take an opportunity of making a remark or two on our friendship, and on all your good offices to me. I have a natural timidity of mind in these matters ; liking better to take the feeling between us for granted, than to speak of it. But, good God ! what a short while you have known me ! I feel it a sort of duty thus to recapitulate, however unpleasant it may be to you. You have been living for others more than any man I know. This is a vexation to me, because it has been depriving you, in the very prime of your life, of pleasures which it was your duty to procure. As I am speaking in general terms, this may appear nonsense ; you perhaps will not understand it ; but if you can go over, day by day, any month of the last year, you will know what I mean. On the whole however this is a subject that I cannot express myself upon — I speculate upon it frequently ; and believe me the end of my speculations is always an anxiety for your happiness. This anxiety will not be one of the least incitements to the plan I purpose pursuing. I had got into a habit of mind of looking towards you as a help in all difficulties — This very habit would be the parent of idleness and difficulties. You will see it is a duty I owe myself to break the neck of it. I do nothing for my subsistence — make no exertion — At the end of another year you shall applaud me, not for verses, but for conduct. While I have some immediate cash, I had better settle myself quietly, and fag on as others do. I shall apply to Hazlitt, who knows the market as well as any one, for something to bring me in a few pounds as soon as possible. I shall not suffer my pride to hinder me. The whisper may go round ; I shall not hear it. If I can get an article in the Edinburgh, I will. One must not be deli-

cate — Nor let this disturb you longer than a moment. I look forward with a good hope that we shall one day be passing free, untrammelled, unanxious time together. That can never be if I continue a dead lump. I shall be expecting anxiously an answer from you. If it does not arrive in a few days this will have miscarried, and I shall come straight to —— before I go to town, which you I am sure will agree had better be done while I still have some ready cash. By the middle of October I shall expect you in London. We will then set at the theatres. If you have anything to gainsay, I shall be even as the deaf adder which stoppeth her ears.

· · · · · · · ·

134. TO THE SAME

Winchester, September 23, 1819.

· · · · · · ·

Do not suffer me to disturb you unpleasantly : I do not mean that you should not suffer me to occupy your thoughts, but to occupy them pleasantly; for I assure you I am as far from being unhappy as possible. Imaginary grievances have always been more my torment than real ones — You know this well — Real ones will never have any other effect upon me than to stimulate me to get out of or avoid them. This is easily accounted for — Our imaginary woes are conjured up by our passions, and are fostered by passionate feeling : our real ones come of themselves, and are opposed by an abstract exertion of mind. Real grievances are displacers of passion. The imaginary nail a man down for a sufferer, as on a cross; the real spur him up into an agent. I wish, at one view, you would see my heart towards you. 'T is only from a high tone of feeling that I can put that word upon paper — out of poetry. I ought to have waited for your answer to my last before I wrote this. I felt however compelled to make a joinder to yours. I had written to Dilke on the subject of my last, I scarcely know whether I shall send my letter now. I think he would approve of my plan ; it is so evident. Nay, I am convinced, out and out, that by prosing for a while in periodical works I may maintain myself decently.

. . . .

135. TO CHARLES WENTWORTH DILKE

Winchester, Friday, October 1 [1819].

MY DEAR DILKE — For sundry reasons, which I will explain to you when I come to Town, I have to request you will do me a great favour as I must call it knowing how great a Bore it is. That your imagination may not have time to take too great an alarm I state immediately that I want you to hire me a couple of rooms (a Sitting Room and bed room for myself alone) in Westminster. Quietness and cheapness are the essentials : but as I shall with Brown be returned by next Friday you cannot in that space have sufficient time to make any choice selection, and need not be very particular as I can when on the spot suit myself at leisure. Brown bids me remind you not to send the Examiners after the third. Tell Mrs. D. I am obliged to her for the late ones which I see are directed in her hand. Excuse this mere business letter for I assure you I have not a syllable at hand on any subject in the world.

Your sincere friend   JOHN KEATS.

136. TO BENJAMIN ROBERT HAYDON

Winchester, Sunday Morn [October 3, 1819].

MY DEAR HAYDON — Certainly I might : but a few Months pass away before we are aware. I have a great aversion to letter writing, which grows more and more upon me ; and a greater to summon up circumstances before me of an unpleasant nature. I was not willing to trouble you with them. Could I have dated from my Palace of Milan you would have heard from me. Not even now will I mention a word of my

affairs — only that ' I Rab am here ' but shall not be here more than a Week more, as I purpose to settle in Town and work my way with the rest. I hope I shall never be so silly as to injure my health and industry for the future by speaking, writing or fretting about my non-estate. I have no quarrel, I assure you, of so weighty a nature, with the world, on my own account as I have on yours. I have done nothing — except for the amusement of a few people who refine upon their feelings till anything in the understandable way will go down with them — people predisposed for sentiment. I have no cause to complain because I am certain anything really fine will in these days be felt. I have no doubt that if I had written Othello I should have been cheered by as good a mob as Hunt. So would you be now if the operation of painting was as universal as that of Writing. It is not : and therefore it did behove men I could mention among whom I must place Sir George Beaumont to have lifted you up above sordid cares. That this has not been done is a disgrace to the country. I know very little of Painting, yet your pictures follow me into the Country. When I am tired of reading I often think them over and as often condemn the spirit of modern Connoisseurs. Upon the whole, indeed, you have no complaint to make, being able to say what so few Men can, ' I have succeeded.' On sitting down to write a few lines to you these are the uppermost in my mind, and, however I may be beating about the arctic while your spirit has passed the line, you may lay to a minute and consider I am earnest as far as I can see. Though at this present ' I have great dispositions to write ' I feel every day more and more content to read. Books are becoming more interesting and valuable to me. I may say I could not live without them. If in the course of a fortnight you can procure me a ticket to the British Museum I will make a better use of it than I did in the first instance. I shall go on with patience in the confidence that if I ever do anything worth remembering the Reviewers will no more be able to stumble-block me than the Royal Academy could you. They have the same quarrel with you that the Scotch nobles had with Wallace. The fame they have lost through you is no joke to them. Had it not been for you Fuseli would have been not as he is major but maximus domo. What Reviewers can put a hindrance to must be — a nothing — or mediocre which is worse. I am sorry to say that since I saw you I have been guilty of a practical joke upon Brown which has had all the success of an innocent Wildfire among people. Some day in the next week you shall hear it from me by word of Mouth. I have not seen the portentous Book which was skummer'd at you just as I left town. It may be light enough to serve you as a Cork Jacket and save you for a while the trouble of swimming. I heard the Man went raking and rummaging about like any Richardson. That and the Memoirs of Menage are the first I shall be at. From Sr. G. B.'s, Lord Ms [54] and particularly Sr. John Leicesters good lord deliver us. I shall expect to see your Picture plumped out like a ripe Peach — you would not be very willing to give me a slice of it. I came to this place in the hopes of meeting with a Library but was disappointed. The High Street is as quiet as a Lamb. The knockers are dieted to three raps per diem. The walks about are interesting from the many old Buildings and archways. The view of the High Street through the Gate of the City in the beautiful September evening light has amused me frequently. The bad singing of the Cathedral I do not care to smoke — being by myself I am not very coy in my taste. At St. Cross there is an interesting picture of Albert Dürer's — who living in such warlike times perhaps was forced to paint in his Gauntlets — so we must make all allowances.

I am, my dear Haydon, Yours ever
JOHN KEATS.

Brown has a few words to say to you and will cross this.

137. TO FANNY BRAWNE

College Street.
[Postmark, October 11, 1819.]

MY SWEET GIRL — I am living today in yesterday : I was in a complete fascination all day. I feel myself at your mercy. Write me ever so few lines and tell me you will never for ever be less kind to me than yesterday.— You dazzled me. There is nothing in the world so bright and delicate. When Brown came out with that seemingly true story against me last night, I felt it would be death to me if you had ever believed it — though against any one else I could muster up my obstinacy. Before I knew Brown could disprove it I was for the moment miserable. When shall we pass a day alone ? I have had a thousand kisses, for which with my whole soul I thank love — but if you should deny me the thousand and first — 't would put me to the proof how great a misery I could live through. If you should ever carry your threat yesterday into execution — believe me 't is not my pride, my vanity or any petty passion would torment me — really 't would hurt my heart — I could not bear it. I have seen Mrs. Dilke this morning ; she says she will come with me any fine day. Ever yours JOHN KEATS.

Ah hertè mine !

138. TO THE SAME

25 College Street.
[Postmark, October 13, 1819.]

MY DEAREST GIRL — This moment I have set myself to copy some verses out fair. I cannot proceed with any degree of content. I must write you a line or two and see if that will assist in dismissing you from my Mind for ever so short a time. Upon my Soul I can think of nothing else. The time is passed when I had power to advise and warn you against the unpromising morning of my Life. My love has made me selfish. I cannot exist without you. I am forgetful of everything but seeing you again — my Life seems to stop there — I see no further. You have absorb'd me. I have a sensation at the present moment as though I was dissolving — I should be exquisitely miserable without the hope of soon seeing you. I should be afraid to separate myself far from you. My sweet Fanny, will your heart never change? My love, will it? I have no limit now to my love. . . . Your note came in just here. I cannot be happier away from you. 'T is richer than any Argosy of Pearles. Do not threat me even in jest. I have been astonished that Men could die Martyrs for religion — I have shudder'd at it. I shudder no more — I could be martyr'd for my Religion — Love is my religion — I could die for that. I could die for you. My Creed is Love and you are its only tenet. You have ravish'd me away by a Power I cannot resist; and yet I could resist till I saw you; and even since I have seen you I have endeavoured often 'to reason against the reasons of my Love.' I can do that no more — the pain would be too great. My love is selfish. I cannot breathe without you.

Yours for ever   JOHN KEATS.

139. TO FANNY KEATS

Wentworth Place [October 16, 1819].

MY DEAR FANNY — My Conscience is always reproaching me for neglecting you for so long a time. I have been returned from Winchester this fortnight, and as yet I have not seen you. I have no excuse to offer — I should have no excuse. I shall expect to see you the next time I call on Mr. A. about George's affairs which perplex me a great deal — I should have to-day gone to see if you were in town — but as I am in an industrious humour (which is so necessary to my livelihood for the future) I am loath to break through it though it be merely for one day, for when I am inclined I can do a great deal in a day — I am more fond of pleasure than study (many men have preferr'd the latter) but I have become resolved to know something which you will credit when I tell you I have left off animal food that my brains may never henceforth be in a greater mist than is theirs by nature — I took lodgings in Westminster for the purpose of being in the reach of Books, but am now, returned to Hampstead being induced to it by the habit I have acquired in this room I am now in and also from the pleasure of being free from paying any petty attentions to a diminutive house-keeping. Mr. Brown has been my great friend for some time — without him I should have been in, perhaps, personal distress — as I know you love me though I do not deserve it, I am sure you will take pleasure in being a friend to Mr. Brown even before you know him. — My lodgings for two or three days were close in the neighbourhood of Mrs. Dilke who never sees me but she enquires after you — I have had letters from George lately which do not contain, as I think I told you in my last, the best news — I have hopes for the best — I trust in a good termination to his affairs which you please God will soon hear of — It is better you should not be teased with the particulars. The whole amount of the ill news is that his mercantile speculations have not had success in consequence of the general depression of trade in the whole province of Kentucky and indeed all America. — I have a couple of shells for you you will call pretty.

Your affectionate Brother JOHN——.

140. TO FANNY BRAWNE

Great Smith Street.
Tuesday Morn.
[Postmark, College Street, October 19, 1819].

MY SWEET FANNY — On awakening from my three days dream ('I cry to dream again') I find one and another astonish'd at my idleness and thoughtlessness. I was miserable last night — the morning is always restorative. I must be busy, or try to be so. I have several things to speak to you of tomorrow morning. Mrs. Dilke I should think will tell you that I purpose living at Hampstead. I must impose chains upon myself. I shall be able to do nothing. I should like to cast the die for Love or death. I have no Patience with anything else — if you ever intend to be cruel to me as you say in jest now but perhaps may sometimes be in earnest, be so now — and I will — my mind is in a tremble, I cannot tell what I am writing.

Ever my love yours   JOHN KEATS.

141. TO JOSEPH SEVERN

Wentworth Place, Wednesday
[October 27 ? 1819].

DEAR SEVERN — Either your joke about staying at home is a very old one or I really call'd. I don't remember doing so. I am glad to hear you have finish'd the Picture and am more anxious to see it than I have time to spare : for I have been so very lax, unemployed, unmeridian'd, and objectless these two months that I even grudge indulging (and that is no great indulgence considering the Lecture is not over till 9 and the lecture room seven miles from Wentworth Place) myself by going to Hazlitt's Lecture. If you have hours to the amount of a brace of dozens to throw away you may sleep nine of them here in your little Crib and chat the rest. When your Picture is up and in a good light I shall make a point of meeting you at the Academy if you will let me know when. If you should be at the Lecture to-morrow evening I shall see you — and congratulate you heartily — Haslam I know 'is very Beadle to an amorous sigh.'

Your sincere friend   JOHN KEATS.

142. TO JOHN TAYLOR

Wentworth Place, Hampstead,
November 17 [1819].

MY DEAR TAYLOR — I have come to a determination not to publish anything I have now ready written : but, for all that, to publish a poem before long, and that I hope to make a fine one. As the marvellous is the most enticing, and the surest guarantee of harmonious numbers, I have been endeavouring to persuade myself to untether Fancy, and to let her manage for herself. I and myself cannot agree about this at all. Wonders are no wonders to me. I am more at home amongst men and women. I would rather read Chaucer than Ariosto. The little dramatic skill I may as yet have, however badly it might show in a drama, would, I think, be sufficient for a poem. I wish to diffuse the colouring of St. Agnes's Eve throughout a poem in which character and sentiment would be the figures to such drapery. Two or three such poems, if God should spare me, written in the course of the next six years, would be a famous Gradus ad Parnassum altissimum — I mean they would nerve me up to the writing of a few fine plays — my greatest ambition, when I do feel ambitious. I am sorry to say that is very seldom. The subject we have once or twice talked of appears a promising one — The Earl of Leicester's history. I am this morning reading Holinshed's 'Elizabeth.' You had some books a while ago you promised to send me, illustrative of my subject. If you can lay hold of them, or any others which may be serviceable to me, I know you will encourage my low-spirited muse by sending them, or rather by letting me know where our errand-cart man shall call with my little box. I will endeavour to set myself selfishly at work on this poem that is to be.

Your sincere friend
JOHN KEATS.

143. TO FANNY KEATS

Wednesday Morn —
[November 17, 1819].

MY DEAR FANNY — I received your letter yesterday Evening and will obey it tomorrow. I would come to-day — but I have been to Town so frequently on George's Business it makes me wish to employ to-day at Hampstead. So I say Thursday without fail. I have no news at all entertaining — and if I had I should not have time to tell them as I wish to send this by the morning Post.

Your affectionate Brother
JOHN.

144. TO JOSEPH SEVERN

Wentworth Place, Monday Morn —
[December 6 ? 1819].

MY DEAR SEVERN — I am very sorry that on Tuesday I have an appointment in the City of an undeferable nature ; and Brown on the same day has some business at Guildhall. I have not been able to figure your manner of executing the Cave of despair,[55] therefore it will be at any rate a novelty and surprise to me — I trust on the right side. I shall call upon you some morning shortly, early enough to catch you before you can get out — when we will proceed to the Academy. I think you must be suited with a good painting light in your Bay window. I wish you to return the Compliment by going with me to see a Poem I have hung up for the Prize in the Lecture Room of the Surry Institution. I have many Rivals, the most threatening are An Ode to Lord Castlereagh, and a new series of Hymns for the New, new Jerusalem Chapel. (You had best put me into your Cave of despair.)

Ever yours sincerely
JOHN KEATS.

145. TO JAMES RICE

Wentworth Place [December 1819].

MY DEAR RICE — As I want the coat on my back mended, I would be obliged if you would send me the one Brown left at your house by the Bearer — During your late contest I had regular reports of you, how that your time was completely taken up and your health improving — I shall call in the course of a few days, and see whether your promotion has made any difference in your Behaviour to us. I suppose Reynolds has given you an account of Brown and Elliston. As he has not rejected our Tragedy, I shall not venture to call him directly a fool ; but as he wishes to put it off till next season, I cannot help thinking him little better than a knave. — That it will not be acted this season is yet uncertain. Perhaps we may give it another furbish and try it at Covent Garden. 'T would do one's heart good to see Macready in Ludolph. If you do not see me soon it will be from the humour of writing, which I have had for three days continuing. I must say to the Muses what the maid says to the Man — 'Take me while the fit is on me.' Would you like a true story ? 'There was a man and his wife who being to go a long Journey on foot, in the course of their travels came to a river which rolled knee-deep over the pebbles — In these cases the man generally pulls off his shoes and stockings, and carries the woman over on his back. This man did so. And his wife being pregnant and troubled, as in such case is very common, with strange longings, took the strangest that ever was heard of. Seeing her husband's foot, a handsome one enough, looked very clean and tempting in the clear water, on their arrival at the other bank, she earnestly demanded a bit of it. He being an affectionate fellow, and fearing for the comeliness of his child, gave her a bit which he cut off with his clasp knife — Not satisfied, she asked for another morsel. Supposing there might be twins, he gave her a slice more. Not yet contented she craved another piece. "You wretch," cries the man, "would you wish me to kill myself? Take that" — upon which he stabbed her with the knife, cut her open, and found three children in her Belly : two of them very comfortable with their mouths shut, the third with its eyes and mouth stark staring wide open. "Who would have thought it?" cried the widower, and pursued his journey.' Brown has a little rumbling in his stomach this morning.

Ever yours sincerely   JOHN KEATS.

146. TO FANNY KEATS

Wentworth Place, Monday Morn — [December 20, 1819].

MY DEAR FANNY — When I saw you last, you ask'd me whether you should see me again before Christmas. You would have seen me if I had been quite well. I have not, though not unwell enough to have prevented me — not indeed at all — but fearful lest the weather should affect my throat which on exertion or cold continually threatens me.—By the advice of my Doctor I have had a warm great Coat made and have ordered some thick shoes — so furnish'd I shall be with you if it holds a little fine before Christmas day. — I have been very busy since I saw you, especially the last Week, and shall be for some time, in preparing some Poems to come out in the Spring, and also in brightening the interest of our Tragedy. — Of the Tragedy I can give you but news semigood. It is accepted at Drury Lane with a promise of coming out next season: as that will be too long a delay we have determined to get Elliston to bring it out this Season or to transfer it to Covent Garden. This Elliston will not like, as we have every motive to believe that Kean has perceived how suitable the principal Character will be for him. My hopes of success in the literary world are now better than ever. Mr. Abbey, on my calling on him lately, appeared anxious that I should apply myself to something else — He mentioned Tea Brokerage. I supposed he might perhaps mean to give me the Brokerage of his concern which might be executed with little trouble and a good profit ; and therefore said I should have no objection to it, especially as at the same time it occurred to me that I might make over the business to George — I questioned him about it a few days after. His mind takes odd turns. When I became a Suitor he became coy. He did not seem so much inclined to serve me. He described what I should have to do in the progress of business. It will not suit me. I have given it up. I have not heard again from George, which rather disappoints me, as I wish to hear before I make any fresh remittance of his property. I received a note from Mrs. Dilke a few days ago inviting me to dine with her on Xmas day which I shall do. Mr. Brown and I go on in our old dog trot of Breakfast, dinner (not tea, for we have left that off), supper, Sleep, Confab, stirring the fire and reading. Whilst I was in the Country last Summer, Mrs. Bentley tells me, a woman in mourning call'd on me, — and talk'd something of an aunt of ours — I am so careless a fellow I did not enquire, but will particularly : On Tuesday I am going to hear some Schoolboys Speechify on breaking up day — I 'll lay you a pocket piece we shall have 'My name is Norval.' I have not yet look'd for the Letter you mention'd as it is mix'd up in a box full of papers — you must tell me, if you can recollect, the subject of it. This moment Bentley brought a Letter from George for me to deliver to Mrs. Wylie — I shall see her and it before I see you. The Direction was in his best hand written with a good Pen and sealed with a Tassie's Shakspeare such as I gave you — We judge of people's hearts by their Countenances ; may we not.

judge of Letters in the same way ? — if so, the Letter does not contain unpleasant news — Good or bad spirits have an effect on the handwriting. This direction is at least unnervous and healthy. Our Sister is also well, or George would have made strange work with Ks and Ws. The little Baby is well or he would have formed precious vowels and Consonants — He sent off the Letter in a hurry, or the mail bag was rather a warm berth, or he has worn out his Seal, for the Shakspeare's head is flattened a little. This is close muggy weather as they say at the Ale houses.

I am ever, my dear Sister, yours affectionately   JOHN KEATS.

147. TO THE SAME

Wentworth Place, Wednesday.
[December 22, 1819.]

MY DEAR FANNY — I wrote to you a Letter directed Walthamstow the day before yesterday wherein I promised to see you before Christmas day. I am sorry to say I have been and continue rather unwell, and therefore shall not be able to promise certainly. I have not seen Mrs. Wylie's Letter. Excuse my dear Fanny this very shabby note.

Your affectionate Brother   JOHN.

148. TO GEORGIANA AUGUSTA KEATS

Thursday, January 13, 1820.

MY DEAR SIS.: By the time you receive this your trouble will be over. I wish you knew they were half over. I mean that George is safe in England and in good health. To write to you by him is almost like following one's own letter in the mail. That it may not be quite so, I will leave common intelligence out of the question, and write wide of him as I can. I fear I must be dull, having had no good-natured flip from Fortune's finger since I saw you, and no sideway comfort in the success of my friends. I could almost promise that

if I had the means I would accompany George back to America, and pay you a visit of a few months. I should not think much of the time, or my absence from my books ; or I have no right to think, for I am very idle. But then I ought to be diligent, and at least keep myself within the reach of materials for diligence. Diligence, that I do not mean to say ; I should say dreaming over my books, or rather other people's books. George has promised to bring you to England when the five years have elapsed. I regret very much that I shall not be able to see you before that time, and even then I must hope that your affairs will be in so prosperous a way as to induce you to stop longer. Yours is a hardish fate, to be so divided among your friends and settled among a people you hate. You will find it improve. You have a heart that will take hold of your children ; even George's absence will make things better. His return will banish what must be your greatest sorrow, and at the same time minor ones with it. Robinson Crusoe, when he saw himself in danger of perishing on the waters, looked back to his island as to the haven of his happiness, and on gaining it once more was more content with his solitude. We smoke George about his little girl. He runs the common-beaten road of every father, as I dare say you do of every mother: there is no child like his child, so original, — original forsooth! However, I take you at your words. I have a lively faith that yours is the very gem of all children. Ain't I its uncle?

On Henry's marriage there was a piece of bride cake sent me. It missed its way. I suppose the carrier or coachman was a conjuror, and wanted it for his own private use. Last Sunday George and I dined at Millar's. There were your mother and Charles with Fool Lacon, Esq., who sent the sly, disinterested shawl to Miss Millar, with his own heathen name engraved in the middle. Charles had a silk handkerchief belonging to a Miss Grover, with whom he pretended to be smitten, and for her sake kept exhibiting and adoring the handkerchief all the evening. Fool Lacon, Esq., treated it with a little venturesome, trembling contumely, whereupon Charles set him quietly down on the floor, from where he as quietly got up. This process was repeated at supper time, when your mother said, 'If I were you Mr. Lacon I would not let him do so.' Fool Lacon, Esq., did not offer any remark. He will undoubtedly die in his bed. Your mother did not look quite so well on Sunday. Mrs. Henry Wylie is excessively quiet before people. I hope she is always so. Yesterday we dined at Taylor's, in Fleet Street. George left early after dinner to go to Deptford; he will make all square there for me. I could not go with him — I did not like the amusement. Haslam is a very good fellow indeed; he has been excessively anxious and kind to us. But is this fair? He has an innamorata at Deptford, and he has been wanting me for some time past to see her. This is a thing which it is impossible not to shirk. A man is like a magnet — he must have a repelling end. So how am I to see Haslam's lady and family, if I even went? for by the time I got to Greenwich I should have repell'd them to Blackheath, and by the time I got to Deptford they would be on Shooter's Hill; when I came to Shooter Hill they would alight at Chatham, and so on till I drove them into the sea, which I think might be indictable. The evening before yesterday we had a pianoforte hop at Dilke's. There was very little amusement in the room, but a Scotchman to hate. Some people, you must have observed, have a most unpleasant effect upon you when you see them speaking in profile. This Scotchman is the most accomplished fellow in this way I ever met with. The effect was complete. It went down like a dose of bitter, and I hope will improve my digestion. At Taylor's too, there was a Scotchman, — not quite so bad, for he was as clean as he could get himself. Not hav-

ing succeeded in Drury Lane with our tragedy, we have been making some alterations, and are about to try Covent Garden. Brown has just done patching up the copy — as it is altered. The reliance I had on it was in Kean's acting. I am not afraid it will be damn'd in the Garden. You said in one of your letters that there was nothing but Haydon and Co. in mine. There can be nothing of him in this, for I never see him or Co. George has introduced to us an American of the name of Hart. I like him in a moderate way. He was at Mrs. Dilke's party — and sitting by me; we began talking about English and American ladies. The Miss —— and some of their friends made not a very enticing row opposite us. I bade him mark them and form his judgment of them. I told him I hated Englishmen because they were the only men I knew. He does not understand this. Who would be Braggadochio to Johnny Bull? Johnny's house is his castle — and a precious dull castle it is; what a many Bull castles there are in so-and-so crescent! I never wish myself an unversed writer and newsmonger but when I write to you. I should like for a day or two to have somebody's knowledge — Mr. Lacon's for instance — of all the different folks of a wide acquaintance, to tell you about. Only let me have his knowledge of family minutiæ and I would set them in a proper light; but, bless me, I never go anywhere. My pen is no more garrulous than my tongue. Any third person would think I was addressing myself to a lover of scandal. But we know we do not love scandal, but fun; and if scandal happens to be fun, that is no fault of ours. There were very good pickings for me in George's letters about the prairie settlement, if I had any taste to turn them to account in England. I knew a friend of Miss Andrews, yet I never mentioned her to him; for after I had read the letter I really did not recollect her story. Now I have been sitting here half an hour with my invention at work, to say something about your mother or Charles or Henry, but it is in vain. I know not what to say. Three nights since, George went with your mother to the play. I hope she will soon see mine acted. I do not remember ever to have thanked you for your tassels to my Shakspeare — there be hangs so ably supported opposite me. I thank you now. It is a continual memento of you. If you should have a boy, do not christen him John, and persuade George not to let his partiality for me come across. 'T is a bad name, and goes against a man. If my name had been Edmund I should have been more fortunate.

I was surprised to hear of the state of society at Louisville; it seems to me you are just as ridiculous there as we are here — threepenny parties, halfpenny dances. The best thing I have heard of is your shooting; for it seems you follow the gun. Give my compliments to Mrs. Audubon, and tell her I cannot think her either good-looking or honest. Tell Mr. Audubon he 's a fool, and Briggs that 't is well I was not Mr. A.

Saturday, January 15.

It is strange that George having to stop so short a time in England, I should not have seen him for nearly two days. He has been to Haslam's and does not encourage me to follow his example. He had given promise to dine with the same party to-morrow, but has sent an excuse which I am glad of, as we shall have a pleasant party with us to-morrow. We expect Charles here to-day. This is a beautiful day. I hope you will not quarrel with it if I call it an American one. The sun comes upon the snow and makes a prettier candy than we have on twelfth-night cakes. George is busy this morning in making copies of my verses. He is making one now of an 'Ode to the Nightingale,' which is like reading an account of the Black Hole at Calcutta on an iceberg.

You will say this is a matter of course. I am glad it is — I mean that I should like

your brothers more the more I know them. I should spend much more time with them if our lives were more run in parallel; but we can talk but on one subject — that is you.

The more I know of men the more I know how to value entire liberality in any of them. Thank God, there are a great many who will sacrifice their worldly interest for a friend. I wish there were more who would sacrifice their passions. The worst of men are those whose self-interests are their passion; the next, those whose passions are their self - interest. Upon the whole I dislike mankind. Whatever people on the other side of the question may advance, they cannot deny that they are always surprised at hearing of a good action, and never of a bad one. I am glad you have something to like in America — doves. Gertrude of Wyoming and Birkbeck's book should be bound up together like a brace of decoy ducks — one is almost as poetical as the other. Precious miserable people at the prairie. I have been sitting in the sun whilst I wrote this till it 's become quite oppressive — this is very odd for January. The vulcan fire is the true natural heat for winter. The sun has nothing to do in winter but to give a little glooming light much like a shade. Our Irish servant has piqued me this morning by saying that her father in Ireland was very much like my Shakspeare, only he had more colour than the engraving. You will find on George's return that I have not been neglecting your affairs. The delay was unfortunate, not faulty. Perhaps by this time you have received my three last letters, not one of which had reached before George sailed. I would give twopence to have been over the world as much as he has. I wish I had money enough to do nothing but travel about for years. Were you now in England I dare say you would be able (setting aside the pleasure you would have in seeing your mother) to suck out more amusement for society than

I am able to do. To me it is all as dull here as Louisville could be. I am tired of the theatres. Almost all the parties I may chance to fall into I know by heart. I know the different styles of talk in different places, — what subjects will be started, how it will proceed like an acted play, from the first to the last act. If I go to Hunt's I run my head into many tunes heard before, old puns, and old music ; to Haydon's worn-out discourses of poetry and painting. The Miss —— I am afraid to speak to, for fear of some sickly reiteration of phrase or sentiment. When they were at the dance the other night I tried manfully to sit near and talk to them, but to no purpose ; and if I had it would have been to no purpose still. My question or observation must have been an old one, and the rejoinder very antique indeed. At Dilke's I fall foul of politics. 'T is best to remain aloof from people and like their good parts without being eternally troubled with the dull process of their every-day lives. When once a person has smoked the vapidness of the routine of society he must either have self-interest or the love of some sort of distinction to keep him in good humour with it. All I can say is that, standing at Charing Cross and looking east, west, north, and south, I can see nothing but dulness. I hope while I am young to live retired in the country. When I grow in years and have a right to be idle, I shall enjoy cities more. If the American ladies are worse than the English they must be very bad. You say you should like your Emily brought up here. You had better bring her up yourself. You know a good number of English ladies ; what encomium could you give of half a dozen of them? The greater part seems to me downright American. I have known more than one Mrs. Audubon. Her affectation of fashion and politeness cannot transcend ours. Look at our Cheapside tradesmen's sons and daughters — only fit to be taken off by a plague. I hope now soon to come to the time when I shall never be forced to walk through the city and hate as I walk.

Monday, January 17.

George had a quick rejoinder to his letter of excuse to Haslam, so we had not his company yesterday, which I was sorry for as there was our old set. I know three witty people all distinct in their excellence — Rice, Reynolds, and Richards. Rice is the wisest, Reynolds the playfulest, Richards the out-o'-the-wayest. The first makes you laugh and think, the second makes you laugh and not think, the third puzzles your head. I admire the first, I enjoy the second, I stare at the third. The first is claret, the second ginger-beer, the third crême de Byrapymdrag. The first is inspired by Minerva, the second by Mercury, the third by Harlequin Epigram, Esq. The first is neat in his dress, the second slovenly, the third uncomfortable. The first speaks adagio, the second allegretto, the third both together. The first is Swiftean, the second Tom-Crib-ean, the third Shandean. And yet these three eans are not three eans but one ean.

Charles came on Saturday but went early ; he seems to have schemes and plans and wants to get off. He is quite right ; I am glad to see him employed at business. You remember I wrote you a story about a woman named Alice being made young again, or some such stuff. In your next letter tell me whether I gave it as my own, or whether I gave it as a matter Brown was employed upon at the time. He read it over to George the other day, and George said he had heard it all before. So Brown suspects I have been giving you his story as my own. I should like to set him right in it by your evidence. George has not returned from town ; when he does I shall tax his memory. We had a young, long, raw, lean Scotchman with us yesterday, called Thornton. Rice, for fun or for mistake, would persist in calling him Stevenson. I know three people of no wit at all, each distinct in his excellence — A, B, and C. A is the foolishest, B the sulkiest, C is a negative. A makes you yawn, B makes you hate, as for C you never see him at all though he were six feet high — I bear the first, I forbear the second, I am not certain that the third is. The first is gruel, the second ditch-water, the third is spilt — he ought to be wip'd up. A is inspired by Jack-o'-the-clock, B has been drilled by a Russian serjeant, C, they say, is not his mother's true child, but she bought him of the man who cries, Young lambs to sell.

Twang-dillo-dee — This you must know is the amen to nonsense. I know a good many places where Amen should be scratched out, rubbed over with ponce made of Momus's little finger bones, and in its place Twang-dillo-dee written. This is the word I shall be tempted to write at the end of most modern poems. Every American book ought to have it. It would be a good distinction in society. My Lords Wellington and Castlereagh, and Canning, and many more, would do well to wear Twang-dillo-dee on their backs instead of Ribbons at their button-holes; how many people would go sideways along walls and quickset hedges to keep their 'Twang-dillo-dee' out of sight, or wear large pig-tails to hide it. However there would be so many that the Twang-dillo-dees would keep one another in countenance — which Brown cannot do for me — I have fallen away lately. Thieves and murderers would gain rank in the world, for would any of them have the poorness of spirit to conde-scend to be a Twang-dillo-dee? 'I have robbed many a dwelling house; I have killed many a fowl, many a goose, and many a Man (would such a gentleman say) but, thank Heaven, I was never yet a Twang-dillo-dee.' Some philosophers in the moon, who spy at our globe as we do at theirs, say that Twang-dillo-dee is writ-ten in large letters on our globe of earth; they say the beginning of the 'T' is just on the spot where London stands, London

being built within the flourish; 'was' reaches downward and slants as far as Timbuctoo in Africa; the tail of the 'g' goes slap across the Atlantic into the Rio della Plata; the remainder of the letters wrap around New Holland, and the last 't' terminates in land we have not yet di-covered. However, I must be silent; these are dangerous times to libel a man in — much more a world.

Friday, 27 [for 28th January, 1820].

I wish you would call me names: I de-serve them so much. I have only written two sheets for you, to carry by George, and those I forgot to bring to town and have therefore to forward them to Liverpool. George went this morning at 6 o'clock by the Liverpool coach. His being on his journey to you prevents my regretting his short stay. I have no news of any sort to tell you. Henry is wife bound in Camden Town; there is no getting him out. I am sorry he has not a prettier wife: indeed 'tis a shame: she is not half a wife. I think I could find some of her relations in Buffon, or Capt⁴ Cook's voyages or the hierogly-glyphics in Moor's Almanack, or upon a Chinese clock door, the shepherdesses on her own mantelpiece, or in a *cruel* sampler in which she may find herself worsted, or in a Dutch toyshop window, or one of the daughters in the ark, or any picture shop window. As I intend to retire into the country where there will be no sort of news, I shall not be able to write you very long letters. Besides I am afraid the postage comes to too much; which till now I have not been aware of.

People in military bands are generally seriously occupied. None may or can laugh at their work but the Kettle Drum, Long Drum, Do. Triangle and Cymbals. Think-ing you might want a rat-catcher I put your mother's old quaker-colour'd cat into the top of your bonnet. She's with kitten, so you may expect to find a whole family. I hope the family will not grow too large for its lodging. I shall send you a close written sheet on the first of next month, but for fear of missing the Liverpool Post I must finish here. God bless you and your little girl.

Your affectionate Brother
JOHN KEATS.

149. TO FANNY BRAWNE

DEAREST FANNY, I shall send this the moment you return. They say I must remain confined to this room for some time. The consciousness that you love me will make a pleasant prison of the house next to yours. You must come and see me frequently: this evening, without fail — when you must not mind about my speaking in a low tone for I am ordered to do so though I *can* speak out.

Yours ever, sweetest love. —
J. KEATS.

turn over

Perhaps your Mother is not at home and so you must wait till she comes. You must see me tonight and let me hear you promise to come tomorrow.

Brown told me you were all out. I have been looking for the stage the whole afternoon. Had I known this I could not have remain'd so silent all day.

150. TO FANNY KEATS

Wentworth Place, Sunday Morning.
[February 6, 1820.]

MY DEAR SISTER — I should not have sent those Letters without some notice if Mr. Brown had not persuaded me against it on account of an illness with which I was attack'd on Thursday. After that I was resolved not to write till I should be on the mending hand; thank God, I am now so. From imprudently leaving off my great coat in the thaw I caught cold which flew to my Lungs. Every remedy that has been applied has taken the desired effect, and I have nothing now to do but stay within

doors for some time. If I should be confined long I shall write to Mr. Abbey to ask permission for you to visit me. George has been running great chance of a similar attack, but I hope the sea air will be his Physician in case of illness — the air out at sea is always more temperate than on land — George mentioned, in his Letters to us, something of Mr. Abbey's regret concerning the silence kept up in his house. It is entirely the fault of his Manner. You must be careful always to wear warm clothing not only in frost but in a Thaw. — I have no news to tell you. The half-built houses opposite us stand just as they were and seem dying of old age before they are brought up. The grass looks very dingy, the Celery is all gone, and there is nothing to enliven one but a few Cabbage Stalks that seem fix'd on the superannuated List. Mrs. Dilke has been ill but is better. Several of my friends have been to see me. Mrs. Reynolds was here this morning and the two Mr. Wylie's. Brown has been very alert about me, though a little wheezy himself this weather. Everybody is ill. Yesterday evening Mr. Davenport, a gentleman of Hampstead, sent me an invitation to supper, instead of his coming to see us, having so bad a cold he could not stir out — so you see 't is the weather and I am among a thousand. Whenever you have an inflammatory fever never mind about eating. The day on which I was getting ill I felt this fever to a great height, and therefore almost entirely abstained from food the whole day. I have no doubt experienced a benefit from so doing — The Papers I see are full of anecdotes of the late King : how he nodded to a Coalheaver and laugh'd with a Quaker and lik'd boiled Leg of Mutton. Old Peter Pindar is just dead: what will the old King and he say to each other ? Perhaps the King may confess that Peter was in the right, and Peter maintain himself to have been wrong. You shall hear from me again on Tuesday.

Your affectionate Brother JOHN.

151. TO THE SAME

Wentworth Place, Tuesday Morn.
[February 8, 1820.]

MY DEAR FANNY — I had a slight return of fever last night, which terminated favourably, and I am now tolerably well, though weak from the small quantity of food to which I am obliged to confine myself: I am sure a mouse would starve upon it. Mrs. Wylie came yesterday. I have a very pleasant room for a sick person. A Sofa bed is made up for me in the front Parlour which looks on to the grass plot as you remember Mrs. Dilke's does. How much more comfortable than a dull room up stairs, where one gets tired of the pattern of the bed curtains. Besides I see all that passes — for instance now, this morning — if I had been in my own room I should not have seen the coals brought in. On Sunday between the hours of twelve and one I descried a Pot boy. I conjectured it might be the one o'Clock beer — Old women with bobbins and red cloaks and unpresuming bonnets I see creeping about the heath. Gipsies after hare skins and silver spoons. Then goes by a fellow with a wooden clock under his arm that strikes a hundred and more. Then comes the old French emigrant (who has been very well to do in France) with his hands joined behind on his hips, and his face full of political schemes. Then passes Mr. David Lewis, a very good-natured, good-looking old gentleman who has been very kind to Tom and George and me. As for those fellows the Brickmakers they are always passing to and fro. I mus'n't forget the two old maiden Ladies in Well Walk who have a Lap dog between them that they are very anxious about. It is a corpulent Little beast whom it is necessary to coax along with an ivory-tipp'd cane. Carlo our Neighbour Mrs. Brawne's dog and it meet sometimes. Lappy thinks Carlo a devil of a fellow and so do his Mistresses. Well they may — he would sweep 'em all down at a run; all for

the Joke of it. I shall desire him to peruse the fable of the Boys and the frogs: though he prefers the tongues and the Bones. You shall hear from me again the day after to-morrow.

Your affectionate Brother
JOHN KEATS.

152. TO FANNY BRAWNE

MY DEAREST GIRL, — If illness makes such an agreeable variety in the manner of your eyes I should wish you sometimes to be ill. I wish I had read your note before you went last night that I might have assured you how far I was from suspecting any coldness. You had a just right to be a little silent to one who speaks so plainly to you. You must believe — you shall, you will — that I can do nothing, say nothing, think nothing of you but what has its spring in the Love which has so long been my pleasure and torment. On the night I was taken ill — when so violent a rush of blood came to my Lungs that I felt nearly suffocated — I assure you I felt it possible I might not survive, and at that moment thought of nothing but you. When I said to Brown 'this is unfortunate' I thought of you. Tis true that since the first two or three days other subjects have entered my head. I shall be looking forward to Health and the Spring and a regular routine of our old Walks.

Your affectionate   J. K.

153. TO THE SAME

My sweet love, I shall wait patiently till tomorrow before I see you, and in the mean time, if there is any need of such a thing, assure you by your Beauty, that whenever I have at any time written on a certain unpleasant subject, it has been with your welfare impress'd upon my mind. How hurt I should have been had you ever acceded to what is, notwithstanding, very reasonable ! How much the more do I love you from the general result ! In my present state of Health I feel too much separated from you and could almost speak to you in the words of Lorenzo's Ghost to Isabella

' Your Beauty grows upon me and I feel
  A greater love through all my essence steal.'

My greatest torment since I have known you has been the fear of you being a little inclined to the Cressid ; but that suspicion I dismiss utterly and remain happy in the surety of your Love, which I assure you is as much a wonder to me as a delight. Send me the words ' Good night ' to put under my pillow.

Dearest Fanny,
Your affectionate   J. K.

× 154. TO FANNY KEATS

Wentworth Place [February 11, 1820].
MY DEAR FANNY — I am much the same as when I last wrote. I hope a little more verging towards improvement. Yesterday morning being very fine, I took a walk for a quarter of an hour in the garden and was very much refresh'd by it. You must consider no news, good news — if you do not hear from me the day after to-morrow.

Your affectionate Brother   JOHN.

155. TO THE SAME

Wentworth Place, Monday Morn.
[February 14, 1820.]
MY DEAR FANNY — I am improving but very gradually and suspect it will be a long while before I shall be able to walk six miles — The Sun appears half inclined to shine ; if he obliges us I shall take a turn in the garden this morning. No one from Town has visited me since my last. I have had so many presents of jam and jellies that they would reach side by side the length of the sideboard. I hope I shall be

well before it is all consumed. I am vexed that Mr. Abbey will not allow you pocket money sufficient. He has not behaved well — By detaining money from me and George when we most wanted it he has increased our expenses. In consequence of such delay George was obliged to take his voyage to England which will be £150 out of his pocket. I enclose you a note — You shall hear from me again the day after to-morrow.

Your affectionate Brother   JOHN.

156. TO FANNY BRAWNE

MY DEAREST GIRL — According to all appearances I am to be separated from you as much as possible. How I shall be able to bear it, or whether it will not be worse than your presence now and then, I cannot tell. I must be patient, and in the mean time you must think of it as little as possible. Let me not longer detain you from going to Town — there may be no end to this imprisoning of you. Perhaps you had better not come before tomorrow evening: send me however without fail a good night.

You know our situation —— what hope is there if I should be recovered ever so soon — my very health will not suffer me to make any great exertion. I am recommended not even to read poetry, much less write it. I wish I had even a little hope. I cannot say forget me — but I would mention that there are impossibilities in the world. No more of this. I am not strong enough to be weaned — take no notice of it in your good night.

Happen what may I shall ever be my dearest Love
Your affectionate   J. K.

157. TO THE SAME

MY DEAREST GIRL — how could it ever have been my wish to forget you? how could I have said such a thing? The utmost stretch my mind has been capable of

coach in the winter full against the wind, bring me down with a brace of bullets, and I promise not to 'peach. Remember me to Reynolds, and say how much I should like to hear from him; that Brown returned immediately after he went on Sunday, and that I was vexed at forgetting to ask him to lunch; for as he went towards the gate, I saw he was fatigued and hungry.

I am, my dear Rice, ever most sincerely yours

JOHN KEATS.

I have broken this open to let you know I was surprised at seeing it on the table this morning, thinking it had gone long ago.

160. TO FANNY KEATS

[February 19, 1820.]

MY DEAR FANNY — Being confined almost entirely to vegetable food and the weather being at the same time so much against me, I cannot say I have much improved since I wrote last. The Doctor tells me there are no dangerous Symptoms about me, and quietness of mind and fine weather will restore me. Mind my advice to be very careful to wear warm cloathing in a thaw. I will write again on Tuesday when I hope to send you good news.

Your affectionate Brother JOHN ——.

161. TO FANNY BRAWNE

MY DEAREST FANNY — I read your note in bed last night, and that might be the reason of my sleeping so much better. I think Mr. Brown is right in supposing you may stop too long with me, so very nervous as I am. Send me every evening a written Good night. If you come for a few minutes about six it may be the best time. Should you ever fancy me too low-spirited I must warn you to ascribe it to the medicine I am at present taking which is of a nerve-shaking nature. I shall im-

pute any depression I may experience to this cause. I have been writing with a vile old pen the whole week, which is excessively ungallant. The fault is in the Quill: I have mended it and still it is very much inclin'd to make blind es. However these last lines are in a much better style of penmanship, tho' a little disfigured by the smear of black currant jelly; which has made a little mark on one of the pages of Brown's Ben Jonson, the very best book he has. I have lick'd it but it remains very purple. I did not know whether to say purple or blue so in the mixture of the thought wrote purple which may be an excellent name for a colour made up of those two, and would suit well to start next spring. Be very careful of open doors and windows and going without your duffle grey. God bless you Love!

J. KEATS.

P. S. I am sitting in the back room. Remember me to your Mother.

162. TO THE SAME

MY DEAR FANNY, — Do not let your mother suppose that you hurt me by writing at night. For some reason or other your last night's note was not so treasureable as former ones. I would fain that you call me Love still. To see you happy and in high spirits is a great consolation to me — still let me believe that you are not half so happy as my restoration would make you. I am nervous, I own, and may think myself worse than I really am; if so you must indulge me, and pamper with that sort of tenderness you have manifested towards me in different Letters. My sweet creature when I look back upon the pains and torments I have suffer'd for you from the day I left you to go to the Isle of Wight; the ecstasies in which I have pass'd some days and the miseries in their turn, I wonder the more at the Beauty which has kept up the spell so fervently. When I send this round I shall be in the front parlour watching to see you show yourself for a minute in the garden. How illness stands as a barrier betwixt me and you! Even if I was well —— I must make myself as good a Philosopher as possible. Now I have had opportunities of passing nights anxious and awake I have found other thoughts intrude upon me. 'If I should die,' said I to myself, 'I have left no immortal work behind me — nothing to make my friends proud of my memory — but I have lov'd the principle of beauty in all things, and if I had had time I would have made myself remember'd.' Thoughts like these came very feebly whilst I was in health and every pulse beat for you — now you divide with this (may *I* say it?) 'last infirmity of noble minds' all my reflection.

God bless you, Love.   J. KEATS.

163.   TO THE SAME

MY DEAREST GIRL, — You spoke of having been unwell in your last note : have you recover'd? That note has been a great delight to me. I am stronger than I was : the Doctors say there is very little the matter with me, but I cannot believe them till the weight and tightness of my Chest is mitigated. I will not indulge or pain myself by complaining of my long separation from you. God alone knows whether I am destined to taste of happiness with you : at all events I myself know thus much, that I consider it no mean Happiness to have lov'd you thus far — if it is to be no further I shall not be unthankful — if I am to recover, the day of my recovery shall see me by your side from which nothing shall separate me. If well you are the only medicine that can keep me so. Perhaps, aye surely, I am writing in too depress'd a state of mind — ask your Mother to come and see me — she will bring you a better account than mine.

Ever your affectionate JOHN KEATS.

164.   TO JOHN HAMILTON REYNOLDS

[February 23 or 25, 1820.]

MY DEAR REYNOLDS — I have been improving since you saw me : my nights are better which I think is a very encouraging thing. You mention your cold in rather too slighting a manner — if you travel outside have some flannel against the wind — which I hope will not keep on at this rate when you are in the Packet boat. Should it rain do not stop upon deck though the Passengers should vomit themselves inside out. Keep under Hatches from all sort of wet.

I am pretty well provided with Books at present, when you return I may give you a commission or two. Mr. B[arry] C[ornwall] has sent me not only his Sicilian Story but yesterday his Dramatic Scenes — this is very polite, and I shall do what I can to make him sensible I think so. I confess they tease me — they are composed of amiability, the Seasons, the Leaves, the Moons, etc., upon which he rings (according to Hunt's expression), triple bob majors. However that is nothing — I think he likes poetry for its own sake, not his. I hope I shall soon be well enough to proceed with my faeries and set you about the notes on Sundays and Stray-days. If I had been well enough I should have liked to cross the water with you. Brown wishes you a pleasant voyage — Have fish for dinner at the sea ports, and don't forget a bottle of Claret. You will not meet with so much to hate at Brussels as at Paris. Remember me to all my friends. If I were well enough I would paraphrase an ode of Horace's for you, on your embarking in the seventy years ago style. The Packet will bear a comparison with a Roman galley at any rate.

Ever yours affectionately
J. KEATS.

165. TO FANNY BRAWNE

MY DEAREST GIRL — Indeed I will not deceive you with respect to my Health. This is the fact as far as I know. I have been confined three weeks and am not yet well — this proves that there is something wrong about me which my constitution will either conquer or give way to. Let us hope for the best. Do you hear the Thrush singing over the field ? I think it is a sign of· mild weather — so much the better for me. Like all Sinners now I am ill I philosophize, aye out of my attachment to every thing, Trees, flowers, Thrushes, Spring, Summer, Claret, &c. &c. — aye every thing but you. — My sister would be glad of my company a little longer. That Thrush is a fine fellow. I hope he was fortunate in his choice this year. Do not send any more of my Books home. I have a great pleasure in the thought of you looking on them.

Ever yours my sweet Fanny   J. K.

166. TO FANNY KEATS

Wentworth Place, Thursday,
[February 24, 1820.]

MY DEAR FANNY — I am sorry to hear you have been so unwell : now you are better, keep so. Remember to be very careful of your clothing — this climate requires the utmost care. There has been very little alteration in me lately. I am much the same as when I wrote last. When I am well enough to return to my old diet I shall get stronger. If my recovery should be delay'd long I will ask Mr. Abbey to let you visit me — keep up your Spirits as well as you can. You shall hear soon again from me.

Your affectionate Brother JOHN ——

167. TO FANNY BRAWNE

MY DEAREST FANNY — I had a better night last night than I have had since my attack, and this morning I am the same as when you saw me. I have been turning over two volumes of Letters written between Rousseau and two Ladies in the perplexed strain of mingled finesse and sentiment in which the Ladies and gentlemen of those days were so clever, and which is still prevalent among Ladies of this Country who live in a state of reasoning romance. The likeness however only extends to the mannerism, not to the dexterity. What would Rousseau have said at seeing our little correspondence ! What would his Ladies have said ! I don't care much — I would sooner have Shakspeare's opinion about the matter. The common gossiping of washerwomen must be less disgusting than the continual and eternal fence and attack of Rousseau and these sublime Petticoats. One calls herself Clara and her friend Julia, two of Rosseau's heroines — they all the same time christen poor Jean Jacques St. Preux — who is the pure cavalier of his famous novel. Thank God I am born in England with our own great Men before my eyes. Thank God that you are fair and can love me without being Letter-written and sentimentaliz'd into it. — Mr. Barry Cornwall has sent me another Book, his first, with a polite note. I must do what I can to make him sensible of the esteem I have for his kindness. If this north east would take a turn it would .be so much the better for me. Good bye, my love, my dear love, my beauty —

love me for ever   J. K.

168. TO THE SAME

MY DEAREST GIRL — I continue much the same as usual, I think a little better. My spirits are better also, and consequently I am more resign'd to my confinement. I dare not think of you much or write much to you. Remember me to all.

Ever your affectionate
JOHN KEATS.

169. TO THE SAME

MY DEAR FANNY — I think you had better not make any long stay with me when Mr. Brown is at home. Whenever he goes out you may bring your work. You will have a pleasant walk today. I shall see you pass. I shall follow you with my eyes over the Heath. Will you come towards evening instead of before dinner? When you are gone, 't is past — if you do not come till the evening I have something to look forward to all day. Come round to my window for a moment when you have read this. Thank your Mother, for the preserves, for me. The raspberry will be too sweet not having any acid; therefore as you are so good a girl I shall make you a present of it. Good bye

My sweet Love!   J. KEATS.

170. TO THE SAME

MY DEAREST FANNY — The power of your benediction is of not so weak a nature as to pass from the ring in four and twenty hours — it is like a sacred Chalice once consecrated and ever consecrate. 'I shall kiss your name and mine where your Lips have been — Lips! why should a poor prisoner as I am talk about such things? Thank God, though I hold them the dearest pleasures in the universe, I have a consolation independent of them in the certainty of your affection. I could write a song in the style of Tom Moore's Pathetic about Memory if that would be any relief to me. No — 't would not., I will be as obstinate as a Robin, I will not sing in a cage. Health is my expected heaven and you are the Houri —— this word I believe is both singular and plural — if only plural, never mind — you are a thousand of them.

Ever yours affectionately my dearest,
     J. K.

You had better not come to day.

171. TO THE SAME

MY DEAREST LOVE — You must so long in the cold — I have been ing that window to be open. — Y half-cured me. When I want son oranges I will tell you — these à propos. I am kept from food rather weak — otherwise very well do not stop so long upstairs — it m uneasy — come every now and tl stop a half minute. Remember Your Mother.

Your ever affectionate   J. K

172. TO THE SAME

SWEETEST FANNY — You fear times, I do not love you so much wish? My dear Girl I love you e ever and without reserve. The have known the more have I lo every way — even my jealousies ha agonies of Love, in the hottest fit had I would have died for you. vex'd you too much. But for Lo I help it? You are always new. of your kisses was ever the sweet last smile the brightest; the las ment the gracefullest. When yo my window home yesterday, I w with as much admiration as if I h seen you for the first time. You u half complaint once that I only lo beauty. Have I nothing else then in you but that? Do not I see naturally furnish'd with wings imp self with me? No ill prospect has b to turn your thoughts a moment fi This perhaps should be as much a of sorrow as joy — but I will not that. Even if you did not love me not help an entire devotion to y much more deeply then must I you knowing you love me. My M been the most discontented and res

er was put into a body too small for
never felt my Mind repose upon any-
with complete and undistracted en-
at — upon no person but you. When
'e in the room my thoughts never fly
t window: you always concentrate
ole senses. The anxiety shown about
oves in your last note is an immense
re to me: however you must not
such speculations to molest you any
nor will I any more believe you can
he least pique against me. Brown is
ut — but here is Mrs. Wiley — when
gone I shall be awake for you. —
nbrances to your Mother.

r affectionate   J. KEATS.

. TO CHARLES WENTWORTH DILKE

[Hampstead, March 4, 1820.]

DEAR DILKE — Since I saw you I
een gradually, too gradually perhaps,
ring; and though under an interdict
espect to animal food, living upon
) victuals, Brown says I have pick'd
ittle flesh lately. If I can keep off
mation for the next six weeks I
[shall do very well. You certainly
have been at Martin's dinner, for
g an index is surely as dull work
graving. Have you heard that the
eller is going to tie himself to the
r eat or not as he pleases. He
Rice shall have his foot on the
· notwithstanding. Reynolds is go-
sail on the salt seas. Brown has
mightily progressing with his Ho-
A damn'd melancholy picture it
l during the first week of my illness
) me a psalm-singing nightmare, that
me almost faint away in my sleep. I
I am better, for I can bear the Pic-
I have experienced a specimen of
politeness from Mr. Barry Cornwall.
s sent me his books. Some time ago
d given his first publish'd book to

Hunt for me; Hunt forgot to give it and
Barry Cornwall thinking I had received it
must have thought me a very neglectful
fellow. Notwithstanding he sent me his
second book and on my explaining that I
had not received his first he sent me that
also. I am sorry to see by Mrs. D.'s note
that she has been so unwell with the spasms.
Does she continue the Medicines that bene-
fited her so much? I am afraid not.
Remember me to her, and say I shall not
expect her at Hampstead next week unless
the Weather changes for the warmer. It
is better to run no chance of a supernumer-
ary cold in March. As for you, you must
come. You must improve in your penmanship; your writing is like the speaking
of a child of three years old, very understandable to its father but to no one else.
The worst is it looks well — no, that is not
the worst — the worst is, it is worse than
Bailey's. Bailey's looks illegible and may
perchance be read; yours looks very legi-
ble and may perchance not be read. I
would endeavour to give you a facsimile of your word Thistlewood if I were
not minded on the instant that Lord Ches-
terfield has done some such thing to his son.
Now I would not bathe in the same River
with Lord C. though I had the upper hand
of the stream. I am grieved that in writing and speaking it is necessary to make
use of the same particles as he did. Cobbett is expected to come in. O that I had
two double plumpers for him. The minis-
try are not so inimical to him but it would
like to put him out of Coventry. Casting
my eye on the other side I see a long word
written in a most vile manner, unbecoming
a Critic. You must recollect I have served
no apprenticeship to old plays. If the only
copies of the Greek and Latin authors had
been made by you, Bailey and Haydon they
were as good as lost. It has been said that
the Character of a Man may be known by
his handwriting — if the Character of the
age may be known by the average good-

ness of said, what a slovenly age we live in. Look at Queen Elizabeth's Latin exercises and blush. Look at Milton's hand. I can't say a word for Shakspeare's.

Your sincere friend   JOHN KEATS.

174. TO FANNY BRAWNE

MY DEAR FANNY — I am much better this morning than I was a week ago : indeed I improve a little every day. I rely upon taking a walk with you upon the first of May : in the mean time undergoing a babylonish captivity I shall not be jew enough to hang up my harp upon a willow, but rather endeavour to clear up my arrears in versifying, and with returning health begin upon something new: pursuant to which resolution it will be necessary to have my or rather Taylor's manuscript, which you, if you please, will send by my Messenger either today or tomorrow. Is Mr. D. with you today? You appeared very much fatigued last night : you must look a little brighter this morning. I shall not suffer my little girl ever to be obscured like glass breath'd upon, but always bright as it is her *nature to*. Feeding upon sham victuals and sitting by the fire will completely annul me. I have no need of an enchanted wax figure to duplicate me, for I am melting in my proper person before the fire. If you meet with anything better (worse) than common in your Magazines let me see it.

Good bye my sweetest Girl.   J. K.

175. TO THE SAME

MY DEAREST FANNY — Whenever you know me to be alone, come, no matter what day. Why will you go out this weather? I shall not fatigue myself with writing too much I promise you. Brown says I am getting stouter. I rest well and from last night do not remember any thing horrid in my dream, which is a capital symptom, for

any organic derangement always occasions a Phantasmagoria. It will be a nice idle amusement to hunt after a motto for my Book which I will have if lucky enough to hit upon a fit one — not intending to write a preface. I fear I am too late with my note — you are gone out — you will be as cold as a topsail in a north latitude — I advise you to furl yourself and come in a doors.

Good bye Love.   J. K.

176. TO THE SAME

MY DEAREST FANNY — I slept well last night and am no worse this morning for it. Day by day if I am not deceived I get a more unrestrain'd use of my Chest. The nearer a racer gets to the Goal the more his anxiety becomes; so I lingering upon the borders of health feel my impatience increase. Perhaps on your account I have imagined my illness more serious than it is: how horrid was the chance of slipping into the ground instead of into your arms — the difference is amazing Love. Death must come at last; Man must die, as Shallow says; but before that is my fate I fain would try what more pleasures than you have given, so sweet a creature as you can give. Let me have another opportunity of years before me and I will not die without being remember'd. Take care of yourself dear that we may both be well in the Summer. I do not at all fatigue myself with writing, having merely to put a line or two here and there, a Task which would worry a stout state of the body and mind, but which just suits me as I can do no more.

Your affectionate   J. K.

177. TO THE SAME

MY DEAREST FANNY — Though I shall see you in so short a time I cannot forbear sending you a few lines. You say I did

ou yesterday a minute account of
h. Today I have left off the
which I took to keep the pulse
I find I can do very well without
is a very favourable sign, as it
re is no inflammation remaining.
: I may be wearied at night you
my best time; I am at my best
ht o'Clock. I received a Note
Procter today. He says he can-
ne a visit this weather as he is
 an inflammation in the Chest.
horrid climate this is? or what
ahabitants it has? You are one
My dear girl do not make a joke
not expose yourself to the cold.
e Thrush again — I can't afford
 run me up a pretty Bill for
esides he ought to know I deal
ti's. How can you bear so long
onment at Hampstead? I shall
member it with all the gusto that
izing carle should. I could build
o you for it.

Your affectionate
J. K.

178. TO FANNY KEATS

[March 20, 1820.]

ιR FANNY — According to your
rrite to-day. It must be but a
for I have been attack'd several
ι a palpitation at the heart and
ιr says I must not make the
exertion. I am much the same
: have been for a week past. They
hing but debility and will entirely
ιy recovery of my strength which
ect of my present diet. As the
ll not suffer me to write I shall
rown to let you hear news of me
:ure if I should not get stronger
iope I shall be well enough to
see your flowers in bloom.
ur most affectionate Brother
JOHN ——.

179. TO FANNY BRAWNE

MY DEAREST GIRL — As, from the last
part of my note you must see how gratified
I have been by your remaining at home,
you might perhaps conceive that I was
equally bias'd the other way by your going
to Town, I cannot be easy to-night without
telling you you would be wrong to suppose
so. Though I am pleased with the one, I
am not displeased with the other. How
do I dare to write in this manner about my
pleasures and displeasures? I will tho'
whilst I am an invalid, in spite of you.
Good night, Love! J. K.

180. TO THE SAME

MY DEAREST GIRL — In consequence of
our company I suppose I shall not see you
before tomorrow. I am much better to-
day — indeed all I have to complain of is
want of strength and a little tightness in
the Chest. I envied Sam's walk with you
today; which I will not do again as I may
get very tired of envying. I imagine you
now sitting in your new black dress which
I like so much and if I were a little less
selfish and more enthusiastic I should run
round and surprise you with a knock at
the door. I fear I am too prudent for a
dying kind of Lover. Yet, there is a great
difference between going off in warm blood
like Romeo, and making one's exit like a
frog in a frost. I had nothing particular
to say today, but not intending that there
shall be any interruption to our correspondence (which at some future time I propose
offering to Murray) I write something.
God bless you my sweet Love! Illness is
a long lane, but I see you at the end of it,
and shall mend my pace as well as possible. J. K.

181. TO THE SAME

DEAR GIRL — Yesterday you must have
thought me worse than I really was. I

assure you there was nothing but regret at being obliged to forego an embrace which has so many times been the highest gust of my Life. I would not care for health without it. Sam would not come in — I wanted merely to ask him how you were this morning. When one is not quite well we turn for relief to those we love : this is no weakness of spirit in me: you know when in health I thought of nothing but you; when I shall again be so it will be the same. Brown has been mentioning to me that some hint from Sam, last night, occasions him some uneasiness. He whispered something to you concerning Brown and old Mr. Dilke which had the complexion of being something derogatory to the former. It was connected with an anxiety about Mr. D. Sr's death and an anxiety to set out for Chichester. These sort of hints point out their own solution: one cannot pretend to a delicate ignorance on the subject: you understand the whole matter. If any one, my sweet Love, has misrepresented, to you, to your Mother or Sam, any circumstances which are at all likely, at a tenth remove, to create suspicions among people who from their own interested notions slander others, pray tell me: for I feel the least attaint on the disinterested character of Brown very deeply. Perhaps Reynolds or some other of my friends may come towards evening, therefore you may choose whether you will come to see me early today before or after dinner as you may think fit. Remember me to your Mother and tell her to drag you to me if you show the least reluctance —

.   .   .   .

182. TO FANNY KEATS

Wentworth Place, April 1 [1820].

MY DEAR FANNY — I am getting better every day and should think myself quite well were I not reminded every now and then by faintness and a tightness in the Chest. Send your Spaniel over to Hampstead, for I think I know where to find a Master or Mistress for him. You may depend upon it if you were even to turn it loose in the common road it would soon find an owner. If I keep improving as I have done I shall be able to come over to you in the course of a few weeks. I should take the advantage of your being in Town but I cannot bear the City though I have already ventured as far as the west end for the purpose of seeing Mr. Haydon's Picture, which is just finished and has made its appearance. I have not heard from George yet since he left Liverpool. Mr. Brown wrote to him as from me the other day — Mr. B. wrote two Letters to Mr. Abbey concerning me — Mr. A. took no notice and of course Mr. B. must give up such a correspondence when as the man said all the Letters are on one side. I write with greater ease than I had thought, therefore you shall soon hear from me again.

Your affectionate Brother JOHN ——,

183. TO THE SAME

[April 1820.]

MY DEAR FANNY — Mr. Brown is waiting for me to take a walk. Mrs. Dilke is on a visit next door and desires her love to you. The Dog shall be taken care of and for his name I shall go and look in the parish register where he was born — I still continue on the mending hand.

Your affectionate Brother JOHN ——,

184. TO THE SAME

Wentworth Place, April 12, [1820].

MY DEAR FANNY — Excuse these shabby scraps of paper I send you — and also from endeavouring to give you any consolation just at present, for though my health is tolerably well I am too nervous to enter into any discussion in which my heart is concerned. Wait patiently and take care of your health, being especially careful to keep yourself from low spirits which are great enemies to health. You are young and have only need of a little patience. I am not yet able to bear the fatigue of coming to Walthamstow, though I have been to Town once or twice. I have thought of taking a change of air. You shall hear from me immediately on my moving anywhere. I will ask Mrs. Dilke to pay you a visit if the weather holds fine, the first time I see her. The Dog is being attended to like a Prince.

Your affectionate Brother   JOHN.

185. TO THE SAME

[Hampstead, April 21, 1820.]

MY DEAR FANNY — I have been slowly improving since I wrote last. The Doctor assures me that there is nothing the matter with me except nervous irritability and a general weakness of the whole system, which has proceeded from my anxiety of mind of late years and the too great excitement of poetry. Mr. Brown is going to Scotland by the Smack, and I am advised for change of exercise and air to accompany him and give myself the chance of benefit from a Voyage. Mr. H. Wylie call'd on me yesterday with a letter from George to his mother : George is safe at the other side of the water, perhaps by this time arrived at his home. I wish you were coming to town that I might see you ; if you should be coming write to me, as it is quite a trouble to get by the coaches to Walthamstow. Should you not come to Town I must see you before I sail, at Walthamstow. They tell me I must study lines and tangents and squares and angles to put a little Ballast into my mind. We shall be going in a fortnight and therefore you will see me within that space. I expected sooner, but I have not been able to venture to walk across the country. Now the fine Weather

is come you will not find your time so irksome. You must be sensible how much I regret not being able to alleviate the unpleasantness of your situation, but trust my dear Fanny that better times are in wait for you.

Your affectionate Brother JOHN ——.

186. TO THE SAME

Wentworth Place, Thursday [May 4, 1820].

MY DEAR FANNY — I went for the first time into the City the day before yesterday, for before I was very disinclined to encounter the scuffle, more from nervousness than real illness ; which notwithstanding I should not have suffered to conquer me if I had not made up my mind not to go to Scotland, but to remove to Kentish Town till Mr. Brown returns. Kentish Town is a mile nearer to you than Hampstead — I have been getting gradually better, but am not so well as to trust myself to the casualties of rain and sleeping out which I am liable to in visiting you. Mr. Brown goes on Saturday, and by that time I shall have settled in my new lodging, when I will certainly venture to you. You will forgive me I hope when I confess that I endeavour to think of you as little as possible and to let George dwell upon my mind but slightly. The reason being that I am afraid to ruminate on anything which has the shade of difficulty or melancholy in it, as that sort of cogitation is so pernicious to health, and it is only by health that I can be enabled to alleviate your situation in future. For some time you must do what you can of yourself for relief; and bear your mind up with the consciousness that your situation cannot last for ever, and that for the present you may console yourself against the reproaches of Mrs. Abbey. Whatever obligations you may have had to her you have none now, as she has reproached you. I do not know what property you have, but I will enquire into it : be sure however that beyond the obligation that a lodger may have to a landlord you have none to Mrs. Abbey. Let the surety of this make you laugh at Mrs. A.'s foolish tattle. Mrs. Dilke's Brother has got your Dog. She is now very well — still liable to Illness. I will get her to come and see you if I can make up my mind on the propriety of introducing a stranger into Abbey's house. Be careful to let no fretting injure your health as I have suffered it — health is the greatest of blessings — with *health* and *hope* we should be content to live, and so you will find as you grow older.

I am, my dear Fanny, your affectionate Brother,   JOHN ——.

187. TO CHARLES WENTWORTH DILKE

[Hampstead, May 1820.]

MY DEAR DILKE — As Brown is not to be a fixture at Hampstead, I have at last made up my mind to send home all lent books. I should have seen you before this, but my mind has been at work all over the world to find out what to do. I have my choice of three things, or at least two, — South America, or Surgeon to an Indiaman ; which last, I think, will be my fate. I shall resolve in a few days. Remember me to Mrs. D. and Charles, and your father and mother.

Ever truly yours   JOHN KEATS.

188. TO FANNY BRAWNE

MY DEAREST GIRL — I endeavour to make myself as patient as possible. Hunt amuses me very kindly — besides I have your ring on my finger and your flowers on the table. I shall not expect to see you yet because it would be so much pain to part with you again. When the Books you want come you shall have them. I am very well this afternoon. My dearest. . . .

[Signature cut off.]

189. TO THE SAME

Tuesday Afternoon.

MY DEAREST FANNY — For this Week past I have been employed in marking the most beautiful passages in Spenser, intending it for you, and comforting myself in being somehow occupied to give you however small a pleasure. It has lightened my time very much. I am much better. God bless you.

Your affectionate   J. KEATS.

190. TO THE SAME

Tuesday Morn.

MY DEAREST GIRL — I wrote a letter for you yesterday expecting to have seen your mother. I shall be selfish enough to send it though I know it may give you a little pain, because I wish you to see how unhappy I am for love of you, and endeavour as much as I can to entice you to give up your whole heart to me whose whole existence hangs upon you. You could not step or move an eyelid but it would shoot to my heart — I am greedy of you. Do not think of anything but me. Do not live as if I was not existing. Do not forget me — But have I any right to say you forget me ? Perhaps you think of me all day. Have I any right to wish you to be unhappy for me ? You would forgive me for wishing it if you knew the extreme passion I have that you should love me — and for you to love me as I do you, you must think of no one but me, much less write that sentence. Yesterday and this morning I have been haunted with a sweet vision — I have seen you the whole time in your shepherdess dress. How my senses have ached at it ! How my heart has been devoted to it ! How my eyes have been full of tears at it ! I[n]deed I think a real love is enough to occupy the widest heart. Your going to town alone when I heard of it was a shock to me — yet I expected it —

promise me you will not for some time till I get better. Promise me this and fill the paper full of the most endearing names. If you cannot do so with good will, do my love tell me — say what you think — confess if your heart is too much fasten'd on the world. Perhaps then I may see you at a greater distance, I may not be able to appropriate you so closely to myself. Were you to loose a favourite bird from the cage, how would your eyes ache after it as long as it was in sight; when out of sight you would recover a little. Perhaps if you would, if so it is, confess to me how many things are necessary to you besides me, I might be happier; by being less tantaliz'd. Well may you exclaim, how selfish, how cruel not to let me enjoy my youth! to wish me to be unhappy. You must be so if you love me. Upon my soul I can be contented with nothing else. If you would really what is call'd enjoy yourself at a Party — if you can smile in people's faces, and wish them to admire you *now* — you never have nor ever will love me. I see *life* in nothing but the certainty of your Love — convince me of it my sweetest. If I am not somehow convinced I shall die of agony. If we love we must not live as other men and women do — I cannot brook the wolfsbane of fashion and foppery and tattle — you must be mine to die upon the rack if I want you. I do not pretend to say that I have more feeling than my fellows, but I wish you seriously to look over my letters kind and unkind and consider whether the person who wrote them can be able to endure much longer the agonies and uncertainties which you are so peculiarly made to create. My recovery of bodily health will be of no benefit to me if you are not mine when I am well. For God's sake save me — or tell me my passion is of too awful a nature for you. Again God bless you.

J. K.

No — my sweet Fanny — I am wrong — I do not wish you to be unhappy — and yet I do, I must while there is so sweet a Beauty — my loveliest, my darling! good bye! I kiss you — O the torments!

191. TO JOHN TAYLOR

[Wesleyan Place, Kentish Town]
June 11, [1820.]

MY DEAR TAYLOR — In reading over the proof of St. Agnes's Eve since I left Fleet Street, I was struck with what appears to me an alteration in the seventh stanza very much for the worse. The passage I mean stands thus —

> her maiden eyes incline
> Still on the floor, while many a sweeping train
> Pass by

'T was originally written —

> her maiden eyes divine
> Fix'd on the floor, saw many a sweeping train
> Pass by.

My meaning is quite destroyed in the alteration. I do not use *train* for *concourse of passers by*, but for *skirts* sweeping along the floor.

In the first stanza my copy reads, second line —

> bitter *chill* it was,

to avoid the echo *cold* in the second line.
Ever yours sincerely JOHN KEATS.

192. TO CHARLES ARMITAGE BROWN

[Wesleyan Place, Kentish Town, June, 1820.]
MY DEAR BROWN — I have only been to ——'s once since you left, when —— could not find your letters. Now this is bad of me. I should, in this instance, conquer the great aversion to breaking up my regular habits, which grows upon me more and more. True, I have an excuse in the weather, which drives one from shelter to shelter in any little excursion. I have not heard from George. My book is coming out with very low hopes, though not spirits, on my part. This shall be my last

trial ; not succeeding, I shall try what I can do in the apothecary line. When you hear from or see —— it is probable you will hear some complaints against me, which this notice is not intended to forestall. The fact is, I did behave badly ; but it is to be attributed to my health, spirits, and the disadvantageous ground I stand on in society. I could go and accommodate matters if I were not too weary of the world. I know that they are more happy and comfortable than I am ; therefore why should I trouble myself about it ? I foresee I shall know very few people in the course of a year or two. Men get such different habits that they become as oil and vinegar to one another. Thus far I have a consciousness of having been pretty dull and heavy, both in subject and phrase; I might add, enigmatical. I am in the wrong, and the world is in the right, I have no doubt. Fact is, I have had so many kindnesses done me by so many people, that I am cheveaux-de-frised with benefits, which I must jump over or break down. I met —— in town, a few days ago, who invited me to supper to meet Wordsworth, Southey, Lamb, Haydon, and some more ; I was too careful of my health to risk being out at night. Talking of that, I continue to improve slowly, but I think surely. There is a famous exhibition in Pall-Mall of the old English portraits by Vandyck and Holbein, Sir Peter Lely, and the great Sir Godfrey. Pleasant countenances predominate ; so I will mention two or three unpleasant ones. There is James the First, whose appearance would disgrace a ' Society for the Suppression of Women ; ' so very squalid and subdued to nothing he looks. Then, there is old Lord Burleigh, the high-priest of economy, the political save-all, who has the appearance of a Pharisee just rebuffed by a Gospel bon-mot. Then, there is George the Second, very like an unintellectual Voltaire, troubled with the gout and a bad temper. Then, there is young Devereux, the favourite, with every appearance of as

slang a boxer as any in the Court ; his face is cast in the mould of blackguardism with jockey-plaster. I shall soon begin upon ' Lucy Vaughan Lloyd.' [56] I do not begin composition yet, being willing, in case of a relapse, to have nothing to reproach myself with. I hope the weather will give you the slip ; let it show itself and steal out of your company. When I have sent off this, I shall write another to some place about fifty miles in advance of you.

Good morning to you. Yours ever sincerely.   JOHN KEATS.

193. TO FANNY KEATS

Friday Morn [Wesleyan Place, Kentish Town, June 26, 1820.]

MY DEAR FANNY — I had intended to delay seeing you till a Book which I am now publishing was out, expecting that to be the end of this week when I would have brought it to Walthamstow : on receiving your Letter of course I set myself to come to town, but was not able, for just as I was setting out yesterday morning a slight spitting of blood came on which returned rather more copiously at night. I have slept well and they tell me there is nothing material to fear. I will send my Book soon with a Letter which I have had from George who is with his family quite well.

Your affectionate Brother JOHN ——.

194. TO FANNY BRAWNE

Wednesday Morning.

MY DEAREST FANNY — I have been a walk this morning with a book in my hand, but as usual I have been occupied with nothing but you : I wish I could say in an agreeable manner. I am tormented day and night. They talk of my going to Italy. 'T is certain I shall never recover if I am to be so long separate from you : yet with all this devotion to you I cannot persuade myself into any confidence of you. Past

ce connected with the fact of my
aration from you gives me agonies
e scarcely to be talked of. When
ther comes I shall be very sudden
rt in asking her whether you have
Mrs. Dilke's, for she might say no
me easy. I am literally worn to
hich seems my only recourse. I
forget what has pass'd. What?
with a man of the world, but to
iful. I will get rid of this as much
ble. When you were in the habit
g with Brown you would have left
d your own heart have felt one
one pang mine did. Brown is a
t of Man — he did not know he
ng me to death by inches. I feel
t of every one of those hours in
now; and for that cause, though
ione me many services, though I
love and friendship for me, though
ioment I should be without pence
iot for his assistance, I will never
ieak to him until we are both old
we are to be. I *will* resent my
ving been made a football. You
this madness. I have heard you
it *was* not unpleasant to wait a
s — you have amusements — your
iway — you have not brooded over
as I have, and how should you?
to me an object intensely desira-
e air I breathe in a room empty of
inhealthy. I am not the same to
io — you can wait — you have a
l activities — you can be happy
me. Any party, any thing to fill
iay has been enough. How have
s'd this month? Who have you
rith? All this may seem savage
You do not feel as I do — you do
r what it is to love — one day you
'our time is not come. Ask your-
r many unhappy hours Keats has
you in Loneliness. For myself I
in a Martyr the whole time, and
reason I speak; the confession is
:om me by the torture. I appeal

to you by the blood of that Christ you believe in : Do not write to me if you have
done anything this month which it would
have pained me to have seen. You may
have altered — if you have not — if you
still behave in dancing rooms and other
societies as I have seen you — I do not
want to live — if you have done so I wish
this coming night may be my last. I cannot live without you, and not only you but
chaste you ; virtuous you. The Sun rises
and sets, the day passes, and you follow
the bent of your inclination to a certain
extent — you have no conception of the
quantity of miserable feeling that passes
through me in a day. — Be serious ! Love
is not a plaything — and again do not
write unless you can do it with a crystal
conscience. I would sooner die for want
of you than —

Yours for ever

J. KEATS.

195. TO FANNY KEATS

Mortimer Terrace, Wednesday [July 5, 1820]..

MY DEAR FANNY — I have had no return of the spitting of blood, and for two
or three days have been getting a little
stronger. I have no hopes of an entire
reëstablishment of my health under some
months of patience. My Physician tells
me I must contrive to pass the Winter in
Italy. This is all very unfortunate for us
— we have no recourse but patience, which
I am now practising better than ever I
thought it possible for me. I have this.
moment received a Letter from Mr. Brown,
dated Dunvegan Castle, Island of Skye.
He is very well in health and spirits. My
new publication has been out for some days
and I have directed a Copy to be bound
for you, which you will receive shortly.
No one can regret Mr. Hodgkinson's ill
fortune : I must own illness has not made
such a Saint of me as to prevent my rejoicing at his reverse. Keep yourself in as
good hopes as possible ; in case my illness.

should continue an unreasonable time many of my friends would I trust for my sake do all in their power to console and amuse you, at the least word from me — You may depend upon it that in case my strength returns I will do all in my power to extricate you from the Abbeys. Be above all things careful of your health which is the corner stone of all pleasure.

Your affectionate Brother JOHN ——.

196. TO BENJAMIN ROBERT HAYDON

[Mortimer Terrace, July, 1820.]

MY DEAR HAYDON — I am sorry to be obliged to try your patience a few more days when you will have the Book [Chapman's *Homer*] sent from Town. I am glad to hear you are in progress with another Picture. Go on. I am afraid I shall pop off just when my mind is able to run alone.

Your sincere friend
JOHN KEATS.

197. TO FANNY KEATS

Mortimer Terrace [July 22, 1820.]

MY DEAR FANNY — I have been gaining strength for some days : it would be well if I could at the same time say I am gaining hopes of a speedy recovery. My constitution has suffered very much for two or three years past, so as to be scarcely able to make head against illness, which the natural activity and impatience of my Mind renders more dangerous. It will at all events be a very tedious affair, and you must expect to hear very little alteration of any sort in me for some time. You ought to have received a copy of my Book ten days ago. I shall send another message to the Booksellers. One of the Mr. Wylie's will be here to-day or to-morrow when I will ask him to send you George's Letter. Writing the smallest note is so annoying to me that I have waited till I shall see him. Mr. Hunt does everything in his

power to make the time pass as agr with me as possible. I read the g part of the day, and generally tak half-hour walks a-day up and dov terrace which is very much pester'(cries, ballad singers, and street music have been so unfortunate for so long every event has been of so depress nature that I must persuade mys think some change will take place aspect of our affairs. I shall be up< look out for a trump card.

Your affectionate Brother
JOHN —

198. TO FANNY BRAWNE

MY DEAREST FANNY — My head is zled this morning, and I scarce know I shall say though I am full of a hu things. 'Tis certain I would rath writing to you this morning, notwith ing the alloy of grief in such an occup than enjoy any other pleasure, with to boot, unconnected with you. Upo soul I have loved you to the extren wish you could know the Tendernes which I continually brood over your ent aspects of countenance, action and I see you come down in the morning you meet me at the Window — I see thing over again eternally that I eve scen. If I get on the pleasant clue in a sort of happy misery, if on th pleasant 't is miserable misery. You plain of my illtreating you in word, th and deed — I am sorry, — at times bitterly sorry that I ever made yo happy — my excuse is that those have been wrung from me by the ness of my feelings. At all event in any case I have been wrong ; c believe that I did it without any ca should be the most sincere of Pen I could give way to my repentant fe now, I could recant all my suspici could mingle with you heart and though absent, were it not for some parts of your Letters. Do you suppose it possible I could ever leave you? You know what I think of myself and what of you. You know that I should feel how much it was my loss and how little yours. My friends laugh at you! I know some of them — when I know them all I shall never think of them again as friends or even acquaintance. My friends have behaved well to me in every instance but one, and there they have become tattlers, and inquisitors into my conduct : spying upon a secret I would rather die than share it with any body's confidence. For this I cannot wish them well, I care not to see any of them again. If I am the Theme, I will not be the Friend of idle Gossips. Good gods what a shame it is our Loves should be so put into the microscope of a Coterie. Their laughs should not affect you (I may perhaps give you reasons some day for these laughs, for I suspect a few people to hate me well enough, *for reasons I know of*, who have pretended a great friendship for me) when in competition with one, who if he never should see you again would make you the Saint of his memory. These Laughers, who do not like you, who envy you for your Beauty, who would have God-bless'd me from you for ever: who were plying me with disencouragements with respect to you eternally. People are revengeful — do not mind them — do nothing but love me — if I knew that for certain life and health will in such event be a heaven, and death itself will be less painful. I long to believe in immortality. I shall never be able to bid you an entire farewell. If I am destined to be happy with you here — how short is the longest Life. I wish to believe in immortality — I wish to live with you for ever. Do not let my name ever pass between you and those laughers ; if I have no other merit than the great Love for you, that were sufficient to keep me sacred and unmentioned in such society.

If I have been cruel and unjust I swear my love has ever been greater than my cruelty which last [*sic*] but a minute whereas my Love come what will shall last for ever. If concession to me has hurt your Pride God knows I have had little pride in my heart when thinking of you. Your name never passes my Lips — do not let mine pass yours. Those People do not like me. After reading my Letter you even then wish to see me. I am strong enough to walk over — but I dare not. I shall feel so much pain in parting with you again. My dearest love, I am afraid to see you ; I am strong, but not strong enough to see you. Will my arm be ever round you again, and if so shall I be obliged to leave you again? My sweet Love! I am happy whilst I believe your first Letter. Let me be but certain that you are mine heart and soul, and I could die more happily than I could otherwise live. If you think me cruel — if you think I have sleighted you — do muse it over again and see into my heart. My love to you is 'true as truth's simplicity and simpler than the infancy of truth' as I think I once said before. How could I sleight you? How threaten to leave you? not in the spirit of a Threat to you — no — but in the spirit of Wretchedness in myself. My fairest, my delicious, my angel Fanny! do not believe me such a vulgar fellow. I will be as patient in illness and as believing in Love as I am able.

Yours for ever my dearest
JOHN KEATS.

199. TO THE SAME

*I do not write this till the last,
that no eye may catch it.*

MY DEAREST GIRL — I wish you could invent some means to make me at all happy without you. Every hour I am more and more concentrated in you ; every thing else tastes like chaff in my Mouth. I feel it almost impossible to go to Italy — the fact is I cannot leave you, and shall never taste one minute's content until it pleases chance to let me live with you for good. But I will not go on at this rate. A person in health as you are can have no conception of the horrors that nerves and a temper like mine go through. What Island do your friends propose retiring to ? I should be happy to go with you there alone, but in company I should object to it ; the back-bitings and jealousies of new colonists who have nothing else to amuse themselves, is unbearable. Mr. Dilke came to see me yesterday, and gave me a very great deal more pain than pleasure. I shall never be able any more to endure the society of any of those who used to meet at Elm Cottage and Wentworth Place. The last two years taste like brass upon my Palate. If I cannot live with you I will live alone. I do not think my health will improve much while I am separated from you. For all this I am averse to seeing you — I cannot bear flashes of light and return into my gloom again. I am not so unhappy now as I should be if I had seen you yesterday. To be happy with you seems such an impossibility ! it requires a luckier Star than mine ! it will never be. I enclose a passage from one of your letters which I want you to alter a little — I want (if you will have it so) the matter express'd less coldly to me. If my health would bear it, I could write a Poem which I have in my head, which would be a consolation for people in such a situation as mine. I would show some one in Love as I am, with a person living in such Liberty as you do. Shakespeare always sums up matters in the most sovereign manner. Hamlet's heart was full of such Misery as mine is when he said to Ophelia 'Go to a Nunnery, go, go !' Indeed I should like to give up the matter at once — I should like to die. I am sickened at the brute world which you are smiling with. I hate men, and women more. I see

nothing but thorns for the future — wherever I may be next winter, in Italy or nowhere, Brown will be living near you with his indecencies. I see no prospect of any rest. Suppose me in Rome — well, I should there see you as in a magic glass going to and from town at all hours, —————— I wish you could infuse a little confidence of human nature into my heart. I cannot muster any — the world is too brutal for me — I am glad there is such a thing as the grave — I am sure I shall never have any rest till I get there. At any rate I will indulge myself by never seeing any more Dilke or Brown or any of their Friends. I wish I was either in your arms full of faith or that a Thunder bolt would strike me.

         God bless you.   **J. K.**

209. TO FANNY KEATS

         Wentworth Place [August 14, 1820].

MY DEAR FANNY — 'T is a long time since I received your last. An accident of an unpleasant nature occurred at Mr. Hunt's and prevented me from answering you, that is to say made me nervous. That you may not suppose it worse I will mention that some one of Mr. Hunt's household opened a Letter of mine — upon which I immediately left Mortimer Terrace, with the intention of taking to Mrs. Bentley's again ; fortunately I am not in so lone a situation, but am staying a short time with Mrs. Brawne who lives in the house which was Mrs. Dilke's. I am excessively nervous : a person I am not quite used to entering the room half chokes me. 'T is not yet Consumption I believe, but it would be were I to remain in this climate all the Winter : so I am thinking of either voyaging or travelling to Italy. Yesterday I received an invitation from Mr. Shelley, a Gentleman residing at Pisa, to spend the Winter with him : if I go I must be away in a month or even less. I am glad you

ike the Poems, you must hope with me
hat time and health will produce you some
more. This is the first morning I have
een able to sit to the paper and have many
etters to write if I can manage them.
God bless you my dear Sister.

Your affectionate Brother JOHN ——.

201. TO PERCY BYSSHE SHELLEY

Wentworth Place, Hampstead, August, 1820.]

MY DEAR SHELLEY — I am very much
ratified that you, in a foreign country,
ad with a mind almost over-occupied,
hould write to me in the strain of the let-
er beside me. If I do not take advan-
tge of your invitation, it will be prevented
y a circumstance I have very much at
eart to prophesy. There is no doubt that
a English winter would put an end to
e, and do so in a lingering hateful man-
er. Therefore, I must either voyage or
urney to Italy, as a soldier marches
p to a battery. My nerves at present
re the worst part of me, yet they feel
othed that, come what extreme may,
shall not be destined to remain in one
ot long enough to take a hatred of
ty four particular bedposts. I am glad
u take any pleasure in my poor poem,
hich I would willingly take the trou-
e to unwrite, if possible, did I care so
ach as I have done about reputation. I
eeived a copy of the Cenci, as from your-
lf, from Hunt. There is only one part
f it I am judge of — the poetry and
ramatic effect, which by many spirits
wadays is considered the Mammon. A
odern work, it is said, must have a purse, which may be the God. An artist
ust serve Mammon; he must have "self-
ncentration"—selfishness, perhaps. You,
am sure, will forgive me for sincerely
marking that you might curb your mag-
aimity, and be more of an artist, and
d every rift of your subject with ore.

The thought of such discipline must fall
like cold chains upon you, who perhaps
never sat with your wings furled for six
months together. And is this not extraordinary talk for the writer of Endymion,
whose mind was like a pack of scattered
cards? I am picked up and sorted to a pip.
My imagination is a monastery, and I am
its monk. I am in expectation of Prome-
theus every day. Could I have my own
wish effected, you would have it still in
manuscript, or be but now putting an end
to the second act. I remember you advising me not to publish my first blights, on
Hampstead Heath. I am returning advice
upon your hands. Most of the poems in
the volume I send you have been written
above two years, and would never have
been published but for hope of gain; so
you see I am inclined enough to take your
advice now. I must express once more
my deep sense of your kindness, adding
my sincere thanks and respects for Mrs.
Shelley.

In the hope of soon seeing you, I remain
most sincerely yours   JOHN KEATS.

202. TO JOHN TAYLOR

Wentworth Place [August 14, 1820].

MY DEAR TAYLOR — My chest is in such
a nervous state, that anything extra, such
as speaking to an unaccustomed person, or
writing a note, half suffocates me. This
journey to Italy wakes me at daylight
every morning, and haunts me horribly. I
shall endeavour to go, though it be with the
sensation of marching up against a battery.
The first step towards it is to know the expense of a journey and a year's residence,
which if you will ascertain for me, and let
me know early, you will greatly serve me.
I have more to say, but must desist, for
every line I write increases the tightness of
my chest, and I have many more to do. I
am convinced that this sort of thing does

not continue for nothing. If you can come, with any of our friends, do.

Your sincere friend   JOHN KEATS.

203. TO BENJAMIN ROBERT HAYDON

Mrs. Brawne's Next door to Brown's, Wentworth Place, Hampstead, [August] 1820.

MY DEAR HAYDON — I am much better this morning than I was when I wrote the note: that is my hopes and spirits are better which are generally at a very low ebb from such a protracted illness. I shall be here for a little time and at home all and every day. A journey to Italy is recommended me, which I have resolved upon and am beginning to prepare for. Hoping to see you shortly

I remain your affectionate friend

JOHN KEATS.

204. TO JOHN TAYLOR

Wentworth Place [August 15, 1820].

MY DEAR TAYLOR — I do not think I mentioned anything of a Passage to Leghorn by Sea. Will you join that to your enquiries, and, if you can, give a peep at the Berth if the Vessel is [in] our river.

Your sincere friend   JOHN KEATS.

P. S. — Somehow a copy of Chapman's Homer, lent to me by Haydon, has disappeared from my Lodgings — it has quite flown I am afraid, and Haydon urges the return of it so that I must get one at Longman's and send it to Lisson Grove — or you must — or as I have given you a job on the River — ask Mistessey [Mr. Hessey]. I had written a Note to this effect to Hessey some time since but crumpled it up in hopes that the Book might come to light. This morning Haydon has sent another messenger. The copy was in good condition with the head. Damn all thieves! Tell Woodhouse I have not lost his Blackwood.

Testamentary paper enclosed in the foregoing.

My chest of Books divide among my friends.

In case of my death this scrap of paper may be serviceable in your possession.

All my Estate real and personal consists in the hopes of the sale of books publish'd or unpublish'd. Now I wish *Brown* and you to be the first paid Creditors — the rest is in nubibus — but in case it should shower pay my Taylor the few pounds I owe him.

205. TO CHARLES ARMITAGE BROWN

[Wentworth Place, August 1820.]

MY DEAR BROWN — You may not have heard from ——, or ——, or in any way, that an attack of spitting of blood, and all its weakening consequences, has prevented me from writing for so long a time. I have matter now for a very long letter, but not news : so I must cut everything short. I shall make some confession, which you will be the only person, for many reasons, I shall trust with. A winter in England would, I have not a doubt, kill me; so I have resolved to go to Italy, either by sea or land. Not that I have any great hopes of that, for, I think, there is a core of disease in me not easy to pull out. I shall be obliged to set off in less than a month. Do not, my dear Brown, tease yourself about me. You must fill up your time as well as you can, and as happily. You must think of my faults as lightly as you can. When I have health I will bring up the long arrear of letters I owe you. My book has had good success among the literary people, and I believe has a moderate sale. I have seen very few people we know. —— has visited me more than any one. I would go to —— and make some inquiries after you, if I could with any bearable sensation ; but a person I am not quite used to causes an oppression on my chest. Last week I received a letter from Shelley, at Pisa, of a very kind nature, asking me to pass the winter with him. Hunt has behaved very kindly to me. You shall hear from me again shortly.

Your affectionate friend JOHN KEATS.

206. TO FANNY KEATS

Wentworth Place, Wednesday morning
[August 23, 1820].

MY DEAR FANNY — It will give me great Pleasure to see you here, if you can contrive it; though I confess I should have written instead of calling upon you before I set out on my journey, from the wish of avoiding unpleasant partings. Meantime I will just notice some parts of your Letter. The seal-breaking business is over blown. I think no more of it. A few days ago I wrote to Mr. Brown, asking him to befriend me with his company to Rome. His answer is not yet come, and I do not know when it will, not being certain how far he may be from the Post Office to which my communication is addressed. Let us hope he will go with me. George certainly ought to have written to you: his troubles, anxieties and fatigues are not quite a sufficient excuse. In the course of time you will be sure to find that this neglect is not forgetfulness. I am sorry to hear you have been so ill and in such low spirits. Now you are better, keep so. Do not suffer your Mind to dwell on unpleasant reflections — that sort of thing has been the destruction of my health. Nothing is so bad as want of health — it makes one envy scavengers and cinder-sifters. There are enough real distresses and evils in wait for every one to try the most vigorous health. Not that I would say yours are not real — but they are such as to tempt you to employ your imagination on them, rather than endeavour to dismiss them entirely. Do not diet your mind with grief, it destroys the constitution; but let your chief care be of your health, and with that you will meet your share of Pleasure in the world — do

not doubt it. If I return well from Italy I will turn over a new leaf for you. I have been improving lately, and have very good hopes of 'turning a Neuk' and cheating the consumption. I am not well enough to write to George myself — Mr. Haslam will do it for me, to whom I shall write to-day, desiring him to mention as gently as possible your complaint. I am, my dear Fanny,

Your affectionate Brother JOHN.

207. TO CHARLES ARMITAGE BROWN

[Wentworth Place, August 1820.]

MY DEAR BROWN — I ought to be off at the end of this week, as the cold winds begin to blow towards evening; — but I will wait till I have your answer to this. I am to be introduced, before I set out, to a Dr. Clark, a physician settled at Rome, who promises to befriend me in every way there. The sale of my book is very slow, though it has been very highly rated. One of the causes, I understand from different quarters, of the unpopularity of this new book, is the offence the ladies take at me. On thinking that matter over, I am certain that I have said nothing in a spirit to displease any woman I would care to please; but still there is a tendency to class women in my books with roses and sweetmeats, — they never see themselves dominant. I will say no more, but, waiting in anxiety for your answer, doff my hat, and make a purse as long as I can.

Your affectionate friend
JOHN KEATS.

208. TO ——

[September, 1820.]

The passport arrived before we started. I don't think I shall be long ill. God bless you — farewell.

JOHN KEATS.

209.　TO CHARLES ARMITAGE BROWN

Saturday, September 28 [1820], *Maria Crowther*,
Off Yarmouth, Isle of Wight.

MY DEAR BROWN — The time has not yet come for a pleasant letter from me. I have delayed writing to you from time to time, because I felt how impossible it was to enliven you with one heartening hope of my recovery ; this morning in bed the matter struck me in a different manner ; I thought I would write ' while I was in some liking,' or I might become too ill to write at all ; and then if the desire to have written should become strong it would be a great affliction to me. I have many more letters to write, and I bless my stars that I have begun, for time seems to press, — this may be my best opportunity. We are in a calm, and I am easy enough this morning. If my spirits seem too low you may in some degree impute it to our having been at sea a fortnight without making any way.[57] I was very disappointed at not meeting you at Bedhampton, and am very provoked at the thought of you being at Chichester to-day. I should have delighted in setting off for London for the sensation merely, — for what should I do there ? I could not leave my lungs or stomach or other worse things behind me. I wish to write on subjects that will not agitate me much — there is one I must mention and have done with it. Even if my body would recover of itself, this would prevent it. The very thing which I want to live most for will be a great occasion of my death. I cannot help it. Who can help it ? Were I in health it would make me ill, and how can I bear it in my state ! I daresay you will be able to guess on what subject I am harping — you know what was my greatest pain during the first part of my illness at your house. I wish for death every day and night to deliver me from these pains, and then I wish death away, for death would destroy even those pains which are better than nothing.

Land and sea, weakness and decline, are great separators, but death is the great divorcer for ever. When the pang of this thought has passed through my mind, I may say the bitterness of death is passed. I often wish for you that you might flatter me with the best. I think without my mentioning it for my sake you would be a friend to Miss Brawne when I am dead. You think she has many faults — but for my sake think she has not one. If there is anything you can do for her by word or deed I know you will do it. I am in a state at present in which woman merely as woman can have no more power over me than stocks and stones, and yet the difference of my sensations with respect to Miss Brawne and my sister is amazing. The one seems to absorb the other to a degree incredible. I seldom think of my brother and sister in America. The thought of leaving Miss Brawne is beyond everything horrible — the sense of darkness coming over me — I eternally see her figure eternally vanishing. Some of the phrases she was in the habit of using during my last nursing at Wentworth Place ring in my ears. Is there another life ? Shall I awake and find all this a dream ? There must be, we cannot be created for this sort of suffering. The receiving this letter is to be one of yours. I will say nothing about our friendship, or rather yours to me, more than that, as you deserve to escape, you will never be so unhappy as I am. I should think of — you in my last moments. I shall endeavour to write to Miss Brawne if possible to-day. A sudden stop to my life in the middle of one of these letters would be no bad thing, for it keeps one in a sort of fever awhile. Though fatigued with a letter longer than any I have written for a long while, it would be better to go on for ever than awake to a sense of contrary winds. We expect to put into Portland Roads to-night. The captain, the crew, and the passengers, are all ill-tempered and weary. I shall write to Dilke. I feel as if I was closing my last letter to you.

My dear Brown, your affectionate friend
JOHN KEATS.

210. TO MRS. BRAWNE

October 24 [1820], Naples Harbour.

MY DEAR MRS. BRAWNE — A few words will tell you what sort of a Passage we had, and what situation we are in, and few they must be on account of the Quarantine, our Letters being liable to be opened for the purpose of fumigation at the Health Office. We have to remain in the vessel ten days and are at present shut in a tier of ships. The sea air has been beneficial to me about to as great an extent as squally weather and bad accommodations and provisions has done harm. So I am about as I was. Give my Love to Fanny and tell her, if I were well there is enough in this Port of Naples to fill a quire of Paper — but it looks like a dream — every man who can row his boat and walk and talk seems a different being from myself. I do not feel in the world. It has been unfortunate for me that one of the Passengers is a young Lady in a Consumption — her imprudence has vexed me very much — the knowledge of her complaints — the flushings in her face, all her bad symptoms have preyed upon me — they would have done so had I been in good health. Severn now is a very good fellow but his nerves are too strong to be hurt by other people's illnesses — I remember poor Rice wore me in the same way in the Isle of Wight — I shall feel a load off me when the Lady vanishes out of my sight. It is impossible to describe exactly in what state of health I am — at this moment I am suffering from indigestion very much, which makes such stuff of this Letter. I would always wish you to think me a little worse than I really am ; not being of a sanguine disposition I am likely to succeed. If I do not recover your regret will be softened — if I do your pleasure will be doubled. I

dare not fix my Mind upon Fanny, I have not dared to think of her. The only comfort I have had that way has been in thinking for hours together of having the knife she gave me put in a silver-case — the hair in a Locket — and the Pocket Book in a gold net. Show her this. I dare say no more. Yet you must not believe I am so ill as this Letter may look, for if ever there was a person born without the faculty of hoping I am he. Severn is writing to Haslam, and I have just asked him to request Haslam to send you his account of my health. O what an account I could give you of the Bay of Naples if I could once more feel myself a Citizen of this world — I feel a spirit in my Brain would lay it forth pleasantly — O what a misery it is to have an intellect in splints ! My Love again to Fanny — tell Tootts I wish I could pitch her a basket of grapes — and tell Sam the fellows catch here with a line a little fish much like an anchovy, pull them up fast. Remember me to Mr. and Mrs. Dilke — mention to Brown that I wrote him a letter at Portsmouth which I did not send and am in doubt if he ever will see it.

My dear Mrs. Brawne, yours sincerely and affectionate   JOHN KEATS.
Good bye Fanny ! God bless you.

211. TO CHARLES ARMITAGE BROWN

Naples, November 1 [1820].

MY DEAR BROWN — Yesterday we were let out of quarantine, during which my health suffered more from bad air and the stifled cabin than it had done the whole voyage. The fresh air revived me a little, and I hope I am well enough this morning to write to you a short calm letter ; — if that can be called one, in which I am afraid to speak of what I would fainest dwell upon. As I have gone thus far into it, I must go on a little ; — perhaps it may relieve the load of WRETCHEDNESS which presses upon me. The persuasion that I shall see her no more will kill me. My dear Brown, I should have had her when I was in health, and I should have remained well. I can bear to die — I cannot bear to leave her. Oh, God! God! God! Every thing I have in my trunks that reminds me of her goes through me like a spear. The silk lining she put in my travelling cap scalds my head. My imagination is horribly vivid about her — I see her — I hear her. There is nothing in the world of sufficient interest to divert me from her a moment. This was the case when I was in England; I cannot recollect, without shuddering. the time that I was a prisoner at Hunt's, and used to keep my eyes fixed on Hampstead all day. Then there was a good hope of seeing her again — Now! — O that I could be buried near where she lives! I am afraid to write to her — to receive a letter from her — to see her hand-writing would break my heart — even to hear of her anyhow, to see her name written, would be more than I can bear. My dear Brown, what am I to do? Where can I look for consolation or ease? If I had any chance of recovery, this passion would kill me. Indeed, through the whole of my illness, both at your house and at Kentish Town, this fever has never ceased wearing me out. When you write to me, which you will do immediately, write to Rome (poste restante) — if she is well and happy, put a mark thus +; if ——

Remember me to all. I will endeavour to bear my miseries patiently. A person in my state of health should not have such miseries to bear. Write a short note to my sister, saying you have heard from me. Severn is very well. If I were in better health I would urge your coming to Rome. I fear there is no one can give me any comfort. Is there any news of George? O that something fortunate had ever happened to me or my brothers! — then I might hope, — but despair is forced upon me as a habit. My dear Brown, for my sake be her advocate for ever. I cannot say a word about Naples; I do not feel at all concerned in the thousand novelties around me. I am afraid to write to her — I should like her to know that I do not forget her. Oh, Brown I have coals of fire in my breast — It surprises me that the human heart is capable of containing and bearing so much misery. Was I born for this end? God bless her, and her mother, and my sister, and George, and his wife, and you, and all!

Your ever affectionate friend

JOHN KEATS.

[Thursday, November 2.]

I was a day too early for the Courier. He sets out now. I have been more calm to-day, though in a half dread of not continuing so. I said nothing of my health; I know nothing of it; you will hear Severn's account from Haslam. I must leave off. You bring my thoughts too near to Fanny. God bless you!

212. TO THE SAME

Rome, November 30, 1820.

MY DEAR BROWN — 'T is the most difficult thing in the world to me to write a letter. My stomach continues so bad, that I feel it worse on opening any book, — yet I am much better than I was in quarantine. Then I am afraid to encounter the pro-ing and con-ing of anything interesting to me in England. I have an habitual feeling of my real life having passed, and that I am leading a posthumous existence. God knows how it would have been — but it appears to me — however, I will not speak of that subject. I must have been at Bedhampton nearly at the time you were writing to me from Chichester — how unfortunate — and to pass on the river too! There was my star predominant! I cannot answer anything in your letter, which followed me from Naples to Rome, because I am afraid to look it over again. I am so weak (in mind) that I cannot bear the sight of any handwriting of a friend I love so much as I do you. Yet I ride the little horse, and at my worst even in quarantine, summoned up more puns, in a sort of desperation, in one week than in any year of my life. There is one thought enough to kill me ; I have been well, healthy, alert, etc., walking with her, and now — the knowledge of contrast, feeling for light and shade, all that information (primitive sense) necessary for a poem, are great enemies to the recovery of the stomach. There, you rogue, I put you to the torture ; but you must bring your philosophy to bear, as I do mine, really, or how should I be able to live ? Dr. Clark is very attentive to me ; he says there is very little the matter with my lungs, but my stomach, he says, is very bad. I am well disappointed in hearing good news from George, for it runs in my head we shall all die young. I have not written to Reynolds yet, which he must think very neglectful ; being anxious to send him a good account of my health, I have delayed it from week to week. If I recover, I will do all in my power to correct the mistakes made during sickness ; and if I should not, all my faults will be forgiven. Severn is very well, though he leads so dull a life with me. Remember me to all friends, and tell Haslam I should not have left London without taking leave of him, but from being so low in body and mind. Write to George as soon as you receive this, and tell him how I am, as far as you can guess ; and also a note to my sister — who walks about my imagination like a ghost — she is so like Tom. I can scarcely bid you good-bye, even in a letter. I always made an awkward bow.

God bless you !

JOHN KEATS.

NOTES AND ILLUSTRATIONS

I. POEMS

Page 1. IMITATION OF SPENSER.
A transcript of this poem in a copy-book of Tom Keats contains two variations from the text of 1817. Line 12 reads,

> 'Whose silken fins, and golden scales light'

and in line 29 *glassy* for *glossy*. The first reading is required by the rhythm; but the absence of the mark of the possessive case leads one to think that the accent mark may have been a hasty reading of the proper mark as printed.

Page 9. ON FIRST LOOKING INTO CHAPMAN'S HOMER.
That it was Balboa and not Cortez who first saw the Pacific Ocean, an American school-boy could have told Keats; but it is not such slips as these that unmake poetry.

Page 9. EPISTLE TO GEORGE FELTON MATHEW.
Line 75. The quotation is from *The Faerie Queene*, I. iii. 4.

Page 11. To ——
The original valentine of which these lines are an enlargement was as follows: —

> 'Hadst thou lived in days of old,
> Oh, what wonders had been told
> Of thy lively dimpled face,
> And thy footsteps full of grace:
> Of thy hair's luxurious darkling,
> Of thine eye's expressive sparkling,
> And thy voice's swelling rapture,
> Taking hearts a ready capture.
> Oh! if thou hadst breathed then,
> Thou hadst made the Muses ten.
> Couldst thou wish for lineage higher
> Than twin sister of Thalia?
> At least for ever, ever more
> Will I call the Graces four.'

Then follow lines 41-68, and the valentine closes, —

> 'Ah me! whither shall I flee?
> Thou hast metamorphosed me.
> Do not let me sigh and pine,
> Prythee be my valentine.'

Page 13. SONNET: TO ONE WHO HAS BEEN LONG IN CITY PENT.
Mr. Forman points out Keats's echo in the first line of Milton's line,

> 'As one who long in populous city pent'
> *Paradise Lost*, ix. 445.

Page 14. 'I STOOD TIP-TOE UPON A LITTLE HILL.'
Line 115. Lord Houghton gives this varied reading for this and the next line: —

> 'Floating through space with ever-living eye,
> The crowned queen of ocean and the sky.'

Page 18. SLEEP AND POETRY.
Line 274. Rhythm seems to require the emendation proposed by Mr. Forman: —

> 'Ere the dread thunderbolt could reach me? How'

Page 27. SPECIMEN OF AN INDUCTION TO A POEM.
Line 61. *Libertas* is the name which his friends gave to Leigh Hunt. See later the EPISTLE TO CHARLES COWDEN CLARKE, line 44. Mrs. Clarke confirms the application.

Page 28. CALIDORE.
Line 40. In a transcript in Tom Keats's copy-book, this and the next line read: —

> 'Its long lost grandeur. Laburnums grow around
> And bow their golden honours to the ground.'

Page 33. ADDRESSED TO BENJAMIN ROBERT HAYDON.
The references in the first sonnet are to Wordsworth and Hunt.

Page 35. ON THE GRASSHOPPER AND CRICKET.
Leigh Hunt's competing sonnet is as follows:

> 'Green little vaulter in the sunny grass
> Catching your heart up at the feel of June,
> Sole voice that's heard amidst the lazy noon,
> When ev'n the bees lag at the summoning brass;
> And you, warm little housekeeper, who class
> With those who think the candles come too soon,
> Loving the fire, and with your tricksome tune
> Nick the glad silent moments as they pass;
> Oh sweet and tiny cousins, that belong,
> One to the fields, the other to the hearth,
> Both have your sunshine; both though small are strong
> At your clear hearts; and both were sent on earth
> To sing in thoughtful ears this natural song, —
> In doors and out, summer and winter, Mirth.'

Page 40. LINES ON THE MERMAID TAVERN.
Sir Charles Dilke has a manuscript copy of which the four closing lines are: —

'Souls of Poets dead and gone,
Are the winds a sweeter home,
Richer is uncellar'd cavern
Than the merry Mermaid Tavern?'

Page 41. ROBIN HOOD.
Line 36. *Grenè shaw* = green wood. Shaw
frequently appears in the termination of English
local names.

Page 49. ENDYMION.
The variations here noted in Book I. are from
the manuscript copy supplied to the printer, and
are furnished by Mr. Forman in his edition of
Keats. They were discarded by the poet either
before he gave his copy in, or in his proofs.

Line 13.
From our dark Spirits, and before us dances
Like glitter on the points of Arthur's Lances.
Of these bright powers are the Sun, and Moon.

Line 24. Telling us we are on the heaven's
brink.

Line 94. And so the coming light in pomp
receive.

Line 153.
From his right hand there swung a milk white
vase
Of mingled wines, outsparkling like the stars.

Apparently Keats gave the broad sound to *a*
in *vase*, but rejected the false rhyme. See the
lines To ———, p. 12, where *vase* rhymes with
pace.

Line 208. *Needments*. See the *Faery Queene*,
Book I. canto vi., stanza 35, lines 55, 56,

'and eke behind,
His scrip did hang, in which his needments he did
bind.'

Line 232. It is interesting to note that the
Hymn to Pan beginning here was recited by
Keats to Wordsworth when he met the elder
poet at Haydon's house, December 28, 1817.

Lines 407–412.
Now happily, there sitting on the grass
Was fair Peona, a most tender Lass,
And his sweet sister; who, uprising, went
With stifled sobs, and o'er his shoulder leant.
Putting her trembling hand against his cheek
She said: 'My dear Endymion, let us seek
A pleasant bower where thou may'st rest
apart,
And ease in slumber thine afflicted heart:
Come, my own dearest brother: these our
friends
Will joy in thinking thou dost sleep where
bends

Our freshening River through yon birchen
grove;
Do come now!' Could he gainsay her who
strove,
So soothingly, to breathe away a Curse?

Lines 440–442.
When last the Harvesters rich armfuls took.
She tied a little bucket to a Crook,
Ran some swift paces to a dark well's side,
And in a sighing-time return'd, supplied
With spar-cold water; in which she did squeeze
A snowy napkin, and upon her knees
Began to cherish her poor Brother's face;
Damping refreshfully his forehead's space,
His eyes, his Lips: then in a cupped shell
She brought him ruby wine; then let him
smell,
Time after time, a precious amulet,
Which seldom took she from its cabinet.
Thus was he quieted to slumbrous rest:

Line 466.
A cheerfuller resignment, and a smile
For his fair Sister flowing like the Nile
Through all the channels of her piety,
He said: 'Dear Maid, may I this moment die,
If I feel not this thine endearing Love.

Lines 470–472.
From woodbine hedges such a morning feel
As do those brighter drops, that twinkling steal
Through those pressed lashes, from the blos-
som'd plant

Lines 494, 495.
More forest-wild, more subtle-cadenced
Than can be told by mortal; even wed
The fainting tenors of a thousand shells
To a million whisperings of lily bells;
And mingle too the nightingale's complain
Caught in its hundredth echo; 't would be
vain:

Lines 539, 540.
And come to such a Ghost as I am now!
But listen, Sister, I will tell thee how.

Lines 545, 556.
And in this spot the most endowing boon
Of balmy air, sweet blooms, and coverts fresh
Has been outshed; yes, all that could enmesh
Our human senses — make us fealty swear
To gadding Flora. In this grateful lair
Have I been used to pass my weary eves.

Line 555. *Ditamy*. So Keats unmistakably in
manuscript and print. The prevailing form is
dittany.

Line 573. Mr. Forman says that in the manuscript something was written over this line in pencil, but then rubbed out. He suggests that after all Keats decided to leave the reader to accent the first syllable of *enchantment*, and so correct the otherwise faulty rhythm.

Lines 600, 601.
And to commune with them once more I rais'd
My eyes right upward: but they were quite
    dazed.

An example of the freedom of accent which Keats uses in common with other poets who have a mastery of line.

Line 632. Handfuls of bud-stars.

Line 646.
But lapp'd and lull'd in safe deliriousness;
Sleepy with deep foretasting, that did bless
My Soul from Madness, 't was such certainty.

Line 651.
There hollow sounds arous'd me, and I died.

Line 665.
Our feet were soft in flowers. Hurry o'er
O sacrilegious tongue the — best be dumb;
For should one little accent from thee come
On such a daring theme, all other sounds
Would sicken at it, as would beaten hounds
Scare the elysian Nightingales.

Line 722.
This all? Yet it is wonderful — exceeding —
And yet a shallow dream, for ever breeding
Tempestuous Weather in that very Soul
That should be twice content, twice smooth,
    twice whole,
As is a double Peach. 'T is sad Alas!

Lines 896, 897.
In the green opening smiling. Gods that keep,
Mercifully, a little strength of heart
Unkill'd in us by raving, pang and smart;
And do preserve it like a lily root,
That, in another spring, it may outshoot
From its wintry prison; let this hour go
Drawling along its heavy weight of woe
And leave me living! 'T is not more than
    need —
Your veriest help. Ah! how long did I feed
On that crystalline life of Portraiture!
How hover'd breathless at the tender lure!
How many times dimpled the watery glass
With maddest kisses; and, till they did pass
And leave the liquid smooth again, how mad!
O 't was as if the absolute sisters had
My Life into the compass of a Nut
Or all my breathing   and shut
To a scanty straw. To look above I fear'd

Lest my hot eyeballs might be burnt and
    sear'd
By a blank naught. It moved as if to flee —
Line 964.
Most fondly lipp'd. I kept me still — it came
Again in passionatest syllables,
And thus again that voice's tender swells:

Not quite content with *passionatest*, Keats tried again:

'Again in passionate syllables: saying'

Book II. The variations in this and the succeeding books are recorded by Mr. Forman and are derived from two sources, — the first draft made by Keats, and the manuscript afterward sent by him to the printer. Those here noted are from the first draft, unless otherwise noted.

Line 13. *Close*, i. e., embrace.
Lines 27–30.   Juliet leans
Amid her window flowers, sighs, — and as she
    weans
Her maiden thoughts from their young firstling
    snow,
What sorrows from the melting whiteness grow.

Line 31. The *Hero* is that of Shakespeare's *Much Ado about Nothing*, the *Imogen* the heroine in his *Cymbeline*.
Line 32. *Pastorella*. See *Faerie Queene*, VI. ii.
Line 38. *Rest* in the sense of remaining inactive, not the rest of restoration.

Line 49.
Through wilderness, and brittle mossed oaks.

Line 56.
Bends lightly over him, and he doth see.

Line 83.
Went swift beneath the flutter-loving guide.

Lines 93, 94.
Endymion all around the welkin sped
His anxious sight.

Lines 96, 97.
His sullen limbs upon the grass — what tongue,
What airy whisperer spoilt his angry rest?

Line 102.
And carelessly began to twine and twist.

Lines 143, 144.
His soul to take a city of delight
O what a wretch is he: 't is in his sight.

Line 227.
Whose track the venturous Latmian follows
    bold.

Lines 253, 254.
The mighty ones who 've shone athwart the day
  Of Greece and England.

Lines 270-272.
Himself with every mystery, until
His weary legs he rested on the sill
Of some remotest chamber, outlet dim.

Lines 278-280.
Whose flitting Lantern, through rude nettle-
  beds,
Cheats us into a bog, — cuttings and shreds
Of old Vexations plaited to a rope
Wherewith to haul us from the sight of hope,
And bind us to our earthly baiting-ring.

Line 285. The reading *raught* is derived from
the manuscript, though the first edition has
caught.

Line 363. Originally this imperfect line
read, —

    ' To seas Ionian and Tyrian. Dire

and then followed a weak passage, which was
afterward thrown out and the better lines that
follow substituted; but in making the change
Keats apparently overlooked this defect.

Line 376 *et seq.* Compare this passage with
Spenser's account of the garden of Adonis in
Faerie Queene, Book III. canto vi.

Lines 396, 397.
And draperies mellow-tinted like the peach,
Or lady peas entwined with marigolds.

Line 400. *Tenting swerve,* as Keats informed a
friend who did not at once perceive the meaning,
is a swerve in the form of the top of a tent.

Line 416.
The creeper, blushing deep at Autumn's blush.

Line 436.
For 't is the highest reach of human honour.

Lines 461-464.
Who would not be so bound, but, foolish elf,
He was content to let Divinity
Slip through his careless arms — content to see
An unseized heaven sighing at his feet.

It is not easy to see why Keats should substitute ' amorous plea faint through ' for ' Divinity slip through.'

Line 482.
Over this paly corse, the crystal shower.

Lines 505, 506.
Cupids awake ! or black and blue we 'll pinch
Your dimpled arms.

Lines 526-533.
Queen Venus bending downward, so o'ertaken,
So suffering sweet, so blushing mad, so shaken

That the wild warmth prob'd the young sleep-
  er's heart
Enchantingly ; and with a sudden start
His trembling arms were out in instant time
To catch his fainting love. — O foolish rhyme,
What mighty power is in thee that so often
Thou strivest rugged syllables to soften
Even to the telling of a sweet like this.
Away ! let them embrace alone ! that kiss
Was far too rich for thee to talk upon.
Poor wretch ! mind not those sobs and sighs !
  begone !
Speak not one atom of thy paltry stuff,
That they are met is poetry enough.

Line 541. The finished manuscript reads *dies;*
the first edition has *dyes.* The former seems the
more poetic reading, and yet the construction
would introduce a new image rather abruptly.

Line 578. The text reads, —

    ' Thou shouldst mount up to with me. Now adieu !'

But the word ' to ' so destroys both rhythm and
sense, that I have ventured to throw it out as
an overlooked error.

Line 589. By throwing the emphasis strongly
on *all,* the meaning of the line is made evident.

Line 628. Keats tried *massy, blackening,* and
bulging, before he settled on *jutting.*

Lines 642-657.
About her majesty, and her pale brow
With turrets crown'd, which forward heavily
  bow
Weighing her chin to the breast. Four lions
  draw
The wheels in sluggish time — each toothed
  maw
Shut patiently — eyes hid in tawny veils —
Drooping about their paws, and nervy tails
Cowering their tufted brushes to the dust.

Lines 657-660.
To cloudborne Jove he bent: and there was
  tost
Into his grasping hands a silken cord
At which without a single impious word
He swung upon it off into the gloom.

Lines 668-671.
With airs delicious. Long he hung about
Before his nice enjoyment could pick out
The resting place: but at the last he swung
Into the greenest cell of all — among
Dark leaved jasmine: star flower'd and be-
  strown
With golden moss.

Lines 756, 757.
Enchantress ! tell me by this mad embrace.
By the moist languor of thy breathing face.

'60, 761.
:nderest — and by the breath — the
e
on — nectar — Heaven! — 'Jove above !

)0.
llas self not love ? she must — she
ust !

49, 850.
: the strange voice is on the wane —
but guess'd from the departing sound.

rman makes a very plausible surmise
ts had a half purpose to go on with a
:iption of this voice and he prints the
at follow. They are not in the draft,
y of the annotated copies to which he
it appear in Leigh Hunt's *The Indica-*
) January, 1820. They are well worth
g, since if they are not by Keats they
ely have been penned by some one in
nd Hunt's circle who had an extraor-
iack at imitation of Keats.

t a voice is silent. It was soft
in-echoes, when the winds aloft
a winds of summer) meet in caves ;
i sheltered places the white waves
i'd into music, as the breeze
id stems the current : or as trees
eir green locks in the days of June :
: girls when to the maiden moon
harmonious pray'rs : or sounds that come
near) like a faint distant hum
grass, from which mysterious birth
the busy secrets of the earth.
i low voice of Syrinx, when she ran
irest from Arcadian Pan ;
one's, when she pined away
or (and yet 't was not so gay)
i whisper when she came to Troy,
'd to wander with that blooming boy.
uch'd harps in flowery casements hung ;
lovers' ears the wild woods sung
bowers at twilight ; like the sound
when he takes his nightly round
see the roses all asleep :
i dim strain which along the deep
iid utters to the sailors' ear,
tempests, or of dangers near.
emona, who (when fear was strong
ioul) chaunted the willow song,
before she perish'd : or the tone
pon the waters heard alone :
i that come upon the memory
friends departed ; or the sigh
irl breathes when she tries to hide
er eyes betray to all beside.'

i0.
ls outswelling their faint tinged curls.

BOOK III. 'Keats said with much simplicity,' reports Woodhouse, ' "It will be easily
seen what I think of the present ministers, by
the beginning of the third Book." ' Keats may
have had Milton and Lycidas in mind when he
thus covertly made a poem serve as a scourge.

Lines 31, 32.
In the several vastnesses of air and fire :
And silent as a corpse upon a pyre.

Lines 41. Keats was wont to record the date
when he finished a book, but he wrote against
this line, 'Oxford, Septr. 5, [1817] as if to register his oath and connect the opening of the
book with the immediate time.

Lines 56, 57.
Thou dost bless all things — even dead things
    sip
A midnight life from thee.

Lines 89, 90.
Enormous sharks from hiding-holes and fright-
    'ning
The whale's large eyes with unaccustomed
    lightning.

Lines 445–447.
Their music came to my o'ersweeten'd sense
And then I felt a hovering influence
A breathing on my forehead.

Lines 581–583.   Great Jove,
What fury of the three could harm this dove ?
Dear youth ! see how I weep, hear how I sigh.

Line 752.
And bound it round Endymion : then stroke.

Lines 864, 865.
At his right hand stood winged Love, elate,
And on his left Love's fairest mother sate.

Lines 954–956.
When thy bright diadem a silver gleam
O'er blue dominion starts. Thy finny team
Snorts in the morning light, and sends along.

Line 979.
Who is not full of heaven when thou hast
    smil'd ?

BOOK IV.
Lines 48–54.   No eyelids meet
To twinkle on my bosom ! false ! 't was false.
They said how beautiful I was ! Who calls
Me now divine ? Who now kneels down and
    dies
Before me till from these enslaving eyes
Redemption sparkles. Ah me, how sad I am !
Of all the poisons sent to make us mad —
Of all death's overwhelmings.' — Stay, beware,
Young Mountaineer !

Lines 76, 77.
Sweet shadow, be distinct awhile and stay
While I speak to thee — trust me it is true.

Lines 85–87.
Of passion from the heart — where love is not
Only is solitude — poor shadow! what
I say thou hearest not! away, begone
And leave me, prythee, with my grief alone!'
The Latmian lean'd his arm upon a bough,
A wretched mortal: what can he do now?
Must he another Love? O impious.

Line 94.
While the fair moon gives light, or rivers flow
My adoration of thee is yet pure
As infants prattling. How is this — why sure
I have a triple soul.

Line 104.
Shut softly up alive — ye harmonies
Ye tranced visions — ye flights ideal:
Nothing are ye to life so dainty real.
O Lady, pity me!

Lines 136–138.
Canst thou do so? Is there no balm, no cure?
Could not a beckoning Hebe soon allure
Thee into Paradise? What sorrowing
So weighs thee down? what utmost woe could bring
This madness? — Sit thee down by me, and ease
Thine heart in whispers — haply by degrees
I may find out some soothing medicine.' —
'Dear Lady,' said Endymion, 'I pine —
I die — the tender accents thou hast spoken
Have finish'd all — my heart is lost and broken.

Line 154.
The lustrous passion from a lover's eye

Line 157. An instance of *spry* for *spray* is cited by Mr. Forman from Sandys's *Ovid*, Book XI., verses 498, 499.

Line 247.
Arch infant crews in mimic of the coil.

Line 341. For *wild* the expressive *wide* occurs in the draft and printer's copy.

Line 539. The rightful tinge of health.

Line 700. After this line, and before the next these two lines appear in the finished manuscript. —

'And by it shalt thou sit and sing, hey nonny!
While doves coo to thee for a little honey.'

Lines 749–741.
Me, dear Endymion, were I to weave
My own imaginations to sweet life
Thou would'st o'ertop them all.

Line 769.
Por'd on its hazel carpet of shed leaves.

Line 774. *Hyperion* apparently had already occurred to Keats as subject for a poem.

Lines 811–813.
Were this sweet damsel like a long neck'd crane,
Or an old rocking barn owl half asleep,
Some reason would there be for thee to keep
So dull-eyed — but thou know'st she 's beautiful:
Yes, yes! and thou dost love her well — I 'll pull.

Page 110. ISABELLA, OR THE POT OF BASIL. Stanza xxx., line 5. A manuscript variation is: —

'What might have been too plainly did she see,'

Stanza xxxv., lines 4–7, another reading: —

'Had marr'd his glossy hair, that once could shoot
Bright gold into the Sun, and stamp'd his doom
Upon his soiled lips, and took the mellow Lute
From his deep voice, and down past his loamed ears.'

Stanza xxxviii., the last two lines in the manuscript read: —

'Go, shed a tear upon my heather bloom
And I shall turn a diamond in my tomb.'

Stanza liv., last line. *Leqfits* seems to be a word of Keats's coinage.

Stanza lxiii. Mr. Forman in the Appendix to the second volume of his edition of Keats has a long note on the 'sad ditty' born of the story of Isabella, in which he shows that the air of the Basil Pot song, though not now current, was common enough in mediæval manuscripts and printed collections of popular poetry.

Page 123. TRANSLATION FROM A SONNET BY RONSARD.
The following is the original: —

'Nature, ornant Cassandre, qui deuoit
De sa douceur forcer les plus rebelles,
La composa de cent beautez nouuelles,
Que dès mille ans en espargne elle anoit : —
De tous les biens qu' Amour au ciel connoit
Comme un trésor cherement sous ses ailes
Elle enrichit les graces immortelles
De son bel œil qui les Dieux esmouuoit. —
Du Ciel à peine elle estoit descenduë
Quand ie la vey, quand mon ame esperduë
En dueint folle, et d'un si poignant trait,
Amour coula ses beautez en mes veines,
Qu'autres plaisirs ie ne sens que mes peines
Ny autre bien qu'adorer son portrait.

Page 123. SONNET: TO A LADY SEEN FOR A FEW MOMENTS AT VAUXHALL.

The form given to this sonnet in *Hood's Magazine*, where it was published, April, 1844, varies slightly from that in Lord Houghton's publication. The first line reads : —

'Life's sea hath been five times at its slow ebb'

and the closing lines are : —

'Other delights with thy remembering
And sorrow to my darling joys doth bring.'

Page 124. FANCY.
The poem as sent by Keats to his brother and sister was revised when he came to include it in his volume, and the following are the more interesting variations : —

Line 5.
Towards heaven still spread beyond her —

Line 10. Cloys with kissing. What do then ?

Line 24. To banish vesper from the sky.

Line 33.
All the faery buds of May,
On spring turf or scented spray ;

Line 57.
And the snake all winter shrank
Cast its skin on sunny bank ;

Line 66. This line was followed by two afterward omitted : —

'For the same sleek-throated mouse
To store up in its winter house.'

Line 68.
Every joy is spoilt by use ;
Every pleasure, every joy
Not a mistress but doth cloy.
Where 's the cheek that doth not fade,

Line 89. The following lines were dropped out, the two drafts agreeing again at line 90 : —

'And Jove grew languid. Mistress fair !
Thou shalt have that tressed hair
Adonis tangled all for spite ;
And the mouth he would not kiss,
And the treasure he would miss ;
And the hand he would not press
And the warmth he would distress.
  O the Ravishment — the Bliss !
Fancy has her where she is —
Never fulsome, never new,
There she steps ! and tell me who
Has a mistress so divine ?
Be the palate ne'er so fine
She cannot sicken. Break the mesh.'

Page 125. ODE : BARDS OF PASSION AND OF MIRTH.
In the copy made for George and Georgiana Keats are the following variations : —

Line 19.
But melodious truth divine,
Philosophic numbers fine ;

Line 23. Thus ye live on Earth, and then

Line 30.
To mortals of the little week
They must sojourn with their cares

Page 127. THE EVE OF ST. AGNES.
The following letter from Keats to his publisher, John Taylor, written June 11, 1820, is interesting for its textual criticism : ' In reading over the proof of *St. Agnes's Eve* since I left Fleet Street, I was struck with what appears to me an alteration in the seventh stanza very much for the worse. The passage I mean stands thus —

"her maiden eyes incline
Still on the floor, while many a sweeping train
Pass by."

'T was originally written : —

"her maiden eyes divine
Fix'd on the floor, saw many a sweeping train
Pass by."

My meaning is quite destroyed in the alteration. I do not use *train* for *concourse of passers by*, but for *skirts* sweeping along the floor.
'In the first stanza my copy reads, second (sic) line : —

"bitter *chill* it was,"

to avoid the echo *cold* in the second line.'
In a manuscript version, Lionel was the name given to the hero instead of Porphyro.
Page 134. ODE ON A GRECIAN URN.
Line 9. Both in the original manuscript and in the *Annals* the line reads : —

'What love ? what dance ? what struggle to escape ?'

Line 16. The *Annals* reading is : —

'Thy song, nor ever bid the spring adieu.'

a line which had no rhyme and very likely was transferred by mistake from the next stanza.
Line 34. The manuscript reads *sides* for *flanks*.
Page 139. LA BELLE DAME SANS MERCI.
The text given is that of *The Indicator*, but Lord Houghton, when reprinting the poem in *Life, Letters and Literary Remains* used another form apparently. The variations below are from Lord Houghton's copy.

Line 1. O what can ail thee, knight-at-arms

Line 3.
The sedge has wither'd from the lake.

Line 5. O what can ail thee, knight-at-arms.
Line 19.

'For sidelong would she bend, and sing.'

stanzas v. and vi. are transposed.
Line 30.
And there she wept, and sigh'd full sore.

Line 32. With kisses four.

Line 33. And there she lulled me asleep

The version sent to George and Georgiana
Keats agrees, with but trifling variation, with
that given by Lord Houghton.
Page 140. CHORUS OF FAIRIES.
In Lord Houghton's version this is called
Song of Four Fairies. There is one variation
to be noted in line 46, where he reads,

'Beyond the nimble-wheeled quest.'

Page 142. ON FAME.
The copy sent by Keats to his brother and
sister shows these variations.
Line 7.
As if a clear Lake meddling with itself
Should cloud its clearness with a muddy gloom.
Line 14.
Spoil his salvation by a fierce miscreed.

Page 142. TO SLEEP.
In line 5. Lord Houghton's copy reads *lulling*
for *dewy* which is found in a manuscript of Sir
Charles Dilke. In another draft of twelve lines
by Keats which was copied in *The Athenæum,*
October 26, 1872, the first three lines are the
same as printed; the next nine are as follows:

'As wearisome as darkness is divine
O soothest sleep, if so it please thee close
My willing eyes in midst of this thine hymn
Or wait the amen, ere thy poppy throws
Its sweet death dews o'er every pulse and limb —
Then shut the hushed Casket of my soul
And turn the key round in the oiled wards
And let it rest until the morn has stole,
Bright tressed from the grey east's shuddering
bourn.'

Page 142. ODE TO PSYCHE.
The copy sent by Keats to his brother and
sister varies from that printed in the 1820 volume in at least one important particular, and it
is not quite clear why Keats, when he substituted *roof* for *fan* in line 10, did not mend the
rhyme also. In line 14 the copy in the letter
reads *Syrian.*
Page 146. LAMIA.
The manuscript copy, presumably the one
given to the printer, is in existence, and Mr. Forman notes amongst others the following readings, changed apparently in the proof.

PART I. line 48.
Cerulean spotted, golden-green, and blue.
Line 69.
I had a silver dream of thee last night.
Line 78.
And, swiftly as a mission'd phœbean dart.
Line 104. Pale wax her immortality far woe
Line 114.
Warm, tremulous, devout, bright-tom'd, psalte-
rian.
Ravish'd, she lifted up her Circean head.
Line 132.
To the swoon'd serpent, and with languorous arm.
Line 155.
A deep volcanian yellow took the place.
Line 167.
And her new voice, softlisting in the air
Cried 'Lycius! gentle Lycius, where, ah where!
Line 185.
Ah! never heard of, delight never known
Save of one happy mortal! only one. —
Lycius the happy: for she was a Maid.
Line 260. A line was added to this, —

'Thou to Elysium gone, here for the vultures I'

Line 378. A royal-squared lofty portal door.
PART II. line 45. Two lines were here
added : —

'Too fond was I believing, fancy fed
In high deliriums, and blossoms never shed!'

Lines 82-84.
Became herself a flame — 't was worth an age
Of minor joys to revel in such rage.
She was persuaded, and she fixt the hour
When he should make a Bride of his fair Par-
amour.
After the hottest day comes languidest
The colour'd Eve, half-hidden in the west;
So they both look'd, so spake, if breathed
sound,
That almost silence is, hath ever found
Compare with nature's quiet. Which lov'd
most,
Which had the weakest, strongest heart so lost,
So ruin'd, wreck'd, destroy'd : for certes they
Scarcely could tell   they could not guess
Whether 't was misery or happiness.
Spells are but made to break. Whisper'd the
Youth.
Line 174.
Fill'd with light, music, jewels, gold, perfume.

Line 231. In Tom Taylor's *Autobiography of Haydon*, vol. i. p. 354, is a passage which is a slight comment on these lines. 'He then, in a strain of humor beyond description, abused me for putting Newton's head into my picture. "A fellow," said he, "who believed nothing unless it was as clear as three sides of a triangle." And then he and Keats agreed he had destroyed all the beauty of the rainbow, by reducing it to the prismatic colors. It was impossible to resist him, and we all drank Newton's health and confusion to mathematics.'

Line 293.
From Lycius answer'd, as he sunk supine
Upon the couch where Lamia's beauties pine.

Line 296.   'from every ill
That youth might suffer have I shielded thee
Up to this very hour, and shall I see
Thee married to a Serpent? Pray you mark,
Corinthians! A Serpent, plain and stark!'

At the close of the poem, Keats appended the passage from Burton which had given him his theme: —

'Philostratos, in his fourth book, *de Vita Apollonii*, hath a memorable instance in this kind, which I may not omit, of one Menippus Lycius, a young man twenty-five years of age that, going betwixt Cenchreas and Corinth, met such a phantasm in the habit of a fair gentlewoman, which, taking him by the hand, carried him home to her house, in the suburbs of Corinth, and told him she was a Phœnician by birth, and if he would tarry with her, he should hear her sing and play, and drink such wine as never any drank, and no man should molest him; but she, being fair and lovely, would die with him, that was fair and lovely to behold. The young man, a philosopher, otherwise staid and discreet, able to moderate his passions, though not this of love, tarried with her awhile to his great content, and at last married her, to whose wedding, amongst other guests, came Apollonius; who, by some probable conjectures, found her out to be a serpent, a lamia; and that all her furniture was, like Tantalus' gold, described by Homer, no substance, but mere illusions. When she saw herself descried, she wept, and desired Apollonius to be silent, but he would not be moved, and thereupon she, plate, house, and all that was in it, vanished in an instant; many thousands took notice of this fact, for it was done in the midst of Greece.' — Burton's *Anatomy of Melancholy*, Part III., Sect. 2, Memb. I. Subs. I.

Page 199. HYPERION.

Since the introductory note to this poem was printed, a letter from Canon Ainger has appeared in *The Athenæum* (26 August, 1899), in which he states that he has seen a copy of the 1820 volume, given by Keats to a Hampstead friend and neighbor, and bearing on the title page 'with J. Keats's compliments.' He adds, 'Keats has with his own hand scored out, in strong ink lines, the publisher's preface. . . . At the head of this preface Keats has written, "I had no part in this; I was ill at the time." And after the concluding sentence about *Endymion*, which he has carefully bracketed off, he has written, "This is a lie!"' This is interesting testimony, especially if Canon Ainger's opinion as to this being in Keats's handwriting is correct.

Page 232. THE LAST SONNET.
A manuscript reading of the last line is: —

'Half-passionless, and so swoon on to death.'

II. LETTERS

1. Page 255. 'God 'ield you.' Mr. Colvin calls attention to the frequency with which Keats, in his early letters, falls into Shakespearian phrases.

2. Page 255. 'Endymion.' The reference is not to the poem of that name, but to the verses beginning 'I stood tiptoe upon a little hill.' See p. 14.

3. Page 255. 'Your kindness.' Reynolds had addressed Keats in a sonnet as follows: —

'Thy thoughts, dear Keats, are like fresh gathered leaves,
  Or white flowers pluck'd from some sweet lily bed;
  They set the heart a-breathing, and they shed
Tho glow of meadows, mornings, and spring eves
O'er the excited soul. — Thy genius weaves
  Songs that shall make the age be nature-led,
  And win that coronal for thy young head
Which time's strange hand of freshness ne'er bereaves.
Go on! and keep thee to thine own green way,
  Singing in that same key which Chaucer sung;
Be thou companion of the summer day,
  Roaming the fields and older woods among:
So shall thy Muse be ever in her May,
  And thy luxuriant spirit ever young.'

4. Page 257. 'Aunt Dinah's counterpane.' The letter was crossed, after a fashion more common in days of heavy postage than now.

5. Page 259. Hazlitt had reviewed in *The Examiner* for May 4, 1817, Southey's *Letter to William Smith Esq., M. P.*, and had been excessively severe.

6. Page 259. 'The Nymphs.' A mythological poem, on which Hunt was at this time engaged.

, 7. Page 259. 'Does Shelley go on telling strange stories of the death of kings?' Gilfillan, in his *Gallery of Literary Portraits*, tells the story of Shelley amusing himself and Hunt, when they were travelling in a stage coach, and startling an old lady travelling with them, by suddenly crying out to Hunt, 'For God's sake, let us sit upon the ground and tell sad stories of the death of kings.' *King Richard II.*, iii. 2.

8. Page 261. 'I long to see Wordsworth's as well as to have mine in.' Haydon was painting his Christ's Entry into Jerusalem, and was introducing likenesses of his friends into the picture.

9. Page 262. 'Bertrand,' *i. e.*, General Bertrand, who was one of Bonaparte's petty court at St. Helena.

10. Page 263. Jane Reynolds afterward married Thomas Hood. The Reynolds family lived in Little Britain, so quaintly sketched by Washington Irving.

11. Page 263. 'Hampton,' *i. e.*, Little Hampton, a quiet watering place at the mouth of the Arun, on the south coast of Sussex, a little more than halfway between London and Portsmouth.

12. Page 265. 'Miss Taylor's essays in Rhyme.' Fanny Keats was fourteen years old at this time, and the Norwich ladies, Ann and Jane Taylor, were in the height of their popularity with young readers.

13. Page 266. 'Tell Dilke.' The Dilkes were friends living in Hampstead whom Reynolds had introduced to Keats. Charles Wentworth Dilke was at the time a clerk in the Navy Pay-Office, and a disciple of Godwin and warm friend of Hunt. Later he became a man of great consequence in the literary world as editor and chief owner of *The Athenæum*. The W. D. mentioned below is William Dilke, a younger brother, who had served in the Commissariat department. He was at this time about forty-two years old.

14. Page 268. 'Northern Poet.' See Wordsworth's *Personal Talk*, beginning —

'I am not one who much or oft delight
To season my fireside with personal talk.'

15. Page 269. Hazlitt had just collected and published his *The Round Table*, which he first printed in *The Examiner*.

16. Page 271. 'You and Gleig.' Mr. Colvin makes this note: 'G. R. Gleig, son of the Bishop of Stirling: born 1796, died 1888: served in the Peninsular War and afterwards took orders. Chaplain-General to the Forces from 1846 to 1875: author of the *Subaltern* and many military tales and histories.'

17. Page 271. 'The two R's.' Reynolds and Rice.

18. Page 274. 'The little Song.' See headnote to 'Lines,' p. 37. The allusion just below in Adam's waking is to *Paradise Lost*, Book VIII., lines 478–484.

19. Page 275. 'Christie.' Jonathan H. Christie, a college friend of Lockhart, who took up Lockhart's quarrel with John Scott, fought the latter in a duel and killed him.

20. Page 277. 'Wells.' Charles J. Wells, a schoolmate of Tom Keats. See the Sonnet, p. 13, 'To a Friend who sent me some Roses.' The family of Wells lived in Featherstone Buildings, from which Letter 24 was written.

21. Page 277. 'Shelley's poem.' *Laon and Cynthia*, renamed *The Revolt of Islam*.

22. Page 277. The tragedy was *Retribution, or the Chieftain's Daughter;* the pantomime was *Don Giovanni*. The articles, as the postscript to this letter shows, did appear in *The Champion*.

23. Page 278. 'We played a concert.' A burlesque affair. Keats, his brothers and friends, were wont to entertain themselves with imitating musical instruments, vocally.

24. Page 278. Haydon's *Autobiography*, I. 384, gives a more detailed account of this supper party. Ritchie, here referred to, Mr. Colvin tells us, was Joseph Ritchie, who 'started on a Government mission to Fezzan in September, 1818, and died at Morzouk the following November. An account of the expedition was published by his travelling companion, Captain G. F. Lyon, R. N.' Ritchie wrote a poetical *Farewell to England*, which was printed by A. A. Watts in his *Poetical Album*.

25. Page 278. 'Medal of the Princess,' *i. e.*, Princess Charlotte, who died November 6, 1817.

26. Page 278. 'Bob Harris,' the manager of Covent Garden Theatre.

27. Page 279. 'Miss Kent's.' Mr. Forman notes that the article was not by Miss Bessy Kent, Hunt's sister-in-law, but by Shelley, who used the initials E. K. for 'Elfin Knight.'

28. Page 279. 'Mr. Abbey.' Mr. Richard Abbey, a tea-merchant, one of the guardians of the Keats family. See above, p. xv.

29. Page 283. See a lively refutation of this conjecture of Hunt's, and a general statement of the relations of the 'Cockney school' with the Edinburgh critics in Lang's *The Life and Letters of John Gibson Lockhart*, I. 150–155.

30. Page 285. 'As the old song says.' Mr. Forman here quotes the 'old song,' which is 'Sharing Eve's Apple,' given in the Appendix, p. 248, on Mr. Forman's authority as by Keats. Mr. Colvin merely indicates a break. It is quite possible that Keats in the jesting mood with which his letter opens, wrote these nonsense lines and, in Scott's fashion, palmed them off as an 'old song.'

31. Page 285. 'For the sum of twopence.' See the head-note to 'Robin Hood,' p. 41.

32. Page 287. 'Mr. Robinson.' Henry Crabbe Robinson. This delightful diarist does not record this visit, nor in the two or three references to Keats speak as if he knew him. In an entry for December 8, 1820, he records reading some of Keats's poems, and adds: 'There are a force, wildness, and originality in the works of this young poet which, if his perilous journey to Italy does not destroy him, promise to place him at the head of the next generation of poets.'

33. Page 293. Haydon had written with enthusiasm about a seal with a true lover's knot and the initials W. S., found in a field at Stratford-on-Avon.

34. Page 293. 'Dentatus' was the subject of a picture by Haydon.

35. Page 295. 'Claude's Enchanted Castle.' Mr. Colvin has this interesting note: 'The famous picture now belonging to Lady Wantage, and exhibited at Burlington House in 1888. Whether Keats ever saw the original is doubtful (it was not shown at the British Institution in his time), but he must have been familiar with the subject as engraved by Vivarès and Woollett, and its suggestive power worked in his mind until it yielded at last the distilled poetic essence of the "magic casement" passage in the "Ode to a Nightingale." It is interesting to note the theme of the Grecian Urn ode coming in also amidst the "unconnected subject and careless verse" of this rhymed epistle.'

36. Page 296. 'Posthumous works.' Haydon had written Keats: 'When I die I'll have Shakespeare placed on my heart, with Homer in my right hand and Ariosto in the other, Dante at my head, Tasso at my feet, and Corneille under my —.'

37. Page 300. 'Worsted stockings.' Keats hints at the neighborhood of the children of the Postman Bentley, at whose house in Wellwalk he lodged.

38. Page 306. 'The opposite,' i. e., a leaf with the name and 'from the Author.'

39. Page 315. 'A scrap of paper.' The book was a copy of 'Endymion,' and Keats had left

in London a scrap of paper bearing 'from the Author,' to be pasted in.

40. Page 316. 'The Swan and two necks' was the name of the coach office in Lad Lane, London.

41. Page 320. '3 little volumes.' The several references to these books indicate Cary's Translation of Dante, which was so published by Taylor and Hessey and advertised on the fly-leaf of 'Endymion.'

42. Page 328. 'A Woman.' Mr. Colvin notes: 'Miss Charlotte Cox, an East Indian cousin of the Reynoldses — the "Charmian" described more fully' in Letter 74.

43. Page 328. 'Slip-shod Endymion.' John Scott wrote of the poem in *The Morning Chronicle*, October 3, 1818: 'That there are also many, very many passages indicating both haste and carelessness I will not deny; nay, I will go further, and assert that a real friend of the author would have dissuaded him from immediate publication.'

44. Page 338. 'I have scarce any hopes of him.' Thomas Keats died a few hours later, on the same day this letter was written. As noted in the biographical sketch, Keats now removed to Wentworth Place.

45. Page 339. 'This thin paper.' Mr. Colvin notes: 'A paper of the largest folio size, used by Keats in this letter only, and containing some eight hundred words a page of his writing.'

46. Page 340. 'Her daughter senior.' Fanny Brawne, of whom this is the first mention in the letters.

47. Page 354. 'Henrietta Street,' the residence of Mrs. Wylie.

48. Page 355. 'The silk tassels,' Mr. Colvin explains, were the gift of Georgiana Keats.

49. Page 366. 'Am I all wound with Browns.' Mr. Colvin reminds the reader of the origin of the phrase in Caliban's mouth:

'Sometimes am I
All wound with adders, who with cloven tongues
Do hiss me into madness.'

The little Brown boys, brothers of Charles Armitage Brown, are the 'Boys' referred to above, p. 364.

50. Page 368. This discreet notice of Reynolds's parody appeared with some alteration in *The Examiner*, April 26, 1819.

51. Page 378. James Elmes was the editor of *Annals of the Fine Arts*, in which first appeared the 'Ode to a Nightingale.' See p. 144.

52. Page 383. 'An oriental tale of a very beautiful color.' Mr. Forman, on the authority of Dr. Reinhold Köhler, Librarian of the Grand-

ducal Library of Weimar, identifies the story, which is a variant of the Third Calender's story in *The Arabian Nights*, as the 'Histoire de la Corbeille,' in the *Nouveaux Contes Orientaux* of the Comte de Caylus.

53. Page 399. 'Hunt's triumphal entry into London.' Mr. Forman makes the following note on this passage : 'Henry Hunt, of Manchester Massacre fame, ended an imprisonment of two years and a half on the 30th of October, 1822, and made an "entry into London" on the 11th of November, 1822 ; but the trial of which his imprisonment was the issue had not taken place till the spring of 1820; and the entry alluded to by Keats was one which took place between the massacre and the trial.'

54. Page 413. 'From Sr. G. B.'s, Lord M.' Sir George Beaumonts and Lord Musgraves.

55. Page 416. 'The Cave of despair.' Spenser's Cave of Despair was the subject of the picture (see Letter 141) with which Severn won the Royal Academy premium.

56. Page 438. 'Lucy Vaughan Lloyd.' The name under which Keats proposed to publish 'The Cap and Bells.' See p. 216.

57. Page 446. 'Without making any way.' Mr. Colvin appends this note : 'The *Maria Crowther* had in fact sailed from London, September 18 : contrary winds holding her in the Channel, Keats had landed at Portsmouth for a night's visit to the Snooks of Bedhampton.'

BIBLIOGRAPHICAL LIST OF KEATS'S POEMS

In this list the contents are given in their order of the three volumes published by Keats. Then follow the poems gathered by Lord Houghton, and those printed for the first time in the Letters, collected by Mr. Forman, Mr. Colvin, and Mr. Speed. The few instances of independent periodical publication of poems, and of those gathered by Mr. Forman, are noted in the head-notes to those poems.

I. POEMS, | BY | JOHN KEATS. | 'WHAT MORE FELICITY CAN FALL TO CREATURE, | THAN TO ENJOY DELIGHT WITH LIBERTY ' | *Fate of the Butterfly.* — SPENSER. | LONDON: | PRINTED FOR C. & J. OLLIER, 3 WELBECK STREET, | CAVENDISH SQUARE. | 1817.
Dedication. To Leigh Hunt, esq.
'I stood tip-toe upon a little hill.'
Specimen of an Induction to a Poem.
Calidore. A Fragment.
To Some Ladies.
On receiving a curious shell, and a Copy of Verses from the same Ladies.
To ——. [Hadst thou liv'd in days of old].
To Hope.
Imitation of Spenser.
'Woman! when I behold thee flippant, vain.'
Epistles:
 To George Felton Mathew.
 To my Brother George.
 To Charles Cowden Clarke.
Sonnets:
  I. To my Brother George.
  II. To —— ['Had I a man's fair form, then might my sighs.']
  III. Written on the day that Mr. Leigh Hunt left prison.
  IV. 'How many bards gild the lapses of time.'
  V. To a Friend who sent me some roses.
  VI. To G. A. W.
  VII. 'O Solitude, if I must with thee dwell.'
  VIII. To my Brothers.
  IX. 'Keen, fitful gusts are whisp'ring here and there.'
  X. 'To one who has been long in city pent.'
  XI. On first Looking into Chapman's Homer.
  XII. On leaving some friends at an early hour.
  XIII. Addressed to Haydon.
  XIV. Addressed to the same.
  XV. On the Grasshopper and Cricket.
  XVI. To Kosciusko.
  XVII. 'Happy is England.'
Sleep and Poetry.

II. ENDYMION: | A POETIC ROMANCE. | BY JOHN KEATS. | 'THE STRETCHED METRE OF AN ANTIQUE SONG.' | LONDON: | PRINTED FOR TAYLOR AND HESSEY, | 93, FLEET STREET, | 1818.

III. LAMIA | ISABELLA, | THE EVE OF ST. AGNES, | AND OTHER POEMS. | BY JOHN KEATS, | AUTHOR OF ENDYMION. | LONDON: | PRINTED FOR TAYLOR AND HESSEY, | FLEET STREET | 1820.
Lamia.
Isabella; or the Pot of Basil.
The Eve of St. Agnes.
Ode to a Nightingale.
Ode on a Grecian Urn.
Ode to Psyche.
Fancy.
Ode [' Bards of Passion and of Mirth'].
Lines on the Mermaid Tavern.
Robin Hood. To a Friend.
To Autumn.
Ode on Melancholy.
Hyperion : a Fragment.

IV. LIFE, LETTERS AND LITERARY REMAINS OF JOHN KEATS. EDITED BY RICHARD MONCKTON MILNES [AFTERWARD LORD HOUGHTON].

[The following were incorporated in the biographical portion.]

To Spenser.
To Chatterton.
To Byron.
On seeing the Elgin Marbles.
To Haydon, with the above.
On seeing a lock of Milton's Hair.
A Draught of Sunshine.
What the Thrush said.

On sitting down to read *King Lear* once again.
To the Nile.
Epistle to John Hamilton Reynolds.
Fragment of an Ode to Maia.
On visiting the Tomb of Burns.
Written in the Cottage where Burns was born.
Meg Merrilies.
On Ailsa Rock.
Lines written in the Highlands after a visit to Burns's cottage.
At Fingal's Cave.
Written upon the top of Ben Nevis.
A Prophecy: To George Keats in America.
Translation from a Sonnet of Ronsard.
Spenserian stanzas on Charles Armitage Brown.
Spenserian stanza written at the end of Canto II. Book V. of *The Faerie Queene*.
Fragments:
'Where 's the Poet? show him! show him!'
Modern Love.
The Castle Builder.
'Welcome joy, and welcome sorrow.'
Ode to Fanny.
[The following were grouped in the section *Literary Remains*]: —
Otho the Great.
King Stephen.
The Cap and Bells.
Ode to Apollo.
Hymn to Apollo.
On ——— : 'Think not of it, sweet one, so.'
Lines: 'Unfelt, unheard, unseen.'
Song : 'Hush, hush! tread softly.'
Song : 'I had a dove and the sweet dove died.'
Faery song : 'Shed no tear! O, shed no tear.'
Song : 'Spirit here that reignest.'
Faery song : 'Ah! woe is me.'
Extracts from an Opera.
La Belle Dame sans Merci.
Song of Four Faeries.
Ode on Indolence.

The Eve of St. Mark.
To Fanny: 'Physician Nature! let my spirit blood.'
Stanzas : 'In a drear-nighted December.'
Sonnets :
'Oh, how I love on a fair summer's eve.'
'To a Young Lady who sent me a laurel crown.'
'After dark vapours have oppress'd our plains.'
Written on the Blank space at the end of Chaucer's Tale of *The Floure and the Lefe.*
On the Sea.
On Leigh Hunt's poem *The Story of Rimini.*
'When I have fears that I may cease to be.'
To Homer.
Written in answer to a sonnet.
To J. H. Reynolds.
To ——— : 'Time's sea hath been five years at its slow ebb.'
To Sleep.
On Fame.
Another on Fame.
'Why did I laugh to-night?'
A Dream, after reading Dante's Episode of Paolo and Francesca.
'If by dull rhymes our English must be chain'd.'
'The day is gone, and all its sweets are gone.'
'I cry your mercy — pity — love! — aye, love.'
The Last Sonnet.
V. THE LETTERS OF JOHN KEATS:
Acrostic: Georgiana Augusta Wylie.
At Teignmouth.
Mrs. Cameron and Ben Nevis.
The Devon Maid.
A Little Extempore.
The Gadfly.
The Human Seasons.
To Thomas Keats.
A Party of Lovers.
A Song about Myself.
Two or Three Posies.

INDEX OF FIRST LINES

INDEX OF TITLES

[The titles of major works and general divisions are set in SMALL CAPITALS.]

INDEX TO LETTERS

CPSIA information can be obtained at www.ICGtesting.com
Printed in the USA
LVOW06*1607230215

428003LV00012B/336/P

9 781163 462058